GLOBAL STUDIES

RUSSIA, THE EURASIAN REPUBLICS, AND CENTRAL/EASTERN EUROPE

FIFTH EDITION

STAFF

Ian A. Nielsen	Publisher
Brenda S. Filley	Production Manager
Lisa M. Clyde	Developmental Editor
Diane Barker	Editorial Assistant
Roberta Monaco	Editorial Assistant
Charles Vitelli	Designer
Cheryl Greenleaf	Permissions Coordinator
Shawn Callahan	Graphics Coordinator
Lara M. Johnson	Graphics
Steve Shumaker	Graphics
Libra Ann Cusack	Typesetting Supervisor
Juliana Arbo	Typesetter

GLOBAL STUDIES

RUSSIA, THE EURASIAN REPUBLICS, AND CENTRAL/EASTERN EUROPE

FIFTH EDITION

Minton F. Goldman
Northeastern University

The Dushkin Publishing Group, Inc., Sluice Dock, Guilford, Connecticut 06437

Russia, the Eurasian Republics, and Central/Eastern Europe

OTHER BOOKS IN THE GLOBAL STUDIES SERIES

Africa
China
India and South Asia
Japan and the Pacific Rim
Latin America
The Middle East
Western Europe

Library of Congress Cataloging in Publication Data
Main entry under title: Global studies: Russia, the Eurasian Republics, and Central/Eastern Europe.
    1. Russia—History–1994. 2. Eurasian Republics—History–1994. 3. Central Europe—History–1994.
    4. Eastern Europe—History–1994.
I. Title: Russia, the Eurasian Republics, and Central/Eastern Europe. II. Goldman, Minton F., *comp.*
ISBN 1–56134–293–9   94–071537

Fifth Edition

Printed in the United States of America

 Printed on recycled paper

Russia, the Eurasian Republics, and Central/Eastern Europe

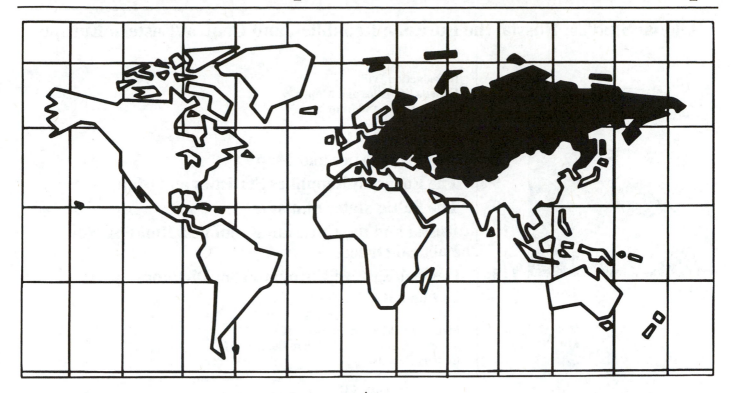

AUTHOR/EDITOR

Dr. Minton F. Goldman

The author and editor of *Global Studies: Russia, the Eurasian Republics, and Central/Eastern Europe* is associate professor of political science at Northeastern University in Boston, Massachusetts. He has published book reviews and articles on European diplomacy and Soviet foreign policy in the *Journal of Southeast Asian Studies, Revue d'Histoire Maghrebine, Polity, East European Quarterly, Il Politico,* and *Comparative Strategy.* He has contributed chapters to *Dynamics of the Third World, The Presidency and National Security Policy,* and *President Carter and Foreign Policy.* Dr. Goldman has traveled extensively in Central/Eastern Europe and the former Soviet Union and has presented numerous papers on panels of professional conferences in the United States and abroad. He is also the recipient of Northeastern University's "Excellence in Teaching" award.

SERIES CONSULTANT

H. Thomas Collins
Washington, D.C.

Contents

Global Studies: Russia, the Eurasian Republics, and Central/Eastern Europe

Page 14

Page 74

Page 89

Introduction   viii
Canada Statistics and Map   x
U.S. Statistics and Map   xi
World Map   xii
Regional Map   2

4   **Russia Statistics and Map**

5   **The Eurasian Republics Statistics and Map**

9   **The Baltic States Statistics**

10   **Russia and the Eurasian Republics: Building New Political Orders**

113   **Central/Eastern Europe: From Dictatorship to Democracy**

Map: Central/Eastern Europe   113
Regional Essay: Central Eastern Europe   114
Country Reports:

    Albania   137
    Bulgaria   143
    Czechoslovakia (The Czech Republic and Slovakia)   150
    Hungary   160
    Poland   169
    Romania   183
    Yugoslavia (The Republics of the former Yugoslavia)   191

208   **Articles From the World Press**

Annotated Table of Contents for Articles   208
Topic Guide   210

Page 166

Page 175

Articles:

Russia

1. **Why the Soviet Economy Failed,** H. Brand, *Dissent,* Spring 1992. 212
2. **Russia: Yeltsin's Kingdom or Parliament's Playground?** Stephen White, *Current History,* October 1993. 222
3. **No Reason to Cheer,** Jill Smolowe, *Time,* December 27, 1993. 227
4. **Privatization in the Former Soviet Empire,** Stephen S. Cohen and Andrew Schwartz, *The American Prospect,* Spring 1993. 229
5. **Social Problems in Russia,** David E. Powell, *Current History,* October 1993. 235
6. **Will Russia Disintegrate into Bantustans?** Bogdan Szajkowski, *The World Today,* August/September 1993. 241
7. **Sacrificed to the Superpower,** Michael Dobbs, *Washington Post National Weekly Edition,* September 20–26, 1993. 248

Eurasian Republics

8. **Active Leadership: Russia's Role in Central Asia,** Vitaly Naumkin, *Harvard International Review,* Spring 1993. 252
9. **On Its Own: Islam in Post-Soviet Central Asia,** Shirin Akiner, *Harvard International Review,* Spring 1993. 255
10. **Russia and the Caucasus: Empire in Transition,** Daniel Sneider, *Christian Science Monitor,* December 13, 1993. 259
11. **Estonia Leads Baltic States into New Era,** Daniel Sneider, *Christian Science Monitor,* January 25, 1993. 263

Central and Eastern Europe

12. **Nationalism Redux: Through the Glass of the Post-Communist States Darkly,** Steven L. Burg, *Current History,* April 1993. 265
13. **Albania's Road to Democracy,** Elez Biberaj, *Current History,* November 1993. 270
14. **Bulgaria: Stable Ground in the Balkans?** Luan Troxel, *Current History,* November 1993. 275
15. **After the Uncoupling, Slovakia Seems Unnerved,** Jane Perlez, *New York Times,* July 30, 1993. 280
16. **Hungary: Counting the Social Cost of Change,** Rudolf Andorka, *The World Today,* April 1993. 281
17. **Poland Turns the Corner,** Francine S. Kiefer, *Christian Science Monitor,* May 26, 1993. 285
18. **Communism's Staying Power in Romania,** Mike Maturo, *The World & I,* May 1993. 287
19. **Why Yugoslavia Fell Apart,** Steven L. Burg, *Current History,* November 1993. 291

Credits 298
Glossary of Terms and Abbreviations 299
Bibliography 301
Sources for Statistical Summaries 303
Country Review Form 304
Index 305

Introduction

THE GLOBAL AGE

As we approach the end of the twentieth century, it is clear that the future we face will be considerably more international in nature than ever believed possible in the past. Each day print and broadcast journalists make us aware that our world is becoming increasingly smaller and substantially more interdependent.

World food shortages, the arms trade, and regional conflicts in Central America, the Middle East, the dissolution of communism in what was the Soviet Union and Eastern Europe, and other areas that threaten to involve us all make it clear that the distinctions between domestic and foreign problems are all too often artificial—that many seemingly domestic problems no longer stop at national boundaries. As Rene Dubos, the 1969 Pulitzer Prize recipient stated: "[I]t becomes obvious that each (of us) has two countries, (our) own and planet Earth." As global interdependence has become a reality, it has become vital for the citizens of this world to develop literacy in global matters.

THE GLOBAL STUDIES SERIES

It is the aim of this Global Studies series to help readers acquire a basic knowledge and understanding of the regions and countries in the world. Each volume provides a foundation of information—geographic, cultural, economic, political, historical, artistic, and religous—that will allow readers to better understand the current and future problems within these countries and regions and to comprehend how events there might affect their own well-being. In short, these volumes attempt to provide the background information necessary to respond to the realities of our Global Age.

Author and Editor
Each of the volumes in the Global Studies series has been crafted under the careful direction of an author/editor—an expert in the area under study. The author/editors teach and conduct research and have travelled extensively through the countries about which they are writing.

In this *Russia, the Eurasian Republics, and Central/Eastern Europe* volume, the author/editor has written the regional essays and the country reports. In addition, he has been instrumental in the selection of the world press articles that relate to each of the regional sections.

Contents and Features
The Global Studies volumes are organized to provide concise information and current world press articles on the regions and countries within those areas under study.

Regional Essays
Global Studies: Russia, the Eurasian Republics, and Central/Eastern Europe, Fifth Edition, covers Russia, the Eur-

(United Nations photo/Yutaka Nagata)
The global age is making all countries and all people more interdependent.

asian republics, the Baltics (Estonia, Latvia, and Lithuania), and Central/Eastern Europe—Albania, Bulgaria, Czechoslovakia (now the Czech Republic and Slovakia), Hungary, Poland, Romania, and the republics of the former Yugoslavia (Bosnia-Herzegovina, Croatia, Macedonia, Serbia, Montenegro, and Slovenia). For Russia and the Eurasian republics region, as well as European regions, the author/editor has written narrative essays focusing on the cultural, sociopolitical, and economic differences and similarities of the countries and people in the regions. The purpose of the regional essays is to provide readers with an effective sense of the diversity of the areas as well as an understanding of their common cultural and historical backgrounds. Accompanying the regional essays are full-page maps showing the political boundaries of each of the countries within the regions.

Country Reports
Concise reports are written for each of the countries within the region under study. These reports are the heart of each Global Studies volume. *Global Studies: Russia, the Eurasian Republics, and Central/Eastern Europe, Fifth Edition*, contains seven country reports, covering the Central/Eastern European countries.

The country reports are comprised of five standard elements. Each report contains a small map visually positioning the country amongst its neighboring states; a summary of statistical information (in the case of the Eurasian republics, the Baltics, Czech Republic/Slovakia, and the republics of the former Yugoslavia, the statistics have been abbreviated due to the lack of available figures); a current essay providing important historical, geographical, political, cultural, and economic information; a historical timeline offering a convenient visual survey of a few key historical events; and four graphic indicators, with summary statements about the country in terms of development, freedom, health/welfare, and achievements, at the end of each report.

A Note on the Statistical Summaries

The statistical information provided for each country has been drawn from a wide range of sources. The nine most frequently referenced are listed on page 303. Every effort has been made to provide the most current and accurate information available. However, occasionally the information cited by these sources differs to some extent, and, all too often, the most current information available for some countries is dated. Aside from these discrepancies, the statistical summary of each country is generally quite complete and reasonably current. Care should be taken, however, in using these statistics (or, for that matter, any published statistics) in making hard comparisons among countries. We have also included comparable statistics on Canada and the United States, which follow on the next two pages.

World-Press Articles

Within each Global Studies volume are reprinted a large number of articles carefully selected by our editorial staff and the author/editor from a broad range of international periodicals and newspapers. The articles have been chosen for currency, interest, and their differing perspectives on the subject countries and regions. There are a total of nineteen articles in *Global Studies: Russia, the Eurasian Republics, and Central/Eastern Europe, Fifth Edition.*

The articles section is preceded by a *Topic Guide* as well as an *Annotated Table of Contents.* The Annotated Table of Contents offers a brief summary of each article, while the Topic Guide indicates the main theme(s) of each article. Thus, readers desiring to focus on articles dealing with a particular theme, say, human rights, may refer to the Topic Guide to find those articles.

Glossary, Bibliography, Index, and Appendices

At the back of each Global Studies volume, readers will find a *Glossary of Terms and Abbreviations*, which provides a quick reference to the specialized vocabulary of the area under study and to the standard abbreviations (KGB, CMEA, etc.) used throughout the volume.

Following the Glossary is a *Bibliography*, which is organized into general-reference volumes, national and regional histories, current-events publications, and journals that provide regular coverage on Russia and Central/Eastern Europe.

The *Index* at the end of the volume is an accurate reference to the contents of the volume. Readers seeking specific information and citations should consult this standard index.

Currency and Usefulness

This fifth edition of *Global Studies: Russia, the Eurasian Republics, and Central/Eastern Europe,* like other Global Studies volumes, is intended to provide the most current and useful information available necessary to understand the events that are shaping the cultures of the region today.

We plan to issue this volume on a regular basis. The statistics will be updated, regional essays rewritten, country reports revised, and articles completely replaced as new and current information becomes available. In order to accomplish this task we will turn to our author/editor, our advisory boards and—hopefully—to you, the users of this volume. Your comments are more than welcome. If you have an idea that you think will make the volume more useful, an article or bit of information that will make it more current, or a general comment on its organization, content, or features that you would like to share with us, please send it in for serious consideration for the next edition.

(United Nations photo/P. Teuscher)
Understanding the problems and lifestyles of other countries will help make us literate in global matters.

Canada

GEOGRAPHY

Area in Square Kilometers (Miles):
9,976,140 (3,850,790) (slightly larger than the United States)
Capital (Population): Ottawa (920,000)
Climate: from temperate in south to subarctic and arctic in north

PEOPLE

Population
Total: 27,797,000
Annual Growth Rate: 1.28%
Rural/Urban Population Ratio: 23/77
Ethnic Makeup of Population: 40% British Isles origin; 27% French origin; 20% other European; 1.5% indigenous Indian and Eskimo; 11.5% mixed
Languages: both English and French are official

Health
Life Expectancy at Birth: 75 years (male); 82 years (female)
Infant Mortality Rate (Ratio): 7/1,000
Average Caloric Intake: 127% of FAO minimum
Physicians Available (Ratio): 1/449

Religion(s)
46% Roman Catholic; 16% United Church; 10% Anglican; 28% others

Education
Adult Literacy Rate: 99%

COMMUNICATION

Telephones: 18,000,000
Newspapers: 96 in English; 11 in French

TRANSPORTATION

Highways—Kilometers (Miles):
884,272 (549,133)
Railroads—Kilometers (Miles):
146,444 (90,942)
Usable Airfields: 1,142

GOVERNMENT

Type: confederation with parliamentary democracy
Independence Date: July 1, 1867
Head of State: Queen Elizabeth II
Head of Government: Prime Minister Jean Chrétien
Political Parties: Progressive Conservative Party; Liberal Party; New Democratic Party; Reform Party; Bloc Québécois
Suffrage: universal at 18

MILITARY

Number of Armed Forces: 88,000
Military Expenditures (% of Central Government Expenditures): 8.7%
Current Hostilities: none

ECONOMY

Currency ($U.S. Equivalent): 1.27 Canadian dollars = $1
Per Capita Income/GDP: $19,600/$537.1 billion
Inflation Rate: 1.5%
Total Foreign Debt: $247 billion
Natural Resources: petroleum; natural gas; fish; minerals; cement; forestry products; fur
Agriculture: grains; livestock; dairy products; potatoes; hogs; poultry and eggs; tobacco
Industry: oil production and refining; natural-gas development; fish products; wood and paper products; chemicals; transportation equipment

FOREIGN TRADE

Exports: $124 billion
Imports: $118 billion

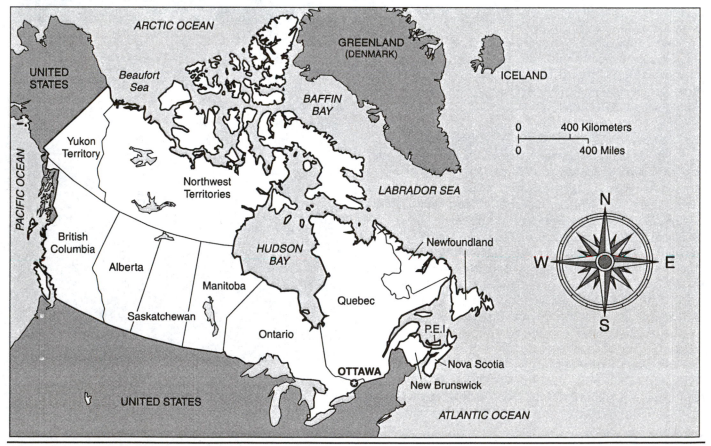

The United States

GEOGRAPHY

Area in Square Kilometers (Miles):
9,578,626 (3,618,770)
Capital (Population): Washington,
D.C. (606,900)
Climate: temperate

PEOPLE

Population
Total: 258,103,700
Annual Growth Rate: 1.02%
Rural/Urban Population Ratio: 26/74
Ethnic Makeup of Population: 80%
white; 12% black; 6% Hispanic; 2%
Asian, Pacific Islander, American Indian, Eskimo, and Aleut
Languages: predominantly English; a
sizable Spanish-speaking minority

Health
Life Expectancy at Birth: 72 years
(male); 79 years (female)
Infant Mortality Rate (Ratio):
8.3/1,000
Average Caloric Intake: 138% of
FAO minimum
Physicians Available (Ratio): 1/404

Religion(s)
55% Protestant; 36% Roman Catholic; 4% Jewish; 5% Muslim and others

Education
Adult Literacy Rate: 97.9% (official)
(estimates vary widely)

COMMUNICATION

Telephones: 182,558,000
Newspapers: 1,679 dailies; approximately 63,000,000 circulation

TRANSPORTATION

Highways—Kilometers (Miles):
7,599,250 (4,719,134)
Railroads—Kilometers (Miles):
270,312 (167,974)
Usable Airfields: 12,417

GOVERNMENT

Type: federal republic
Independence Date: July 4, 1776
Head of State: President William
("Bill") Jefferson Clinton
Political Parties: Democratic Party;
Republican Party; others of minor political significance
Suffrage: universal at 18

MILITARY

Number of Armed Forces: 1,807,177
*Military Expenditures (% of Central
Government Expenditures):* 22.6%
Current Hostilities: none

ECONOMY

Per Capita Income/GDP:
$23,400/$5.95 trillion
Inflation Rate: 3%
Natural Resources: metallic and nonmetallic minerals; petroleum; arable
land
Agriculture: food grains; feed crops;
oil-bearing crops; livestock; dairy
products
Industry: diversified in both capital-
and consumer-goods industries

FOREIGN TRADE

Exports: $442 billion
Imports: $544 billion

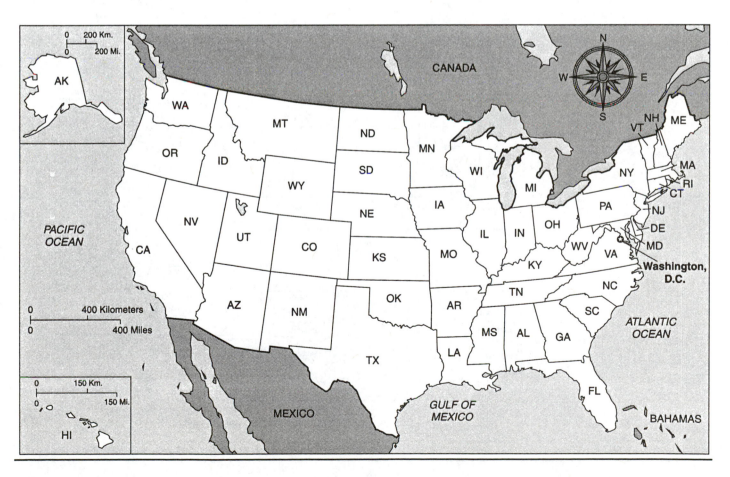

GLOBAL  STUDIES

This map of the world highlights Russia, the Eurasian Republics, and Central/Eastern European countries that are discussed in this volume. All of the following essays are written from a cultural perspective in order to give the readers a sense of what life is like in these countries. The essays are designed to present the most current and useful information available. Other books in the Global Studies series cover different global areas and examine the current state of affairs of the countries within those regions.

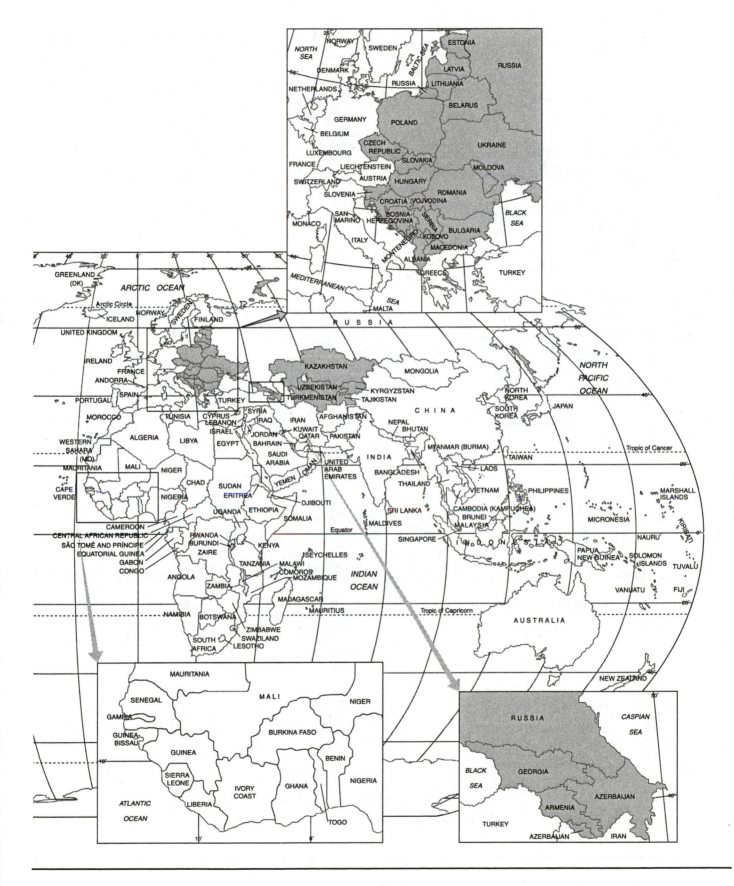

Russia, the Eurasian Republics, and Central/Eastern Europe

0 Kilometers 2000

0 Miles 2000

NORTH ATLANTIC OCEAN

NORWEGIAN SEA

BARENTS SEA

KARA SEA

RUSSIA

NORTH SEA

NORWAY

SWEDEN

FINLAND

Tallin
1

Riga
2

Vilnius

Moscow

UNITED KINGDOM

GERMANY

POLAND

Warsaw

5 Minsk

KAZAKHSTAN

FRANCE

Prague 6

Bratislava

7 8

Budapest

UKRAINE

Kiev

19 Kishinev

Alma-Ata

Bashkik

UZBEKISTAN

23

9

ROMANIA

Bucharest

11

13

Sofia 18

Tbilisi

Tashkent

Dushanbe

TURKMENISTAN

24

10

ITALY

14 15 17

Yerevan 21 22 Baku

Ashkhabad

AFGHANISTAN

PAKISTAN

SPAIN

16

20

SYRIA

IRAN

TURKEY

GREECE

IRAQ

SAUDI ARABIA

ALGERIA

LIBYA

EGYPT

INDIAN OCEAN

1. ESTONIA
2. LATVIA
3. LITHUANIA
4. RUSSIA
5. BELARUS
6. CZECH REPUBLIC
7. SLOVAKIA
8. HUNGARY
9. SLOVENIA (Ljubljana)
10. CROATIA (Zagreb)
11. BOSNIA-HERZEGOVINA (Sarajevo)
12. VOJVODINA (Novi Sad)

13. SERBIA (Belgrade)
14. MONTENEGRO (Titograd)
15. KOSOVO (Pristina)
16. ALBANIA (Tirana)
17. MACEDONIA (Skopje)
18. BULGARIA
19. MOLDOVA
20. GEORGIA
21. ARMENIA
22. AZERBAIJAN
23. KYRGYZSTAN
24. TAJIKISTAN

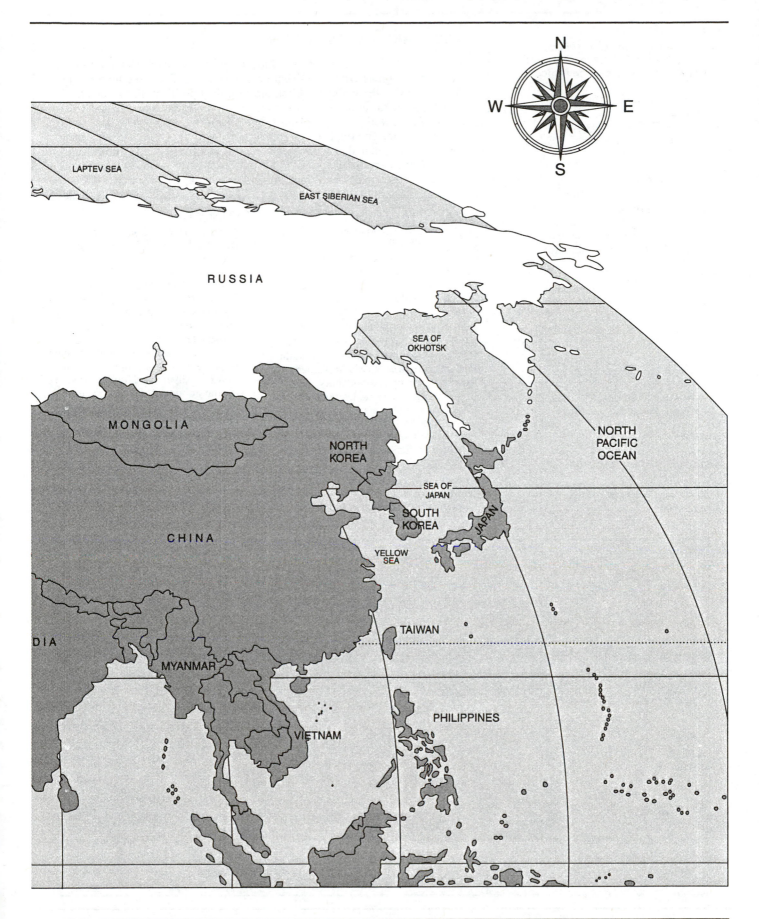

Russia (Russian Federation)

GEOGRAPHY

Area in Square Kilometers (Miles):
17,075,200 (6,591,027) (slightly more than 1.8 times the size of the United States)
Capital (Population): Moscow (8,800,000)
Climate: varied; generally, long, cold winters and short summers

PEOPLE

Population
Total: 149,300,400
Annual Growth Rate: 0.21%
Rural/Urban Population Ratio: 26/74
Ethnic Makeup of Population: 82% Russian; 4% Tatar; 3% Ukrainian; 1% Chuvash; 1% Bashkir; 1% Belarussian; 1% Moldavian; 7% others

Health
Life Expectancy at Birth: 64 years (male); 74 years (female)
Infant Mortality Rate (Ratio): 27.6/1,000
Average Caloric Intake: 130% of FAO minimum
Physicians Available (Ratio): 1/222

Religion(s)
18% Russian Orthodox; 9% Muslim; 3% Jewish, Protestant, Georgian Orthodox, or Roman Catholic; 70% atheist

Education
Adult Literacy Rate: 99% (official)

COMMUNICATION
Telephones: 24,400,000
Newspapers: 8,285

A DYNAMIC PLACE IN HISTORY

A man of Mikhail Gorbachev's achievements is not ready for retirement, although his job as Soviet president no longer exists. For more than 8 years Gorbachev was the world's boldest, most original political thinker and tactician. He made the arms race an anchronism, he ended the cold war, and he led his people, as well as the people of Central/Eastern Europe, to abandon faith in communism. The ripple effect of that move will be seen in not only those nations still committed to communism, in particular China, Cuba, North Korea, and North Vietnam, but also in the West, which no longer has to mobilize enormous resources to contain Soviet political and military aggrandizement.

TRANSPORTATION
Highways—Kilometers (Miles): 893,000 (553,660)
Railroads—Kilometers (Miles): 158,100 (98,022)
Usable Airfields: 964

GOVERNMENT
Type: federation
Independence Date: August 24, 1991
Chief of State: Boris Nikolayevich Yeltsin
Political Parties: Christian Democratic Party; Democratic Russia Movement; Russia's Choice; Russian Unity; Republic Party; Liberal Democrats; Civic Union; Labor Party; Russian Communist Worker's Party; Russian Party of Communists; others
Suffrage: universal over 18

MILITARY
Number of Armed Forces: n/a
Military Expenditures (% of Central Government Expenditures): n/a
Current Hostilities: none

ECONOMY
Currency ($ U.S. Equivalent): 1,772 rubles = $1 (official); actual value is a fraction of this figure
Per Capita Income/GDP: n/a
Inflation Rate: 25% per month
Natural Resources: fossil fuels; waterpower; timber; manganese; lead; zinc; nickel; mercury; potash; phosphate
Agriculture: wheat; rye; oats; potatoes; sugar beets; cotton; sunflowers; flax
Industry: diversified: highly developed capital goods industries; consumer goods industries comparatively less developed

FOREIGN TRADE
Exports: $39.2 billion
Imports: $35 billion

The Eurasian Republics

ARMENIA

GEOGRAPHY
Area in Square Kilometers (Miles):
29,800 (11,503) (slightly larger than Maryland)
Capital (Population): Yerevan (n/a)

PEOPLE

Population
Total: 3,481,000
Annual Growth Rate: 1.23%
Ethnic Makeup of Population: 93% Armenian; 3% Azerbaijani; 2% Russian; 2% others
Major Languages: Armenian; Azeri; Russian; others

Health
Life Expectancy at Birth: 68 years (male); 75 years (female)
Infant Mortality Rate (Ratio): 28/1,000

Religion(s)
94% Armenian Orthodox; 6% others

Education
Adult Literacy Rate: 100% (official)

GOVERNMENT
Type: republic
Head of State: President Levon Akopovich Ter-Petrosyan
Political Parties: Armenian National Movement; National Democratic Union; National Self-Determination Association; Armenian Democratic Liberal Organization; Armenian Revolutionary Federation; Christian Democratic; others

ECONOMY
Currency ($ U.S. Equivalent): 415 rubles = $1 (subject to wide fluctuations)
Per Capita Income/GDP: n/a
Inflation Rate: 20% per month

FOREIGN TRADE
Exports: $30 million
Imports: $300 million

AZERBAIJAN

GEOGRAPHY
Area in Square Kilometers (Miles):
86,600 (33,428) (slightly larger than Maine)
Capital (Population): Baku (n/a)

PEOPLE

Population
Total: 7,573,500
Annual Growth Rate: 1.5%
Ethnic Makeup of Population: 83% Azerbaijani; 6% Russian; 6% Armenian; 3% Daghestani; 2% others
Major Languages: Azeri; Russian; Armenian; others

Health
Life Expectancy at Birth: 67 years (male); 75 years (female)
Infant Mortality Rate (Ratio): 35/1,000

Religion(s)
87% Muslim; 6% Russian Orthodox; 6% Armenian Orthodox; 1% others

Education
Adult Literacy Rate: 100% (official)

GOVERNMENT
Type: republic
Head of State: President Geidar Aliyev
Political Parties: New Azerbaijan Party; Musavat Party; National Independence Party; Social Democratic Party; Party of Revolutionary Revival (successor to the Communist Party); Party of Independent Azerbaijan

ECONOMY
Currency ($ U.S. Equivalent): 1 manat = 10 Russian rubles (U.S. $1 equivalency n/a)
Per Capita Income/GDP: n/a
Inflation Rate: 20% per month

FOREIGN TRADE
Exports: $821 million
Imports: $300 million

BELARUS

GEOGRAPHY

Area in Square Kilometers (Miles):
207,600 (80,134) (slightly smaller than Kansas)
Capital (Population): Minsk (1,600,000)

PEOPLE

Population

Total: 10,370,300
Annual Growth Rate: 0.34%
Ethnic Makeup of Population: 79% Belarussian; 13% Russian; 4% Polish; 3% Ukrainian; 1% others
Major Languages: Belarussian; Russian; others

Health

Life Expectancy at Birth: 66 years (male); 76 years (female)
Infant Mortality Rate (Ratio): 19/1,000

Religion(s)

Eastern Orthodox; others

Education

Adult Literacy Rate: 100% (official)

GOVERNMENT

Type: republic
Head of State: Chairperson of the Supreme Soviet Mechislav Grib
Political Parties: Belarussian Popular Front; United Democratic Party; Social Democratic Party; Belarus Workers Union; Communist Party; others

ECONOMY

Currency ($ U.S. Equivalent): 1 ruble = 10 Russian rubles (U.S. equivalency n/a)
Per Capita Income/GDP: n/a
Inflation Rate: 30% per month

FOREIGN TRADE

Exports: $1.1 billion
Imports: $751 million

GEORGIA

GEOGRAPHY

Area in Square Kilometers (Miles):
69,700 (26,904) (slightly larger than South Carolina)
Capital (Population): Tbilisi (1,200,000)

PEOPLE

Population

Total: 5,634,000
Annual Growth Rate: 0.85%
Ethnic Makeup of Population: 70% Georgian; 8% Armenian; 6% Russian; 6% Azerbaijani; 10% Ossetian, Abkhaz, and others
Major Languages: Georgian; Russian; Armenian; Azeri; others

Health

Life Expectancy at Birth: 69 years (male); 76 years (female)
Infant Mortality Rate (Ratio): 16/1,000

Religion(s)

65% Georgian Orthodox; 11% Muslim; 10% Russian Orthodox; 8% Armenian; 6% unknown

Education

Adult Literacy Rate: 100% (official)

GOVERNMENT

Type: republic
Head of State: President Eduard A. Shevardnadze
Political Parties: All-Georgian Merab Kostava Society; All-Georgian Traditionalists; Georgian National Front; Georgian Social Democratic Party; Green Party; Georgian Popular Front; National Democratic Party; National Independence Party; others

ECONOMY

Currency ($ U.S. Equivalent): (currently retaining Russian ruble) 1,772 rubles = $1 (official)
Per Capita Income/GDP: n/a
Inflation Rate: 50% per month

FOREIGN TRADE

Exports: n/a
Imports: n/a

KAZAKHSTAN

GEOGRAPHY

Area in Square Kilometers (Miles):
2,717,300 (1,048,878) (slightly larger than 4 times the size of Texas)
Capital (Population): Almy (formerly Alma-Ata) (1,100,000)

PEOPLE

Population

Total: 17,156,500
Annual Growth Rate: 0.65%
Ethnic Makeup of Population: 42% Kazakh; 37% Russian; 5% Ukrainian; 5% German; 2% Uzbek; 2% Tatar; 7% others
Major Languages: Kazakj; Russian

Health

Life Expectancy at Birth: 63 years (male); 73 years (female)
Infant Mortality Rate (Ratio): 8/1,000

Religion(s)

47% Muslim; 15% Russian Orthodox; 2% Protestant; 36% others

Education

Adult Literacy Rate: 100% (official)

GOVERNMENT

Type: republic
Head of State: President Nursultan A. Nazarbayev
Political Parties: People's Congress; Kazakh Socialist Party (former Communist Party); December Movement; Freedom Party

ECONOMY

Currency ($ U.S. Equivalent): (currently retaining Russian ruble) 1,772 rubles = $1 (official)
Per Capita Income/GDP: n/a
Inflation Rate: 28% per month

FOREIGN TRADE

Exports: $1.5 billion
Imports: $500 million

KYRGYZSTAN

GEOGRAPHY
Area in Square Kilometers (Miles):
198,500 (76,621) (slightly smaller than
South Dakota)
Capital (Population): Bishkek
(631,000)

PEOPLE

Population
Total: 4,626,000
Annual Growth Rate: 1.56%
Ethnic Makeup of Population: 52%
Kirghiz; 22% Russian; 13% Uzbek;
4% Ukrainian; 2% German; 7% others
Major Languages: Kirghiz; Russian

Health
Life Expectancy at Birth: 63 years
(male); 72 years (female)
Infant Mortality Rate (Ratio): 49/1,000

Religion(s)
70% Muslim; Russian Orthodox (n/a)

Education
Adult Literacy Rate: 100% (official)

GOVERNMENT
Type: republic
Head of State: President Askar Akayev

Political Parties: Kyrgyz Democratic
Movement; Civic Accord; National
Revived Asaba Party; Communist Party

ECONOMY
Currency ($ U.S. Equivalent):
(currently retaining Russian ruble)
1,772 rubles = $1 (official)
Per Capita Income/GDP: n/a
Inflation Rate: 29% per month

FOREIGN TRADE
Exports: n/a
Imports: n/a

MOLDOVA

GEOGRAPHY
Area in Square Kilometers (Miles):
33,700 (13,008) (slightly more than
twice the size of Hawaii)
Capital (Population): Chisineau
(formerly Kishinev) (753,000)

PEOPLE

Population
Total: 4,456,000
Annual Growth Rate: 0.4%
Ethnic Makeup of Population: 65%
Moldovan/Romanian; 14% Ukrainian;
13% Russian; 8% Gagauz, Bulgarian,
and others
Major Languages: Moldovan;
Romanian; Russian

Health
Life Expectancy at Birth: 64 years
(male); 72 years (female)
Infant Mortality Rate (Ratio): 31/1,000

Religion(s)
99% Eastern Orthodox; 1% Jewish

Education
Adult Literacy Rate: 100% (official)

GOVERNMENT
Type: republic
Head of State: President Mircea
Ivanovich Snegur

Political Parties: Christian Democratic
Popular Front; Yedinstvo Movement;
Social Democratic Party; Agrarian
Democratic Party; Democratic Party;
Democratic Labor Party; others

ECONOMY
Currency ($ U.S. Equivalent):
(currently using Russian ruble until
Moldovan lei is introduced)
1,772 rubles = $1 (official)
Per Capita Income/GDP: n/a
Inflation Rate: 27% per month

FOREIGN TRADE
Exports: $100 million
Imports: $100 million

TAJIKISTAN

GEOGRAPHY
Area in Square Kilometers (Miles):
143,100 (55,237) (slightly smaller than
Wisconsin)
Capital (Population): Dushanbe (n/a)

PEOPLE

Population
Total: 5,836,000
Annual Growth Rate: 2.72%
Ethnic Makeup of Population: 65%
Tajik; 25% Uzbek; 3% Russian; 7%
others
Major Languages: Tajik; Russian

Health
Life Expectancy at Birth: 66 years
(male); 71 years (female)
Infant Mortality Rate (Ratio): 64/1,000

Religion(s)
80% Sunni Muslim; 5% Shia Muslim;
15% others

Education
Adult Literacy Rate: 100% (official)

GOVERNMENT
Type: republic
Head of State: Acting President and
Assembly Chairperson Emomili
Rakhmanov

Political Parties: Tajik Democratic
Party; Tajik Socialist Party; Islamic
Revival Party; others

ECONOMY
Currency ($ U.S. Equivalent):
(currently retaining Russian ruble)
1,772 rubles = $1 (official)
Per Capita Income/GDP: n/a
Inflation Rate: 35% per month

FOREIGN TRADE
Exports: $100 million
Imports: $100 million

TURKMENISTAN

GEOGRAPHY
Area in Square Kilometers (Miles):
488,100 (188,407) (slightly larger than California)
Capital (Population): Ashkhabad (Ashgabat) (416,000)

PEOPLE

Population
Total: 3,915,000
Annual Growth Rate: 2.04%
Ethnic Makeup of Population: 73% Turkmen; 10% Russian; 9% Uzbek; 2% Kazakh; 6% others
Major Languages: Turkmen; Russian; Uzbek; others

Health
Life Expectancy at Birth: 61 years (male); 69 years (female)
Infant Mortality Rate (Ratio): 8/1,000

Religion(s)
87% Muslim; 11% Eastern Orthodox; 2% unknown

Education
Adult Literacy Rate: 100% (official)

GOVERNMENT
Type: republic
Head of State: President Saparmurad Niyazov
Political Parties: Democratic Party (formerly Communist Party); Party for Democratic Development; Agzybirlik Party

ECONOMY
Currency ($ U.S. Equivalent): (manat to be established; currently using Russian ruble) 1,772 rubles = $1 (official)
Per Capita Income/GDP: n/a
Inflation Rate: 53% per month

FOREIGN TRADE
Exports: $100 million
Imports: $100 million

UKRAINE

GEOGRAPHY
Area in Square Kilometers (Miles):
603,700 (233,028) (slightly smaller than Texas)
Capital (Population): Kiev (2,637,000)

PEOPLE

Population
Total: 51,821,000
Annual Growth Rate: 0.06%
Ethnic Makeup of Population: 73% Ukrainian; 22% Russian; 5% others
Major Languages: Ukrainian; Russian; Romanian; Polish

Health
Life Expectancy at Birth: 65 years (male); 75 years (female)
Infant Mortality Rate (Ratio): 21/1,000

Religion(s)
Ukrainian Orthodox; Kiev Patriarchate; Ukrainian Autocephalous Orthodox; Ukrainian Catholic; Protestant; Jewish (percentages unknown)

Education
Adult Literacy Rate: 100% (official)

GOVERNMENT
Type: republic
Head of State: President Leonid M. Kravchuk
Political Parties: Green Party; Liberal Party; Liberal Democratic Party; Democratic Party; People's Party; ·Social Democratic Party; Ukrainian Christian Democratic Party; Ukrainian Conservative Party; Ukrainian Republican Party; others

ECONOMY
Currency ($ U.S. Equivalent): 3,000 karbovantsi = $1
Per Capita Income/GDP: n/a
Inflation Rate: 20%–30% per month

FOREIGN TRADE
Exports: $13.5 billion
Imports: $16.7 billion

UZBEKISTAN

GEOGRAPHY
Area in Square Kilometers (Miles):
447,440 (172,696) (slightly larger than California)
Capital (Population): Tashkent (n/a)

PEOPLE

Population
Total: 22,128,000
Annual Growth Rate: 2.17%
Ethnic Makeup of Population: 71% Uzbek; 8% Russian; 5% Tajik; 4% Kazakh; 2% Tartar; 2% Karakalpak; 8% others
Major Languages: Uzbek; Russian; others

Health
Life Expectancy at Birth: 65 years (male); 75 years (female)
Infant Mortality Rate (Ratio): 21/1,000

Religion(s)
88% Muslim (mostly Sunni); 9% Eastern Orthodox; 3% others

Education
Adult Literacy Rate: 100% (official)

GOVERNMENT
Type: republic
Head of State: President Islam Karimov
Political Parties: People's Democratic Party (formerly the Communist Party); Democratic Party; People's Movement; others

ECONOMY
Currency ($ U.S. Equivalent): (currently retaining Russian ruble) 1,772 rubles = $1 (official)
Per Capita Income/GDP: n/a
Inflation Rate: 17% per month

FOREIGN TRADE
Exports: $900 million
Imports: $900 million

The Baltic States

ESTONIA

GEOGRAPHY

Area in Square Kilometers (Miles):
45,100 (17,409) (slightly larger than Vermont and New Hampshire combined)
Capital (Population): Tallinn (502,000)

PEOPLE

Population
Total: 1,608,500
Annual Growth Rate: 0.52%
Ethnic Makeup of Population: 62% Estonian; 30% Russian; 3% Ukrainian; 2% Belarussian; 2% Finnish; 1% others

Major Languages: Estonian; Latvian; Lithuanian; Russian; others

Health
Life Expectancy at Birth: 65 years (male); 75 years (female)
Infant Mortality Rate (Ratio): 19/1,000

Religion(s)
primarily Lutheran

Education
Adult Literacy Rate: 100% (official)

GOVERNMENT

Type: republic
Head of State: President Lennart Meri
Political Parties: Popular Front; Christian Democratic Party; Estonian Christian Democratic Union; Estonian Heritage Society; National Independence Party; Social Democratic Party; Independent Estonian Communist Party; People's Centrist Party; Estonian Royalist Party; others

ECONOMY

Currency ($ U.S. Equivalent): 12 Estonian kroon = $1
Per Capita Income/GDP: n/a
Inflation Rate: 1%–2% per month

FOREIGN TRADE

Exports: n/a
Imports: n/a

LATVIA

GEOGRAPHY

Area in Square Kilometers (Miles):
64,100 (24,743) (slightly larger than West Virginia)
Capital (Population): Riga (910,000)

PEOPLE

Population
Total: 2,735,600
Annual Growth Rate: 0.5%
Ethnic Makeup of Population: 52% Latvian; 34% Russian; 5% Belarussian; 5% Ukrainian; 2% Polish; 2% others
Major Languages: Latvian (official); Lithuanian; Russian; others

Health
Life Expectancy at Birth: 69 years (male); 75 years (female)
Infant Mortality Rate (Ratio): 22/1,000

Religion(s)
Lutheran; Roman Catholic; Russian Orthodox

Education
Adult Literacy Rate: 100% (official)

GOVERNMENT

Type: republic
Chief of State: Chairman Supreme Council Anatolijs V. Gorbunovs
Political Parties: Democratic Labor Party of Latvia; Inter-Front of the Working People of Latvia; Latvian Democratic Party; Social Democratic Workers' Party; Latvian People's Front; Liberal Party; others

ECONOMY

Currency ($ U.S. Equivalent): 1.32 lats = $1 (official)
Per Capita Income/GDP: n/a
Inflation Rate: n/a

FOREIGN TRADE

Exports: n/a
Imports: n/a

LITHUANIA

GEOGRAPHY

Area in Square Kilometers (Miles):
65,200 (25,167) (slightly larger than West Virginia)
Capital (Population): Vilnius (597,000)

PEOPLE

Population
Total: 3,819,700
Annual Growth Rate: 0.76%
Ethnic Makeup of Population: 80% Lithuanian; 9% Russian; 8% Polish; 3% others
Major Languages: Lithuanian (official); Polish; Russian

Health
Life Expectancy at Birth: 71 years (male); 76 years (female)
Infant Mortality Rate (Ratio): 17/1,000

Religion(s)
Roman Catholic; Lutheran; others

Education
Adult Literacy Rate: 100% (official)

GOVERNMENT

Type: republic
Chief of State: Seimas Chairperson and Acting President Algirdas Mykolas Brazauskas
Political Parties: Christian Democratic Party; Democratic Labor Party of Lithuania; Lithuanian Democratic Party; Lithuanian Green Party; Lithuanian Independence Party; Lithuanian Nationalist Union; Lithuanian Social Democratic Party; others

ECONOMY

Currency ($ U.S. Equivalent): using talonas as temporary currency; planning introduction of convertible litas; U.S. equivalency n/a
Per Capita Income/GDP: n/a
Inflation Rate: 10%–20% per month

FOREIGN TRADE

Exports: n/a
Imports: n/a

Russia and the Eurasian Republics: Building New Political Orders

WHY STUDY RUSSIA AND THE EURASIAN REPUBLICS?

A study of the newly independent Russia and the Eurasian republics casts the Soviet Communist experience in a new light. Soviet communism for generations was able to survive and maintain itself, despite its many flaws, by whatever means. People abroad as well as within the Soviet Union came to believe that Soviet communism would endure indefinitely. But the collapse of the Soviet state suggests that Soviet communism was a transitional political order that held the seeds of its own self-destruction and which led to the emergence in the republics of the former Soviet Union of a new political order called, for lack of a more precise term, post-Communist.

The former Soviet republics that, for the time being at least, now form what is known as the *Commonwealth of Independent States,* are experimenting to find an ideal or, at least, a workable and improved political order. So far they have retained some of the egalitarianism and paternalism of the old Soviet system while trying to adopt some of the political and economic liberalism of the parliamentary democracies in the West. Their attempts are complicated by the fact that the peoples of the republics that have emerged from the Soviet Union inhabit an enormous landmass that stretches across 2 continents and contains more than 286 million people with well over 100 ethnic groupings, 100 nationalities, and about 130 different languages.

The Soviet Union was the second—or possibly the first, depending on one's viewpoint—most militarily powerful political entity in the world, the leading rival and antagonist of the United States. With its enormous military power, including the most technologically advanced conventional and nuclear weapons, the former Soviet state controlled most of Central/Eastern Europe and exerted influence throughout the developing Third World. And, as the first country to develop Marxist ideas and practices, it was a role model for other societies that suffered from the same hardships that had inspired the Communist ascendancy in Russia in 1917 and the subsequent establishment of the Soviet state. How Russia and the new Eurasian republics will manage and allocate this vast military resource is now a source of considerable discussion and disagreement.

Russia and the Eurasian republics are important to the outside world, especially the West, also because international peace and stability depend on the success of their movement away from socialist authoritarianism toward political and economic democracy; the West does not want a return to Soviet-style imperialism. At the same time, the newly emancipated peoples of the former Soviet republics are not only a huge potential market for the goods and services of foreign countries, especially those that are highly industrialized, but also a reservoir of opportunities for the development of new and extensive cultural and scientific interactions that can benefit the entire world.

HOW TO STUDY RUSSIA AND THE EURASIAN REPUBLICS

Before one can understand and evaluate the region, one must understand the past, especially the recent past, of the traditional Soviet system. This essay analyzes that system, in particular its roots, how it worked, its performance problems, its effort at profound restructuring to resolve those problems, called *perestroika,* and its collapse. Following this analysis is a discussion of major problems confronting Russia and the Eurasian republics and of the chances of their survival.

A WORD ON TERMS

For decades many foreigners failed to differentiate between the terms *Russia* and *Soviet Union.* Russia referred to the largest, most populous, and most politically influential of the 15 constituent union-republics that comprised the Union of Soviet Socialist Republics, commonly known as the Soviet Union. Thus, Russia was part of the Soviet Union, not synonymous with it.

The Soviet Union was a federation that was formally established by the Soviet Communist Party in 1922. The word *Soviet* referred to the conciliar or parliamentary type of government of the federation and its constituent union-republics. The Soviet type of government prevailed in all levels of administration in the Soviet Union, down to small villages and towns. *Soviet* derived from a Russian word meaning "council." It came into popular usage in the Russian Revolutions of 1905 and 1917, when insurgent workers, peasants, and soldiers formed soviets or councils in St. Petersburg, Moscow, and other Russian cities to oppose Czarist authority and create an alternative to it.

Sometimes people intentionally used the word *Russia* when they really meant the *Soviet Union.* They did this because Russians in fact created the Soviet state and retained control of it from 1917, despite the multinational character of its society.

THE TRADITIONAL SOVIET SYSTEM

ROOTS

The roots of Soviet communism include the pre-Communist past, notably the historic, economic, and sociocultural characteristics of the Czarist political system; the principles of communist ideology; and the birth and evolution of the Soviet Communist system following the 1917 Bolshevik Revolution. A look at how the Soviet system worked, which shows how Russian Marxists used power to achieve socialism (the prerequisite for communism), describes methods of popular political participation, such as voting, interest groups, and the role of the Soviet Communist Party; and the formal structures of the Soviet government, such as the executive, legislative, and judicial branches, the bureaucracy, the economy, the social welfare system, and foreign policy making.

The "traditional Soviet political system" refers to the Marxist-Leninist polity established by the Bolsheviks (Russian followers of Karl Marx led by Vladimir Lenin in the early years of the twentieth century) after their successful revolution against the Czarist empire in November 1917. This new polity, called *socialist* and committed to the ultimate development of a communist society, transformed rural and agrarian Russia into an industrialized, semiurbanized modern society under the rule of the Communist Party until the collapse of party rule 74 years later, at the end of 1991. Much of the traditional Soviet system prevails today in Russia and the other former Soviet republics.

CZARISM

In the 3 centuries preceding the 1917 Bolshevik Revolution and the Marxist seizure of power, the Czarist government was relentlessly authoritarian. The first czar of the Romanov family, Michael, ascended the Russian throne in 1614. Nicholas II, the last Romanov czar, abdicated in 1917. Throughout these 3 centuries of Romanov rule, the power of the Czarist regime remained as autocratic, centralized, and extensive as the technology of the times permitted. The political theory of the Czarist regime—that the czar could do no wrong and accounted only to God—remained unchanged for 300 years.

The Romanov czars devised a variety of administrative measures to enforce political obedience, including a gargantuan bureaucracy and a ruthless secret police. Their power was nearly absolute, and the vast majority of their subjects had almost no way to influence them. Late-nineteenth-century czars, notably Alexander III (1881–1894) and Nicholas II (1894–1917), also had an obsessive drive to unify their multinational empire and reinforce their autocratic rule. They tried to impose the Russian language and the Russian Orthodox faith on non-Russian minorities under their rule. This "Russification" also involved harassment of Russian Jews to induce their abandonment of Judaism and to oblige them to accept Russian culture.

Czarism was especially oppressive during the nineteenth and early twentieth centuries, as a result of the industrial revolution, which brought to Russia the same social miseries it had caused in the West. The last Romanov czars were indifferent to the plight of the growing Russian proletariat, who endured terrible living and working conditions as a result of the factory system in the cities of European Russia. These czars shared the assumption of other laissez-faire societies

(Eugene Gordon)

The Winter Palace in St. Petersburg, Russia (known in the Soviet era as Leningrad) is famous as the home of Romanov czars from the mid-eighteenth century to the end of their reign in 1917.

that the misery of the workers was inevitable, that the industrialization process was good for the entire society, and that government should not interfere to remedy its problems.

Why Czarism Endured

Why did the Czarist system endure past the time when other European political systems had begun to transform themselves into liberal democracies? One reason was a pervasive sense of insecurity, a result of the vulnerability of the enormous Russian landmass to the intrusions of hostile neighbors such as Swedes, Poles, Lithuanians, Mongols, Turks, and Germans. The Russian people tolerated the Czarist autocracy because it was the only certain means of assuring their defense and survival.

Serfdom also reinforced Czarism. Most of the landless Russian peasantry had been serfs since the thirteenth century. Serfdom, which was really a form of slavery, kept Russians impoverished, ignorant, and servile. As long as serfdom flourished, the Russian people were politically, economically, and psychologically incapable of challenging Czarism. Serfdom provided the Russian landed aristocracy with a cheap source of labor and rendered that class loyal to and supportive of the czar.

The peculiar development of the Russian entrepreneurial middle class is another explanation for the endurance of Czarism. Since the money for industrial development in Russia at the end of the nineteenth century came from the czars, the Russian middle class, which was the beneficiary of industrialization, was beholden to the Czarist system and, like the aristocracy, supportive of it. Moreover, political reforms sought by the middle class were limited and of little practical value to the poverty-stricken Russian peasantry and workers who craved radical social and economic change.

Finally, the Russian Orthodox Church buttressed Czarism. The church taught lessons that encouraged the deeply religious Russian people to accept and obey the Czarist order. Orthodox clergy preached the subordination of the individual to the congregation or group, the inevitability of suffering, the promise of a life after death in return for endurance and passivity, the evil of dissent and disobedience, and the sanctity of secular as well as spiritual authority.

Opposition to Czarism

While there was much to explain the endurance of Czarism, it is also true that there was a continuing opposition to it during the rule of the Romanovs. Opposition was at first sporadic, ineffectual, and ruthlessly suppressed by a regime fearful of change. In the seventeenth and eighteenth centuries, this opposition consisted of periodic outbursts of rebellion by a depressed peasantry seeking relief from the burdens and cruelties of serfdom.

In the early nineteenth century, the intelligentsia, including some military officers, offered some resistance. Influenced by liberal ideas developing in Western Europe during and after the French Revolution, they sought political and social change in Russia. But these critics had little impact on the regime's behavior until the reign of Alexander II (1855–1881).

Sympathetic to complaints that serfdom had destroyed peasant incentive and thus undermined Russian agricultural output, Czar Alexander II decreed the emancipation of the serfs in 1861. The newly emancipated serfs also received allotments of land purchased by the Russian government. They were to pay for this land on the "installment plan," over a 49-year period, and therefore did not really own it. Nor were they assured of enough land to support their families.

Czar Alexander II carried out major political reforms in the countryside in order to permit some self-government in the form of local legislatures, called *zemstvos*, and a more rational court system, modeled after judicial systems in Western Europe. But there was no liberalization of the Czarist government. Consequently, opposition to the Czarist order continued in the 1870s and involved young political activists called *narodniki* ("nationalists"), who worked with the peasantry to pressure the czar to introduce further agricultural reform to relieve their poverty. The narodniki, however, found the peasantry more angry about their staggering indebtedness to landlords than about the conservatism of the czar. More violent political groups began to appear. They were fervently hostile to the regime because of its stubborn resistance to reform; some were called terrorists. They openly attacked Czar Alexander II and finally succeeded in assassinating him in March 1881.

The Russian Social Democratic Party (RSDP) was another kind of opposition to Czarism. Founded in 1898 and inspired by Marxist ideas, it sought to improve the living and working conditions of the depressed wage-earning proletariat who appeared in the cities of European Russia during the second half of the nineteenth century. Because of Czarist repression, the RSDP remained underground until legitimized in 1906 by Czar Nicholas II. A wing of the party made up of revolutionary Marxists believed in violence as the only way to improve the condition of the workers.

The Bolshevik Challenge

By 1912 the revolutionary Marxists had become a majority within the RSDP; hence, they were called *Bolsheviks*, from the Russian word meaning "greater." Their cohesiveness and sheer persistence under the leadership of Vladimir Lenin had enabled the Bolsheviks to expand their influence within the RSDP.

Czar Nicholas II's refusal to consider major social and economic reforms for workers helped to vindicate the Bolshevik commitment to violence. Indeed, he responded to the demands of the workers with excessive brutality. A workers' peaceful protest, led by a Russian Orthodox priest, Father Gapon, ended in a massacre on Sunday, January 22, 1905.

Bolshevik radicalism also gained support within the RSDP as a result of the Revolution of October 1905, when workers in St. Petersburg and other cities waged a general strike to improve working conditions. The Revolution, in which the Bolsheviks actively participated, brought few concessions for the poor. Instead, Czar Nicholas II promised political reforms sought by the middle class, namely, a constitution, a new national Parliament (called the *Duma*), and the introduction of ministerial accountability.

Another opportunity for the Bolsheviks to challenge the Czarist order came during World War I, which greatly increased the hardships of workers and peasants. In March 1917 workers expressed their discontent by a general strike in St. Petersburg and other Russian cities. This massive popular action, along with the dissatisfaction of middle-class political groups in the Duma over the failure of Czar Nicholas to liberalize his rule despite the promises of reform in 1905, led to his abdication.

A provisional government of liberals and moderate socialists succeeded the czar. But this new government, of which Alexander Kerensky became prime minister in May, could not make real changes in Russian society. It refused to accommodate popular demands for an end to the war, for further redistribution of land to poor peasants, and for immediate alleviation of widespread food shortages. It lasted only from March to November 1917.

During this 7-month period, the Bolsheviks waited for the right moment to seize power. They were ready not only to destroy the provisional government but also to oppose any groups, no matter how reformist, that did not support their revolutionary strategy. Their ultimate goal was the creation of a communist society.

The Bolshevik moment of action came on November 7, 1917, a point at which the provisional government was at its weakest because of the tremendous strain on all sectors of Russian life caused by the country's continuing involvement in the world war. The Bolsheviks seized control of key centers of administration and communication in St. Petersburg and other Russian cities. The provisional government, lacking popular support, collapsed.

To this day the success of the Bolsheviks seems miraculous. After all, the Bolsheviks were only a very small minority of the Russian opposition to Czarism; the Russian state was the largest landmass of any European country; and previous revolutionary groups that had tried desperately to obtain change, let alone the destruction of the Czarist system, had failed.

Several reasons explain the success of the Bolsheviks. The most important, perhaps, was the leadership of Vladimir

Lenin, who was not only a masterful strategist but also an inspiring unifier and energizer of those who accepted his revolutionary beliefs. In his commitment to destroy Czarism and achieve communism in Russia, Lenin at all times believed that the end justified the means. This meant a willingness to take whatever steps necessary to win and hold power.

The Bolsheviks were successful also because of their highly disciplined, cohesive internal organization, which always had given them a strength out of proportion to their numbers. They loyally accepted Lenin's strictures about the need for unity, laid down in his famous 1902 treatise on the nature of the revolutionary party, called *What Is to Be Done?*

In addition, the events of 1917 played into the hands of the Bolsheviks. The most important for Bolshevik success were

(New York Public Library)

Nicholas II (r. 1894–1917), the last of the Romanov czars, with his family. The czar, who abdicated in March 1917, his wife, and his children were murdered by the Bolsheviks on July 16, 1918.

the intensification of material hardship as a result of World War I and the failure of the provisional government to alleviate it and to address major political and socioeconomic problems, including popular demands that Russia leave the war. Another factor was the absence of any viable reformist alternative to the Bolsheviks. Other political opponents of Czarism were in disarray.

COMMUNIST IDEOLOGY

Following their seizure of power from the provisional government, the Bolsheviks quickly established a new political and socioeconomic order based upon their Marxist ideology. This ideology, Soviet communism, explained the purposes and methods of the Soviet state from its inception in 1917.

Soviet communist ideology was the inspiration for much Soviet political organization and behavior. It was the political language of all Soviet citizens and their government. It encouraged unity within the ethnically and culturally diverse Soviet society. It also legitimized the structure and behavior of the Soviet political system in the eyes of Soviet citizens and provided them with a basis for judging societies committed to other ideologies.

The Marxian Critique of Capitalism

The core of Soviet communist ideology was the Marxian critique of capitalism and advocacy of violent revolution by workers to replace capitalism with a stateless and classless society. In the mid-nineteenth century, Karl Marx, a German, addressed the problems of Western industrial societies. But his ideas appealed to Russian revolutionaries, since the Czarist regime stubbornly refused to reform Russian society. By 1917 Russia was a fertile place for Marxist ideas.

According to Marx, those who own the means of production (capitalists) exploit those who are without property (workers). Capitalists, motivated by greed and selfishness, will not do anything for workers that might diminish profits. Since those who own the means of production dominate the governments of capitalist societies, Marx argued, workers have no chance of relief. Thus, he said, to end their misery, workers must destroy not only the capitalistic economy but also the political system that protects it.

Marx also believed that workers in different national societies can unify against capitalists because they share a class consciousness, a common economic complaint that can override differences of religion, country, and ethnic background. A workers' movement, therefore, can be international and become a truly broad, unified opposition to capitalism. Marx also assumed that the workers have the physical and intellectual wherewithal to make a successful revolution against capitalism.

Marx described the ideal communist society, which would follow the workers' revolution against capitalism. It would have no social classes because there would be common own-

ership of the means of production. And since there would be no exploitation, there also would be no need for a state. Communist society would be egalitarian and democratic.

Socialism vs. Communism

The political and socioeconomic conditions in Russia caused Lenin to modify Marxism. According to Lenin, Russia would need a transition period of undetermined length before the achievement of communism, during which there would be a socialist system wherein the workers would create preconditions for the communist society, such as unity, social equality, economic prosperity, and political stability.

In the Russia of 1917, unity meant bringing Russian and non-Russian peoples together under a centralized administration that would permit cultural diversity but simultaneously assure the administrative unity essential to developing socialism and ultimately communism. Social equality involved the elimination of distinctions based on wealth, religion, race, and other causes of societal conflict.

Prosperity meant a redistribution of economic wealth through the elimination of private ownership of farms and the nationalization of industry and trade. It also meant creation of a comprehensive social security and welfare system for all

(New York Public Library)

Karl Marx had more influence on underdeveloped, agrarian Russia, of which he knew little, than on his native Germany and its developed industrial neighbors, whose social and economic ills were the focus of his many ideas and writings.

citizens that would end the misery of workers once and for all.

To achieve these conditions, Lenin believed that the workers would have to establish a dictatorship similar in some respects to the recently overthrown Czarist government. The socialist dictatorship would be coercive. It would suppress all protest and dissent. But politics in this new workers' state would be different from that in the old Czarist order. The new government would be of, by, and for workers and peasants and, hence, "democratic."

Lenin's socialism also called for a single political party of dedicated Marxists to lead the workers to their promised land of communism. This party always would be a small, highly disciplined organization of motivated revolutionaries who had successfully fought capitalism and were committed to the construction of a new socialist order essential to the achievement of communism. Since this party represented the workers, it would tolerate no rivals.

The Soviet Union was a socialist state striving to achieve communism. Therefore, it was not, strictly speaking, communist—it was socialist. Communism was not what the Soviet Union had but what it *hoped* to have.

Official Ideology and Popular Beliefs

While the principles of socialism were the basis on which Soviet administrative organization and behavior rested, other popular political beliefs, derived from the official ideology, helped to explain the values and attitudes of ordinary Soviet citizens. The most widely held beliefs were the superiority of the community over the individual; the responsibility of the state to assure Soviet citizens a minimum level of material well-being in the areas of education, employment, health care, and housing; the notion that politics was not the job of ordinary private citizens but of the Soviet Communist Party; and the importance of societal order and stability.

These beliefs explained many well-known characteristics of the Soviet population, in particular the difficulty Soviet citizens had in understanding the self-reliance of ordinary people in the West and the Soviet citizenry's apparent willingness to accept with little question the Communist Party's monopoly of power. It is also apparent why Soviet citizens had a strong sense of pride in the achievements of their socialist society; and why Soviet society had very strong conservative instincts, seen clearly in the popular suspicion of political dissent and deviance.

POLITICAL EVOLUTION FROM 1917

The Soviet political system experienced six phases from 1917. Four of these coincided with the leaderships of Vladimir Lenin, Joseph Stalin, Nikita Khrushchev, and Leonid Brezhnev. The fifth phase, the post-Brezhnev phase, coincided with the leaderships of Yuri Andropov and Kon-

stantin Chernenko. The sixth phase coincided with the leadership of Mikhail Gorbachev.

There was enormous continuity in Soviet political development. Yet a close look at what happened to Soviet institutions established in the early years of the Soviet system suggests that there also was much change. Indeed, the Soviet political system of the 1980s was far different from what it was in the 1920s and 1930s.

The Lenin Phase (1917–1927)

Under Lenin the Bolsheviks sought legitimacy by destroying enemies, creating a new political system, and inaugurating socioeconomic change in accordance with ideology. It was a harsh and brutal phase in terms of the condition of the individual, who was ruthlessly subordinated to the system's commitment to radical change and reform.

(New York Public Library)

Vladimir Lenin strikes a familiar pose, haranguing workers and other Soviet citizens in 1919. Leon Trotsky stands listening at the right of the platform.

The achievements of the Soviet regime during the Lenin phase, however, were monumental. The Bolsheviks concluded a long civil war against military remnants of the Czarist system. They established institutions of government. They affirmed the Communist Party's supremacy in Soviet politics and abolished all other political parties.

The Bolsheviks suppressed criticism and dissent outside the Communist Party by means of censorship and the subordination of interest groups, including the trade unions. Inside the party criticism and dissent were discouraged by curtailment of discussion and debate and the imposition of a militarylike discipline of its membership.

The Soviet leadership took the first steps toward socialism. First it tried, but quickly abandoned, a plan called War Communism to eliminate private enterprise: The Soviet leaders did too much too fast, and there was great popular resistance. Lenin then decided to move more slowly and cautiously in the development of socialism. The new regime established a mixed economy in which some private ownership of the means of production continued, especially in agriculture. But other sectors of the economy, notably industry, were nationalized. The creation of this mixed economy was termed the New Economic Policy (NEP).

When Lenin died, in 1924, the change of leadership took place with virtually no popular involvement. There was competition among prominent political figures like Leon Trotsky, Lev Kamenev, Nikolai Bukharin, Gregori Zinoviev, and Joseph Stalin for the position of party general secretary. Stalin was successful because he isolated, discredited, and ultimately destroyed those who opposed him. He advocated policies (notably a continuation of Leninist initiatives like the NEP) that he knew the party rank-and-file supported, even if he himself preferred alternatives. Finally, Stalin had the advantage of a political machine of supporters.

The Stalin Phase (1927–1953)

In the Stalin phase, which began with the Soviet Communist Party's endorsement of Stalin's victory at its 15th Congress, in December 1927, many administrative characteristics of the later political system developed. The process of autocratization begun by Lenin continued, and ultimately the system became totalitarian.

Under Stalin the Soviet system came under the rule of a single, omnipotent leader. Through his personal control of the major instruments of political power, especially the Communist Party and the secret police, Stalin became the object of intense fear and respect. He also became something of a religious symbol.

Real and suspected critics and opponents of Stalin's policies were liquidated during Stalin's "Great Purge" of the 1930s. The Great Purge depended upon police use of unprecedented powers of investigation and interrogation. A politically subservient court system also played a significant role in the purges. Defendants had little protection against a state bent on destroying all challenges to its power. Arrests during the Great Purge ran into the millions. The targets were people as diverse as top political figures with whom Stalin had worked in earlier years (like Trotsky, Kamenev, Zinoviev, and Bukharin), high-ranking military officers, lower-level Communist Party members, government workers, and ordinary citizens. Indeed, anyone even suspected of criticism of the regime was caught up in this terrifying nightmare.

Stalinist totalitarianism had other dimensions. One was a highly centralized bureaucracy. Another was the virtual extinction of representative institutions. Legislatures on both national and local levels of government lost political influence. They did not meet regularly and were subordinated to executive bodies. The judiciary became a pliant tool of the executive and of the Communist Party, dutifully obeying the will of the leadership.

The justification for this totalitarianism was social discipline to accelerate the process of socialist development, which required enormous material sacrifice by an already impoverished society. Some people believe also that Stalin accumulated enormous power for personal reasons, to make himself a "Marxist czar."

Stalin presided over a profound socioeconomic transformation of the Soviet Union. He was responsible for the destruction of whatever capitalism remained in Soviet agriculture. Under Stalin's first 5-Year Plan, begun in 1928,

(New York Public Library)

The famous and forbidding Soviet leader Joseph Stalin at a meeting with other Soviet leaders in 1937, the time of the purges. The man at the far right is V. M. Molotov, who would become Soviet foreign minister in March 1939, at the time of the German dismemberment of Czechoslovakia.

privately owned farms were seized and converted into self-governing collective farms or state-controlled farms on which farmers worked for regular wages like workers in factories. Those who resisted collectivization, notably well-off peasant farmers called *kulaks* who had benefited from the reforms of Lenin's NEP, were arrested and imprisoned.

Stalin also undertook a crash program to industrialize the Soviet Union, which was predominantly agrarian at the time of the 1917 Revolution. He pursued industrialization not only because it was a necessary component of socialist development (industrialization would lessen the Soviet Union's dependence on foreign manufacturers) but also because it would strengthen Soviet military power.

Soviet society experienced great hardships in the Stalin phase. Agricultural output declined, causing severe food shortages. The regime intensified the shortages by exporting food in order to pay for industrial imports. In addition, Stalin gave priority to the production of so-called producer goods, such as machine tools, rather than to consumer goods, like clothing and other necessities.

Stalin led the Soviet state in World War II, during which it is believed that 20 million Soviet citizens perished. Although the war was a terrible drain on an already impoverished and exhausted society, it resulted, paradoxically, in strengthening the Soviet dictatorship. The war distracted the Soviet people from Stalin's excesses of the 1930s. It generated patriotism and national unity. It also greatly strengthened the Soviet military machine. The Soviet Union emerged from the war as second in power only to the United States.

The Khrushchev Phase (1953–1964)

When Stalin died, in March 1953, no one in the leadership had the equivalent of his power. Consequently, several influential senior party officials, including Nikita Khrushchev, shared power. Khrushchev was the most influential because of his power base in the popular and resource-rich Ukraine; his administrative expertise in agriculture, a critical area of the Soviet economy; and his apparent closeness in earlier years to Stalin. Moreover, there was support for his becoming Stalin's successor as party general secretary (Khrushchev subsequently changed the name of this office to first secretary) on the understanding that he would continue to share power with others; that decision making in the party would be by consensus; and that there would be an end to some of Stalin's abusive policies, particularly mass purges and indiscriminate use of terror.

In the mid-1950s Khrushchev consolidated his power base shrewdly and carefully, making appointments of his supporters to key positions in the upper echelons of the party bureaucracy. He adopted a platform calculated to appeal to the party rank-and-file, promising a new concern with the quality of life, and he tried to cultivate a grass-roots popularity to strengthen his power within the party.

(United Nations photo)

The late Soviet leader Nikita Khrushchev, addressing the 21st Congress of the Soviet Communist Party in 1959.

Khrushchev's accumulation of power climaxed in June 1957, when he crushed the opposition of the so-called anti-party group. This group consisted of several of Khrushchev's earlier colleagues whom he had pushed out of power because of their criticisms of him. They tried, but failed, to oust Khrushchev. With the help of supporters like the influential minister of defense, Marshal G. D. Zhukov, Khrushchev defeated the anti-party group and had its members expelled from the party. He then forced the resignation of Premier Nikolai Bulganin. Khrushchev's power now reached its apex.

Under Khrushchev Soviet society moved away from—and Khrushchev even denounced—the most rigid aspects of Stalinism. The new Soviet leadership recognized that many of Stalin's actions had been unnecessary, perhaps even counterproductive.

The most conspicuous change occurred in politics. Khrushchev openly discredited Stalin's policies in order to change or abandon them. For example, to mitigate Stalinist repressiveness, he condemned the personality cult, removed known supporters of Stalin from positions of responsibility in the Communist Party apparatus, and placed the secret police under party control, affording a relief from terror. There was limited opportunity for mild criticism of government policy in the press.

There was also an increase in popular involvement in government, although the essence of the dictatorship remained. For example, Khrushchev called for the reinvigoration of legislative bodies on all levels of administration. They were to increase their roles in monitoring the economy, especially the performance of farms and factories; they were to report production problems to higher authorities.

Modest changes in the judicial system provided individuals with more opportunity to defend themselves in trials. Defense attorneys were allowed to be more aggressive in their protection of clients and judges were occasionally allowed to find for the defendant in political trials.

Khrushchev initiated economic change as well. The regime expressed concern for the material well-being of the individual. Khrushchev tried to increase food supplies, to make available more manufactured goods like home appliances and automobiles, and to provide more housing.

The Khrushchev leadership showed a new interest in efficiency and quality in economic production. Khrushchev divided the Communist Party bureaucracy into separate industrial and agricultural hierarchies. He fostered a measure of administrative decentralization, giving line officials, such as factory managers and collective farm directors, more autonomy in the running of their production units.

The Khrushchev phase ended in 1964, with the first secretary's sudden ouster by the Central Committee, which had become dissatisfied with not only his domestic and foreign policies but also his political style. Despite his condemnation of the personality cult, Khrushchev had begun to re-create it around himself. Following the anti-party crisis, he took both the offices of premier and first secretary in 1958. He thereby ended the collegialism (shared authority) in top-level decision making that he had agreed to accept when he first took power.

Other factors contributed to Khrushchev's ouster. Acute shortages of grain and dairy products in the early 1960s were an embarrassment. His efforts to streamline party organization produced chaos and conflict among party administrators. And he was blamed for alienating China, letting the United States get the better of the Soviet Union in the Cuban Missile Crisis, and accomplishing nothing toward the reunification of Berlin under East German rule.

The Brezhnev Phase (1964–1982)

Leonid Brezhnev succeeded Khrushchev as Soviet Communist Party general secretary (the term first secretary was dropped) in October 1964. His personal and political closeness to Khrushchev had not stopped him from mobilizing the support of Khrushchev's critics. Brezhnev was the choice of his Politburo/Presidium colleagues because he seemed to be the kind of quiet, professional, and conservative leader they wanted.

Under Brezhnev there was a reappraisal and alteration of Khrushchevian policies. Brezhnev considered many of Khrushchev's policies to be impractical and ineffective, such as his administrative decentralization and the division of the Communist Party into industrial and agricultural hierarchies. The Brezhnev regime sought to discredit Khrushchev—in a way that calls to mind Khrushchev's criticisms of Stalin years earlier—as a means of ridding the party and state bureaucracies of some of Khrushchev's close supporters.

Brezhnev also cautiously "rehabilitated" Stalin. His purpose was a discreet restoration of some Stalin-like discipline in Soviet society. Stalin was now praised as a war hero; his hometown of Gori, in Georgia, was made into a museum. Some Stalinists imprisoned by Khrushchev were released. High-ranking party figures who had been associated with Stalinism, like Central Committee secretary Mikhail Suslov, were kept on in positions of power.

Along with this renewal of interest in Stalin were more direct measures to reemphasize political discipline and ideological orthodoxy inside the Communist Party. Brezhnev extended the activities of party control commissions on the union and regional levels.

There was an equivalent tightening up outside the party. The Brezhnev regime began an all-out attack on dissident members of the literary and scientific intelligentsia. There were sudden invasions of the privacy of suspected dissidents by KGB agents; prolonged imprisonment of convicted dissidents in labor camps, penitentiaries, and insane asylums; pressures on some of the dissidents to emigrate from the Soviet Union into permanent exile; and all kinds of harassment of individuals.

Brezhnev did not completely de-Khrushchevize Soviet society; nor did he thoroughly re-Stalinize it. For example, the top party leadership remained collegial. Brezhnev never really became more than "first among equals" in the party Politburo. Brezhnev also tolerated development of what has been termed "institutional pluralism," namely, wider discussion and debate in newspapers, periodicals, and books; regime sensitivity to bureaucratic interests on different levels of the party organization; and an increasing articulation of special interests seeking to influence policy making. Finally, Brezhnev called for a larger measure of independence for local legislative bodies.

Now known as "the period of stagnation," the last years of Brezhnev's rule witnessed a slowdown of economic growth. The regime stubbornly refused to abandon Stalinist policy. With its traditional emphasis on expansion of *quantity* rather than on *quality* of output, Brezhnev's adherence to this outmoded growth model of the 1930s made for inefficient use of the country's land, labor, and capital resources. Another cause of the economic slowdown was political. An indulgent Brezhnev regime paid for the loyalty of bureaucrats by allowing them to place personal interests ahead of the public good.

By the early 1980s, there was a marked deterioration of living conditions for most Soviet citizens. A new generation of Soviet citizens—well educated, articulate, and knowledgeable about better conditions in the West—was disgusted by the regime's perceived failure to deliver the material well-being promised in the ideology of communism. A growing number of strikes and demonstrations against the authorities threatened the stability of the country and a collapse of what in the West has been called a "social contract" between the rulers and ruled. According to this contract, which seems to prevail in most socialist societies, the Soviet people gave up many political rights to the party and state leadership in return for a guarantee of security, free health care, and a minimum material well-being, including guaranteed employment. By the time of Brezhnev's death and during the brief tenures of his successors Andropov and Chernenko, there was the possibility of a major social upheaval in the Soviet Union.

The Post-Brezhnev Phase (1982–1985)
Two successions quickly followed Brezhnev's death in November 1982: Yuri Andropov (1982–1984), and Konstantin Chernenko (1984–1985). Andropov and Chernenko were in power for too brief a time to leave their imprint on Soviet society; there were no significant changes in the structure and functioning of the Soviet system under their leaderships.

The Gorbachev Phase (1985–1991)
Following his promotion within the Communist Party Politburo in March 1985 to the position of general secretary, Gorbachev spoke often of a "pre-crisis" in Soviet society. By this he meant the flaws and errors of his predecessors, notably Brezhnev. Gorbachev predicted social upheaval unless the country addressed this pre-crisis by a program of broad and profound systemic reform. This *perestroika,* or restructuring, at first focused on the economy with a view to raising the depressed Soviet standard of living. But Gorbachev discovered that economic improvement depended on the introduction of other changes—notably, a more tolerant and open political environment; greater popular influence over the civil and military institutions of government and over the organization and behavior of the Communist Party; and a foreign policy responsive to domestic needs and priorities.

Perestroika was meant to be a long-term program to transform the Soviet Union into a completely different kind of polity, a change comparable in scope to the transformation of Czarist Russia by Lenin and Stalin into the Soviet Union. Soviet citizens as well as people abroad were pessimistic about the chances of Gorbachev's success and even of his political survival, but nobody expected that life in the Soviet Union would ever go back to what it was before Gorbachev. However, few imagined the scope of the changes that would explode in the late 1980s and early 1990s.

THE SOVIET SYSTEM

Major components of any political system are instruments of popular political participation and institutions of government. Citizens of a state participate in politics through voting, interest groups, and political parties. Institutions of government are concerned with policy making and include executives, legislatures, judiciaries, and bureaucracies. In socialist countries other important aspects of government are the planned, regimented, centralized economy and the comprehensive social security and welfare systems.

POPULAR PARTICIPATION

Soviet citizens were educated to perform a political role essential to the achievement of socialism and communism. "Ideal" Soviet citizens were supposed to place the well-being of the community ahead of individual self-interest and personal gain. Most willingly accepted the view of government that opposition to its policies was immoral and illegal and that those who opposed them were criminals. They also accepted the Communist Party's monopoly of political power. They were expected to be self-disciplined and devoted to work and to contribute to civic activities.

The Soviet system used a variety of methods to foster these characteristics, not least of which was the pervasive use of political symbols and messages. These glorified the progress of the Soviet state toward socialism and exhorted the Soviet people to work harder for further socialist development. Slogans and ubiquitous pictures of Marx and Lenin and the current leadership everywhere evoked the pride of Soviet citizens and reminded them of what was expected.

The mass media were an important means by which Soviet citizens received lessons on behavior. Television and radio programs, newspapers, magazines, and books told Soviets the political values and attitudes that they were expected to have as members of a society that was building socialism. This relentless education by the media was reinforced by restrictions on foreign travel, which discouraged Soviet citizens from contact with non-Soviet ideas, and by heavy-handed censorship, which prevented widespread dissemination of domestic criticism and dissent.

Soviet citizens were taught proper political behavior also by a comprehensive system of punishment and rewards. Rewards were given to those citizens whose behavior in the workplace, neighborhood, and elsewhere in society was above reproach; who were never "troublemakers," in the sense of shirking work or being nonconformist or socially deviant in personal lifestyle; and who thereby had some or all of the ideal characteristics of the "new Soviet person." Exemplary Soviet citizens could obtain more easily than would otherwise be the case improved living conditions in preferred areas; promotion to higher rank, greater responsibility, and more pay on the job; and the award of medals and honors that called public attention to them and improved their status.

The process of political education started early in life and continued to the end. It took place everywhere and was truly impossible to escape. For example, ideological and political education occurred on the preschool, elementary school, and high school levels, and in universities. The classroom and the teacher fostered the collective mentality by group learning. Children were taught not only the importance of submerging

(UN photo/Philip Teuscher)

Moscow's Red Square was the main square of the capital of the Soviet Union, not only for the military parades regularly held there but also because it was the symbolic political center of the Soviet state. On the left is the Kremlin Wall.

the individual personality to that of the group but also responsiveness to peer pressure for conformity. Indeed, by belaboring the individual's obligation to conform, schools and teachers discouraged children from questioning commonly accepted norms and saying what they really thought.

Political education occurred in such official youth organizations as the Young Pioneers and the Komsomol as well as in other social groups. It went on in the workplace—in factories, farms, mines, and business offices—where time was regularly set aside for "study sessions" on political and ideological issues conducted by members of the Communist Party. Political education took place also in apartment houses, recreation facilities, and in all military units at home and abroad.

Voting

The most frequent opportunity for popular political participation was voting in legislative elections on the national and local levels of government. The important phase of these elections seemed to be the nomination process, which until the Gorbachev era was carefully supervised by the Communist Party to assure that candidates for office were politically reliable and not critical of the regime and its policies. Several kinds of organizations were legally authorized to nominate candidates: local agencies of the Communist Party, the Kom-

somol, trade unions, cooperatives, work collectives, and meetings of servicemen in their military units.

Although voting for most of the Soviet Union's history did not provide citizens with the opportunity to change leadership and policies, as it does for citizens in Western democracies, it was not inconsequential. Voting provided at least the illusion of popular involvement in the political system. It helped to legitimize the system, its leaders, and its policies by giving to citizens the appearance of having some say in how the country developed socialism.

Interest Group Activity

Pre-perestroika interest group activity, another opportunity for popular political participation, was limited, primarily because the Communist Party jealously guarded its political monopoly and was sensitive to challenges of its policies. Well-defined organizations committed to the special interests of particular groups, such as industrial workers, educators, jurists, economists, physicians, and writers, certainly did exist in the Soviet Union. But while their leaders may have been listened to, the organizations had little independence and could not aggressively pressure the Soviet regime to pursue policies favorable to their supporters.

On the other hand, some special interest groups did have substantial influence over policy making by the top Soviet leadership. The most important of them were the army and the KGB. Their leaders were in the top echelons of the party, where they could lobby for preferred policy alternatives.

Some interest groups were illegal. Among these were the Helsinki Watch Group, which was concerned with human rights in the Soviet Union; Jewish émigrés who sought freedom to leave the Soviet Union; and antinuclear peace demonstrators. When members of these groups tried to influence government policy by public demonstrations or even by peaceful written petitions, they frequently were arrested or otherwise harassed.

Finally, there were amorphous interest groups within the rank-and-file of the Soviet military, civilian bureaucracies, and legislatures. Soldiers, civil servants, and elected political officials constituted a potential source of interest articulation. But these people had no organization, no leadership, and no independent funding to enable them to express grievances and influence policy making.

The Communist Party

The Communist Party of the Soviet Union (CPSU) was the most important vehicle of popular participation. According to Soviet ideology, the Communist Party was the agent of the working masses, charged with leading them to communism. It took responsibility for all successes and failures of Soviet political development. Few Soviet Marxists believed that the achievement of socialism and communism was possible without the leadership of the party.

The party enjoyed a central, dominant, and omnipotent role in Soviet life. It was the real source of power and leadership in Soviet society. It had something to say about almost every aspect of Soviet life and was the ultimate source of all policies. The party was the object of reverence and admiration of most ordinary Soviet citizens, who trusted its judgment in the management of Soviet national affairs.

Party Membership

Communist Party membership was elitist, in accordance with Marxist-Leninist ideology. Its membership rarely exceeded 12 percent of the total Soviet population. While the party claimed that more than half of its membership were drawn from workers and farmers, after several years members become bureaucrats within the party organization and no longer had the outlook of the larger social groups in which they grew up. As this happened the party became less a reflection of the people it served. Furthermore, party membership did not represent all of Soviet society because its membership tended to be overwhelmingly Russian and male. For a long time, its top leaders were mostly over age 60.

It was also true that some people joined the Communist Party less out of ideological fervor than out of the desire for career advancement, which the party could assure. Nonideological incentives for joining the Communist Party were the vast array of perquisites available to many party members. Attractive perks were access to scarce items of food, clothing, and appliances imported from abroad and beyond the reach of most Soviet citizens and a top spot on a long waiting list for good apartments in preferred locations or for scarce new automobiles, for which many ordinary Soviet citizens had to wait up to 10 years.

Party Organization: Leadership Organs in Moscow

Essential to its leadership of Soviet society was the Communist Party's traditionally disciplined and cohesive internal organization. It was based upon the principles of democratic centralism, which stipulated that leading party bodies on all levels of organization were elected and must account for their behavior in periodic reports to their constituents and to higher bodies within the party. Democratic centralism called for strict party discipline and subordination of minority to majority. It also required the obedience of lower party agencies to higher agencies.

Democratic centralism was much more restrictive in fact than the theory implied. Before the late 1980s, the top leadership was not elected; it self-selected its membership, and there were no limits on the time of service in office. The top leadership's reports to the party were not open to criticism and debate, and factionalism within the rank-and-file was strictly forbidden. In effect, the practice of democratic centralism made the internal organization of the Soviet Communist Party highly autocratic, with the selection and behavior of the leadership not subject to any real influence from or control by the rank-and-file membership.

The All-Union Party Congress. According to party rules, the All-Union Party Congress was the supreme organ of the party, the locus of sovereignty, and the agency that selected the party leadership and determined party policy. The Congress was supposed to meet at least once every 4 to 5 years. It consisted of delegates chosen by party agencies on all levels of organization.

In practice the Congress did little of substance before the perestroika era. It rarely discussed but always approved the general secretary's report. It had little choice in the election of the Central Committee. It had virtually no role in the selection of either the membership of the Politburo or the general secretary, the titular head of the party. The proceedings of the Congress, however, were important symbolically, in the sense of helping to legitimize the leadership and its policies by giving the appearance of all-party support. The Congress also provided the party leadership with an opportunity to communicate with rank-and-file members to obtain their support of its policies. And because representatives of foreign Communist parties attended—but did not participate in—the Soviet Communist Party Congress, the leadership had an opportunity to engage in shoulder-rubbing diplomacy to help achieve foreign policy objectives.

The Central Committee. A somewhat more important organ of the Communist Party was the Central Committee, which was elected by and accountable to the Congress. The rules of the party charged the Central Committee with appointing the leading functionaries of the party, with directing their work, and in particular with originating and executing the party budget. The Central Committee was also supposed to direct the work of administrative agencies and nonparty organizations throughout the country in which party members participated.

The authority of the Central Committee was broad and significant—at least on paper. In practice, however, the role of the Central Committee was much more restricted than the rules of the party prescribed. This was partly because it had become a very large and unwieldy body since Lenin's time. In the 1930s Stalin had packed it with his supporters. As its membership expanded and its capacity to deliberate declined, it was obliged to delegate day-to-day decision-making authority to a small group made up of its most influential members: the Politburo. In the Khrushchev and Brezhnev years, however, the Central Committee regained some influence over policy making.

The Politburo. The Politburo consisted of 12 to 17 of the most senior party leaders, who served as a collective leadership of the Communist Party. The presiding officer of the Politburo was the general secretary, who was usually the de facto choice of the Politburo.

The Politburo's members were influential primarily because they held other important posts in either the party or the state. The Politburo included key members of the Secretariat. The Politburo membership also included high-ranking government officials. The chief of the Leningrad party organization, which was responsible for supervising a substantial portion of Soviet heavy and defense industries, sometimes was in the Politburo. Other members usually were the premier of the Russian Soviet Federative Socialist Republic (R.S.F.S.R.), the largest and most populous of the 15 constituent Soviet republics; and the first secretary of the Ukrainian party organization in Kiev, who was in charge of the most fertile and productive agricultural region of the Soviet Union.

Given the influence of its individual members, Politburo decision making was based upon consensus. It was no longer possible for a single person, say, the general secretary, to dictate policy. The Politburo and the Central Committee no

(Gamma-Liaison/Bernard Charlou)

The top Soviet leadership appearing in a familiar pose in front of the Lenin Mausoleum in Red Square, observing the traditional May Day parade. Foreigners could gauge the political influence of particular leaders by their locations relative to that of the Soviet Communist Party general secretary, who in this photograph was Leonid Brehznev (standing fourth from the right).

longer tolerated a Stalin-like leader. The best a general secretary could do was to mediate and persuade.

The Secretariat.   The Central Committee's Secretariat had the critical responsibility of directing the party bureaucracy. In theory the Secretariat's membership was selected by and accountable to the Central Committee, but in practice the Politburo made the appointments. According to party rules, the Secretariat selected the personnel of the party bureaucracy, supervised its behavior to ensure execution of Politburo decisions, and in general supervised the ebb and flow of party life throughout the Soviet Union.

The General Secretary.   The head of the Secretariat, who was also the leader of the Soviet Communist Party, was the general secretary (called first secretary in the time of Khrushchev). His leadership authority came from the support of colleagues in the Secretariat, the Central Committee, and the Politburo. While the general secretary was supposed to be elected by the All-Union Party Congress, in fact he was the choice of his colleagues in the other leading organs of the party. The Congress simply ratified their choice.

Party Organization on the Local Level

Party organization on the intermediate and local levels of Soviet administration followed the model of organization at the top. There was a congress on the republic level; its equivalent on the city and district levels was the conference. On the local level, the equivalent was the general meeting. Accompanying these legislative bodies were executive organs comparable to the Central Committee and Secretariat in Moscow. Below the republic level, executive organs were called executive committees and bureaus. As was true of the top level, legislative bodies did not meet for long periods of time; they generally allowed executive bodies to transact business in their name.

Local party organization proliferated everywhere. There was hardly a village, town, urban center, factory, farm, neighborhood, large apartment house, military unit, organization meeting, or other gathering place where the party did not have some kind of official presence. The larger the number of people in a particular place, the more complex the party organization there was likely to be.

The Party and the Government Bureaucracy

The Soviet Communist Party monitored and controlled the government bureaucracy on all levels of Soviet administration, from the top of the bureaucratic pyramid in Moscow to the local, grass-roots level. The party thus maintained its supremacy over government and made sure that state administrators carried out its policies.

On all administrative levels of the Soviet government, there was an interlocking relationship between party and state agencies, which one might refer to as *parallelism*. There were two important features of parallelism. First, for most agencies of local administration, there was an equivalent party agency that continually surveilled, supervised, and scrutinized its government counterpart to assure conformity and obedience to decisions of higher party authorities. Second, in many instances, local party officials held positions in the government agencies they were supervising in the same manner that party leaders in the Politburo simultaneously held top positions in the national governments.

Finally, the Communist Party assured a continuing subordination of the government bureaucracy on all administrative levels by its control of appointments to both civilian and military positions of responsibility, through a system called *nomenklatura*. This was the list of government positions over which the party legally had control of appointments. The party used its appointment power to make sure that people in responsibility in the government bureaucracy were politically loyal, or properly "red," as well as professionally qualified, or adequately expert.

In sum, the Soviet Communist Party had enormous influence over the workings of the government bureaucracy. It is not an exaggeration to say that there was very little that bureaucrats could do that was outside of party purview or beyond its control.

The Party and Trade Unions

Soviet trade unions confined their activities to helping workers increase fringe benefits and to interceding with management on behalf of workers who had gotten into trouble as a result of absenteeism, poor performance on the job, or some other unsatisfactory conduct that could have led to punishment. Soviet trade unions also were expected to mobilize workers to expand output to meet goals set by the party. Unions were expected to ensure that workers make their contribution to socialist development and to resolve problems that interfere with stable labor/management relations. The Soviet Communist Party closely controlled Soviet trade union organizations. The general secretary of the All-Union Council of Trade Unions was usually a high-ranking member of the Communist Party.

The Party and the Army

Party ties to the army and other military services were equally important. But they were somewhat more complex and uncertain than ties to the trade unions, if only because the Soviet Army was a powerful and influential institution in its own right.

The party/army relationship went through several phases of evolution, although the party leadership was nearly always suspicious of the military. In the 1920s and early 1930s, the army was still officered by personnel trained under the czars. Its leadership was suspected of the same self-interest characteristic of military organizations everywhere else and aroused party doubts about its loyalty to communist ideology. Officers suspected of political unreliability were eliminated during Stalin's purges of the 1930s.

Party distrust of the military decreased considerably in the era of World War II. The Soviet Army proved its loyalty by expelling the Nazi invaders and extending Soviet control into Central/Eastern Europe. Subquently, it acquired new political influence and was given responsibility for directing Soviet space exploration and developing nuclear weapons. In the 1950s, 1960s, and 1970s, the army's influence increased as a result of the Sino–Soviet dispute and a perceived Chinese threat to Soviet territory in East Asia as well as because of growing Soviet political and military difficulties in Central/Eastern Europe.

Beginning in the late 1950s, the army leadership saw opportunities to make allies within the party and thereby to gain a role in policy making. In the July 1957 anti-party crisis, which threatened the political dominance of Khrushchev, Army chief Marshal Zhukov supported Khrushchev against his rivals and critics, enabling Khrushchev to retain power.

Army leaders in Brezhnev's time, in particular the late marshals Andrei Gretchko and Dimitri Ustinov, supported the general secretary's policies in return for his commitment to an expansion of the country's conventional and nuclear capabilities. The army wanted to avoid the kind of humiliation suffered in the Cuban Missile Crisis in 1962, when military weakness required Soviet accommodation of U.S. demands for a withdrawal of offensive missiles from Cuba. The party, however, still monitored and controlled the army and the other military services carefully.

FORMAL STRUCTURES OF GOVERNMENT

The formal structures of government in the Soviet Union were in appearance not unlike those of many other modern political systems, in particular those in the West. But the Soviet government was, from the Western vantage point, a highly centralized dictatorship. The starting point of an analysis of this discrepancy between appearance and reality is the Soviet Constitution.

The Soviet Constitution
There were four Soviet constitutions, although the substance of them did not change much. The constitutions described, legitimized, and reinforced the administrative order. The constitutions signified where the Soviet regime perceived itself to be in the process of socialist development and were intended to serve as a guide to where Soviet society would go in the future.

The last Soviet Constitution, promulgated in 1977, was distinctive in several ways. It identified the Soviet Union as a developed socialist state, signifying the achievement of a new, higher level of socialist development. It confirmed the Communist Party as the leading and guiding force in Soviet society in much more explicit terms than were used in the earlier documents. The 1977 Constitution indicated the continuing need for social discipline. It stressed the citizen's responsibility for meeting obligations as a prerequisite for the enjoyment of political rights and privileges.

Soviet Federalism
The Soviet Union had a federal type of administrative system in which there was at least the appearance of a dispersal of power between central (federal) administration in Moscow and local administrative agencies. The country was divided into 15 *constituent republics,* which in turn were subdivided into smaller units of government called *autonomous republics*; and into *national areas,* which were further subdivided into districts, cities, towns, and villages. The constituent republics were each inhabited by the largest of the many—more than 100—culturally and linguistically diverse national groups that comprised Soviet society. Autonomous republics and national areas were inhabited by somewhat smaller ethnic groups.

Established in 1922, this Soviet federal structure recognized the separate cultural identities of the large national groups that the Soviet state inherited from the Czarist empire. To this end Soviet federalism provided for "cultural autonomy," which meant the right of local inhabitants to use their own language in local administration (although local party and government officials were supposed to be fluent in Russian as well) and the right of newspapers and schools to use the local language. To reinforce cultural autonomy, the Soviet federal system guaranteed the inviolability of union-republic boundaries and the representation of the constituent union-republics and other ethnically based administrative units in the national government at the center, notably in the Council of Nationalities of the Supreme Soviet, which was the second chamber of the national Legislature in Moscow.

Soviet federalism was intended to encourage the loyalty to the new Soviet system of the different national groups that had made up the old Russian empire. It was also intended to provide for a substantial administrative unity to assure socialist development throughout the Soviet landmass. Thus Soviet federalism did not allow for the kind of political autonomy enjoyed by constituent units in the federal systems of Western countries like West Germany and the United States. Despite the appearance of a dispersal of authority, the Soviet federal system was characterized by a high degree of administrative centralization. Decision-making authority was concentrated at the center of the country—in Moscow—where the federal organs of government and the party were located.

The Federal Government
As is true of most modern governments, the Soviet federal government in Moscow was divided into three branches: the executive, legislative, and judicial. The bureaucracy, a fourth aspect of the national government, was sufficiently important

Built between 1838 and 1849, inside the Kremlin Wall, the Kremlin Palace became the meeting place of the Supreme Soviet and the soviet of the Russian republic. The flag of the Soviet Union or of the Russian republic was flown when either of these bodies was in session.

to merit separate discussion here, even though in a technical sense it belonged with the executive.

The Executive Branch

Before changes enacted into law in December 1988, the Soviet executive branch consisted of a president and a Council of Ministers. The Council of Ministers was a body of approximately 180 members who were responsible for running the bureaucratic departments that were in charge of almost every aspect of Soviet life.

Inside the Council of Ministers was a Presidium, or inner group, of the most senior, most experienced, and most politically influential members of the state apparatus. Members of this inner group were the premier, the minister of foreign affairs, the defense minister, the agriculture minister, the chief of the KGB, and heads of other key departments of government.

The Presidium of the Council of Ministers was the day-to-day leadership of the state. Its members were powerful administrators, not only because of their authority as heads of critical government departments but also because some of them simultaneously were top-ranking members of the Communist Party leadership, in either the Politburo or the Central Committee.

The Soviet Council of Ministers' responsibilities for management of the state bureaucracy were broad and complex because of the country's commitment to socialist development. The Council of Ministers performed all the functions of executives in Western democracies. In addition, it control-

led those aspects of economic, social, and cultural life that are normally left to the private sector in Western societies. The Soviet Council of Ministers, therefore, was one of the most powerful executive bodies in the world.

Although theoretically chosen by and accountable to the Supreme Soviet, in practice the membership of the Council of Ministers was determined partly by its own inner leadership and partly by the Communist Party's Politburo, of which some ministers were members. The Council of Ministers functioned quite autonomously of the Supreme Soviet, and there was little accountability.

The Legislative Branch

Until changes were enacted into law in December 1988, the national, or federal, Legislature in Moscow had always been the Supreme Soviet, which was bicameral. Its two houses were the Council of the Union and the Council of the Nationalities. The primary purpose of bicameralism seemed to be to give the different national groups in Soviet society representation at the center. But this representation was never very meaningful because the Legislature never played a significant role in the working of government; it was virtually a rubber stamp, approving and ratifying policies presented to it with little discussion or debate. Votes taken were almost always unanimous.

Several factors explain the weakness of the Supreme Soviet as a legislative body. To begin with, the Supreme Soviet was always too big to accomplish anything of consequence. The two houses of the Supreme Soviet had a combined member-

The Supreme Soviet, the Soviet Union's national Parliament housed in the great Kremlin Palace, visible from Red Square, in session. The seating arrangement of parliamentary deputies in the audience with the top party and government leaders on raised platforms in the front (directly under the statue of Lenin) suggested that deputies were supposed to be the listeners and leaders were supposed to be the performers.

ship of about 1,500. The Supreme Soviet met for only a few days at a time, usually twice a year. There was little opportunity for legislative deputies to become deeply involved in and knowledgeable about anything brought to their attention. Another weakness was the exclusion of mavericks, critics, and would-be opponents of the regime, who found it impossible to be elected to seats. Once candidates who had been elected took their seats, they were subject to rigorous in-house discipline, which discouraged spontaneous outbursts or expressions of assertiveness.

Having said all this, it is also true that the Supreme Soviet did play a positive role. Its convening on a regular basis helped to legitimize the Soviet system by giving at least the appearance of popular involvement. Moreover, it could and sometimes did provide a forum, albeit a very restricted one, for the expression of concerns that citizens had on the grassroots levels of administration.

The Presidium of the Supreme Soviet was more important in the administrative process than its parent body. The Presidium's membership reflected the diversity of Soviet society. It had 36 members in addition to a chairperson (who was also the president of the Soviet Union), a first vice chairperson, and 15 other vice chairpersons representing the constituent republics. These vice chairpersons usually were themselves chairpersons of the supreme soviets of their own republics. The membership of the Presidium also included a variety of party and state notables and famous personalities.

While the Presidium theoretically was elected by the Supreme Soviet, in practice it determined its own replacements, who, of course, had the approval of the Communist Party leadership. Also, the Presidium acted independently of the parent body to which, in theory, it was accountable.

The Presidium of the Supreme Soviet had a great deal of power, and its activities were extensive. It issued enforceable decrees and ordinances, thereby acting as an interim legislature. It could amend the Constitution. It supervised the work of the Council of Ministers and could dismiss its members, although in practice dismissal was done on signal of the Politburo. It ratified treaties and received ambassadors. The Presidium could deprive individuals (for example, political dissidents) of their Soviet citizenship. It supervised the military, which involved removal of the high command and the ordering of a partial mobilization—again, however, on signal from the top party leadership. The Presidium also received complaints and criticism from citizens throughout the country, enabling it to collect much information about administra-

(UN photo/Saw Lwin)
Then–Soviet foreign minister Andrei Gromyko addressing the UN General Assembly in New York in 1984.

tion on the local levels. Finally, the activities of all local governing bodies, called soviets, were subject to its supervision and control.

The chairperson of the Presidium or Soviet president was very powerful. This individual not only presided over and directed its proceedings but also could simultaneously hold the position of general secretary of the Communist Party.

Brezhnev used this position to strengthen his influence within the government apparatus. Because Brezhnev's successors as president, Andropov and Chernenko, held office for very short periods, it was difficult to know if they were able to increase their power as a result of holding simultaneously the office of Soviet president and party general secretary. Unlike Brezhnev, Gorbachev initially refrained from seeking the presidency, which was held by former foreign minister Andrei Gromyko from 1985 to 1988. But in October 1988, after Gromyko's resignation, Gorbachev finessed his own election to the presidency, presumably for the same reason as Brezhnev in 1977: to strengthen his personal political power and leadership authority, in this instance to facilitate implementation of his sweeping reform program.

Law and the Judicial Branch

Soviet law had a very broad application and dealt with aspects of personal behavior that in Western societies are usually the concern of the private individual. Soviet law was intended to promote a respect for the process of socialist development on the part of both private citizens and public agencies. Soviet law was supposed to inculcate a sense of the moral rightness of behavioral norms established by the regime and of the impropriety—indeed, the absolute wrongness—of violating those norms.

Law in the Soviet Union traditionally was closely connected to and supportive of economic planning and development; thus, it had a much wider area of concern than public law in Western democracies. Soviet law included a variety of economic subjects having to do with the running of collective farms, employee/employer relations in factories, and worker behavior. For example, Soviet law forbade what was called a "parasitic way of life," which meant avoidance of what the regime termed "socially useful work." Therefore, the law could make criminals of citizens who did not fulfill the state's expectations of their roles in the national work force.

Legal procedure worked differently in the Soviet Union from how it does in the West. For example, the role of Soviet judges was unique. There was much more give-and-take between judges and witnesses. Judges might criticize witnesses and defendants in a court trial. While judges were elected for 5-year terms, they were subject to the same kinds of political scrutiny as other state officials and could not act with an independent mind.

People's assessors, who were lay individuals, assisted judges and in theory provided them with the opinion of the ordinary person. People's assessors were elected for 2 years and might not have had any judicial training. Because they were frequently overshadowed by judges, who were better trained and more aggressive, their real role seemed to be political and symbolic. They gave the impression of popular involvement in a judicial process that had the reputation of being compulsive and severe. Their involvement, however, helped to increase popular sensitivity and obedience to the law.

The behavior of Soviet attorneys was quite different from that of their counterparts in the West, especially in handling a defense. Lest they become targets of the court's wrath, Soviet defense attorneys had to be very careful not to appear overzealous in the protection of clients who were fighting the state. The most that defense attorneys could hope to do for their clients was to present a balanced case.

From a Western vantage point, perhaps the most striking feature of Soviet law and legal procedure was the inequity that apparently occurred whenever the exercise of individual rights challenged the purported interests of the state. Soviet courts, in the Western view, were political instruments of the Soviet leadership. Public trials rarely involved state officials who might have abused their authority. The Soviet regime often ignored the constitutional rights of citizens, as seen in dissident Alexander Solzhenitsyn's arrest, expulsion, and loss of citizenship in 1974 without any judicial hearing or procedure.

The KGB.   The Committee for State Security, or KGB, one of the most publicized instruments of Soviet law enforcement, was responsible for protecting Soviet society against its real or imagined enemies everywhere. The KGB's powerful and pervasive influence in Soviet society was a result not only of its extensive intelligence-gathering apparatus and its exaggeration of the dangers and threats to Soviet domestic and external security but also of the climate of intense distrust and watchfulness that governed the Soviet state's relations with its citizens and citizens' relations among themselves.

The KGB could be very abusive because of operatives who were not always accountable for their behavior and who were not always easily controlled by their superiors. Examples of the KGB's abuses of power were the pervasiveness of its surveillance activity, its threats and annoying searches, and its use of entrapment devices, blackmail, and intimidation. It could arrange an individual's loss of employment, eviction from housing, and other forms of harassment. It was especially aggressive in dealing with dissidents in the late 1970s, virtually crushing the entire dissident movement.

A practice developed in the Brezhnev era was KGB incarceration of political dissidents in mental hospitals. With the help of unscrupulous doctors, KGB operatives badgered political inmates to the point where they confessed error or truly went insane. All this was done, of course, without a costly and potentially embarrassing trial.

The Soviet regime traditionally defended this KGB behavior, saying that the interests of the party were synonymous with those of society and that there was no reason to tolerate the behavior of a few people seeking to obstruct socialist development and prevent Soviet workers from achieving their ultimate goal of communism. Indeed, from the Soviet vantage point, the workers, through their state and in particular its security and police apparatus, had to take whatever steps necessary to resist their enemies.

The Bureaucracy

The Soviet bureaucracy was unique for many reasons, not the least being the sheer enormity of its responsibilities and personnel, the result of the nation's commitment to the socialist transformation of its socioeconomic environment. Indeed, the regime eventually became self-conscious about this gargantuan administrative machine, which contradicted the Marxist promise of a withering away of the state.

Perhaps the most publicized evil of the Soviet bureaucracy was bribery. It had been with the Soviet system since its inception; Lenin called it the worst enemy of the revolution. Bribery may have even worsened over the years because the Soviet bureaucracy expanded substantially to cope with accelerated socioeconomic change.

The persistence and pervasiveness of bribery in the Soviet bureaucracy were the result of many factors endemic to the Soviet system. Shortages of food, apartments, automobiles, and many other necessities and luxuries encouraged bureaucrats to accept bribes for favors rendered. The temptation to accept bribes was increased by the poor salary and poor living conditions of many state employees, especially in the service industries. But even highly paid bureaucrats wanted more and found it difficult to resist the temptation to accept "tips."

Furthermore, bribery was a way of life that generally was not considered bad, if only because it always had been done. And because it was so ingrained and so pervasive, it was difficult to stamp out completely, no matter how determined the regime was. The most that any Soviet leadership could accomplish against bribery was an isolated attack for symbolic and educative purposes.

A serious flaw in the bureaucracy under Brezhnev was the manipulation of information or, simply, the telling of lies about conditions in the society. To satisfy their superiors, bureaucratic managers on all levels of administration transformed the dissemination of misleading and deceptive information, called *paradnost*, into a fine art. Each year lies were piled on top of lies about the true state of affairs, in a veil of impenetrable secrecy—to the point where, when Gorbachev became general secretary, the government and party leadership had no precise idea of the true state of the economy.

This "government by officials" had other problems. Employees often relied on family-type relationships that involved mutual accommodations at the expense of the state. There were widespread efforts to hoodwink superiors in order to conceal fraud, ineptitude, pilfering, cronyism, and nepotism.

To cope with some of these problems, the state made superiors responsible for the levels of achievement of their subordinates, and all state employees were responsible for damage done to state property by their negligence or carelessness. They were obliged to pay back to the state up to 3 months of their wages as compensation. But, ironically, these remedies worsened the problems that they were supposed to resolve. For example, to protect their own positions, managers concealed the failures of their subordinates and of entire units for which they were responsible.

To control its bureaucracy, the Soviet regime developed a multiplicity of party and nonparty controls. There were five different types of control: by party agencies, by government agencies other than the Ministry of Finance, by the Ministry of Finance, by the procuracy, and by the local soviets. Administrators could be called upon at any time by one or more of these control agencies to account for their behavior or that of the people working for them. These extensive controls, however, did not correct the problems from which the Soviet bureaucracy suffered. The sheer size and complexity of the bureaucracy made it difficult and many times impossible for control personnel to track down the source of a problem and remedy it. Sometimes controls were counterproductive, in

(United Nations photo)

Collective farm villages were compact and self-contained, with cooperative banks and post offices. Farm families had their own homes, with backyards where they could raise ducks, pigs, chickens, and vegetables for their own consumption or for sale in local markets.

that they were intrusive and disruptive of routine and to that extent contributed to bureaucratic inefficiency.

It is not surprising that the last Soviet leaders gave much attention to the problem of corruption and incompetence in the bureaucracy. Gorbachev went after abuses like bribe taking, concealment, falsification, and the display of indifference to citizens as part of his campaign to improve the Soviet administrative efficiency. There were other reasons why so much publicity was given to corruption and other ills of the Soviet bureaucracy. Accusing managers and ministers of incompetence or malfeasance and forcing their removal from office—and even their arrest, conviction, and imprisonment—provided the leadership with an opportunity to dispose of critics or enemies who might otherwise use their authority to sabotage policies they secretly opposed.

THE ECONOMY

The scope of Soviet economic control was staggering by Western standards. The Soviet state ran most of the economy and had much to say about the few economic areas not under its direct control. The state controlled allocation of land, labor, and capital; production; distribution; and a very large aspect of consumption.

The basis of state control of the Soviet economy was the "state plan," which determined all phases of Soviet economic life. The state plan, which was drawn up by the Gosplan (State Planning Agency), set the goals of most areas of Soviet production. These goals were based on decisions made by the

Communist Party leadership. However, the Gosplan also took into account input from production units like factories and farms.

To carry out the provisions of the state plan, the Soviet economy was divided into the following units of economic organization:

- *Institutions*—all government administrative, financial, and commercial agencies.
- *Industrial enterprises,* which resembled the manufacturing companies and corporations of capitalist economies, consisted of factories, mines, and other basic units of production.
- *Agricultural cooperatives,* which were divided into 1) *collective farms,* which were large, self-governing farm communities with some decision-making autonomy and with remuneration to farmers based on earnings of the farm as a whole; and 2) *state farms,* which were run directly by the state and which paid farmers a regular wage. Both types of farms could be very large, consisting of thousands of acres and incorporating several villages.
- *Societal organizations,* including trade unions, professional associations, and social clubs and groups.

The economy had a very limited private sector. It consisted of small garden plots owned by farmers employed by collective and state farms, who worked on their plots part-time and marketed what they produced for extra income. The private garden plots were embarrassingly efficient as compared to collective and state farms. By the end of the 1970s, more than half of the Soviet Union's potato crop and almost a third of vegetables, meat, and milk came from the cultivation of private plots.

The Soviet economic system had impressive accomplishments. In little over half a century it achieved a radical redistribution of wealth and transformed an agricultural country to a highly industrialized and urbanized one. It raised the standard of living of the overwhelming majority of Soviet citizens as compared to the lifestyles of their parents in the 1920s and 1930s and their grandparents before the Revolution of 1917.

SOCIAL SECURITY AND WELFARE

The scope of the Soviet social security and welfare system went beyond anything in Western societies. It guaranteed the usual benefits of modern state welfare systems, like insurance for illness, unemployment, and retirement. Soviet citizens also enjoyed guaranteed housing and cradle-to-grave health care.

Housing

The state was able to guarantee housing to all citizens because it owned most of the housing facilities in the country. Rents were very low for most apartments in state housing. There was also cooperative housing built by financially self-sustaining cooperatives of renters who were willing to pay higher rents in return for better-quality accommodation.

Soviet housing policy, however, was flawed. The regime was not always able to provide living quarters when people needed them. There was always a housing shortage, mainly because of the unwillingness of the Soviet leadership to invest sufficiently in housing construction. People frequently had to wait a long time for the assignment of an apartment, especially one located in a preferred urban area. Because of a steady influx of people from the countryside, housing shortages were so acute in cities like Moscow and Leningrad that authorities had to restrict private movement to those cities.

Guaranteed housing, moreover, did not always mean high-quality and comfortable housing. Much of Soviet housing was shabby by Western standards. New construction often showed careless workmanship, the use of cheap materials, and faulty planning. Older units were not in good repair. When something went wrong, it was very difficult for Soviet workers to repair and restore it. Hence, the state found it necessary to allow more construction of housing by private cooperatives and, in a very few instances, by private individuals.

Health Care

Like Soviet housing policy, the health care system was comprehensive. It provided an extensive network of hospitals and clinics. There was unlimited hospitalization, and the ratio of physicians to population was among the highest in the world.

The achievements of the Soviet health care system were impressive. Life expectancy increased; infant mortality declined; and epidemic and endemic diseases like malaria, cholera, and typhus, to which the country had been prone years ago, were brought under control.

On the other hand, the system also had many weaknesses. Participating physicians were overworked; they had to see a requisite number of patients per hour to meet quantitative targets set by authorities in Moscow. When there were mistakes or problems, physicians were always held responsible to superiors in the usual bureaucratic manner. The health care system was highly centralized and thus a bureaucratic nightmare.

As was true of other areas of Soviet life having to do with the material well-being of the individual, the depth of stated official concern was never matched by an equivalent willingness to spend and improve. The expansion of health care facilities, especially the construction and maintenance of clinics and the acquisition of technical equipment, did not receive the same priority as, say, defense industries. There was a scarcity not only of costly medical equipment standard in most large American hospitals, such as kidney dialysis machines, but also of low-cost and simple equipment, like needles and tubing.

The health care system seemed geared more to curing illness than to preventing it. Some diseases that are easily controlled in other countries ran rampant in the Soviet Union. Influenza, for example, killed tens of thousands of Soviet babies. Rickets continued to be a childhood scourge. Whereas 70 percent of cervical cancers were detected in their early and potentially treatable stages in the United States, 60 percent of the Soviet Union's cases were not recognized until they were terminal.

Despite these criticisms one must commend the Soviet health care system for revolutionizing medical treatment and for doing so in a relatively brief period, considering the size and diversity of the Soviet population as well as the country's broad territorial expanse. As far as is known in the West, there were no major breakdowns in the medical system and no major cutbacks in medical care expenditures.

The cost of this welfare program was substantial and borne by the beneficiaries themselves, primarily in the form of low wages and a pervasive tax, the "turnover tax," which was levied on almost everything the consumer needed and used. By forgoing the discretionary income that workers can earn in capitalist societies, the Soviet citizens paid a high price for their extensive social benefits. Thus, Soviet citizens had more protection but lower living standards than the citizens of capitalist societies.

FOREIGN POLICY

Communist ideology influenced Soviet international behavior. The Soviets always believed that capitalist countries were inherently expansionist and thus threatened Soviet security and that capitalism inevitably would collapse in consequence of its own inherent weaknesses and flaws, especially if Marxists aggressively fought against it. This belief explained the

(Intourist, Moscow)

Kalanin Prospect, one of the major downtown Moscow thoroughfares. The architecture of the high-rise office buildings built in Khrushchev's era contrasts with the Stalinist architectural style of the Hotel Ukraine in the foreground.

traditional undercurrent of suspicion and hostility in Soviet relations with the West. It also helped to explain the special relationship of the Soviet state with the socialist countries of Central/Eastern Europe and with Communist parties elsewhere. Finally, it provided some understanding of the intense Soviet interest in the developing societies of the Third World that were searching for ways to achieve modernization.

But nonideological considerations also played a role in explaining Soviet policy toward the West; toward ruling and nonruling Communist parties; and toward the developing countries of Asia, Africa, and Latin America. These considerations included protection of Soviet security abroad, the need for extensive foreign trade to promote economic development and modernization, and the craving for prestige and recognition as a global superpower.

The West

The Soviet Union pursued détente with the West from the 1950s. *Détente* involved occasional summit meetings between Soviet and Western leaders and treaty-making diplomacy, which led to the conclusion of agreements on trade, arms control, cultural and scientific exchanges, and other political matters. Détente diminished the likelihood of confrontation and conflict with the West, thus allowing the Soviet

regime to focus attention on other places in the world where its interests were threatened, such as the Middle East, Central Asia, and along the Soviet frontier with China. In making possible the conclusion of arms control agreements like SALT II, détente allowed the Soviets to protect advantages they had acquired vis-à-vis the West in the development of weapons arsenals and to minimize unnecessary and costly weapons production so that scarce investment capital could be invested elsewhere in the Soviet economy.

Détente was essential to an expansion of Soviet trade with the West. The Soviets wanted to purchase high technology products that they could not produce themselves but which they needed to increase the quality and quantity of their industrial and agricultural output. Improvement of Soviet economic performance was essential to the success of overall Soviet socialist development and in particular to the achievement of societal material well-being to assure political stability.

Only through détente could the Soviets induce the West, in particular the United States, to recognize them as a global superpower. The Soviet leadership always sought international respect, because it contributed to the legitimization of the Soviet system not only in the international community but also with the Soviet people.

The Soviets may have had an ulterior and, arguably, a sinister motive for their pursuit of détente in the Khrushchev and Brezhnev years: namely, to lull the West into a false sense of security and diminish its sensitivity to a Soviet arms buildup. The Soviets may also have wanted an opportunity to exploit differences between the United States, which believed that détente had a worldwide application, and the North Atlantic Treaty Organization (NATO) allies in Western Europe, which argued at times that détente applied mainly to Europe.

The Soviets showed, however, that when détente was an obstacle to the protection of their interests, they were willing to ignore it. Hence, they virtually destroyed political dissent in the Soviet Union in the late 1970s, despite U.S. president Jimmy Carter's aggressive campaign in support of human rights. They simultaneously tightened restrictions on the emigration of Soviet Jews, despite strong American opposition. And they assisted Marxists and other left-wing political groups in Third World countries, in the name of socialist internationalism. In their pursuit of détente, therefore, the Soviets seemed willing to risk a heightening of tensions in their relations with the West and to forfeit benefits of détente in order to obtain other advantages.

Socialist Countries in Central/Eastern Europe

For reasons of security, the Soviets insisted upon substantial loyalty among the socialist countries established in Central/Eastern Europe after World War II. Central/Eastern Europe was a historic invasion route to the Soviet Union; this route had been used most recently by Nazi Germany in World War II. The socialist countries of Central/Eastern Europe were a strategic buffer between the Soviet state and the capitalist West.

The Soviet Union also insisted that the socialist political systems of Central/Eastern Europe conform to the Soviet model, in particular the single-party dictatorship. The Soviets believed that a liberal political order in Central/Eastern Europe could lead to an erosion of their commitment to socialist development and a westward shift of foreign policy orientation, to the detriment of Soviet security.

To assure the loyalty of the Central/Eastern European states to Soviet foreign and domestic policies between the 1940s and 1980s, Moscow maintained close ties with their leaderships. The Soviets conferred with them in periodic bilateral summit meetings and at either local party congresses or international party gatherings; they maintained strong links with them through the Soviet-led regional military and economic organizations like the Warsaw Pact and the Council for Mutual Economic Assistance (CMEA).

The Kremlin had other means of influencing the behavior of its allies to assure conformity with Soviet policy. There always was the option of military intervention, which was used in August 1968 to prevent the Czechoslovak govern-

(United Nations photo)
Eduard Shevardnadze, once the Soviet foreign minister under Mikhail Gorbachev. Later he became the president of the independent republic of Georgia.

ment from experimenting with liberal reforms. The so-called Brezhnev Doctrine asserted the right of socialist countries to intervene in one anothers' internal affairs to protect socialism against internal as well as external challenges. Gorbachev repudiated the doctrine by saying that the Soviet Union would never use force in Central/Eastern Europe, but what a conservative successor might do if confronted with a threat to Soviet security in Central/Eastern Europe was another matter.

The Soviets had powerful sources of leverage other than outright military force. The Kremlin dominated the Warsaw Pact command structure, paying 80 percent of the operating costs and cycling allied commanders through mid-career training in Soviet military academies. Moscow also controlled promotion to high ranks within the Soviet bloc military establishments and monitored political loyalty and morale through the Main Political Administration of the Soviet Army and Navy. Furthermore, although the Central/Eastern European armies were equipped with all the latest conventional weaponry to enable them to fulfill their role vis-à-vis NATO, they were kept short of ammunition and operated with a command and communications structure that would have been ineffective without Soviet control. Finally, various status-of-forces agreements with Soviet bloc nations governing the movement of Soviet troops allowed for their mobilization and deployment without prior approval of the host governments.

The Soviet Union also had substantial economic leverage over the countries, to discourage domestic or international policies the Kremlin considered prejudicial to Soviet interests. The Soviets provided the countries with cheap raw materials, especially oil and gas, without demanding precious hard currency and bought their less-than-world-class products.

At times the Soviets tolerated a limited amount of Central/Eastern European deviance from their wishes. Sometimes enforcement of conformity was physically impossible, as in the case of Yugoslavia and Albania. In other instances deviance did not threaten the domestic commitment to the single-party dictatorship and to continuing membership and support of the Warsaw Pact military alliance, as in the case of Romania. The Soviets said in 1956 that they were willing to acknowledge the legitimacy of "different paths to socialism" which individual Central/Eastern European countries wanted to follow for reasons of national self-interest, as long as they did nothing to jeopardize their commitment to socialism and/or their loyalty to the socialist community and to the Soviet Union.

China

China was a relentless competitor of the Soviet Union in the world communist movement from the late 1950s. China not only refused to acknowledge Soviet leadership of the world's Communist parties but also challenged and rejected important principles of Soviet ideology. China rivaled the Soviet Union for influence not only in Asia and elsewhere in the

Third World but also in the European movement of Communist parties. At times this rivalry was quite dangerous, because of China's geographic proximity to the Soviet Union, its expanding military capability, especially in the nuclear arena, and its ties with the United States.

The Third World

The Soviets always understood that Third World countries were reluctant to embrace Marxist-Leninism, despite their commitment to sweeping socioeconomic reform and their opposition to laissez-faire capitalism. Thus, in their relations with Third World countries, the Soviets did not make a fetish of ideology—they were never out to "communize the world."

Communist ideology nevertheless did influence Soviet behavior toward the Third World. In the 1960s and 1970s, the Soviets wanted Third World countries to expand their public sectors and limit capitalism. They also supported political parties and groups that were on the ideological left, especially Marxist and other groups waging wars of national liberation against local and/or foreign capitalist forces. Indeed, the Soviets said they had an obligation to support Marxists whenever they were fighting capitalists.

The Soviet Union also had important nonideological ambitions in the Third World. The Kremlin wanted the friendship and cooperation of Third World governments in the United Nations, where it needed votes to block measures sponsored by rivals and opponents. In the economic realm, the Soviets wanted sources of raw materials and markets for manufactured exports.

Strategic considerations helped to explain Soviet policy in the Third World. Countries near Soviet territory, such as Iran, Afghanistan, and Pakistan, along with neighboring countries in the Middle East and around the Persian Gulf, were important to Soviet security. The Soviets never wanted dangerous antagonists like the Americans or the Chinese to obtain a foothold in these places. At the same time, the Soviets saw opportunities to shift the balance of strategic forces vis-à-vis the United States to their advantage by cultivating certain Third World countries.

The Soviets tried to achieve their ambitions in Third World countries by giving them economic and technical assistance on very easy terms. They granted loans with low interest rates and with few strings attached and provided easy means of repayment by accepting local currency or export commodities. Sometimes Soviet economic aid led directly to an expansion of Soviet political influence, as when, for example, the recipient country appointed Soviet advisers to key administrative positions to help it make the best use of sophisticated equipment the Soviets had given it. And the sale of arms to Third World countries not only resulted in a weapons dependency that gave Moscow some political leverage but also facilitated trade beneficial to the Soviet Union.

Political diplomacy was still another instrument of Soviet policy in the Third World. The Soviets signed treaties of friendship, cooperation, consultation, and mutual defense. The exchange of visits by Soviet officials with leaders of Third World governments was useful in flattering them and enhancing Soviet influence with them. Sometimes Soviet diplomacy also supported Third World causes, such as black nationalism in Southern Africa, Palestinian self-determination in the Middle East, and opposition to U.S. initiatives in the United Nations.

As a measure of last resort to protect their vital interests in the Third World, the Soviets intervened militarily in Third World countries. They did so directly, as in Afghanistan in 1979; and indirectly, by means of proxies like Cuba, in Angola and Ethiopia in the mid- and late 1970s.

These methods did not always assure success. Indeed, the Soviets confronted many obstacles to the achievement of their ambitions in the Third World. Some obstacles had to do with the attitudes and policies of the Third World countries themselves; other obstacles were thrown up by the United States, China, and other countries with opposing interests. Additional obstacles to Soviet success in the Third World were the Soviet Union's limited capabilities.

Third World governments sometimes found the Soviets to be pushy, overbearing, rude, even prejudiced. This was true not only because the Soviets occasionally may have behaved in these ways but also because leaders of the Third World countries may have been hypersensitive to their countries' newly won independence and resented pressure on them. Moreover, governments that were recipients of Soviet weapons lost patience if the weapons did not work properly. They also became flustered when Soviet diplomacy did not seem adequately supportive of their interests abroad, especially in relations with the United States. Finally, many Third World leaders governed deeply religious societies that were offended by the atheism of Soviet communism. This was especially true of Islamic countries.

The Soviets always were constrained in what they could do in the Third World by their own finite political, economic, military, and strategic capabilities. It is an oversimplification to say that, because there were constraints on the formation of a critical public opinion within the Soviet Union, Moscow could pursue any policy it wished. The regime could never ignore the possibility that costly, belligerent, and dangerous excursions into the Third World could arouse popular dissatisfaction, provide encouragement to dissidents, and excessively burden its problem-ridden economy. The regime nearly always had to give priority to domestic needs, especially in moments of economic scarcity.

Large-scale strategic considerations also limited Soviet policy in the Third World. Soviet leaders had to be wary of the way in which a distraction in the Third World encouraged Chinese political and territorial ambitions in Asia at the Soviet Union's expense. The Soviets had to be careful not to allow their policies in the Third World to compromise their freedom of action in Soviet bloc countries, where they had substantial security interests. Soviet leaders had to be sensitive to the way in which Central/Eastern European countries could exploit Soviet distractions in the Third World to seek more autonomy and to increase their orientation toward the West. Nor could they ever dismiss the possibility of a clash with the West, in particular the United States.

Foreign Policy Making

The Politburo and Secretariat were intimately involved in foreign policy making. The Politburo deliberated on important foreign policy initiatives. Its role seemed to be to set the large principles of policy. It relied on the Secretariat and other agencies for information and for implementation of its decisions.

The Central Committee itself had only an occasional involvement in foreign policy making. It did not have a policy-originating role. Its major responsibility appeared to be concerned with ratification and communication. On the other hand, the Politburo would seek Central Committee approval of a major foreign policy initiative carrying substantial risk, such as the decision to intervene in Czechoslovakia in 1968.

The Ministry of Foreign Affairs was the chief state agency concerned with foreign policy. It was organized for that purpose in much the same way as foreign affairs ministries in other modern political systems. It had a large bureaucracy of experts in Moscow, and it controlled the embassies and consulates of the Soviet Union abroad. The Ministry of Defense was involved when the implementation of foreign-policy decisions required military support.

Other state agencies that cooperated with the Ministry of Foreign Affairs in the implementation of foreign policy were the Ministry of Foreign Trade and the KGB. The Ministry of Foreign Trade was concerned with most economic measures needed to carry out foreign policy. The KGB did what most strategic intelligence-gathering agencies do: It acquired information about foreign countries, especially secret data, and engaged in espionage and counterespionage activities. The KGB also monitored the Soviet frontier.

Another important state agency that exerted influence on foreign policy making was the Institute for the Study of the United States and Canada, located within the Soviet Academy of Sciences. This so-called USA Institute provided party and state leaders with up-to-date, accurate, and jargon-free explanations of American domestic and international behavior.

PERFORMANCE PROBLEMS

Serious problems threatened the Soviet Union's domestic tranquillity and external security. The most intractable of these were interethnic tensions, social problems, political dissent, economic underperformance, and deterioration of the environment.

INTERETHNIC TENSIONS

Relations among the different ethnic groups that comprised Soviet society were characterized by suspicion, resentment, and sometimes open hostility. There are many reasons for this disharmony among the nationalities, especially the largest ones. Not least were the weakness of their sense of belonging to the large Soviet national community in which they resided since the Bolshevik Revolution in 1917; the strength of their separate cultural identities, which, paradoxically, the Soviet regime sought to preserve in order to conciliate the nationalities and encourage their loyalty to the Soviet system; and different levels of material well-being, which were the result of different levels of economic development and wealth endowment. But the most serious cause of interethnic tensions was the dominant influence of Russians over key institutions of the Soviet national government and its insistence on the use of the Russian language almost everywhere in society.

Russian Dominance

Russians predominated in leading party and state agencies. Sixty percent of all Soviet Communist Party members were Russian. The All-Union Party Congress, which convened periodically in Moscow, was dominated by Russians and transacted its business in Russian, even though many party members were ethnically non-Russian. A substantial majority of the party Politburo consisted of Russians. Russians also held key party and government posts in the non-Russian republics.

The Soviet leadership tried to strengthen this Russian influence. The regime encouraged Russians to colonize, or settle, areas inhabited predominantly by non-Russian peoples, and it aggressively promoted the Russian tongue as the first language of all Soviet peoples. Despite the official policy of cultural autonomy, Soviet authorities in Moscow went to excessive and sometimes controversial lengths to foster the use of Russian in non-Russian areas. Large amounts of money were spent for the instruction of Russian in the schools and universities of the non-Russian republics. The Russian language became the official language of administration throughout the country and had to be used in all official communications between local areas and Moscow.

Russian dominance resulted also from the absence of any meaningful opportunities for the non-Russian peoples to influence the policy-making process at the center. This was true because the institutions in which the non-Russian national groups were represented by law—namely, the Council of Nationalities in the old Supreme Soviet and the All-Union Party Congress—actually had very little power.

Apart from the selfish, ethnocentric desire of Russian Marxists to perpetuate Russian control of the Soviet system, Soviet leaderships promoted Russian dominance to develop a new Soviet nationality based on Russian culture. This Soviet-nationality policy took advantage of communist ide-

(Intourist, Moscow)

The Mother Armenia Monument, located in Akhtanak Park in Yerevan, Armenia, built to commemorate the 50th anniversary of Soviet power in Armenia.

(Intourist, Moscow)

This monument to the victims of the massacre of more than 1 million Armenians by Turks in 1915 contains an open-air mausoleum in which an eternal flame burns. A column to its right symbolizes eternal life and brotherhood. The monument is sacred to Armenians.

ology, which held that national differences were a relic of the discredited bourgeois-capitalist society to be replaced by socialism. But it was also intended to strengthen administrative unity essential to successful economic development and the establishment of an effective defense of the country against foreign subversion.

The Soviet leadership was determined to maintain Russian dominance also because of a declining birth rate among Russians. In the 1980s the Russian population slipped somewhat, from about 54 percent to about 52 percent of the total population, while the birth rates of non-Russian groups, especially those of the Muslim peoples of the Central Asian republics, rose.

Russian dominance of the Soviet system aroused the anger of many non-Russian peoples who resented Russification of their cultures, especially in the area of language. The non-Russian peoples also resented political control by Russians as well as an absence of ways to resist it except by protest and dissent. They were frustrated by the contradiction between Russian dominance and the constitutional commitment of the Soviet system to respect their separate cultural identities. The

Baltic peoples of Estonia, Latvia, and Lithuania, who were very nationalistic, and the Muslim peoples of the Soviet Central Asian republics, who were very sensitive about their Islamic cultural traditions, reacted strongly against Russian dominance; in response, the Soviet regime tried in a variety of ways to counter and control these perceived anti-Russian feelings. The result was conflict and tension between non-Russian and Russian peoples.

Baltic Nationalism

Estonians, Latvians, and Lithuanians who remembered the days of independence before annexation by the Soviet Union in April 1940 were very nationalistic and resentful of the highly centralized rule imposed upon them by Moscow. They tried in a variety of ways to exploit the limited amount of autonomy they did enjoy. They stubbornly preserved their languages and local customs. Indeed, local Communist Party newspapers in the Baltic republics perennially complained about popular indifference to the Russian language and a lack of fluency in it. In a gesture of protest—albeit a mild one—many Estonians in the 1979 Supreme Soviet elections either did not participate in voting or, when they did, they actually marked their ballots against the official candidate. In that election Estonia had the highest "no-vote" of any socialist republic.

Muslim Grievances

Another source of interethnic tensions was the resentment of Muslim citizens of the former Soviet Union's Central Asian republics over the presence in their local governments of Russians. The Russians sometimes seemed to Soviet Muslims to be abrasive, especially when they put on airs of superiority and acted as if they were civilizers of a primitive people. Some Soviet Muslims were concerned by the possibility of large-scale population transfers to inhospitable places elsewhere in the country where there were labor shortages. On one occasion the regime moved a number of Central Asian Muslims to the north. The Muslims had such difficulty becoming acclimated to the new environment because of climatic contrasts and Russification pressures that other plans to move large numbers of people from the south to the north were abandoned.

Moscow's worst fear was that Pan-Islamic sympathies encouraged by broadcasts from Iran, Pakistan, and Saudi Arabia would encourage a spirit of independence in Central Asia. At the least the Islamic revival abroad, spearheaded by Iran, was likely to stimulate a demand of Soviet Muslims for more national and religious freedom and for greater political and cultural autonomy.

But most Soviet Muslims showed no serious signs of alienation, and there seemed to be no major movements for secession in the Muslim republics. The Soviet government tried to encourage Muslim acceptance of Marxist rule by an intensive socialization of the youth. Soviet propaganda constantly compared the relative modernization and affluence of Soviet Central Asia with the underdevelopment and poverty in Iran, Afghanistan, and Pakistan.

Still, the Gorbachev regime did have cause for anxiety and was not complaisant about sources of Muslim dissatisfaction with the central government. Because the birth rate of the Muslims was increasing at a much faster rate than that of other national groups and because of the innumerable contacts Soviet Muslims began to have with coreligionists in Afghanistan and other neighboring Islamic societies in the 1980s, the Soviet regime expected Muslim pressures for a larger role in the Soviet political system to become more intense.

SOCIAL PROBLEMS

The persistence of deep-rooted social problems not only belied what the Soviets said about the achievements of their socialist society but also threatened its political stability. One problem involved religion. Other problems were alcoholism, juvenile delinquency and adult crime, discrimination against women, and weaknesses in the education and health care systems.

Religious Harassment

Before the Gorbachev phase, the Soviet regime was consistently hostile to religion, which was considered a relic of the society's bourgeois past. The official attitude toward religion was also the result of history. The complaisance of Russian orthodox clerics toward, and their profit from, Czarism discredited the Russian Orthodox Church in Soviet eyes.

The Soviets saw religion also as a potential threat to political stability. Soviet officials considered the church, synagogue, and mosque to be rivals of the Communist Party and a threat to its monopoly of power. They also believed that religion could undermine loyalty and obedience of citizens to the party and state.

But from the beginning of the Stalinist era, the Soviet leadership gave up trying to annihilate religion. The Soviet government allowed the major religions—Russian Orthodoxy, Islam, and Judaism—to exist. However, party and state agencies relentlessly disseminated the message of atheism to remind those who were religious of the official attitude and to discourage people, especially the youth, from being religious. School textbooks were laced with antireligious propaganda, describing faith in God as antiquated and antiscientific. The hope of officials was that in the long term organized religion would disappear.

Russian Orthodoxy

The Soviet state permitted the Russian Orthodox Church's religious practice, paid its maintenance costs, and provided seminaries to train clergy. The government had to give permission for any religious activity such as fund raising, publications, and the organization of a congregation.

At the same time, however, the regime discriminated against and harassed the Orthodox Church. It converted many churches into museums instead of keeping them as places of worship. Those open for religious services were in disrepair and frequently were located in out-of-the-way places. The regime also made it awkward or uncomfortable for people who openly professed religious commitment. Religion was something you didn't talk about in public if you wanted to get ahead in your career.

These efforts to discredit and discourage religious practice among those who professed the Orthodox faith were not successful. People packed existing churches at holiday times, especially at Christmas. And many young couples sought a religious marriage ceremony along with the required secular administrative one performed by a state official. Historical fascination with the divine and supernatural seemed to be an indestructible trait of the Russian people.

Islam

While Islam had the second-largest religious following in the Soviet Union, it was potentially the most troublesome for the Soviet state. The Soviets faced a dilemma with Islam that they had with no other religion. They had to be careful in their domestic antireligion policies to avoid antagonizing foreign Islamic countries, especially influential ones like Saudi Arabia, concerned with the condition of Muslims living under Communist rule.

Nevertheless, the Soviets continued unabashedly to try to weaken the Islamic faith by extensive and unrelenting pressures. Local party agencies actively promoted atheism, not only in schools, newspapers, and exhibits in former mosques converted to museums, but also by usurping old customs, creating new rituals extolling Soviet life, and enlisting elder *asksals,* or venerable storytellers, to talk about "the falsehood of religious concepts, the futility and harm in the worship of dark forces invented by clergymen for their own enrichment." Schoolteachers also helped the party in attacking Islamic religious practice.

The Soviet state tried to make attendance in mosques difficult. The number of mosques remained small. Those used for worship were left in disrepair and were located in hard-to-reach places. Official figures showed only 200 mosques for all of Soviet Central Asia's more than 20 million people of Muslim faith. The regime also restricted pilgrimages and the pursuit of formal religious study. Muslim pilgrims were apparently hand-picked by Soviet authorities, and some of them were actually KGB agents.

Another means of discouraging Islamic religious practices was a contrived scarcity of Korans. In a 1976 printing, only 10,000 copies were made and were available only in Arabic, not in Russian or any other languages and alphabets that young Soviet citizens in the Muslim constituent republics could read and write. A religious official obviously sympathetic—at least outwardly so—to regime policy on the printing of Korans explained that confining the book to an Arabic edition was a way of preserving its purity.

The Soviet regime did not succeed in smothering the Islamic religion. Older people with influence over the youth continued to practice some Islamic traditions in the privacy of the home. And Muslims in the Soviet Army in Afghanistan apparently were repelled by commands to kill Afghan coreligionists. These soldiers had to be replaced by military personnel from non-Muslim parts of the Soviet Union.

Judaism

Many Soviet Jews, as well as Jews in the United States and other parts of the world, spoke of an official Soviet discrimination that went beyond anything endured by other religious groups. They accused the Soviets of discriminating against Jews in much the same way as their Czarist predecessors did. Many Soviet Jews likened their situation to that under czars Alexander III and Nicholas II, who persecuted and harassed Russian Jews in the 1880s and 1890s, causing many to emigrate to the United States.

Alleged Soviet discrimination against Jews involved the same kind of policies the regime pursued toward other religions. Jewish synagogues fell into disrepair because little public money was made available for maintenance. There were restrictions on the training of rabbis, the publication of books in Hebrew, and the production and distribution of special foods like matzos. Synagogues, like mosques and many Orthodox churches, were located in hard-to-find places. It was easy for a foreign visitor seeking a synagogue to pass it by because of the absence of distinctive markings.

There was, allegedly, official discrimination of a more sinister kind. It was said to occur when Jews sought entry into and advancement in the professions, especially education and the bureaucracy. They met roadblocks at every turn, starting with their efforts to gain admission to universities and graduate schools. Some Soviet Jews said that it was impossible to climb the professional ladder if they practiced their religion.

The problem of discrimination was complicated by the impossibility of discussing it openly. People of influence refused to acknowledge its existence. There was an implicit threat that forceful efforts to bring it out into the open would invite retribution, such as dismissal from a job and harassment of family and even of friends who showed sympathy. Ultimately, the only escape was emigration.

Discrimination against Jews provoked an aggressive interest group of Soviet Jews who wanted to emigrate from their homeland. In an angry, perhaps vengeful, response to this embarrassing phenomenon, an image-conscious Soviet leadership from time to time tightened restrictions on emigration by all kinds of impediments, including repeated denial of exit visas and the payment of an exorbitant departure tax. The regime considered emigration to be an act of disloyalty and punished not only those who applied for exit visas but also others, like employers for whom would-be emigrants worked.

Soviet discrimination led to international complications, especially with the United States, which showed great sensitivity to the condition of Soviet Jewry. Influential American Jews lobbied aggressively and persuasively with their government to put pressure on Moscow to liberalize its policy on Jewish emigration.

Alcoholism

Alcoholism predominated among Soviet peoples. It was chronic and caused serious political, economic, and social problems. Alcoholism contributed to disorderliness and crime, resulted in missed hours at work, and made people weak, docile, and subservient. Many Soviet citizens seemed to drink for the express purpose of getting drunk and would drink until they were in a stupor.

A major reason for excessive drinking seemed to be escape from the monotony and deprivation of everyday life in the

Soviet Union. The shabby and crowded living quarters, the limited means of recreation affordable for the average citizen, the perennial shortages of necessities and the few luxury items—in short, the harshness and drabness of everyday life—led people to seek distraction through drinking. The problem of excessive drinking, therefore, was linked closely to living and working conditions that could not easily be changed by the Soviet government. Without distracting people with alcohol, the state would have had to spend heavily on the development of alternative means of public relaxation, such as expensive sports facilities. Consequently, while Moscow spent a lot of money to discourage alcoholism, it carefully refrained from going all out to make alcohol unavailable.

The Soviet government was ambivalent on the issue of controlling alcohol consumption for another reason: The state imposed high taxes on hard liquor. It did not want to lose this lucrative source of revenue. Still, the Gorbachev leadership seemed bent on continuing the efforts of its predecessors to reduce at least heavy consumption of alcohol. In 1985 there were sharp increases in the prices of liquor, beer, and wine. The long lines of Soviet citizens outside the wine shops on the eve of the announced price increases confirmed the widely held view that people would find a way to continue past drinking habits, because "the nip" remained the only easy and certain means of achieving relief from the stress of everyday Soviet life. Indeed, as a result of strong popular antipathy to the regime's antidrinking campaign, Gorbachev relented and made alcoholic beverages a bit more accessible.

Juvenile Delinquency and Adult Crime

Juvenile delinquency and adult crime were embarrassments to the Soviet leadership because they confirmed the existence of problems and imperfections found in other, nonsocialist, "inferior" bourgeois polities. With some reluctance the Soviet regime began to acknowledge that the causes of juvenile delinquency and adult crime in the Soviet Union were not so different from the causes in nonsocialist societies. The Soviets themselves said that juvenile delinquency was caused by parental neglect and indifference, narcotic and alcohol addiction, boredom, and a profound amorality and lack of belief in Marxist-Leninism.

To some extent primary schools were implicated by encouraging difficult, misbehaving youngsters to leave school after the eighth grade. Thus, some teenagers were thrown onto the street. Since those under 16 could not hold full-time jobs, some young people were beyond the supervision of parents and society. They became prone to drug addiction and drinking.

The Soviets railed against three kinds of misbehavior that had serious impact on society: hooliganism, parasitism, and economic crime.

Hooliganism was a mindless violation of public order by young people as well as others. It was said by the Soviets to be inspired by a contempt for society.

Parasitism was a reluctance to work or study or in some other way to avoid the performance of one's responsibilities to the family and the state. Parasitism was a willingness to live at the expense of others. People who did not want to do a job assigned to them because they did not like it or were not trained for it ran the risk of being charged with parasitism. People who intentionally evaded employment also were liable to charges of parasitism. Soviet authorities took a dim view of parasitism because of the lengths to which the state went to prepare people for gainful employment and because of the loss to the economy due to unemployment.

Economic crimes were considered to be the most serious and consisted of stealing state property, falsification, and embezzlement of state funds for private use. The state mandated the death penalty for some economic crimes. Crimes were a source of embarrassment to the Soviets because they suggested that Soviet citizens possessed the same acquisitiveness characteristic of citizens of capitalistic societies.

Discrimination against Women

Marxist ideology preached equality, but in Soviet society women were not equal. They were the object of a systematic and pervasive discrimination outside the home. They were expected to work at a job while simultaneously discharging their traditional responsibility for home management and childrearing. Women in the Soviet Union confronted inequities everywhere. Most educated women could find jobs only in prestigious but low-paying jobs, like family practice in medicine. They were grossly underrepresented in the party and state bureaucracies, and there were no women in the party Politburo.

Several factors accounted for discrimination against women. While Soviet husbands needed and expected their wives to work in order to survive, never mind obtain a longed-for but very expensive luxury like an automobile, they did not want to do housework to help their working mates. They looked forward to the day when they could afford to have their wives stay at home and confine their work to family. There was a strong tradition of male chauvinism in the Soviet Union that was only barely affected by the egalitarianism of communist ideology. Assumptions of male superiority and female subservience endured.

In the predominantly Muslim republics of Soviet Central Asia, the Islamic religion discouraged female assertiveness and female employment in jobs outside the home. There were examples of families everywhere in the Soviet Union—not only in the Islamic republics—that, for reasons of tradition, did not want their daughters to receive a higher education and enter as equals the world of men. And some educated women who held responsible and well-paying jobs voiced privately a preference for part-time work and more time for family life.

The Soviet state tried to diminish discrimination. Women were given maternity and child care leave to lessen the disadvantage of caring for family while developing a career. The state also provided stipends to encourage women to have more children without detriment, at least in theory, to their economic status. (Indeed, the state recognized and rewarded fecundity. Mothers of 10 or more children were designated "heroines of socialist labor.") And Soviet women made important gains. They accounted for one-quarter of the Soviet equivalent of Ph.D.'s. Nearly one-third of ordinary judges were women, and almost one-third of the 1,500 members of the Supreme Soviet were women. Seventy percent of all physicians were women.

But discrimination persisted. For example, in the late 1980s, there was still a striking absence of women from positions of leadership. Only a very small percentage of collective farm directors, factory managers, and construction supervisors were women. And while women had a much higher representation in the teaching profession, they held only about one-fourth of school principalships. Even more striking evidence of discrimination was the fact that women continued on average to earn lower salaries than their male counterparts.

Despite the bitterness and cynicism of many Soviet women, there appeared to be little feminist activism. On the surface most women were satisfied with their roles and were unwilling to lobby aggressively for equal treatment by the system. Women who did enter positions of responsibility and leadership seemed to want to avoid the controversy that would result from championing women's equality. Moreover, government censors would not allow blunt charges of sex discrimination by the regime.

Education

The school system was another area of Soviet society where there were problems, although they were less subversive of domestic tranquillity than religious harassment, abuse of alcohol, and juvenile delinquency. One weakness of Soviet schools was the way in which they fostered a tension-producing inequality, despite the regime's commitment to the ideological goal of egalitarianism. The best schools, those with better-trained teachers and up-to-date equipment for classroom instruction, were located in the large cities, especially in the European regions of the Soviet Union. Because of their locations, the best schools were not always open to citizens from all parts of the country and from all walks of life. Children of farmers and workers had to attend the schools close to where their parents worked.

One aspect of the school system that caused considerable tension was the ritual of assigning students employment following their graduation. Graduates had to accept the jobs assigned them and had to hold those jobs for at least 3 years. One rejected an assignment at great peril to one's future career development. Consequently, there was much personal anxiety as graduation neared. Students were not above trying to influence the assignments by bribery or "pulling strings" with officials responsible for making assignments. Sometimes disappointment with one's assignment was so great that it led to depression, demoralization, even suicide. The price of a secure job after graduation thus came very high.

Another problem in Soviet education—and one that was admitted by Soviet authorities—was the way in which emphasis on education led many young people to disparage the kind of manual work that required only a minimum of schooling. A large portion of Soviet young people did not express much interest in becoming workers on the assembly line. They preferred jobs that required more education and had greater prestige than those held by manual workers. As a result the authorities had to propagandize the importance of assembly-line work in this proletarian society.

Health Care

The Soviets acknowledged massive shortcomings in their health care system, symbolized by a gradual decrease in life expectancy and a steady worsening of the infant mortality rate. In the 1980s there was a slow erosion in hospital services and general health care. Other weaknesses of the health care system included the very poor state of Soviet hospitals and polyclinics. They were underequipped, lacked modern facilities, and did not have sufficient pharmaceutical supplies. Doctors' and nurses' salaries were too low.

Poor standards of sanitation and public hygiene and high levels of alcoholism caused a striking increase in death rates in the Soviet Union, especially among working males. By the late 1980s, the average Soviet male could expect to live for only about 60 years—some 6 years less than he could in the mid-1960s. Conditions of maternity care were unsatisfactory, especially in Soviet Central Asia. Only 30 percent of maternity hospitals in the Soviet Union met acceptable hygiene standards, and only a few maternity wards in all of Central Asia were properly equipped.

Nearly as shocking was infant mortality. The infant mortality rate for the entire Soviet Union was 25.2 deaths per 1,000 births. In some underdeveloped regions in the Central Asian republics, the rate was 60 and sometimes even more than 100 deaths for every 1,000 births.

These shortcomings were mainly the result of inadequate funding in consequence of the Kremlin's application of the "leftover" principle in Soviet investment policy. According to this principle, heath care received whatever was left of investment after other priorities, such as defense and domestic heavy industry, had been met. As a result there was a continuous reduction in the share of national income allocated to medical services. In 1989 it was below 4 percent, as compared to the 8 to 12 percent allocated to medical services in other countries.

POLITICAL DISSENT

Dissent was a logical consequence of the Soviet regime's intolerance of most forms of criticism and protest. It was inevitable in a society that promised in its ideology a paradise on Earth and in its propaganda insisted upon the need of citizens to make great personal sacrifices to achieve that paradise, while delivering far less than what people needed and wanted simply to survive, never mind thrive. The complexity, intensity, and relentlessness of the Soviet dissident movement, despite the regime's best efforts to obliterate it—and sometimes the Soviet authorities came close to that—were in proportion to the regime's flaws and its failure to mitigate them.

Major Groups of Dissidents

In the Brezhnev phase, there were at least five well-known groups of Soviet dissidents. One large and somewhat diverse group included people like the late Andrei Sakharov and human rights activists Yuri Orlov and Anatolyi Shcharansky. This group was critical of the Soviet dictatorship, in particular its refusal to allow serious criticism or opposition to its policies, and sought liberalization along Western democratic lines. They asked for civil liberties, truly representative government, relaxation of censorship, and establishment of a system of checks and balances to limit governmental power and prevent abuses. Human rights activists also demanded Soviet compliance with the human rights provisions of the 1975 Helsinki agreements.

A second group of dissidents included Jews seeking to emigrate because of official discrimination. They were concerned primarily with pressuring the Soviet government to give them exit visas.

A third group of dissidents advocated the causes of the non-Russian nationalities against the Russifying and homogenizing policies of the central government. In this group were Georgian, Ukrainian, and Baltic national dissidents.

A fourth group consisted of people who protested the regime's harassment of them for religious reasons. Catholic, Lutheran, Baptist, and Pentecostal dissidents demanded a lessening of regime discrimination and the right to emigrate.

Finally, other dissidents, notably Alexander Solzhenitsyn, advocated a return to historic Russian values and traditions. These people sought a separation of Russia from the non-Russian peoples, whom they distrusted. (They have been called "chauvinistic reactionaries.") They also displayed a somewhat un-Marxist admiration of the Russian Orthodox Church.

External Stimulants of Political Dissent

International circumstances encouraged Soviet dissident groups. The Helsinki agreements of 1975, signed by the Soviet Union and other socialist countries in Central/Eastern Europe as well as by Western democracies, focused international attention on alleged violations of human rights of Soviet citizens by their government. Washington and Paris frequently accused the Soviet Union of violating the human rights of its citizens. This international concern inspired Soviet dissidents to publicize their complaints.

Dissident groups in other socialist countries also inspired dissent. The Charter 77 movement in Czechoslovakia, which protested human rights violations by the Communist government in Prague, and the emergence of the Committee for Social Self Defense in Poland, which tried to help workers arrested by the Warsaw authorities for their role in the 1976 food strikes, attracted the attention of Soviet dissidents. The Eurocommunist phenomenon of the 1970s, in which Western Marxists, notably the leaders of the French, Italian, and Spanish Communist parties, advocated a liberal parliamentary path to socialist development and criticized the Soviet system for its violations of human rights, also influenced and encouraged dissent in the Soviet Union. The independent Polish trade union, Solidarity, in the 1980s had an impact on Soviet dissidents, especially in the Baltic republics, although it was not clear how much influence Solidarity had on Soviet workers.

Soviet workers—who had much to complain about—traditionally were a source of only very mild and restrained dissidence in the Soviet Union for several reasons. Spontaneous and illegal union activities were ruthlessly suppressed by the state. Soviet industrial centers were widely dispersed, discouraging communication and cooperation among workers in different factory locations. Soviet workers themselves were divided along nationality lines. Moreover, Soviet workers had no allies in other social groups, such as farmers, the intelligentsia, and the Russian Orthodox clergy. The intelligentsia, from which most Soviet dissidents came, seemed to have little interest in helping workers obtain redress of their grievances against the system.

Dissident groups in the Soviet Union were always weak, lacking strong and cohesive organization and effective leadership. They showed little of the discipline and unity that the Marxists of Lenin's time had in their opposition to Czarism. Many dissidents tended to be individualistic, absolutist in their thinking, and antagonistic toward one another as well as to other social groups. Their very Russian-like dogmatism, in particular the intolerance some had of alternative ideas and positions, contradicted their professed affection for Western-style liberalism and political pluralism.

Forms of Political Dissent

Political dissent had many forms from its apparent beginnings during the Khrushchevian "cultural thaw." It first appeared in literary expression, perhaps because literature provided an opportunity to express criticism obliquely and with minimum risk. The *Samizdat,* or materials reproduced privately and clandestinely (the opposite of *Gosizdat,* which meant government-published and thus officially sanctioned), included literature not likely to pass Soviet censors.

An important watershed in the early development of political dissent through literature was the Andrei Sinyavsky-Yuli Daniel trial in 1966. These two Soviet writers were arrested for having their works, which were critical of the regime, published abroad under pseudonyms. They were accused of anti-Soviet agitation and were convicted in a trial that provoked opposition in Western Europe as well as at home. Indeed, many Soviet dissidents, notably Alexander Ginzburg, who published an unofficial record of the trial, dated their participation in the movement from this time.

Shortly after the trial, the most important Samizdat publication, *The Chronicle of Current Events,* was launched. The *Chronicle* was an underground journal that covered a variety of political criticism. Other Samizdat publications focused on specific nationality and religious grievances. There was also a spate of terrorism, such as a 1977 bomb explosion in a Moscow subway train by disgruntled Armenians, airplane hijackings, and even self-immolations. But the most persistent, and possibly the most embarrassing, forms of dissidence were the less violent ones. The frequent public criticisms of Soviet policy by Andrei Sakharov and the activities of human rights activists known as the Helsinki Watch Group received publicity in the Western press.

Regime Responses to Political Dissent

The Soviets always reacted vehemently to the behavior of dissidents because of deep-seated hostility to and fear of opposition of any kind. This attitude toward opposition was historical, dating back to Czarist Russia. There was always a characteristically Russian fear of things different, of alien ideas, and of popular challenges to the established order.

A measure of anti-intellectualism contributed to regime hostility to dissent. Those in positions of administrative authority and responsibility for the day-to-day operation of the Soviet system, notably censors, police, and many members of the Communist Party, were usually not intellectuals. Many had only the minimum of formal education and little sympathy for people with ideas they did not understand.

One never knew—and perhaps the regime itself did not know—what might happen to particular dissidents until they were actually taken in hand by the authorities. Official reactions depended upon circumstances of the moment, such as the particular kind of dissent being dealt with, the state of the economy, the international situation, and relations with the United States.

Specific regime reactions to dissent occasionally included warnings to dissidents by legal officials. Other, more draconian, responses consisted of arrest, conviction, and punishment by imprisonment, ranging from a few years in an ordinary penitentiary to many years at hard labor, under difficult and even life-threatening physical conditions, in maximum-security institutions. The regime also resorted to the ancient punishment of forced exile to either obscure places in the Soviet Union or abroad.

There were also unofficial and informal responses to dissent, such as harassment of individuals by KGB agents, who could intrude on any aspect of a citizen's life with near impunity. This intrusion might involve an unexpected rifling of an apartment, constant surveillance, or "trailing" and entrapment. The KGB also could arrange for the confinement of dissidents in mental hospitals for indefinite periods, where they would be harassed until they recanted. Another indirect means of dealing with dissidents was contrived discrimination against them and their families in the workplace, at school, and elsewhere.

In 1983 the Andropov regime went beyond its predecessor in trying to reduce dissent. It revived old laws that limited the contact that Soviet citizens could have with foreigners. This move was intended to curtail the practice of Soviet dissidents meeting with Western visitors, especially journalists, and informing them of their complaints and grievances against the regime, which would then, in some instances, promptly appear on the front pages of major Western newspapers. The regime also revived laws that extended the terms of troublesome prisoners in labor camps.

ECONOMIC UNDERPERFORMANCE

Economic underperformance plagued the Soviet system from its inception. It was dangerous because it prevented the regime's fulfillment of its elaborate promises to improve the material well-being of the Soviet peoples and thereby contributed to societal discontent and the possibility of political instability.

Agriculture

The most intractable and perhaps most serious aspect of economic underperformance was in agriculture, especially in the failure of agricultural output to meet food needs. While every Soviet leader did much to cope with this problem, none succeeded in correcting it.

The inadequacy of Soviet agricultural output resulted from many different and complex factors. At the head of the list was a scarcity of arable land. Only about 10 percent of the enormous Soviet landmass was designated arable; and much of this was not ideal for farming because of climatic extremes, water erosion, and other problems that undermine soil fertility.

Another reason was incentive—or, rather, the lack of it. Most Soviet farmers were little more than wage earners with no stake in excelling. Moreover, many Soviet farmers did not earn as much as industrial workers, and the fact that they were better off than were earlier generations was little consolation.

Soviet agriculture also suffered from an inadequacy of machinery. That which Soviet farmers did have was either underutilized or abused. Many machines in need of repair stood idle because of the absence of spare parts, and there was poor maintenance and storage. Finally, the Soviet leadership diminished the supply of agricultural machinery available for domestic use by exporting abroad. There were poor storage facilities for grain harvests that exceeded anticipated requirements. About 20 percent of the harvests, even in bad periods, was lost to rot, partly because storage was inadequate. Invariably, grain reserves were low and never sufficient to make up for unexpected shortfalls of annual harvests.

Distribution was another problem. Perishable food products could not be moved swiftly to market and frequently rotted on freight platforms while awaiting shipment. Part of the distribution problem had to do with the inefficiency of the Soviet railway system as well as the lack of first-class roads needed by heavy trucks.

Soviet agriculture also lacked enough good mineral fertilizers. Soviet farmers were obliged to use smaller amounts of fertilizer than their American counterparts, and the quality of Soviet fertilizers was lower than in the West. Consequently, it was difficult to maximize yield.

Another and by no means insignificant factor that contributed to inadequate agricultural output was the conservatism of Soviet leaders who showed great reluctance to inaugurate changes that might improve productivity. When reforms were discussed and tried, as Khrushchev found, to his dismay, there was much resistance from the bureaucracy, which had a vested interest in preserving the centralized agricultural decision-making process. Indeed, the bureaucracy bitterly resisted any leadership efforts, however slight, to boost food production by encouraging private garden plots that were beyond its control. The bureaucracy also resisted any efforts to increase the autonomy of collective and state farms.

Finally, the Soviet leadership was reluctant to commit to agriculture the level of investment needed to achieve a significant improvement in output. There was an increase in agricultural investment between 1961 and 1975 over that of the preceding period, but the total investment only involved a decrease in the traditional investment advantage of industry over agriculture. It did not bring agriculture up to parity with industry.

Industry

Soviet industry suffered from underperformance in the form of poor quality, high costs, and economic waste, for some of the same reasons as agriculture. Chief among these reasons was an excessively centralized decision-making apparatus. Managerial personnel had little decision-making discretion. They also were obsessed with protecting themselves against criticism and punishment by superiors. They were evasive and defensive. They hesitated to use what little discretion allowed them by central planners and administrators to innovate or develop improved technology to increase the quality and quantity of output.

Furthermore, central planners, who had the bulk of decision-making authority, tended to ignore consumer demand. They set targets for output based upon somewhat arbitrary assessments of need. They also determined output goals in many industries in terms of number of tons or in ruble value and paid little attention to the quality and marketability of what was to be produced. This helps to explain why much of Soviet industrial output, when measured by Western standards, was shoddy and why there was much waste of scarce resources. At the same time, the Soviet industrial machine lacked labor-saving automation based on modern computer technology. In general, it simply took too many people too long to make decisions at the center and to implement them in the production unit.

Disproportionate growth caused by overinvestment in some industries and underinvestment in others was another reason for underperformance. The Soviet leadership tended to overinvest in heavy industry for reasons of ideology and defense. But profits in heavy industry were small when compared to the profits that could be made in the production of consumer goods. Furthermore, the regime continued to invest in inefficient units of production for the sake of full employment. This unbalanced investment policy encouraged poor quality, to say nothing of high production costs.

Perhaps a critical reason for underperformance had to do with the behavior of workers. Soviet workers protested low wages and the absence of goods they needed and wanted by slackening their pace of work, because the unions to which they belonged were controlled by the Communist Party and did not provide them with adequate means of obtaining satisfaction of grievances.

Strict obedience to the decisions of the Gosplan led to disastrous economic losses. For example, billions of rubles were spent building the Baikur-Amur extension of the Trans-Siberian railway before there was anything to haul on it; it soon fell into disrepair. The highly centralized method of determining prices also produced absurdities. Arbitrarily low prices for fuel and raw materials in the past stimulated excessive use, creating waste and inefficiency in industry and agriculture and raising real costs of production. Ultimately, a very costly program of price subsidies was required to avoid penalizing the consumer.

The Consumer

Not surprisingly, another economic problem potentially threatening to political stability involved the Soviet consumer, who suffered from inadequate quantity and quality of goods. There was never enough food, housing, clothing, and durable goods like automobiles and household appliances. Soviet citizens became inured to long lines in grocery stores and long waiting periods for cars, housing, and appliances.

Some of the reasons for consumer neglect in the Soviet Union already have been identified in our discussion of the problems of production in Soviet agriculture and industry. Other causes of this neglect were political. Consumers never had an effective interest group able to lobby for government policies to improve their lot. And while in its final years the

Soviet government began to study poverty levels, noting that some segments of the society were "underprovisioned," very little was done to address the large problem of consumer neglect.

Neglect of consumer goods compromised other sectors of the economy by discouraging workers from expanding output. Because consumer goods were not produced and made available for sale to the workers, the bonus and extra pay given for increased productivity were meaningless and provided no incentive for workers to excel.

Shortages of consumer goods also encouraged workers to patronize the black market, which thrived in Soviet society because most shortages were chronic. The black market experienced constantly rising prices for continuously scarce commodities, with the long-term effect of encouraging the development of barter. In barter, citizens traded their talents and possessions and paid no taxes on any of this activity.

Remedies

While Soviet leaderships made many promises to improve economic performance, for a long time they did little to fulfill them beyond a mere tinkering with existing institutions and policies. For example, agricultural shortfalls were dealt with by allowing expansion of the private garden plots and by massive importation of foreign grain. Underperformance in industry was addressed by modest amounts of administrative decentralization, which involved small increases in the discretionary authority of factory managers in such areas as plant renewal, wages, and working hours. Even these gestures were bitterly resisted by a bureaucracy determined to oppose any change that involved reducing its authority.

On the other hand, there was evidence in the mid-1980s of official interest in a major overhaul of the Soviet economy. A confidential memo, prepared by a group of economists associated with the Siberian division of the Soviet Academy of Science in Novisibirsk and circulated in the Soviet economic administration, supported market-driven planning, flexible prices, and incentives to workers. The memo said that economic bureaucrats (the personnel of the Gosplan, the industrial ministries, and other state economic agencies) had to be restricted and their opposition to innovation curtailed. It charged that the bureaucracy frequently blocked reform because change would have required a high level of competence many bureaucrats did not possess and would have resulted in their loss of privilege.

The recommendations apparently inspired a joint Central Committee–Council of Ministers decree in 1984 giving plant managers authority over their budgets and discretion in matters of investment, wages, bonuses, and profit retention. To spur technological innovation, management was to have authority to reward innovative engineers and workers. The criteria for measuring factory performance were simplified in order to emphasize production of goods that would sell, particularly abroad. This meant lower priority for the traditional performance indicators in Soviet industry, notably the overall value of output, which encouraged factories to turn out large volumes of goods regardless of quality or need.

THE ENVIRONMENT

A major socioeconomic problem that only in the late 1980s began to arouse both official and public concern was industrial pollution of the environment. For example, Soviet writers and scientists complained about the pollution of Lake Baikal, an inland sea of fresh water in Siberia. For years a large pulp plant on the southwest tip of the lake had spilled contaminants into its waters, disrupting the fragile ecological balance and endangering public health. In response to this and other expressions of concern about pollution, the Soviet government enacted new laws to protect forests, air quality, water resources, and animal life. In 1987 the Communist Party ordered a halt to the pulp plant's polluting of Lake Baikal.

Another major environmental problem with very serious political implications involved the cotton economy in Uzbekistan, in Soviet Central Asia. Moscow's obsession with expanding cotton production caused an enormous amount of environmental deterioration, in particular pollution with pesticides, defoliants, and fertilizers, and the shriveling of the Aral Sea.

The ravaging of the Aral Sea by pollutants was especially striking. Soviet authorities diverted its waters to irrigate the cotton fields of Uzbekistan and Turkmenistan. As a result of the diversion, the sea began shrinking and its pollutants condensed, turning the two rivers that feed it, the Amu Darya and the Syr Darya, into little more than sewers. The contaminated water—the only potable water in some places—spread infection and disease, especially among the weakest infants. Moreover, the chemical pesticides and defoliants used in cotton growing were absorbed by the people who worked in the fields, and they were washed into the river water that the people drank.

The Environment and Nuclear Energy: Chernobyl

Beginning in the Brezhnev phase, the Soviet leadership gave a high priority to the development of nuclear power in order to diminish dependence on limited oil and natural-gas reserves. By the end of 1985, Soviet nuclear facilities had achieved a total generating capacity of 20,000 megawatts. Nuclear fuel power-generating plants were responsible for 11 percent of the nation's total power output, placing the Soviet Union in third place among countries with nuclear-generated electricity, after the United States and France. But in the spring of 1986, the meltdown of a nuclear reactor in the Chernobyl nuclear plant in Ukraine brought home to Soviet authorities the dangers of its commitment to double the Soviet Union's nuclear power-generating capacity by 1990.

The Chernobyl nuclear accident on April 26, 1986, was the world's worst civil nuclear disaster. A cloud of radioactive fallout drifted hundreds of miles northward and westward beyond Ukraine into other parts of the Soviet Union, Scandinavia, and Central/Eastern Europe, ultimately affecting areas as far away as Italy, France, Britain, and even North America.

Soviet investigators accused workers and managers at the plant of negligence, incompetence, complacency, irresponsibility, and lack of discipline—in sum, a carelessness born of a conviction, untempered by careful and thoughtful supervision from above, that what did happen could not happen. Western scientists concluded that there had been serious flaws in the construction of the number-four reactor at the Chernobyl plant, which had outdated technology and inadequate safety devices.

The accident had a profound effect on the health and well-being of people within the immediate area of the plant. Radiation levels within that area were 2,500 times greater than normal. Medical treatment was difficult because Soviet doctors lacked the technical skills needed to handle cases of extreme radiation. No one knew what the long-term health consequences would be.

Evacuation of residents in highly contaminated areas was difficult because there had been little preparation for a disaster of Chernobyl proportions. In the month after the meltdown, it was necessary to move 92,000 people and provide them with food, clothing, and shelter. Local authorities had to disperse hundreds of thousands of children in Kiev and nearby cities to contamination-free areas in summer camps located in the south. Authorities also had to worry about other people who voluntarily left their homes out of fear of contamination to stay with friends or in temporary housing, where they waited to hear from officials when it was safe to return. Not since World War II had Soviet authorities had to deal with the movement of so many people.

Contamination of the rich food-producing topsoil of a large region surrounding the Chernobyl plant destroyed most of the Ukrainian grain crop for 1986. The Soviets were unprepared for this agricultural calamity, because of their limited grain storage capacity. There also was a temporary loss of nuclear-generated energy output.

The task of decontamination was horrendous in cost and complexity. Major cleanup activities included protection of the Pripyat River and the groundwater in the area against contamination; prevention of the spread of radioactive dust around the plant, in part by paving the ground with concrete; reduction of the spread of contamination through runoff of rain water, achieved by seeding clouds before they reached the power-plant area; the extinguishing of a large number of small fires around the reactor building; and the construction of a concrete containment structure, which would permanently encase the number-four reactor while ensuring ventilation so that residual heat would not build up. Some of these remedial activities continued well into 1987; problems and complications slowed down the processes of repair and reconstruction.

While the Chernobyl accident did not appear to dampen the enthusiasm of Soviet leaders for continued expansion of nuclear generating capability, it at least increased their sensitivity to safety in the construction and maintenance of nuclear facilities. They also knew better the problems likely to occur in a Chernobyl-type disaster, notably the care of large numbers of potential victims of a nuclear disaster. They may also have become more aware of the liabilities of secrecy in nuclear development and thus more willing to interact with other countries in this area of policy making.

THE FINAL ERA BEGINS

THE IMPACT OF PERESTROIKA

Beginning in 1986 the Gorbachev leadership embarked upon a radical program of reform called *perestroika,* or restructuring, which eventually involved all aspects of the Soviet political system: the economy, political environment, party, government, military, society, and foreign policy. The purpose of perestroika was to enable the system to improve the quality of life of average Soviet citizens and thereby assure their loyalty to and the survival of socialism. Perestroika profoundly transformed—and ultimately destroyed—the traditional Soviet polity.

In countless and endlessly long public and party speeches in the mid-1980s Mikhail Gorbachev spoke of a "pre-crisis" in the Soviet state, brought on by a long period of economic stagnation for which his predecessor Brezhnev was responsible. Gorbachev spoke of the urgency of resolving this pre-crisis situation, first, so he said, by accelerating output. Subsequently, when he realized that underperformance was the result of profound flaws in the system's organization and behavior, he advocated restructuring to make it function more efficiently. Gorbachev warned that failure to restructure the system would eventually jeopardize it by provoking a violent social turmoil, an oblique reference to the popular uprising in Poland in the summer of 1990. That crisis theatened Polish socialism and in the long term was the cause of its demise.

Writers in the West identified this pre-crisis as a failure of the so-called social contract, an implicit understanding between Communist leaderships and their societies that, in return for popular loyalty and obedience to party rule, citizens would obtain a radical improvement in the standard of living. By the time of Gorbachev's ascendancy in the Soviet Union in 1985, it was plain to all Soviet citizens that the utopian ideal was far from having been achieved and that, while life was tolerable for most, the standard of living was still low as compared to not only the West but also other socialist countries—and even, embarrassingly, to some countries in the Third World.

In particular, it was obvious to most Soviet citizens that the system had not redeemed its promises of improvement in the areas of food, clothing, housing, medical care, and other amenities important in daily life. And it was an open secret that many party and state managers, the lieutenants of the ruling elite, were abusive to the point of irrationality in their treatment of the citizenry they were supposed to serve. They were also personally corrupt, incompetent, apathetic, dishonest, and, worse, obsessed more with career building than with socialist development—this despite the enormous perquisites available to them that in effect made them a privileged class in a society that was supposed to eschew class distinctions.

Gorbachev and his close advisers knew that the time had come for systemic reform. This, they believed, was necessary to assure the Soviet system's legitimacy at home, to enforce its claims to superpower status abroad, and to protect and further its global interests. They believed that unless the Soviet system was thoroughly overhauled to make it serve its citizens better it would never be able to achieve the place that its size and wealth justified in the international community.

The time for radical reform had come also because the people in power in the Kremlin in the mid-1980s were of a new generation, sensitive to the flaws of the past and confident in their ability to improve the system once and for all. This was Gorbachev's generation, born well after the Revolution of 1917 and coming of age in the post-Stalin era, sensitive to the excesses of the earlier formative period of Soviet development. They were also proud of the new Soviet society because of the essentially humanitarian rationale on which it was based. They did not accept the long-held view of early Soviet leaders, notably Lenin and Stalin, that the end justified the means. They were in these as well as other respects very different in their political outlook and behavior from their tyrannical predecessors.

From the 27th party Congress in early 1986 to the collapse of the Soviet state in December 1991, perestroika affected all major areas of Soviet national life. Most of the changes that took place involved a loosening of state control and an increase in individual initiative and responsibility—a new respect for individuals in their relationship with the state.

The first area of Soviet life to experience change was the economy, perhaps the area most in need of profound alteration to improve performance. The next area of Soviet life affected by perestroika was the political environment; this involved changes called *glasnost,* or openness and candor. Gorbachev and his advisers believed that a relaxation of the political environment must accompany change in the economy. Changes in the political environment inevitably required changes in the party, in terms of not only personnel (Gorbachev removed from positions of power those who resisted perestroika) but also the style and substance of party behavior. Eventually there had to be changes in the structure and performance of government, called *democratization.* Finally, perestroika had a large impact on foreign policy, requiring changes in past thinking about and actions in the international arena, to the point where it was possible to speak of a revolution in Soviet foreign policy accompanying the revolutionary events at home.

Perestroika and the Economy

Gorbachev's restructuring of the Soviet economy had several dimensions: 1) substantial curtailment of the power of central administrators to control agriculture, industry, prices, and foreign trade; 2) the use of profitability as an economic indicator in the functioning of economic enterprises, with provision for their contraction or liquidation on the basis of their profit-and-loss records; 3) expansion of worker participation in the management of enterprises that employed them; 4) official acceptance and encouragement of a limited private entrepreneurialism in selected areas of the economy having to do with consumer services and food production; 5) the introduction of major agricultural reform, involving a gradual movement away from the traditional system of collectivization toward private control and ultimately private ownership of land as the most efficient way of expanding food output; 6) the closing of a massive gap between production and consumption to raise the standard of living of Soviet citizens in areas of health, education, and welfare, an effort sometimes referred to as the "human factor" in Soviet perestroika; and 7) the pursuit of joint ventures with foreign enterprises to facilitate Soviet acquisition of investment capital and technology needed to improve both production and distribution of goods and services.

Decentralization

The most conspicuous targets of Gorbachev's program of decentralization were the historically sacrosanct administrative control agencies known as Gosplan (the Soviet government's central planning agency) and Gosnab (its sister agency, in charge of fixing prices for all goods produced by state-run enterprises). Gorbachev asked for and received in June 1987 Central Committee approval to transfer the Gosplan's responsibility for determining the quality and quantity of all Soviet economic output to lower administrative levels, in particular to enterprise managers themselves; and to overhaul the elaborately controlled and subsidized system of pricing that set the value of more than 200,000 goods and services.

Unfortunately, the decentralization of economic decision making did not go far enough. Central authorities still had too much opportunity to interfere. Central ministries, which were supposed to be primarily reservoirs of research and technology with overall responsibility for quality control, still meddled in enterprise-level decision making through so-called state orders, or government contracts, which got top priority. This back-door way of running the economy from Moscow required enterprises to manufacture a certain amount of goods regardless of need, for the sake of attaining "notorious gross output levels," as Gorbachev put it; and undermined factory managers who were supposed to be in charge of production, buying, selling, and the disposition of profits.

Nor was there a real decentralization of pricing. Extensive state subsidies kept prices artificially low. Soviet leaders feared that freely fluctuating prices would generate inflation and provoke a violent popular reaction. Moreover, the government intended to cushion the negative impact of price reform on Soviet consumers by increasing availability of consumer goods in the short term by importing more of them from abroad.

Profitability

The use of profitability as a determinant of an enterprise's survival was a striking departure from the traditional practice of keeping production units going when they were demonstrably inefficient and unprofitable, simply to assure the continuing employment of their workers and managers. In June 1987 the Central Committee approved new rules whereby unprofitable enterprises were to be closed down even at the risk of causing unemployment. Enterprises that had difficulty in making ends meet were supposed to control costs not only by technological innovation to increase efficiency of production but also by cutting wages. Enterprises were supposed to meet a standard of financial accountability. They were to work closely with banks to obtain credit and to use it efficiently. Financial accountability was to encourage enterprises to meet delivery dates and to promote quality control to meet standards assuring sales and profits.

Although in theory by 1990 all of Soviet industry was to function according to financial accountability, in practice this did not occur. Ministries did not allow crucial enterprises, like those belonging to the military industrial complex, to declare bankruptcy; they also ensured that important but unprofitable enterprises continued to receive subsidies. Another problem in achieving financial accountability was unemployment caused by failed enterprises. Soviet workers had never experienced massive layoffs; the Kremlin, anticipating unrest, in 1988 provided for the establishment of job-placement centers, a system of retraining for workers who lost their jobs as a result of restructuring, and continuation of pay for at least 2 months. The Soviet regime had never acknowledged the existence of an unemployment problem and had no experience in dealing with one.

Worker Incentives

To encourage workers to improve their productivity, the Central Committee in 1987 authorized a significant expansion of existing opportunities for workers to participate in the management of the enterprises that employed them. A new rule required workers to elect all members of their enterprise's management teams, from the director down. The rule also established a new workers' institution, the labor collective council, a continuing executivelike body of the labor collec-

tive, to be elected by its members and to function on a day-to-day basis. These requirements were supposed to increase the opportunity of Soviet workers to influence management.

Another effort to provide workers' incentives involved a reversal of the traditional policy of wage leveling. This policy, which maintained the fiction that everyone was economically equal, brought a measure of political stability, but it alienated the most industrious members of society.

Under Gorbachev the Soviet regime sought to link pay to performance. In 1986 a decree on reforming the wage system in the production sector stipulated that workers' pay had to be linked to job performance and that raises and bonuses must be paid for out of enterprise profits.

The issue of wage differentials proved particularly controversial. The economic inequality resulting from increased wage differentials was anathema to Soviet ideologists. Furthermore, it threatened the stable and secure employment arrangement to which the Soviet labor force had become accustomed.

Private Entrepreneurialism

In still another effort to increase the quality and quantity of Soviet output in the consumer goods sector, Gorbachev asked for and received the Communist Party's approval for the legitimization and extension of existing private entrepreneurial activities. According to new laws, Soviet citizens could work for themselves instead of for the state as owners of cafés, tailoring establishments, repair shops, and other areas of business where there was pent-up demand for service.

In 1988 private entrepreneurial undertakings, referred to as "cooperatives," assumed increased importance in economic restructuring. Soviet economic planners, frustrated by the prospects of reviving the industrial sector, began to turn to cooperatives as a way of delivering a jolt of competition to stimulate a sluggish economy. A new law allowed cooperatives to conduct business with foreign companies and to receive hard currency as payment, to own property, to hire consultants, and to receive guarantees against government interference in their day-to-day operation. This law also gave prospective cooperatives the opportunity to appeal government rejection of their applications to start a business and established the right of state-run enterprises to join cooperatives.

Problems hindered rapid development of cooperatives in the service sectors. With the almost total absence of wholesale trade, it was hard to obtain necessary resources and materials. The credit system for cooperatives was not developed. There was also mounting popular hostility to the new entrepreneurialism because of alleged price gouging; because of the appearance of a new group of egregiously affluent promoters and hustlers in the new cooperatives; and because there was little sympathy for the entrepreneurial spirit, which, in emphasizing rugged individualism and initiative, contradicted the moral teachings of the socialist system of the previous 7 decades against personal aggressiveness in economic and social life.

In response to the growing and pervasive popular resentment against the new entrepreneurialism—especially the way in which it was leading to an accumulation of individual wealth—the Soviet government announced in April 1989 imposition for the first time of a progressive income tax. The government also curtailed development of medical cooperatives, ordering state hospitals to cease renting expensive medical equipment to private doctors. While not against medical cooperatives in theory, the government was critical of them in practice because they "abused the system." For example, they leased valuable state equipment and used it to "extract personal gain."

Nevertheless, expansion of private entrepreneurialism occurred in March 1990, when the Supreme Soviet passed a law giving private citizens the right to own small-scale factories and other businesses for the first time since the 1920s. The controversial term *private property* was not used, and the law was framed in accordance with prevailing Marxist terms, including a prohibition against the exploitation of one person's labor by another. Still, the law represented a striking departure from more than a half century of Soviet policy. Furthermore, one of Gorbachev's chief economic advisers, Leonid Abalkin, promised other advances toward private entrepreneurialism, like the creation of a new banking system to help underwrite new privately owned businesses.

Agricultural Reform

Gorbachev's agricultural reform program involved a gradual transfer of farms from collective to individual control and ownership. By expanding private farming he hoped to foster the personal initiative and diligence of rural workers essential to an expansion of their productivity.

Beginning in 1985 Gorbachev began to shift decision-making power from central and republic ministries to local agricultural enterprises. He encouraged different kinds of entrepreneurial activities, such as farm cooperatives and contractual leasing arrangements by individual farmers for the renting of land on long-term leases from state authorities. He also increased state support for personal auxiliary farming. In addition, most farms moved to so-called contract leasing, in which brigades of workers managed plots of land within a vast state farm.

In 1989 the leadership decided to carry agricultural reform a step further and approved the most far-reaching departure yet from the traditional collectivized and state farm system: Individual farmers were now allowed to lease state land for life and to pass on the leasehold to their children. Thus, the farm population had a chance at independent land management for the first time since the 1920s. In 1990 Gorbachev finally obtained legislation that gave farmers who chose to lease land and engage in private farming equal legal and financial footing to compete with the big state farms. Other changes included a restructuring of the existing collectives and state farms, which were to continue to be the mainstay of Soviet agriculture. These farms, as well as farms on private leaseholds, were free to sell whatever was not purchased by the state in private markets (although the percentages of what could be sold privately were not defined). The state, however, continued to be the largest purchaser and had priority of purchase, leaving only a small amount of output for non-state-controlled distribution.

The Human Factor

Gorbachev said that the success of economic restructuring depended on the human factor. This referred to the need to provide Soviet citizens with adequate food, clothing, shelter, and other amenities of life. The efficiency of workers was linked to their satisfaction with living standards.

In developing policy to address the human factor Gorbachev seemed to be listening to the advice of reform economists like Nikolai Shmelyev and Vasily Selyunin, who urged that he disavow the country's traditional obsession with industrial growth and shift emphasis to expanding the quality and quantity of consumer goods. The regime now spent precious gold and hard currency for imports of foreign-produced consumer goods and expanded investment in its own consumer industries, especially housing construction; increased investment in health care; and paid more attention to the plight of impoverished groups such as elderly people, whose pensions in many cases placed them below even the regime's meager measure of "poverty level."

Another effort to improve the human condition in Soviet society was the government's decision to reverse policy and allow private charity organizations to work among the elderly and poor. These organizations began to appear in 1988.

Joint Ventures

Joint ventures permitted foreigners to share in the equity and management of both private and state-owned Soviet industrial and service enterprises. They were intended to bring into the Soviet Union the kind of technology and management experience needed to expand local consumer goods production. The program of joint ventures was both radical and controversial. It represented a departure from the Soviet Union's historic protection of its domestic economy against competition from the highly efficient capitalist economies of the West. It also ended a long period of economic isolation, because joint ventures engaged in a kind of international division of labor that involved joint production with firms outside the Soviet bloc.

Joint ventures were formed in a wide range of economic activities, with hotel and restaurant services for foreign tourists presenting a natural area for cooperation. Typical industrial agreements between Soviet and Western firms involved the production of machinery and computer software for managing petroleum production in Soviet refineries, the equipping of Soviet fertilizer plants with high-technology machinery manufactured in the United States, and the development of plastic manufacturing in the Soviet Union for food packaging.

Problems in the operation of joint ventures were numerous. For example, Soviet domestic prices were artificial, and the ruble was not convertible. Therefore, it was not clear how the Soviet share of a joint venture could be measured to make sure that the reliability and quality of what the Soviets contributed could equal that of the other side. Other questions had to do with the ability of the foreign partner to select and retain the Soviet engineers and workers it wanted. Another problem involved the need of foreigners to deal with the Soviet bureaucratic maze. Finally, no one knew what would happen if a joint venture had to be liquidated.

In the absence of arrangements that provided otherwise—and such arrangements were difficult to make with the Soviet foreign trade bureaucracy—foreign investors had to take their profits in rubles, for which U.S. and other Western companies had little use. Some American companies found ways around this currency problem. Pepsi-Cola Company, which built two Pizza Hut shops in Moscow, accepted rubles at one outlet and collected foreign currencies at another one in a tourist neighborhood. Occidental Petroleum, on the other hand, exported 25 percent of the plastics produced in Soviet factories for sale in Western Europe and other markets and was allowed to take out of the Soviet Union hard currency earnings equivalent to returns from sales outside the Soviet market.

Insofar as Soviet joint ventures with American firms were concerned, there were specific difficulties, not least of which were American regulations governing the export of certain kinds of technology, the acquisition of licenses, and the extension of credit. U.S. firms did not always find Washington receptive to joint ventures, on grounds of national security.

Problems and Limits of Economic Restructuring in 1990

Soviet citizens had difficulty being enthusiastic about economic restructuring because they did not understand and therefore did not have much sympathy for the changes it was supposed to bring about. Soviet society was inherently conservative, fearful of the new and unknown. This was especially true if change involved a deemphasis of the system's traditional paternalism, in particular subsidized prices, egalitarian wages, and protection from unemployment. Indeed, the benefits of economic restructuring were not at all apparent to many Soviet citizens.

Conservatives warned that efforts to liberalize the Soviet economic system would fail because the economy could not be half free and half controlled. They worried that Gorbachev's policies, by encouraging individualism and group interests at the expense of collectivism, would lessen social

discipline, encourage anarchy, and compromise socialism and the struggle to achieve communism. There also was a silent but nonetheless effective opposition of middle-level party and state bureaucrats likely to lose power and influence, and in some instances their jobs, as a result of the reduction of central control over the country's economic life.

Making matters worse for economic restructuring were two major tragedies that befell the Soviet Union in this critical era of change: the 1986 Chernobyl nuclear accident and the 1988 Armenian earthquake. They caused an unexpected and severe drain on already scarce goods and services and increased the hardship of Soviet citizens as they grappled with the changes wrought by economic restructuring.

Perestroika and the Political Environment: Glasnost

Perestroika led to a liberalization of the repressive Soviet political environment through the set of policies known as glasnost, which called for full, frank, and public discussion of what Soviet citizens thought was wrong with their society. This was a stunning departure from the rigid and repressive control over thought and speech practiced by all previous Soviet leaderships. Glasnost also called upon party and state officials to respond to public inquiries and public criticisms about policy making in different sectors of the administration, from economic enterprises to the KGB. Glasnost thus called upon state officialdom to abandon the secrecy practiced by all Soviet political officials as a matter of course throughout the history of the Soviet state.

The purpose of glasnost was to foster a new dialogue between citizens and the state to identify problems, especially in the economic sphere, to build public support for radical reforms of the economy and other sectors of Soviet soviety and to pressure the bureaucracy to accept and implement changes it might not like. Glasnost was supposed to have many advantages for perestroika: 1) more open mass media would better reflect the leadership's commitment to reform; 2) public discussion of social and economic problems by individuals in the party, bureaucracy, and state apparatus would pressure officials to keep pace with the times and to be accountable for mistakes and abuses; 3) more open media would act as a barometer, providing Soviet reformers with necessary feedback on the general acceptance or rejection of their policies; and 4) glasnost would facilitate popular political participation and therefore be linked closely with policies designed to promote democratization.

In the late 1980s, glasnost led to a substantial expansion of the permissible limits of public debate on national problems. For example, the Soviet press published criticisms of economic slackness and some of its causes, such as alcoholism, drug abuse, bureaucratic corruption, and economic waste. There was more media coverage of major accidents and disasters, injustices of the court system, and homosexuality. Perhaps one of the most striking aspects of the new candor of the official press involved public discussion of national problems such as poverty and homelessness, which former Soviet officials had always insisted were absent from Soviet socialism and found only in capitalist societies.

Glasnost also included historical revisionism, or the rewriting of history. Gorbachev condemned Stalinism anew; cast the Khrushchev era in a much more favorable light than Brezhnev did; and referred in noncondemnatory ways to early Soviet revolutionary figures reviled by Stalin, like Trotsky and Bukharin, anticipating the official rehabilitation of these antiheroes and their ideas and policies.

Glasnost and Religion

Glasnost involved a new Soviet tolerance of religion. Leading newspapers reported on religious conferences and congresses in the Soviet Union. They even published stories about the infringement of rights of people seeking to practice their religion openly. Many presented the Russian Orthodox Church in a favorable light, describing its key role in Russian history; its emphasis on values of family, work, and environmental protection; and its potential contributions to charity work and to world peace.

The Soviet government made significant concessions to the Orthodox Church. It returned three monasteries to church jurisdiction. It granted permission to the All-Union Council of Evangelical Christian Baptists to receive 100,000 Bibles from England; and approved a visit of Mother Teresa in 1987 to Moscow, Kiev, and the area around Chernobyl. In 1988 the Gorbachev leadership also approved of and participated in the extensive publicity given to the celebrations of the millennial anniversary of the establishment of Christianity in Russia. Gorbachev used the occasion of the celebrations to tell church leaders of his opposition to past religious repression and of the government's intention to guarantee religious freedom.

Gorbachev wanted to enlist the support of the Russian Orthodox Church in his perestroika policies, and he undoubtedly wanted the church's assistance to alleviate the suffering of ordinary people from the hardships of economic reforms. The regime, moreover, had no reason to fear that its new indulgence of the church would lead to unwanted consequences, at least insofar as the clerical hierarchy was concerned. The leadership of the church remained conservative—conditioned to obedience and accommodation under the long, repressive rule of Stalin, Khrushchev, and Brezhnev—and therefore reluctant to go further than expanding church influence in Soviet society.

Atheistic feeling continued to permeate the Soviet political establishment, suggesting that liberalization of policy toward the church was based more on expediency than on alteration of the historic aversion to religion inspired by Leninism. In 1987 there was still some official discrimination against minority religious groups, such as the Lithuanian Catholics, Pentecostals, and Baptists, that may well have been ignored by a church leadership sensitive to the competition coming from other religious groups.

The Soviet regime's softer approach toward religion had a mixed impact on Soviet Jews. On the positive side was an effort to improve cultural conditions for Soviet Jewry. The regime legalized the instruction of Hebrew in 1988 and agreed in 1989 to the establishment of a Jewish Cultural Center in Moscow, the first in the Soviet Union in 50 years. On the negative side was a new outbreak of anti-Semitism among the public at large, as seen in the emergence of a new chauvinistic movement called *Pamyat* ("Memory" in Russian). Pamyat encouraged popular prejudice against Soviet Jews by blaming them as well as other non-Russian groups for the Soviet regime's repressive policies in the 1920s and 1930s.

Glasnost and Dissent

Under glasnost the Gorbachev leadership seemed willing to tolerate new, unofficial, and critical organs of public political expression. A new magazine, *Glasnost,* addressed Soviet national problems as did discussion groups in Moscow and Leningrad, like the Perestroika Club, which was composed primarily of intellectuals, especially scientists working for Soviet government research institutions.

The most prominent and pervasive of the new unofficial journals, independent of party and state control, was *Ogonyok*, which was started by Vitaly Korotich, a Ukrainian physicist-turned-editor. With revelatory articles on the seamier side of Soviet life, such as fascist tendencies among Soviet youth, corruption in Soviet sports, and the torturing of a criminal suspect by police—subjects that had been taboo in the official press—*Ogonyok* circulation increased in 1987 to 1.5 million copies.

But as it applied to political criticism and dissent, glasnost had limitations. Gorbachev always viewed glasnost as a means to an end rather than an end in itself. The freer political environment existed to serve a purpose: economic reform. Glasnost-inspired dissent was limited by the Communist Party, which still controlled the media. Official censorship severely reduced the ability of the press, radio, television, and journals to pursue a truly open information policy. Communist Party secretary Yegor Ligachev, a critic of the more tolerant political environment fostered by glasnost, deplored the new permissiveness of the Soviet media, calling upon them to show restraint and responsibility in publishing material that reflected negatively on the country's socialist system. He also criticized historical revisionism, saying that there was too much stress on negative aspects of past Soviet development. The KGB was another obstacle to real freedom of expression. KGB operatives throughout the country, in cooperation with conservatives in the party and state bureaucracies, watered down or circumvented directives from the top leadership aimed at increasing personal political freedom.

Gorbachev himself would have been the first to acknowledge the shortcomings of the permissiveness engendered by glasnost. And he shared, to a degree, Ligachev's view that at times glasnost encouraged an all-too-aggressive criticism of national problems and policies. Gorbachev believed that by emphasizing the negative aspects of his reform program, the press discouraged and demoralized the Soviet public.

Glasnost and the Nationalities

One of the most important consequences of glasnost was an increase of nationalism and ethnic self-consciousness among the major non-Russian peoples of the Soviet Union. With more freedom of the press, these peoples expressed their needs, desires, and values, exploding with pent-up feelings of resentment and hostility toward Russians. They openly demanded liberalization, autonomy, and an eventual complete independence of Moscow in administrative, cultural, and economic affairs.

Not surprisingly, the non-Russian groups welcomed the introduction of glasnost and took advantage of it to lobby for greater recognition by Moscow of their special needs and interests. For example, in June 1988 representatives of six non-Russian national movements met in the former Polish city of Lvov in Ukraine and founded a coordinating committee of Patriotic Movements of the Peoples of the U.S.S.R. The committee was supported by national rights campaigners from Ukraine, Lithuania, Estonia, Latvia, Georgia, and Armenia. It called for political and economic decentralization of the Soviet Union as well as the eventual transformation of the Soviet Union into a confederation of separate sovereign states. The Kremlin reacted more tolerantly than ever before to demands of the national minorities, listening extensively, tolerantly, and sympathetically to their complaints and their demands for change. But Gorbachev resisted their demands for changes that would have significantly altered the highly centralized Soviet administrative system, still dominated by Russians.

The challenge for Gorbachev was to remain sensitive to the nationalistic susceptibilities of the ethnic minorities while at the same time to assure the administrative unity he needed for the success of perestroika. In looking for a moderate long-term solution to the problem of controlling the increasing assertiveness of the large and small minorities, Gorbachev was willing to allow the minorities an extremely large amount of control over their local affairs, in return for their acceptance of nominal Soviet authority and continued membership in the Soviet federal union.

Glasnost and Baltic Nationalism

When glasnost began there was a veritable explosion of nationalist-inspired protest and dissent in the Baltic republics. In 1987 thousands of people in Estonia, Latvia, and Lithuania publicly protested the anniversary of the 1939 Hitler–Stalin pact in which Germany gave the Soviets a green light to annex the Baltic states that had received their independence from Russian rule at the end of World War I. These demonstrations were significant in two respects. First, they affirmed the intensity of anti-Russian feelings among the Soviet Union's Baltic citizens, despite Moscow's efforts to integrate them into Soviet society. Second, they revealed Moscow's hypersensitivity to the way such public expressions of anti-Russian sentiment were reported—and, in the Kremlin's view, sensationalized—by the Western media, which were accused by Soviet authorities of gratuitous mischief making, as if to suggest that the existence of hostility toward Russia in non-Russian areas like the Baltic republics was the result of outside interference rather than of popular discomfort over subordination to Russian rule.

A proliferation of nationalist organizations emerged from cultural groups and professional unions. These organizations fielded candidates in local and national parliamentary elections in 1988 and 1989. They also publicly commemorated important historical events that were anniversaries of national tragedies. They staged a dramatic cross-border "hand holding" of several hundred thousand citizens of Estonia, Latvia, and Lithuania in August 1989 to mark the 50th anniversary of the Nazi–Soviet Non-aggression Pact and to protest continuing communism and Soviet control. Representatives from these republics lobbied directly with the Soviet leadership for political, economic, and sociocultural change.

Baltic nationalist organizations—the Estonian Popular Front, the Latvian Popular Front, and the Lithuanian Sajudis and Movement for the Support of Perestroika—publicized a long list of grievances against Moscow. Their most important grievance was that the Soviet Union had unlawfully destroyed the independence of the Baltic countries with the complicity of Nazi Germany in April 1940. A commission of the Lithuanian Legislature in August 1989 publicly declared the Soviet annexation of Lithuania illegal, the first official effort of the Baltic republics to lay the legal groundwork for declarations of independence.

Baltic nationalists also complained that Moscow's excessive centralization of economic power stifled economic life and forced the Baltic peoples to endure a low standard of living. Lithuanian nationalists in particular advocated the equivalent of states' rights; and the republic's government approved a constitutional amendment establishing a right—opposed by Moscow—to reject national laws with which they did not agree, a measure that violated the Soviet Constitution, which established the supremacy of national over republic law.

Baltic nationalists called for the deployment of Baltic soldiers of the Soviet Army in their native republics rather than to posts elsewhere in the Soviet Union. They insisted that Baltic soldiers be under the command of Baltic officers. In effect, they sought a breakup of the Soviet Army into nationality-based divisions.

In the economic sphere, they demanded and obtained a near-total independence from Moscow's administrative and planning agencies. They also sought policies to address environmental issues long ignored by Moscow and advocated freedom to develop closer economic ties with Western Europe.

In addition, Baltic nationalists criticized the past influx of Russians into their republics. In Latvia, where ethnic Latvians numbered less than 50 percent of the republic's total population, they sought both to curtail Russian immigration and to limit the political influence of Russians on local government. Estonians enacted a law defining residency requirements for voting in local elections that discriminated against recent Russian immigrants. And nationalists in all three republics lobbied aggressively to establish the local language as the state language, in place of Russian. (The Russian minorities protested this action as a violation of their rights under the Soviet Constitution.)

These explicitly anti-Russian gestures provoked a backlash by Russians living and working in Estonia, in the form of strikes and demonstrations against local authorities. Estonian citizens of Russian origin and other non-Estonian groups formed their own popular front organization, the Intermovement, to resist the discriminatory policies of the Estonian majority and the majority's efforts to achieve autonomy of Moscow. One of Intermovement's first acts was to protest a law requiring non-Estonians working in Estonia to learn the language within 4 years or face dismissal.

Gorbachev sympathized with legitimate Baltic demands for reform. He approved the promotion of reform-minded party members to positions of leadership in the Baltic branches of the Soviet Communist Party. He made striking concessions in the economic sphere, granting most of the Baltic demands for near-total local control over their economic life. In another conciliatory gesture, in 1989 the Kremlin acknowledged the existence of the secret protocols of the 1939 pact with Germany assigning the Soviet Union paramouncy in the Baltic states, on which basis the Soviet forces had invaded and occupied them in 1940.

Gorbachev's conciliatory approach stemmed from his commitment to glasnost and his belief that the political ferment in the Baltic republics was a logical and healthy consequence of glasnost and democratization—healthy, that is, as long as it did not get out of control and lead to secession (as it eventually did). Also important in understanding Gorbachev's policy was his view that the Baltic peoples, with their already high degree of overall socioeconomic development as compared to other parts of the Soviet Union, were the most likely to make a success of his economic restructuring policies, which, incidentally, they strongly endorsed.

Gorbachev hoped that Soviet flexibility in regard to Baltic nationalism would help to keep the region inside the Soviet administrative system. Many Baltic nationalist figures were sensitive to Moscow's anxiety over the possible loss of the Baltic republics and for a time avoided demands for immediate independence. There was a strong economic logic for postponing discussion of secession: Baltic economists believed that most of the region's trade would continue to be with the Soviet Union.

But Gorbachev always opposed Baltic secession, which would have set a dangerous precedent for other national minorities in the Soviet Union. Indeed, the mere prospect of secession strengthened the hand of skeptics, especially conservatives in the top party leadership, the state security establishment, and the army high command, who were determined to preserve the integrity of the historic Soviet domain bequeathed by Lenin and Stalin.

On several occasions in 1988 and 1989 the Kremlin warned Baltic nationalist leaders against promoting secession and against policies that violated the Soviet Constitution, such as discriminatory behavior by local authorities toward Russians and other minorities. And in 1989 Soviet Politburo member Yacovlev publicly declared that there was no link between the Nazi–Soviet pact and the current status of the Baltic republics and therefore no legal basis for secession.

The Lithuanian Crisis. A crisis over secession did occur, on March 11, 1990, when the newly elected Lithuanian Supreme Soviet voted a declaration of independence from the Soviet Union. This momentous act was predictable after the independence movements in Central/Eastern Europe and after the overwhelming victory of candidates who supported independence in the February 1990 Lithuanian parliamentary elections.

In the weeks immediately following the elections, the Lithuanian Legislature enacted laws to reinforce the republic's independence. The Parliament called for the issuance of Lithuanian identity cards and for the rejection of the Soviet military draft. Moreover, Lithuanian authorities refused to cooperate in the apprehension and prosecution of young Lithuanian men who had defected from the Soviet Army. Lithuanian president Vytautas Landsbergis made a point of addressing Gorbachev as if he were the head of a foreign state.

The Soviet reaction to this challenge was swift but also, at least initially, restrained. After declaring the Lithuanian action a violation of the Soviet Constitution and therefore illegal, Gorbachev told the Lithuanian government that Moscow would not oppose eventual secession if it occurred within the framework of the Constitution, which was in the process of being amended to provide the means for secession, which always had been accepted in principle if not in practice. He also appealed to the Lithuanians, as supporters of perestroika, to remain part of the Soviet Union to help him implement his reform program from which they, as well as the rest of the country, stood to benefit. Finally, he promised all of the republics a new "union treaty" giving real autonomy to republic governments in return for their acceptance of central government control over defense.

The Lithuanian Parliament refused to go back on its declaration of independence, and eventually Gorbachev threatened Lithuania. Gorbachev exerted tremendous psychological pressure. He criticized the Lithuanian Parliament for voting on independence precipitously—only hours after its election and without having provided all of the republic's citizens, including minorities like the Russians, who constituted about 9 percent of the republic's 3.7 million inhabitants, an opportunity to express their point of view, such as in the form of a republic-wide referendum.

Gorbachev warned of dire economic consequences if the Lithuanians implemented secession. He reminded Lithuania of its dependence on trade with the Soviet Union and the difficulties of developing economic links with the West. An independent Lithuania would have to pay $33 billion for economic property in the republic that technically belonged to the Soviet state. Lithuania would also lose territory transferred to Lithuania following its admission to the Soviet Union in 1940. Furthermore, Gorbachev expressed deep concern for the well-being of the Russian minority in Lithuania, suggesting a moral as well as a political justification for a possible military interference in Lithuania to preserve its legal membership in the Soviet Union.

By the end of March 1990, Gorbachev had moved toward more stringent actions to sway the Lithuanians from their independence course. He sealed off the republic to prevent outsiders, including tourists and journalists, from entering the republic, thus isolating it from the West. He sent limited military contingents into the republic to protect federal buildings and installations as well as to intimidate the local populace and the government in Vilnius. Federal authorities moved to establish control over local law enforcement and criminal justice agencies in the republic. In April Gorbachev threatened an economic boycott of the republic if its government did not rescind various legislative enactments that violated the Soviet Constitution.

Gorbachev's responses to Lithuania were influenced by several considerations. One was fear that the Lithuanian steps might set off the feared chain reaction of secessionist movements, not only in the other Baltic republics but in any republics where there was nationalist agitation. What was also at stake was the possible disintegration of the traditional Soviet state. In particular, the Soviet military worried about the strategic liabilities of the Soviet Union's loss of control over Lithuania and perhaps the Baltic republics. Indeed, the reduction of Soviet political influence and military power in Central/Eastern Europe in 1989, while possibly encouraging the Lithuanian independence movement, probably strengthened the Kremlin's determination to maintain control over the Baltic republics, which would have had to take the place of the former Soviet bloc countries as the first line of Soviet defense against a threat from the West.

In its confrontation with the Kremlin over independence, the political leadership of Lithuania did not have much support from the West. Most of Western Europe remained silent on the issue. The Bush administration responded cautiously, despite the United States' past refusal to acknowledge the legality of the Soviet incorporation of the Baltic republics in 1940. Washington, however, did urge Gorbachev to resolve Moscow's differences with Vilnius peacefully. Both then-president Bush and secretary of state James Baker warned the Kremlin of very negative consequences for Soviet–American relations if it tried a forceful Brezhnev-style Soviet crackdown in Lithuania. The U.S. Congress was more adamant than Bush and wanted the United States to recognize Lithuanian independence; its views undoubtedly strengthened the impact of the Bush administration's warnings to Moscow about restraint in dealing with Vilnius. This position discouraged the more aggressive elements in the Soviet leadership and to that extent was of some help to the Lithuanians.

Nevertheless, the disappointed nationalist leadership correctly concluded that the United States and other Western nations were reluctant to take up the cause of Baltic nationalism. With Gorbachev making extraordinary changes in Soviet foreign and domestic policies, the West did not want to risk strengthening the hand of Communist Party conservatives and rivals of Gorbachev who might challenge his leadership if he could not control Lithuania. Moreover, Washington argued (with some plausibility) that the new Lithuanian government had yet to demonstrate the reality of its independence of the Soviet Union. It had no effective control over the country and, therefore, recognition at this juncture was premature. The Bush administration also expressed its desire to avoid the mistake that it believed the Eisenhower administration had made in Hungary in 1956, when it led the Hungarian opposition to expect that the United States would help in resistance to Communist rule but never fulfilled that expectation, even when the Soviets invaded Budapest.

Nor did Lithuania receive strong support from other Baltic republics. While both Estonia and Latvia sympathized with Lithuania, they carefully refrained from imitating its confrontational approach. They took to heart Gorbachev's strong warnings against precipitous efforts to secede from the Soviet Union. They also were sensitive to the absence of effective Western support. They proceeded cautiously on the issue of separation from the Soviet Union and watched events in Lithuania to see how fast they themselves might be able to move toward independence.

The Lithuanian cause was also weak among reformers in the Congress of People's Deputies and the Supreme Soviet, in particular the Interregional Group, which had often sided with deputies from the Baltic republics on issues of economic and political freedom. They voted along with Gorbachevists to declare the republic's secession illegal and invalid. Like Gorbachev, they deplored the Lithuanian Parliament's haste in declaring independence and its apparent unwillingness to consult all the Lithuanian public.

The Lithuanian crisis dramatized for the Kremlin the urgency of addressing the larger problem of reconciling ethnocultural nationalism to Soviet unity. The Supreme Soviet, despite misgivings, approved changes in the Soviet Constitution that created a strong presidential office capable of dealing directly and decisively with threats to unity. It also enacted a new law on union-republic relations that provided for the secession of a republic. The law provided for a complex and therefore difficult process would-be secessionist republics would need to pursue in order to gain independence of the Soviet Union, which made secession practically impossible. According to this law, the secession of a republic could occur only after the holding of a republic-wide referendum in which two-thirds of the voters agreed to secession, after formal approval by the Soviet Congress of People's Deputies and passage of a 5-year period in which issues connected with secession were resolved to the satisfaction of both the central and local authorities, including the payment of resettlement expenses for those who opposed secession and opted to leave the republic that seceded.

Ukrainian Nationalist Activity. Ukraine, with the second-largest population (52 million) of the union-republics, a fifth of Soviet industry, and the reputation of being the Soviet Union's breadbasket because it provided one-fifth the Soviet Union's agricultural output, experienced a glasnost-encouraged nationalism. Sources of Ukrainian nationalism were the historic prejudice against the Russians, who obtained control of the region by conquest; economic and social grievances, not least of which were anger at the Chernobyl disaster in 1986 and the new lease on life given the Catholic Church, which looked to the Vatican for leadership and recently had been allowed new freedom to function.

In republic-level and local-level government legislative elections in March 1990, candidates favoring independence won seats. These nationalists, many of whom belonged to a popular front organization known as Rukh, along with many young people, in particular a new anti-Communist organization calling itself the Union of Independent Ukrainian Youth, admired and supported the movement toward independence in the Baltic republics. The Rukh issued a declaration urging the conversion of its loose alliance of human rights activists, environmental activists, and radical Communists into a full-fledged political party. Rukh president Ivan Drach declared that the new party would seek the full sovereignty of Ukraine, which meant, he said, secession from the Soviet Union.

But Ukrainian nationalist politicians were more cautious than their Lithuanian counterparts. They spoke about "eventual" independence, in 5 years or so, and of the importance of laying the groundwork for separation gradually and incrementally. For example, some Ukrainian nationalists said that a start toward independence should be demands on Moscow to allow Ukrainian soldiers to do their military service in Ukraine.

Tatar, Georgian, Moldovan, Armenian, and Azerbaijani Agitation. Forcibly exiled to Central Asia from their homeland on the Crimean peninsula during World War II because of collaboration with Germans by some of their number, the Tatars fought quietly for the first several decades to regain their original homeland. In the summer of 1987, they demonstrated in Red Square and subsequently held rallies and demonstrations for the re-creation of an autonomous republic in the Crimea.

Consistent with glasnost, Soviet authorities reacted with a measure of sympathy and promised in July a hearing with then-Soviet president Andrei Gromyko, who had recently been named to head a commission to examine Tatar complaints. A commission report in October 1987 called for cultural concessions to the Tatars and criticized discrimination against them in matters of housing, employment, and schooling. The Soviets subsequently announced in February 1988 that a limited number of Crimean Tatars would be able to return to the Crimea.

But the commission did not make any significant changes in boundaries, and it officially denied the request of the Crimean Tatars for an autonomous republic. The Gromyko commission argued that the administrative territorial division of the country made it possible to give ethnic groups an independent voice and that the population in the Crimea had trebled in the postwar period and was now overwhelmingly Russian and Ukrainian. These groups would object strongly to the formation of a Tatar republic there.

Georgians also expressed ethnocultural nationalism. They were sensitive about their history and culture, given the fact that for much of their past they had lived under the control of powerful invaders: Greeks, Romans, Turks, Mongols, and now Russians. They were as much the victims of the culture-destroying Russification policies of the late-nineteenth-century czars as other non-Russian peoples conquered and administered by the czars. Religion was an important ingredient of Georgian nationalism. Since the third century A.D., the Georgian people had had their own branch of the Orthodox Church, with its own patriarch.

Georgians also were defensive about their language, which belongs to the Caucasian family, is distinct from the Indo-European system and highly inflected, and which they considered threatened by the efforts of the central authorities to promote cultural homogenization. When Moscow tried in 1978 to remove a clause from the Georgian Constitution proclaiming Georgian the official language, thousands of demonstrators poured into the streets, forcing the authorities to back down.

Finally, Moscow had helped, quite inadvertently, to heighten Georgian nationalistic sensitivities by fostering economic growth and development. Moscow had brought industry, expanded educational opportunities, groomed a native party and government apparatus, and had tolerated a flourishing of Georgian culture, all of which had raised aspirations of

Georgian autonomy. Moscow also had stimulated Georgian eagerness for economic reform, which would allow an expansion of private enterprise and individual initiative, thereby increasing Georgian impatience with economic regimentation.

Georgian nationalists in the late 1980s were divided over the long-range goals of their antigovernment actions. Some would have been satisfied by an extensive autonomy; others favored complete separation from the Soviet Union. The Georgian nationalist movement, consequently, did not develop the kind of unity of purpose and organization characteristic of nationalism in the Baltic republics.

In Moldavia (or Moldova, as it is known today, and called Bessarabia when the area was under Romanian control before World War II), there was also a growing spirit of autonomy. The Moldovans started to campaign for greater popular control over their local economic and political affairs.

This desire for greater autonomy in Moldova was fueled in part by policies of Moscow. In the spirit of glasnost, the Soviet authorities quietly began to undo one of the great cultural hoaxes of the twentieth century—namely, the historic Soviet insistence that Moldovans were a unique ethnic group, independent of the Romanian nationality to which they really belonged. As a consequence, Moldovans were forced to write their Romanian language in the Cyrillic alphabet. In January 1989 the Moldovan Communist Party leadership agreed to three demands of intellectuals in the republic: 1) it declared that Romanian and Moldovan tongues were identical; 2) it restored the Latin script; and 3) it established the Moldovan tongue as the official state language of the republic.

These gestures heightened Moldovan sensitivity to their Romanian origins. Informal nationalist-minded political groups sprung up and demanded limits on Russian migration into Moldova, a halt to environmentally harmful industrial projects, and the replacement of leaders considered holdovers from a corrupt and conservative past.

Armenian nationalism came from a strong sense of community based on a shared memory of the 1915 massacre, the influence of the Armenian Church, the contribution of Armenians living abroad to a view of Soviet Armenia as a homeland, and the fact that Soviet Armenia was the most ethnically homogeneous of the 15 constituent republics, with more than 90 percent of its population Armenian. Taking advantage of the more tolerant political atmosphere inspired by glasnost as well as by Gorbachev's call for grass-roots political initiative, Armenian nationalism found its voice early in 1988, when a group of Armenian intellectuals raised an old Armenian demand for the return to Armenian control of the autonomous region of Nagorno-Karabakh.

Nagorno-Karabakh, a mountainous enclave situated in the neighboring republic of Azerbaijan, was inhabited predominantly by Armenian people. Historically, this area was under Armenian control. It would have remained so after the Bolshevik Revolution had Stalin not given it to Azerbaijan in 1923. The local Azerbaijani administrative authorities discriminated against the Armenian population living in Nagorno-Karabakh.

At the root of Azerbaijani discrimination were religious and ethnic prejudices. Many Azerbaijani people were Muslims and of Persian or Turkish extraction, while the Armenians were Christians. And in light of their demands for the return of Nagorno-Karabakh to Armenia, the Azerbaijani considered the Armenians land-grabbers.

Azerbaijani discrimination against Armenians in Nagorno-Karabakh took many forms. For example, the local Azerbaijani authorities converted Armenian Christian churches to mosques and curtailed Christian religious training in the state-run school system. And they pursued investment policies that left the region's infrastructure underdeveloped and its Armenian population poverty-stricken.

While the Kremlin was sympathetic to the Armenian position, it steadfastly refused to allow the transfer of Nagorno-Karabakh from Azerbaijan to Armenia. Soviet authorities in Moscow were afraid of provoking the wrath of the Azerbaijani population and of setting a dangerous precedent for boundary changes elsewhere in the Soviet state.

The Armenians resented Moscow's refusal to support the cause of annexation; the Azerbaijanis resented Moscow's perceived pro-Armenian sympathies. And both groups resented the failure of the 19th Communist Party Conference in 1988 to disavow Soviet cultural homogenization and Russian assimilationist policies. The Conference offered no solution to the problem of Nagorno-Karabakh beyond acknowledging its seriousness and the existence of interethnic conflict elsewhere in the Soviet Union.

Infuriated by Moscow's unwillingness to sanction the transfer of Nagorno-Karabakh to the Armenian republic, the Armenians, otherwise sympathetic to Gorbachev's perestroika, now turned against the Soviet leader. A few Armenian activists, representing the intelligentsia and other social groups, created the so-called Karabakh Committee, not only to spearhead annexation of the disputed region to Armenia but also to lobby aggressively with Moscow for increased economic sovereignty, priority for the Armenian language in republic schools and public affairs, and a veto over federal projects in the republic.

This activity in turn provoked the Azerbaijanis to violence against Armenians living not only in Nagorno-Karabakh but elsewhere in Azerbaijan, including Baku, its capital. By the summer of 1989, it seemed as if the two republics were about to go to war—the Armenians to get Nagorno-Karabakh, and the Azerbaijanis to keep it. Each side increased discrimination against the people of the other living under its jurisdiction. In June and July, there was a mass exodus of Armenian residents of Nagorno-Karabakh to the Armenian republic. In late 1989 Azerbaijani workers blockaded rail lines carrying food and fuel into Armenia.

Amidst this escalating nationalism was an earthquake in Armenia on December 7, 1988, killing more than 25,000

Armenian citizens. Armenians blamed the Soviet authorities for taking too long to get necessary equipment to the republic to unearth victims. They also complained that Gorbachev was using the occasion of the disaster to suppress the nationalist protest by arresting nationalist figures, such as the members of the Karabakh Committee.

In early 1989 the Soviet leadership, in the spirit of glasnost and democratization, tried hard to conciliate Armenia. First, it allowed relatively open coverage of the earthquake. Second, it invited foreign help in the pursuit of relief and recovery efforts. Third, it acceded to demands by the Armenians for their increased economic and environmental autonomy of Moscow. Finally, it released interned members of the Karabakh Committee, which subsequently transformed itself into a kind of Armenian popular front organization.

These Soviet gestures, however, did little to lessen Armenian hostility to Moscow or to Baku. Moreover, Soviet policy seemed to strengthen Azerbaijani nationalism by confirming suspicions of a pro-Armenian bias in Moscow. By late 1989 an Azerbaijani popular front organization emerged, not only championing the republic's claims to Nagorno-Karabakh but also demanding increased administrative autonomy. Moscow seemed to incline toward the Azerbaijani position on Nagorno-Karabakh, restoring the region to the control of Baku, an action that heightened Armenian hostility.

Perestroika and the Communist Party

The Soviet Communist Party underwent profound change under perestroika, because Gorbachev believed that the party, more than any other institution, was responsible for the pre-crisis situation inherited from the Brezhnev phase. In his view the party had to liberalize its highly authoritarian structure; loosen its stranglehold over the Soviet economy and society; and rid itself of a self-interested, unresponsive, and corrupt managerial elite. He was convinced that a successful economic revival depended on party reform in at least three areas: internal organization, party–state relations, and the behavior of individual party members.

Internal Organization

To bring new blood to the party's leadership positions, Gorbachev recommended adoption of new rules for electing leadership on the local and national levels of the party organization. The 19th Communist Party Conference in June 1988 agreed to limit terms of first secretaries, who were in effect the bosses of a local party agency, and of the general secretary, who was the leader of the whole party, to two 5-year terms. Gorbachev was excluded from this new ruling. The Conference also agreed to the introduction of multiple candidacies in party elections.

Gorbachev wanted as well to allow more freedom for rank-and-file discussion of critical issues. Party leaders initially were not receptive to this change, fearing that a liberal environment in the party would encourage divisiveness, undermine discipline, and compromise the unity of the party and its ability to act as a cohesive force in leading the country. While there was increased internal party debate, there was no formal agreement to modify democratic centralism.

Party–Government Relations

The 19th Conference limited the party's involvement in the day-to-day administration of the country. It abolished party departments that duplicated the activities of the government. The work of the party's central apparatus became concentrated in two departments or sectors, each supervised by a secretary: the ideological–propaganda department, and the organization–personnel department. The first department supervised party schooling and promoted the ideological line in primary party organizations and in the country at large. The second department dealt with internal party organization and with personnel matters within both the party and state bureaucracies.

While a great deal of change was implemented, much of the way the party traditionally operated remained the same. The party bureaucracy continued to influence appointments and promotions within the government. Furthermore, to assure continuing party influence over local government, Gorbachev required that party leaders simultaneously run in elections for local government. Gorbachev was extremely sensitive to the way in which incompetent party officials had created the illusion of success while concealing the reality of failure. Enraged by extensive corruption, including embezzlement and bribery, Gorbachev insisted that party bureaucrats change their behavior or risk losing their jobs. He said that party officials had to show humility and undertake periodic self-criticism to identify where they may have gone wrong in the performance of their responsibilities.

In addition, Gorbachev called for scaling down the extraordinary extent of privileges and perquisites that party officials had accumulated over the years. They had special stores, hospitals, and sanatoria and possessed "certificate rubles"—a special currency that made possible the purchase of goods not available to people with ordinary rubles. Soviet citizens had long been aware of this new class of bureaucrats who lived better than ordinary people and they did not like it, as they made clear under glasnost.

The Party and Glasnost

The Communist Party's commitment to glasnost was evident at the 19th Conference. Delegates, elected for the first time in a relatively free and open manner by the party rank-and-file, openly and on occasion severely criticized past party behavior. The frankness and intensity of the 4-day proceedings startled both the Soviet viewing public (numbering in the tens of millions) and the party delegates who attended and participated in it. One delegate was quoted as saying that he had witnessed a revolution.

What was stunning was not only the dynamic character of discussion but also the participation of ordinary delegates. Many interacted with the party leadership, interrogating and criticizing it in a way that had never been possible at earlier congresses and conferences. The spontaneity of the conference showed how glasnost had changed the party itself.

Under glasnost new political organizations, called *popular fronts,* emerged. These offered an alternative to the party, and eventually they opened the way to development of political pluralism and the emergence of a multiparty system. The popular fronts were independent of the party and were committed to an array of political, economic, and cultural reforms. Occasionally they were critical of the Communist Party and its leadership, including Gorbachev. Glasnost allowed these organizations to demonstrate publicly, to nominate candidates for public office along with the Communist Party, and to lobby aggressively for radical change. The most active and influential of the popular fronts appeared in the Baltic republics and Armenia, where they became popular vehicles for expression of ethnocultural nationalism.

Another quasi-political party organization that emerged under glasnost was the Democratic Union (DU), established in 1988. The DU was a truly radical organization of young activists, mostly in their mid-thirties, that called openly for the end of one-party rule and the establishment of a multiparty system. The DU nominated candidates for national public office, held public demonstrations in favor of democratic reform, and displayed distinct anti-Communist tendencies; for example, in March 1989 DU members unfurled the old blue and red flag of Czarist Russia.

The party's tolerance of this new political activism foreshadowed the emergence of competitive political parties. Prominent and influential figures, including Gorbachev, were willing at least to mention and discuss such a radical idea. Articles appeared in the official media in the early months of 1989 severely criticizing the Communist Party, charging it with responsibility for helping Stalin create a ruthless police state, a tyrannical bureaucracy, and an enormously inefficient centralized economy. These commentaries were a prelude to an attack on the party's monopoly that led to a decline of party influence and the genesis of other political parties to compete for leadership of the Soviet state.

Finally, glasnost encouraged development of factionalism within the Soviet Communist Party, especially within the top party leadership. From 1988 onward Gorbachev had to confront skepticism, criticism, and sometimes not-so-covert opposition to his reforms from both a left and a right in what seemed to be a serious erosion of democratic centralism. The left wanted the general secretary to go faster in reforming the Soviet system. The most notable representative of this position was Boris Yeltsin, the former head of the Moscow city party organization. The right wanted Gorbachev to move slowly and cautiously—and in some areas not at all. Its

leading advocate was Yegor Ligachev, a member of the Politburo and of the Secretariat.

The Left and Boris Yeltsin

Yeltsin's position in 1987 and 1988 was that perestroika could not succeed unless Gorbachev broadened and accelerated radical political and economic reforms. He tried to do so in his own district, Moscow. Yeltsin became very popular among the citizens of Moscow for trying to address their complaints about local economic problems and for holding the party responsible for them. He criticized party leaders, including Gorbachev, at a meeting of the Central Committee in October 1988. He was subsequently reprimanded for violating the rules of democratic centralism; he eventually was replaced as head of the Moscow party organization. Although they did not come to his support, many in the Central Committee, including, perhaps, Gorbachev himself, were sympathetic to his complaints. Moreover, the citizens of Moscow rallied behind him and saw him as a hero against the conservative bureaucrats.

The Right and Yegor Ligachev

Ligachev, the chief spokesperson and defender of the conservative point of view about perestroika in the late 1980s, had the respect of the party apparatus, in which he had served longer and probably enjoyed a higher standing than Gorbachev. He did not break with Gorbachev's policies and, indeed, praised economic restructuring. However, Ligachev urged restraint in the political sphere, criticized the discussion of party privilege, complained about negative news coverage, and warned against a permissiveness toward public dissent.

By the summer of 1989, Ligachev's personal power to challenge Gorbachev had declined. For example, Gorbachev's proposed changes in the traditional agricultural system (in particular the expansion of private leaseholds, tantamount to private ownership of farm land) were diametrically opposed to the collective system, which Ligachev staunchly defended. Furthermore, nothing lowered Ligachev's stature so much as the growing popularity and political influence of Yeltsin, whose attacks on Ligachev measurably increased the Moscow chief's public support.

Although Yeltsin called regularly for Ligachev's resignation, and although Gorbachev looked on during these assaults and did not support Ligachev publicly, allowing him to defend himself as best he could, the Soviet leader did not force his ouster or punish him for his criticism. Despite the differences between Gorbachev and Ligachev, there seemed to be an agreed-upon division of labor, in which Gorbachev pressed for change while Ligachev tried to prevent too great a deviation from socialist doctrine and practice.

Perestroika and the Government

Another important aspect of perestroika involved reforms of national and local government called *democratization,* which

Gorbachev defined as the need for everybody to participate in shaping society. Democratization was intended to give a sense of common purpose to the Soviet people and to engage them in a process of self-monitoring of their political and economic activity. Gorbachev especially wanted to mobilize people against the all-too-comfortable and conservative bureaucracy. Finally, democratization was supposed to end the alienation of people from government, which now was blamed for the hardships of daily life. Democratization provided mechanisms to allow the regular, nonviolent, popular-based change of leaders to assure their responsiveness to social needs.

Gorbachev's democratization, however, was not the same as Western democracy. It did not involve abandonment of the traditional authoritarian system that had governed since Lenin's time. Democratization did not call for a reduction of the enormous power concentrated in the hands of party and state leaders; nor did it provide for all the individual rights and liberties guaranteed in Western democratic systems.

Democratization initially affected several aspects of the Soviet governmental aparatus, in particular legislative institutions on the national and local levels; the Soviet presidency; the relationship between the republics and the Central government in Moscow; and the criminal justice system, including the KGB, the bureaucracy, and the military. In all these instances, democratization involved either increasing popular influence over state agencies or assuring their responsiveness to popular interests and needs.

Legislative Reform

The Supreme Soviet in December 1988 approved major changes in the Soviet legislative system on both the national and local levels, in order to increase voter influence over legislative behavior. The most important changes were the introduction of multiple candidacies in the nomination and election of members of all legislative bodies; the reinvigoration of the local soviets; and the replacement of the old Supreme Soviet with two new bodies, the Congress of Peoples' Deputies and a new, small, bicameral Supreme Soviet.

Multicandidacies were intended to allow the election of mavericks, critics, and dissidents. The Communist Party now had to compete with nonparty groups and individuals; the party could no longer monopolize the nomination and election processes.

The reinvigoration of the local soviets, organizations that traditionally had done little more than ratify decisions made elsewhere, involved a substantial expansion of their authority. Members of local soviets now were to work full time instead of part time on their legislative duties, thereby strengthening their expertise and eventually their power. The local soviets taxed enterprises within their jurisdiction to provide the revenue they needed to function full time. These bodies assumed responsibilities formerly performed by local party agencies, such as monitoring the performance of farms and factories in their geographic area.

The attempt to reinvigorate the local soviets, however, did not appreciably increase their activities. They had little success in solving problems in agriculture, housing construction, and the environment in their regions. Moreover, they were subject to party influence and control because of Gorbachev's insistence that the first secretary of the local party organization seek leadership of the local legislature—Gorbachev apparently wanted to conciliate the local party apparatus and avoid a dangerous provocation of its already resentful bosses.

The Congress of Peoples' Deputies. The most important change in the national Legislature was the creation of a new legislative body in Moscow, the Congress of Peoples' Deputies. The Congress was made up of 2,250 members, 1,500 of them elected from territorial and national districts and 750 from the governing bodies of party, youth, artistic, and other organizations. Elections were to be held once every 5 years. The Congress was to convene yearly to discuss constitutional, political, social, and economic issues. But its real task was to select from its membership a Supreme Soviet—smaller and more influential than the old one—a Constitutional Review Committee, and a chairperson of the Supreme Soviet, who also would be the president of the Soviet Union. This new chief executive was to preside over the Supreme Soviet, serve as chairperson of the national Defense Council, the country's highest national security agency, and have broad authority to shape both domestic and foreign policy. The term of office was limited to two 5-year periods.

The 1989 Elections to the Congress. Elections for membership in the Congress were held on March 26, 1989. They were open and hectic, with much campaigning by candidates of non-party-controlled groups and individuals as well as by party-sponsored people. In that respect they were unprecedented in recent Soviet political history, with even Soviet voters themselves exhilarated—or befuddled—by the enormous freedom of choice.

In the elections the Communist Party tried, somewhat unsuccessfully, to undermine those whom it disliked, in particular the now very popular party maverick Boris Yeltsin and the political dissident Andrei Sakharov. Eventually both were elected to seats in the Congress and emerged as influential spokespeople for the opposition.

Indeed, despite the efforts of the party to influence the outcome of the nomination and election of candidates for seats in the Congress, the results were a stunning statement of voter opposition to the political establishment. Wherever they could voters rejected candidates associated with the local party and state administration. Many party candidates rejected by the voters in favor of reformers ultimately lost their jobs within the party, in accordance with Gorbachev's insistence that the party had to be responsive to public will.

Still, a majority of the deputies elected were party members (albeit outspoken reformers) and therefore were obliged in their advocacy of reform to adhere to party requirements, under the rules of democratic centralism of loyalty and obedience to the top leadership.

When the Congress of Peoples' Deputies convened for the first time, in May 1989, to fulfill its mandate of electing the Soviet president and a new Supreme Soviet, there was an explosion of discussion about complaints against the regime and its leadership, including Gorbachev. Before long there was a demand for Congress itself to become the chief lawmaking body and to deal directly with key problems like the economy. There seemed to be a move among some of the deputies, especially those from Moscow, to draft a new and comprehensive agenda for the Congress that would make it much more than the nominating and oversight body it was originally intended to be.

But the Congress demurred and proceeded to complete the business for which it was charged: It elected both the new, more influential Soviet president and the new Supreme Soviet. The deputies overwhelmingly voted Gorbachev as president of the Soviet Union and elected Anatolyi Lukyanov, a kind of chief of staff and chief adviser to Gorbachev, as vice president. It then proceeded to elect the smaller Supreme Soviet.

In its first session, the Congress, in conjunction with the new Supreme Soviet, completed an impressive agenda, including approval of the leasing of farms and factories; the introduction of cost accounting in the Baltic republics as a start toward capitalism; and discussion of many other important issues, such as press freedom, conversion of defense plants to consumer production, and private ownership of property. While there was no action on these issues, the mere discussion of them was noteworthy.

The New Supreme Soviet. In June and July 1989, the newly established Supreme Soviet convened and was asked to approve a slate of ministers submitted by President Gorbachev. Aggressive reformers like Yeltsin and Sakharov worked hard to assure that the new Supreme Soviet would not be like its complaisant and deferential predecessor. The new body, charged with the responsibility of ratifying ministerial appointments, took its business very seriously, perhaps more so than Gorbachev expected.

For example, while the new Legislature approved the reappointment of Premier Nikolai Ryzkhov and Foreign Minister Eduard Shevardnadze without much controversy, its committees cross-examined and vigorously investigated the past record of Ryzkhov's nominees, rejecting eight despite previous party approval of them. The premier ended up dropping six of them; the other two withdrew voluntarily. He subsequently came up with acceptable alternatives—people who were quickly approved by the Legislature.

The Legislature ultimately endorsed the reappointment of Defense Minister Dmitri Yazov, but he had so little support

that it was necessary to change the voting rules to allow a simple majority of those present and voting to suffice for endorsement, as opposed to an absolute majority, because Yazov might not have survived a vote by absolute majority. During the debate over his reappointment, critics attacked waste, corruption, and poor living standards in the military and said that the 65-year-old general should make way for a more progressive generation of leadership. Deputies from the Baltic republics had been among the opponents of his reappointment because he fiercely opposed their proposal to let young people from non-Russian republics serve in separate units deployed in their native regions.

The Legislature's assertive behavior in approving the new Council of Ministers was both novel and very significant. The refusal to approve of certain party nominees suggested a historic turning point, a demonstration to the government that in the future it might be dependent on the elected deputies—a situation that would be without precedent in the history of Communist Party rule.

The New Soviet Presidency

On March 13, 1990, the Congress of Peoples' Deputies strengthened the presidential office, making the new Soviet president far more powerful than was originally intended. Now the president was to be elected directly by Soviet citizens. The president had the authority—subject only to notification of the Supreme Soviet and to existing constitutional law—to declare a state of national emergency and to impose martial law. The president could veto enactments of the Supreme Soviet, which could override the veto only by a two-thirds majority.

There was some opposition in the Congress to accommodating Gorbachev's demands for a stronger presidency. Many deputies believed that there were not enough limits and restraints to prevent abuse of power and a possible return to Stalinism. But Gorbachev won the support of the Congress by arguing that the country needed strong national leadership to preserve unity in the face of mounting interethnic conflict and the emergence of secessionist movements. He also argued the need of strong leadership to resolve worsening economic problems and to move forward with perestroika. Moreover, many deputies acknowledged that their fears about the new presidential office did not apply to Gorbachev as much as to his unknown successors.

In deference to Gorbachev and as a sign of its continued backing of his leadership despite reservations about and criticisms of his behavior, the Congress of Peoples' Deputies also agreed that the first presidential election would be held in the old way—namely, the president would be chosen by the Congress. In the latter part of March 1990, it elected Gorbachev (who, incidentally, had no opponents) president of the Soviet Union. With his newly strengthened power base in the state apparatus and increased independence of the Communist Party, where his critics had been able to undermine and block his policies, Gorbachev accelerated the loosening of the party's still substantial grip over the national economy.

In retrospect, however, Gorbachev's unwillingness to run for president in a direct election was a gross tactical error in his strategy to implement perestroika. In the short term, he did strengthen his authority. But in the long term, he was weakened because he eventually came to lack the popular base needed to pursue his reformist policies, which increasingly were challenged by the leaders of the republics who were popularly elected and able to speak for their constituencies in a much more authoritative way. Had Gorbachev run for the Soviet presidency in a direct election in March 1990, he probably would have won because of enormous popularity with ordinary people who still hoped his perestroika would indeed improve their living conditions. By the following year, he had lost that popularity, as people were disillusioned and angry over the perceived failure of perestroika to change daily life for the better.

Reforms of the Justice System

Perestroika-inspired reforms of the Soviet government included new criminal and civil codes as well as a new code of legal procedures. The office of public prosecutor was separated from the courts, which were now part of a single institution, the Ministry of Justice. This was intended to give greater independence to the courts and greater rights to the accused.

Gorbachev promised to raise the status of lawyers, but his pledge left details to be filled in by the Ministry of Justice. This secretive organization controlled or at least decisively influenced many of the 100,000 Soviet lawyers, either by directly employing them or through its links with the procuracy and the Supreme Court. The ministry at first resisted Gorbachev's ideas but eventually became more receptive to change; in early 1989 it allowed the establishment, for the first time, of an independent Soviet bar group (the Soviet Advocates' Association).

Other changes in the criminal justice system aimed at softening treatment of political dissidents. These changes included imposition of shorter terms of detention, curtailment of political interference in court trials of dissidents, a narrowing of the definition of political crimes, and a requirement of fuller proof for conviction. An amendment to the Soviet criminal code replaced a statute that outlawed, with little definition, "anti-Soviet agitation and propaganda" and defamation of the Soviet state or political system.

The Soviet government showed a new determination to eliminate psychiatric abuses, whereby healthy but politically dissident people were locked up in mental hospitals by the KGB for political dissidence. In January 1988 a new corrective statute, passed by the Presidium of the Supreme Soviet, contained legal guarantees against errors and malpractices in psychiatric cases. It provided rules for examination and for the commitment of mental patients to psychiatric hospitals as well as specification that chief psychiatrists of health agencies, rather than doctors working for the police or the KGB, must exercise control over medical treatment of mental patients. The new Presidium order also provided for appeal by patients of a confinement decision and guarantee of legal assistance.

Perestroika and the Bureaucracy

The 19th Conference acknowledged complaints against the bureaucracy, which Gorbachev considered one of the most important obstacles to perestroika. The Conference formally condemned the bureaucracy's "high-handedness" in the economy and in the social and spiritual spheres, its indifference to the rights and needs of the people, and its disdainful attitude toward public opinion and the social experience of the working people. The Conference called for an end to this behavior, demanding that state and public institutions and party committees become fully accessible to people; that managers refrain from delays and formalism; and that departmental instructions and bureaucratic contrivances cease to encroach upon the legitimate rights of citizens.

Gorbachev replaced top party and government leaders who had condoned bureaucratic abuses and obstructionism. He also used glasnost-inspired public criticism of bureaucrats to make them more responsive and responsible. He expected that recourse to market forces would weaken and eventually supplant bureaucratic managers by ending their stranglehold over the country's economic life.

Perestroika and the Military

Gorbachev undertook major reforms of the military. Reforms involved almost all aspects of its operation and required it to accept and cooperate with the reforms in other areas of Soviet life. For example, as a result of the new emphasis on improving the quality of life of Soviet consumers, it was necessary to persuade the army to get used to the fact that it would no longer have first claim on national resources and that it would no longer get whatever it said it needed to perform its strategic and security-related functions. Gorbachev made it very clear to the top Soviet military leadership that henceforth, in light of the demands of restructuring in the economic sphere, the army and the navy must make do with less. To achieve this goal, Gorbachev told the military that it had to pay more attention to managerial skills and in particular to improve the traditionally harsh and unpleasant living conditions experienced by recruits.

The military was obliged to accept a new strategic doctrine that emphasized defense rather than offense. Gorbachev reduced the traditionally heavy role of the military in foreign policy making and excluded its participation, except in an advisory capacity, in decision making on arms reduction.

Perestroika also required the army to accept with grace growing popular criticism of many aspects of its behavior, from its involvement in Afghanistan to its management of human resources at home. The army was obliged to cooperate with glasnost and to accept a new degree of public scrutiny. Needless to say, the military leadership was uneasy about perestroika, even though it welcomed economic restructuring, which it believed would ultimately benefit not only the country at large but also the armed forces.

To maintain civilian control over the army, in order to assure its cooperation with perestroika, Gorbachev tried to diminish the military's exaggerated stature in Soviet society. For example, he reduced the ceremonial role of the military as seen in the less conspicuous presence of its leadership in the review of the annual November 7 pageants in Red Square to celebrate the anniversary of the Bolshevik Revolution.

The most important means of keeping the armed services on a tight leash involved personnel changes at the top. In the spring of 1987 Gorbachev found an opportunity to replace Defense Minister Marshal Sokolovsky, in the flap over the incursion of Soviet air space by a young West German pilot, who had flown his small Cessna aircraft through the Soviet air defense system and landed in the middle of Red Square. This incident was terribly embarrassing, to say the least, to the Kremlin. Gorbachev complained about the ineptitude of certain officers and promptly fired Sokolovsky, appointing in his place Dmitri Yazov, at that time a known supporter of Gorbachev's effort to improve management skills in the Soviet military. With Yazov in place, Gorbachev was now in a position—or so he thought, with some justification—to move forward with policies to overhaul the military's inefficient administrative apparatus, to develop new arms control initiatives, and to reduce Soviet military deployments around the world in order to divert new resources toward domestic development.

Perestroika and Foreign Policy

Perestroika inspired striking changes in Soviet foreign policy. Gorbachev referred to these changes as "New Thinking" about future Soviet international behavior. Gorbachev and his foreign policy advisers, such as Eduard Shevardnadze, Anatoli Dobrynin, and Aleksandr Yacovlev, rejected the old two-camps theory of ideological conflict between socialist and capitalist countries. Insisting that technology had brought nations closer together and fostered interdependence, Gorbachev argued that national interests could no longer be defined in strictly ideological terms and that nations with different ideological commitments must cooperate to resolve common economic, strategic, and environmental problems.

Because nuclear weapons can obliterate civilization and conventional weapons are almost as destructive, Soviet foreign policy strategists asserted that war was no longer a rational instrument of policy. They contended that war must be replaced by political and diplomatic instruments such as arms control agreements, confidence-building measures, and a strengthening of international law and organization. It therefore followed, according to Gorbachev, that the military

had to be subordinate to political instruments of foreign policy. Force capabilities had to be reduced to levels of "reasonable sufficiency," and the primary purpose of the military had to be defensive, not offensive.

Gorbachev and his advisers also believed that past emphasis on military strength and excess security had been counterproductive: the costly arms race burdened an already debilitated Soviet economy; suspicion of Soviet intentions prevented good relations with the capitalist West; and Soviet readiness to use massive military power to achieve foreign policy goals discredited socialism as an attractive alternative to capitalism.

New Thinking affected Soviet foreign policy in many areas. Soviet relations with the West steadily improved; Moscow showed a new leniency and restraint in dealing with its Central/Eastern European allies and included an explicit Soviet renunciation of force in relations with them. The Soviets also began to pull back military involvement in many areas of the Third World. Finally, the Soviets demonstrated new interest in the United Nations as well as other international organizations involved in conflict resolution.

Still, it was also true that New Thinking did not replace traditional Soviet ambitions, interests, and goals in the international community. The Soviet state continued to be extremely security-conscious; it continued to harbor ideological prejudices and suspicious in its dealings with the outside world; it still was not above acting in response to so-called targets of opportunity or to achieve an important goal when the cost of doing so was low and the chances of success great. Furthermore, its policy abroad was still influenced by economic, societal, and military capabilities, which helped to determine objectives as well as limits.

Past Soviet foreign policies would have been altered or reversed starting in the late 1980s, even in the absence of New Thinking, because of their evident weaknesses. Indeed, by the time Gorbachev came to power in March 1985, the Kremlin could not ignore the counterproductive consequences for Soviet well-being of many policies pursued in the 1960s and 1970s. For example, Soviet military and ideological expansion in the last years of Brezhnev's rule, especially the Soviet invasion of Afghanistan in December 1979, had led to a deterioration of relations with the United States and a denial of much-needed American technology. Soviet heavy-handed interference in Central/Eastern Europe had exacerbated latent anti-Russian feelings and undermined the credibility and legitimacy of socialist regimes, thus compromising the Soviet goal of permanent Soviet security vis-à-vis the West. And Soviet hostility toward China, at its height under Brezhnev, had pushed China closer to Japan and the United States, thereby raising the possibility of a triple entente against Soviet interests in Asia. It had obliged the Soviets to maintain huge and costly deployments of conventional and nuclear forces along the Sino–Soviet frontier in Asia and had complicated the task of protecting the interests of Soviet clients and friends in Asia (North Vietnam, North Korea, Afghanistan, and India).

Relations with the West
Gorbachev gave priority in the late 1980s to improved Soviet relations with the West. He saw many advantages in East–West cooperation, not least of which was an expansion of trade, which would give the Soviet Union access to the financial, economic, and technological resources needed to make perestroika successful. He did not share the view his predecessors had of the West as a threat to Soviet security.

The United States. In Soviet strategy toward the West, relations with the United States assumed central importance. Gorbachev sought a reversal of the deterioration of relations between the superpowers that had occurred in the late 1970s and early 1980s. The Soviets discussed outstanding issues with the Americans, like regional conflicts in Afghanistan and Angola, arms reduction, human rights, and trade. The conclusion in December 1987 at the Washington summit of the Soviet–American treaty eliminating intermediate-range nuclear missiles from Europe and a number of Soviet unilateral reductions in conventional and other nuclear weapons and troop deployments; the Soviet military withdrawal from Afghanistan in February 1989 and support for an end of the civil war in Angola; and the increased tolerance of political dissent and diversity with assurances of further change in human rights policy sought by the United States—all seemed to confirm a turning point in relations between the two superpowers.

Many differences remained, however. The Soviets were upset over the continuing American commitment to the Strategic Defense Initiative (SDI, or Star Wars), the planned U.S. deployment of defense weapons in space. While the Kremlin suspected that the Bush administration would never deploy such sophisticated and expensive weaponry, the Soviets did not dismiss the possibility of SDI becoming a reality. This would have necessitated matching it with a Soviet equivalent, which would have drained Soviet resources.

Western Europe. Gorbachev aggressively strengthened Soviet relations with the Western European allies. As he gradually diminished the Soviet military presence in Central/Eastern Europe, thereby weakening Soviet security in that region, the importance of good relations with Western Europe increased. At the same time, Gorbachev emphasized the commonality of past traditions and current needs between the Soviet Union and Western Europe, referring to their membership in a "common European home."

He intensified Soviet efforts to encourage disarmament in Europe as a means of enhancing Soviet security without having to invest in a costly military buildup; to decouple the Western European countries from the United States, thereby driving a wedge in NATO; and to increase Soviet access to

Western European financial, economic, and technological resources. Gorbachev exploited the growth of neutralist and pacifist tendencies in many Western European societies and especially among the youth; the eagerness of Western European countries, especially West Germany, to encourage perestroika and respond sympathetically to it by expanding trade; and the desire of Western European governments to develop a measure of independence vis-à-vis the United States in relations with the Soviet Union.

Gorbachev's most dramatic and persuasive gestures toward Western Europe involved unilateral concessions on arms reduction. In 1987 the Kremlin agreed to exclude the nuclear defense forces of Britain and France from coverage in the INF treaty. In 1988 Gorbachev announced a decision to cut Soviet armed forces in Europe by more than 12 percent and to reduce conventional weapons deployed in Central/Eastern Europe. In 1989 the Soviets offered to make cuts in their short-range nuclear missiles deployed in Central/Eastern Europe.

Gorbachev particularly went out of his way to cultivate West Germany and France. Soviet relations with these countries steadily improved as Gorbachev skillfully played on their interest in expanding trade with the Soviet Union and in developing independence in relations with Moscow. They wished ultimately to obtain Soviet support of their own objectives in Europe, especially an expansion of political and economic ties with the Soviet bloc allies.

Ties with Central/Eastern Europe
Gorbachev introduced major changes in Soviet policy toward Central/Eastern Europe. He accepted (in fact, he actively encouraged) major departures from the Soviet model of socialism. The most important of these departures were increased political pluralism, involving abandonment of the Communist Party's monopoly of power; and the expansion of market principles and private entrepreneurialism, leading to a radical reduction of the traditional state control over national economic life. Gorbachev thus presided over the decommunization and desatellization of the Soviet bloc countries.

Under Gorbachev the Soviet Union renounced the use of force in the region, thereby repudiating the Brezhnev Doctrine, which was used to justify the 1968 Soviet-led Warsaw Pact intervention in Czechoslovakia. Indeed, in late 1989 the Soviet leadership formally admitted the error of this act and apologized for it.

Gorbachev refrained from interfering with the changes that took place in Poland, Hungary, East Germany, Czechoslovakia, and Romania in late 1989, despite anxiety in the Kremlin over the unanticipated speed and scope of these departures from traditional Soviet bloc socialism. The Kremlin did not succumb to the temptation to block changes involving the curtailment of Communist party control, on which Soviet power and influence in Central/Eastern Europe had depended since World War II.

Gorbachev's leniency in dealing with the upheaval in Central/Eastern Europe was the result of conditions inside the Soviet Union. The Soviets could no longer afford to spend the money and resources needed to maintain close control of the Soviet bloc political systems. Heavy troop deployments, never mind a full-scale military invasion, were no longer feasible from an economic point of view. Furthermore, maintaining the close Soviet control utilized by Stalin, Khrushchev, and Brezhnev no longer made sense—a perceived threat from the West, as the Soviets believed existed in the past and used as a justification for demanding Soviet bloc unity with and subordination to Moscow, had diminished.

The argument that Central/Eastern European departures from the Soviet model would encourage equivalent and unwanted change in the Soviet Union and therefore had to be prevented at all costs (a justification for Soviet suppression of the 1968 Czechoslovak reform program) was no longer valid. Soviet socialism itself was reforming; in fact, Soviet leaders were looking at change in Central/Eastern Europe to see what aspects could be adopted in their own country.

The Gorbachev leadership was more confident, more flexible, more pragmatic, and more intellectual in its thinking about Soviet–Central/Eastern European relations. Gorbachev and his foreign policy advisers were quite unlike past Soviet leaders, who always were on the defensive, suspicious, stubborn, and crude in their handling of problems with Soviet bloc allies.

Conditions in Central/Eastern Europe influenced Gorbachev's departures from past Soviet policies. The socialist dictatorships, which Soviet policy had so assiduously supported, had not served Soviet interests effectively. They had failed to maintain the internal stability necessary to achieve the legitimacy on which their long-term survival—and therefore the survival of Soviet influence and power—depended. They had failed to inculcate a pro-Soviet orientation among peoples who were traditionally hostile to Russia.

Past Soviet policies of intrusion had exacerbated anti-Russian feelings in many Soviet bloc societies. To that extent they had weakened and discredited the socialist systems closely linked to Moscow, which were therefore viewed in the public mind as little more than servile agents of a despised national enemy. Certainly past Soviet harshness toward the Soviet bloc countries did little to help—and, in fact, undermined—the efforts of local Communist party leaders to diminish popular antipathy to the Soviet state.

At the same time, pervasive and irresistible pressures for radical change in politics, the economy, and society had been steadily mounting in Soviet bloc countries. Because the logic of profound change had become as overwhelming in Central/Eastern Europe as it was in the Soviet Union, it would have been foolhardy for the Kremlin to support Soviet bloc conservatives, with whom the Gorbachevian leadership had little in common in their opposition to change. Gorbachev favored the development of perestroika-like reforms in the Soviet bloc countries to revive their enfeebled economies, which were closely linked to the Soviet economy and a potential source of help for the Soviet Union's own economic recovery.

Finally, Gorbachev's new approaches to Central/Eastern Europe have to be understood within the context of Soviet relations with the West. The new Soviet restraint was conducive to the strong ties that Gorbachev wanted with Western Europe and the United States.

The well-being of Central/Eastern Europe, compromised, to say the least, by the imposition of Soviet and Communist power after World War II, had always been important to Western Europe, for economic and strategic reasons: Central/Eastern Europe was a potentially large and profitable market for Western industrial and agricultural output and at the same time was important to the security of West Germany and Scandinavia. Thus, as Gorbachev had correctly calculated, the West was bound to respond in a positive way to any Soviet effort to foster the health and stability of Central/Eastern Europe.

The Kremlin understood the inevitability of a severe setback in Soviet relations with the West in the event of a return to the coercive and interventionist policies of the past in Central/Eastern Europe. The resumption of intrusive Soviet policies would surely have compromised any chances the Soviets had of persuading the West to liberalize trade and sell the high technology so desperately needed to reinvigorate as well as reform the Soviet economy and to make possible an improvement in living conditions essential to social stability. It would also have compromised the ongoing process of East–West arms reduction, which Gorbachev wanted in order to reduce defense expenditures.

There were both opportunities and dangers in Gorbachev's shifts away from past Soviet policy in Central/Eastern Europe. By allowing the countries to reject their socialist systems and move toward democracy and capitalism, Gorbachev encouraged new popular sympathy for the Soviet Union. The citizens of most Soviet bloc countries saw Gorbachev as a hero, perhaps even a savior, who had facilitated their liberation from conservative, hard-line, and corrupt leaders responsible for the dreadful conditions of daily life. Thus he had a chance of achieving genuine friendship and cooperation between Central/Eastern Europe and the Soviet Union, which had eluded his predecessors.

However, Gorbachev's new policies of leniency and restraint carried liabilities for the enfeebled Soviet Union. As reforms led to a curtailment of Soviet physical power in Central/Eastern Europe, the Kremlin faced competition for influence with West Germany. Bonn had developed a dense network of human, cultural, and economic ties with individual Soviet bloc countries. The West German economic presence also seemed to be greater than that of other Western countries. Other aspects of West German influence-building in Central/Eastern Europe involved arms control policies, such as Bonn's stated reluctance in the spring of 1989 to modernize NATO's nuclear capability, as well as progress toward reunification. West German chancellor Helmut Kohl, in the aftermath of political changes in East Berlin in the fall of 1989, called for closer economic and social relations between the two Germanys as preconditions for reunification.

To offset West German initiatives, Gorbachev looked to France. After years of inactivity, punctuated by occasional denunciations of human rights violations, French president François Mitterrand had resolved to make Central/Eastern Europe one of the top foreign policy priorities of his new term. In December 1988 he visited Czechoslovakia; in January 1989 he visited Bulgaria. The impulse behind the French initiative was partly to recover export markets that, however small, were important for key sectors of the French economy. But the most compelling imperative was, as French diplomats discreetly put it, to accompany West Germany into Central/Eastern Europe as Soviet influence declined. In this effort Paris may well have had the tacit backing of Moscow.

Gorbachev perceived an increase of U.S. interest in Central/Eastern Europe as he reduced Soviet military power in the region. He noted the groundswell of public support in the United States for an active American role in helping Poland and Hungary to democratize; he expressed concern over the apparent readiness of the Bush administration to develop a high American profile in those countries. Gorbachev also was in no rush for the reunification of the two Germanys, although he did not rule it out and eventually accepted it. Indeed, the prospect of a reunified Germany might have provided an incentive to the newly independent Central/Eastern European systems, especially Poland, Hungary, and Czechoslovakia, to support continuation of the Warsaw Pact and good relations with the Soviet Union as the only effective means of lessening their vulnerability to a powerful united German state. In February 1990, in response to evident anxieties in Moscow about the implications for Soviet security in Europe, Gorbachev insisted that German reunification had to proceed gradually, with due consideration to the interests of Germany's neighbors, especially Poland and the Soviet Union. He eventually retreated from demands that a united German state be neutral, partly in response to the opposition of the United States as well as of Poland, Hungary, and Czechoslovakia. He agreed that a unified Germany could belong to NATO, given that that was what the West as well as most Germans wanted. The Kremlin also supported Poland's insistence on a German guarantee of existing borders and on its participation in any international unification agreement.

Relations with the Third World

Gorbachev and his advisers made a fundamental reassessment of past Soviet policy in the Third World. By the early 1980s, it had become clear that earlier hopes for strong clients and lasting influence resulting from the promotion of Marxist-Leninist vanguard party-states had not been achieved. By late in that decade, the Soviets had realized the flaws of past policy toward Third World countries, acknowledging that the export of their political and economic structures to the Third World had not worked out well.

Although Marxist-Leninist allies had willingly cooperated with Moscow both politically and militarily, they were very poor, even by Third World standards. The introduction of such socialist measures as collectivization of agriculture and wholesale nationalization of foreign and domestic private property had only made them poorer. Moreover, the populations of these leftist countries viewed their Marxist rulers as illegitimate. Several regimes—including those in Angola, Mozambique, Afghanistan, Cambodia, and Nicaragua— faced internal guerrilla insurgencies. As the need for Moscow's assistance grew, the Soviet Third World "empire" became a substantial drain on Soviet resources.

As the Soviets concentrated on perestroika, therefore, they had to redefine their Third World policy. There was new emphasis on technological and economic cooperation; deemphasis of Soviet military assistance; and priority given to the settlement of regional conflicts in such places as Afghanistan, Cambodia, Angola, and Nicaragua.

This shift from military expansion to political diplomacy in policy toward the Third World under Gorbachev can be seen in a number of Soviet initiatives, notably the military withdrawal from Afghanistan and the effort to promote a political settlement in Angola. The Soviets pursued a policy of caution and restraint in the Middle East, with attempts at reconciliation with Israel balanced by support for the Palestinian cause and friendship with the Palestine Liberation Organization (PLO) and Yasir Arafat. They also attempted to balance ties with conservative states, such as Egypt and Jordan, with political and military links to very radical states, like Syria, Iraq, and Iran. Finally, the Soviets attempted to support Cuba and Nicaragua while cultivating good relations with conservative, somewhat pro-American states like Brazil, Mexico, and Argentina.

Relations with East Asia

Gorbachev took important steps to improve Soviet relations with China, Japan, and other countries in the Pacific Basin. Moscow wanted legitimacy as a political and economic participant in East Asia; territorial security in the region; and a lessening of American influence there to prevent a three-way political entente between China, Japan, and the United States, which Gorbachev believed would threaten Soviet strategic interests. Gorbachev's policy was largely economic and diplomatic in order to reverse Moscow's military image, which had been counterproductive. It had not led to an appreciable increase of Soviet political influence. Indeed, it had led the Chinese to do exactly what the Soviets opposed: namely, to draw closer to the United States and Japan and inadvertently to bolster American influence in the region.

Relations with China

Gorbachev aggressively pursued reconciliation with China to enable the Soviets to withdraw some of the 53 divisions deployed along the 3,900-mile Sino–Soviet frontier. This would allow a savings in defense costs deeper than any arms-control agreement with the United States might have produced. To promote this reconciliation, the Kremlin downplayed ideological differences between the two countries and acknowledged similarities between the Chinese and Soviet systems. The Kremlin also paid attention to long-standing Chinese complaints against Soviet policies in Asia: Gorbachev offered to reduce Soviet troop and missile deployments along the Sino-Soviet frontier; he acknowledged the Chinese claim that the border between the two countries ran down the center of the Amur River in its path to the Pacific; he withdrew Soviet military forces from Mongolia and from Afghanistan; and, finally, he interceded successfully with the Soviet Union's Vietnam ally to undertake a political and military disengagement from Cambodia.

The Chinese and Soviet leaders held a summit in Beijing in June 1989. In a grand gesture of reconciliation, Gorbachev offered the Chinese an apology for the long period of tension in Sino–Soviet relations, acknowledging that to a certain extent "we bear responsibility." The most tangible results of that summit included the signing of agreements on normalization of relations on both party and state levels and the removal of 120,000 Soviet troops from the frontier.

Relations with Japan

The Soviets had much to gain from stable relations with Japan. They wanted an expansion of Japanese investment in the exploitation of Siberian mineral deposits and joint ventures with Soviet enterprises, within which the Japanese could provide capital and high technology. But the Soviets were not as forthcoming with Japan as with China. Some obstacles to close ties included Japan's continuing political and diplomatic intimacy as well as close military cooperation with the United States; its expanding economic ties with China; the interest of the Japanese public in strengthening Japan's military defense; and Japan's persistence in demanding Soviet return of the islands taken from Japan after World War II.

The dispute over these islands (Kunashir, Shikotan, Etorofu, and the Habomais group, located in the Kurile chain north of the Home islands) was the biggest stumbling block. The Kremlin was unwilling to give the islands back to Japan, at least at that time, for three reasons: resentment over a perceived Japanese prejudice toward the Soviet Union, the prestige for the Soviet Union of retaining the islands, and their strategic importance to the Soviet military as a result of their proximity to Soviet Navy and Air Force installations headquar-

tered in the Far East. As long as the Kremlin would not accommodate Tokyo on this issue, Tokyo would not expand trade and in other ways improve ties with the Soviet Union.

Interest in the United Nations

Under Gorbachev the Soviet Union showed a renewed interest in the United Nations, in particular in its peacekeeping responsibilities, which in the past the Kremlin had frequently criticized and refused to support. Now UN efforts to reduce tensions and improve the general international environment complemented Soviet policy, especially Soviet efforts to strengthen ties with the United States and China and to wind down regional conflicts.

In addition to advocating expanded peacekeeping activities, Gorbachev suggested that the United Nations could verify compliance with arms control agreements and peace treaties and investigate acts of international terrorism. He also proposed an increase of UN authority in other areas, such as economic relations and the environment, and he called for enhancing the power of the International Court of Justice and the authority of the International Atomic Energy Agency to decide international disputes. The Soviet Union also evidenced new support of UN activities on behalf of human rights.

Changes in the Foreign Policy Machinery

Gorbachev introduced several changes in the foreign policy-making apparatus, including a reduction of military influence, a strengthening of civilian policymakers, a strengthening of the national Legislature's role, an increase in popular influence over foreign policy making, and development of a special role for himself. These changes were to make possible departures from policies that Gorbachev considered mistaken and counterproductive.

THE COLLAPSE OF THE SOVIET UNION

At least five circumstances in 1990 and 1991 contributed to the collapse of the Soviet Union in December 1991. They were: 1) a precipitous decline in agricultural and industrial production; 2) intensification of ethnocultural nationalism and separatism; 3) the pluralization of Soviet politics, in particular the emergence of a democratic opposition and a steady erosion of the Communist Party's monopoly of power; 4) the emergence of a "commonwealth" of Slavic countries to replace the Soviet Union; and 5) the resignation of President Gorbachev.

DECLINE OF PRODUCTION

Soviet economic output declined overall by 4 percent in 1990 and by 10 to 15 percent in the first half of 1991. In the first 3 quarters of 1991, Soviet national income fell by at least 13 percent, if not more (some Soviet economists suggested that it declined between 18 and 25 percent). Here was a phenomenon akin to the West's economic depression of the 1930s.

Agricultural output suffered in part because of Gorbachev's ultimate failure to upgrade the inefficient collectivized Soviet agricultural system by expanding private entrepreneurialism. Many farmers liked the security of the collective farms and resented those who struck out on their own. If they applied for a piece of land, peasants living on state farms were often threatened with eviction. The few farmers who did farm independently faced insurmountable obstacles. They often got poor land miles from the village, inaccessible to roads and power lines. The collective farms had almost all the livestock and machinery, and their managers refused to rent or sell to private farmers, having found that private farming could wipe out the collective farms. Also, a private farmer who needed extra hands to bring the harvest had to approach the very people who opposed him: the collective farm managers.

The failure of economic restructuring to provide adequate storage and distribution of goods contributed to the decline in agricultural output in 1990 and 1991. There still were not enough grain elevators to store surplus grain and not enough refrigerated railway cars to get perishable goods to market before spoilage began. In early 1992 many collective farms used grain to fatten livestock in anticipation of promised increases in meat prices; these farms reneged on 1991 contracts with state authorities, expecting that the longer they waited, the higher the prices they would receive for their produce or livestock. State warehouses experienced theft on a grand scale, reckoned by Soviet officials at about 10 to 15 percent of stock.

Steadily diminishing output was also attributable to land degradation. At least 1.5 billion tons of topsoil in the Soviet Union eroded each year, with production losses estimated at $31 billion to $35 billion. Industrial pollution also lowered crop yields. By unhappy coincidence, the major sources of pollution in the former Soviet Union, such as metallurgical centers indiscriminately depositing lead, cobalt, and zinc wastes into the soil, were located in agricultural areas. Inappropriate use of fertilizers and pesticides were another cause of the environmental pollution responsible for undermining agricultural productivity. Prices for these agricultural inputs were heavily subsidized, leading farmers to dump more and more of them on the land, regardless of whether they were raising yields commensurately.

Industrial output in 1990 and 1991 declined when the centralized system of allocation of resources broke down. Factories were unable to obtain supplies and had to shut down. This in turn disrupted the production schedules of other factories. The new, only fitfully functioning system of limited self-management and self-financing had destroyed the chain of command without creating a replacement system for a market-driven exchange of goods and services. Factories had difficulty in getting supplies also because trade among the republics throughout 1991 was in chaos.

Byelorussia (now called Belarus), Estonia, and eventually Ukraine and Russia, the wealthiest of the Soviet republics, declared themselves sovereign, took control of their own resources, and proceeded to restrict exports of their products.

Another cause of the decline in industrial output throughout 1990 and 1991 was Gorbachev's difficulties in making state enterprises self-financing. Managers of state enterprises had no idea of costs and earnings. Consequently, when they were told to operate at a profit and threatened with bankruptcy proceedings if they failed, they were thoroughly confused. Production suffered.

Difficulties with privatization also contributed to the Soviet economy's decline in 1990 and 1991. Despite the enactment of laws opening the way for privatization, little progress had been made; most industry was still under state control. The vast state bureaucracy was still attempting to control instead of easing regulation. For example, one new regulation required cooperatives to be "affiliated" with state enterprises in order to engage in business, but affiliation really meant an obligation of the privately owned business to share its profits with a state enterprise. Would-be entrepreneurs also feared that the government might one day reverse free market policy and make private business firms illegal again.

The Kremlin's failure in the late 1980s to lure foreign investment through its policy of joint ventures also explains the economic problems of 1990 and 1991. Although the Kremlin in 1990 liberalized rules governing foreign investment in the Soviet economy, allowing majority ownership of joint ventures by foreigners, many potential investors stayed away because of uncertainty about earning profits and repatriating them. This was complicated by the fact that the ruble was not freely convertible to dollars or other Western money and that bartering in commodities or settling accounts in convertible currency was almost always illegal. Western banks hesitated to invest because, despite moves toward privatization and away from central planning and control of economic life, there was still no clear Soviet legal concept of ownership.

Finally, the economic slowdown must be blamed on certain cultural characteristics. Apathy, indifference toward work, pessimism about the future, and inertia led many simply to stop working and live by their wits. After years of Communist mismanagement, industriousness, discipline, and efficiency did not rank high with most citizens. Aleksandr Yacovlev, one of Gorbachev's closest and most influential advisers, believed that psychological dependence on the state, nurtured by subsidies of food, housing, education, and medical care, had led to a mass inertia, a habit of mind he considered the most serious obstacle to reform. Workers were now being asked to behave in new ways that they did not understand and with which they had little sympathy.

Dramatic evidence of the economic decline was the acute shortages of food, in particular staples such as milk, eggs, cheese, butter, and sausage. Diets moved away from meat and dairy products in short supply to potatoes, cabbages, and wheat porridge. Long lines required shoppers to wait at least 3 hours; workers relied on older retired relatives to do the shopping for them.

Shortages of food and other commodities, especially clothing, provoked a sharp rise in inflation. The currency became almost worthless; bartering became the norm in 1990. The ruble's rate fell to 60 to the dollar—way down from the traditional official value of $1.55 to a ruble in the mid-1980s. Many people in the cities and the rural areas had so little faith in the ruble that they refused to use it as a medium of exchange.

With gross national product in decline, the Soviet Union had difficulty in servicing its foreign debt of almost $80 billion. This was complicated by a decline of exports. Natural gas and oil output dropped in 1990 and 1991. Meanwhile, imports of consumer goods rose as the state tried to ease shortages resulting from the slack in domestic production. The decline in GNP also fed unemployment.

Other economic problems made life difficult in 1991. The burgeoning budget deficit grew as the Soviet government increased subsidies to try to keep real incomes from falling. The republic governments led by independence-minded nationalist politicians refused to make payments to the central government, depriving it of the revenue necessary to implement its policies. And the Soviet military continued to be expensive, probably accounting for some 40 percent of the national budget and consuming 18 percent of GNP in 1990 and 1991.

Last-Minute Remedies

President Gorbachev initially relied upon the exercise of central authority to curb the decline. In September 1990 the Supreme Soviet granted him decree power to force sectors of the economy to comply with previously passed reform laws meant to force government enterprises to deliver the raw materials and finished goods that they had been holding back in order to sell them on the black market.

Since this failed, Gorbachev attempted a liberal approach. He gave tentative backing to the so-called 500 Day Plan, authored by his chief economic advisers Stanislav Shatalin and Nikolai Petrakov. This plan aimed to move the country, in 500 days, to a market-based economy by stabilizing the budget, making the ruble convertible, decontrolling prices, and accelerating privatization of enterprises.

But conservatives in the central government and the Soviet Communist Party, including then–prime minister Nikolai Ryzkhov, opposed this plan. Gorbachev also feared moving away too quickly from the old order, with its risks of increasing hardships and provoking social turmoil. In order to strike a balance between the liberals and conservatives, in October 1990 Gorbachev offered his own plan. This kept the central government in Moscow in control of transportation, communication, defense industries, energy, credit, and monetary policy and gave supervision of national economic develop-

ment to a committee consisting of representatives of the republics. The Gorbachev plan gave the republics broad latitude in setting the pace for price deregulation, privatization of state enterprises, and setting rules governing wages and social security. However, it denied them control over their mineral wealth and autonomy in regulating their economic life, which most of them were now demanding.

Gorbachev's economic plan for a "prudent revolution" was passed by the Supreme Soviet on October 19, 1990. Shatalin and Petrakov were critical and warned that the longer the Soviet president delayed in introducing truly radical change, the worse the economic situation would become. The republics did not like this plan either. Russia said that it would follow the Shatalin plan and dissociate itself from the central government. Ukraine announced a plan to introduce its own crude currency, in the form of special coupons to be used in conjunction with rubles in the purchase of consumer goods. Some republic leaderships, fearful of a popular backlash against reform, increased pensions and wrote off the debts of failing collective farms, thereby enlarging rather than reducing the horrendous budget deficit.

In the spring of 1991, however, Gorbachev again edged toward the left. He cautiously backed a plan by Yevgeni Primakov, a close political adviser, and Grigory Yavlinsky, an economic adviser to Russian president Boris Yeltsin, to ask the Bush administration for massive U.S. assistance, worth about $30 billion annually, to help the Soviet Union move from the centrally planned economy to one based on market forces. The Kremlin would pledge to decontrol prices, privatize state-controlled enterprises, and abandon central planning. This plan, supported by 9 of the 15 Soviet republics, including Russia, was never adopted because of strenuous conservative opposition.

Following the August 1991 coup attempt, with the hard-liners swept from positions of influence, the liberal reformers made several proposals. A plan by Yavlinsky provided for a strong union, with cooperation among the republics on the issues of price decontrol and reduction of expenditures to ease the budget deficit. Yavlinsky's plan won Gorbachev's support because it emphasized a strong center, to which Gorbachev was deeply committed. An economic treaty signed by 8 republics on October 18, 1991, put the plan in place, but it failed because the republics refused to cooperate in the acceptance and implementation of radical change.

By the end of 1991, the economy of the Soviet state was in limbo. The Gorbachev leadership seemed to have lost control over the economic destiny of the country. It had no plan to reverse the steady deterioration of the Soviet economy.

INTENSIFICATION OF ETHNOCULTURAL NATIONALISM AND SEPARATISM

A second major cause of the Soviet Union's collapse was the intensification of nationalist movements among the large ethnic groups that controlled republic governments and pushed them to seek increased autonomy—and, in some instances, complete independence of the Soviet central government in Moscow. At the same time, there were "micro" nationalist movements among the many small ethnocultural groups living in some of the republics that wanted the same autonomy and independence as the large, "macro" nationalist movements. Thus, not only the unity of the Soviet state was threatened but also the unity of republics that had ethnically heterogeneous societies.

"Macro" Movements

In the 1990 elections for republic legislatures, voters consistently supported candidates who voiced popular historic resentments toward central control. Non-Russian leaderships in particular wanted independence for their republics, an end to Russification, and the establishment of the local tongue as the official language of politics and education. The opposition won power in seven republics. Other republics, still run by Communists, also wanted greater autonomy of Moscow.

The newly elected republic leaders and their parliaments quickly asserted a right to their own political systems and constitutions and to diminish, or even to eradicate, central government control. They laid claim to all the land and property within their borders and to all natural and other resources, including labor, and in some cases the right to their own currencies. Republic leaderships also sought control of local police and challenged central authority over border troops, secret police, and intelligence. They demanded the right to direct relations, particularly economic ties, with other countries and insisted that local draftees into the Soviet Army should serve only on their own territory. Some republics began to establish their own armies.

Gorbachev tried, with little success, to accommodate these demands for autonomy within the framework of a reformed union. In November 1990 he presented a draft treaty providing for greater autonomy for the republics. The powers of the central government were to continue in place. The treaty stated no specific method of secession—a point of dispute with the Baltic republics—and did not give the republics control over wealth located inside their boundaries. When only 8 of the 15 republics accepted the draft, Gorbachev, in March 1991, offered a new draft, which provided for greater autonomy and a less intrusive central government. The new draft recognized the declarations of state sovereignty passed by all 15 republics; recognized the right of the republics to full diplomatic relations with other countries; provided for the right of secession; and gave the republics a share of control in the defense and energy industries and a role in the writing and adoption of a new Soviet constitution. Because the revised draft still preserved a strong federal union, many independence-minded republics rejected it and called for a very loose confederation to replace the old union.

In mid-March 1991 Gorbachev held a popular referendum throughout the Soviet Union on the issue of the union. Six republics boycotted the referendum, and the outcome of the vote was far from decisive. While the Central Asian republics voted overwhelmingly in favor of preserving the union, voters in other republics approved by only a slim majority. But the Gorbachev leadership spoke of an "impressive majority" in favor of the union and tried to persuade all the republics to accept the revised draft of the union treaty. To get their support, Gorbachev yielded significantly to the demands of the republics for increased power sharing.

Nine republics, including Russia, agreed in April 1991 to join the central government in producing a confederative union and a new national constitution providing for an extensive decentralization of administrative authority by the Kremlin, as well as the holding of national elections for the new agencies created in the constitution. This Nine Plus One Agreement (nine republics and the central government) gave more to the nine than to the one. The nine republics had the right to secede, significant economic and administrative power, and the promise of a new constitution and genuinely democratic elections throughout the union by 1992. By July 1991 the nine republics that were party to the April agreement had produced a draft treaty that in effect transformed the union into a loose confederation.

But at this point progress toward a reformed union stalled, and the political situation deteriorated over the summer. The explanation for this lay in the internal politics within three key republics: Russia, Lithuania, and Georgia. They reinforced their independence of the central government and complicated Gorbachev's effort to preserve the Soviet Union, even in a confederative form.

Russia

In mid-June 1990 the Russian Parliament declared its sovereignty, including the right to veto any federal law on Russian territory. Russian Communists established their own independent branch of the parent organization that could lobby aggressively with the national party leadership on behalf of Russian interests. These actions strengthened Russian president Yeltsin's administrative authority within the republic. Yeltsin refused to allow the Russian government to transfer any funds to the central government without a strict accounting; he called for a transfer of the bulk of economic decision making from the center to the republics; and he campaigned for the ouster of conservative Soviet prime minister Ryzkhov. Yeltsin also challenged the central government by establishing a Russian-controlled branch of the KGB.

In early April 1991, the Russian Parliament called for the direct election of the republic powers, enabling Yeltsin to continue his challenge to the authority of the center and to Gorbachev's leadership. No progress toward union could occur until after the elections.

Lithuania

The Baltic republics, especially Lithuania, had become increasingly uncompromising about their independence because the Soviet government had treated them so harshly. For example, in mid-January 1991, Soviet troops and armor had taken up key positions in Vilnius in an effort to force the Landsbergis government to retreat from its campaign for independence. The Kremlin hoped that this move would cause Latvia and Estonia to pull back from their own challenges to Soviet authority. But the Landsbergis government refused to reverse course, and a full-blown military confrontation began. Soviet military and Interior Ministry special forces ("Black Berets") invaded Lithuanian government buildings, including those housing the local television station and the press, causing a dozen Lithuanian deaths.

Something of a climax was reached when a bogus provisional government of local conservatives linked to Kremlin hard-liners, calling itself the National Salvation Front, proclaimed itself in control of Lithuania. This failed, but the political consequences for Gorbachev's attempt to preserve the union were serious. Gorbachev's credibility with nationalists and democrats everywhere in the Soviet Union was undermined and provoked an even stronger nationalism among the Baltics.

On February 9, 1991, Lithuanians voted overwhelmingly for independence of the Soviet Union. On March 3, 1991, the peoples of Estonia and Latvia voted overwhelmingly for independence. Ethnic Russians in Latvia supported the republic's independence, giving the Kremlin pause and discouraging ideas for more coercion.

Georgia

The situation in Georgia had developed by April 1991 to the point where its government was reluctant to be part of a confederation. In February 1990 the Georgian Communist Party had called for complete political, economic, and cultural self-determination for the Georgian republic. It supported full sovereignty for all the republics and only a limited role for central government in defense, foreign policy, and for problems most important to the whole country.

On March 9, 1990, the Georgian Parliament declared illegal and invalid agreements of 1921 and 1922 between the Georgian and Soviet Russian governments establishing Soviet control over Georgia after the invasion of Georgian territory by the Soviet Army. This gesture was intended to create a legal basis for independence. In November 1990 the Georgian Parliament terminated the Soviet military draft on Georgian territory and created the equivalent of a republic army, called the Georgian National Guard.

In October 1990 elections for the Georgian republic's Supreme Soviet gave nationalist groups a majority, with Zviad Gamsakhurdia named chairperson. The Parliament accepted Gamsakhurdia's proposal to create a new post of president of the republic, to be elected directly by the voters, a move that would not only strengthen his bid for Georgian independence of Moscow but also increase his already immense personal authority. Gamsakhurdia, a vehement anti-Communist and champion of Georgian nationalism in the Brezhnev era who had become the spokesperson for the Georgian movement for independence, won the presidency in the May 26, 1991, elections.

The Gamsakhurdia leadership gradually escalated a boycott of the central government by refusing to participate in the meetings of central bodies in which Georgia had a seat. Georgia, like the Baltic republics and Armenia, held its own referendum on independence, on March 31, 1991, as a substitute for Gorbachev's March 17 referendum on preserving a renewed union. Independence was approved by 98 percent of voters. Interestingly, the large Russian, Armenian, and Azerbaijani minorities strongly supported independence. The republic's leadership also repeatedly stated that Georgia would refuse to sign a new union treaty, in any form, and that any such treaties were invalid unless the signatories possessed equal status under international law.

"Micro" Autonomist and Independence Movements

Exacerbating the divisiveness caused by the nationalism of the large ethnic groups in the Soviet state throughout 1990 and 1991 was a resurgence of nationalism among the small ethnic groups in several of the heterogeneous republics, such as Russia, Moldova, and Georgia. These groups demanded increased autonomy of their republic governments and, in a few instances, complete independence, imitating the assertiveness that the republic governments had shown the central authorities in Moscow.

Bashkir, Tatar, and Chechen-Ingushetia in Russia

In 1990–1991 some 25 million non-Russians were concentrated in autonomous republics or regions within the Russian republic. Several major groups challenged the authority of the Yeltsin government, demanding independence or at least substantially increased autonomy from Moscow.

In the center of the highly industrialized Ural Mountains, the autonomous republic of Bashkir declared its independence of both the Soviet Union and Russia in October 1990, although only 25 percent of the 4 million inhabitants of the republic are Bashkir. The Tatar autonomous republic, perhaps the most restive of the non-Russian minorities within the Russian republic, threatened Russian unity by demanding greater autonomy of Moscow in the fall of 1991.

Finally, the Muslim population of the Chechen–Ingushetia national area in southwestern Russia near the Caspian Sea demanded independence in November 1991. Yeltsin declared a state of emergency in Grozny, the capital, and wanted to use force against the local nationalists, but he was restrained by his Parliament. A disturbing aspect of Chechen–Ingush nationalism was the support it sought from neighbors.

Gagauz and Russians in Moldova

In resistance to a law in 1990 making Romanian the republic's official language and requiring people in dozens of jobs, from doctors to hairdressers, to pass Romanian language tests, two small minorities in Moldova, the Gagauz, a group of about 150,000 Turkic Christians living in the southern reaches of the republic, and a larger group of about 300,000 Russians and Ukrainians living in the east near the Dniester River, proclaimed their own Gagauz and Trans-Dniester autonomist republics. Both the former Soviet central government and the Moldovan republic government in Kishinev called these declarations illegal, but the issue was by no means settled.

Abkhazians, South Ossetians, and Meskhetians in Georgia

As Georgia proposed independence of the Soviet Union in 1991, leaders of the Abkhazian and South Ossetian minorities there feared that an independent Georgia would not respect their cultural rights and that they would no longer be able to turn to Moscow for protection. Both groups pushed for secession from Georgia and declared their loyalty to Moscow. Nationalists in both regions boycotted the October 1990 republic elections. In December 1990 Abkhazian and South Ossetian leaders refused to participate in the voting on these issues. South Osseta declared a self-styled "Supreme Soviet of the South Ossetian Soviet Republic," which voted to subordinate the republic directly to the Soviet Union, a move that Moscow, as well as Tbilisi, refused to accept. Gamsakhurdia responded forcefully and suspended Ossetian autonomy, imposing direct rule of Tbilisi. Open warfare between Georgian and Ossetian armed groups broke out despite the presence of Soviet military forces in the region. It continued throughout 1991, as the South Ossetians tried to associate themselves more explicitly and more closely to the rapidly deteriorating Soviet central government in Moscow. And when Moscow hard-liners staged their coup in August 1991, the Abkhazian Communist Party immediately supported their actions, a gesture that provided the Georgian nationalist government with a pretext to shut down the Abkhazian Communist organization.

A wild card in Georgian nationalist politics was the attempt by Meskhetian Turks, exiled to Central Asia by Stalin during World War II, to return to their homeland in the Caucasus. Unwelcome and attacked in Uzbekistan and elsewhere, the Meskhetians wanted to reclaim their homeland in Georgia. Many Georgians, however, feared that the Meskhetians had lost all ties to Georgia, including knowledge of the Georgian language, and would ultimately want to separate their territory from Georgia and perhaps seek to become part of Turkey. To prevent their return, Georgian officials reportedly went to the extreme of faking a landslide on the Georgian military highway, the only entrance point to Georgia from the northeast. In other key points of entry to the republic, Georgian "volunteers" prevented the return of the Meskhetians. In late 1990 Meskhetian refugees massed on the Georgian border near Sochi and threatened to force their way into Georgia. They eventually relented in hopes of obtaining a negotiated settlement of their claims. Few Meskhetians had succeeded in returning to Georgia by the end of 1991.

Russians and Ukrainians in Central Asia

In Kazakhstan, populated predominantly by Slavs (Russians and Ukrainians), Kazakh people accounted for only 36 percent of the republic's 17 million people. The Russian population had always thought of the land and its inhabitants as part of Russia, even though it belonged to Kazakhstan; the Russian-dominated Soviet government in Moscow did nothing to discourage such thinking. Once Russians and Ukrainians experienced directly the reality of their administrative subordination to the Kazakh Muslim personnel who ran the republic government in Alma Ata, there could well be turmoil and political conflict.

There was also a potentially explosive situation in Uzbekistan involving the Slavic minority of Russians and Ukrainians, who made up about 8 percent of the population. Uzbeks resented the strong Russian influence in their local Communist party. This was corrected by a gradual process of Uzbekization from 1959 to 1983, resulting in the ascendancy of non-Russians. Now, in the post-Soviet era, many Russians are scared of discrimination and have spoken of an imminent mass exodus back to the Russian republic.

PLURALIZATION OF SOVIET POLITICS

Another major circumstance surrounding the collapse of the Soviet Union was the pluralization of Soviet politics during the late 1980s. The many democratic reform groups that had appeared as a result of glasnost undermined the historic single-party system that had kept glued together the extraordinarily diverse and conflict-ridden Soviet society.

Rise of Democratic Groups

With glasnost in the late 1980s, radical intellectuals spoke out against the Soviet system. Arguing that Soviet society had been swindled by "seventy years on the road to nowhere," they delegitimized the Soviet system, which was a factor in its collapse, especially as the scope and pace of their activities expanded significantly in 1990 and 1991.

This nascent democratic opposition took advantage of the partially open elections allowed by Gorbachev in 1989 to help him create a power base for reform communism. For example, as a result of the March 1989 elections for the Congress of Peoples' Deputies, there emerged independent blocs, such as the Inter-regional Group of Andrei Sakharov, Gavril Popov, and Anatoli Sobchak, which began to lobby for radical liberalization of the Soviet political system.

These groups eventually went far beyond reform of the system, to outright repudiation of it. Tension mounted between the government and the opposition as the country moved toward local elections, set for the spring of 1990. Although the radicals did not publicize their intentions, it became increasingly clear, especially in private conversation, that their goal was to wrest power from the party and to move toward genuine constitutional government, a market economy, and private property.

Throughout 1990 and 1991, the Democrats got a significant lift from Boris Yeltsin. Dismissed in earlier times as a "maverick populist" with little prospect of mounting an effective challenge to Gorbachev's power and influence, Yeltsin quickly emerged as a central, perhaps decisive figure in the emergence of a vibrant democratic opposition. He strengthened his democratic credentials enormously when, in July 1990, he dramatically resigned from the Communist Party during its televised 28th Congress, thus publicly distancing himself from those who were increasingly receiving the blame of the people for the perceived failure of perestroika and the worsening of economic conditions.

In August 1990 Yeltsin placed himself firmly in the camp of the radical reformers when he called for Russia's adoption of the economic program of Stanislav Shatalin. A measure of his extraordinary popularity was the way in which, on March 28, 1991, several hundred thousand Muscovites defied a ban on rallies in order to demonstrate their support of Yeltsin against the effort of conservatives in the Russian Parliament to impeach him. This massive explosion of popular wrath was unprecedented in recent Russian history and suggested the kind of power that an alienated citizenry could use to influence the political system. Finally, Yeltsin became a powerful force within the reform movement when, in June 1991, he was elected by an overwhelming popular majority to the presidency of the Russian republic.

Yeltsin was, perhaps, the most influential figure in the democratic movement, having brought real democratic reform to the Russian government through the establishment of a directly elected chief executive. However, he could not bring unity to the democratic forces because of their deep divisions, their lack of experience with party organization other than that of the highly centralized and autocratic Communist Party, and their extraordinary diversity of aims and ambitions. Nevertheless, in the beginning of July 1991, the Democrats finally announced the formation of a new political organization, called the Movement of Democratic Reforms, under the leadership of former Soviet foreign minister Eduard Shevardnadze. The Democratic Movement was unique in that it included not only outside dissidents but also Communist Party members who had been alienated by conservatives in the top party leadership. Although the Movement had a long way to go in mounting an effective challenge to the Communists, its establishment put the Communist Party on the defensive and accelerated the decline of its influence and power.

Moreover, with the formation of the Movement, party members like Shevardnadze and Yacovlev who once had hoped, as Gorbachev still did, that the Communist Party could eventually reform itself, now gave up that hope once and for all. Shevardnadze left the party with stinging criticisms of it, calling it intolerant, nostalgic for the discredited past, and doomed to oblivion because of its stubborn conservatism.

The Decline of the Communist Party

While the influence of democratic forces increased, that of the Communist Party diminished during 1990 and 1991. In this period the party lost power for several reasons. During the February 7, 1990, plenum of the Soviet Communist Party's Central Committee, it voted to end its historic monopoly of power in the Soviet Union. This decision reversed Lenin's policy—adopted following the Bolshevik seizure of power in November 1917—of establishing a single-party state under Marxist leadership. It was an about-face for Gorbachev, who had reaffirmed his support of the party's monopoly of power as late as December 8, 1989. At that time he declared, "It is essential to maintain the one-party system" during a heated discussion of demands by Andrei Sakharov and other reformers in the Congress of Peoples' Deputies to revoke Article 6 of the Soviet Constitution, which guaranteed the Communist Party's supremacy.

Several reasons explain Gorbachev's change of position. His call for the abandonment of the party's monopoly of power was consistent with other steps taken to curtail party influence over the running of the Soviet system in favor of the state apparatus, which became more influential and more powerful in policy making. Gorbachev benefited personally from a strengthened state apparatus as public criticism of and hostility toward the party increased in consequence of continued deteriorioration of economic conditions and interethnic rivalries.

Furthermore, as then–premier Ryzkhov asserted during the plenum, the Communist Party had already lost its political monopoly because of the de facto existence of pluralism in the form of new political organizations. Mass defections of old and young party members to these new organizations, perceived to have a more promising political future than the Communists, also influenced Gorbachev's new willingness to move faster toward a multiparty system—which, incidentally, he never had explicitly precluded.

The formal termination of the party's political monopoly did not automatically mean the end of its influence and power. The party plenum stopped short of demands for full pluralism in the form of a dialogue with opposition groups, which conceivably could lead to Central/Eastern European–style coalition regimes. Indeed, the party remained the single most well-endowed reservoir of administrative expertise in the country. Thus, the February 7 vote did not mean an immediate emergence of a Western–style pluralistic political system.

The party preserved the bulk of its leadership authority. Despite the fact that the party remained one of the most serious obstacles to the reform and improvement of Soviet life, because of its strong conservative instincts borne out of not only ideology but also the self-interest of its membership, Gorbachev had acknowledged in September 1989 that the Soviet Communist Party "was and remains the main organizing and coordinating force capable of leading the people along the path of . . . Socialist change, of playing an integrating and rallying role in society and, let us be blunt about it, of preventing an undesirable, dramatic turn of events."

Another reason for the decline and disintegration of the Soviet Communist Party was the March 1989 elections for the Congress of Peoples' Deputies, which put anti-Communists in positions of power for the first time. In some places newly elected non-Communist officials confiscated party property. Seeing the handwriting on the wall, several million party members retired; others joined reformist political groups. Yeltsin showed his power when he banned political organizations in the workplace and effectively ended the long tradition in which party members dominated the leadership of offices, factories, and farms.

The party suffered also as Gorbachev tried to transform it into a conventional reformist organization modeled after the Socialist parties in the west. At the end of July 1991, in a plenum of the party's Central Committee, Gorbachev asked the party to give up its Marxist ideology. He supported other reformers and said that the party would lose any claim to participate in the political life of the country if it did not break with the past. In his view it had lost contact with reality when it set unachievable goals based on "raw ideology" regardless of the concerns of Soviet citizens. Gorbachev also called upon the party to accept power sharing with non-Communist leaderships and organizations in the republics. The Central Committee eventually endorsed Gorbachev's proposals to transform the party into a broad-based reform organization, effectively abandoning its monopoly of politics.

One consequence was that the Russian branch split into two organizations, one of reformers and the other of hard-liners. Since the Russian branch was the most influential of local organizations, the split tended to undermine further the party's hold on power. Russian Communists were fragmented even more at the beginning of August 1991, when a subbranch of the reform Communists, called the Democratic Party of Russian Communists, emerged, an alternative organization founded by Russian vice president Aleksandr Rutskoi.

Hard-liners in the party leadership were appalled by the party's decline. They made no secret of their alarm at the decline of centralized authority or their willingness to prevent it. They headed institutions whose power was vested in the old order of state ownership, centralized planning, and the coherence of the union.

On August 19, 1991, Prime Minister Valentin Pavlov, Interior Minister Boris Pugo, KGB chairperson Vladimir Kryuchkov, Defense Minister Dmitri Yazov, and managers of the military–industrial complex, notably Oleg Baklanov, first deputy chairperson of the Defense Council, called up their resources and tried to force Gorbachev out of power. They believed that the people would support them. Economic conditions had not improved under perestoika. The hard-liners thus had the psychological as well as the political wherewithal to go on the offensive against perestroika and, if necessary, against Gorbachev himself.

The Ascendancy of Hard-line Conservatives

Gorbachev understood these feelings and may have tried to contain them. As early as December 1990, he had replaced his liberal interior minister, Vadim Bakatin, with the former KGB general Boris Pugo, and replaced Nikolai Ryzkhov as prime minister with Valentin Pavlov, a command administrative economist deeply hostile to radical reforms.

Hard-liners had gained again at a session of the Congress of Peoples' Deputies, in December 1990, when Gorbachev named a colorless career Communist aparatchik, Gennadi Yanev, to be his vice president, a move that stunned reformers, including some of his closest supporters like Shevardnadze and Yacovlev. Indeed, Shevardnadze was shocked by the way in which Gorbachev seemed to be allowing the ascendancy of hard-liners who he knew opposed further progress in his reform program. Shevardnadze also was angry that his long-time friend did not defend him against virulent public attacks from the hard-liners who deplored his arms-control initiatives. He eventually resigned as foreign minister in December 1990, predicting a rightist offensive to block the perestroika-inspired transformation of the Soviet Union.

The hard-liners now tried to force Gorbachev to the right on the issue of Lithuanian separatism. They authorized KGB special forces, army paratroopers, and Interior Ministry Black Berets to force Lithuania and Latvia to curtail their campaigns for independence. Although the hard-liners suffered a setback when Gorbachev refused to oust the Landsbergis government by force, Pugo, Pavlov, Kryuchkov, and others renewed their pressure on Gorbachev to pursue a conservative course. Pavlov claimed in January 1991 that Western aid to the Soviet Union was designed to destabilize and destroy Soviet socialism. Obviously, Pavlov did not want the West to help Gorbachev move forward with perestroika-inspired reforms. He sought to discredit the West in the eyes of the Soviet public. In another effort to move the country in a conservative direction, Pavlov ordered the confiscation of all ruble bills larger than 50, ostensibly to reduce the monetary excess but instead, perhaps, to prepare the country for a shift to the right with a command administrative shock therapy to remedy the country's now desperate economic crisis.

In March 1991 the hard-liners lashed out at Yeltsin after the Russian leader publicly called for a "declaration of war" against Gorbachev for having betrayed perestroika by appointing them. They called for Yeltsin's impeachment. When several hundred thousand Muscovites demonstrated on March 28 and strikes in support of him at the Siberian coal mines occurred, the impeachment failed. Hard-liners felt desperate.

The August 1991 Coup

For the first time, the hard-liners now turned on Gorbachev. Infuriated by Gorbachev's support of the so-called Nine Plus One Agreement of April 23, 1991, providing for a radical devolution of administrative power from the central government in Moscow to the republics, effectively emasculating the old union, the hard-liners tried to get the Communist Party's Central Committee to replace him as general secretary. They proposed Anatoli Lukyanov, a long-time friend of Gorbachev's, for chairperson of the Supreme Soviet, second in line for the succession.

The hard-liners, however, were checkmated temporarily when Gorbachev beat back their effort against him by threatening to resign from the party if it did not endorse the Nine Plus One Agreement. The Central Committee supported Gorbachev, with some misgivings, to avoid a devisive conflict over the succession.

The hard-liners were determined to force Gorbachev to curtail his reforms. They correctly sensed that Gorbachev had been weakened in these battles because the democrats wanted once and for all to stop his shifting between left and right on reform and lead their campaign to democratize and decentralize Soviet political and economic organization.

Grievances of the Military

Among the hard-line faction in the Kremlin in the spring and summer of 1991 was the top Soviet military leadership, in particular Defense Minister Yazov, who deplored Gorbachev's policies of retrenchment internationally, especially in Central/Eastern Europe, a region of prime importance for the security of the Soviet state. He also thought that Gorbachev's decision in 1988 to withdraw Soviet forces from Afghanistan before the achievement of a victory over the Mujahideen was a mistake, not only because it weakened Soviet security in Central Asia but also for reasons of pride. He opposed the shrinking budgets that required severe cutbacks in defense equipment and personnel. And he and other top-ranking Soviet officers were especially resentful of Gorbachev's apparent willingness to tolerate abuse of the military from the new political and national opposition groups and in the public media. They were incensed at the verbal insults and outright theft of military property by lawless gangs of dissidents in places like Georgia, by revelations in a critical press of increased defections, and by charges of brutality in the ranks. They also regretted the downgrading of ideology, which had helped to promote a docile and obedient society.

The Prelude to the Coup

The hard-liners were emboldened when, in June, Pavlov attempted to outmaneuver Gorbachev by asking the Supreme Soviet for the transfer of decree powers to the prime minister's office to allow it to deal with what was termed the country's "imminent collapse." Such a move would have put Pavlov in control of the country. Instead of firing Pavlov and like-minded members of his government for their evident disloyalty to him, Gorbachev skirted this issue, left them in power, and called upon the Parliament simply to reject Pavlov's demands.

Meanwhile, in late July, Yeltsin, eight other republic presidents, and Gorbachev accepted a draft union treaty that went even further than the Nine Plus One Agreement in transforming the union into a confederation of near sovereign constituent republics. This presented a real threat of disintegration, because it involved the breakup of a single economic plan, a single plan for civil rights, a single defense, and a single foreign policy. Under these circumstances, Pavlov insisted, he and his associates had no choice other than to take decisive measures to stop the slide of the country to catastrophe. They decided to force Gorbachev out of power, through a coup.

The chief plotters were Pavlov, Pugo, Kryuchkov, Yazov, Yanev, and Baklanov. Less well known plotters were V. A. Starodubstev, chairperson of the U.S.S.R. Farmers' Union, and A. I. Tizyakov, president of the Association of State Enterprises and Industrial, Construction, Transportation, and Communications Facilities of the Soviet Union. The plotters gave Gorbachev an ultimatum on Sunday, August 18, at his vacation home in the Crimea, demanding that he reject the latest draft of the union treaty. When he refused, they put him under house arrest, cut his telephone lines, and proceeded to take control of the administrative offices in Moscow of both the Soviet and Russian governments. They established a Committee on the State of Emergency under Vice President Yanev, who was theoretically in command of the Soviet government and ready to exercise the powers of Gorbachev, who was said to be "incapacitated."

The Failure of the Coup

Beginning on Monday, August 19, 1991, the plotters met popular resistance, led by Russian president Yeltsin. Yeltsin called upon hundreds of thousands of Muscovites to surround and defend him and the Russian Parliament buildings. At the same time, Ukraine declared the orders and decrees of the Committee null and void.

Meanwhile, the plotters failed to ensure that the members of a special KGB unit would follow their orders to arrest Yeltsin and other leaders and to take over the Russian Parliament building, which they did not do. Local KGB commanders had mixed feelings about the coup, apparently unknown to Kryuchkov, and refused to go after Yeltsin.

The military also was unreliable, despite its grievances against Gorbachev and eagerness to replace him. Yazov apparently had no stomach for massive civilian bloodshed. Unlike KGB chief Kryuchkov, who was an alarmist convinced of imminent disaster unless a firm hand took control of the Soviet system and blocked further change, Yazov, whose concerns centered primarily on the perceived negative impact of perestroika on the army, was reluctant to mobilize the army's resources behind the coup.

Moreover, many middle-level military leaders had strong reformist instincts and wanted, rather, to repair the army's image and professionalism. Typical was Air Force commander in chief Yevgeni Shaposhnikov, who refused to participate in the coup. Shaposhnikov had been very vocal about the need for economic reform, a market economy, and the integration of the Soviet Union into the world economy after 70 years of debilitating and counterproductive isolation.

Conscripts deployed in Moscow, who were uneasy over the role of the army in the attempted seizure of power, went so far as to assure civilians that they would not obey orders to shoot. The plotters also did not have the support of regional commanders, whose willingness to obey orders varied from place to place. In Georgia, for example, the independence-seeking president, Zviad Gamsakhurdia, persuaded the local commander not to deploy his troops. And Leningrad mayor Sobchak persuaded the military commander there to allow mass demonstrations in the center of the city by promising not to call for a strike (which went ahead anyway at several plants). The coupmakers' inability to secure the country's second city was a significant cause of their failure.

Inexplicably, the plotters neglected to call on the independent right-wing group of deputies in the Soviet Legislature. Members of Soyuz were strongly supportive of the traditional Soviet Union and critical of Gorbachev's willingness to decentralize administrative authority and thereby strengthen the power and influence of the Soviet government in Moscow.

The plotters also botched the mobilization of the party out of a desire to exclude the deputy general secretary, Vladimir Ivachoko, who was thought unreliable. This meant that the Central Committee Secretariat did not immediately support the coup after the Emergency Committee's televised press conference. These missteps were catastrophic because they provided Yeltsin with the opportunity to mobilize the Moscow public.

In sharp contrast to the plotters, who had no blueprint for change beyond vague promises to inspire mass support, the loyalists knew exactly how they should act. On Monday, August 19, while the Soviet cabinet, with only one dissenting voice, endorsed the coup, and while the Soviet Communist Party's Central Committee Secretariat sat in silence, Yeltsin, along with Popov, Sobchak, and others, publicly called for resistance. They did not move to take power themselves; they called instead for the restoration of Gorbachev as the legitimate president, both to ensure continuity of state power and to give constitutional legitimacy to their own de facto exercise of that power, a gesture that was useful domestically and internationally in the heat of the crisis.

The beginning of the end of the coup occurred when representatives of Yeltsin went on Wednesday, August 21, to the Crimea, where the hard-liners had kept Gorbachev under house arrest and incommunicado. They brought Gorbachev and his family back to Moscow. Shortly after his arrival, the Supreme Soviet formally reinstated him as president. The coup was now officially over.

MOVEMENT TOWARD A COMMONWEALTH

In the weeks following the collapse of the coup and the arrest of its leaders, Yeltsin liberally exploited Gorbachev's legitimacy as well as his new majority in the Russian Parliament to demolish the old Soviet order. He appeared on national television reiterating a series of decrees he had issued during the coup, including one suspending the Soviet Communist Party and its propaganda instrument, *Pravda*. Dominated by Yeltsin, Gorbachev changed the leadership of the KGB and the army. He appointed Yevgeni Shaposhnikov as minister of defense and Vadim Bakatin, Pugo's liberal-minded predecessor at the Interior Ministry, as head of the KGB. Shaposhnikov and Bakatin began at once an extensive purge of their respective institutions, reducing their size, dissolving existing party cells, and putting them under the control of state authority. Meanwhile, in Russia, Yeltsin systematically rid the Russian government (and ultimately those parts of the Soviet government under Russian control) of the old nomenklatura, replacing them with young, liberal, and modernizing professionals who would drastically reform the economy.

Following his return from the Crimea to Moscow, Gorbachev exhorted the government to avoid a "Yugoslavization" of the Soviet Union's conflict-ridden multinational society and to preserve the union. On September 2, 1991, the Congress of Peoples' Deputies approved a plan essentially similar to the provisions of the Nine Plus One draft treaty. But while Russia favored preservation of the union in a new confederative form, there was now much opposition to it from other republics, in particular the Baltic republics and Ukraine.

The Baltic republics wanted nothing to do with efforts to salvage the Soviet system. Estonia and Latvia had declared their independence on August 20 and 21; and after the coup all three Baltic republics, with support from the West, demanded complete separation from the Soviet Union. On September 6 the Kremlin decreed the complete independence of the Baltic states. Encouraged by this break in the union, separatists in other republics began to plan their own independence.

Ukraine announced on October 17 that it would not sign the new plan because popular sentiment wanted more autonomy of the Soviet Union than this treaty called for. Indeed, Ukraine was skeptical of a union of any kind, given its fears of a resurgent and powerful Soviet central government. It would wait for the outcome of a referendum, scheduled for December 1, 1991, on the issue of independence. On that date Ukrainian voters overwhelmingly approved a declaration of

(Novosti Photo)

Mikhail Gorbachev became general secretary of the Communist Party of the Soviet Union in March 1985. His endorsement by the Politburo was immediate and indicated the power of his influence. Under his administration, the Soviet Communist Party as well as the entire Soviet Union experienced monumental changes. His policies of perestroika and glasnost brought about changes that would eventually lead, in December 1991, to his resignation from office.

independence and elected their nationalist leader Leonid Kravchuk to the Ukrainian presidency.

Support for preserving the Soviet Union in any shape or form was now minimal. When Gorbachev proposed that there should be economic agreement, those who supported the proposal on November 14 insisted on sending it to their respective parliaments for ratification. By this time Russia itself had lost interest in preserving the union, however loose it might be, because Yeltsin believed that Russia could do better alone. In his view the central government was the biggest obstacle to economic reform. Frustrated by Gorbachev's failure to bring the republics together on issues of unity and economic improvement, Yeltsin now thought that each republic would have to carry through reform on its own, in its own way, and at its own pace.

On December 8, 1991, the presidents of Russia, Ukraine, and Belarus, which together controlled 73 percent of the Soviet population and 80 percent of the territory of the Soviet Union, signed an agreement in the Belarus capital of Minsk to create a new confederation of republics, called the *Com-monwealth of Independent States,* or C.I.S. They declared the Soviet Union at an end. This agreement was made quite independently of Gorbachev, whom they did not even bother to consult.

In many respects the powers of the new Commonwealth defined at Minsk resembled those that Gorbachev had been seeking for a reformed union with joint control over foreign policy, trade, customs, transportation and communications systems, currency, emigration, the environment, and fighting organized crime. A separate statement at Minsk declared that the preservation and development of close economic ties among the republics were important to the national economy and should continue. Ukraine and Belarus agreed to follow the lead of Russia in decontrolling prices.

THE RESIGNATION OF GORBACHEV

Gorbachev quickly and forcefully denounced the C.I.S. as illegal, denying that the three presidents had the authority to terminate the Soviet state, an action he said could be taken only by the Congress of Peoples' Deputies. Gorbachev predicted that the dissolution of the Soviet Union would lead to chaos and anarchy and eventually to civil war. He clearly was devastated by this irrefutable punctuation of his failure to save the union, in which he still had faith, as well as by the prospect of his imminent political collapse.

The Slavic presidents ignored Gorbachev. They submitted the Minsk agreement for ratification by their parliaments. The Commonwealth came into being on December 10, 1991. Other republics subsequently sought entry into the C.I.S., and on December 20, 1991, a formal agreement was signed at Alma Ata, in Kazakhstan, by leaders of 8 republics. The "Minsk" republics accorded the others the cofounder status they demanded. The Alma Ata signatories recognized one another's sovereign independence and agreed to determine shortly the disposition of the Soviet military, with Soviet defense minister Shaposhnikov in charge of an interm military command. By December 22, 3 more republics—Armenia, Azerbaijan, and Moldova—joined the Commonwealth, to bring the total membership to 11 former Soviet republics. Only Georgia refrained from seeking admission, because of its Civil War as well as its strong urge to have complete independence after the fashion of the Baltic republics.

On December 20 the government of the Russian republic assumed formal jurisdiction over the Soviet Foreign Ministry, the KGB, the Supreme Soviet, and even Gorbachev's presidential office. With a disquieting agressiveness, the Russians took over the Soviet money supply and Soviet trade in oil, gold, diamonds, and foreign currency, fueling suspicion, jealousy, and animosity among the other republics, in particular Ukraine.

With no support among the republics for his leadership, Gorbachev resigned as president of the Soviet state. On December 26 the Supreme Soviet passed a resolution acknowledging the demise of the Soviet Union. Russia subsequently was assigned the Soviet Union's seat in the Security Council of the United Nations, and the former Soviet Union's embassies abroad replaced the Soviet flag with that of the Russian republic.

PROBLEMS, POLICIES, AND PROSPECTS

Russia and the Eurasian republics confronted monumental problems. The most important were: 1) promoting stable, efficient, and popular democratic government; 2) moving toward a market economy; 3) disposing of the former Soviet Union's military establishment; 4) controlling nationalist rivalries within and among the former Soviet republics; and 5) protecting and furthering the external interests of the republics. We close the essay with a discussion of future prospects.

PROMOTING DEMOCRATIC GOVERNMENT

Although they rejected Soviet dictatorship, the peoples of the new Commonwealth were far from embracing Western-style democratic government. Russian president Yeltsin, for example, despite his democratic rhetoric, acted in most undemocratic ways during and after the August 1991 coup attempt against Gorbachev. Yeltsin issued decrees that exceeded his legal prerogatives, confiscating property, invading the homes of parliamentary deputies, and suppressing a literary association of right-wing writers. He hectored Gorbachev after his return from captivity, demonstrating an inability to distinguish between the friends and foes of democracy and forgetting that without Gorbachev's leadership since 1985, there would have been no popularly elected President Yeltsin to symbolize resistance, no Russian Parliament to give him refuge and support, and few, if any, anticoup protesters in the streets.

The Soviet Communist Party still had its adherents. On August 30, 1991, just 8 days after the coup, Nina Andreeya, the author of the famous 1988 letter defending conservatism in the Soviet Union to party hard-liner Ligachev, declared publicly that the party was not dead, that the decline of the party was a temporary phenomenon, and that it would return to power someday. Alexander Kabanov, vice rector of Moscow's higher Party School, predicted in September 1991 that the party would change its name, break up into several factions, and function through normal political parties. This was historically inevitable, he insisted.

Many long-time party members remain important functionaries in the ministries of the different republics, including Russia, that still control the bulk of the economy. Ex-Communists continue to predominate in the legislative and executive bodies of the republics. They are not schooled in democratic ideology and practice; some may not be sympathetic to democracy. Former Communist leaders continue to manage factories and farms in Russia and remain in powerful political positions in some of the Central Asian republics. Neither the late Soviet nor the current Russian authorities have formally outlawed Communist party groups; charters have transformed them into conventional political organizations willing to compete in open elections for governmental office.

Many leaders of the republics whose power has rested on a patronage-based network of interpersonal relations were not interested in democratizing their systems. They feared losing their personal political power and inviting an explosion of popular protest and dissent, which could lead to anarchy and revolution. Uzbekistan's President Islam Karimnov said publicly in September 1991 that his republic was not ready for democracy and that he preferred the Chinese model of limited economic reform and a prohibition against popular political manifestations. Indeed, authoritarianism continues to prevail despite the trappings of parliamentary and democratic proceedings.

POLITICAL DEVELOPMENT IN RUSSIA

Russian president Yeltsin himself was skeptical about moving immediately toward Western-style democracy. He said in April 1992 that Russia needed a "presidential government," not a parliamentary democracy. He warned that to move prematurely to democratic government would be "suicide," given the difficult transition when "we still have to deal with a seriously ill society." He spoke of parliamentary democracy as a highly politicized form of politics that would paralyze policy making. But Yeltsin had another reason for championing "presidential government" in Russia for the next few years. A strengthened Russian Parliament might favor the Communist holdovers elected in 1989, whom Yeltsin wanted to push out of power because of their resistance to his economic reforms.

The overwhelming majority of ordinary citizens in the republics are not democratically inclined but, rather, passive or focusing on economic rather than political conditions. Moreover, opinion polls show a popular yearning for a strong government that will improve living conditions. Real opposition to the August 1991 coup came only from several hundred thousand people living primarily in the city areas of Russia. And in the weeks and months following the coup and well into 1992, there were many popular demonstrations in Moscow and elsewhere in Russia calling for a return of the old centralized Soviet state and a restoration of the power and influence of the Soviet Communist Party. Some of these demonstrations reflected a strong anti-Semitic bias, with people blaming the Jews as well as Yeltsin for hard times, a tendency hardly conductive to the development of liberal democracy.

The Russian KGB, even though different from its Soviet predecessor in some respects, is hardly a democratic institution. It was given a mandate to curtail its operations; to transform itself into a small intelligence-gathering institution; and to shed its responsibilities for border security, executive protection, government communications, and control of dissidence. By December 1991 it looked as if the KGB was becoming little more than a shadow of its old imposing self. But some people charge that the KGB has not really changed, that it has not experienced an "ideological perestroika."

In December 1991 Yeltsin issued a presidential decree to create a "super ministry" of internal affairs and public security. This act horrified his liberal supporters, and Russia's new constitutional court rejected it. Next Yeltsin created a new Russian Agency for Federal Security, with some of the responsibilities of the old KGB, and named Yevgeny Savostyanov to head the Moscow branch. Although the real role of the KGB's successor is by no means clear, Savostyanov indicated that he would like to do "political investigations." There is the possibility of a return in Russia at least to a KGB-like institution, despite widespread popular hostility to the KGB.

Yeltsin versus the Russian Legislature

Democracy in Russia has been hampered by severe economic problems as well as excessive politicization of the government. For example, Yeltsin's determination to move forward with economic reform eventually led to a showdown with the Russian Congress of Peoples' Deputies that was heavily influenced by 300 to 400 conservative deputies. These deputies blocked Yeltsin's effort to free up the state-controlled diminished economy. They succeeded because a large group of deputies sympathetic to Yeltsin's goals still wanted to proceed slowly with reform; mostly they supported the conservatives. The remaining 400 or so deputies who wanted rapid and substantial steps toward a free market economy were usually outnumbered.

The Conservative Challenge

Conservatives (as well as centrists) opposed an abrupt dismantling of the state-controlled economy from which they and their supporters drew their power and influence in Russian society. They spoke for the managers of the giant Russian military–industrial complex, former Communists, and a large constituency of bureaucrats on the national and local levels of government administration. These bureaucrats did everything they could to sabotage Yeltsin's efforts, just as they had undermined Gorbachev and his policies of economic restructuring in the late 1980s.

Conservatives also disliked Yeltsin's authoritarian style of leadership. In their view Yeltsin violated the spirit of the democracy that he said he wanted to establish in Russia.

Many conservatives were strong Russian nationalists. They considered Yeltsin to be too supportive of the West and to be jeopardizing Russia's strategic interests abroad. They thought that Yeltsin should resist Western pressures to speed up domestic economic reform, which caused hardships for ordinary Russian citizens. Nor did they want him to cooperate with the West's anti-Serb policies in the Bosnian Civil War. They also wanted him to resist the efforts of Central/Eastern Europe countries to join NATO. The nationalists dreamed of reconstituting the Soviet state and wanted Yeltsin to expand Russian political, economic, and military influence in the ex-Soviet republics, starting with the Baltic republics, Ukraine, and Georgia.

Finally, many conservatives did not want Yeltsin at all; they wanted a president who shared their ideas about the future of Russia's domestic policies and foreign relations. They thought vice president Aleksandr Rutskoi was a credible replacement for Yeltsin.

Yeltsin's foes in the Congress in 1992 and 1993 were justified to some degree in their opposition to Yeltsin's leadership. Aggressive and independent in the pursuit of reform policies and given to circumventing the Legislature by issuing decrees, Yeltsin did act contrary to the spirit and the letter of the Russian Constitution, which gave the president only limited power. The conservatives, however, certainly were not democrats either; many were ex-Communists. Thus, under these circumstances, ordinary people did not think much of their complaints that Yeltsin's presidency disregarded principles of checks and balances, limited government, and legislative sovereignty.

Russians did listen, though, when conservative deputies criticized Yeltsin's economic policies. Moves toward a free market had caused increasing hardship for too many people, who said, when asked, that they believed themselves better off under the old Soviet economic system. In addition, conservative complaints that Yeltsin's foreign policies were too pro-West tapped into the unhappiness many felt that Russia apparently had lost power and influence abroad and seemed inferior to the West in its military and diplomatic policies. Soldiers and officers of the old Red Army, in particular, were bitter over the loss of Afghanistan and Central/Eastern Europe, areas of historic importance to Russia's international security and prestige.

In December 1992 conservatives in the Congress of Peoples' Deputies attempted to overthrow Yeltsin's government by a vote of no-confidence. But there was not enough support for a vote, and the government continued to be in the hands of reformist ministers. In the face of such pressures, however, Yeltsin had to sacrifice his reformist prime minister, Yegor Gaidar, an advocate of rapid change to private enterprise. In his place Yeltsin appointed Viktor Chernomyrdin, a Soviet-era technocrat with strong conservative instincts.

Throughout 1993 Yeltsin argued that he had a right to act independently of the Congress and the Supreme Soviet in his domestic and foreign policy making: Having been chosen by a plurality of Russian voters in free, open, and competitive presidential elections in June 1991, he had an obligation to set policy. He also argued that while he had a plan to improve the country's material well-being, the Parliament had no plan beyond that of a "gradual transition." This, Yeltsin said, was a disguised commitment to maintain the majority of remaining wage and price controls, subsidies, and other policies of the discredited Communist regime.

Yeltsin's Weaknesses

Yeltsin was at a disadvantage in dealing with the Congress of Peoples' deputies and the Supreme Soviet. He lacked the support of a cohesive, disciplined party organization that could put forward his policies. While a number of political party groups were committed to political democracy, economic reform, and Yeltsin's leadership of the country—they collectively identified themselves as the Presidential Party—they were divided on many issues and could not form the kind of integrated parliamentary bloc he needed to manage the Legislature effectively. Although the conservatives and centrists were also deeply divided over policy and ideology, they usually united when it came time to oppose Yeltsin's initiatives.

The Russian Constitution, promulgated in 1977, was of little help in defining the ground rules for this battle between executive and Legislature. Amended in 1991 to create the office of president, the Constitution made the office very weak while giving primacy to the Congress, which had the power to confirm the prime minister and cabinet, to impeach the president, and to amend the Constitution. Moreover, the Supreme Soviet, drawn from the Congress, controlled the Central Bank, which was responsible for monetary policy and therefore played a pivotal role in the enactment of economic reform.

After Yeltsin was elected Russia's first president, things got off to a good start; the president and Congress agreed on the critical issue of Russia's separation from the Soviet Union. Before long, however, they were at each other's throats. Yeltsin, committed to reform and to strong leadership, had to work against the Constitution. The Congress, dominated by conservatives in favor of the status quo, had the Constitution on its side and wanted a weak president to forestall reform.

A Showdown between President and Parliament

In late March 1993, Yeltsin, faced with a constitutional and political stalemate, claimed special powers to rule by decree. He called for a new constitution and a new Parliament. Until these were in place, he said, the Legislature and the Constitutional Court could not overturn his decrees.

The Congress opposed Yeltsin's maneuver, calling it unconstitutional. Conservatives tried to impeach him. They failed because most members of the Congress of Peoples' Deputies did not want such radical action, especially since there was no one with Yeltsin's stature to replace him. Moreover, a vote to oust Yeltsin conceivably could lead to a civil war if the president decided to fight the Congress.

Yeltsin retreated a bit as well. He agreed to omit the words "special powers" in his announcement of presidential rule by decree and said that a legislative rejection of his decrees would be possible if backed by the Constitutional Court.

The April 25, 1993, Referendum

Yeltsin also called for a referendum to be held at the end of April 1993. The referendum would ask Russian voters to say whom they wished to govern the country: Yeltsin or the deputies. The Congress didn't like the referendum proposal: Yeltsin appeared to be popular with many Russians, who would support him and vote against the Congress. For his part, Yeltsin believed that a majority of voters would support him, if not his reformist policies.

Shortly after the showdown with the Congress, Yeltsin left for a summit meeting in Vancouver, British Columbia, Canada, with U.S. president Bill Clinton. Yeltsin hoped that this meeting and Clinton's backing of him would help strengthen his standing with many Russians as well as supporters in the government. (Conservatives later pointed to this meeting as a sign that Yeltsin was much too eager to please the Americans for the sake of getting their economic help in promoting his reform program.)

The Russian Congress eventually approved the referendum, but only after the conservatives structured it to suit their own interests. They agreed on four referendum questions: 1) Do you have confidence in Yeltsin? 2) Do you approve of the present reform program? 3) Do you want early parliamentary elections? and 4) Do you want early presidential elections? The deputies hoped that voters angry over the decline of their living standards would deny Yeltsin the confidence he sought and would back the Congress and settle in their favor, once and for all, who the people thought should rule Russia. The Congress also undoubtedly concluded that a referendum might be easier than trying to negotiate the complex balance of authority between president and Parliament. Moreover, they tacked on the requirement that 50 percent of all eligible voters must participate in the referendum to make it valid. Given the level of popular skepticism, this requirement was a high hurdle for Yeltsin to jump.

Public opinion polls taken by Russian agencies as well as by Radio Free Europe seemed to vindicate both sides. Of those polled, 51 percent favored a strong leader while only 31 percent favored democracy; 50 percent believed that the state should guarantee full employment; 63 percent believed that the state should maintain control over prices; 59 percent believed that state control over private business was useful; and, finally, 65 percent felt that inflation was the number-one economic problem. Interestingly, 44 percent of those polled did not believe that capitalism would help them, 46 percent said that Marxism also was of no use, and 50 percent opposed the private ownership of land.

The campaign for the referendum in the first three weeks of April 1993 was bitter. Both sides denounced each other in the most accusatory rhetoric and with much scandal mongering directed at the chief spokesperson for each side: Yeltsin and Rutskoi. Rutskoi emerged from the campaign as the standard-bearer of all Russians opposed to Yeltsin's reformism.

Russians were peculiarly calm, perhaps indifferent, even pessimistic about the referendum. Demonstrators on behalf of both sides came out in Moscow, but most voters dismissed the referendum, believing that it would make little difference in their lives.

As the date of the referendum approached, Yeltsin's popularity seemed to increase. Hoping for stability in government, on April 25 people voted in larger numbers than anticipated and supported Yeltsin, whatever misgivings they may have had about the substance of his policy. At least Yeltsin *had* a policy—the conservatives had no coherent program beyond calling for the ouster of the reformers. Moreover, Yeltsin had been helped by a decision shortly before the referendum of the Constitutional Court, which so far had tended to support positions of the conservatives, to invalidate the Congress's rule that all questions had to win a 50 percent majority of all eligible voters. It ruled that only questions 3 and 4 required the approval of an absolute majority of Russia's 106 million eligible voters.

Sixty-six percent of eligible voters participated in the referendum, and most supported Yeltsin, his reform program, and his wish for early parliamentary elections. Most voters also opposed early presidential elections, as Yeltsin had wanted. The strongest support for Yeltsin came from Moscow and St. Petersburg, from young and educated segments of Russian society. But Yeltsin received support everywhere in Russia.

The referendum did not end the confrontation between president and Parliament, however. Conservatives continued to oppose Yeltsin, to try to force the removal of reformers from his government, and to block his efforts to privatize industrial and agricultural enterprises. They also tried again to impeach him. In response Yeltsin simply issued decree after decree to implement his policies, effectively ignoring the Parliament. The confrontation between the two branches intensified in the summer of 1993.

Frustrated and angry, in August 1993 Yeltsin asked the Supreme Soviet to approve the early parliamentary elections that Russian voters had said they wanted (the tenure of the existing Legislature would not legally expire until 1995). Conservatives, led by Rutskoi and Congress chairperson Ruslan Khasbulatov, refused, fearing a loss of influence, although some would agree to early Parliamentary elections if presidential elections were held simultaneously.

A budget crisis forced the issue. At the end of August, the Supreme Soviet rejected the government's belt-tightening budget; passed its own budget, which provided for a deficit twice the size that allowed in the government's budget; and gave an ultimatum to the government to get the money needed to implement its spending policies, presumably by printing it. Yeltsin responded by temporarily suspending Rutskoi from the vice presidency. He charged that Rutskoi was the beneficiary of a transfer of $3 million to a Swiss bank and could not stay in office while under investigation. Khasbula-

tov immediately denounced Yeltsin's act as "unconstitutional." The Russian Constitution, he pointed out, gave no authority to the president to suspend his vice president. Rutskoi called the suspension a "coup," and the Supreme Soviet voted overwhelmingly to countermand Yeltsin's action. It turned the whole issue of removal over to the Constitutional Court, which, under its conservative chairperson Valery Zorkin, was expected to be more sympathetic.

In mid-September 1993 Yeltsin brought Gaidar back to the government as first deputy prime minister for economic affairs. This act signaled not only the conservatives, but also the West, which had been holding back the distribution of credit promised to help Russia in its pursuit of free market reforms because of government instability, that the president was as determined as ever to move forward with his reform program. Then, on September 22, Yeltsin, not waiting for the Court to respond and in a new effort to get the upper hand once and for all, ordered the dissolution of both the Supreme Soviet and the Congress of Peoples' Deputies. He suspended the existing Constitution and announced elections for two new parliamentary bodies, a State Duma and a Confederation Council. These elections were to be held in mid-December with presidential elections 6 months later.

Yeltsin's acts clearly went beyond his constitutional powers. He also ignored an amendment passed by the Congress earlier in 1993, declaring that if the president should dissolve the Parliament, he automatically would lose his powers. But, Yeltsin had little use for the old Constitution. He had been ready for this step for several months.

The September–October 1993 Parliamentary Crisis
Yeltsin's dissolution of the Supreme Soviet and Congress momentarily threatened civil war. Supreme Soviet deputies, led by Khasbulatov and Rutskoi, refused to disband, hoping to convene the larger Congress of Peoples' Deputies to reply to Yeltsin's challenge. On September 23, 400 Congress deputies, 289 fewer than required for a quorum, met in the Parliament building known as the White House. They voted out Yeltsin and elected Rutskoi to replace him. Rutskoi created a rump government, including ministers of interior and defense. The Constitutional Court, meanwhile, ruled Yeltsin's dissolution illegal.

Anticipating Yeltsin's anger, the deputies immediately set up barricades around the White House to protect it against an attack by Yeltsin. They were armed with assault rifles, machine guns, and grenade launchers that apparently had been accumulated and stored in the White House in recent months in anticipation of an eventual violent showdown with the president. For the next 12 days there was a tense standoff, almost a mini-war between the deputies and Yeltsin, who demanded that they leave the building, give up their weapons, and cease their resistance.

Though he had the White House surrounded by police, Yeltsin tried to avoid bloodshed. He tried to get the deputies to surrender peacefully. He turned off the electricity and water to the building and refused to allow any supplies inside. These tactics as well as others had some success. Each day a number of deputies left the building, either out of fear for their survival or because they had been bribed with cash or plane tickets. By the end of the first week, the only people left in the White House were Khasbulatov, Rutskoi, followers of the radical nationalist Vladimir Zhirinovsky, some neo-Bolsheviks, fundamentalists, and thugs trying to protect them.

On October 4 Yeltsin changed tactics and ordered troops to evacuate the remnants of the Congress, including Rutskoi and Khasbulatov, who were promptly jailed. The fight was over. The Legislature was defeated. Yeltsin was now the sole source of administrative power in Russia until the election of a new Parliament in mid-December.

Rutskoi, Khasbulatov, and their conservative supporters in the Supreme Soviet had grossly overestimated their support in the Congress and among the people. The Congress never had been unanimously in favor of resisting the president. Moreover, popular support for the parliamentary side never materialized. Despite misgivings about Yeltsin, the public was more concerned with preserving the symbol, if not the substance, of strong leadership.

The grievances of the Russian military were certainly real, but Rutskoi and Khasbulatov could not bring the military to their side. Rutskoi, a highly decorated Army commander in Afghanistan, had been at odds with Defense Minister Pavel Grachev, whom the Congress had unwisely antagonized earlier by accusing him of corruption. Conservative deputies had wanted to discredit Grachev and force him out for someone more sympathetic to the Parliament. Nor could the conservatives mobilize the internal security apparatus, whose leadership was loyal to Yeltsin.

Finally, Rutskoi and Khasbulatov had neither the skill nor the opportunity to prepare for a forceful showdown with Yeltsin. They had allowed themselves to be misled by Yeltsin's frequent temporizing with them in the past and apparently concluded that once again they could get the better of him in a face-down.

From the outset Yeltsin had decisive advantages that would assure his victory over the Congress. He was, after all, the leader of Russia, a society that deeply respected leadership and had a certain mystical faith in it when it acted with determination and strength. Furthermore, unlike his rivals in the Parliament, Yeltsin had gone out of his way to cultivate and win the support of the military and security leaders. He was willing to pay special attention to the military and to accommodate its special needs and interests. For example, he agreed to pay increases for officers, toured military installations to indicate his awareness of military needs and wants, and adopted a new assertiveness in dealing with the West in the fall of 1993. All of this worked to Yeltsin's advantage by strengthening his relationship with Defense Minister Gra-

chev. During the crisis army leaders ignored calls from Rutskoi to support the Congress against Yeltsin.

Yeltsin had been shrewd in cultivating the army. Given the low morale among the troops, there might have been some real opposition to him during the showdown with Parliament. As it was, some officers who disliked Yeltsin's leadership—and there were many of them—did support Rutskoi, Khasbulatov, and the others resisting presidential authority in the White House showdown. For example, General Albert Makashov sided with the legislature and commanded armed groups inside the Parliament building during the siege by the government. He also led an assault on the television station outside of Parliament. The degree of military loyalty also varied in different parts of the country. The army's reliability was complicated further by a host of interpersonal rivalries.

Throughout the crisis some of the leaders of Russia's 88 provinces and autonomous republics supported the Parliament. Many were ex-Communists, conservative, and highly particularistic in defense of their region's economy and relations with Moscow. For example, local leaders in the city of Bryansk, about 200 miles southwest of Moscow, believed that Yeltsin had indeed acted unconstitutionally and feared that he planned to restore a Soviet-style dictatorship. Leaders of regional legislative bodies also saw a dangerous precedent being set in Moscow in Yeltsin's dismissal of the deputies. If Yeltsin succeeded, their own government leaders might try the same thing in their political jurisdictions. When Yeltsin called on regional legislative bodies to follow the national example by scheduling new elections and dissolving themselves, they hardened their opposition to Yeltsin.

Regional executives, however, argued in favor of Yeltsin, either because he had done them some favor in the past or because they agreed that he had been abused too long by the Congress. They reasoned that his act against the Supreme Soviet was fully justified, especially in light of the ambiguity of the already obsolete Russian Constitution. Some reasoned that they might have to follow Yeltsin's example in a confrontation with their own conservative legislative bodies. And in some instances, such as in St. Petersburg, local government leaders proposed a compromise, asking for election of a new Parliament and a new president immediately and simultaneously, a formula sternly rejected by Yeltsin.

While some regional leaders perceived the turning of the tide in favor of Yeltsin and became afraid of retribution once the crisis was over if they tried to oppose him, others agreed with Yeltsin that conservative legislative bodies everywhere in the country were impediments to change and should give way to avoid a replication of the kind of paralysis that had afflicted the national government in recent years. In the end the regions remained neutral. Local populations, though interested in what was happening in Moscow, refused to be distracted from their daily routines.

An Authoritarian Interlude

In the weeks following the crisis, Yeltsin ruled the country with a firm hand in order to assure social peace. He was determined not to repeat past mistakes of temporizing with political opponents by tolerating the kind of dissent that had paralyzed his government.

Apart from imprisoning Khasbulatov and Rutskoi, and charging them with provoking mass disorder, a crime punishable by up to 15 years in prison, Yeltsin banned radical opposition organizations, like the National Salvation Front and the Union of Officers, whose members had helped to defend the deputies against Yeltsin's forces, as well as newspapers. He also sent censors to mainstream newspapers like *Nezavisimaya Gazeta,* demanding that they dismiss personnel who had opposed the president. *Pravda* and *Sovetskaya Rossiya,* which had been critical of Yeltsin, were told to fire their editors and change their names. Eventually more than a dozen newspapers were ordered to shut down permanently. There was an explosion of popular anger over the apparent return to censorship on television that symbolized how far Russians had come in their enjoyment of press freedom.

Yeltsin also tried to bring conservative regional administrations into line, firing the powerful leaders of the Amur and Novisibirsk regions, who had opposed his dissolution of the Congress and the Supreme Soviet. He made clear that henceforth he was not going to tolerate political challenges from ambitious and aggressive regional leaders seeking to enhance their autonomy of Moscow. Yeltsin also dissolved city and town councils throughout Russia, most of which were filled with members who were Communist and elected before the collapse of the Soviet state. He called for elections of new regional councils, which would be smaller in size and be called assemblies or dumas, as they were in Czarist times. Although local governing bodies discussed, criticized, and, in a few instances, rejected Yeltsin's dissolution order, most complied.

Yeltsin's dictatorial manner in the period leading to the parliamentary elections in December 1993 provoked controversy at home and discomfort abroad. At home Yeltsin was accused by democrats of betraying the new liberal order; abroad, supporters like U.S. president Bill Clinton were concerned by what seemed a lapse in democratic development; Clinton continued to back Yeltsin in the hope that his restrictive measures were temporary expedients.

Ordinary Russians seemed to accept the government's hard line stoically, believing that there was some legitimacy for it in their new democracy. Most Russians, especially in Moscow, had been appalled by the violence surrounding the controversy between Yeltsin and the deputies and now wanted no more of it, even if they had to endure a loss of personal freedom. Yeltsin kept in place a state of emergency, with a curfew in Moscow, until October 17. Citizens hoped that the new return of quiet to the streets would enable the president to give his undivided attention to improving the country's economic life, creating a new constitution that would work, and getting the country ready for the parliamentary elections.

The December 12, 1993, Parliamentary Elections

On October 12, Yeltsin laid out some of the ground rules for the December 12 elections. He said that there would be election of members to both a lower house, to be called the State Duma, which would represent the Russian people by population, and an upper house, which would represent the population by region and would be called the Federation Council. Members in both houses would be elected directly by the voters for a 4-year term. The Duma would consist of 250 members, half of whom would be elected from single member districts on a "winner take all" basis and the other half from multicandidate national party lists with proportional representation, whereby each party list would win a percentage of seats in the new Duma based on the percentage of popular votes for that list. The Council would consist of 2 delegates from each of the 88 regions into which Russia was administratively divided; an earlier plan to have 1 of these 2 delegates appointed by Moscow to assure substantial influence of the central government on the Council was discarded in favor of the direct popular election of both delegates. Other details concerning the organization and powers of these legislative bodies were worked out during the campaign within a new constitution, which also would be put before Russian voters on December 12.

Voter Options. While voters were offered an extraordinary variety of political choices, representing a broad political spectrum of interests, including those of Communists, Fascists, ecologists, industrialists, feminists, reformists, and others, six party groups stood out as favorites with the most likely chance of winning seats: 1) Russia's Choice, led by Yegor Gaidar and other top government officials committed to radical economic reform and loyal to Yeltsin; 2) Russian Unity, led by Sergei Shakrai, a Yeltsin aide who favored a slower pace of reform and more subsidies for national industry; 3) the Republican Party, led by Grigory Yavlinsky, a reform economist who also supported gradualism in Russian economic reform; 4) the Russian Communist Party, an organization that played no part in the October 1993 parliamentary crisis, led by Gennadi Zyuganov and opposed to privatization of industrial and agricultural property; 5) the Liberal Democratic Party, led by Vladimir Zhirinovsky, a populist and radical nationalist who spoke admiringly of Stalin, Hitler, and Saddam Hussein, and capitalized on Russia's wounded pride and economic misery; and 6) Civic Union, the main centrist party, led by Arkady Volsky, who spoke for industrial managers of state-owned enterprises and advocated continued state control over a substantial part of the national economy, especially enterprises concerned with defense.

The Yeltsin government tried to make sure that the parties allowed to compete in the election would have a truly national rather than local constituency of support by requiring that no more than 15 percent of the signatures needed to field candidates could be taken in any one region. The government also required parties to receive at least 5 percent of the vote to seat their successful candidates. Thirteen parties eventually were allowed to field candidates.

Yeltsin's Role.   During the campaign Yeltsin stayed aloof from the race, neither forming a party nor endorsing any of the groups fielding candidates. When he did address the nation, he appealed for voter support of the new constitution that had been drafted. Although voters surmised that he backed Russia's Choice, Yeltsin never endorsed this party. His only advice to voters with regard to the election was to support responsible and honest candidates. Indeed, he chose to go abroad during the last few days of the campaign, so he was not even in the country as voters prepared to go to the polls.

Yeltsin's behavior could be explained in several ways. First, he wanted to be the president of all Russia, not simply the representative of a special constituency, no matter how large it might be. In this respect his approach resembled that of Czech Republic president Vaclav Havel, who also tried to eschew strong party affiliations. Both no doubt were inspired by the French Fifth Republic president Charles de Gaulle, who always had insisted that he was above politics and the leader of all Frenchmen, not just those who shared his particular ideology and political program. Furthermore, Yeltsin was eager for popular support of his new constitution, even if voters disagreed with him personally.

It is also possible that Yeltsin, along with many other top politicians, did not really understand the crucial role of political parties in a parliamentary system, especially their role as agents of the leadership in the legislature to facilitate policy making. Russians had little knowledge of Western-style parties. Their only experience with parties was the Communist Party. But it may also be true, as Yavlinsky reportedly has suggested, that Yeltsin did understand quite well the role of parties and intentionally abstained from supporting any of them to encourage conflict and fragmentation in the new Parliament, which would weaken it and thereby strengthen further his policy-making role and allow him to serve out the rest of his term (until June 1996). Perhaps he also wanted to encourage support for extremists in Parliament so that he could pose as the real guarantor of stability and progress.

The Campaign.   There was a lack of the public enthusiasm and involvement that usually are part of elections in Western democracies. Ordinary Russian citizens showed some of the same indifference and the same pessimism evident in the campaign leading up to the April 30 referendum. They seemed to have little interest in the reformist parties, in the

belief that they probably would make little difference in their lives even if elected to power. A poll taken by the Russian Center for Public Opinion on December 8 showed that 40 percent of those questioned were undecided about which politicians and party groups deserved to wield power. While people desperately wanted politicians who would improve the country's economy, they did not believe that any politicians could achieve this goal.

Moreover, the groups fielding candidates were not Western-style parties, though they tried to look and act like them, using symbols to identify themselves to voters and making use of television to communicate their messages and promises. They had no large organization in rural Russia; they had no defined programs; and they had no internal cohesion, discipline, and unity. They consisted mainly of professional politicians headquartered in Moscow who were using the new open and competitive system to advance not just their own ideas on policy but also their professional careers, more so, perhaps, than politicians in the more developed parliamentary systems.

Election Results.   Finally, the reformist parties were split four ways, between the followers of Geidar, Yavlinsky, Shakrai, and St. Petersburg's mayor, Anatolyi A. Sobchak, ensuring that no one of them could get a plurality, never mind a majority, needed to support a cabinet. These reformist leaders had different views about the scope and pace of reform as well as conflicting ambitions to obtain power. For example, Geidar supported Yeltsin while Yavlinsky and Shakrai, critical of his authoritarianism, wanted a change in leadership; Yavlinski apparently wanted the presidency for himself. Not surprisingly, the reformist groups did not do as well as they had hoped. While together they won a plurality (152 seats), they were so divided that they could not make a coalition to back Yeltsin and enable him to move forward with his free market reform program. In effect they had lost the opportunity given them by Yeltsin's disbanding of the old legislative bodies to lead the country.

The conservative parties, however, notably the Communists and Liberal Democrats, did better than anyone had expected. The Liberal Democrats ended up with 24 percent of the popular vote and about 78 seats in the State Duma, the second-largest party group. The Communists won 13.25 percent and 64 seats.

The Zhirinovsky Phenomenon

The success of the Liberal Democratic Party, led by Vladimir Zhirinovsky, who campaigned on a platform of antireformism, law and order, and a nationalistic foreign policy, was troublesome to the reformists as well as to outsiders, in particular to the West and to Russia's neighbors in Central/Eastern Europe. In 1991 Zhirinovsky had been a candidate in the Russian presidential elections but won only about 7 percent of the popular vote. He supported the anti-Gorbachev coup in

August 1991 and subsequently became one of the strongest and most vitriolic critics of Yeltsin's reformist policy at home and conciliatory behavior abroad, referring to Yeltsin on one occasion as a lackey of the Americans.

Zhirinovsky apparently had accumulated an enormous amount of wealth, which enabled him to run an expensive campaign in November and early December 1993, involving a generous and skillful use of television. He said a lot of things that average Russian citizens wanted to hear. He proposed an immediate liquidation of the 5,000 criminal organizations that had sprung up in the wake of the reforms that terminated government control over the economy. He called for the immediate expulsion of non-Russians from ex-Soviet republics like Armenia and Georgia who had come to Moscow to make a killing by selling scarce goods, especially food, at exorbitant prices. Zhirinovsky also advocated the restoration of Russia's imperial legacy of control over territory that stretched from the Baltic Sea to the Black Sea, from Finland to Alaska. He argued that Russia could be prosperous again if it ceased giving assistance to other ex-Soviet republics, exported weapons abroad to former clients like Iraq, and called a halt to the conversion of military enterprises to the production of consumer goods. He not only pandered to the popular sense of abandonment and personal humiliation caused by the precipitous decline of living standards caused by the government's reform program but also tapped into a xenophobic and messianic nationalism that Russians have felt for at least a century.

The votes for Zhirinovsky signaled the alienation of a large sector of the Russian population as a result of the destruction of the Soviet Union, which Russia had always dominated, and the miserable economic conditions that had ensued. Russian voters showed their anger, their frustration, and their pessimism in their support for Zhirinovsky, but most of all their fear of and opposition to harsh and rapid economic change regardless of its justification by the reformers.

The obvious questions raised by Zhirinovsky's showing in the elections were: Did Russians want democracy? Did they want economic reform? While most voters probably did not want a restoration of the old Soviet dictatorship and its costly and dangerous empire, they did want the stability, security, and material well-being that Zhirinovsky promised.

Problems for Yeltsin

The results of the election were a mixed blessing for Yeltsin. On the one hand, he did not receive the mandate to move the country quickly to a free market economy. Indeed, the results of the election clearly indicated widespread opposition to anything in the nature of a Polish–style shock therapy approach to reform. Lacking a cohesive plurality of reformists in the new State Duma and obliged to conciliate moderates and conservatives, Yeltsin reappointed Chernomyrdin as prime minister and Gerashchenko as head of the Central Bank because of their conservative, anti–shock-therapy ap-

proach to reform. Chernomyrdin made very plain at the outset the direction in which his policy initiatives would go: He chastised Geidar and other reformers for their poorly thought out reform experiments and especially for their failure to take adequate account of the hardships that ordinary people were enduring as a result of moves toward the free market. He said that his government would focus less on tight money policies and spending controls to reduce Russia's steadily escalating inflation and more on social protection, especially job creation to mitigate increasing unemployment. Yeltsin had no alternative to political cohabitation with Chernomyrdin and others like him in 1994.

While Yeltsin failed to get the support he wanted for his reform policies, he did get voter approval of his Constitution. The absence of a real constitution had been a major cause of the turmoil in executive–legislative relations. This constitution gave the president substantial power, at least in theory, to manage the Legislature and govern independently of it. Public support of the new Constitution was a triumph for Yeltsin given his personal commitment to it.

The New Russian Constitution

The new Constitution, drafted in the summer and fall of 1993 by a special Constituent Assembly comprised of representatives from local government and the Congress of Peoples' Deputies in Moscow, provided for the kind of executive-oriented parliamentary democracy that Yeltsin had wanted and that resembled in some respects the governmental organization of the French Fifth Republic.

Under the new Constitution, the president of the republic was head of state and commander in chief of Russian military forces, with the responsibility for protecting the Constitution and setting basic domestic and foreign policy guidelines. The president can be elected for a maximum of two 4-year terms. The president has extensive power to implement policy: The president can nominate and dismiss the prime minister, the cabinet, and the head of the Central Bank, which is no longer under the jurisdiction of the Legislature; can dissolve the State Duma; can call for elections after 1 year has elapsed since the preceding elections and for a referendum; can declare martial law and a state of emergency and issue decrees; and can propose legislation and veto it. Finally, the president can be impeached only on a charge of treason or other grave crime by the Parliament.

The government, which consists of the prime minister and cabinet, is responsible for the day-to-day administration of the country. While the prime minister is nominated by the president, the nominee must be approved by the Duma, which is subject to dissolution if it fails to approve a presidential choice three times in succession. The cabinet is nominated by the prime minister and approved by the president. The cabinet drafts the national budget, which must then be approved by the Duma.

The Legislature is bicameral and is known as the Federal Assembly. The upper house is called the Federation Council and consists of two representatives from each of the 88 members (regions or republics) of the Russian Federation. It confirms changes in internal boundaries, a presidential declaration of martial law or state of emergency, and the president's use of the armed forces abroad. It has the power to remove the president from office in the event the president is found guilty of a criminal act. It has the power to appoint top judges, including the prosecutor general; and, along with the Duma, the lower house of the Assembly, it can override a presidential veto by a two-thirds majority.

The State Duma, the lower house, represents the citizens of the federation by population. It approves legislation and the state budget. It confirms the president's choice to head the cabinet and the Central Bank and the appointment of senior judges. It can file charges to impeach the president; it can vote no-confidence in the government; and it can override a presidential veto, along with the Federation Council, by a two-thirds majority of its membership.

The Constitution provides for a federal pattern of intergovernmental relations that gives local administration a substantial discretion, which local political leaders demanded in return for their support of the Constitution and of the unity of the federation, which some of them had questioned and in some instances rejected. Sixty-nine primarily Russian-inhabited administrative provinces and territories have the right to pass their own laws and charters and to levy their own taxes. They are represented in the Federation council, which has real policy-making authority in cooperation with other federal governing institutions, like the president, the cabinet, and the State Duma. Republics inhabited by non-Russian minorities of the federation continue to enjoy the special condition of cultural autonomy that they had in the old Soviet system. This cultural autonomy includes separate legislatures, flags, and languages. But the influence they have in the functioning of the national government in Moscow is equal to that of the primarily Russian-inhabited administrative provinces and territories.

Finally, the Constitution has an elaborate Bill of Rights that includes freedom of conscience, freedom from a governing ideology, freedom of movement, freedom of the press, and the right to private property. These rights do not seem to be encumbered by the qualifications and exceptions stipulated in the 1977 Soviet Constitution that in effect left Soviet citizens with little protection from abuse by government. The new Constitution also calls for the protection of social privileges like free education, housing, medical care, and protection against unemployment enjoyed by Russians under the Soviet system. In this respect the new Constitution preserves some of the paternalism of the old regime.

The Constitution provides also that the first Legislature will serve only 2 years, this short term to coincide with the remainder of Yeltsin's term as president. This means that at the end of 1995, Russians will have an opportunity to choose a completely new leadership while having a reasonable period of transitional political development to determine exactly what kind of leaders they want.

What this Constitution really means for the working of the Russian government remains to be seen. On the one hand, it creates the strong executive-oriented, administratively unified Russian government that Yeltsin insisted was needed to enable the country to proceed successfully through the transition from Communist rule to a liberal political and economic order. Despite charges by his enemies that he is an autocrat and that the strong presidency allows him to introduce another dictatorship in Russia, Yeltsin himself seems to be genuinely committed to democracy as he understands it: namely, popular government appropriately constrained to prevent political anarchy and dissolution.

But there are problems in assuring the permanence of its popular character. In the hands of an autocrat, the Russian government as described in the new Constitution could degenerate into a dictatorship through a presidential abuse of power encouraged by the inability of the other institutions to function properly. The Legislature could be paralyzed by endless political conflict among its members. And the intergovernmental relationship could be disrupted by an explosion of particularism and separatism arising out of economic- and/or ethnocultural-based grievances. Skeptics argue that in the absence of established political parties, the parliamentary democracy will quickly become a creature of the strong president and eventually become the dictatorship that nobody wants.

While a majority of Russian voters did approve the Constitution, they did so more because they supported Yeltsin than because they understood and appreciated what the Constitution provided for. As 1993 came to an end, it was clear that most Russians wanted more than anything else an improvement in their miserable living conditions; that they thought Yeltsin rather than the politicians in the Russian Legislature could accomplish this goal; and that, for these reasons, they were willing to give Yeltsin almost everything he wanted.

Russians are skeptical about the success of the Constitution. Both politicians and ordinary people have had little or no experience with the kind of Western-style parliamentary government the Constitution seems to have established for them. They are suspicious of guarantees about their political and/or economic well-being pledged verbally or in written form, since for so long in history they were abused by those who had made such pledges. And they were not involved directly or indirectly in the creation of the new Constitution, which was handed down to them from on high with a mandate to accept or reject it, a situation not conducive to a popular legitimization of it.

Of course, if the new system of government that it establishes enables Russia's political leadership to solve the country's economic crisis, people will accept it. The key to its survival, after all, may be economics rather than politics.

Postelection Politics: Yeltsin versus Chernomyrdin
By February 1994 the political makeup of the new Russian government was clear and, contrary to what some people in Russia and abroad anticipated, Yeltsin was not dominant. Indeed, Prime Minister Chernomyrdin began to overshadow him, especially in the area of cabinet appointments. Yeltsin was unable to keep reformers like Yegor Gaidar and Boris Fyodorov in key positions. Rather, the new Russian government, starting with the prime minister and the head of the Central Bank, was heavily tilted in the direction of caution and restraint regarding further movement toward the free market economy. The new government, despite warnings of hyperinflation, decided to approve huge disbursements of cash to bankrupt industrial enterprises and collective farms.

It remains to be seen whether Yeltsin can emerge from the political aftermath of the December 12 parliamentary elections as the strong leader the new Constitution encourages him to be. Much depends on his relationship with Prime Minister Chernomyrdin, with whom he must cooperate in the formulation of policy.

TOWARD A MARKET ECONOMY: THE RUSSIAN MODEL

In early 1992 Yeltsin's Russia adopted the radical economic reforms inspired by Shatalin, Yavlinsky, and Gaidar. Gaidar advocated a rapid, Polish–style dismantling of socialism as the only means of expanding output to relieve severe shortages, especially of food, and to raise the standard of living. The Yeltsin–Gaidar program had three general dimensions: decontrol of prices; acceleration of privatization in the agricultural, industrial, and service sectors of the Russian economy; and the transformation of the ruble into a convertible currency.

Decontrol of Prices
Beginning January 2, 1992, Yeltsin allowed prices on most, though not all, consumer goods to rise to their natural levels based upon supply and demand. Producers could set whatever price they pleased on these goods, with distributors allowed to add another 25 percent. Prices on these goods subsequently quadrupled as food producers tried to make the most of the new opportunity for windfall profits. The Russian reformers hoped that by letting prices rise, all producers would soon take their products to market, ease shortages, and bring about lower prices.

Yeltsin tried to soften the impact of the price hikes. Food reserves were made available to the elderly and to people on low fixed pensions. Price controls were still in effect for milk, some kinds of bread, sugar, vodka, cooking oil, and medicine. Pensioners, students, and the disabled received help from soup kitchens as well as stipends and special discounts. Regional authorities in Russia could use local money to provide limited subsidies, as some of them in fact did, to ease hard-

ships. The Russians intended to use Western credits to buy additional goods.

The impact of price deregulation, nevertheless, was brutal. The Moscow Statistical Service announced in January 1992 that an individual now needed 1,944 rubles a month for a bare minimum of subsistence—most Russian workers earned about 400 to 800 rubles a month. The skyrocketing prices for food and fuel provoked angry reactions from ordinary Russian people and also politicians. Ruslan Khasbulatov, the speaker of the Russian Parliament, and many parliamentary deputies wanted a respite from the price reform, calling the program unwise and unrealistic. They argued that price increases before the implementation of privatization of business were premature and provocative. Yeltsin's response also had some merit: He said that price reforms were being undermined by conservative bureaucrats holding back production of consumer necessities in order to torpedo his policies.

Yeltsin's expectation that, after an initial spurt of inflation, supply would catch up with demand and prices would level off was not fulfilled by the end of the first quarter of 1992. Indeed, scarcity and near hyperinflation continued. Production was still dominated by monopolies that were only minimally responsive to supply and demand, and methods of distribution were still inadequate and inefficient.

This Russian experience explains why the leaders of other ex-Soviet republics were not eager to move quickly to a market economy. They worried about the destabilizing effects of rapid change, the danger of social turmoil, and the inevitability of a threat to their power base by angry consumers. Nevertheless, other republics did decontrol some prices after the fashion of Russia. But by the end of January 1992, in response to loud protests by students and low-paid workers, the leaderships retreated and restored most price controls. In Uzbekistan, for example, there was an explosion of public outrage over price hikes in mid-January, when students, enraged by soaring prices and bread shortages, went on a rampage in Tashkent.

Ukraine, like some other republics, feared a deluge of Russians paying rubles for goods that were far less expensive than at home. As a temporary preventive measure, the government in Kiev introduced a system of ration coupons which had to be used along with currency for the purchase of Ukrainian goods. In January 1992 Ukraine became the first ex-Soviet republic to move toward a local currency—ostensibly, Ukrainian leaders asserted, in response to the Russian Central Bank's failure to send Ukraine new supplies of rubles. The Kiev government converted the ration coupons into a quasi-medium of exchange. Ukraine paid salaries to workers partly in rubles and partly in coupons, with 1 coupon deemed equal to 1 ruble at the official rate. Prices for food and other items were soon stated in coupons. By mid-February the coupons served as an alternative to the ruble, which slowly disappeared from circulation. The coupons were traded for U.S. dollars, with 16 to the dollar.

A climax of price decontrol came in mid-October 1993, when the government decided to end subsidies on bread that would cause at least a 100 percent increase in bread prices. The subsidy had escaped the initial phase of price decontrol in January 1992 because Yeltsin had been afraid of provoking opposition in the Parliament. Yet the subsidy had been a tremendous drain on the impoverished Russian treasury, involving, for example, state purchases of grain at sometimes double the market price, imports of costly foreign grain, and payments to collective farms to keep them operating despite their inefficiency and difficulty in earning a profit. The people likely to suffer the most from the inevitable rise in prices were pensioners.

Currency Stabilization and Convertibility

In early 1992 the International Monetary Fund requested that the Russian ruble be made convertible, one of several conditions that Russia would have to meet to qualify for financial assistance. This requirement had serious political liabilities for the Yeltsin government. The exchange rate of the ruble had risen in 1991 from 60 rubles to the dollar to 170 rubles by January 1992. With this rate Russian assets could be purchased cheaply, a dangerous development, given latent Russian suspicions and fear of foreigners. In addition, the ruble was unstable. In January there was near hyperinflation, caused by the decontrol of prices and by budget deficits.

The Yeltsin government tried to meet the budget problem by calling for deep spending cuts, especially in the military sector, where spending already had been reduced to the equivalent of 4.5 percent of GNP, down from about 25 percent under Gorbachev. Yeltsin planned a tight monetary policy to reduce hyperinflation.

Privatization of Industry

One of the most important aspects of Russia's move toward a free market economy is privatization, which, according to Harvard University economics professor Jeffrey Sachs, an adviser to President Yeltsin, is the chief means of improving living conditions. Privatization of consumer service enterprises like retail stores has proceeded smoothly and quickly. But privatization of the huge state-controlled industrial sector has proceeded very slowly, with 90 percent of Russian industry still under state control at the end of 1993. Much of this industry was inefficient, unprofitable, and a tremendous drain on the national wealth, especially the nonproductive military–industrial complex on which the Communist governments had lavished enormous amounts of precious resources until the rethinking of this policy by Gorbachev within the context of his perestroika.

Privatization of heavy industry is problematical because there is no investor class in the poverty-stricken Russian society except the ex-Communist enterprise managers. These are the only people with both the skill and the resources needed to buy out the firms. In other cases workers have pooled their meager savings to join with management to buy out and control the enterprises that had always employed them, an effort to ensure job security. But these transactions affect only a very small part of the state-controlled economy. Foreign investors are potential buyers in cooperation with Russian partners, but foreign investment has been very slow in coming to Russia, much slower than to Poland, Hungary, and the Czech Republic, partly because of political instability, partly because of the still formidable difficulties foreign investors have in dealing with the corrupt, inefficient, and conservative Russian bureaucracy. The explosion of crime has also played a role.

Privatization of heavy industry has been slow also because in many instances enterprise managers and their superiors in the local bureaucracies do not want to risk losing their jobs. They in turn have had the backing of influential members of the Congress of Peoples' Deputies, such as Arkady Volsky, leader of the Civic Union. Volsky spoke for the interests of the military–industrial complex, a vast array of large industrial enterprises employing hundreds of thousands of people. At the same time, many in the Russian Legislature and executive branches have opposed privatization for ideological reasons related to their Marxist-Leninist beliefs. The idea of tinkering with the economy to improve its productivity is accepted, but they strongly condemn systemic change to free enterprise as impractical and immoral. These and other opponents of privatization believe that at the least it would lead to an uncontrollable unemployment that would throw Russian society into chaos and revolution. And, finally, even those people sympathetic to privatization agree that certain industries should never be privatized under any circumstances, like defense, energy-producing, and natural resources industries.

Nevertheless, under pressure from reformers in and out of his government as well as from potential foreign backers like the Group of Seven countries and the IMF, Yeltsin tried to move ahead with privatization of heavy industry in 1992 and 1993. For example, he tried to get ordinary Russian citizens interested in becoming small investors by giving them so-called vouchers, in October 1992, to buy shares in enterprises being privatized. Each voucher was worth 10,000 rubles at the time it was distributed by the government; but the vouchers lost more than 50 percent of their value within a 12-mounth period because many Russians did not understand what to do with them and sold or traded them for whatever could be gotten from speculators who realized how the vouchers could someday make possible inexpensive ownership of a government enterprise. Ordinary Russians, to the dismay of the economic reformers advising Yeltsin, simply had little if any idea of the meaning of investment and ownership. Nevertheless, by July 1993, according to then–privatization minister Anatoli Chubais, much progress had been made in privatization of state-controlled industries, with every third worker in Russian industry employed by a privatized or privatizing enterprise and with millions of citizens now shareholders and owners.

Privatization of Agriculture

Yeltsin tried to speed up the privatization of agriculture. In November 1991 the Russian Parliament approved an agricultural reform program that set February 1, 1992, as a deadline for local governments to decide on farm sizes and other standards for collective farm workers to shift to family farming. The law set heavy fines for bureaucrats who dragged their feet and interfered with these changes. In December 1991 Yeltsin also signed an executive order giving collective farm workers greater rights to buy and sell individual plots and giving nonfarmers small country gardens. Yeltsin was way ahead of the Russian Parliament, which was wary of private ownership of land and the dismantling of the collective farm system.

Further land privatization in Russia and other Soviet republics faced other problems. The lack of land records and assessments of quality variations prevented the easy and equitable distribution of land. There was also a mismatch of equipment; the massive size of existing collectives meant that the heavy tractors designed for them were unsuitable for the new small farms.

Nevertheless, in Russia, at least, limited private farming had thrived since it was first allowed by Gorbachev as part of perestroika. By 1993 there were 184,000 private farmers. But private farmers functioned under tight restrictions. They were prohibited from selling land for 10 years and from owning plots larger than 50 acres. These restrictions effectively ruled out mortgages, large-scale farms, and the creation of a real estate market. They also made it difficult to achieve efficiency and profitability. Even so, these private farms, which comprised only 4 percent of Russia's arable land, were 40 to 50 percent more efficient than the massive collective farms.

President Yeltsin strengthened the land-owning rights of Russians through a decree in October 1993, shortly after his dissolution of the Congress of Peoples' Deputies and Supreme Soviet, which had opposed liberalizing the rules governing land ownership to protect collective farms from competition. The decree allowed Russian citizens to buy, sell, exchange, and give away land. It also provided for the assignment of title ownership of shares of collective or state farms granted to each farm worker 2 years earlier, in order to protect property rights in business transactions. But this and other decrees still do not allow land sales to foreigners, and they require that farm lands be restricted to agricultural use.

Although it has been legally possible to obtain land for private cultivation since 1989, in practice it is very difficult. Would-be private farmers can obtain land only from the collective farm, which is not eager to sell to a competitor. Other obstacles include the difficulty of getting credit to start up farming until harvest time, and equipment is scarce and

prices of seed exorbitant. Ukraine, like much of the rest of the former Soviet Union, especially Central Asia, is well behind Russia in the development of privatization in the agricultural sector.

The Russian Money Crisis

In the latter half of 1992, Yegor Gaidar, then acting prime minister, was in the middle of a political and constitutional crisis over his free market economy reform. Gaidar wanted to limit resource-draining subsidies to inefficient and unprofitable state-owned industrial enterprises. But the Russian Central Bank, which was responsible to the Supreme Soviet and led by Viktor Gerashchenko, an antireformist conservative and closet Marxist-Leninist, opened the credit spigot in the hope of dampening unemployment. Gerashchenko reportedly issued during July and August 1992 alone credits of some $5 billion to various enterprises that otherwise would have gone bankrupt. The credits were loans to be repaid at artificially low interest rates, if at all.

The Bank extended these enormous credits without consulting Prime Minister Gaidar, who, obviously, had he had the opportunity, would have strenuously objected. The Bank's action not only undercut the Gaidar cabinet's reform program but embarrassed it with the IMF, which was demanding a sharp reduction of the Russian budget deficit and other moves to stabilize the inflated Russian currency as a prerequisite for disbursement of credit promised earlier by Western leaders. The IMF insisted on a budget deficit of no more than 5 percent of gross national product and inflation in single digits by the end of 1992. But by that time, because of the Bank's liberal credit policy as well as because of the entry of large quantities of rubles printed by other ex-Soviet republics that Moscow chose to honor in order to prevent the breakdown of interrepublic trade, inflation in Russia was running about 30 percent a month.

While Gaidar warned that the country was on the verge of a hyperinflation that would bring the economy to its knees, Yeltsin's reformist finance minister Boris Fyodorov tried to undo some of Gerashchenko's damage by curtailing the Bank's inflationary policies. By April 1993 Yeltsin seemed to have brought the Central Bank's behavior into line with his reform policies. Possibly in anticipation of a Yeltsin victory in the April 25 referendum, the Bank made a concession to the reformers, agreeing to phase out credits for ailing industries and to cooperate with the government in reducing the inflation rate to 10 percent by the end of 1993.

But the Bank continued independently to do mischief to the economy. In July 1993 it suddenly and without warning announced the withdrawal from circulation of all banknotes issued before the beginning of the year. Russians with huge supplies of this currency stored at home were told that they could exchange up to 35,000 rubles, a relatively small amount, within 2 weeks; the balance could be deposited in savings banks at low interest rates, and withdrawals would not be allowed for at least 6 months.

The Central Bank's action did not address the causes of inflation and therefore was bound to have little or no remedial effect while increasing the hardship of Russian consumers who had hoped to buy dollars with their accumulated rubles. Moreover, other Soviet republics would find it extremely difficult to unload their rubles in Russia, and those private business enterprises that had amassed larger currency reserves from profitable deals would be caught with a lot of demonetized currency.

President Yeltsin, Prime Minister Chernomyrdin, and Finance Minister Fyodorov saw the Bank's behavior as arbitrary and insensitive to the potential backlash of the very people—ordinary Russian consumers—who conservatives said they wanted to protect. Reformers, in particular Fyodorov, also saw the Bank's move as a serious obstacle to the privatization and stabilization of the Russian economy. Finally, the government was annoyed over the way in which the Bank's policy undercut their efforts to accommodate the IMF.

Yeltsin decided to modify the Bank's policy. On July 26 he issued a decree that Russians could exchange up to 100,000 old rubles, or about $100, for new ones until the end of August, instead of the 35,000 old rubles by August 7. He also decreed that 10,000-ruble banknotes marked 1992 could be exchanged for new ones above the limits and that banknotes of 10 rubles or less could be used until the end of August, no matter when issued, which was a great help to the myriad of kiosk entrepreneurs in Moscow and other cities.

Abuses of the New Private Entrepreneurialism

The lack of regulation, in particular the absence of restrictions on profit making and the primitive methods of tax collection, have contributed to a kind of anarchy in the recent explosion of private businesses in big cities like Moscow. The most serious—indeed, socially dangerous—side effect of the new private entrepreneurialism has been the appearance of an alarming gap between a small, aggressive, and ostentatious class of hyper-wealthy people and the rest of the population. Ordinary Moscow wage earners are stuck in low-paying state jobs (in October 1993 the average monthly wage of workers in Moscow was $50) and barely able to get by; many pensioners, especially old women, are begging everywhere in cities just for food money. Other people, meanwhile, perhaps hundreds of thousands of them, are making, investing, and spreading around cash with a spirit of adventure, risk, freedom, and tawdriness that would make the most aggressive Western entrepreneurs blush.

The glitz of the new era is evident on the once drab Tverskaya Street (formerly Gorky Street), which has become a flourishing, neon-lit shopping boulevard. Mobs of people crowd into the newly rebuilt and redecorated GUM department store to buy Western goods, especially clothing, at astronomical prices by the standards of ordinary Russian wage earners. Expensive cars, especially Mercedes Benz cars, never seen in the Communist era, are now zipping up and down the main thoroughfares of downtown Moscow. And the many foreign currency food stores, originally opened for Westerners and known in the Soviet era as *beriozka* shops, now are frequented mainly by Russians. While many Russians do not complain about the contrasts in wealth and seem to accept with equanimity the influx of imported luxuries they cannot possibly afford, others, perhaps the majority, are sullen and angry, and it may be only a matter of time before their patience wears out.

Sources of the New Wealth

A major source of the new wealth is speculation in real estate. Russian entrepreneurs with cash buy up newly privatized communal apartments, resettle the occupants in larger and more attractive quarters elsewhere in the city, refurbish the vacated run-down tenements, and resell them to foreigners or Russians at enormous profit.

Another source of wealth is currency speculation. Because the banking system is so ramshackle, the value of the ruble varies widely from one part of Russia to the next. A speculator in Moscow with foreign currency will trade it for rubles in another Russian city and change it back to dollars in Moscow at a 20 to 40 percent profit, minus several hundred dollars in bribes to keep suspicious authorities from inspecting his belongings.

The new wealth also comes from the sale of commodities, like metals, where the domestic price for acquiring them remains under state control and well below the world market level. These commodities frequently come from state supplies released by corrupt government bureaucrats and industrial managers in return for generous bribes. Black-metal wire, for example, sells in Russia for about $70 a ton, yet the world price for the same ton of wire is $222. The profits to be made from the sale of black-metal wire, thus, are exorbitant. Again, however, profits are diminished by bribes that must be paid to a variety of local and national authorities, such as state bureaucrats, factory managers, railroad officials, and customs officers.

Some taxation of profits has been enacted into law by the Russian Parliament, but tax liability can be reduced to a minimum by concealing the extent of earnings. Much of the profits is kept in foreign banks, beyond the reach of government officials. Thus, despite heavy bribes and some taxation as well as a ceiling on profit margins decreed by the Russian government in January 1993, profits can still be enormous. This situation will continue until the government can regulate and impose taxes on the turnover.

An Explosion of Crime

This extraordinary accumulation of wealth has given rise to a new, well-organized criminal element known as the Russian Mafia, which demands its share of the new opulence. Although Mafia gangs are involved in every conceivable kind of criminal activity, from money laundering and trafficking in narcotics to the disposal of expensive automobiles stolen in the West, a favorite and familiar activity is protection, which is having a devastating impact on the economy. As private enterprise gets started, crooks seek a cut for themselves in the profits of new businesses by offering them "protection" against destruction of property. If individuals refuse to buy protection, the Mafia uses violence against them and their property.

This drives Russian investors to go to great lengths to conceal their wealth, but in doing so, they forfeit whatever protection the authorities could provide. The authorities have little idea of the extent of private business and virtually no control over its behavior. Indeed, Major General Aleksandr Gurov, director of the Russian Security Ministry's research institute, has frankly admitted that the Russian state cannot ensure the safety of businesses. In part this is the result of a lack of money, personnel, and surveillance technology. Another key weakness of Russian law enforcement agencies is corruption, with many officials in league with the criminals they are supposed to control.

The Mafia is scaring off both would-be big investors from abroad and potential small Russia-based investors. New private concerns from banks to retail stores have become the target of well-organized, highly professionalized, and heavily armed bandits willing and able to use the most brutal methods, including wanton killings, to extort money. Russia is reckoned to have more than 3,000 such gangs, and criminal types proliferate in Moscow, giving parts of the city the appearance of Chicago or New York in the Prohibition Era, when gangs were rampant.

The Collapse of the Russian Oil Industry

It would be hard to overstate the importance of oil, either to the old Soviet Union or to Russia today. In the 1970s the huge oil profits helped to keep the inefficient Soviet economy functioning. In the 1980s, however, oil prices dropped and Moscow's oil exports could no longer pay for purchases of Western technology and American grain.

When the Soviet Union collapsed, the oil industry suffered as well. Production took a nose dive as the incompetence of Soviet oil producers and bureaucrats took its toll. In the early 1990s, pumps began to break down and oil fields began drying up from drilling practices that have plugged the pores in oil-bearing rock and fouled oil reservoirs with water. Across Siberia, there are lakes of spilled oil and 18,000 idle wells. The companies, all state owned, ran on budgets unrelated to the oil they produced. When they managed to find oil and bring it to the surface, Russian oil producers lost a third of it through leaking pipes and wasteful refineries.

One serious problem for the industry has been a chronic shortage of oil field equipment, which had been manufactured in Azerbaijan. It was bad enough that the equipment had

to be shipped several thousand miles northeast to Siberia. But the supply of equipment dried up in the wake of the war between Azerbaijan and Armenia that has been going on intermittently for over five years. Supplies of equipment from other republics also disappeared following the disintegration of the Soviet state in 1991. With the lack of equipment along with inept drilling practices and colossal mismanagement, Russian oil production declined 28 percent between 1988 and 1993.

The collapse of the Russian oil industry has been a disaster for the Russian economy, complicating and slowing down Yeltsin's efforts to move Russia toward a market economy. Chronic fuel shortages have left cities without heat and machines without fuel, making it especially difficult for farmers to harvest their grain. Oil available for export has declined, hurting countries formerly dependent on Russia for cheap energy and severely reducing Russia's hard currency earnings.

The situation for Russian oil output in the near future is not promising. Russia desperately needs foreign investment to modernize its oil extracting and refining facilities. But foreign oil companies, which would like to help rehabilitate the decrepit Russian oil industry and at the moment are competing for contracts with Russian enterprises, are reluctant to invest significant amounts of money until there is more financial and political stability. The results of the December 12, 1993, parliamentary elections, which gave Vladimir Zhirinovsky's radical right political party, the Liberal Democrats, 25 percent of the popular vote, are not very encouraging to foreign investment in Russian oil. Zhirinovsky has echoed the view of other conservatives that foreigners should not be allowed to exploit Russia's precious natural resources. The new Russian State Duma, under the influence of conservatives and a large centrist group that seems more sympathetic to the economic views of hard-liners like Zhirinovsky than to reformers like Gaidar and Fyodorov, is unlikely to remove bureaucratic obstacles to large-scale foreign investment in Russia.

A Bright Spot: The Boom in Private Housing

To avoid concluding this discussion of post-Communist economic development in Russia on a pessimistic note, we turn to the boom in private housing construction that is enlivening the otherwise drab Russian landscape and indicating real, if limited, progress toward realization of the market economy.

Around the outskirts of Moscow, an emerging market economy is altering the landscape with a housing boom. Instead of waiting decades for the state to grant a cramped room or two in a high-rise apartment building with a tenement's air of dirt and decay, thousands of Muscovites are buying newly privatized plots of land on which they are building their own homes. The legal framework now makes this buying spree possible, in particular a new law legalizing land sales, another allowing villages to "hand out" lots, and a third repealing rules limiting rural construction to one-story cottages usually no larger than a Western garage. And Russians are stretching the rule that forbids building any structure more elaborate than a summer shelter on thousands of small plots that people already own and are buying in the suburbs of the capital.

Real estate prices vary dramatically, from as little as $900 for a small plot with no utilities, to $2,000 for a do-it-yourself cabin kit, to $300,000 for a four-bedroom villa with European fixtures and greenhouse in a walled-in community with 24-hour guards.

Russian home buyers cannot purchase property as easily as their American counterparts, because there is no such thing as a mortgage. People must pay cash. Those who have no cash to buy a finished home can still build, but everything is a headache if they do it themselves. They must serve as their own general contractor, recruiting plumbers, electricians,

(UPI/Bettmann)

Russian president Boris Yeltsin emerged as a dominant figure in the developing democratic movement in the Soviet Union. During and after the coup attempt of August 1991, Yeltsin made decisive moves to thwart the hard-liners. After Mikhail Gorbachev was returned from house arrest, Yeltsin took him to task over not being able to distinguish friends from foes. Yeltsin is generally considered important to the development of democracy in the former Soviet republics, but his own political survival is not certain.

masons, and the like, bribing them and then sleeping on the site to prevent theft of expensive materials—which, incidentally, they frequently have to scour the city to obtain, since much of what they need is scarce.

Nevertheless, private homes are rising everywhere, not just in Moscow, where most of them currently are because the capital has more entrepreneurs, foreigners, and other people who earn substantial salaries. In the rush for new homes, a new industry in Russia is emerging that includes land developers, real estate agencies, lumber yards, plumbing suppliers, and skilled craftspeople. Fueling the boom beyond the change in laws making private ownership possible is a greater availability of construction materials than ever before, though most are still scarce by Western standards. If local officials begin to free up state-controlled land for private development, the legendary housing shortage in Russia might appreciably diminish. But, in this as in other business deals, it helps to know appropriate state officials and have money ready to pay them in return for short-circuiting cumbersome bureaucratic procedures.

REORGANIZATION OF THE EX-SOVIET MILITARY

Although the republic defense ministers agreed in principle in Moscow, at the end of December 1991, to create a joint armed force and appointed Shaposhnikov to a 2-month term as interim Commonwealth commander, C.I.S. unity of action on military matters was difficult, partly because the republics wanted territorial armies, an inevitable desire given the fragmentation of the former Soviet military along ethnic lines and the much-resented domination of the officer corps by Russians. The republic leaders agreed that individual members could form separate armies, although strategic weapons would remain under a single command.

Still, Commonwealth leaders did have strong incentives to preserve some kind of central control over the former Soviet military. Many ex-Soviet Army officers opposed the breakup of the army into republic-controlled units and wanted a unified, if leaner, force under central command. They argued that the security of the republics required a central military organization, given the reality of a nuclear world and the fact that almost every neighbor of the former Soviet Union is likely to harbor territorial ambitions and be ready to exploit differences among the republics. Former Soviet officers have argued also that republic armies might be able to fight against unarmed peasants but would be no match for a modern army.

In a gesture of desperation, 5,000 officers of all ranks from the former Soviet military gathered in the Kremlin on January 17, 1992, to demand of C.I.S. leaders that the Soviet armed forces remain intact. The gathering was called by local assemblies in all branches of the military. Nothing on the scale of this meeting ever took place in the Soviet Union. The officers condemned a perceived civilian hostility toward the army, the murderous weapons raids by armed Georgian bands, and Ukraine's insistence on splitting the army and navy into territorial branches. The officers adopted a resolution expressing concern over the hasty and "unreasonable" division of the army and navy, called on the Commonwealth politicians to preserve the army's unity with a single unitary command for a transitional period, and agreed to set up a coordinating council to represent the interests of the armed services.

In mid-February 1992, C.I.S. leaders met in Minsk to set up the council. Three republics (Ukraine, Moldova, and Azerbaijan) rejected the idea of a unified military force. Ukrainian president Kravchuk intoned that unified armed forces could logically only exist in a unified state, which the Commonwealth of Independent States had not yet become. Ukraine did not want the C.I.S. to become a quasi-union reminiscent of the late Soviet Union and feared that a Commonwealth army would still be dominated by Russians. Azerbaijan opposed a Commonwealth army because it wanted to have an independent force to deal with Armenian opposition to its administration of Nagorno-Karabakh. It had discovered that Russian troops, the remnants of the Soviet Army, deployed in Nagorno-Karabakh, had been cooperating with the Armenian side.

Problems in the Russian Military

The Russian Army faces many problems that come with the fall of the Soviet state and of communist ideology. The military now has less money, fewer personnel, and a much diminished role in national affairs with the decline of Russian influence in Central/Eastern Europe, Central Asia, and the Middle East. In many instances earning lower pay than minimally educated factory workers, soldiers lack adequate housing and basic necessities. Russian officers are suffering economic hardship along with everyone else. Many officers and soldiers are driven to corruption, for example, selling military equipment, ranging from small handguns to sophisticated weapons.

Conditions for Russian draftees are especially tough. They could easily make much more as civilians, and they are subjected to ruthless hazing. They dread eventual assignment for duty in areas where there is fighting, such as the Caucasus, Tajikistan, Georgia, and Moldova. Draft dodging is common; only about 30 percent of draftees show up for induction. Many are ready to do anything, with the help of family and friends, to escape the draft. Parents will even go to induction centers and argue openly with military personnel about the dangers of military life.

Especially painful for morale is the fact that the army has shrunk in size. In 1988 the Soviet Army had 5 million people in uniform. The Russian Army, its successor, is about 1.5 million, with many officers convinced that what is left of the army lacks the strength to defend and protect the Russian state. Some military and political leaders probably believe that its rival, the United States, no longer takes it seriously, no longer considers it a mortal threat.

Russian officers are also angry over the way in which Yeltsin has backed off a more aggressive foreign policy. They feel that Yeltsin has done little to counter hostile American policies toward former Soviet allies like Iraq. They have argued forcefully against return of the offshore islands to Japan before any substantial Japanese economic and financial assistance is forthcoming. Army leaders are also riled by alleged discrimination against Russian minorities in areas that once belonged to the Soviet state, such as the Baltic republics.

What most disturbs and demoralizes the Russian military, in particular its officers corps, is the deterioration of their status in Russian society. In their view the military has been stripped of its mission; and its history of greatness dating back to the Czarist era, when it was the chief instrument of Russian national growth, has been forgotten.

Recently, Yeltsin has gone out of his way to appease the military and keep it loyal. He has opposed membership of the Central/Eastern European countries in NATO, resisted Western pressures on Russia to support anti-Serb actions in the Bosnian Civil War, and has kept lines of communication open with Saddam Hussein and Muammar al-Qadhafi. He has also gotten German money to build housing for officers and other military personnel; and he agreed to an increase in pay for officers, despite pressure from his reformist advisers to control government spending in the interest of reducing inflation.

Nevertheless, the army and the navy are wild cards in the future development of politics in Russia. No one really knows, for example, how military personnel voted in the December 12, 1993, parliamentary elections. Many undoubtedly gave their votes to the Liberal Democratic Party of Zhirinovsky because they like what he said about restoring Russia's influence abroad, especially along border areas.

It is clear that the military leadership does not like the conflict now taking place among the politicians. Like the military in other unstable national environments, the Russian military may sometime decide to step in and bring order, in the form of a dictatorship that would set about recovering Russia's lost influence and power in the world community. Some military intervention is already taking place. In many regions of the former Soviet Union, Russian troops on patrol have taken sides in the fighting among ethnic groups, with or without Moscow's blessing. Usually they are trying either to keep certain areas from spinning further away from Russian influence or protecting the interests of Russian minorities. In the Baltic republics, for example, senior commanders, acting independently of the Kremlin, delayed the scheduled withdrawal of their forces. The Russian military is also involved in the bitter tug-of-war between Russia and Ukraine over control of the Black Sea fleet and enforcement of agreements providing for the transfer of Ukraine's nuclear capacity to Russia.

NATIONALIST RIVALRIES WITHIN AND AMONG REPUBLICS

The ex-Soviet republics have experienced internal conflicts sparked by a resurgence of ethnocultural nationalism among minorities following the collapse of the Soviet state. Conflicts among republics also have occurred; these have grown out of economic, strategic, and territorial issues. Conflicts within and among the ex-Soviet republics have undermined their internal stability and have weakened the already fragile unity of the Commonwealth of Independent States.

Russia

Many non-Russian peoples in Russia have agitated for greater administrative autonomy of Moscow and, in some cases, complete independence. In addition, Russia has had difficulties with other ex-Soviet republics, especially Ukraine, but also with Kazakhstan and Tajikistan, provoking a fear that Moscow wants to reconstitute something very close to the old Russian-dominated Soviet state.

Moscow and Non-Russian Minorities

The most dangerous outbreak of ethnic conflict inside Russia has occurred in the Caucasus, whose mountains are home to many tribes divided by language, religion, and a history of feuding. Since the collapse of Soviet authority, there has been continuous unrest. In late 1992 fighting broke out in North Ossetia between Ossetians, who are Christian, and Ingush, who are Islamic. During Soviet rule the Ingush had been part of the Chechen-Ingushetia autonomous republic. After the collapse of the Soviet Union, the Chechens declared their independence of Russia. The Ingush preferred to continue under Moscow's rule, but the Chechens refused to allow the Ingush to separate and still consider Ingush territory as part of their republic.

The Ingush want direct control over the so-called Prigordony region of North Ossetia, an area that historically had belonged to the Ingush but was taken away from them by Stalin in 1944 and then administered by Ossetians within Russia. Yeltsin wanted a quick end to the fighting and, in November 1992, declared a state of emergency in both North Ossetia and the territory inhabited by the Ingush. He sent 3,000 Russian *spesnatz* troops to both Ossetia and Ingushetia to help separate the warring sides.

Yeltsin's anxiety over what to the outside world seemed like a small ethnic tempest in a teapot was well founded. The Ingush had the sympathy of Muslim peoples elsewhere in Russia. The continued fighting could provoke an explosion of anti-Russian nationalism among Russia's Muslim minorities. According to Emil Payin, a leading specialist on ethnic conflicts, the Ossetian–Ingushetian conflict, fought on Russian territory, set a dangerous precedent for the future course of agitation by the non-Russian minorities for greater autonomy of Moscow.

Within days the worst fears of the Russian leadership about the spread of the conflict seemed to be vindicated. The leader of the self-proclaimed Chechen republic, former Soviet Air Force general Dzhokhar Dudayev, alarmed by the presence of a large Soviet military force in nearby Ingush territory, declared that the Russians had violated the territorial integrity of the Chechen republic. He threatened to enter the Ossetian conflict if Russian troops were not immediately withdrawn. To avoid a spread of the conflict, the Yeltsin government decided to move Russian troops away from the Chechen frontier. The Russian forces now began a long and arduous effort to disarm the combatants, an effort that so far has had only partial success. The region remains a cauldron of conflict and a serious threat to Russia's continuing administrative control.

In the meantime the fate of the Chechen republic remains in limbo. Neither Russia nor any other republic is ready to recognize its independence. Given its distance from Moscow, however, there is little that the Yeltsin government can do to restore Moscow's control. Nevertheless, aware of his isolation and vulnerability, Chechen leader Dudayev might be willing to establish some administrative links with Russia if Moscow would recognize Chechen sovereignty. But the chances of that are now slim, given the influence of nationalists in the Russian government. These people are opposed to the weakening of Moscow's control over any part of Russian territory.

An equally troublesome threat to the unity and integrity of the Russian federation comes from the Tatars, a Turkic-speaking Muslim people living at the confluence of the Volga and Kama rivers, about 500 miles east of Moscow, with their capital in Astrakhan. The Tatars, who had enjoyed the status of an autonomous republic in the Russian federation during the Soviet period, seized the opportunity of the collapse of the Soviet state to emancipate themselves from Russian rule. In March 1992 they voted overwhelmingly in a referendum in favor of complete independence of Moscow, which Moscow refused to recognize.

The Yeltsin government was reluctant to allow the Tatars to go their own way. The territory they inhabit is rich in oil, heavily industrialized, and part of the route of natural gas pipelines originating in Tyumen. Furthermore, 43 percent of the population of Tatarstan are Russian. The Tatar leadership realizes that complete independence of Russia is not possible and, like Dudayev and the Chechens, the Tatars may be willing to accept administrative links to Russia provided their sovereignty is recognized. But the Yeltsin government is not likely to accept Tatar sovereignty, which would limit Moscow's influence over internal Tatar policy and threaten the territorial integrity of the Russian federation. In February 1994 the Russian government reached a compromise with the Tatar autonomists. President Yeltsin signed an agreement with Tatarstan president Mintimer Shaimiyev giving Tatarstan a large measure of control over its local affairs.

Russian Influence in Other Republics

Ukraine and other republics have taken issue with Russia's claim to be the equivalent of the legal heir to the Soviet state and, therefore, first among equals in the Commonwealth. In their view Yeltsin railroaded them into an acceptance of Russian predominance in the C.I.S. and of Russia's right to the spoils of the Soviet state. Ukraine has assailed Russia for laying claim to all Soviet missions abroad and, in particular, for raising the Russian tricolor to the exclusion of the flags of other republics over those missions.

Ukrainian anxieties about Russia have not been without justification. In the period following the August 1991 coup, Russia took control of many former Soviet ministries. Russia turned the august Soviet Academy of Sciences into a Russian academy. And in March 1993, Yeltsin asked the international community, in particular the United Nations, to recognize Russia's "special responsibility" in the post-Soviet era to maintain peace and stability in the former Soviet Union and approve of its exercising "special powers" throughout the region. Though Yeltsin did not explain the meaning of "special powers," the term was widely understood to refer to the use of military force to stop interethnic conflicts. The Baltic republics, which were outside the Commonwealth, and Ukraine were especially sensitive to this new phase of Russia's perceived campaign to restore its influence over neighboring countries.

Equally intimidating to other ex-Soviet republics is Russia's quiet policy of using its trade in raw materials to promote a Moscow-oriented, perhaps Moscow-led union of ex-Soviet republics linked together by agreements to cooperate in the economic and strategic areas. Russia supplies most of the oil, natural gas, and timber needed by other ex-Soviet republics but has been reluctant to sell them as much as they want. Russia prefers to export to the West for hard currency, which the republics do not have. But if they accommodate Russia's policy of building unity within the Commonwealth under Moscow's leadership, Russia is ready to furnish low-cost loans to buy its raw materials.

Ukraine

Russia and Ukraine differ over trade, transfer of nuclear weapons the disposition of the former Soviet government's Black Sea naval fleet, and control of the Crimea. Relations between the two republics are strained.

Ukrainian officials complain about Russia's failure, despite bilateral trade agreements, to fulfill promises of oil deliveries. Ukraine depends on Russia for oil and, with the collapse of the centrally managed Soviet oil industry, supplies have become increasingly haphazard. From Ukraine's point of view, the problem starts at the point of production, namely, in Russia, where distributors demand "extras" such as meat, sugar, and grain before they will ship oil.

Russia and Ukraine are at odds over the ultimate disposition of the Black Sea fleet of the former Soviet Navy deployed in Ukrainian waters. In January 1992 Ukraine ordered the entire Black Sea fleet to take an oath of loyalty. Russia is very sensitive about the legendary fleet, for several reasons. It is historically the core of the Russian Imperial Navy, beginning in the eighteenth century; it is responsible for the protection of Commonwealth interests in the Mediterranean, where the U.S. Sixth Fleet is deployed; and half of the Black Sea fleet's ships are capable of carrying nuclear arms. Russians have said that it must remain under the command of the Commonwealth. But Ukraine insisted in the early months of 1992 on its right to command the fleet and to try to enforce the oath of loyalty. By June 1993, however, Ukraine had decided to compromise with Russia on the disposition of the Black Sea fleet. Yeltsin and Ukrainian president Leonid Kravchuk agreed to split the fleet down the middle, with Ukraine selling its portion of the fleet to the Russians. But Ukraine then changed its mind. Despite all this activity, the ultimate disposition of the old Soviet Black Sea fleet remains uncertain.

In March 1992 another military issue surfaced when Kravchuk put a halt to further transfers of former Soviet nuclear weapons to Russia. President Kravchuk said that he wanted to make sure that they were being destroyed properly and were not being redeployed in Russia. He asked the West for financial and technical assistance in disposing of the weapons on Ukrainian soil. In particular he asked the United States for guarantees of Ukrainian security and up to $1.5 billion in compensation for the dismantling and transfer to Russia of Ukraine's nuclear weapons.

In January 1993, to persuade Kravchuk to continue denuclearization of Ukraine's weapons arsenal and to get Ukraine's Parliament to ratify START I, Yeltsin offered him security guarantees against nuclear or conventional attack and promised a slight increase in Russian oil deliveries. When this tactic did not work, Yeltsin tried another: He told Ukrainians that effective July 1, 1993, Russia would charge market prices in its economic dealings with Ukraine—a development that could create economic disaster in Ukraine— unless Ukraine agreed to closer economic and military unity, in particular Kiev's return to a common currency with Russia, coordination of Ukrainian and Russian economic reform policies, and the completion of its transfer of nuclear weapons to Russia.

The Russians had some success with this approach. In July 1993 Ukraine agreed, along with Belarus, to join Russia in an economic union involving the removal of tariffs and other trade barriers to create a single market in goods, services, and capital, with joint policies on prices, investment, and taxation. The three Slavic states also pledged coordination in their common goal to move from centralized economies to capitalism, although Ukraine and Belarus are currently far behind Russia.

In the military sphere, Ukraine remained cautious and somewhat uncooperative, pledging to continue transferring nuclear weapons but not doing much to implement such pledges. By the end of 1993 Russian and Ukrainian leaders acknowledged that little progress had been made on dismantling and disposing of the 1,600 Ukrainian long-range nuclear warheads. Behind this behavior was the Ukrainian Parliament, where nationalists were insisting the Ukraine keep its nuclear capability even though in November 1993 it had ratified the START I agreement. In their view the West had not provided much financial assistance to Ukraine to help offset disposal costs. Moreover, politicians fed on a common distrust of Russia, pointing to the bellicose rhetoric of Vladimir Zhirinovsky following the Russian parliamentary elections.

Closely related to the confrontation between Russia and Ukraine over the Black Sea fleet was control of the Crimea. Russian leaders wanted the Crimea, which was transferred to Ukrainian jurisdiction in 1954 by Nikita Khrushchev, returned to Russia. To them the Crimea remains an inseparable part of Russia, to which it belonged since the late eighteenth century, when Russian czarina Catherine II emancipated it from Ottoman Turkish rule. Moreover, the Crimea is inhabited predominantly by Russians. Complicating the issue, at least for the Russian side, was the division of opinion about the Crimea between Russian vice president Rutskoi and Yeltsin. Yeltsin was less eager than Rutskoi to provoke the Ukrainians.

When the Ukrainians rejected Russian claims, Yeltsin backed off and, in February 1992, acknowledged Ukraine's sovereignty over the Crimea. The Russian government, however, expressed concern when Ukraine decided to allow the return of the Tatars to their old home in the Crimea. The Russian population in the Crimea made it plain that it did not welcome the Tatars and looked to Moscow to protect its economic, political, and cultural interests.

A new dimension of the Crimean issue appeared in May 1992, when the Crimean local government declared its independence of Ukraine. This Crimean nationalism had grown out of ethnic as well as economic circumstances. The overwhelming majority of Crimeans (about 70 percent out of 2.5 million people) are Russian, and as long as Ukraine was part of the Russian-dominated Soviet state, they accepted with equanimity the location of their land in Ukraine. When the Soviet state fell apart and Ukraine became independent, the Crimean Russians worried about being completely cut off from Russia.

Before long their discomfort turned to frustration and anger because their living standards declined sharply under the independent Ukrainian government. Crimea suffered, like the rest of Ukraine, when Kiev replaced the ruble with a new Ukrainian currency, which quickly lost its value. Crimea also has suffered, like Ukraine, from fuel shortages resulting from the decline of oil imports from Russia. About a third of Crimean enterprises shut down and others operated at only 50 percent capacity. The Crimean Russians were disgusted by this Ukrainian administrative ineptitude. At the same time, although Russia was not that much better off than Ukraine, Crimean Russians thought that Russia at least seemed to be making some progress toward a free market economy.

President Kravchuk responded to the Crimean declaration of independence firmly but in a conciliatory manner. He tried to increase Crimean administrative autonomy and agreed in 1993 to allow the Crimeans to elect their own president. But Kravchuk refused to consider secession, which, he insisted, would be unconstitutional. Ukraine's Parliament gave him special powers to overrule any secessionist action by Crimean local authorities, including the new Crimean president. To the chagrin of Kiev, in January 1994 Crimean voters elected as their first president Yuri Meshkov, a separatist committed to merging Crimea with Russia. The Crimean Tatars, who now number about 300,000, along with the small Ukrainian minority, want to remain part of Ukraine.

The assertiveness of Crimea's Russian majority poses a serious and embarrassing problem for Russia, which would like to take the side of the Crimean Russians. There is a lot of sympathy in Moscow for all Russians living in Ukraine. But Russian support for Crimean separatism would surely antagonize the government in Kiev, discouraging its transfer of nuclear weapons. It also would strengthen fears throughout the ex-Soviet lands of Russian expansionism. Finally, Russian support of kin in Crimea could set off a civil war.

Georgia

Since the end of 1991, independent Georgia has been caught up in a multifaceted civil war.

One aspect of the war involved former Georgian president Zviad Gamsakhurdia, forced out of office and succeeded by former Soviet foreign minister Eduard Shevardnadze in early 1992. Gamsakhurdia and his followers in northwestern Georgia tried to oust Shevardnadze and regain power. Gamsakhurdia's insurgency failed because he could not rally public opinion behind him. Despite his role as a dissident when Georgia was part of the Soviet Union, he showed little tolerance of dissidence coming from others. He was seen as a conservative, an autocrat, and an extremist. Georgians preferred the more genteel Shevardnadze, with his many and important connections to the outside world. Moreover, at the end of 1993, Gamsakhurdia suddenly disappeared. In early 1994 there were reports of his death.

A second aspect of the civil war is the secessionist movement in the South Ossetian region of eastern Georgia, where the people want to join with their kin in North Ossetia, which is part of Russia. Although the Ossetians in the summer of 1993 seemed on the verge of freeing themselves from Georgian rule, this campaign for independence eventually failed. They had little sympathy from the Yeltsin government, which wanted to avoid boundary changes that could prove troublesome to Russia. Moscow also saw no gain for Russia from a disintegration of the Georgian state that might well be the result if Ossetia became independent.

A third aspect of the Civil War—and the one presenting the most serious challenge to President Shevardnadze and the integrity of independent Georgia—is the secessionist movement in Abkhazia, in northern Georgia. In July 1992 the Abkhazians declared their independence of Tbilisi. They may have had some encouragement from the local Russian military commander, who personally disliked Shevardnadze for his part in the dissolution of the Soviet Union and seemed ready to help bring him down. At the same time, the Yeltsin government was reluctant to put a stop to the collusion between the local Russian forces deployed in the Caucasus and the Abkhazian separatists. The Kremlin was annoyed by Shevardnadze's refusal to join the C.I.S. and to sign special agreements linking Georgia to Russia; Shevardnadze was afraid of Russian dominance and a loss of independence, in particular opportunities to cultivate relations with the West.

Fearing the disintegration of his country and infuriated by the way in which the Gamsakhurdia forces began using Abkhazia as a refuge and exploiting Abkhazian separatism to weaken him, Shevardnadze began a long military campaign to punish the Abkhazians and bring them back to the rule of Tbilisi. For about a year, Georgian and Abkhazian forces fought each other in and around Sukhumi, on Georgia's Black Sea coast. In July 1993, however, with the help of the Kremlin, which was worried about complaints from abroad as well as from within the Commonwealth that Russia was trying to expand its influence in the ex-Soviet republics by taking sides in local ethnic conflicts, Shevardnadze negotiated a truce with the Abkhazians and asked a reluctant Georgian Parliament to accept it without settling once and for all the issue of Abkhazian separatism. Shortly afterward Shevardnadze withdrew much of the Georgian force from Sukhumi.

But Yeltsin continued to be under pressure by nationalists in the Russian Congress of Peoples' Deputies to nurture links between Russia and the former Soviet republics. To get their support for his economic reforms, he tried to conciliate them in foreign policy. And, when it became clear that he needed the support of the army in his struggle with the Congress, Yeltsin decided to blackmail Shevardnadze into strengthening Georgian political, economic, and military links to Moscow. He indirectly encouraged the Abkhazian seizure of Sukhumi in September 1993.

The Russian tactic was successful. Facing the prospect of losing a critical part of his territory, Shevardnadze now begged Yeltsin for help, offering to bring Georgia into the C.I.S. The Kremlin agreed to help. Yeltsin wanted Shevardnadze's support for closer Georgian ties to Russia. The Kremlin also worried that a continuation and intensification of the conflict between Georgians and Abkhazians could escalate into a region-wide war. A united Georgia at peace with itself was better than a divided Georgia in a perpetual state of civil war. Furthermore, Washington and Bonn, in response to desperate requests for help from Shevardnadze, had been sending messages of concern to Yeltsin, telling him that they had little sympathy for the ill-concealed effort of Russia to treat the ex-Soviet republics as its backyard. Finally, Russia's meddling undermined its claim to a peacekeeping role in the former Soviet Union, to say nothing of the credibility of Yeltsin's proposal in February 1993 that the United Nations grant Russia special powers to play that role.

The Yeltsin government eventually decided to help Georgian forces retake Sukhumi and suppress Abkhazian separatism. In October 1993 several thousand Russian troops, including paratroopers and heavy armor, were deployed in northern Georgia. By December Sukhumi was under Georgian control.

The war in Abkhazia and the rebellion of Gamsakhurdia's followers have had a debilitating effect on Georgia's society. They have contributed substantially to a culture of violence. Crime has increased, the justice system has almost collapsed, and the police cannot protect civilian life and property. The proliferation of crime in Tbilisi has changed the city radically; sidewalk kiosks and the popular coffee houses have all but disappeared because of their vulnerability to theft and vandalism.

War and rebellion have also ruined the once productive Georgian economy, which had been able to provide Georgians with a comparatively good standard of living. By late 1992 inflation had reached 50 percent a month, the result in part of shortages caused by the disruption of railroad service into Russia by Abkhazian vandalism. The cutoff of rail service starved Georgian industry of oil, power, and spare parts and Georgian agriculture of markets. Industrial production dropped in 1992 by two-thirds of what it had been in 1990, and unemployment was steadily increasing, to 20 percent by September 1992. Georgia's new currency, the coupon, issued in April 1993 on a par with the Russian ruble, deteriorated sharply in value. By August it was worth one-sixth of the ruble. The average salary in Georgia by the end of 1993 was less than $3 a month, and as prices of everything, especially food, clothing, and energy, had risen sharply, people have become terrified about the future.

At the same time, there has been no reform to speak of because of the ongoing Civil War. Industry and most of agriculture, including the country's legendary vineyards, remain under state control. There are a few private restaurants in Tbilisi; they are always in danger of going out of business either because of hyperinflation or crime.

Finally, adding to Georgia's misery is a new and horrendous refugee problem as a result of the fighting in and around Sukhumi. Two hundred thousand people fled Abkhazian terrorism in Sukhumi to the neighboring mountains, where many of them have died of cold and hunger. Georgia does not have the resources to handle this problem.

The Georgian political scene is bleak. Shevardnadze's deal with the Russians to rescue Sukhumi and dampen Abkhazian separatism was not well received by the politicians in Tbilisi. They accused him of betraying the country. Moreover, despite his widespread popularity and the view of many politicians in and outside of the Georgian Parliament that without his leadership Georgia would fall apart, Shevardnadze's own political situation has deteriorated. His effort to remain above politics, in particular his failure to build a political party loyal to him, has weakened his ability to transform his enormous popularity into political power. Only recently has he tried to build political support for his leadership by launching a new bloc of small parties, the Citizens' Union, to make a parliamentary majority that will back his policies.

Finally, the presence of Russian troops in Georgia serves as a reminder of the country's weakness and dependence on its giant neighbor, a situation that does not help Shevardnadze's credibility with his followers and the public at large. For the time being, another curse on Georgian politics is the apparent renewal of Moscow's influence over the country.

Moldova

The self-styled Trans-Dneister republic, comprising a narrow strip of territory on the east bank of the Dneister River, not far north of its entry into the Black Sea, and consisting of about 600,000 Russian and Ukrainian people, tried to break away from Moldovan control in early 1992. The problem has continued to fester and disrupt Moldova's domestic politics and foreign relations, especially with Russia and Ukraine. The Russians and Ukrainians in Trans-Dneister are afraid that Romania will annex Moldova, which is inhabited primarily by people of Romanian origin. Both Romanian president Ion Iliescu and Moldovan president Mircea Snegur deny this possibility. But the Slavic peoples of the Trans-Dneister region point out that since the collapse of the Soviet Union, the Romanian-dominated government in Chisineau (formerly Kishinev), the capital of Moldova, has Romanized the alphabet, made Romanian the state language, and adopted a flag and seal almost identical to those of Romania.

Moldova's efforts in 1992 to restore its authority over the Trans-Dneister region were complicated by the Russian 14th Army headquartered in the region. The 14th Army's command, which had become all but independent of Moscow, was made up of Slavic officers who were furious over the disintegration of the Soviet state and Moldova's independence. They sympathized with the local population in the region and supported its resistance to Moldovan control. The Moldovans, for their part, believed that Russia wanted to weaken Moldova; force its entry into the C.I.S., which Moldovan president Snegur had resisted because of the heavy Russian influence over it; and discourage annexation to Romania.

But Yeltsin, as in the case of Georgia, wanted Russia to appear true to its internationally proclaimed role as peacemaker to the region. In mid-1992 he placed a former supporter of his, Lieutenant General Aleksandr Labed, in command of the 14th Army, with instructions to promote peace in the region. With Labed's cooperation a Russo-Moldovan agreement was concluded in which peacekeepers from Moldova, Russia, and the Trans-Dneister would end the fighting in return for Moldova's willingness to grant the Slavic peoples of the Trans-Dneister a special status of autonomy.

However, the peoples of the Trans-Dneister republic still want their independence, and Labed and his forces remain sympathetic and supportive of their ambition. Indeed, Labed believes that all the Slavic peoples of the former Soviet Union will reunite together, including those living in Kazakhstan. His thinking has a lot of support in the Russian political and military establishment in Moscow. For the time being, therefore, Moscow is doing little to discourage Labed's benevolent neutrality toward the Slavic peoples of the Trans-Dneister, even though Moldova seems to have given up on joining Romania.

Civil war in Moldova, as in Georgia, has contributed to economic devastation. Real income for the country's 4.3 million people dropped by two-thirds between 1990 and 1993. By late 1993 inflation was running at 30 percent a month, and living conditions had deteriorated sharply as a result of a severe energy shortage.

The Civil War has aggravated an economic situation that was bad to begin with. Much of the hardship is tied to the disruption of Moldova's economic relations with Russia in the post-Communist era. During the Soviet era, Russia sent oil and gas to Moldova at subsidized prices, but since 1992 Russia has insisted on market prices for its energy exports and payment in hard currency, of which Moldova has little. Also, Moldova's food processing industries have suffered a considerable loss of business with Russia that has not been recovered in other markets—Moldova's exports do not yet meet the standards for sales in the West, and Moldovan producers cannot afford to upgrade the quality of their output to make it competitive. Matters were worsened when Russia imposed tariffs on imports from Moldova as retaliation when President Snegur refused to join the C.I.S. or an economic union with Russia.

Moldova has made a little progress in moving toward a free market economy, but at great cost to its people. To fight inflation, reduce the budget deficit, and make Moldova's currency convertible, President Snegur cut credits to industry. He also has begun privatization of Moldova's state-controlled industrial enterprises. Moldova, however, faces the classic consequences of free market reforms: rising prices, unemployment, and a conservative state bureaucracy manned by old-line Communists. Moldova's immediate prospects for economic improvement, along with internal political peace and stability, are not promising.

Armenia and Azerbaijan

The collapse of the Soviet state coincided with a renewal of violence between Armenians and Azerbaijani in Nagorno-Karabakh. The spark apparently occurred when Armenians allegedly shot down an Azerbaijani helicopter by heat-seeking missiles at the end of January 1992. The intensity of the fighting appeared to mark a new phase in the nearly 4-year-old battle for Nagorno-Karabakh. In response to Armenian requests that the Commonwealth intervene to stop the fighting, Russian foreign minister Andrei Kozyrev hosted a conference with Armenian and Azerbaijani leaders in Moscow in late February. The Russian initiative seemed to have some success, because Armenian and Azerbaijani diplomats agreed to an immediate cease-fire in Nagorno-Karabakh. They agreed to a Russian proposal to set up a negotiating commission, consisting of Russian, Armenian, and Azerbaijani representatives. Presumably in response to the Armenian concession in September 1991, in which Yerevan renounced any claims to the territory of Nagorno-Karabakh, the Azerbaijani side agreed to allow participation in the tripartite discussions of representatives of Nagorno-Karabakh. Armenians, with the knowledge, if not support, of the Armenian republic government in Yerevan, attacked Azerbaijani villages in Nagorno-Karabakh. Thus, while officials in Baku and Yerevan might have compromised over the administration of the Armenian minority concentrated in Nagorno-Karabakh, Armenians in the region took matters into their own hands against Azerbaijani villages, when troops of the former Soviet Ministry of the Interior deployed in the disputed area by Gorbachev were evacuated on orders from the Yeltsin government, which was worried about Russians getting caught between the combatants.

Russia wants a resolution of the conflict between Armenia and Azerbaijan because its continuation is bound to involve Iran, which has a small minority of Azerbaijani people. The Iranian government envisions a crisis that could compromise Iran's stability, security, and reputation in the Islamic world. At the very least, Iran has an interest in mediating between Armenia and Azerbaijan to preclude the interference of Turkey, which also is concerned about the development of ethnic nationalism in the Caucasus.

Developments in 1992 and 1993 underscored the elusiveness of a settlement of Armenian differences with Azerbaijan over Nagorno-Karabakh. In early 1992 Nagorno-Karabakh declared itself independent of Azerbaijan after 99 percent of voters endorsed that course in a referendum. By May 1992 Karabakh forces, backed covertly by Armenia, ousted the remnants of Azerbaijani authority. The Karabakh Armenians then began an offensive to obtain additional Azerbaijani territory outside the enclave to open a territorial link with metropolitan Armenia. By early September 1993, Karabakh forces had secured control of a large portion of southwestern Azerbaijan, bringing them almost to the Azerbaijani border with Iran. The Karabakh military and political leaders are also pushing the besieged Azerbaijani to negotiate with them and agree to Nagorno-Karabakh's independence, which is highly unlikely, given Azerbaijani determination to recover everything they have lost and the sympathy that they have from

Turkey and Iran. Moreover, neither Armenia nor Russia supports Karabakh's bid for complete independence, but they would be satisfied with a compromise that provides for Karabakh's administrative autonomy.

Karabakh Armenian forces tried in 1993 to make the Azerbaijani feel sufficiently desperate to accept, at the least, such a compromise. Already Azerbaijani people living in the path of the Karabakh campaign were suffering terribly, having to flee their homes to avoid what some have called an Armenian version of ethnic cleansing. The Armenian onslaught produced an horrendous Azerbaijani refugee problem with more than 1 million people in flight, not only for Azerbaijan itself but also for Iran.

Armenia and Russia want to avoid at all costs stirring up a crusade on behalf of the besieged Azerbaijani by the Muslim Turkic peoples in the region, fearing an endless and bitter conflict similar to the Civil War raging in Bosnia. Both Turkey and Iran have made their anxiety over the Karabakh offensive against Azerbaijan unmistakably clear: In August 1993 Iran publicly demanded the withdrawal of Karabakh forces from western Azerbaijan; and in September Turkey increased troop deployments along its frontier with Armenia, echoing Iran's call for an immediate withdrawal of foreign troops from Azerbaijan and warning Armenia of war. Turkey is especially sensitive to the Armenian territorial offensive in Azerbaijan. The Turks fear that Armenian territorial expansion into Azerbaijan will interfere with long-term plans to unify the Turkic peoples of Central Asia in the post-Communist era.

The ongoing war in Nagrono-Karabakh has encouraged political extremism in Azerbaijan. In May 1992, in the face of rising popular fury over his government's failure to control Nargorno-Karabakh and protect the Armenian minority there, President Ayaz Mutalibov resigned, only 6 months after a democratic election. He did not want to go along with the demands of nationalist forces in Azerbaijan for an all-out attack on Nagorno-Karabakh to defeat the Armenians once and for all. Popular Front leader Abulfez Elchibey, a radical nationalist committed to a fight to the finish to restore Azerbaijani control over Nagorno-Karabakh, was elected in June 1992 to replace Mutalibov. He wanted absolute independence for Azerbaijan, which meant pulling the country out of the C.I.S.

Elchibey's election, however, did not bring political stability to Azerbaijan. Throughout the remainder of 1992 and during most of 1993, disaffected ex-army officers, who had been relieved of their commands as a result of their failure to halt the Armenian offensive against Azerbaijani territory beyond Nagorno-Karabakh, went on a rampage against the government in Baku. They took top officials hostage and demanded the resignation of Prime Minister Panakh Guseinov. These rebel leaders and their followers, who may well have numbered in the thousands, with arms acquired from departing ex-Soviet forces, found an ally in Geidar Aliyev, a former Soviet Politburo member, KGB chief, and head of the Azerbaijani Communist Party in the 1980s.

Aliyev, the governor of Nakhichevan, the small Azerbaijani enclave in the Armenian republic on the Iranian frontier, made common cause with rebel leader Surat Huseynov, an ex-army officer who had gone into private business and had become a millionaire. Huseynov had the resources to help Aliyev attack Elchibey. By mid-1993 Elchibey was out of favor with the people, largely because of the steady losses to the Armenians. In June the Parliament named Aliyev its chairperson. When Elchibey fled Baku to avoid the possibility of capture by Huseynov's troops, the Parliament gave Aliyev presidential powers. In an August referendum, Azerbaijani voters overwhelmingly expressed no-confidence in Elchibey, opening the way for Aliyev to assume the presidency, with Huseynov as his prime minister. By the end of 1993, Aliyev was in charge of Azerbaijan.

The Yeltsin government had a hand in Aliyev's success. The Kremlin had little affection for Elchibey's nationalism and independence, especially regarding the Commonwealth. By contrast, Aliyev and his supporters were interested in restoring at least economic ties between Russia and Azerbaijan. Russian leaders, especially conservatives seeking to strengthen Russia's links with other ex-Soviet republics (like the resource-rich Azerbaijan) and concerned about a strengthening of Azerbaijani links to the Islamic world, especially Turkey and Iran, supported Aliyev's return to power. The Kremlin now offered to help the Azerbaijani in their war with the Karabakh Armenians. By November 1993 the Kremlin had military advisers in Azerbaijan to reorganize and strengthen the demoralized army.

Even without the effects of the war, the economy of Azerbaijan has been troubled by obsolete technology, decrepit transportation and communications infrastructures, and its extremely poor work ethic, a legacy of the Soviet era.

Economic conditions are no better in Armenia. By early 1993, Armenians were enduring hardships reminiscent of those following the earthquake of December 1988. Homes had no heat or hot water, and electricity was in short supply, rationed to 4 hours of use a day. To stay warm in the winter months, Armenians burned books, furniture, and telephone poles; still, thousands died of cold and starvation, mostly children and the elderly. There were food shortages, and prices were sky-high for everything. Agriculture and industry were almost at a standstill.

While the war in Azerbaijan certainly contributed to Armenia's hardships, trouble for Armenia's economy had started almost from the moment of the Soviet Union's collapse. Traditional patterns of trade were severely curtailed. Azerbaijan imposed an embargo on all trade with Armenia, which, consequently, lost its chief source of natural gas. Oil imports from Russia also declined for the same reason that they declined for other ex-Soviet republics: the Russians raised prices and wanted payment in hard currency. Furthermore, whatever oil was sold to Armenia was difficult to transport because the rail lines carrying Russian oil had to cross Georgia. Trains trying to crossing Georgia were frequently robbed or simply destroyed. The Georgian government taxed goods in transit by 30 percent. Adequate supplies of food could not enter Armenia from Turkey, which had its own grievances against Yerevan and no incentive to ease Armenian economic difficulties, while the war over Nagorno-Karabakh continued. Only an end of the war in Azerbaijan can bring some relief.

Central Asia

The ex-Soviet republics of Central Asia—Kazakhstan, Uzbekistan, Tajikistan, and Turkmenistan—also have experienced internal turmoil, much of it inspired by religiocultural differences long repressed by the Communist authorities. People throughout the region are recalling their religious roots. Indeed, there seems to be a virtual Islamic revival, with religion again playing a central role in both the cultural and political life of the region. As people turn away from Russia, the influence of Russian culture and language is diminishing. Many of the Central Asian peoples of the former Soviet Union dream of a vast Central Asian state, a revival of the old idea of a grand Turkestan.

While democracy is much talked about, there is little popular understanding of it, at least in the Jeffersonian sense of elected leaders and guarantees of basic rights. People talk about "Islamic democracy," in which the principles of equality and brotherhood, which come from Islamic teachings, play an important role. (Many think that Saudi Arabia, which has a monarchical autocracy, is an Islamic democracy.) What the peoples of Central Asia seem to want more than anything else is a government that will respect Islam and not abuse them, as the former Communist regimes did. And yet, having said this, it is also true that the peoples of Central Asia want internal order and security and have continued to support ex-Communist leaders who have renounced their Marxist origins and embraced Islam.

There appears to be a consensus in Central Asia in favor of keeping political pluralism to a minimum to assure stability and economic well-being. Political conservatives with little sympathy for the introduction of Western-style democracy have the power. They insist on political conformity and are ready to punish opponents. As long as they affirm their loyalty to Islam, the peoples of Central Asia seem willing to accept them; and the truly liberal democratic forces remain small, weak, and without much influence.

The Central Asian republics are extremely diverse and potentially conflict-ridden. Unity within some of them has been elusive, and there is certainly little unity among them beyond Islam. They have different political histories, cultural and linguistic characteristics, levels of economic wealth, and domestic and international ambitions. The commitment to economic reform varies from republic to republic. In addition, some of the republics have large ethnocultural minorities that are now demanding the same kind of autonomy—and, in some instances—independence that the republics sought of Moscow in 1991. The region's extraordinary diversity is best seen in a look at individual countries.

Tajikistan

Tajikistan is the most conflict-ridden of the ex-Soviet Central Asian republics. Internal conflicts brought full Civil War to Tajikistan, as neo-Communists and militant Islamic fundamentalists began fighting each other following the collapse of the Soviet State. Democratic elements and discontented poverty-stricken minorities, such as the Garmis and Pamiri Tajiks in the eastern part of the country who suffered under Communist rule, have tended to align with Islamists against the Communists.

From the beginning of the post-Soviet era, the Tajik Communists have been determined to hold power. They have opposed a succession of democratic- and religion-based political groups, in particular the Islamic Rebirth Party. The former head of the Tajik Communist Party, Rakhman Nabiyev, presided over a conservative Parliament beginning in 1991. Democratic-, Islamic-, and rural-based opposition groups relentlessly opposed Nabiyev. They condemned the corruption and repression of the Nabiyev order and spoke for the people living in eastern Tajikistan, who complained about the poverty of their villages and the evident discrimination against them by the Nabiyev regime. They also spoke for Tajiks living in the remote mountainous areas of the country, whose interests had been all but forgotten by the urban Marxist leaders in Dushanbe. Nabiyev drew most of his support from the tribal groups living in the western part of the country in the regions of Kurgan-Tyube, Kulyab, and Khodzhent.

In May 1992 opposition groups consisting of Islamists, democratic secularists, and representatives of the autonomous region of Badakhshan, in the eastern part of the republic, forced Nabiyev to flee the capital. Several days later he agreed to share power with the opposition, now calling itself the Union of Popular Forces, in a coalition cabinet with control of one-third of the ministries, including Defense and Interior, held by non-Communists. Nabiyev also promised to introduce political reforms democratizing the Tajik political system and to hold presidential elections in December 1992.

But very little changed in Tajikistan in the next several months. Demonstrations against the government increased. When no liberalization of the political order and no official acceptance of freedom of religion followed, the opposition demanded that Nabiyev resign.

Meanwhile, Afghan fundamentalists were slipping into Tajikistan with weapons to help the anti-Communists get rid of Nabiyev. In September 1992, when opposition deputies in the Parliament failed to get a no-confidence vote against Nabiyev, militant members of the opposition intercepted him at the airport and forced him to sign his resignation. Legislative and cabinet leaders opposed to Nabiyev now took over the government and promised a democratic political order. But social peace and stability have continued to be elusive.

In October 1992 the ex-Communists attacked the government in Dushanbe to restore Nabiyev to power. For the next few weeks, there was continuous fighting in the capital, forcing thousands to flee. In November 1992 the Communists regained power. Nabiyev decided to retire, and Sagkak Safarov, an ex-convict who had put together a powerful militia organization in the Kulyab region, took his place. He proceeded to take revenge against the religious and democratic opposition leaders, accusing them of treason, and with this policy provoked an escalation of the Civil War. By early 1993 probably 10 percent of the population, or about 500,000 people, had become refugees, and up to 40,000 people had been killed. Many Tajik refugees entered Uzbekistan; others fled into northern Afghanistan, inhabited by ethnic kin.

Russia and other neighboring republics, in particular Uzbekistan, worried that the Civil War could spread quickly throughout the region. At the end of 1992, Russia contributed the major portion of a C.I.S.–sponsored peacekeeping force of about 1,000 troops to try to maintain order in Dushanbe. Subsequently, Russian defense minister Grachev decided to send a much larger Russian contingent to prop up the Communist government. By February 1993 there were about 3,500 Russian troops in Tajikistan and 20,000 Russian military personnel. Grachev pledged to rebuild the Tajik Army and to provide Russian help at the frontier with Afghanistan. Meanwhile the Uzbek leadership, concerned about the safety of the large Uzbek minority in Tajikistan (about 25 percent of the total Tajik population), decided to back the Communists as the only political force capable of preventing the establishment of an Iranian-style fundamentalist regime.

Despite the large Russian military presence in Tajikistan, the Civil War continued, with militant fundamentalists from Afghanistan continuing to filter into Tajikistan to help the Islamic opposition. The Russians seemed unable either to get the Communist government in Dushanbe, now under Emomali Rakhmanov, to negotiate with the Islamists or to stop the infiltration of Afghan insurgents. Under Rakhmanov's leadership the Communist regime seemed determined to punish the opposition wherever it could, hoping eventually to destroy it. For example, progovernment militia forces carried out an ethnic cleansing–like policy against villages in Kurgan-Tyube, where religious-based opposition was suspected, reducing many of them to rubble. Although the government denied it, the evidence overwhelmingly supports the view of government complicity.

Although the Civil War might appear to be between Communists and fundamentalists, it really has to do with secular versus religious control of the country. The government of Tajikistan, made up of many ex-Communist Party members and retaining many of the symbols of the old Communist political order, like the hammer and sickle, is more pragmatic than it is ideologically communist. It has no clearly defined Marxist-Leninist orientation. It is more concerned with staying in power than in maintaining a Soviet-style socioeconomic order. Although the regime maintains state control over the industrial and agricultural sectors of the economy, it does so for practical considerations, such as the need to keep people employed, the absence of investment capital for privatization, and simple ambition to maintain control over the wealth of the country to assure continued political power.

Moreover, it seems that local Tajik Communists have intentionally exaggerated the threat of Islamic fundamentalism in Tajikistan. By talking about their country's vulnerability to subversion by Iranian-style fundamentalism, the leaders in Dushanbe are able to frighten the Russians into spending a lot of money to keep them in power. In fact, the Tajiks, like most other Muslim peoples in the Central Asian republics, belong to the Sunni sect of Islam, which predominates in Saudi Arabia, not the Shia (or Shiite) sect, to which most Iranians belong, thus suggesting that Tajiks as well as other Central Asian Muslims, even though ethnically related to Iranians, are less susceptible to influence building by Iran than appearances might suggest.

Nevertheless, fear of a fundamentalist-led revolution in Tajikistan is not groundless. The Islamic Rebirth Party has support throughout the country, despite the government's brutal efforts to suppress it. Fundamentalist leaders in Afghanistan, such as Gulbuddin Hekmatyar, present another reason for concern about fundamentalism in Tajikistan. Mindful of the porous character of the Tajik-Afghan frontier and aware of the appeal of its ethnic and fundamentalist ties with Tajikistan's Muslims, Russia and other Commonwealth members with large Muslim populations are determined to maintain a visible presence in Tajikistan and to support its secular government, regardless of its conservatism.

Kazakhstan

Post-Communist Kazakhstan, though somewhat less conflict-ridden than Tajikistan, also faces a problem that threatens its stability and material well-being. The large Russian minority, which constitutes 41 percent of Kazakhstan's population, is Christian, Slavic, predominant in the large urban centers, and heavily involved in the Kazakh bureaucracy. The Kazakhs comprise only 36 percent of Kazakhstan's population and are Muslim and Turkic. In the Soviet era, Kazakhs and Russians coexisted with little difficulty. In the post-Soviet era, President Nursultan Nazarbayev has gone out of his way to look out for the well-being of the Russian minority. He maintains Russian as the language of the administration and of business. He also ensured that a new Constitution for Kazakhstan makes the Russian language almost equivalent to the Kazakh language.

Nazarbayev also has tried to keep his political fences with Moscow in good repair. As soon as the Russian-dominated C.I.S. was established, Nazarbayev asked to join it and urged other Central Asian republics to follow his example. Many of his chief advisers are Russians, and he works closely with Moscow on important issues of common concern, like defense.

But there are clouds on the horizon. Kazakhstan, like other Central Asian republics, is vulnerable to ethnic conflict and civil unrest. For example, in June 1992 there was a vast, popular anti-Communist rally in Almy, the capital (formerly Alma-Ata), where thousands of people demanded the resignation of the Communist leadership. Opposition groups, including Islamists, demanded power sharing in the form of a coalition government. They were angry over Nazarbayev's continued dictatorship over the country as well as over the Communist monopoly of power that so far had ignored the views of the opposition.

This opposition to Nazarbayev can tap into latent Kazakh hostility to Russians dating back to the 1930s, when Stalin forcibly and brutally collectivized Kazakh agriculture, killing animals and causing starvation. Almost 50 percent of the republic's ethnic population died. Another potential source of resentment against Russians is Nazarbayev's economic reform program, especially privatization of public housing. Since the Russians have the money to buy state property being sold to private owners, a large-scale privatization program would enrich them enormously, at the expense of the Kazakh population.

Nazarbayev has tried to discourage anti-Russian feelings. For example, despite a willingness to modernize the Kazakh economy by introducing a free market, Nazarbayev has proceeded very slowly, especially with regard to privatization, restricting it to small service enterprises. He has also started to appoint Kazakhs to major posts in government ministries and in some cases has given Kazakhs priority in obtaining government contracts for their private firms.

Working to his advantage is Kazakhstan's geographic distance from Afghanistan and Iran. Also significant is the fact that Kazakhs are moderate Muslims and are at the moment not very susceptible to Islamic fundamentalist influence from Afghanistan and Iran. Also, foreign investors are attracted to Kazakhstan by Nazarbayev's sober leadership and by the prospect that the environment will remain conducive to earning big profits in the near future. Chevron from the United States and Elf from France have begun to sink substantial capital into oil exploration in Kazakhstan. The American cigarette company Phillip Morris is a potential large-scale investor in Kazakhstan's state-owned tobacco company.

Uzbekistan

Uzbekistan is one of the least ethnically diverse Central Asian republics, with 84 percent of its population made up of ethnic Uzbeks who are Sunni Muslim and Turkic in their religious and racial origins. Like Tajiks, Uzbeks, despite their ethnic connection with Iranians, are less interested in close ties to the theocratic Iranian government than to the secular system in Turkey, to which Uzbek president Islam Karimov looks as a model for his country's future political and economic development.

But one major ethnic problem waits to explode. Tajik minorities are restless in two Uzbekistan cities, Sammarkand and Tashkent, located in the easternmost section of Uzbekistan very near its frontier with Tajikistan. While they are called Uzbeks on their identity papers, something that disturbs them, they feel close to Tajikistan. But it has not yet been enough to provoke their active opposition to Karimov.

President Karimov nevertheless rules as if the Tajiks and the Uzbeks might explode into religious fervor and political expansion at any time. He rules Uzbekistan with an iron hand, tolerating no dissent—which, when it does try to manifest itself, is attributed, and wrongly so, to Islamic fundamentalism. There is really no political opposition, and in many ways the behavior of the Karimov regime today calls to mind the Communist dictatorships in the Soviet era. Indeed, post-Communist political development in Uzbekistan has changed very little since the disintegration of the Soviet Union.

The economic system also has changed very little. Karimov has proceeded very cautiously in the area of economic reform. He seems willing to follow the Russian reform model especially as it is now committed to a slow pace of change. He eschews any kind of shock therapy that would provoke economic hardships that could easily lead to political dissidence and challenges to his government. Moreover, Uzbekistan has inherited some severe economic problems from the Soviet era that could cause Karimov serious political problems. The Soviet government required that Uzbekistan grow cotton, but an overemphasis on cotton production prevented cultivation of food commodities. Karimov is now emphasizing the production of fruits and vegetables. Still, food is in short supply and very expensive for ordinary Uzbek workers. The government subsidizes prices for bread, rice, and other staples and cannot possibly consider price decontrol, despite a commitment to introduce the free market economy, without risking an explosion of social discontent. Still, many Uzbeks are depressed and pessimistic about their future well-being.

Like Nazarbayev in Kazakhstan, Karimov wants Western political backing and economic assistance, which will not be forthcoming without progress toward democracy and the free market. Like other leaders of the ex-Soviet republics, Karimov has to walk a fine line between the kind of authoritarian rule needed to lead the country successfully through the post-Communist transition and the expectations of the West for a complete break with the political and economic institutions of the Communist past. As compared to the leaderships of the other ex-Soviet republics Karimov has not done badly. His country has been free of civil war and is moving slowly toward a new liberal order that eventually should provide a better standard of living.

INTERNATIONAL PROBLEMS AND POLICIES

It is still not clear to what extent the leaders of Russia and the other former Soviet republics share the ancient anxieties about powerful neighbors on their frontiers. Some ex-Soviet officers have argued strongly and persuasively that the new independent republics, lacking the cohesion of the old Soviet Union, are indeed fair game for aggressive outsiders.

The former Soviet republics do share a need for economic, financial, and technical aid from the West. Some of the republics that have nuclear weapons, notably Russia, Ukraine, Belarus, and Kazakhstan, must assure the West that the nuclear weapons arsenal of the former Soviet state will be controlled and will not fall into the possession of foreign countries.

In addressing these and other international problems, the policies of Russia and the Eurasian republics are likely to follow the principles of New Thinking adopted by the Gorbachev leadership. This means an aversion to the use of force to further international interests and a readiness to cooperate with foreign countries in the solution of cross-national problems such as environmental decay. Political diplomacy and reliance on international organizations like the United Nations and the World Court are sufficient to protect national interests. The republics will also rely on confidence-building measures designed to improve interstate relations, and on international organizations, starting with the United Nations and including the International Monetary Fund and World Bank.

Nevertheless, each of the former Soviet republics seemed determined to pursue its own foreign policy goals, based on its self-perceived national interests. On the eve of the May 1992 C.I.S. summit in Moscow, a top-level Russian official, when asked if the Commonwealth had a future, replied without thinking twice, "It will scarcely keep in its present state." But he also observed that one could not rule out some sort of new union in the future.

Additional summit meetings took place in the second half of 1992 and during 1993, reflecting the interest of most of the ex-Soviet republics to continue discussing problems of mutual concern. At these meetings the C.I.S. leaders discussed the outbreak of ethnic conflicts and civil war, currency stabilization, interrepublic trade, the disposition of nuclear weapons, relations with the West, and other regional problems. At a July 1992 meeting, they set up a joint peacekeeping force. In March 1993 Russia, Kazakhstan, Uzbekistan, Armenia, Kyrgyzstan, and Tajikistan agreed to consider establishing a NATO-like collective security organization of ex-Soviet republics.

But the prospects of the ex-Soviet republics' developing a coherent approach to foreign relations dimmed considerably in June 1993, when defense ministers meeting in Moscow agreed to discontinue efforts at maintaining a unified defense structure and dissolved the C.I.S. joint military command. They replaced it on a temporary basis with a much down-graded body, called the "joint staff for coordinating military cooperation between the states of the Commonwealth." This led to the transfer of command of C.I.S. peacekeeping forces in places like Tajikistan, Moldova, and the Caucasus to Russia. Still, the ex-Soviet republics continued to discuss a collective security system and in August 1993 agreed to study the possibility of setting up a NATO-like organization with a common air and missile defense network. But by 1994 the C.I.S., in foreign relations as well as in other matters, remained what it had been at its beginning: an entity in which the individual parts were stronger than the whole.

Russian Foreign Policy

Major focal points of the Russian republic's foreign policy have been Europe, the United States, and Japan. The Yeltsin leadership seemed willing to continue the spirit as well as the substance of the conciliatory policies of the late Soviet government under Gorbachev.

Europe

Russia will continue to be concerned with Finland, the ex-Soviet Baltic republics of Estonia, Latvia, and Lithuania, Central/Eastern Europe, and Germany. In the early 1990s Yeltsin tried to strengthen Russia's relations with these countries to enhance Russian security and to obtain needed economic help.

Finland. Yeltsin agreed to abandon the Soviet Union's Finlandization policy, or the neutralization of Finnish international behavior imposed on Helsinki by the Stalinist government after World War II. This attempt to reduce Finish animosity toward Russia, which dates back to the Soviet invasion of Finland in 1939, will set the tone as the Russians develop economic ties with Helsinki.

The Finns welcome improved relations with Russia, for economic as well as strategic reasons. Historically, in the trade relationship between Finland and the former Soviet state, the Finns sent 25 percent of their exports to the Soviet Union. Goods ranging from giant icebreakers to tuxedos worn by Soviet musicians went to the Soviet Union in return for Soviet oil and gas. Finland needs Russia perhaps more than Russia needs Finland, judging from the economic dislocation that the Finns have suffered as a result of the collapse of the Soviet state and the ensuing decline in trade. Moreover, because Finland oriented its export industries toward the Russian market, it has still another incentive to expand trade with Russia.

The Baltic Republics. Post-Communist Russia must carefully and discreetly develop relations with the newly independent Baltic republics. The Baltic peoples, especially Lithuanians, are very sensitive about Russia because of the long and harsh Soviet administration. They have been trying to remove all traces of the Soviet presence, notably signs with the Cyrillic alphabet, statues of Lenin, and pictures of the hammer and sickle.

Trade is chaotic. Russia no longer sells and therefore no longer buys as it did in the past, causing hardship for the Baltic peoples, who are not yet prepared to buy from and sell to Western markets. Historic patterns of trade with Russia and other former Soviet republics have been completely disrupted.

Other Russo–Baltic problems are territorial. The Yeltsin government wants to continue to administer the Russian city of Kaliningrad, once part of Germany and strategically important to Russia because of its naval base on the Baltic. Kaliningrad, however, is territorially cut off from the rest of Russia by Lithuania and Poland. Also, about 128,000 officers and soldiers of the former Soviet Army are in the Baltic republics. These countries want them withdrawn immediately because of their fear that these troops could jeopardize their independence, say, in supporting a coup against the nationalist governments in Vilnius, Riga, and Tallinn.

There are large Russian minorities in each of the three Baltic states. Russia worries that they may face discrimination, especially since they were encouraged by successive Soviet leaderships to colonize the Baltic republics and were given privileged economic positions. Now many Russians in the Baltics consider themselves native and want to stay where their children were born. A possible straw in the wind of change for these Russians is the view of Estonian nationalist Tiit Made, a member of the Estonian Parliament in Tallinn, who said that the current 25 deputies representing Russians in the Parliament ought to be reduced to 7 or 8.

Despite these strains, Russia wants good relations with the Baltic republics to further its economic and strategic interests. Some hope—in vain—to bring the Baltic republics into the Commonwealth. In February 1992, in a conciliatory gesture, Russia agreed to begin an immediate withdrawal of former Soviet forces from Lithuania and to leave some weapons behind to bolster the Vilnius government. Yet the withdrawal of Russian forces has proceeded very slowly and still has far to go. During talks with representatives of the Baltic states, Moscow has argued that it cannot withdraw the troops because there is not enough housing in Russia to accommodate them.

In fact, the troops have remained for other reasons. In October 1992 Yeltsin suspended the Russian troop withdrawals, accusing the countries of infringing on rights of the 25 million Russians who are permanent residents. Russian military commanders have complained bitterly of unprovoked harassment of their troops by Baltic authorities, especially in Latvia and Estonia. Because a new citizenship law in Lithuania allows any residents to become citizens automatically, there is less of a problem for Moscow there than in Estonia and Latvia, which have been enacting rules that discriminate against Russian residents. Estonia and Latvia hope that the Russians will pack up and return to Russia, an unlikely event,

given the deep roots that many Russian residents now have in these countries.

Moscow also has been flustered by the efforts of the Baltic governments to establish economic independence of Russia. They have established their own currencies and tried to reorient their trade westward despite their historic dependence on Russian imports, especially oil and natural gas, and their substantial sales to the Russian market. Perhaps, Moscow may have reasoned, delaying the withdrawal of Russian troops and insisting that some bases remain under Russian control might inspire a rethinking of the Baltic countries' move to sever economic links with Russia. Finally, Yeltsin probably has kept Russian troops in place in response to pressure from influential civilian and military conservatives in the Moscow political establishment, many of whom were members of the Congress of Peoples' Deputies in 1992 and 1993, to do something to retain some Russian influence in the Baltics, if only for reasons of Russian territorial security.

The Baltic leaders and their peoples distrust these explanations, fearing a restoration of Russian political and military influence in the region. In 1992 they accused Yeltsin of playing politics in order to curry favor with his conservative rivals by showing them he can be tough with the Baltics.

The future of Russian relations with the Baltic states, however, may be less bleak for Russia than appearance suggests. The Baltics are and will remain economically weak and strategically vulnerable; they need friendship with Russia. Moreover, despite their shared fight for independence in 1991, the Baltic Republics have a traditional reluctance to cooperate closely with one another as a result of differences in language, culture, and history. In 1992, for example, according to World Bank figures, less than 10 percent of their combined foreign trade volume came from intra-Baltic trade. At the same time, more than 50 percent of their exports went to Russia, and, with the exception of Latvia, more than 50 percent of their imports were from Russia. Moreover, Russia is likely to remain their chief trading partner for a long time, because Baltic exports cannot compete yet in the Western market, and the countries lack the foreign exchange to buy Western goods.

The Russians would like to participate in the region's growing economic strength. The Baltic states, which always enjoyed incomes and living standards higher than those in the rest of the Soviet Union, are moving toward free market economies fairly quickly. Inflation dropped from 600 percent in 1991 to about 10 percent by the end of 1993 in all 3 countries. Local currencies, freed from the ruble, have become stable and freely convertible on Western exchange markets, and shortages are quickly disappearing, through prices for food and other commodities remain quite high.

A straw in the wind of change in Russo–Baltic relations is an apparent decline of anti-Russian feelings in the Baltic countries. In parliamentary and presidential elections in Lithuania, ex-Communists, who wanted to strengthen ties with Moscow, replaced nationalists. In the November 1992 parliamentary elections, the Democratic Labor Party, made up principally of Communists who had supported Gorbachev's perestroika, won an absolute majority. And in presidential elections held in February 1993, Algirdas Brazauskas, the party's leader, who favored a policy of reconciliation with Russia, defeated nationalist President Vytautas Landsbergis.

The shift toward ex-Communists and to Brazauskas reflected a popular interest in having a different leadership try to mitigate some of the hardships that Lithuanians were experiencing as a result of their economic transitions. Lithuanian voters were weary of excessively nationalistic but managerially inept leadership and preferred experienced administrators, most of whom had been Communist. Brazauskas struck a responsive chord in promising to reverse his predecessor's economic isolationism and open the country to foreign investment and slow the rate of change away from socialism. He particularly focused on agriculture, where there was a lot of opposition to the replacement of collective farms with private ones, which had great difficulty getting started. Indeed, conditions were so bad during 1993 that Lithuania, which in the past had supplied meat to much of the Soviet Union, was now importing it from Germany just to meet local demand.

On taking power, Brazauskas moved quickly to improve his country's strained relations with Russia. One of the first steps he took was to drop the provocative demand endorsed by Landsbergis that Russia pay Lithuania $146 billion in reparations for the costs to the country of the Soviet occupation. He insisted that Lithuania look to the future rather than the past in developing relations with Russia. Brazauskas's conciliatory approach facilitated the Russian troop withdrawal in September 1993. In October Lithuania became the first Baltic nation to reach a trade agreement with Russia.

There was evidence of a slight softening of anti-Russian feelings also in Estonia. In late 1993 the Estonian government decided to allow nonresidents to vote in local elections. When local elections were held in October and November 1993, Russian candidates, many of them ex-Communists advocating a policy of reconciliation and accommodation toward Russia, won a substantial number of seats. While some nationalists expressed alarm over the prospect of a resurgence of Communist and Russian influence in Estonia, others saw the election results as a positive step toward the achievement of domestic political stability and a new, productive relationship with Russia.

Nevertheless, relations between Russia and the Baltic states remain problematical. Yeltsin has opposed the membership of Central/Eastern European countries in NATO, although he told Polish president Lech Walesa in August 1993 that Russia would not object to Polish membership in the Western alliance. Many Baltic nationalists now argue that Russia wants to restore its influence in the region. Their fears increased with the election to the Russian Parliament of Vladimir Zhirinovsky along with a number of his followers from the Liberal Democratic Party who have asserted that the Baltic states should be part of Russia.

The Latvian government, which was negotiating to get the Russians to withdraw their remaining troops (about 12,000) in January 1994, was especially alarmed, because Russians outnumbered ethnic Latvians and because Yeltsin was delaying the evacuation of Russian forces. Riga appealed to the Clinton administration for support when the Kremlin demanded that the Skundra radar base and other facilities, such as the port of Liepajua used by the Russian Baltic fleet, remain in Russian hands in return for a full military evacuation. Politicians in Riga insisted that the Russians leave Latvia uncondtionally and completely. Indeed, the Latvians became somewhat hysterical over the continuing presence of the Russian military and complained that the presence of Russian troops discouraged foreign investment and retarded Latvian economic development, to say nothing of offering opportunities for confrontation that could lead to conflict between the two countries.

The Clinton administration has been caught in a dilemma in responding to Baltic appeals for help to get the Russians out. On the one hand, Washington supports Yeltsin and does not want to do anything to strengthen his conservative rivals, say, by expressing support for Baltic nationalism and pressuring the Kremlin to accelerate its military evacuation from the region. At the same time, however, the administration sympathizes with the efforts of the Estonians and Latvians to negotiate the Russian military out of their countries, especially in light of Zhirinovsky's success in the December 12 parliamentary elections, and has stated publicly its support for withdrawal. To avoid antagonizing either side, however, Washington has proceeded cautiously, refusing to go beyond rhetoric.

Central/Eastern Europe. Russia's interests in Central/Eastern Europe parallel those of the late Soviet Union and again center on trade and security. But the former Soviet satellites are hypersensitive to links that in any way would compromise their newly won sovereignty, never mind obstruct their inexorable orientation westward.

Russia and Poland tangled over the speed of Moscow's withdrawal of former Soviet forces from Poland and the rapid decline of Russian trade. While Yeltsin pledged to have all Soviet troops out of Poland by the end of 1992, much earlier than was originally envisaged, the troops were literally stripping the areas they occupied of everything that was removable and leaving the facilities they used in profound disrepair. Polish officials were furious and presented the Russian government with demands for huge monetary compensation. Nevertheless, the Yeltsin government remained true to its pledge on troop withdrawal. The last Russian combat force deployed in Poland pulled out on October 18, 1992, although 6,000 noncombat forces, concerned with transportation and communication, remained in Poland to assist in the Russian troop withdrawal from eastern Germany.

Trade remains a problem in Polish–Russian relations. In the early 1990s the Russian government sharply curtailed the delivery of oil and natural gas to Poland, primarily as a result of a decline of output caused by problems connected with machine maintenance and strikes. The Russian move caused havoc in the already enfeebled Polish economy. Polish factories had to reduce operations, and overall productivity declined. Since the Polish economy had not yet developed new import–export relationships with the West, this problem meant a crippling setback to Poland's plans for economic recovery.

The West. While relations between post-Communist Russia and the West are good, there have been problems. Many conservatives in the Russian Parliament and military are ultra-nationalistic and critical of Yeltsin's friendliness with the West. Upset with the loss of Russian influence and prestige in the international community and with the weakening of the Soviet Army, these nationalists have argued that Russia has different global interests than the West and must chart its own course.

Yeltsin has resisted much of the nationalists' pressure because he needs the West, especially its financial assistance. He needs to stabilize the currency and reduce an enormous budget deficit while trying to preserve a social cushion for the many Russians who suffer as the government moves toward free enterprise. The West, namely, in this case, the so-called Group of Seven (G-7) industrial powers, which includes Japan, has promised more than $28 billion in credit to Russia. But only a small fraction of that amount has actually been disbursed, despite Yeltsin's frequent admonitions that the failure of the West to provide assistance makes real economic reform difficult and supports the cause of the most reactionary political elements.

Unfortunately for Yeltsin and his reformist colleagues, the request for help has come at a very bad time for the West, with its sagging economies besieged by recession and high budget deficits. The discretionary money simply has not been available for foreign aid. Furthermore, Western political leaders and their economic advisers have argued that large-scale financial aid to Russia prior to that country's bringing down inflation and reducing the budget deficit would disappear into a bottomless pit of monetary chaos.

This has left the issue of aid disbursement to the International Monetary Fund and the World Bank. The two credit-granting agencies, however, have found this task too much for them. Acting like the bankers they are, IMF and World Bank officials have insisted that Russia pursue the same belt-tightening policies expected of other would-be clients. Yet Yeltsin could not risk a further decline in already marginal living standards for most Russians and giving support to the radical right. Therefore, he did not receive most of the West-

ern credits promised him. By early 1994 World Bank officials were willing to soften the conditions on which they would advance credits, but they had disbursed only about $1.5 billion to Russia. Ordinary Russians, never mind Yeltsin and his reformist supporters, such as Geidar and Fyodorov, were disappointed and disillusioned. They even spoke of a Western "betrayal" of Russia in moves away from communism.

Another issue in Russian relations with the West has involved NATO. The Russian attitude toward NATO has changed considerably since the end of 1992, when Yeltsin wanted Russian membership. During 1993 the question of Central/Eastern European membership in NATO was raised by Poland, Hungary, and the Czech Republic. At first Russia did not object, but in October 1993, in response to the pressure of nationalistic politicians, including military leaders, Yeltsin reversed himself and insisted that Russia did not want its former allies joining NATO. He warned the Western powers that their relationship with Russia would suffer if they admitted the Central/Eastern European countries.

The NATO issue has for the time being been settled by a compromise. In deference to Moscow, the NATO leadership agreed in January 1994 to defer indefinitely full membership of the Central/Eastern European countries and offered them an innocuous "partnership for peace" that invites their cooperation with the Alliance but denies them security guarantees. Nevertheless, the dispute has created a chill in the East–West relationship.

A real test of the New Russia and its relations with the West has concerned the Civil War in Bosnia-Herzegovina. At first Yeltsin was inclined to cooperate with the West in handling the crisis. He accepted the Western sanctions policy against Serbia, having no real affection for Milosevic's territorial ambitions in the former Yugoslavia despite Russia's historic friendship with Serbia. To Yeltsin, Milosevic was a mischief maker who was interfering with Yeltsin's efforts to strengthen Russian ties to the West.

However, in 1992 and 1993, nationalists in the Russian Congress of Peoples' Deputies and Supreme Soviet insisted that Russia stand by Serbia because of their shared ethnic, religious, and linguistic background. Russian nationalists had little sympathy for the Muslim side in the Bosnian Civil War and equated it with the same kind of Islamic fundamentalism that has threatened Russian political stability in the Caucasus and Central Asia.

Influenced by the power of the nationalists, Yeltsin took several steps that brought Russia into conflict with Western policy in Yugoslavia. In January 1993 Russian military intelligence officers signed a secret agreement to supply $300 million worth of arms, including tanks and sophisticated missiles, to Serbia and Serb-controlled areas of Bosnia and Croatia, even though this violated the international arms embargo that Russia had agreed to support. Then, in April 1993, the Yeltsin government announced that it could not support an American-sponsored proposal at the United Nations to toughen existing sanctions against Serbia. And in June 1993 Russia announced its opposition to any plan to arm the Muslim side, saying that it would veto such action in the UN Security Council. At the same time, Moscow planned to supply the Serb republic with desperately needed natural gas. Although the Russians insisted that the gas was for humanitarian purposes, such as the heating of homes and hospitals, the United States, backed by Britain, vehemently opposed a Russian effort to obtain a UN waiver of the sanctions against Serbia and Montenegro prohibiting such a deal. Since all the decisions of the UN Security Council committee that oversees the operation of the sanctions must be unanimous, the Americans were able to torpedo the Russian effort.

Finally, in the beginning of 1994, Yeltsin's government criticized NATO's decision to use air strikes against the Bosnia Serbs, whose artillery was bombarding Sarajevo and causing tremendous civilian casualties. Yeltsin skillfully used diplomacy with the Bosnian Serbs to avert the threatened air strikes. While the West welcomed his initiatives, it was uncomfortable over the way they favored the Serb side. At the same time, the Yeltsin government never denounced, refuted, or rejected Zhirinovsky's public assertion during a brief visit to Serbia in January 1994 that a Western attack on Serbs would be considered a Western attack on Russians.

Germany.   Yeltsin has looked to Germany for aid. In 1991 he went to Germany to meet with political and economic leaders. He strengthened Russo–German relations by signing a statement with Chancellor Kohl pledging cooperation in a wide range of areas, including arms control, scientific research, and the protection of minorities. Kohl added that Germany was very interested in helping Russia exploit its vast oil and gas reserves and complimented Yeltsin for his stalwart commitment to reform. Yeltsin reciprocated by affirming the end of any hostility between the two nations generated in World War II.

But Yeltsin's effort to deal with the problem of the German minority living in Russia, the so-called Volga Germans, has been difficult. This issue concerns the fate of 2 million ethnic Germans who were deprived by Stalin of their administrative autonomy following the German invasion of the Soviet Union in June 1941. The former Volga German autonomous republic occupied an area straddling the Volga River, in the vicinity of the northwest tip of the Caspian Sea, of about 11,000 square miles. At that time Stalin also moved about 400,000 Volga Germans to Siberia in retaliation for the Nazi invasion. Bonn has asked Yeltsin to honor a pledge he gave Kohl to restore an autonomous republic to the 2 million Volga Germans. Bonn expects that restoration of the old Volga republic, with guaranteed rights for Germans, will discourage their mass migration to Germany.

Yeltsin's main problem in accommodating Bonn on this issue is the resistance of Russians who were transplanted in the late 1940s and afterward and who now oppose German administrative control. Yeltsin has said that the boundaries of any autonomous republic for the Volga Germans will include only the territory where 90 percent of the population are German. He has offered an area that is about 1,900 square miles in size. The Volga Germans have rejected this offer and have looked to Bonn for support of their claim to the original size of their republic.

The United States.   Yeltsin has gone out of his way to cultivate good relations with Washington. In January 1992, in a visit to the United Nations in New York, Yeltsin announced that Russia is an ally of the United States, thus officially declaring an end to the cold war. Washington has responded to Yeltsin's overtures with caution and restraint.

In the weeks and months following the anti-Gorbachev coup and the replacement of the Soviet state with the Commonwealth, the Bush administration let events get ahead of it. The U.S. Congress took the lead, appropriating $100 million for the members of the C.I.S. to dismantle nuclear weapons, to transport emergency supplies of food and medicine, and to catalyze private sector involvement in the post-Soviet economy.

But the Congress certainly did not invest much, considering the mammoth problems of the new Commonwealth. There there remains considerable reluctance to undertake an aid program of Marshall Plan dimensions. Critics say that massive aid programs to the former Soviet republics should await the replacement of all authoritarian structures by genuine democracy. Some U.S. economists have argued that massive short-term aid is not what the Soviets need. In their view, technological and managerial assistance to increase the efficiency of the transportation and communications infrastructure are more important than credits to buy American goods. Moreover, they argue, virtually all the resources for restructuring and rebuilding the Russian economy should come from private foreign investors and from the downsizing of the former Soviet military. Because Russia lacks basic institutions such as property rights, a commercial code, and sound money without which markets cannot work, many Western economists believe that money from abroad would be wasted, stolen, or, worse, would dampen the spontaneous growth of the private sector by strengthening the old bureaucracy.

Another issue in Russo–American relations is how nuclear materials and the know-how of atomic scientists of the former Soviet government will be handled. The old Soviet state exercised a tight and efficient control over the movement of goods and personnel across internal as well as foreign borders, and this meant control over nuclear and other strategic technologies and expertise. To the dismay of U.S. leaders, the Commonwealth seems unable to duplicate this control.

The United States wanted Russian cooperation in the negotiation of further reduction in nuclear arsenals. While Yeltsin assured the United States that he and the leaders of the other republics intended to abide by the arms-control treaties signed by Gorbachev, the Bush administration wanted to go further in arms reduction, especially in multiwarhead missiles, which are the core of each country's nuclear capability. On the eve of the president's State of the Union address in January 1992, U.S. Defense Department officials proposed sharp reductions in U.S. land-based, multiple-warhead missiles without any conditions, while other cuts might be offered if the other republics acted reciprocally.

In June 1992 Bush and Yeltsin signed an agreement providing for the elimination of all of Russia's most powerful SS-18 multiple warhead missiles and the reduction of the warheads of each side to a combined total of 7,000, or 3,500 for each, down from the existing level of 22,500. But shortly afterward the Russians indicated that they wanted to retain some SS-18 missile silos and some SS-19 missiles. In November 1992 the Russian Parliament ratified the START I pact concluded in 1991 by Bush and Gorbachev, providing for substantial reduction in short-range nuclear weapons. Agreement on long-range weapons, however, remained elusive with the Kremlin demanding exceptions and adjustments that would allow them to retain some of the missiles they had originally agreed to destroy.

Once START I is implemented, the way will open for START II, negotiated in the fall of 1993. START II provides for the elimination of all land-based, multiple-warhead missiles, including Russia's SS-18s. It would reduce the number of strategic warheads on both sides, from 22,500 to 6,500. Washington did make some concessions that will allow the Russians to maintain a credible deterrent. But START II cannot become operative until START I does, and START I cannot become operative until it is accepted by the other ex-Soviet republics with nuclear capability. By 1994 Belarus and Kazakhstan had accepted it, but Ukraine was holding out. Nationalists in the Ukrainian Parliament wanted to retain some kind of nuclear arsenal to protect Ukraine from possible Russian expansionism.

Another problem in Russo–American relations is Moscow's influence in the republics of the Caucasus and Central Asia. A transitional Russian military presence in the former Soviet republics to assure stability and the basic rights of the ethnic Russian populations is understandable. But in some places Russian military units have been meddling in the domestic politics of independent states. In the summer of 1993, U.S. foreign policy officials discussed forming a peacekeeping mission in the ex-Soviet lands in cooperation with the United Nations. To this end the Clinton administration created a new post of coordinator of regional affairs within the State Department's Office of Newly Independent States. The post was to be filled by James Collins, deputy chief of the U.S. embassy in Moscow. American economic assistance to Russia would be conditioned on its willingness to resolve disputes with other ex-Soviet states peacefully. This idea gained some strength with the assassination in

August 1993 of Fred Woodruff, a CIA agent working for President Shevardnadze in Georgia.

But, to the relief of Moscow, which was beginning to see this plan as an unjustified intrusion into its affairs, the Clinton administration did not go forward with it, perceiving that too many Russians would see it as humiliating and that it would be politically dangerous to Yeltsin and the reformers.

Russo–American relations have also been strained over Russia's sales of nuclear technology to Third World countries, in particular to China, Iran, Syria, and Libya. These sales, in Washington's view, undermine U.S. nuclear nonproliferation policy and strengthen some of the most troublesome adversaries of the United States. The United States is particularly disturbed by Russian arms sales to China of missile guidance technology, rocket engines, and other advanced weapons systems. Washington worries that the Chinese will use the technology not only for themselves but to improve the design of nuclear plants, making them attractive to Third World buyers.

Typical of this particular problem in the Russo–American relationship was Russian shipment of rocket-fuel ingredients to Libya in 1993. According to U.S. intelligence, the deal with Libya began when Pavoks, a Moscow company, exported to Libya 80 tons of ammonium perchlorate, a chemical used to make solid rocket fuel. The sale of this chemical is forbidden under the international agreement known as the Missile Control Regime, which restricts technology sales. Although Russia is not a party to this agreement, it had said that it was observing its provisions.

The Russo–Libyan deal has presented the Clinton administration with a dilemma. Under U.S. law trade, sanctions must be applied against companies that violate the Missile Control Regime. In addition, the act providing aid to Russia calls for development assistance to be cut off if Moscow violates the controls. Clinton could issue a waiver, but such a move would imply that he is more interested in helping Russia than in promoting weapons control and guarding against potential difficulties with the aggressive Libyan government.

The United States was also annoyed by the Russian sale of rocket-engine technology to India in June 1993, forbidden by international agreements. The Russians said that they had a contract with India worth $400 million that they would fulfill. In any event, they said, Washington had no business interfering with legitimate Russian commercial policy. Yeltsin was open to compromise, however, and in July the Kremlin said that after completion of this deal, it would not make any others.

Russia also has provoked Washington by helping Syria acquire special equipment to operationalize its missile capability. Sometime in the summer of 1993, the Russians provided planes to carry special truck bodies from North Korea to Syria for use in mobile missile launchers. Concerned that the shipment could add to Syria's military potential against

Israel, the Clinton administration asked the Kremlin to stop the planes before they left North Korea. The Russians ignored the American request, saying that a private Russian company was involved and that it had no legal authority to interfere. But the Russian government has officially tried to discourage helping North Korea's export of arms abroad because of Americans' sensitivity on this issue.

The Clinton administration decided to keep the matter under wraps for a while, accepting Moscow's position that it had no authority and acknowledging that the hard currency earnings from the deal were desperately needed. But it was also true that the administration again was protecting Yeltsin in his ongoing conflict with conservative forces in the Congress of Peoples' Deputies by not doing anything that could strengthen the argument that ties with the Americans were not in Russia's best interests. In this spirit the State Department eventually decided that the Russian role deserved no further attention by the U.S. government and that Russia had done nothing illegal. Still, the situation illustrates the problems that Washington has in dealing with Russia in the post-Communist era. Russian central authority is weak, the Russians are trying to earn money wherever they can, given their need of hard currency, and the United States' overriding concern is to avoid weakening or undermining Yeltsin because of his genuine commitment to change. These concerns are also apparent in the debates over U.S. economic aid to Russia as well as the question of full membership in NATO for Poland, Hungary, and the Czech Republic.

Japan.   In early 1992 Japan insisted that it could not extend a major economic aid program to Russia without a settlement of the issue of the offshore islands in the northern Pacific (Etoforu, Kunashiri, Shikotan, and the Habomais group). Japan was willing to provide emergency food and medical assistance to Russia and to go forward with a consortium, led by the Mitsui Corporation, to undertake exploration of reserves of oil and gas off Sakhalin Island. Private Japanese investors, however, were reluctant to go into Russia without government guarantees, which will not be forthcoming unless Russia returns the offshore islands to Japanese sovereignty.

A transfer of the islands to Japan is problematical for strategic and nationalistic reasons. The Russian government, like its Soviet predecessor, considers the islands, despite their small size and population and lack of mineral resources, important to the security of Russia because of their proximity to its Pacific missile and naval deployments.

With billions in loans, technology, and development assistance from Japan at stake, Yeltsin tried to accommodate Tokyo. In March 1992 Russian military officials announced a "demilitarization" of the islands, and a Russian public television program suggested that two of the four disputed islands, Shikotan and Habomai, could be returned. On the other hand, the Kremlin would not agree to a Japanese proposal that Russia acknowledge Japanese sovereignty over the islands, in return for which Japan would accept a later date for the actual restoration of Japanese control. Under continuous pressure from nationalists in the Congress of Peoples' Deputies, Yeltsin refused to let go of the islands. Negotiations over the summer of 1992 led nowhere. Yeltsin complained publicly in August that Japan was the only country that had not yet invested a penny in Russia and asked what kind of relationship could the Japanese expect when they would contribute nothing. To the chagrin of Japanese leaders, Yeltsin postponed a summit set for September 1992.

The issue of the islands seemed way out of proportion to their real importance for either the Russians or the Japanese. The Japanese wondered why, if the Russians had already retreated in Central/Eastern Europe and Afghanistan, couldn't they retreat on the islands, especially if doing so would carry a large financial payoff. The answer lies partly in Russian pride. Giving up the islands seemed to be the last straw of retreat from former greatness. Moreover, Japan had been the historic enemy of Russia and a threat to its security. Now it was acting with what Russians thought was unsurpassed arrogance; after all, the Soviet Union had won the islands in World War II. finally, the Russian political establishment was inclined to be stubborn with the Japanese for another reason: They thought that the Japanese were intentionally exploiting Russia's weakness and vulnerability as it moved through the post-Communist transition.

Relations between Moscow and Tokyo at the end of 1992 consequently were at an all-time low. The issue of the islands seemed in permanent stalemate, with neither side willing to make a major concession. Indeed, in September 1992 Yeltsin announced that the islands were going to be developed by Russia and would be open to foreign investment.

Russo-Japanese relations have since remained unchanged: correct but cool. When Yeltsin went finally to Tokyo for a summit with Japanese leaders in October 1993, both sides were polite. Yeltsin apologized publicly for the Soviet Union's harsh treatment of an estimated 600,000 Japanese prisoners in Siberia after World War II. But the Japanese denied his request for a warming of relations and their participation in Russian economic development. When Yeltsin promised a completed Russian demilitarization of the islands, the Japanese did not react at all.

Japanese political leaders would make no concession on aid, despite much pressure from Japan's allies to do something generous to help out. Some in the Japanese government insisted that unless some help were offered, Yeltsin might not survive, and hence this might be the last time Japan would have an opportunity to improve relations with a moderate, democratically inclined government in Moscow. But, lest there be a misunderstanding about the official Japanese position, a foreign policy official asserted that for Tokyo, the bottom line was a Russian acknowledgment of Japanese sovereignty over the islands.

Ukrainian Foreign Policy

Since Ukraine achieved independence in August 1991, its foreign policy has been driven primarily by a search for security, especially vis-à-vis Russia. Ukrainians fear more than anything else an attempt by Russia to reassert its control over their country. Ukraine's vulnerability arises out of several circumstances, not least is the large non-Ukrainian minority (44 percent of the total Ukrainian population of about 52 million people), most of whom are Russian and a perennial object of Russian concern. Moreover, Ukraine has only one-third the population of Russia and is dependent on Russian energy imports for its economic well-being.

Russia has some responsibility for deterioration of Ukraine's economy in the early 1990s, because of its restrictive policy on energy exports. In addition, Russia is part of the ongoing civil conflicts in the Caucasus and has significant political and military influence in other ex-Soviet republics that threatens Ukraine. Making matters worse for Ukraine is Ukraine's geographic isolation and the fact that its relations with Central/Eastern Europe are not sufficiently good so to make possible an alliance or even an entente with those countries. At the same time, Ukraine does not seem to be a candidate for membership of any kind in NATO, which would be very reluctant to provide even the slightest commitment to protect Ukrainian security, given the likelihood that such a commitment might lead NATO into difficulty with Russia. Under these circumstances, Ukraine has tried to protect its security by keeping as much of the Soviet military machine located on its territory as possible.

In developing its army, Ukraine has had to take into account the large Russian minority in its officer corps. Indeed, some ethnic Ukrainian army officers doubt the reliability of the army in a military crisis with Russia. The government in Kiev has tried to strengthen the army's loyalty by insulating it as far as possible from economic hardship. Nevertheless, the Ukrainian Army is not the preferred, first line of defense at the moment. Rather, Ukrainian political leaders are putting their faith in Ukraine's nuclear arsenal inherited from the former Soviet state—the third-largest nuclear arsenal in the world.

This arsenal, however, has placed the Ukrainian leadership in Kiev in a difficult dilemma. Ukraine has been under tremendous pressure from Russia and the United States to transfer its nuclear weapons to Russia. President Kravchuk has been the focus of these pressures, which he has tried to resist but has been obliged from time to time to accommodate. Kravchuk recognizes that Ukraine would have great difficulty using the ex-Soviet nuclear weapons successfully, for both strategic and technical reasons. He also understands better than most of his countrymen the risks of provoking the frustration and anger of the two powers that are best able to assure Ukraine's security and material well-being.

Kravchuk's readiness to destroy some weapons and transfer others to Russia has been steadily and significantly op-posed by the Ukrainian Parliament. Nationalists have a substantial influence, and they worry that denuclearization will deprive Ukraine of an important means of defense and leverage with other parts of the former Soviet Union. In 1992 and 1993, there was a running battle between Kravchuk and the Parliament, in which Kravchuk would make promises about denuclearization of Ukraine's weapons arsenal to Russia and the United States only to have them stonewalled by the Parliament.

Typical of the stalemate was the Parliaments' treatment of the START I missile pact, which Kravchuk had accepted. The Parliament did conditionally ratify START I in November 1993, but it refused to approve making Ukraine a nuclear-free state. Furthermore, it indicated that it would dismantle the Ukrainian nuclear arsenal only gradually, and only after numerous conditions concerning financial and security guarantees were met. The Parliament wanted several billion dollars in American financial assistance and a Russian pledge to respect the political independence and territorial integrity of Ukraine in terms of population and boundaries in return for complete nuclear disarmament. Short of these conditions, the Parliament insisted, Ukraine would keep missile launchers and warheads. It also refused to make Ukraine party to the nuclear nonproliferation treaty.

But Yeltsin and Clinton kept the pressure up on Kravchuk. In December 1993 Yeltsin signed a treaty with Kravchuk providing for a Russian guarantee of Ukraine's boundaries at the time of independence, thus closing off any legal steps on Russia's part to claim Ukrainian territory inhabited by Russian minorities. And in January 1994, on the eve of his summit meeting in Moscow with Yeltsin, Clinton promised Kravchuk substantial American assistance to offset the costs of nuclear disarmament. In a gesture intended to further gratify the Ukrainian leader, Clinton invited him to ride in Air Force 1 from Kiev to Moscow to meet Yeltsin and confirm these Russian–American concessions. Kravchuk then resubmitted the START I treaty without conditions for the Ukrainian Parliament's approval. There the matter rested in early 1994.

Whether the nationalist politicians in Kiev will acquiesce in Kravchuk's commitment to Ukrainian denuclearization remains to be seen. The bellicose rhetoric of Russian ultra-nationalist Zhirinovsky, who has said that Ukraine belongs back under Russian control, may well reignite Ukrainian fears of Russian aggression and harden the position of Ukrainian nationalists.

The Central Asian Republics and the Outside World

While committed to good relations with the West and with their rich and powerful Slavic neighbors—Russia and Ukraine—the five Central Asian republics of the former Soviet Union (Kazakhstan, Uzbekistan, Turkmenistan, Tajikistan, and Kyrgyzstan) have focused increasing attention on Central Asia and the Middle East. They have special strategic, economic, and religiocultural interests in India, Pakistan, Iran, Turkey, Saudi Arabia, and Afghanistan.

Relations with Other Islamic Countries

The Central Asia republics have found Islamic countries to be very interested in developing close relations with them. Conservative Islamic countries such as Saudi Arabia and other Persian Gulf members of the Gulf Cooperation Council have begun to channel economic assistance to them with the aim of discouraging their orientation toward countries such as Iran. Indeed, a fierce competition for supremacy in Soviet Central Asia seems to be in the making between Turkey and Iran and between Saudi Arabia and Pakistan.

The governments of the Central Asian Republics have a special interest in Turkey. Its Western orientation and its apparent success as a secular state with an Islamic population with democratic institutions and a free market make it a model. While these considerations appeal to the ex-Soviet elites who are not infatuated with Islamic fundamentalism, ordinary people have shown a sympathy for the Iranian model of a state governed by Islamic law. If Western-inspired economic reforms, especially in the smaller and poorer republics such as Tajikistan and Turkmenistan, fail to improve economic output, a susceptibility to Islamic fundamentalism as an alternative to the secular governments that now rule them is likely to increase. If that happens Iran will gain an advantage over other Islamic countries in strengthening ties with ex-Soviet republics in Central Asia.

Working against Iranian interests in the Central Asian republics are their secular legacy from the long period of Communist rule and the fact that many of the region's Muslims are Sunni, not Shia (Shi'ite), as in Iran. Kyrgyzstan president Askar Akayev has denounced Islamic fundmentalism and expressed a preference for links with Turkey. The prospect that Iranian fundamentalism will sweep through the former Soviet republics in Central Asia seems unlikely, since Iran has not been such a success story that everyone wants to emulate it. When former Azerbaijan president Mutalibov was asked about the threat of Iranian influence, he dismissed the question as "stupid."

In February 1992 diplomats from Iran, Pakistan, and Turkey met in Teheran to welcome the leaders of the five Central Asian republics and of Muslim Azerbaijan to a regional summit of Central Asian Islamic countries. They pushed forward an economic cooperation organization with three of the former Soviet republics: Turkmenistan, Uzbekistan, and Azerbaijan.

But cooperation so far remains elusive, with the Turks and Iranians, long rivals, holding different concepts of Islamic solidarity. The Turks want to create an Islamic version of the European Community in Central Asia, while Iran, supported by Pakistan, wants to emphasize the religious and cultural component of the community of Central Asian Islamic states. Nevertheless, discussion of tariff reductions, a common market for agricultural products, and the creation of a common development bank to compete with a Saudi-based Islamic bank already operating in Central Asia comprise the beginning of an Islamic-based cooperation, at least in economic matters.

There is also much interest in and discussion of an EC–type regional confederation, which might be called Turkestan. This would comprise the five Central Asian republics. But the Uzbek nationalist leader and poet Muhammed Salik thinks that this is a dream because the five former Soviet Central Asian republics have more dividing them than bringing them together. Each has acquired a separate national identity which stands in the way of a Turkestani federation. Nevertheless, it is also true, as Salik has said, that the republics cannot live apart from one another. They need one another. When the advantages of unification became evident, union might well occur. A step in the direction of a Muslim economic union occurred in November 1992, when the five ex-Soviet Central Asian republics and Afghanistan joined Iran, Pakistan, and Turkey to create a Muslim economic bloc.

Relations with the United States

The Central Asian republics also want good relations with the United States but, like Russia, have found Washington to be cautious and ambivalent. In February 1992 then–secretary of state James Baker toured the five Central Asian Republics and discussed establishment of formal American ties. He made clear U.S. interests, speaking of the development of democratic government, respect for human rights, and curbs on arms production and deployment. The leaders of the republics were responsive, assuring Baker that their governments would respect human rights and refrain from exporting uranium to other Muslim countries. But it remains to be seen whether the Central Asian leaderships will live up to these assurances. Several of the Central Asian leaders are ex-Communists who have displayed an intolerance of political opposition.

Working to the advantage of the Central Asian leaderships in their dealings with the United States is the enormous mineral wealth some of them have, in particular Kazakhstan and Tajikistan, and their susceptibility to Iranian influence. Washington, therefore, is willing to be cooperative and take the Central Asian leaders at their word on developing liberal and democratic governments.

Kazakhstan is of special interest to the United States because it has nuclear weapons and the largest Soviet-era nuclear test site. Kazakhstan also has one of the largest oil fields outside the Persian Gulf and is rich in chrome, gold, silver, lead, zinc, and iron ore deposits. It has superb potential for American investment. In October 1993 Secretary of State Warren Christopher announced an American aid package of $140 million to deal with the country's extraordinary poverty and to help with the cost of dismantling Kazakhstan's nuclear arsenal.

The Bolshevik-Menshevik split in Russian Social Democratic Party (RSDP); the emergence of a separate party, called the Bolsheviks by 1912	Bloody Sunday Massacre; the Revolution of 1905; the October Manifesto	Abdication of Czar Nicholas II; setup of the provisional government; the Bolshevik Revolution	Founding of the Comintern	The formation of the Soviet Union	Lenin dies
1902	1905	1917	1919	1922	1924

Kazakhstan president Nazarbayev has gone out of his way to cultivate the United States. In 1992 he signed the START I treaty committing Kazakhstan to reducing its strategic nuclear warheads. He also pledged to make Kazakhstan a non-nuclear state, and he told Christopher that he would ask the Kazakhstan Parliament formally to ratify the nuclear nonproliferation treaty, which Kazakhstan already abides by.

Behind Nazarbayev's strong pro-American foreign policy are two considerations: national pride and territorial security. Nazarbayev has made plain to the Americans that he wants them to take him seriously and pay attention to Kazakhstan and not lump it into a general U.S. policy toward the region. He also wants American understanding of and assistance for Kazakhstan's complex security needs. In an October 1993 meeting with Christopher, Nazarbayev explained that Kazakhstan's strategic vulnerability results from the fact that it has powerful neighbors to the north (Russia) and to the east (China) and that it worries about the spread of political unrest in places like the Caucasus and neighboring Tajikistan. He wants to be sure that if he gives up Kazakhstan's nuclear capability, the United States will help guarantee Uzbekistan's security.

While Nazarbayev will obtain the attention he seeks from the Clinton administration, he is unlikely to get its commitment to help Kazakhstan protect its security: The administration has shown elsewhere in the ex-Soviet territories as well as in Central/Eastern Europe that American interest does not automatically mean American involvement.

THE FUTURE OF THE C.I.S.

The chances of the Commonwealth's survival are mixed. On the negative side is a multiplicity of ethnic-based political and cultural nationalisms, which divide the republics against one another and make cooperation among them difficult. Moreover, most of the non-Russian republics of the C.I.S. fear the restoration of a powerful, intrusive, and Russian-dominated central government like that of the Soviet national government. Ukraine sees the Commonwealth as a temporary phenomenon, nothing more than a "breathing space . . . on the way to full independence." As one official observed, Ukraine will stay in the C.I.S. only as long as it takes to stabilize its economy and develop viable government institutions.

Ukraine is not alone in its cautious approach. Leaders of the 11 republics, meeting in Minsk in December 1991 to discuss further development of the Commonwealth, carefully avoided use of the word "union." In their determination to avoid re-creating anything that even faintly resembles the

former Soviet state, they spoke of the C.I.S. as neither a state nor a superstate structure. While they had no trouble agreeing to cooperate in a variety of practical matters, ranging from aviation to joint work on cleaning up the fallout from Chernobyl, there were heated exchanges over issues relating to sovereignty of the republics in the area of defense, economic reform, and the future shape and central structures of the C.I.S. In these discussions Ukraine was the staunchest in rejecting anything that infringed on its claims to sovereignty. This summit failed to produce a charter, a cohesive plan for economic reform, or agreement on a united military force.

But the prognosis is not all bad. The Commonwealth has some strengths. By offering an acceptable framework within which to cooperate and coordinate, the C.I.S. can provide its republics with a basis for the resolution of regional ambitions by nonviolent means. It also offers the republics a chance to start the reform process so desperately needed to reverse economic deterioration.

Despite their strong drives for independence and separate development, members of the C.I.S. are held together by economic interdependencies that go back over several centuries. Members are also joined through the irreversible mixture of peoples in different republics, the result of Soviet policy after World War II of moving ethnic populations across republic borders. Finally, they share a legacy of 70 years of socialist development, which left all the republics impoverished. They need to deal with that legacy collectively rather than individually.

Patterns of Future Development

As the Commonwealth works out its future, there are three kinds of confederative arrangements that it might pursue. One is based on ethnicity. The second is based on economic integration. The third is based on regional cooperation.

Ethnic Union

In one kind of development, the large ethnic constituencies would work together instead of against one another. Members of the C.I.S. need a system that will protect the interests of the small republics against the policies of the large republics. The republics also need enough internal autonomy to run their own affairs. Unfortunately, the prospects for such a model are uncertain. Right now the Russian republic is dominant. Also, the extraordinary proliferation of politically motivated party groups fragments the political environment of individual republics and complicates their participation in the C.I.S. The enormous size of the Commonwealth also is a liability, in the

Stalin's party dominance is affirmed 1927	The beginning of the first 5-year plan to nationalize all industry and collectivize agriculture 1928	Stalin's purges begin 1934	Pact with Nazi Germany 1939	Annexation of the Baltic states 1940	Nazi invasion of the Soviet Union 1941	Formation of CMEA 1949

sense that it is difficult for so many republics to allow decisions to be made centrally.

The great complexity of the challenges facing post-Soviet governments—namely, to create market economies, privatize, reindustrialize, and alleviate consumer shortages—is not conducive to elite cooperation, especially with the extreme ethnic heterogeneity that now prevails in the Commonwealth. The peoples of the C.I.S. lack an overarching political loyalty to a common identity that could mitigate their conflict-producing diversity.

Still another problem for the development of the Commonwealth into an ethnic union concerns the proliferation of small conflict-ridden minorities inside the heterogeneous republics. Some 65 million people live outside their titular national territory or are members of an ethnic group that has no territorial unit. Approximately 25 million Russians live outside Russia, primarily in Ukraine and Kazakhstan. This Russian diaspora presents one of the most serious challenges to any attempt to link ethnic background to a republic's identity. Yeltsin warned in August 1991 that the borders of Ukraine and Kazakhstan might have to be adjusted if those republics decide to be independent. He provoked a sharp response from the leaders of both republics that such attitudes threaten to provoke a civil war.

Economic Union

There is also the possibility that the C.I.S. might develop primarily as an economic community based on economic interdependence and mutual self-interest. Steps in this direction had already been taken in the fall of 1991, with the creation of an Interrepublic Economic Committee to coordinate economic relations among the former republics. A draft treaty for a Eurasian Economic Community, presented to the republics on September 16, 1991, envisioned a common currency and banking system, open trade between republics, free migration of labor, and coordinated tax policies, with each republic allowed to issue its own internal currency but required to use rubles when engaging in interrepublic trade. A further step toward the creation of an economic community was taken when members of the newly created Soviet State Council agreed on the need to coordinate food aid throughout the winter. In October representatives of the 12 Soviet republics and Latvia met in Alma Ata to discuss further details of an economic community and to sign an economic agreement.

But nationalist passions have interfered with economic union. Leaders and their bureaucratic lieutenants are under fire by popularly elected parliaments to act on those passions. For example, Ukraine had been critical of Gorbachev's proposal of an economic union in September 1991, because it would have too much of the old union in it and would give rise to a new, powerful, intrusive central government at the expense of newly gained local sovereignty. Ukraine wanted greater control over the spending of funds that it would contribute to the central government and greater freedom to manage Ukraine's share of the Soviet Union's $68 billion foreign debt. When it eventually did agree, on November 14, to join the economic union, after the Yeltsin government agreed to take responsibility for 60 percent of the Soviet debt, it did so reluctantly, with grave misgivings. Even in Russia, which would surely dominate any economic union of the former Soviet republics, there is a fear that poorer, less developed republics might drain resources from Russia. Throughout 1992 and 1993, some ex-Soviet republics using the ruble as their national currency drew millions of dollars worth of rubles from the Russian Central Bank and spent the money freely, exacerbating inflation in Russia as well as at home.

Despite this strain on its economy, Russia maintained the ruble as the national currency in other ex-Soviet republics because it wanted to maintain the financial and industrial links that had developed over a long period of time in the former Soviet Union. Given their long history of interdependence, many republics welcome this policy. In July 1993 Russia, Belarus, and Ukraine forged an economic union that promised extensive economic cooperation and eventual integration with Armenia, Kazakhstan, Tajikistan, and Uzbekistan. Aimed at currency stabilization, this plan is supposed to encourage cooperation on budgets, taxes, monetary, and credit policy as well as interest rates, tax rates, and customs duties. Whether these efforts at economic union will work remains to be seen. Given its own economic and monetary crises, Russia seems hardly suited to the task of acting as leader and disciplinarian of the ex-Soviet republics.

Regional Cooperation

Should the Commonwealth fail, some of its features will remain as it divides into subsets of former republics, possibly in combination with outside states. Two areas in particular have experienced significant regional cooperation: the Baltics and Central Asia. Since early 1990 the Baltic states have held joint sessions of their parliaments and have coordinated economic policies. Some sentiment also exists for integrating the Baltic states into a transnational Scandinavian community. Since 1990 the Central Asian republics also have engaged in efforts to create a regional organization, with the signing that year of a regional cooperation agreement that envisioned broad-based economic cooperation among the five Central

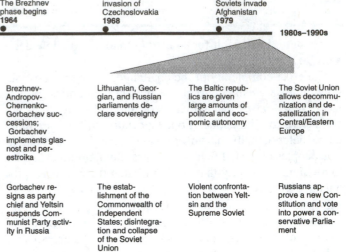

The Khrushchev phase begins
1953

Formation of the Warsaw Pact; cultural thaw
1955

Anti-party crisis; Gromyko becomes the foreign minister
1957

The Brezhnev phase begins
1964

The Soviet invasion of Czechoslovakia
1968

SALT II agreements are signed; the Soviets invade Afghanistan
1979

1980s–1990s

Brezhnev-Andropov-Chernenko-Gorbachev successions; Gorbachev implements glasnost and perestroika

Lithuanian, Georgian, and Russian parliaments declare sovereignty

The Baltic republics are given large amounts of political and economic autonomy

The Soviet Union allows decommunization and desatellization in Central/Eastern Europe

Gorbachev resigns as party chief and Yeltsin suspends Communist Party activity in Russia

The establishment of the Commonwealth of Independent States; disintegration and collapse of the Soviet Union

Violent confrontation between Yeltsin and the Supreme Soviet

Russians approve a new Constitution and vote into power a conservative Parliament

Asian republics of Kazakhstan, Uzbekistan, Turkmenistan, Kyrgyzstan, and Tajikistan. Only days before the August 1991 coup, the leaders of these republics had met in Tashkent and established a permanent commission to coordinate implementation of the cooperation agreement. Azerbaijan has expressed interest in joining the group, which some Central Asian observers have begun to call "Greater Turkestan."

Finally, in June 1992, Russia, Ukraine, Moldova, Georgia, Azerbaijan, and Armenia joined Romania, Bulgaria, Greece, and Turkey in a large conference of Black Sea–Balkan states at Istanbul to discuss political, economic, and strategic problems of mutual concern and to put an end to age-old rivalries. For example, Moldova discussed with Romania and Russia the conflicts over the Moldovan area east of the Dneister River where a Slavic minority had been seeking independence of the majority, which is ethnic Romanian. But the delegates of Armenia and Azerbaijan, which were at war over the disposition of Nagorno-Karabakh, could not see their way clear to meeting and talking. While the disparate members of this new regional group did not achieve any tangilbe results at their first conference, their getting together had great symbolic value, reflecting a strong interest in promoting stability and prosperity throughout the area.

The advantages of regionalism within the C.I.S. are several. Regionalism reduces the complexity involved in managing a community by reducing the number of participants. In some cases, it could also provide a cultural cohesion to transnational organizations which, with a larger number of participants, would otherwise be lacking. On the other hand, regionalism is unlikely to be a workable arrangement for all the former Soviet republics. For example, nationalist passions in the Transcaucasus (Armenia vs. Azerbaijan) make regionalism there impractical, and it is not inconceivable that interethnic rivalries among the Islamic peoples of Central Asia may compromise regionalism in that area as well. While Central Asian elites have moved in the direction of cooperation, at the mass level there has been intense nationalist-inspired violence.

DEVELOPMENT

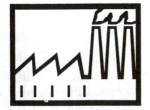

Russia is an example of a country that has made extraordinary progress toward the free market economy. More than half of all small enterprises have been privatized, every third worker is employed by a privatized or privatizing enterprise, and millions of citizens have become shareholders and owners. But Russia still has a long way to go in discarding the old centralized and paternalistic economic order, with most Russian heavy industry and agriculture still under state control; and obstacles to further development of the free market economy abound.

FREEDOM

There remain strong authoritarian and antidemocratic tendencies in the region. For example, to rid himself of a relentless opposition, Russian president Yeltsin illegally dissolved the Russian Supreme Soviet, restored censorship of the press, called upon local legislators who had been defying the central government to resign, ruled by decree until elections for a new Parliament, and reneged on a promise to hold presidential elections.

HEALTH/WELFARE

Only 14% of Russian children can be said to be in good health, according to criteria of the Health Ministry. Up to 20% of preschool children suffer from chronic diseases; up to 60% have rickets, are underweight, and have allergies; more than 10% are anemic; and in some oil- and chemical-producing regions, children are 10 times more likely to get pneumonia and 5 times more likely to have bronchial ailments.

ACHIEVEMENTS

In the midst of economic, social, and political upheaval, in February 1993 Russian scientists and engineers, using a thin aluminum and plastic mirror in space, sent a narrow beam of reflected sunlight flashing across the darkened side of Earth, proving the feasibility of putting much larger mirrors in space that could change night into twilight, saving billions of dollars in electricity and extending planting and harvesting seasons. In another vein Russia made its first private space launch, a strictly commercial venture.

Central/Eastern Europe

NORWAY

SWEDEN

GULF OF BOTHNIA

FINLAND

GULF OF FINLAND

ESTONIA

GULF OF RIGA

LATVIA

LITHUANIA

RUSSIA

BELARUS

NORTH SEA

DENMARK

BALTIC SEA

THE NETHERLANDS

BELGIUM

GERMANY

Warsaw ✪

POLAND

UKRAINE

LUXEMBOURG

Prague ✪

THE CZECH REPUBLIC

SLOVAKIA

FRANCE

LIECHTENSTEIN

AUSTRIA

Bratislava ✪

Budapest ✪

HUNGARY

MOLDOVA

SWITZERLAND

SLOVENIA

Ljubljana ✪

Zagreb ✪

CROATIA

VOJVODINA

Novi Sad ✪

ROMANIA

Bucharest ✪

BLACK SEA

LIGURIAN SEA

ITALY

ADRIATIC SEA

BOSNIA-HERZEGOVINA

Belgrade ✪

Sarajevo ✪

SERBIA

Sofia ✪

MONTENEGRO

Pristina ✪

KOSOVO

BULGARIA

Titograd ✪

Skopje ✪

MACEDONIA

Tirana ✪

ALBANIA

TYRRHENIAN SEA

MEDITERRANEAN SEA

IONIAN SEA

GREECE

AEGEAN SEA

TURKEY

N W E S

0   125   kilometers
0   125 miles

✪ Capital cities

113

Central/Eastern Europe: From Dictatorship to Democracy

WHY STUDY CENTRAL/EASTERN EUROPE?

The countries of Central/Eastern Europe that are covered in this volume—Albania, Bulgaria, the Czech Republic and Slovakia, Hungary, Poland, Romania, and the new republics of the former Yugoslavia—have always been important in world politics. They are the strategic heartland of the great Eurasian landmass that stretches from the Atlantic Ocean in the west to the Ural Mountains in the east. In the past they were the object of intense interest of the large empires on their periphery: Germany, Russia, Austria, and Turkey. Because events in Central/Eastern Europe were at the root of the two world wars in the first half of the twentieth century, political development in the region is important to the security of not only Germany, the Scandinavian countries, and Russia and the Eurasian republics but also of outsiders like other countries of Western Europe and North America.

Central/Eastern Europe is important also because after World War II it came under the rule of Communist parties linked closely to the Soviet Union. In the post–World War II period, most of the Communist party-ruled countries became satellites of Moscow. Satellization meant their acceptance of Soviet political institutions and their subservience to Soviet international policies.

But it is also true that almost all the countries modified their Soviet-style political systems and developed varying degrees of independence of the Soviet Union. While they shared many characteristics with one another and with the Soviet Union because of their common commitment to communist ideology, they also became differentiated in their domestic and foreign policies.

This diversity contradicted popular notions of sameness among the Central/Eastern Europe countries; of slavish pursuit of a single, Soviet-determined path to socialism and communism; and of abject loyalty and obedience to Soviet foreign policy. It was wrong to assume, as many in the West did, the region's absolute acceptance of the Soviet path to socialism and communism. Rather, Communist political development in Central/Eastern Europe was polycentric. The countries developed differentiated domestic and foreign policies based on local needs and interests.

Nevertheless, the Central/Eastern European political systems still resembled the Soviet system and were quite subservient to it. Because of their importance to Soviet territorial security and to Soviet global prestige and influence, the countries became a sphere of Soviet ideological and strategic predominance.

Finally, it is important to study Central/Eastern Europe because of the extraordinary upheavals that occurred throughout the region in late 1989, leading to rapid decommunization and desatellization. Most Central/Eastern European countries are now in a transitional phase of political development in which they are trying to democratize their societies, economies, and political systems. All face severe problems. Some countries will solve these problems more quickly and effectively than will others. There is always the risk of political extremism and of a return to antidemocratic government. In many respects Central/Eastern Europe is a laboratory for political change, with implications for development and modernization in such other regions as Latin America, the Middle East, and South Asia.

HOW TO STUDY CENTRAL/EASTERN EUROPE

There are at least two ways to study Central/Eastern Europe. One is a review of the region as a whole. This approach is important because, as compared to other large geographic regions, such as Western Europe, Latin America, and sub-Saharan Africa, the Central/Eastern European region has many commonalities. A second approach, which involves individual country studies, takes into account contrasts among the different countries, their divergence from the Soviet pattern in the era of Communist rule, and their different patterns of democratic development in the post-Communist era. In this book we look at Central/Eastern Europe in both ways.

The following review of the Central/Eastern European region consists of ten sections: 1) pre-Communist history; 2) Communist party ascendancy after World War II; 3) Soviet satellization in the late 1940s and early 1950s; 4) conformity with the Soviet model; 5) problems with the Soviet model; 6) divergence from the Soviet model; 7) channels of Soviet influence; 8) challenges to Soviet influence in the 1980s; 9) causes and consequences of the revolutionary upheaval that occurred in the region beginning in 1989; and 10) post-Communist development.

PRE-COMMUNIST HISTORY

All the countries of Central/Eastern Europe are new in comparison with those of Western Europe. They gained political independence only in the last 125 years, after a long period of rule by foreigners. Romania became independent in 1878, Bulgaria in 1908, and Albania in 1912. Poland, Czechoslovakia, and Yugoslavia achieved independence at the end of World War I in 1918. (The former East Germany was carved out of modern Germany by the victorious Allies at the end of World War II.)

Foreign Rule
Four great foreign empires occupied most of Central/Eastern Europe for centuries before World War I. The German and Austrian empires partitioned and occupied Poland from the end of the eighteenth century until 1918. The Austrian Empire administered what are now the Czech Republic and Slovakia, Hungary, and the northern region of the former Yugoslavia from the fifteenth century until its demise in

World War I. And the Ottoman Turkish Empire, starting in the late fourteenth century, conquered and occupied Romania, Bulgaria, central and southern Yugoslavia, and Albania. The Turks gradually lost control of these areas during the nineteenth century, when there were periodic rebellions against its rule. The empire disintegrated in World War I.

Although all the Central/Eastern European countries had little autonomy while under the rule of foreign empires, some of them fared better than others. Poland, Czechoslovakia, Hungary, and northern Yugoslavia had a limited amount of self-rule; developed some industrialization, which improved the standard of living; and had more contact with Western ideas and institutions than did the southern or Balkan peoples of Romania, Bulgaria, central and southern Yugoslavia, and Albania. These Balkan peoples suffered under Turkish rule, which was oppressive and abusive. They endured religious persecution, onerous taxation, and remained politically and economically underdeveloped well into the twentieth century.

Political Development (1918–1945)

Between World War I and World War II (1918–1939), all the Central/Eastern European countries had at least the appearance of parliamentary and democratic forms of government. But, with the exception of Czechoslovakia, all the countries had become fascist dictatorships by the end of this 20-year interwar period. Their peoples could not make democracy work because they had had little experience with self-rule. They also lacked national leadership that could achieve discipline and unity without undermining popular government. They faced horrendous social and economic problems that burdened their fragile institutions of self-government. After 1933 some ruling groups increasingly looked to the Nazi model of totalitarian government to solve these problems and to safeguard society against the spread of communism from the Soviet Union.

In one way or another, the countries lost their newly won independence during World War II. Poland, Czechoslovakia, and Yugoslavia were conquered by the Nazis; Romania, Hungary, and Bulgaria became allies and ultimately satellites of the Nazi German state. They were, wittingly or unwittingly, accomplices of Nazi efforts to strengthen German security through political and military control of Central/Eastern Europe and adjacent parts of the Soviet Union. One explanation for this orientation toward Nazi Germany during the 1930s was a strong and long-standing hostility toward the Russians. Most Central/Eastern European peoples disliked the Russians, both for their adoption of communism and for their historic interference in Central/Eastern European affairs.

The Economy

Although there were pockets of industrialization and some urbanization everywhere in Central/Eastern Europe—especially in the north, where there were natural resources for manufacturing, such as coal and iron, and a developed transportation and communications infrastructure—the region as a whole was primarily agricultural and poor. Most of the cultivable land had belonged to a small rural aristocracy. Methods of cultivation remained primitive well into the twentieth century; people and animals continued to do the work that was done by machines in Western Europe. Farming was inefficient not only because of a lack of machines and modern agricultural technology but also because credit was very difficult to come by and many farms were too small to be economical.

Society

On the eve of the Communist takeover, the society of Central/Eastern Europe consisted of four different socioeconomic groups. In addition to a small, affluent landed aristocracy, there was an equally small, new, and well-off entrepreneurial and commercial middle class. This middle class had close ties to the landed aristocracy, out of which it had developed as a result of industrialization. It shared the conservative outlook of the aristocracy, and both classes were political allies. A third class was a small, impoverished, wage-earning proletariat in the cities. This class also was an outgrowth of industrialization.

The largest socioeconomic class was the peasantry. It consisted of two groups: the larger group owned and cultivated small plots of land; other peasants worked on the land of others for a wage.

Most of the societies of the newly independent countries were divided also along ethnocultural lines. The societies of these countries consisted of large and small national groups, many with their own language, religion, and cultural traditions. The new countries inherited multinational societies from the period of foreign rule when large imperial systems administered Central/Eastern Europe and modern boundaries had not yet been drawn.

The largest ethnic groups dominated the political systems of the new countries for several reasons: They usually were the most politically advanced, and they had led nationalist movements or political parties in favor of independence and were confirmed in positions of leadership by the Western powers, notably Britain, France, and the United States. In their new countries, the large ethnic groups used their position of dominance to discriminate against minorities, not only politically but also economically and culturally. This discrimination produced interethnic tensions within a country, weakening democratic government and increasing its vulnerability to foreign attack.

Czechoslovakia and Yugoslavia had the most serious minorities problems. Obsessed with forging a permanent unity of their multinational societies, in the late 1920s and 1930s, Czechoslovak and Yugoslav political leaders strongly resisted the demands of minority groups for ad-

(Novosti photo)

The Kremlin in Moscow. After World War II, despite their historical animosity toward Russians, the Central/Eastern European peoples lived for decades in the shadow of the Soviet Union.

ministrative decentralization, increased representation in national government, and more equitable distribution of national wealth. Instead, the governments went in the opposite direction and tried to promote societal homogenization. Their policies provoked tensions that threatened the stability and ultimately the survival of their countries in the face of Nazi aggression in the late 1930s.

Anti-Semitism

Anti-Semitism was an important aspect of the minorities problem during this pre-Communist period, because Jews were a minority in most of the societies, in particular those of Poland and Romania. Anti-Semitism had existed for centuries and took the form of discrimination against Jews in all aspects of life—in politics, in the economy, and in society. Physical violence against Jews in everyday life, especially in schools, was not unusual.

There were many causes of anti-Semitism in Central/Eastern Europe. The most important were the persistence of religious myths about the Jews; their tendency to ghettoize in the major cities like Warsaw, Bucharest, and Budapest; their accumulation of financial wealth and influence through trade and banking; and their determination to

preserve their cultural identity, especially language, dress, and values, although many Jews did assimilate the Christian culture in which they lived and worked.

There is little doubt, however, that traditional anti-Semitism in Central/Eastern Europe became virulent in the 1930s, as a result of the anti-Semitism of Nazi Germany. The national leadership of several Central/Eastern European countries developed close ties with the Nazi government and voluntarily, or under Nazi pressure, made anti-Semitism official policy.

Hostility to Russians

Most of the peoples of Central/Eastern Europe have always had an abiding dislike and fear of Russians. In part, this anti-Russian sentiment is the result of prejudice, of a sense of superiority, and of a belief in the inferiority of Russian civilization.

Anti-Russian feelings are also, as mentioned earlier, a response to the historic intrusiveness of Russians in the life of Central/Eastern European societies. Poles and Romanians in particular experienced Russian expansionism in the nineteenth and twentieth centuries. Eastern Poland had been conquered and occupied by Czarist Russia from the end of the eighteenth century until World War I, when the modern state of Poland was reconstituted by the Western powers. The northeastern part of Romania known as Bessarabia had been seized by Czarist Russia in 1878, recovered by Romania after World War I, and then seized again and annexed by the Soviet Union in 1940. (Today Bessarabia is known as the Moldova republic.)

The worst nightmare of many Central/Eastern European peoples became a stark reality during and after World War II. The Soviet Union, more powerful than it or its Russian predecessor had ever been in recent history, expanded its political and military power into Central/Eastern Europe, depriving most states of the region of their newly achieved independence.

COMMUNIST PARTY ASCENDANCY

All the Central/Eastern European countries were involved in World War II, either because they were invaded and occupied by Nazi Germany, as was true of Poland, Czechoslovakia, and Yugoslavia (Albania was invaded and occupied by Fascist Italy); or because they were allies and satellites of the Nazis, as was the case in Hungary, Romania, and Bulgaria. The coming of World War II to Central/Eastern Europe was a prelude to the Communist takeover, because it offered the Soviet Union an opportunity to encourage and to assist local Communist parties directly to expand their political influence and ultimately to obtain control of the governments of the Central/Eastern European countries in the period immediately after the war.

Toward the end of the war, the United States and Britain acknowledged the Soviet Union's special interest in Central/Eastern Europe and agreed that the Soviets should have a major influence in the region. Soviet troops occupied most of the Central/Eastern European countries, where they appeared—at least to themselves—as "liberators." They established close contact with local Communist groups, helping them to expand their influence in national politics.

The Origins of Communist Parties

Although Communist parties developed in all the Central/Eastern European countries following the 1917 Bolshevik Revolution in Russia, they did not acquire popularity, and they remained small minority groups. Unlike the Socialist parties before World War I that advocated a nonviolent strategy to achieve economic reforms, the Communists supported revolution and looked to the Russian Marxists for inspiration and guidance. They had little voter support in their countries also because they were too violent and too pro-Russian. Indeed, they remained small organizations with narrow constituencies throughout the interwar period. In a few instances, Communist parties eventually were outlawed.

Soviet Help

During and after World War II, the Soviets helped many of the Central/Eastern European Communist parties to enter the mainstream of politics in their countries. The Soviets wanted to expand Communist influence in an area perceived to be ripe for radical socioeconomic change. After the experience in the 1930s, when several Central/Eastern European states had supported the Nazis or had done little to oppose them, the Soviets also wanted friendly governments in power. They expected the Communists to achieve that objective.

The Soviets enabled Communist parties to acquire cabinet posts in the postwar governments of their countries and to participate in policy making. This helped the Communists to gain political credibility in their societies, thereby increasing their chances of winning popular support in parliamentary elections.

Communist control of certain ministries also gave the parties significant political power. For example, control of ministries of agriculture allowed them to put through long-awaited programs of land redistribution. Control of ministries of education gave them influence over the school systems, and control of ministries of the interior allowed them to obtain influence over the local police apparatus.

At all times the Soviet Union stood ready to provide military support of the Communist parties against popular opposition. Soviet forces that expelled the Nazis in 1944 and 1945 remained in most of Central/Eastern Europe long after the war was over.

Communist Party Strategies and Tactics

Following their own political instincts as well as advice from the Soviets, who wanted to avoid provoking Western suspicions of a Communist takeover, the Central/Eastern European parties, in seeking popularity and electoral victories, carefully avoided both revolutionary rhetoric and gestures of subservience to Moscow. They assured voters of their patriotism and of their commitment to the ballot box to gain power. Their advocacy of a moderate socialism had much appeal in the economically difficult period following the end of the war, when there was unemployment, scarcity, and inflation.

To increase their political constituencies, the Central/Eastern European Communists recruited any reformist-minded people, whether or not they were Marxist-Leninists. They made a special pitch to workers and infiltrated trade unions. They established links with farmers' parties. And, ultimately, they formed parliamentary coalitions that increased their power in cabinets.

Communist parties also gained much benefit from the war. In resisting fascism some Communists became national heroes, like Yugoslav Communist leader Joseph Broz Tito, thus making it easy for people to forget for the moment their close links with the Soviet Union.

The local Communists took advantage of the democratic character of the postwar governments in most Central/Eastern European countries. The Communists had an open political arena in which to campaign for power.

Western Policy

All the Central/Eastern European Communist parties were beneficiaries of the war weariness of the West and, in particular, the unwillingness of the United States to block Soviet and Communist expansion. Although the Americans protested Communist party gains in Central/Eastern Europe following the end of World War II, they did nothing to counter the advance of Communist political influence. The United States wanted to avoid a dangerous confrontation with the Soviet Union, its ally in the recent war with Germany. Moreover, the American government already had agreed at the Yalta and Potsdam conferences to tolerate substantial Soviet and Communist influence in Central/Eastern Europe.

The focus of American interest and action, rather, was Western Europe, which received enormous amounts of economic assistance. The United States wanted to discourage the kind of social conditions that had benefited Communists in Central/Eastern Europe.

The Takeover

The Communist takeover of Central/Eastern Europe was completed by 1948 or 1949 (the precise dates varied from country to country). By that time Communist parties had obtained large pluralities in national parliaments. They dominated cabinets and determined public policy. They used the police power of the state to harass and ultimately to outlaw rival political organizations. They nationalized key sectors of the economy and introduced extensive social security and welfare programs.

By the end of the 1940s, the Communist-controlled governments of Central/Eastern Europe had promulgated new constitutions establishing Soviet-style dictatorships, called in most countries "people's democracy." These new political systems, while committed to the destruction of capitalism and to the development of socialism, were not considered by Moscow to be equivalents of the more advanced socialism of the Soviet Union.

The Yugoslav Exception

The Communist takeover occurred much more quickly in Yugoslavia than in other countries. When the war ended in the spring of 1945, a Communist-led resistance organization called the *Partisans* was the dominant political force in the country and its leader, the Croat Communist Joseph Broz Tito, was a national hero. With the military weapons acquired during the war, the Partisans seized the administrative apparatus of the country, used force to eliminate political opposition, and established control over their country at least 2 years ahead of the Communists elsewhere in

Central/Eastern Europe. They did all this, incidentally, without much Soviet help.

Indeed, the Yugoslavs were able to keep Soviet influence in their country to a minimum. Tito managed to avoid a Soviet military liberation and occupation of his country at the end of the war by singlehandedly expelling the remnants of Nazi occupation forces, presenting the Kremlin with the fait accompli of Partisan political and military dominance of Yugoslavia. He also excluded from positions of leadership within the Yugoslav Communist Party those known to have special links with Moscow.

Other factors helped Tito to limit Soviet influence in Yugoslavia. The great geographic distance between Yugoslavia and the Soviet Union made it difficult for the Kremlin to threaten Tito. The close political ties Tito had had with the Kremlin in the 1930s weakened during World War II. When the war was over, Tito considered himself independent and the equal of Stalin.

By 1947 Tito had established Communist control over local and central administrative authorities in a civil war against political opponents, enabling him to undertake the transformation of Yugoslavia to Soviet-style socialism. This was done despite Soviet advice to the Yugoslav Communists to move slowly lest they arouse Western suspicions and provoke Western interference. Needless to say, Tito ignored this advice.

The Albanian Exception

Albanian Communists, like their Yugoslav counterparts with whom they had developed extensive contacts during the war, had fought fascists and emerged from the conflict as the most powerful political group in their country. With help from the Yugoslavs, the Albanian Communists quickly seized power. Although the new Albanian leadership had good relations with the Soviet Union in the late 1940s and received some assistance from the Soviets, Soviet influence in Albanian politics was minimal because of the absence of Soviet occupation forces and because of the great physical distance between the two countries. Albanian imitation of Soviet socialism was voluntary in this early phase of Communist development; it was not the result of direct Soviet involvement.

SOVIET SATELLIZATION

The Soviets had certain expectations of the new Communist-controlled political systems in Central/Eastern Europe. They wanted the Central/Eastern European Communists to imitate their pattern of political development under Stalin and to pursue domestic and foreign policies that were congenial to Soviet national interests. They did not want Central/Eastern European party leaderships to experiment with the Soviet model, to modify it, and to originate their own national patterns of political development.

Stalin was rigid on Central/Eastern European conformity. He believed that the Soviet model was the only successful way to achieve socialism and communism. Moreover, Central/Eastern European acceptance of Soviet practices reinforced the legitimacy of the Soviet Union's own political system. Conformity also assured the strategic reliability of the new Central/Eastern European systems by strengthening the political, economic, and strategic links they had developed with one another and with the Soviet Union.

Challenges

In the late 1940s, some independent-minded Central/Eastern European leaders tried to deviate from the Soviet model. Polish leader Wladyslaw Gomulka, fearing widespread unrest in the Polish countryside, opposed a Soviet-like forced collectivization of Polish agriculture. In addition, both the Polish and Czechoslovak Communist leaderships wanted to draw closer to the West and to accept Marshall Plan aid from the United States to help their countries recover from the devastation of World War II. Yugoslavia's Tito also wanted to go his own way in socialist development. In addition to proceeding more rapidly than other Central/Eastern European Communist parties to establish Communist control over his country, thereby risking an arousal of Western suspicions and possible Western interference, Tito tried to increase Yugoslavia's territory and political influence in Southeast Europe. He sought Trieste from Italy. He also wanted to establish a union of Balkan Communists, which the Bulgarian Communist Party was on the verge of joining.

Especially disturbing to the Kremlin was Tito's insistence on the principle of national independence of the Soviets in the development of socialism in Yugoslavia and in other countries. For this reason as well as because of his rejection of Soviet advice and his aggressive foreign policies, Tito seemed as a competitor of the Soviet Union and a threat to its influence in the Balkans.

Soviet Responses: The Cominform

The Soviets established the Cominform, a new association of Communist parties. They intended to use the Cominform as a vehicle for disseminating their advice on socialist development and discouraging Central/Eastern European deviation. The Cominform held its inaugural meeting in Poland in September 1947.

Tito defied the Cominform. He did not personally attend the inaugural meeting, and in the following months he reaffirmed his independence of the Soviet Union and his determination to pursue a separate national road to socialism. He also argued the right of other Communist parties to chart their own paths to socialism. He encouraged Polish leader Gomulka to resist the Kremlin's pressure to conform to the Soviet model.

Stalin was infuriated by Tito's challenge. He wanted to punish Tito, to weaken him, and to encourage Tito's col-

leagues to oust him from the party leadership. Stalin also wanted to make an example of Tito to discourage other Central/Eastern European party leaderships from challenging Soviet policy. Stalin demanded and obtained the support of other Central/Eastern European parties for the expulsion of Tito's party from the Cominform and ostracism of the Yugoslav state in the new socialist community. Central/Eastern European accommodation of the Kremlin in this instance foreshadowed the near total subservience of the new Communist party dictatorships to Soviet will in the next few years.

Soviet Pressure on Other Parties

The establishment of the Cominform and the attack on Tito were not enough to induce would-be nationalistic and independent Communist party leaders like those in Poland, Czechoslovakia, and elsewhere to follow slavishly the Soviet line in the mid-1940s. To achieve their subordination, the Kremlin exerted direct pressure on the party leaders. This pressure was primarily political, but there was always an implied threat of military intervention.

One kind of Soviet pressure was Stalin's personal interaction with individual Central/Eastern European Communist leaders in bilateral meetings he held with them in Moscow. In these meetings Stalin conveyed the Soviet line in domestic and foreign policies that the Central/Eastern European party leaders were expected to follow. While his tone was menacing, Stalin also gave them his support and thereby reinforced their power vis-à-vis colleagues back home who might have been tempted to question and oppose adoption of Soviet-inspired policies.

Soviet ambassadors were another channel of Soviet influence. They carefully monitored domestic developments in the countries to which they were accredited. They reported to Moscow any signs of deviation or dissent. It was known to the local party leaderships—and this knowledge undoubtedly intimidated them—that the Soviet ambassadors had the authority to call upon Soviet troops stationed in the host countries.

There also were Soviet nationals in key posts within the Central/Eastern European governments. Soviet secret-police operatives circulated throughout Central/Eastern Europe to monitor daily life and report signs of criticism and opposition.

Diplomatic Links

The Soviets concluded defense treaties with the Central/Eastern European countries. These treaties stressed the common threat of Germany and pledged mutual assistance, and they also prohibited the signatories from joining organizations hostile to the interests of the other signatories. They effectively linked the foreign policies of the Central/Eastern European countries to that of the Soviet Union.

The Soviets concluded cultural and economic treaties as well. Bilateral cultural treaties between the Soviet Union and individual Central/Eastern European countries were intended to diminish historic animosities toward the Russians. The economic treaties fostered dependence of the economies of the Central/Eastern European countries on Soviet foreign trade policies. The Soviets also obliged the Central/Eastern European countries to conclude bilateral treaties with one another.

By 1953 there was a complex network of treaties between the Soviet Union and the Central/Eastern European countries, and between the Central/Eastern European countries themselves. This network effectively limited the foreign policy making of the Central/Eastern European countries; in still another way, it helped to convert Central/Eastern Europe into a Soviet sphere of influence.

Newly created multilateral regional organizations reinforced the treaty system and strengthened in still another way Soviet influence in Central/Eastern Europe. The most important of these organizations were the Council for Mutual Economic Assistance (CMEA) and the Warsaw Treaty Organization (otherwise known as the Warsaw Pact).

The CMEA was created in 1949 to promote economic integration and interdependence to draw the socialist countries closer to one another in the critical area of economic planning and output. In its early years, however, the CMEA did little more than set the Soviet ruble as the standard currency for international transactions and reinforce the economic isolation of Yugoslavia following its ouster from the Cominform. Not many CMEA meetings were held during this period because the Soviet Union wanted to deny the Central/Eastern European countries an opportunity to pressure Moscow for economic assistance to rebuild their dilapidated economies.

The Warsaw Pact was established in 1955, ostensibly in response to West Germany's entry into the North Atlantic Treaty Organization (NATO). But there were other reasons for the Pact. As a collective defense system, it provided a legal justification for the continued deployment of Soviet troops in Central/Eastern Europe. It also linked the defense establishments of the Central/Eastern European countries to one another and to the Soviet Union. The Soviets were able to influence Central/Eastern European defense policies at Pact summit meetings, which were held regularly to discuss political and military matters of common concern; and by Pact maneuvers, which involved the deployment of large numbers of Soviet air, land, and sea forces on the territory of member states.

Satellization Achieved
By 1953 the Kremlin had effectively transformed nearly all the Central/Eastern European political systems into Soviet satellites. By forcing their adoption of the Soviet model of socialism and their subservience to Soviet foreign policy, the Soviet Union deprived these countries of substantial

sovereignty. In this era they were separate and independent states in appearance, not in reality.

Exceptions to Satellization
Yugoslavia was one country that escaped satellization. Tito clearly suffered less from Stalin's ostracism of his party and government in 1948 than the Kremlin had expected. Although Yugoslavia temporarily had few dealings with its socialist neighbors in Central/Eastern Europe, it maintained ties with the West. Tito's position in Yugoslavia became stronger as a result of his successful resistance to the Soviet Union. He was now more popular than ever before. He also continued his independence, and in the 1950s he deviated significantly from the Soviet model.

While Albania also evaded satellization, it nevertheless became a carbon copy of the Soviet political system, and it aligned closely with Soviet international policies in the late 1940s and early 1950s. The Soviet model was congenial to Albania's underdeveloped society. Moreover, Albania benefited from Soviet hostility to Yugoslavia after 1948 because of a fear that Tito's government might try to seize Albanian territory along the Adriatic, to extend the Yugoslav coastline to the strategically important Strait of Otranto. Albanians also worried that Tito might even annex Albania and join it to the territory in southern Yugoslavia known as Kosovo, which was inhabited primarily by Albanian-speaking people.

CONFORMITY WITH THE SOVIET MODEL

As a result of satellization, most of the Central/Eastern European political systems had many characteristics of the Soviet political system in the 1950s and afterward. They all had a monolithic dictatorship by the Communist party, which looked and acted like the Soviet party; a government apparatus that was democratic in appearance but authoritarian in practice; a highly centralized socialist command economy; and a foreign policy based on close relations with one another and with the Soviet Union, opposition to the capitalist West, and support of revolutionary movements and left-wing governments in the Third World.

Dictatorship by the Communist Party
In the Central/Eastern European countries, as in the Soviet Union, the Communist party was the sole source of leadership and policy making. The existence of other political groups in a national front coalition-type organization, a characteristic of some Central/Eastern European socialist systems, in no way compromised the dominant position of the Communist party. Toleration of these "fake" political groups, which were allowed little say in policy making and were prohibited from becoming an opposition, increased the intended illusion of democracy.

The Central/Eastern European Communist parties resembled the Soviet party in the comprehensiveness of their

(Gamma-Liaison/APN)

Soviet Communist Party leader Leonid Brezhnev (right) months before his death in November 1982, with Polish leader Wojciech Jaruzelski, who was in Moscow for talks about his country's political turmoil.

control over not only major institutions—such as the national-front organizations, trade unions, youth and professional associations, and the military—but also over all governmental bureaucracies, from ministers at the top to implementation agencies on local levels of administration. And Central/Eastern European party methods of maintaining this control resembled those of the Soviet party, in particular the so-called interlocking directorate of party and state leaderships, wherein top party figures simultaneously occupied top government posts and the party controlled the appointment of personnel to all important state administrative positions.

The Central/Eastern European parties also resembled the Soviet party in organizational matters. For example, the size of party membership in each country was kept within the range of 6 to 12 percent of the country's population in order to preserve the party's elitist character, which was important for its ideological integrity and internal discipline.

To ensure the discipline of its members, the Central/Eastern European parties uniformly practiced the same organizational principles known as democratic centralism that prevailed in the Soviet Union. For example, leaders of the party were co-opted into power rather than elected democratically; in practice, party leaders had unlimited tenure—only a "palace revolt" or death could remove a party leader from power, which explains why most Communist party leaderships became a gerontocracy and their accountability

to rank-and-file party membership and to the public was minimal. Furthermore, under democratic centralism, rank-and-file members were prohibited from criticizing leadership, from embracing minority points of view and from dividing into factions, and from challenging party policy as defined by the Politburo.

Communist parties in Central/Eastern Europe imitated the Soviet party's insistence on societal conformity with the standard norms of political discipline. Like the Soviet party, they were intolerant of popular dissent and would go to great lengths to suppress it. Their methods, which resembled those in the Soviet Union, included rigorous censorship of the mass media, a readiness to allow the secret-police apparatus to use terror and coercion against suspected deviants, and incessant propaganda calling for popular acceptance of and loyalty to Marxism-Leninism.

All the Central/Eastern European parties were sensitive to the slightest public display of anti-Soviet feeling. They well knew the undercurrent of hostility to the Russians that had always existed in their societies. They also knew that the Kremlin would interfere directly in response to public expressions of anti-Russian sentiment.

Authoritarian Government

Despite the appearance of democratic and parliamentary forms, all the Central/Eastern European governments, like the Soviet government, were autocracies. The Central/Eastern European governments were also highly centralized. Even in Yugoslavia and Czechoslovakia, where there were claims to a federal type of administrative organization in which local authorities supposedly enjoyed a measure of autonomy—similar in some respects to Soviet federalism—public policy making was concentrated at the center; local government had no real independence.

Central/Eastern European heads of state closely resembled the Soviet head of state in their scope of power. However, they differed somewhat in appearance.

The heads of state of Czechoslovakia and Romania were presidents who in theory were chosen by the legislature but who in practice were determined by the party leadership. The Romanian president most closely resembled the Soviet president, in that he simultaneously was the head of the Communist party. The Romanian presidency, like the Soviet presidency, was a very powerful administrative position.

Other countries had a collective chief executive in the form of a state council, as in Poland until 1989, Bulgaria, and Hungary; or a collective presidency, as in Yugoslavia. These agencies were most important for their symbolism than for their decision-making authority, which was minimal. Their memberships were determined by the Communist party, even though formally elected by the legislature, and their scope of administrative power was limited by what the party allowed them to do.

Day-to-day administrative authority was in the hands of a premier and a council of ministers, who also were theoretically elected by the legislature but in practice were chosen by the top party leadership. Although in theory ministers were answerable for their behavior to the legislature and on occasion were questioned by legislative deputies, they actually were quite independent of legislative control. They were accountable only to the premier and to the party leadership to which the premier and the ministers of key departments like interior, agriculture, and foreign affairs belonged.

Central/Eastern European legislatures were subservient to executives. While they could debate and discuss executive measures put before them and could even request alteration of items that they did not like, they could not condemn, oppose, or reject executive policy.

Nor could they aggressively interpellate and challenge ministerial behavior, after the fashion of Western parliaments. They could raise questions about policy, provided they did so in a controlled and "constructive" manner that did not imply political opposition. Legislatures certainly could not oust ministers in a Western-style vote of no-confidence during the years of Soviet dominance.

Thus, while Central/Eastern European legislatures occasionally seemed like they were more active and involved in the process of government, sometimes having longer and livelier debates on government policy than the Soviet Un-

ion's Supreme Soviet, they had as little influence over policy making as did their Soviet counterpart.

The Central/Eastern European governments resembled one another and the Soviet government also in the frequently inept and occasionally dishonest behavior of their bureaucrats. Central/Eastern European governments frequently gave priority in recruitment of bureaucrats to political loyalty rather than expertise. Moreover, bureaucratic managers and their subordinates were under constant surveillance on the job, which made them defensive and encouraged their concealment of error. The low wages of government personnel—an age-old problem of bureaucracies in Central/Eastern Europe and the Soviet Union—encouraged petty theft, fraud, and bribe-taking. Finally, many bureaucrats, like other citizens, viewed the communist system for which they worked as alien, forced upon their countries by the Soviets. This feeling undermined loyalty and efficiency.

Bureaucracies in Central/Eastern Europe shared another characteristic of their Soviet counterpart. Despite close party supervision, they exercised a large personal influence over the policies they were to execute. Bureaucrats in Central/Eastern Europe, like bureaucrats anywhere, could drag their feet in carrying out policy and could sabotage policies they did not like, such as reforms that could lead to a curtailment of their responsibilities and perhaps their retrenchment.

Soviet-Style Command Economies

All the Central/Eastern European countries adopted, in the late 1940s and early 1950s, the highly centralized Soviet economic model. The Soviet model called for a comprehensive and binding national economic plan, nationalization of all industrial activity, complete collectivization of agriculture, and stress on heavy industrial capital goods production. In line with Soviet practice, government planners set prices somewhat arbitrarily and determined production goals primarily in quantitative terms, with little reference to market forces of supply and demand, and they paid insufficient attention to the production of consumer goods.

Social Welfare

The Central/Eastern European countries all imitated the Soviet effort—and some exceeded it—to ensure citizens a minimum level of material well-being in the areas of health, education, and housing. In the late 1940s and early 1950s, the Communist parties introduced comprehensive insurance programs and in many instances established minimum paid-vacation periods to be spent at state-run resorts, where charges were modest.

In 1980 most of the Central/Eastern European countries (Albania was the exception) spent more money per capita on education than on defense. A few countries, notably Po-

(United Nations photo)

The Soviet-style command economy served as the economic model for all the Central/Eastern European countries.

land and Czechoslovakia, spent more on health than on education. In these areas of public policy, the Central/Eastern European countries outdid the Soviet Union, which spent twice as much on defense as on education and 5 times as much on defense as on health.

Foreign Relations

As a result of satellization, the foreign policies of most Central/Eastern European countries conformed with Soviet dictates. Beginning in the late 1940s, the Central/Eastern European Communist leaderships dutifully followed the lead of the Soviet Union and broke relations with Yugoslavia, echoed Soviet cold war rhetoric against the capitalist West, and accepted Soviet positions within CMEA, the Warsaw Pact, and the UN. When the Soviets moved in the direction of détente in the 1950s and 1960s, so did the Central/Eastern European countries. And on signal from the Kremlin, they became increasingly involved in the Third World in the 1960s, providing economic and military assistance to revolutionary groups and leftist governments courted by the Soviet Union.

One must add, of course, that while their sovereignty in foreign policy was limited and they were obliged to accom-modate the Soviet Union, the Communist leaderships derived considerable political, economic, military, and psychological advantages from belonging to a tightly knit bloc of socialist countries guided and protected by Soviet power. Membership in the Soviet bloc ensured domestic stability and external security. It provided new opportunities for economic cooperation and expansion of trade within a diverse and traditionally conflict-ridden region.

PROBLEMS WITH THE SOVIET MODEL

From the mid-1950s onward, some Central/Eastern European countries experienced problems with the Soviet model, which was becoming a straitjacket. These problems threatened the stability and legitimacy of Communist party rule. They occurred in four areas: economic mismanagement, environmental deterioration, political repression, and foreign-policy subservience.

Economic Mismanagement

From the mid-1950s onward, most Central/Eastern European countries began to suffer from the same ills that afflicted the Soviet economy, in particular scarcity of food and other consumer goods, shoddiness of production, low worker productivity, gross waste of resources, rising prices, and declining growth rates.

The cause of these ills was the same kind of conditions found in the Soviet Union. Chief among these were a disregard of the standards of efficiency and rationality in many sectors of the economy; an excess of manpower and the absence of the high technology used in Western industrial production; a colossal waste of resources; an artificial pricing system, which paid little attention to supply and demand; an arbitrary and frequently incentive-diminishing wage scale; and an excessive emphasis on industrial expansion at the expense of agriculture and consumer goods production.

The severity of economic problems varied from north to south. From the beginning of Communist rule, the economies of the northern countries, notably those of Poland, Hungary, and Czechoslovakia, had been stronger, with either a highly developed transportation, communications, and education infrastructure and/or substantial industrialization achieved prior to World War II. They suffered less from adoption in the late 1940s of Soviet-style economic organization than did the poorer, underdeveloped countries of the south—Romania, Bulgaria, Yugoslavia, and Albania.

Some leaders, notably those of Yugoslavia, Hungary, and Czechoslovakia, acknowledged difficulties in the performance of their Soviet-style command economies. They openly admitted that little if any allowance had been made for local economic and social conditions that differed from those in the Soviet Union and that their countries had suffered chronic economic underperformance as a result of their slavish imitation of the Soviet model. But, with the exception of Yugoslavia's Tito, it took Central/Eastern European leaderships a long time after their recognition of the limits of the Soviet model to devise ways of altering it.

Environmental Deterioration

The lack of attention to environmental deterioration in the Soviet Union in the post-Stalinist era carried over into Central/Eastern Europe, where major pollution problems developed as a result of Soviet-imposed, Stalinistic industrialization policies. In addressing these problems, which were occurring at a time of diminishing financial resources, the Central/Eastern European governments received little guidance from the Soviet Union.

The major cause of environmental deterioration was physical contamination of air, land, and water resources as a result of inadequate government control of steel, chemical, and energy-producing industries. Lignite-mining and power-generating industries contaminated the panhandle where East Germany, Czechoslovakia, and Poland met. Industrial debris and sewage clogged the Oder and Vistula rivers. And pollution caused a scarcity of drinking water in Prague and Warsaw.

The governments had other problems controlling the environment. Pollution control was expensive. Industrial enterprises could not rely on government support to pay for making their operation safer but had to do so themselves at the expense of profit. Moreover, because of political restrictions, ordinary citizens affected by pollution could not lobby aggressively for increased government regulation; all they could do was complain to authorities and hope that they would be responsive.

It was also true that while ordinary people complained about environmental pollution, they were not sympathetic to the idea of diverting scarce resources to the task of reducing it. (Governments were under heavy pressure to give priority to housing and food production and did not even want to enforce the environmental regulations already in place.) Furthermore, pollution across national borders was aggravated by interstate political tensions and the lack of interstate cooperation to correct the problem. Thus, while Poland's polluted environment, especially in the highly industrialized area of Silesia, was mainly the result of Polish industry, it also got 45 percent of its air pollution from Czechoslovakia and East Germany.

Finally, none of the countries could expect help from the Soviet Union. Only in the late 1980s did Soviet leaders begin to acknowledge the existence of environmental deterioration; they had little wisdom or resources to share with their allies in this area of socialist development.

Political Repression

In Poland and Czechoslovakia, and to a lesser extent in other Central/Eastern European countries, key groups in society wanted relief from the imposition of Soviet-style societal discipline and the stifling of political expression. These groups included workers, farmers, youths, the scientific and literary intelligentsia, politicians in national legislatures, and the Roman Catholic Church. Different groups at different times in different countries sought major political change.

Those seeking change had their own reform and grievance agenda and, therefore, acted independently of one another. Some were interested mainly in achieving political liberalization in the form of a relaxation of censorship and toleration of dissent, open and competitive elections, and a legislature with real power. Other groups wanted redress of economic grievances, such as higher wages, better living conditions, more food, and the establishment of a responsive trade union organization in contrast to the official party-dominated unions, which did little to protect the interests of workers.

Efforts to obtain change frequently led to political unrest and violence. On some occasions the demand for radical reform caused divisions within the Communist party, in violation of democratic centralism. Invariably, however, the desired reforms did not materialize, and the authorities used coercion to end political turmoil and restore law and order. The Soviet Union invariably had a hand in preserving the status quo against pressures for major alteration of Soviet-style socialism in different Central/Eastern European countries. And the problems that originally caused stress in the society invariably remained to provoke it again at some later time.

Foreign Policy Subservience

A fourth problem for the Central/Eastern European countries concerned foreign policy. In the 1950s, 1960s, and 1970s, several leaders, following in Tito's footsteps, questioned the extent of loyalty and cooperation that the Kremlin expected of them on international issues. Indeed, they believed that continuing subservience to Moscow was a cause of economic and political problems. They knew that their servility to Soviet policies contributed to the undercurrent of popular hostility to the Russians and to the possibility of an outbreak of anti-Soviet sentiment.

Leaderships also were uncomfortable over Soviet-imposed limits on their relations with the West, in particular on efforts to improve political ties and expand trade with Western countries. They wanted to buy from the West industrial goods and technology needed to improve economic performance but not available from either the Soviet Union or from one another. They developed a stake in détente that at times at least seemed, if not in fact was, greater than that of the Soviet Union.

DIVERGENCE FROM THE SOVIET MODEL

A way out of Central/Eastern Europe's problems with the Soviet model of socialism was to reform it. In the years following Stalin's death, in 1953, external circumstances as well as internal problems encouraged the Central/Eastern European countries to alter their Soviet-inspired domestic and foreign policies. The scope of divergence from the Soviet model varied from country to country. Eventually, the Kremlin set and enforced limits to divergence.

External Circumstances

Certain Soviet behavior following the death of Stalin encouraged some Central/Eastern European countries to modify Soviet practices. Other important events also influenced change. They were the Sino–Soviet dispute, Eurocommunism, East–West détente, and the Roman Catholic Church.

Soviet Behavior

In reconciling the Soviet Union with Yugoslavia in 1955 and 1956, Nikita Khrushchev, Stalin's successor as general secretary of the Soviet Communist Party, implied acceptance of Tito's independence of Soviet policy in 1948. Then, at the 20th Congress of the Soviet Communist Party, in 1956, Khrushchev spoke of the legitimacy of "different paths to socialism," implying his country's willingness to tolerate some independence in policy making by other Central/Eastern European parties. Finally, the Soviet Union's own departure, under Khrushchev's leadership, from several Stalinist policies encouraged some Central/Eastern European party leaders at the time and in succeeding years to assume Soviet approval of their own modifications of Stalinism.

The Sino–Soviet Dispute

The outbreak of a long and bitter dispute between the Soviet Union and China in the early 1960s influenced Central/Eastern Europe. This dispute, which grew out of ideological and strategic differences between the two countries as well as a clash between the personalities of their charismatic and compulsive leaderships, undermined Soviet claims to ideological leadership of Communist parties. Coming as it did after the 1948 conflict with Yugoslavia, the Soviet dispute with China affirmed the inability of the Soviet Union to force all Communist parties, even those on its frontiers, to follow its model of socialism.

Eurocommunism

Eurocommunism was a set of ideas and practices of socialist development advocated in the 1970s by Communist parties in Western Europe, notably those of Italy, France, and Spain. The Eurocommunists envisaged a liberal democratic path to socialism that included respect for political freedom, a multiparty system in which the Communist party would move in and out of power in response to the will of the electorate, and a mixed economy that would allow a substantial amount of free enterprise. Eurocommunists also advocated the sovereignty of Communist parties in the determination of national paths to socialist development. Eurocommunism was at odds with Soviet ideology and practice, and it appealed to reformist-minded people in some of the Central/Eastern European countries. Eurocommunism offered an alternative to the Soviet model.

East–West Détente

Beginning with West Germany's *Ostpolitik* (a policy calling for West German reconciliation with Central/Eastern Europe) in the late 1960s, and continuing into the 1970s, the West showed interest in bringing an end to the cold war and improving political and economic relations with the Central/Eastern European countries. This new Western will toward détente, because it offered many advantages to the Central/Eastern European countries, not least of which was an expansion in trade, gave them an incentive to chart their own national paths to socialism. Indeed, through détente the West was able to encourage Central/Eastern Europe to independence of the Soviet Union.

The Roman Catholic Church

The Roman Catholic Church also was responsible for Central/Eastern European divergence from the Soviet model. While the church carefully refrained from criticizing individual governments, it continued to denounce the atheism and totalitarianism of socialist countries. Under Pope John Paul II, the Vatican tried discreetly to encourage Communist party leaderships in Central/Eastern Europe to modify their Soviet-inspired policies against religion. The pope welcomed opportunities to dialogue with Communist leaderships and subtly exploited for this purpose their own interest in interacting with him as another means of legitimizing their rule.

The Scope of Divergence

The extent of divergence from the Soviet model after Stalin's death varied significantly throughout Central/Eastern Europe. Some countries diverged extensively from the Soviet economic model—for example, this was true of Yugoslavia, starting in the 1950s; and of Hungary, starting in the late 1960s. Other countries that attempted substantial divergence in the political sphere, like Poland and Hungary in 1956, Czechoslovakia in 1968, and Poland again in 1980–1981, were less successful, largely because of Soviet opposition.

Other countries, notably Romania, Bulgaria, and Albania, diverged minimally or not at all in the economic and political arenas starting in the 1950s. The Communist party leaderships of these countries were very conservative on the issue of domestic reform. They seemed to share the Kremlin's historic fear that change, especially in politics—say, in the form of liberalization—would jeopardize the Communist party's monopoly of power and eventually subvert the national commitment to socialism.

Three countries succeeded in developing substantial independence of the Soviet Union in their foreign policies: Yugoslavia, Albania, and Romania. Of these, Yugoslavia and Albania displayed the most independence of the Soviet Union; Romania showed the least. While it is true that Romania criticized and opposed Soviet behavior on many occasions, unlike Yugoslavia and Albania it remained closely linked to the socialist community through membership in the Warsaw Pact and CMEA.

The Limits of Divergence

The Soviets under Stalin, Khrushchev, and Brezhnev placed limits on the scope of divergence. Although they never came right out and said as much, they insisted that all of the Central/Eastern European countries remain faithful to three principles of socialist development: 1) a monolithic dictatorship by the Communist party and the party's practice of democratic centralism; 2) socialist control over the means of production; and 3) the preservation of close ties to the socialist community and the Soviet Union through membership in the Warsaw Pact and CMEA.

(UN photo/Yutaka Nagata)

UN General Assembly president Imre Hollai of Hungary (right) greets Romanian foreign minister Stefan Andrei in New York in 1982. The United Nations traditionally acted as a forum in which Central/Eastern European countries like Romania were able to express foreign policy independence of the Soviet Union.

The Soviets also showed little tolerance of political liberalization. They feared that any weakening of political discipline in a Central/Eastern European country, especially within the Communist party itself, was a threat to socialism and to that country's closeness to the socialist community. Thus the Soviet Union interfered to end political liberalization in Poland and Hungary in 1956 and in Czechoslovakia in 1968, and it exerted tremendous pressure on the Polish leadership in 1980 and 1981 to suppress a growing political criticism.

On the other hand, the Soviets tolerated departures from their model of socialism in the economic sphere. They appreciated the Polish Communist Party's decision in the mid-1950s to return some farms to private ownership for the sake of increasing incentives to expand agricultural output. They also accepted the Hungarian Communist Party's decentralization of economic decision making in its New Economic Mechanism of 1968.

The Soviets also appreciated the need for changes in Central/Eastern European economic organization to improve economic conditions as an important means of discouraging outbreaks of social unrest. In the case of Hungary, incidentally, the subsequent success of the 1968 reforms in expanding Hungarian output, which led to a rise in the standard of living, encouraged the Soviet Union to consider its own adoption of a version of those reforms.

The Kremlin also endured Romania's criticisms of the Warsaw Pact and CMEA, neutrality in the Sino–Soviet dispute, and opposition to the Soviet intervention in Czechoslovakia in 1968. The Soviets understood how this independence, inspired by a strong sense of nationalism within Romanian society, strengthened the Romanian leadership. And as long as the Romanian leadership practiced Soviet norms, in particular the Communist party's unchallenged control over society, where they wanted maximum conformity, the Soviets would live with Romania's differences in foreign policy. The Soviet Union was able to do little about the divergence of Yugoslavia and Albania, because they remained beyond its control. The Soviets would have obvious logistical and other difficulties in executing a military intervention in these countries to force their conformity. Moreover, the Soviets knew that they would risk a confrontation with NATO were they to try to limit the independence of Yugoslavia and Albania by military force and thereby disrupt the strategic balance of forces in Europe.

CHANNELS OF SOVIET INFLUENCE

The Soviets wielded extraordinary influence over the development of Central/Eastern Europe until the late 1980s. The channels of this influence were political, economic, and military.

Political Channels

The main political channel of Soviet influence in most Central/Eastern European countries was the first or general secretary of each Communist party. But this was true only as long as the process of leadership selection continued to be dominated by a small group of senior party officials and excluded the influence of the rank-and-file. Moreover, the usefulness of the first or general secretaries as agents of the Kremlin depended upon the loyalty and obedience of party members through the enforcement of democratic centralism.

Economic Channels

CMEA provided the Soviets with additional opportunities to influence the behavior of the Central/Eastern European countries. By encouraging economic interdependence among the states and the Soviet Union through coordination of economic planning and the development of a division of specialization, the Soviet Union exerted some influence over the states' planning processes and strengthened trade and investment links. The Soviets looked to Poles, Czechoslovaks, and Hungarians (as well as East Germans) to expand industrial output and to Bulgarians and Romanians to specialize in the export of raw materials. There was some criticism of this specialization by countries, especially Romania, that wanted to lessen dependence on the Soviet bloc and expand trade with the West. But no Central/Eastern European country defected from CMEA.

The Soviets had additional economic means of influencing the countries. The Soviet Union remained the chief source of energy for the region. It also was the chief purchaser of Central/Eastern European manufactures. Large Soviet purchases helped the countries to offset the cost of high-priced oil imports. Moreover, in many instances the Central/Eastern European countries found Soviet goods more attractive than imports from the West because they were cheaper and could be paid for partly by barter arrangements, which the West rejected.

In the late 1980s, the Soviets looked for support within CMEA for the establishment of currency convertibility to expand trade and strengthen intrabloc economic unity. (A *convertible currency* allows a country to use foreign exchange earned in sales to a second country in order to purchase goods in a third country.) Trade within CMEA consisted mostly of bilateral barter transactions because of the unwillingness of the Central/Eastern European countries to accept one another's currency in payment for exports. But countries like the Soviet Union, Hungary, and Czechoslovakia, which had strong foreign exchange earning capabilities as a result of competitive export industries, were interested in currency convertibility.

Military Channels

The Warsaw Pact remained an important channel of Soviet influence during the 1980s. The Pact always was under the command of a high-ranking Soviet military officer; no Central/Eastern European military officer headed any top-level Warsaw Pact command. Through the Pact the Soviets encouraged standardization of weapons and Central/Eastern European dependence upon Soviet sources of procurement. Warsaw Pact maneuvers in different Central/Eastern European countries served to remind all the countries of the enormous military power that was under Soviet command—power that could be used against the countries to guarantee their loyalty to socialism.

The Soviet-led Warsaw Pact military intervention in Czechoslovakia in August 1968 showed the vulnerability of the Central/Eastern European countries to the collective military might of the Pact in the event of a deviation from the Soviet model considered dangerous to Soviet security. On that occasion the Soviets laid down a doctrine of intervention, as enunciated by Leonid Brezhnev. The Brezhnev Doctrine justified collective military action by socialist countries whenever they were threatened by so-called counterrevolutionary forces. The doctrine meant that the Soviet Union and its Warsaw Pact allies would intervene militarily to prevent any major departures of a Central/Eastern European political system from the single-party dictatorship or any action tantamount to a defection from the alliance system. While Mikhail Gorbachev all but repudiated the Brezhnev Doctrine in a speech on July 6, 1989, to European Community parliamentary deputies in Strasbourg, it would have been foolhardy of Soviet bloc countries to assume that they were no longer vulnerable to Soviet coercion. The Soviet Union might have revived the Brezhnev Doctrine if Gorbachev were replaced as Soviet party leader by a hardliner, or Gorbachev might have been pressured to use force to maintain control by more belligerent Soviet leaders.

The Soviets continued to station troops in Poland, Czechoslovakia, and Hungary (as well as in East Germany) because these countries were the most highly industrialized and the nearest geographically to NATO and therefore of great importance to Soviet security. Although Soviet military personnel in those countries were subject in certain ways to local jurisdiction, in accordance with status-of-forces agreements the Soviet Union concluded with their governments, the Kremlin had considerable latitude in the use of the troops through secret bilateral agreements with the host authorities. The presence of Soviet troops reinforced the political status quo in these countries, making the threat of a Soviet military intervention possible and therefore credible.

CHALLENGES TO SOVIET INFLUENCE IN THE 1980s

Although most of the Central/Eastern European countries remained closely linked to the Soviet Union, in much the same way that they had been since Communist parties achieved power in the late 1940s, developments in the 1980s encouraged some of them—including those that had been most loyal and most deferential to the Soviets in the past—to press for greater autonomy. The most important of these developments were the three Soviet leadership successions in the 1980s, a region-wide slump in economic growth, the sharp deterioration of Soviet–American relations in the aftermath of the Soviet intervention in Afghanistan, the expansion of ties with Western Europe, and perestroika.

The Soviet Leadership Successions

Central/Eastern European Communist leaderships saw uncertainty and ambiguity in the Kremlin in the early 1980s, when there were three leadership successions (from Brezhnev to Andropov in 1982, from Andropov to Chernenko in 1984, and from Chernenko to Gorbachev in 1985). They saw an opportunity in these shifts in the Kremlin to promote their own national interests and ambitions.

For example, in the late summer of 1984, both East Germany and Bulgaria, known for their loyalty and closeness to Moscow, publicized plans of their party leaderships to visit West German Chancellor Helmut Kohl, whose conservative government had just extended a loan of $300 million to East Berlin. Hungary's leadership publicly endorsed this East German policy and encouraged the visit to West Germany.

The Soviets were uneasy, although these initiatives undoubtedly had been cleared in Moscow earlier. (The Kremlin was not unsympathetic to Central/Eastern European countries improving relations with the West to obtain economic help that it was unwilling or unable to provide for its allies.) Moscow did not want its allies to become heavily

indebted to the West. The Soviet leadership clearly was uneasy over what looked like a flurry of East German efforts at the end of the summer of 1984 to court West Germany at the expense of ties to the Soviet Union. Thus, it vetoed East German Communist leader Erich Honecker's planned visit to Bonn at the end of September. The Bulgarian visit also did not occur.

It was also in the summer of 1984 that Honecker made a conciliatory gesture toward Romania. Relations between the two countries had been correct but cool, because of Romanian party leader Nicolae Ceausescu's frequent disagreements with the Kremlin. Honecker congratulated the Romanian Communists on their country's liberation from Nazi German control 40 years earlier, in August 1944. Moreover, Honecker said nothing—to the dismay of the Soviets—about the new Romanian position that the liberation had occurred prior to the entry of Soviet forces into Romania.

In the spring of 1985, while discussing the renewal of the alliance, Warsaw Pact members raised the issues of national sovereignty and noninterference in ways that obliquely challenged the legitimacy of the Brezhnev Doctrine. Furthermore, most of the Central/Eastern European countries favored a short period of renewal, in opposition to the Soviets, who wanted a long renewal period. Although the Pact was renewed for 20 years in April 1985, an apparent victory for the Soviets, the Central/Eastern European countries had communicated to the Kremlin their sensitivity to Soviet intrusiveness and their concern with autonomy in domestic and foreign policy making.

While the Soviets had their way with their allies, they were upset. They did not like the unmistakable tendency of the Central/Eastern European countries to move on their own to improve East–West relations.

Economic Slowdown

The need to remedy an economic slowdown in many parts of Central/Eastern Europe in the early 1980s was another incentive for autonomy. To expand output of consumer goods and of goods exported abroad for hard currency, the countries that were feeling the pinch needed to undertake sweeping reforms toward market-oriented economic structures that would carry them far away from the autarchic Soviet economic model. But they also needed help from the West, in particular Western technology and the financial credit to pay for it. This meant preserving East–West détente when it was being undermined by Soviet–American confrontation.

Because the Central/Eastern European Communist leaderships realized that economic stagnation could lead to political instability, including the kind of unrest Poland experienced, and because they realized the alternative to an expansion of trade with the West was an increased dependency on the Soviet Union, they had a very strong incentive to proceed on their own to keep political and economic ties with the West in good repair. They had a vested interest in diminishing the level of tension between the Soviet Union and the United States.

Soviet–American Relations

It is not an exaggeration to say that the Central/Eastern European countries were very worried throughout the early and mid-1980s about the deterioration of Soviet–American relations and the escalation of the arms race in the form of increased superpower missile deployment in Europe. In response to the American deployment of Pershing II and cruise missiles in Western Europe, the Soviets increased deployment of their SS-20 missiles in East Germany and Czechoslovakia. Other deployment sites were in Poland and Bulgaria.

The Central/Eastern European countries conveyed as pointedly as they could to the Kremlin their concern about the tension-ridden Soviet relationship with the United States. The Soviet–American rivalry threatened their own material well-being, endangering their security and compromising efforts to increase their autonomy of the Soviet Union, which tended to become sensitive about diversity within the Warsaw Pact at times of difficulty with the Americans.

Their enthusiasm over the arms control agreement signed by Mikhail Gorbachev and Ronald Reagan in Washington in December 1987, therefore, was not surprising. They saw the treaty as further evidence of a real improvement in Soviet–American relations. They were gratified by a willingness of the new Soviet leadership to compromise on arms control issues for the sake of promoting superpower détente. And they were relieved that at last the Kremlin would begin to remove Soviet SS-20 missiles from their territory and thereby lessen the risk of their involvement in a nuclear war with the West.

The United States encouraged the countries to move in the direction of greater political and economic freedom. Thus, Poland and other countries increasingly turned to the United States for economic and financial help to facilitate their reform programs.

The United States, however, was reluctant to assume a leading role in fostering change. In July 1989 President George Bush indicated to the NATO allies that the United States envisaged a multilateral approach to the socialist world. In his view, the European Community would coordinate the West's efforts to help Central/Eastern European countries economically. By this policy Bush probably wanted to reassure the Kremlin that the United States was not operating a Western campaign to "decouple" the Warsaw Pact allies from the Soviet Union.

Central/Eastern Europe and Western Europe

In the late 1980s, the Central/Eastern European countries actively sought expanded political and economic ties with Western Europe. Good relations with Western Europe could strengthen their independence of Moscow; could help them to acquire high technology unavailable from the Soviet Union for economic expansion; and could provide opportunities for diplomatic settlement of intra-European problems in the areas of environmental control, arms reduction, and mutual security.

The countries tried to draw closer to Western Europe in several ways. One was through bilateral summitry. Second, the Central/Eastern European countries negotiated with Western Europe to achieve mutual and balanced force reductions in NATO and the Warsaw Pact. And third, through CMEA, the Central/Eastern European countries worked to develop economic links with the European Community, CMEA's counterpart, and to lessen dependence on the Soviet Union. But while Western Europe welcomed the interest of Central/Eastern Europeans in strengthening and expanding détente, it was slow with economic and financial aid, perhaps waiting for further developments and afraid of interfering in Soviet bloc relations and arousing Soviet anxiety.

The Impact of Perestroika

By the mid-1980s all the Central/Eastern European countries were in need of some reformism to correct the many deficiencies in their Soviet-style socialist systems. They had failed to provide their citizens with adequate levels of income, housing, consumer supplies and services, social welfare amenities, education, and job security—the so-called human rights of socialist systems.

The mid-1980s brought evidence of popular unrest provoked by economic crisis. The peoples of Central/Eastern Europe had always tacitly assumed that in return for curtailment of many personal and political freedoms, they would have the material well-being promised by communist ideology and their socialist governments. But by the early 1980s, most peoples of the region believed that their socialist systems would not perform well and would not deliver on ideological promises.

Official reactions between 1985 and 1989 to Soviet perestroika were mixed. While all Soviet bloc Communist leaders dutifully acknowledged that perestroika in the Soviet Union was a welcome development and that an exchange of experience among the allies was good, some were not ready to introduce it in their own societies. On the other hand, ordinary citizens showed much interest in Soviet reform and in some instances insisted that their governments imitate it, or even go beyond it, to improve local conditions.

Hungary and Poland, and to a lesser extent Bulgaria, reacted positively to Soviet perestroika. Hungary and Poland undertook major reforms to carry them far away from the traditional, orthodox, Soviet-style socialism. Bulgaria also attempted reforms, primarily in the economic sphere; but made little change in its traditional political order.

At the same time, Czechoslovakia, while envisaging substantial change in economic organization, initially adopted little substantive change of traditional policies and priorities and seemed determined to prevent any alteration of its political structure. East Germany and especially Romania stalwartly refused either to acknowledge performance problems or make policy changes to resolve them.

Yugoslavia and Albania went their separate and independent ways. Yugoslavia continued a conservative pragmatism of its own design until the Civil War started in 1991, when reform efforts came abruptly to an end. Albania remained indifferent and unresponsive to Soviet perestroika, reasserting its commitment to its own brand of neo-Stalinist organization and behavior.

UPHEAVAL IN 1989

Between October 1 and December 25, 1989, the conservative Communist leaderships of East Germany, Czechoslovakia, Bulgaria, and Romania collapsed. Paradoxically, those countries that at one time had most strongly resisted Gorbachev's call for reform now were in a political revolution. New leaderships, composed of pragmatic and reform-minded Communists, succeeded to power. Responding to the first massive popular demonstrations in 40 years of Communist rule, they were prepared to introduce perestroika-like reforms in their countries and to accommodate other demands for an end to political repression.

The new leaders quickly lifted restrictions on freedom of the press, assembly, speech, and travel. Recognizing the existence of opposition groups, they agreed to share policy-making power with these groups in newly reshuffled coalition-style cabinets. They consented to the formal liquidation of the Communist party's historic monopoly of power, thereby accepting the principle of political pluralism, and they pledged to hold free elections of new parliaments early in 1990. In these elections Communists would compete with other political groups for seats. As the new decade began, the old monolithic and Soviet-dominated authoritarian order appeared to be at an end.

In this new situation, the Communist parties tried to hold on to power. They held emergency "soul-searching" conferences that led to changes in name, to the abandonment of their traditional neo-Stalinistic ideological programs, and to the endorsement of political democratization. Reform-minded Communists criticized and attacked their former conservative leaderships, calling for their punishment for incompetence and corruption.

But the scramble of Communists for political survival was a failure. Popular distrust and dislike of them was pervasive, not only because of their mismanagement of society but also because of recent revelations of the deceit and hypocrisy of their dethroned leaderships. While Erich Honecker, Milos Jakes, Todor Zhivkov, and Nicolae Ceausescu had called for austerity among their citizens and forced them to endure harsh living conditions for the sake of building a better future, these hard-line leaders not only embezzled public wealth for private gain but lived in luxury, enjoying food and other goods that were in many cases unavailable to ordinary citizens and were imported from the West with precious hard currency. As a result the Communist parties and those associated with their policies—or what was left of them—in most of Central/Eastern Europe lost all credibility. It seemed unlikely that, even with the new names, new leaders, and new programs, most would ever enjoy public trust, never mind public support, in a bid to participate once again in national politics.

Roots and Causes

Now that these Communist-controlled systems have fallen so swiftly and dramatically, it is possible to see how fragile the structure was that held them in place. Certainly Gorbachev's clearly stated policy of hands-off regarding the internal politics of the Central/Eastern European countries, along with the model of political reform set by Poland and Hungary earlier in the year, provided the background for the changes in East Germany, Czechoslovakia, Bulgaria, and Romania in the fall and early winter of 1989.

But there were other reasons why these socialist regimes fell so quickly. They had never dug deep roots in their societies. The Central/Eastern Europeans saw their governments as alien, imposed and used by the Kremlin to subject them to Soviet power. Adding to popular dislike of the Communist leaderships was their excessive political repression, at times more harsh than that of the Soviet Union itself and increasingly intolerable in light of the political democratization taking place in Poland and Hungary.

Socialist systems had never obtained legitimacy also because of their failure to provide the material prosperity promised in their communist ideology. Living standards in most of the Central/Eastern European societies had barely improved in the 45-year period of Communist party rule. In some instances living standards had deteriorated in the late 1980s; and they always had been well below those in the West, with which Central/Eastern Europe citizens increasingly compared themselves. In sum, most people, especially the youth, had become fed up with both the political and economic hardships they had endured for the sake of building a utopian society, which they now realized would never materialize.

Thus, despite the appearance of strength, the Communist regimes were in fact weak without Soviet support and therefore unable to suppress forcibly the huge popular demonstrations for democracy—as their conservative leaderships, perhaps tempted by the June 1989 example of the Chinese, initially had been inclined to do. Moreover, the Central/Eastern Europeans were not isolated, as was the Chinese opposition. The societies of East Germany, Czechoslovakia,

Bulgaria, and Romania, because of their geographic proximity to other socialist countries going through reform, and because of the influence of the mass media in communicating events elsewhere in the region, were aware of events throughout Eastern Europe, despite the efforts of their repressive governments to interdict the flow of information.

In addition, Gorbachev advocated and welcomed the kind of change taking place in Poland and Hungary in 1988 and early 1989. He urged other allies in Central/Eastern Europe to adopt their own perestroika-style reform programs to remedy a regionwide stagnation, which affected even the most prosperous socialist countries and threatened an unrest dangerous to socialism and to Soviet influence in Central/Eastern Europe. He brushed aside the Soviet bloc leaders' anxieties about introducing reforms that could and in fact did end by undermining their power and jeopardizing rather than strengthening socialism.

Gorbachev was at least partly responsible for the collapse of Communist party rule in Central/Eastern Europe also because he refused to approve and, indeed, opposed the use of force by East Germany's Honecker, Czechoslovakia's Jakes, Bulgaria's Zhivkov, and Romania's Ceausescu to resist the mounting popular pressures for democracy. In effect, Gorbachev helped seal their doom. Moreover, he ruled out invoking the Brezhnev Doctrine and a Soviet-led military intervention to keep the leaderships in power. Intervention would have alienated the West, might have provoked civil war, and would have sent a dangerous message to the Soviet Union's resistive nationalities. Finally, Gorbachev hoped that the removal of conservative leaders like Honecker, Jakes, Zhivkov, and Ceausescu would make way for reformers, like himself, who would now try to breathe new life into the region's socialist experience. Leaders of the democratic movements in Prague, Leipzig, and Sofia acknowledged that without Gorbachev's policy of leniency and restraint toward Central/Eastern Europe, the political changes that occurred would have been impossible.

Finally, Western European countries, in particular France and West Germany, as well as the United States encouraged and supported the efforts of Soviet bloc countries to abandon communism. It appeared that they would offer large-scale economic and financial assistance, as West Germany and the United States had to Poland and Hungary, should they move away from Communist rule.

Patterns of Political Change

In their opposition to repressive government, the peoples of East Germany, Czechoslovakia, Bulgaria, and Romania showed similar patterns of response. All had massive antigovernment demonstrations in the large urban centers. These were remarkably resilient in the face of brute physical force. Popular determination to achieve change, even if it meant loss of life, apparently was evenly matched against the deadly weapons used by the authorities. Moreover, in

three countries—East Germany, Czechoslovakia, and Bulgaria—the activities of protesting citizens, despite the large numbers of them, were for the most part peaceful, with a minimum of violence and practically no bloodshed. As one commentator observed in Czechoslovakia, "hardly a window was broken." Their example calls into question traditional thinking about the omnipotence of the totalitarian state, in particular its capacity to achieve conformity and obedience for any length of time by coercion.

Romania, however, experienced a very high level of violence in November and December 1989, which culminated with the summary execution of President and party leader Nicolae Ceausescu and his wife, Elena. The violence seemed in proportion to the degree of popular hostility to the regime's political and economic policies in past decades as well as to the stubbornness of its leadership's refusal to heed the writing on the wall, so to speak, in neighboring countries and to respond to the mounting popular pressures, especially among workers, for change. Not surprisingly, in the immediate aftermath of the collapse of the Ceausescu regime, the Romanian people seemed more vengeful in their expression of anti-Communist feelings than were the peoples of other socialist countries.

Whatever the level of violence, though, popular resistance to conservative rule in all four countries during the fall of 1989 cut across class lines. Workers, intellectuals, students, Communist party members, and soldiers cooperated in opposing the leadership of hard-liners. This unprecedented unity of the opposition caught the governments of Honecker, Milos Jakes, Todor Zhivkov, and Ceausescu off guard, unprepared, and more vulnerable than at any time in the past.

In early 1990 the Communist parties rid themselves of their former leaders, who were accused of corruption, dishonesty, and incompetence. The parties changed their names, announced new programs, and agreed to renounce their political monopolies. They also consented to the legalization of multiparty systems, to hold open and competitive elections for parliament before July 1990, and to accept the outcome of these elections, even if doing so meant loss of leadership and exclusion from government. They took these revolutionary steps not only in response to intense popular pressure for an end to Communist dominance but also in the hope that they could salvage some of their political power and play a role in the new democratic order by making timely concessions.

In the immediate postupheaval period, prior to the holding of parliamentary elections in the spring of 1990, the new Communist leaderships made coalitions with recently formed non-Communist organizations to prepare their countries for the transition to pluralistic democracy. These interim regimes also promised and began, albeit cautiously and haltingly, the dismantling of the command economies inherited from their neo-Stalinistic predecessors. They took the first steps to reduce government control over economic life, to increase private entrepreneurialism, to pay more attention to consumer needs, especially in the area of food, and to expand foreign investment in local enterprises.

POST-COMMUNIST DEVELOPMENT

By the summer of 1990, six former Soviet satellites had held free elections for new parliaments and had produced new leaderships committed to liberal democracy. Along with efforts to democratize their political systems, the post-Communist political leaderships have begun to alter radically or even abandon the state-controlled economies that they had been forced to adopt by the Soviet Union. The former Soviet satellites have also undertaken a reorientation of their foreign policies, shifting their focus of international interest from the East to the West.

The newly emancipated Central/Eastern European countries have adopted the Western European style of parliamentary democracy that involves multiparty systems. The unaccustomed openness of the post-Communist political environment has encouraged a proliferation of narrowly focused party organizations. The new democratic systems also have provided for popularly elected presidential executives endowed with substantial leadership authority, enabling them to determine the broad direction of policy.

Another important component taken from the Western European model is ministerial accountability to legislative bodies, which have been given the right to vote no-confidence, thereby enabling them to replace ministerial leadership. Most of the new legislatures have been elected directly by the voters, sometimes in a complex electoral process involving proportional representation. While maximizing representation of the popular will, this has increased the number and competitiveness of the new parties and thereby contributed to a degree of instability that interferes with policy making, especially the enactment of controversial reforms.

At the same time, however, democracy is developing in Central/Eastern Europe in different ways and at different rates of change, based upon the peculiar national character of individual countries. The sharpest contrast is between the less economically developed and more politically conservative Balkan countries in the south and the economically better-off and somewhat more politically mature countries of the north.

For example, throughout 1990 and 1991, Romania, Bulgaria, and Albania moved very slowly in the development of democratic political processes because they lacked a democratic tradition in the pre-Communist era and because under communism their repressive leaderships had destroyed any chances for the emergence of a reformist elite capable of assuming the leadership vacated by the Communists. By contrast, Czechoslovakia, Hungary, and Poland seemed to have more promising futures. They had some

experience with democratic ideas before and during the Communist era. In each of these countries, the Communist party leaderships had tolerated democratic dissidents. Although they were harassed and sometimes severely punished by the authorities, they survived to take the place of their persecutors in 1989 and to implement the political reform that they had been discussing and writing about for many years. Also favorable to the development of democracy in these northern countries was their achievement under Communist rule of a tolerable standard of living (at least by comparison with socialist countries in the south and in the Soviet Union), which provided them with a greater degree of social stability, important to the success of democratic government.

But it is also true that democratic institutions established in the former socialist dictatorships are extremely fragile and, worse, taxed to the breaking point by potentially destabilizing socioeconomic problems. The most important tasks are to introduce a market economy to improve living standards and to promote social peace and harmony, threatened by new sources of ethnocultural conflict, urban violence and anti-Semitism, and over church–state relations.

Trying to solve problems in the short term has tempted the post-Communist leaderships in Central/Eastern Europe to contemplate authoritarian methods that could jeopardize the new democratic experiments by opening the way for a return to an authoritarianism that would enable them to accommodate popular cravings for stability, if not prosperity. Thus far they have resisted this temptation. It remains to be seen how long they can maintain this restraint.

A wild card in the future development of democracy in Central/Eastern Europe is the role of the former Communists. While they certainly remain under a cloud, blamed for almost everything that is wrong with a country in the new era of political independence, they do have the potential for expansion of influence. Their promise for growth lies first in their effort to break as much as they can with past platforms and behavior traits. Many have the veneer of a democratic commitment and loyalty to their countries. They have been helped in this regard by the collapse of the Soviet Union and the Soviet Communist Party. The former Communists also benefit from the role that most of them seem to have adopted of loyal but unrelenting critics of government policies. Also, they exploit the increasing nostalgia that many people in Central/Eastern Europe are beginning to show for the days of order, stability, and predictability during which everybody was guaranteed at least enough food—and, in most cases, a job, a home, and affordable health care, essentials of daily life that no longer are guaranteed.

Introduction of a Market Economy
Economic reformers in the new post-Communist political systems were eager to introduce a market economy, arguing

that while the state-controlled economic systems of the Communist era had restarted economic life after World War II, they had not led to development of modern economies with high-technology industries that depend on innovation and risk taking. In the view of these economists as well as of the new political leaderships, it will take a market-based free enterprise economy to restore economic health, raise living standards, and ultimately ensure political stability in the post-Communist era.

Most Central/Eastern European reform economists believe that this transformation requires the privatization of large and small enterprises in industry, agriculture, and such service areas as banking, insurance, and retail sales; the autonomization of remaining state-controlled industries, with freedom of decision making on prices and wages; and the end of the monopolies and an increase in competitiveness. They are willing to accept bankruptcies and unemployment to encourage rationality in management decision making, improved efficiency, and a reduction of waste. With the termination of centralized control of prices and an end to subsidies to producers and consumers, inefficient industries will go under—and so will distorted prices. The market eventually will determine the real value of what is consumed. To fight the inevitable price inflation when controls are lifted, most governments plan to keep a lid on wages and to use fiscal policy to restrict demand. All the Central/Eastern European countries are in some stage of making their currencies convertible.

In addition, Central/Eastern European governments are trying to establish a legal infrastructure that will define the rules of the marketplace, particularly regarding property, contract, and tort. Other infrastructures—accounting, managerial, statistical—are being installed. Habits of accuracy and full disclosure are slowly taking the place of socialism's tendencies toward false and misleading statistics, cover-ups, and other deceptive economic and financial practices.

There remain several obstacles to meeting these goals. Although state control is diminishing, bureaucratic methods of production and allocation persist. Furthermore, the Central/Eastern Europeans have been hard hit by chaos in relations with their largest trading partner, the former Soviet Union. Trade is now on a hard currency basis, with both sides short of funds. Thus, the countries must pay in hard currency for Soviet oil. Moreover, CMEA is gone, along with its guaranteed markets for even poor-quality manufactured exports. As yet there is no alternative mechanism to facilitate interstate trade and the development of market-based national economies.

There are still other problems in moving toward free enterprise. The only people who have the financial resources to buy or to start up their own businesses are in many instances former Communist party officials. Also, investment banks and stock exchanges are not yet strong enough to finance large businesses. State decontrol of enterprises will

continue at a snail's pace, in part because of price distortion, which makes it very difficult for a buyer to determine the value of what is being purchased.

A further obstacle to capitalist development is psychological. Many Central/Eastern European peoples still have a socialist mind-set about the role of the state in safeguarding their well-being. They expect cheap medical care, housing, and education, as well as full-employment policies that guarantee people a job for life. These are expensive expectations that will take time to change. Until this occurs people are going to view the movement toward a free enterprise economy with suspicion, hostility, and resistance—especially as thus far they have gotten mostly depressed living standards and increased personal hardships rather than the radical improvement in living standards that they anticipated.

According to the International Monetary Fund, the only way to solvency for the post-Communist governments in Central/Eastern Europe is a harsh austerity, involving a reduction of consumption so that a greater part of gross national product can be earmarked for debt repayment. This approach requires keeping real wages down; closing inefficient centralized industries; and developing efficient, competitive, productive industries. But the costs of such austerity are high, especially for the average person. Nevertheless, the reformist leaderships seem determined to continue austerity to facilitate development of a market economy.

Nowhere are the problems of economic reformers more evident than in their efforts to privatize state-owned enterprises. There are hardly any local buyers for these state properties for sale; few citizens have the resources needed to purchase even small enterprises, never mind large concerns. The only people who seem to have the wealth to buy state industries are a small elite, in many instances the former Communist party officials who had managed the industries now being sold. They have bought some industries, thereby denying ownership to new entrepreneurs.

Furthermore, commercial banks and stock exchanges have not yet taken hold, and price distortion makes it very difficult for a buyer to determine the value of what is being purchased. Continuing price controls on raw materials and on finished products have made it virtually impossible for would-be entrepreneurs to figure out exactly what they are getting in a business.

A significant drag on privatization has to do with the fact that the state in many instances is not the uncontested owner of an enterprise and therefore lacks the authority to cede it. Many of these enterprises were confiscated after World War II, and claims against them are now being raised. Before privatization can proceed, the various owners have to resolve their claims for control—claims suppressed over decades of Communist rule. The struggle for "ownership" in nations that do not understand or are unsympathetic to the concept of property titles is taking a special form. The owner turns out to be the individual or group that commands an enterprise's operations and revenue. So far managers appear to have the upper hand, since they can fire workers.

Promoting Social Peace and Harmony

Since the collapse of Communist rule, the Central/Eastern European countries have experienced a revival of intense interethnic antagonisms, which had been held in check by the local Marxist leaderships. The new conditions of free speech, pluralism, and democracy have allowed hate to flourish along with free expression.

To some extent Communist rule can be blamed for the reigniting of nationalist-inspired political passions in the post-Communist era. While condemning nationalism because of its bourgeois inspiration, the Communist parties failed to homogenize the multiethnic societies of many former Soviet bloc countries, because the task of doing so was so horrendous and beyond their capabilities, as in Tito's Yugoslavia; or because it was inconvenient, in that there were political advantages, say, to allowing Czechs and Slovaks to retain their separate cultural identities in order to discourage their urge to have a separate political existence.

Ethnic-based conflict has changed the map of Central/Eastern Europe, causing the breakup of Czechoslovakia into two separate and independent administrative states, the Czech Republic and Slovakia, as well as of Yugoslavia, which has been replaced by the independent republics of Slovenia, Croatia, Bosnia-Herzegovina, and Macedonia, and by a new "rump state" of Yugoslavia, consisting of Serbia and Montenegro. Other areas seem on the threshhold of ethnic-based civil conflict, like the provinces of Kosovo and Vojvodina in Serbia, Transylvania in northwest Romania, and eastern Slovakia, where ethnic minorities chafe at real or imagined discrimination by the ethnic majorities who administer them.

The societies also have experienced a surge of public anti-Semitism, an extraordinary phenomenon, given that few Jews survived the Holocaust in Central/Eastern Europe. The explanation seems to lie in the fact that while the freer, pluralistic political environment has allowed the Central/Eastern European peoples to express the cultural prejudices they always have had about Jews, the Communist leaderships helped to keep those prejudices alive. Many Communist leaders were anti-Semitic and willing to launch anti-Semitic campaigns to gain popularity and legitimacy on the cheap—that is, without having earned it by public policy achievements.

Reorientation of Foreign Policies

To help solve the economic and social problems, the new democratic leaderships are looking to the West. They believe that they deserve and should receive assistance, in

Marshall Plan proportions, because they have done what the West had always wanted them to do. They abandoned socialism and established their independence of Moscow. They now argue that if these reforms are to last, they will need aid to cushion the traumatic impact of change on the daily lives of their citizens. Replacing paternalistic socialism with a new societal order based on individualism and self-reliance, they point out, needs the full help of the West.

Western European countries, and Germany in particular, have been responsive to the needs of the new Central/Eastern European leaderships. They have extended credits, revised export controls to allow purchase of many new high-technology items like computers, civil air navigation, and telecommunication equipment (previously restricted), and encouraged extensive World Bank lending.

Viewing the stability, prosperity, and friendship of the Central/Eastern European peoples as important to its material well-being, Germany has taken the lead in pressing for a substantial aid program to Central/Eastern Europe. The Bonn government has a sense of moral obligation, now that the Berlin Wall is down, not to abandon the peoples of Central/Eastern Europe but, rather, to foster a new economic cooperation between the former socialist societies and the democratic and well-off societies in the West.

But the 12-nation European Community (EC) has been ambivalent about admitting the former Soviet satellites to membership. Although British prime minister John Major has argued for broadening the Community to include the new democracies "as soon as they are ready politically and economically," he is the exception. French president François Mitterrand has warned that Central/Eastern Europe may be decades away from full membership in the EC.

Mitterrand's position derives in part from a concern that the admission of the Central/Eastern European countries would strengthen Germany's already substantial influence in the organization, given existing German political and economic links to the former Communist region. France also has economic reasons for proceeding cautiously: Paris does not want Western Europe markets flooded with cheap agricultural products from Central/Eastern Europe. Also, EC nations fear mass migrations westward to escape economic hardship at home. They want to block such migrations in light of their adoption of a single regional market, which will make movement within and between member nations difficult to control.

Nevertheless, in response to unrelenting pressure from Poland, Hungary, the Czech Republic, and Slovakia, and in an effort to reward these countries for their progress toward political pluralism and the market economy, the EC allowed Central/Eastern European agricultural and other exports into the European market despite opposition from France. Pablo Benavides, the EC's chief negotiator with the Central/Eastern European countries, acknowledged that the agreements

Establishment of the Comintern 1919	World War II begins in Central/Eastern Europe with the invasion of Poland 1939	Abolition of the Comintern 1943	Important decisions on boundaries and governments are made at the Yalta and Potsdam conferences 1945	Establishment of the Cominform 1947	The Cominform expels the Yugoslav party 1948	Establishment of CMEA 1949

with the above-mentioned countries opened the way for their full membership in the Community.

Military integration of Central/Eastern Europe with Western Europe has been slower than political and economic integration. Beginning in 1990 Poland, Hungary, and the then-Czechoslovakia signaled interest in joining NATO. Czech president Vaclav Havel has explained why the ex-Communist nations should belong to NATO: Central/Eastern Europe has always had very close cultural, diplomatic, and geostrategic links with Western Europe, and the destinies of the two regions are linked closely together. The ex-Communist countries, despite the half-century-long intimacy with the Soviet Union, have contributed to and share the values upon which NATO was founded and which it is pledged to defend. Finally, World War II revealed the vulnerability of Central/Eastern Europe to outside aggression, and the region desperately needs to be part of NATO's well-established collective security system.

NATO responded with some modest links with Central/Eastern Europe that provided some limited security against a resurgence of Soviet and post-Soviet Russian influence. In June 1991 the NATO foreign ministers agreed to tell the former Soviet bloc countries that NATO would not accept any coercion against emerging democracies, to offer wider cooperation between East and West in military matters, and to acknowledge close linkages between the security of Western countries and that of the Central/Eastern European countries.

At least for the time being, however, NATO does not contemplate giving membership to any Central/Eastern European country. NATO members do not want to antagonize the Kremlin, which remains very sensitive to the loss of influence in the region. Moreover, the Alliance prefers to wait on the issue of new members until it is sure about its new role and responsibilities in the post-Communist era.

Central/Eastern Europe and the United States

The United States has responded to the new political situation in Central/Eastern Europe with sympathy and encouragement but also with caution. While pleased with the abandonment of socialism and with the emancipation from Soviet control, the American government since 1989 has worried about the will and the capacity of the non-Communist leaderships to adopt capitalism and democracy. Not without some justification, Washington is sensitive to the continuing role of Communists in some countries. American caution also derives from a conviction that it is better for

those countries in the long term to help themselves rather than to rely on large infusions of foreign capital.

And yet there has been some support for aid to Central/Eastern Europe, especially in the U.S. Congress. There are also large numbers of Americans who have roots in the region and who constitute a persuasive voting bloc. Finally, Western Europeans, especially German chancellor Helmut Kohl and former foreign minister Hans Dietrich Genscher, have lobbied aggressively with Washington for generous Western aid to the former Soviet bloc.

In the early 1990s, the United States diminished restrictions on trade with Central/Eastern Europe, offered occasional but modest amounts of economic and financial assistance, and strengthened political ties with the new leaderships. It continued to warn some of the new governments about American sensitivity to perceived violations of human rights, especially conditions that interfered with the holding of truly free and open parliamentary elections. However, Washington did not give the region the attention it deserves. Crises in Yugoslavia, the Middle East, and Somalia in the early 1990s consumed American attention, as did the very visible need for aid to Russia. Under President Bill Clinton, American domestic problems in the mid- to late 1990s will probably also distract Washington from problems in the region.

Central/Eastern Europe and the
Soviet Union/Commonwealth

Central/Eastern European relations with the former Soviet Union in the early 1990s focused on getting the Soviets to withdraw troops and to consent to the dissolution of the Warsaw Pact and CMEA. Bilateral discussions between Central/Eastern European countries that still had large numbers of Soviet troops deployed on their territory, notably East Germany, Poland, Hungary, and Czechoslovakia, were successful in producing agreements on the conditions of final evacuation, which the Kremlin honored. There were some temporary difficulties, reflecting a measure of bitterness on both sides, but these difficulties did not interrupt the withdrawal process. The Kremlin also accommodated demands of the Central/Eastern European countries for the termination of the Warsaw Pact.

At the same time, the Central/Eastern European countries tried to keep their political fences mended with the Kremlin to ensure that the end of Communist rule would not be a liability for the Soviet Union. They discreetly lobbied with the West for aid to the Soviet Union, on the assumption that political and economic crises in the Soviet Union endangered their own security and stability. They also pro-

Establishment of
the Warsaw Pact;
Khrushchev
announces
"different paths to
socialism"
1955

A crisis in Polish
and Hungarian
relations with the
Soviet Union
1956

The Soviet-led
Warsaw Pact
intervention in
Czechoslovakia
1968

Challenges to
Soviet authority
and the Soviet
political and
economic models
gain momentum

Communist rule
collapses in
Central/Eastern
Europe

1980s–1990s

The Yugoslav
Civil War intensi-
fies and threat-
ens regional
stability; CMEA
and the Warsaw
Pact are dis-
solved

Central/Eastern
Europe seeks
closer ties to EC
and NATO; mob-
sters from Italy
and Russia infil-
trate former East
bloc societies

Region-wide pes-
simism and fears
of a return to dic-
tatorship; Rus-
sian troops are
withdrawn from
Central/Eastern
Europe

ceeded cautiously on the issue of Baltic independence, in which they had a substantial interest. Concerned that they might jeopardize the Soviet troop withdrawal process, they were careful not to chastise Moscow when it cracked down on Lithuania in early 1991. And in the Soviet political crisis of August 1991, they were careful not to take sides, even though they were fearful that if the anti-Gorbachev coup had succeeded, they might again have been at risk, especially if conservative military leaders who regretted the collapse of Communist rule came to power.

The post-Communist leaderships also watched with trepidation the conflict in Russia between President Boris Yeltsin and his reformist supporters in the Russian government and the conservative and ultra-nationalist forces in the Russian Congress of Peoples' Deputies and Supreme Soviet. The Central/Eastern European leaders fear the political ascendancy in Russia of politicians and military people committed to a restoration of Russian influence in the region.

Finally, the issue of normal trade relations with Russia and other ex-Soviet republics is still evolving. Trade declined sharply in the early 1990s and has not yet resumed; Moscow simply does not have the money to buy much. Moreover, the political and economic turmoil throughout Russia has paralyzed its capacity to produce and sell abroad, even the oil that is so desperately needed. The Central/Eastern European countries have been in a bind. Their industries had been dependent on Soviet purchases, and even the most advanced cannot make up for the loss of this market. Their exports to Western Europe are not yet competitive.

The Central/Eastern European countries also are frightened of the prospect of huge numbers of desperate citizens facing famine and other hardships migrating westward should chaos occur. They have no resources to cope with such an event and do not know how to prevent it except by urging the West to offer food and other help to the former Soviet Union in the short term.

One significant means of responding to problems with the former Soviet Union is a new emphasis on regional cooperation. Contacts have increased between Central/Eastern European countries and individual former Soviet republics, especially to consider problems of each country's ethnic minorities. The Central/Eastern European countries also have tried to diminish the historic animosities toward one another and to build a strong foundation for friendship and cooperation in solving shared economic, strategic, and environmental problems. The importance of this initiative is obvious as Central/Eastern Europe confronts the most serious regional problem since the revolutions of 1989: the Yugoslav Civil War.

"Central" vs. "Eastern" Europe

The geographic term *Eastern Europe* was always understood, in the Communist past, as a term that implied acceptance of Soviet domination. But without the threat of Soviet domination, at least part of the region (made up of Poland, Hungary, the Czech Republic, and Slovakia) wants the new name of *Central Europe.*

Central Europe has a special meaning in history. It was known as *Middle Europe,* and its capitals were Berlin, Prague, Budapest, and Vienna, cities encompassing the most affluent and most highly developed part of the old Eastern Europe. But the Balkan countries of Eastern Europe, notably Romania, Bulgaria, and Albania, fear that the term *Central Europe* will come to refer to the better-off, western part of the former Soviet bloc, giving the Balkans an inferior status.

This seems to be a distinction already in the making. At the beginning of 1994, in both the domestic and external spheres, Poland, Hungary, the Czech Republic, and Slovakia have made the greatest strides away from the authoritarian and socialist past; while Romania, Bulgaria, and Albania have moved very slowly and haltingly toward a non-Communist political and socioeconomic order. Indeed, these latter countries now display traits of the old Communist order.

Albania

GEOGRAPHY

Area in Square Kilometers (Miles):
28,489 (11,097) (slightly larger than Maryland)
Capital (Population): Tirana (243,000)
Climate: varied temperate

PEOPLE

Population

Total: 3,334,000
Annual Growth Rate: 1.2%
Rural/Urban Population Ratio: 65/35
Ethnic Makeup of Population: 90% Albanian (Geg and Tosk); 10% Greek, Vlach, Gypsy, and Bulgarian
Languages: Albanian (Tosk is the official dialect); Greek

Health

Life Expectancy at Birth: 70 years (male); 76 years (female)
Infant Mortality Rate (Ratio): 32/1,000
Average Caloric Intake: 112% of FAO minimum
Physicians Available (Ratio): 1/574

Religion(s)

70% Muslim; 20% Albanian Orthodox; 10% Roman Catholic

Education

Adult Literacy Rate: 72%

COMMUNICATION

Telephones: 15,000
Newspapers: 42 dailies; 62,400,000 circulation yearly

STILL EUROPE'S "LEAST DEVELOPED COUNTRY"

Albania has no economy to speak of, an unemployment rate of 40 percent, few public services, a primitive economic infrastructure, and a pervasive poverty not seen in Europe since the end of World War II. The average wage is less than $30 a month, and salaries for top jobs are not much higher. Government revenues cover only 20 percent of the national budget of $300 million, with the remainder financed by outside aid and the "printing press."

The task of building a new liberal political order in this "least developed nation" in Europe is daunting. Yet Albanians are glad to be rid of the Communists and are optimistic about the future: A 1993 poll showed that 77 percent of Albanians believed that their country was moving in the right direction, and 71 percent believed that economic conditions would improve by 1994.

TRANSPORTATION

Highways—Kilometers (Miles): 16,700 (10,370)
Railroads—Kilometers (Miles): 543 (337)
Usable Airfields: 10

GOVERNMENT

Type: pluralistic parliamentary democracy
Independence Date: November 28, 1912
Head of State: President Sali Berisha; Prime Minister Alexander Meksi
Political Parties: Socialist Party; Democratic Party; Social Democratic Party; Republican Party; Omonia; Democratic Alliance Party; others
Suffrage: universal and compulsory at 18

MILITARY

Number of Armed Forces: 48,000
Military Expenditures (% of Central Government Expenditures): 11.4%
Current Hostilities: none

ECONOMY

Currency ($ U.S. Equivalent): 97 leks = $1
Per Capita Income/GDP: $760/$2.5 billion
Inflation Rate: 210%
Total Foreign Debt: $500 million
Natural Resources: oil; gas; coal; chromium
Agriculture: wheat; corn; potatoes; sugar beets; cotton; tobacco
Industry: textiles; lumber; fuels; semiprocessed minerals

FOREIGN TRADE

Exports: $45 million
Imports: $120 million

ALBANIA

Since its independence from Turkey in 1912, Albania has been threatened by foreign enemies seeking to partition and annex it. Albania is vulnerable because of its small size; its lack of natural resources needed for an effective military defense; and the sharp differences between the country's largest social groups, the Gegs and the Tosks. Moreover, its strategically significant location astride the Strait of Otranto, which links the Adriatic Sea to the Mediterranean, has made Albania a tempting target of its powerful neighbors, Italy and Yugoslavia.

Albania's existence was threatened only 3 years after gaining independence from the Turkish Empire. In 1915 the Allied powers concluded a secret agreement—which they never executed—to partition Albania at the end of World War I. In the 1920s and 1930s, Benito Mussolini's Italy had designs on Albania; Italy expanded its political influence in Tirana, the Albanian capital, until in 1939 it finally invaded and occupied the country. And when Albania regained its independence, after Italy left the war in 1943, a new threat came from the Yugoslav Communists who helped the newly formed Albanian Communist Party to take over the country at the end of World War II.

The Albanian Communist Party, founded in 1941, understandably had an obsession with security that bordered on paranoia. The worry about security explains the speed with which the Communists adopted the Soviet style of political dictatorship, which would assure the unity and defense of Albania. By 1953 the Albanian Communists had transformed their country into a socialist police state.

Although the Albanian Communists were on very good terms with the Soviets, who already had begun to expand their influence in Tirana, Albania never became a true Soviet satellite. It was too geographically distant from the Soviet Union for the Kremlin to coerce and control.

ECONOMIC BACKWARDNESS, POLITICAL REPRESSION

Albania, predominantly agrarian, is still the most economically backward of the Central/Eastern European countries. It has the lowest standard of living in the region. While other Central/Eastern European countries began experimenting with and diverging from the Soviet model after 1953, Albania continued to be rigidly conformist. It never veered away from the police-state character it acquired in the late 1940s, nor did it diminish in any signifi-

cant way the highly centralized Soviet-style command economy also developed during that period.

Indeed, the Soviet Union's departures from Stalinism and the growing diversity in Central/Eastern European countries frightened the conservative Albanian leadership. In the 1960s, inspired partly by Chinese policies at that time, Albania pursued a mini-cultural revolution to reinforce Stalinist norms of socialist behavior. There were ruthless purges of political moderates both in and out of the Communist Party; people living in the cities were moved to the countryside; and there was a campaign to obliterate foreign influence of any kind, especially printed materials. Much emphasis was placed on ideological conformity and political obedience.

FOREIGN POLICY

There was a tendency toward extremes also in the area of foreign policy. After World War II, the Albanian Communist leadership gradually weaned itself away from its Yugoslav patrons, fearing an eventual Yugoslav takeover of the country. Albanian leaders were comforted by Stalin's anger with Joseph Broz Tito, Yugoslavia's Communist Party leader, and looked to the Soviet Union for protection. There was thus a reversal in Albania's relations with the Soviet Union following Joseph Stalin's death, largely in consequence of the Kremlin's decision to reconcile with Tito.

At the same time, there was an expansion of Albanian ties with China. Despite the huge geographic distance between the countries, they gravitated diplomatically toward each other because of strategic and sociopolitical commonalities. Thus, during the 1960s and early 1970s there was a Sino–Albanian entente. But it never developed into an alliance, and it collapsed shortly after Mao Zedong's death in 1976; the relationship ended 2 years later, when the Chinese government announced a termination of economic aid to Albania. The Albanians once again were isolated.

In the next phase of Albanian foreign relations, beginning in the late 1970s, the Albanian leadership tried to diminish its isolation in world affairs, for reasons of economic expediency as well as security. Albania moved in a variety of directions: toward Yugoslavia and Greece, the capitalist West, and the Soviet Union.

Premier Shehu apparently was sympathetic to the idea of a reconciliation with Yugoslavia, but he was opposed by party leader Hoxha, who was vehemently anti-Yugoslav and feared a resurgence of Yugoslav influence over the Albanian Communist Party. Hoxha feared especially the spread

of Yugoslav ideas on administrative decentralization to Albania. Another obstacle was Yugoslavia's alleged discrimination against the Albanian-speaking people of its Kosovo autonomous republic.

In the conflict over the issue of reconciliation with Yugoslavia within the top Albanian leadership, Shehu lost out to Hoxha, and no reconciliation between the two countries materialized. Shehu died under mysterious circumstances in 1981. Although the official explanation for his death was suicide, there were suspicions that Hoxha, who tried to discredit Shehu after his death (calling the former premier a spy for the United States, the Soviet Union, and Yugoslavia), had him executed.

Albania sought to improve relations with its southern neighbor, Greece, which renounced claims on Albanian territory in 1984. But a major obstacle to any effort to improve relations with Greece was the Greek government's concern about the living conditions of the Greek minority in Albania, though the Greek minority lived no worse than the Albanians. While Greece's left-leaning Papandreou government continued to be interested in an improvement in relations, it was unlikely to move closer toward Albania without some satisfaction on this issue.

Albania expressed some interest in developing ties with other Western nations, notably Canada, but was restrained. The Albanian approach to international affairs was very ideological, and the long-time suspicion of the West remained.

Albania's foreign policy initiatives in the 1980s did not diminish its isolation in the world community. Albania was the only socialist country in Central/Eastern Europe—or anywhere else—to have no close ties with any other socialist country or with the West.

THE END OF THE HOXHA ERA

Hoxha's death, on April 11, 1985, did not lead to any major change in the country's domestic and foreign policies. His successor, Ramiz Alia, reiterated the policy of isolation. The Albanian leadership rejected all Soviet overtures for a reconciliation.

Nor were there significant improvements in Albanian political relations with the United States, although contacts between the two countries that had the potential of positive political significance for the future increased. Notable among these were Albanian exports to the United States and visits to Albania by U.S. citizens of Albanian ancestry.

In the domestic sphere, the Albanian regime remained one of the most repressive in Europe and, according to the UN Commission on Human Rights, a "gross violator" of the rights of individuals. Religious persecution and political oppression did not abate under Ramiz Alia.

The regime faced problems, however, that eventually changed its neo-Stalinistic character. Albanian youth had become restive—they sought a relaxation of political control and a let-up of emphasis on behaviorial conformity. Three circumstances underlay this discontent: a sharp generation conflict (one-third of the Albanian population were under 15, and the median age of Albanians was 25); the influence of Western radio and television broadcasts; and the inability of the Albanian economy to absorb new workers.

To promote economic growth, the Albanian leadership emphasized incentives, in particular increased remuneration of highly productive or "model" workers to stimulate greater worker productivity. It allowed a limited open criticism of bureaucratism, corruption, and nepotism and began to reexamine the role of privately owned plots of land and livestock. There also was administrative decentralization and some wage differentials.

In an unusual acknowledgment of Albania's economic difficulties, Premier Adil Carcani in 1986 spoke of shortages of energy and imported raw materials and condemned mismanagement of economic enterprises. While he insisted on an increase of control everywhere and over everything to increase efficiency, he also called for an emphasis on enterprise profitability and an increase in foreign trade to earn foreign exchange. In 1987 Alia echoed these sentiments, criticizing poor planning and control by enterprise managers. He complained about a serious decline of output in the chrome industry, a source of hard currency earnings, and accused the Ministry of Industry and Mines of poor planning and poor management.

Not surprisingly, given the country's economic malaise, the Albanian leadership continued to diminish—albeit only modestly and very gradually—its xenophobia-inspired isolation. Greece apparently helped to bring Albania to a Balkan summit in 1988. Indeed, Greece responded rather generously to Albanian signals of interest in developing relations between the two countries, even though Albania continued to discriminate against its Greek-speaking minority in southern Albania. Greece in 1988 abandoned claims to the territory inhabited by Albania's Greek minority, known in the past as northern Epirus, and formally terminated a technical state of war that had existed since Italy struck at Greece from Albania in 1940. There were also efforts to strengthen ties with the West. In 1987 Albania normalized relations with West Germany.

DOMESTIC REFORM BEGINS

Evidence of interest in domestic reform existed, even if it was difficult to assess. Some Albanian party members openly discussed the need to introduce reforms—provided that Communist Party dominance and control of Albanian society continued.

Albanian authorities acknowledged difficulties with the country's young people, especially with their "anti-social" tendencies, such as disinterest in the study of Marxism-Leninism and their growing interest in religious activity. They also complained about other kinds of aberrant behavior, such as willful destruction of socialist property and violent behavior on the streets. The mere discussion of these problems suggested the beginning of a reassessment of national life that could provide the justification for reform at a later date.

Albania's reaction to the political upheaval in the rest of Central/Eastern Europe in the summer and fall of 1989 initially was defensive and negative. President Alia declared on January 1, 1990, that the uprisings that had ended Communist control in most Central/Eastern European countries would not affect Albania. He pledged to continue the policies of the past, which, he insisted, had served the country well.

Nevertheless, later that month, at the 9th Plenum of the Albanian Communist Party's Central Committee, Alia outlined a number of changes that have been called a democratization of the country's political, economic, and social changes. Alia seemed to be suggesting two reasons for change. One was preservation of the essence of socialism—or, to put it another way, to reform and thereby reinvigorate an administrative system that had become obsolete and illogical and contributed to economic stagnation and latent social tensions, especially among the country's youth. Another reason was a determination to avoid a replication in Albania of the revolutions against Communist party rule in Central/Eastern Europe.

Meaningful change in Albania, however, was slow in coming. President Alia enacted some of the reforms discussed in the Plenum: he decontrolled prices for some consumer goods and allowed private enterprise, mostly in the service area. The government also allowed farmers, who made up 60 percent of the total population, to cultivate private plots and sell their produce in open markets. But Alia proceeded very slowly in other areas of national life. The Albanian leadership had no interest in relinquishing the Communist Party's monopoly of power in Albania for a system of political pluralism. In recognition of the changing times, however, the government said that it would allow freedom of religion, of movement, and of speech. But there would be no political opposition, forbidden under Albania's Stalinist Constitution.

Alia had to deal with a large and influential conservative constituency, mostly in the bureaucracy, which wanted a traditional Stalinist system for its own self-interest rather than for ideology. Thousands of bureaucrats, at all levels of society, resisted change. Despite a new, more liberal emigration policy, the bureaucracy grudgingly processed requests for passports by citizens seeking to travel abroad. Xheli Gjoni, a prominent spokesperson for the conservative point of view and a candidate member of the party Politburo, severely condemned Albanians seeking to emigrate, calling them enemies of their country.

COMMUNIST RULE WEAKENS

Events soon went beyond Alia's cautious change. The country's small intelligentsia began to speak out critically about the government's repression, lamenting its frequent violations of human rights. They advocated genuine political change. Albanian youth shared these sentiments and voted with their feet against the regime. As soon as it was possible to obtain travel visas, during the summer of 1990, more than 4,000 Albanians tried to leave. Alia responded in early July 1990 with promises of more reforms. He announced the imminent enactment of a law on parliamentary elections and reminded Albanians that they were free to travel abroad wherever they wanted and therefore there was no reason for so many to be in a rush to seek entry to foreign countries.

But these reforms were still not enough, and popular pressure for radical political change mounted. By the latter part of 1990, many Albanians, especially those in the large urban centers, were aware of the profound changes that had taken place throughout Central/Eastern Europe. They wanted equivalent change in their own country. Some even discussed the possibility of having to imitate the bloody Romanian revolution against Ceausescu to achieve the decommunization of Albania.

Although lower-level Communist Party officials deplored this new political assertiveness, the top leadership was cautiously sympathetic. In a major speech to the Albanian Parliament, on November 13, 1990,

Alia declared that the Constitution would be revised to guarantee human rights, permit foreign investments, and allow the government to accept foreign credits. He also said that the party would give up its constitutionally guaranteed monopoly of power. Furthermore, the Parliament subsequently approved a law allowing mass organizations to field their own candidates in parliamentary elections.

Again, however, there were limits to these changes. As 1990 drew to an end, people attacked the symbols of dictatorship, such as monuments and buildings illustrative of the Stalinist era and of the late Enver Hoxha, including even the headquarters of the Communist Party. In December dissident students led antigovernment demonstrations in Tirana, Shkoder, Albasan, and Durres. These events reached a climax with the formation of Albania's first opposition party under Communist rule, the Democratic Party. One of its founders was economics professor Gramoz Pashko, a self-styled "dissident," who declared the Democratic Party's commitment to a multiparty system, protection of human rights, a free market economy, good relations between Albania and its neighbors, and integration with Europe. The national trade union declared its independence of the Communists in the last week of December, asserting that it would no longer act as a party lever, and promised to fight for higher pay and better conditions for workers.

Demanding a role in parliamentary elections, scheduled for February 10, 1991, the new political organizations sought a postponement of election day for at least a month and a half in order to give them an opportunity to cultivate voter support. The Alia government agreed and provided the opposition parties (there were now several, although they still were quite small) with space for campaign headquarters, some telephones, and some automobiles. Moreover, on the eve of the elections, Alia said that the Communist Party would accept defeat if that were the will of the people.

PARLIAMENTARY ELECTIONS

Parliamentary elections, held on March 31, 1991, were the first contested elections Albania had had since 1923. The two major contenders were the Communist and Democratic parties. To the dismay of voters in the large urban centers, who voted overwhelmingly for the candidates of the Democratic Party, the Communists won a comfortable majority of 162 out of 250. Albanians living in the countryside had voted overwhelmingly for the Communists because they were used to Commu-

nist rule and feared an outbreak of lawlessness and anarchy if reformers were elected to lead the country. Indeed, Alia lost his seat in Parliament to the hard-liner Gjoni. The Communists had also benefited from the enormous resources at their disposal: they had run a well-coordinated campaign against the opposition, and they had exploited their tight control over radio, television, and printed media. They had made it very difficult, by virtue of the government's control over the distribution of newsprint supplies, for the opposition to publish its organs, *Rilindja Demoktatie* and *Republika*. The Communists also used the old electoral trick of bribing voters in the countryside to win their support: on the eve of the elections, the regime announced decisions to allow enlarged private farms and unlimited ownership of livestock.

Furthermore, the opposition Democrats had not had enough time to develop a rural constituency or to develop their electoral organization. Rural voters, who made up a majority of the electorate, knew little, if anything, about the noncommunist organizations challenging the Communist Party in the election. According to Sali Berisha, now the leader of the Democrats, the Communists had cheated. He told members of the U.S. Congress in May 1991 that there had been killings and beatings of opposition candidates as well as severe restrictions on opposition access to news outlets.

The election intensified the split between town and country, creating rifts between parents and children, between officers and ordinary soldiers, and between the northern and southern parts of the country, which were inhabited by Gegs and Tosks, respectively. The elections did, however, tend to confirm what was already evident: a steady and seemingly irreversible Albanian movement away from communism. Although the conservative Gjoni intoned that the election results showed that Albanians still had faith in Marxism-Leninism, the opposite was more true, given the fact that the Democratic Party, only 4 months old and hamstrung in so many ways by the Communists, had been able to win 38 percent of the popular vote.

Hard-liners inside the party made a last desperate effort, following the March 1991 elections, to block further departures from the old order. Gjoni was elevated in April from candidate to full membership in the party Politburo. The hard-liners published in the party's *Zeri i Populit* an editorial hailing the late Enver Hoxha as a great leader and saying that there was no need for the party to apologize to the

Albanian people, since it had done its job.

THE END OF COMMUNIST RULE

Reformers pressed on, and finally even Gjoni was prepared for compromise. In the hope of being elected leader of the Communist Party at its 10th Congress, in June 1991, Gjoni, in the keynote address, now disparaged Hoxha's leadership and promised further reform. This political about-face did not fool the reformers, who succeeded in electing former prime minister Fatos Nano as the new chairperson. The Congress criticized the Politburo and replaced it with a 15-member party presidency. It also changed the name of the Communist Party. Henceforth it was to be known as the Socialist Party, with no reference to communism. Subsequently, *Zeri i Populit* dropped the hammer-and-sickle insignia from its masthead and published startling criticisms of Hoxha and his family.

In early July 1991, following post-Communist political patterns in other Central/Eastern European countries, the former Albanian Communists affirmed their break with Marxism-Leninism. A new party program formally abandoned the goal of creating a communist society. It also called for a market economy with a safety net that would minimize the hardships of the new system. While advocating privatization, the Socialists favored preservation of agricultural cooperatives and retention of state control over vital industries, such as those involving national defense.

Chosen president of the republic by the newly elected Parliament, Alia accepted the job and resigned as head of the Communist Party. The Parliament approved a Law on Constitutional Powers, which temporarily superseded the existing Constitution until a new one could be written. The Law on Constitutional Powers endorsed political pluralism and the establishment of a multiparty political system, and it guaranteed human rights and the equality of all forms of private ownership—state, collective, and private. Finally, the Law on Constitutional Powers explicitly banned party activity in the government ministries of defense, internal affairs, justice, and foreign affairs.

Alia took the lead in dismantling the old socialist order. He called for an Albanian version of democracy in national life, involving freely contested elections for managers of industrial enterprises, farms, and Parliament; public debate on changes in higher education; and economic decentralization, in order to give more policymaking authority to district authorities.

Alia also intended to ease conservative bureaucrats out of power through the introduction of elections with multiple candidates and a secret ballot for municipal councils, Parliament, and internal party positions. He wanted limits of 10 years on terms of office in the government, with a fifth-year review of performance and the possibility of dismissal by peers, and limits of 5 years for holding party office. But strikes and street demonstrations in Tirana against the government forced the resignation of Prime Minister Nano in June 1991. Alia replaced him with Ylli Bufi, a nonpartisan, nonideological economist. Bufi formed a coalition cabinet in which half of the 24 ministers were drawn from newly formed opposition groups and half from the Communists.

The final collapse of Communist rule occurred in March 1992, when Albanians voted to elect a new Parliament. Berisha's Democratic Party won an overwhelming majority of the popular vote. While support for the Democrats in the city areas was expected, because they were strongholds of reform, support for them in the countryside, which had voted for the Communists in the March 1991 parliamentary elections, came as a pleasant surprise. People in the small towns and villages of rural Albania were disappointed by the failure of the Communists to improve conditions while they put through major reforms, such as decollectivization. Albanian farmers said they were disgusted, now that they had their own land, over their inability to cultivate it—they complained about the lack of tools, fertilizer, and seed. Other reasons for the nationwide support for the Democrats included the hope that they would once and for all end Albania's international isolation and open up the country to European ideas and values; Berisha's recent visits to Western countries, in particular the United States, had been publicized on the national radio and television. Albanians hoped that with new ties to the West, their country might receive much-needed economic and financial help.

ECONOMIC PROBLEMS

As the Albanian Communist government, with a factionalized democratic opposition, moved toward pluralism and other internal reforms in the early 1990s, it had to cope with a severely debilitated economy. Albania remained the poorest country in Europe. Most Albanians lived with ox- and donkey-drawn carts, grimy steam-powered factories, and threshers dating back to the 1950s. Towns and villages had few shops, and workers either walked to their jobs or traveled on rickety buses. (These conditions persist today.)

In 1990 a drought forced factories to close down for several months for lack of spare parts, raw materials, and power, causing increased unemployment. This in turn drained the state treasury, because of the government's obligation to pay idled workers 80 percent of their normal wages. Albania ended up having to import 70 percent of its energy supplies at high prices because of the Persian Gulf crisis. Inflation rose to 30 percent and agricultural production fell into a slump, with food reserves dangerously low. (In July 1991 many peasants seized land and livestock in a veritable revolution against the old collectivist order.) Making matters worse was a brain drain through emigration, depriving the country of valuable technical and managerial expertise. There was also a drastic decline in revenue from hard-currency exports such as oil, electricity, and chromium; and the foreign debt, which previously was nonexistent, climbed to the equivalent of $500 million.

Waves of impoverished unemployed Albanian young people tried to emigrate to Italy, beginning in the summer of 1990. In March 1991 some 24,000 Albanians went to Italy; in the summer another 10,000 Albanians in desperate straits sought refuge in Italy, in the hope of finding work and better living conditions, but they were turned away.

Albanian reformers were ready to accept the prospect of shock treatment. In the summer of 1991 they proposed to move forward with plans for a market economy. Bufi also proposed an immediate and extensive reduction of government expenditures for administration, the military, and price subsidies and an acceleration of privatization of small- and medium-size enterprises. And in September 1991 the government announced preparations for a reform of the banking and currency systems.

THE END OF ISOLATION

To help facilitate reform of the country's dilapidated economy—in particular to obtain much-needed foreign investment—the Alia leadership initiated a dramatic foreign policy shift. In June 1990 it asked to join the European Conference on Security and Cooperation and said that it would adopt the principles of the 1975 Helsinki Accords on which the ECSC is based. Other incentives to expand ties with neighboring countries were the collapse of Communist regimes throughout Central/Eastern Europe in 1989 and the efforts of the new governments to draw closer to the West, thereby accentuating Albania's psychological as well as diplomatic isolation in Europe.

Alia was especially interested in improving relations with the United States. In April 1990 the government opened negotiations with Washington, and in March 1991 Washington announced a restoration of ties between the two countries. When then–U.S. secretary of state James Baker visited Tirana in June 1991, an estimated 300,000 Albanians gathered in central Tirana to welcome him, a display, incidentally, that was not only anti-Communist but also a strong expression of faith that somehow the United States could and would help Albania. Baker offered a modest program of economic aid, worth about $6 million—not the aid of Marshall Plan dimensions that the Albanians said they needed to implement their reform program. Baker cautioned the Alia leadership that the future of Albanian–U.S. relations would depend on its continued pursuit of political and economic liberalization.

Alia also wanted to improve Albanian relations with Greece, which had been strained for a long time because of alleged discrimination by the Communist government in Tirana against the Greek minority living in southern Albania (in a region the Greek government had frequently called "northern Epirus" and had at times claimed should go to Greece). The Albanian response to Greek territorial claims had been efforts to homogenize the Greek minority under its jurisdiction. This policy led to an exodus of about 6,000 Greek Albanians into Greece in 1990, a migration that the Greek government charged in early 1991 was provoked by Tirana to rid the country of a potentially threatening minority and to weaken the political opposition in view of the first multiparty elections scheduled for February of that year.

Greece took the initiative in trying to improve relations between the two countries. In January 1991 Prime Minister Constantine Mitsoakis announced a visit to Tirana to discuss the problem of the Greek minority, though he was pessimistic about the chances of getting the Alia government, which denied charges of discrimination, to become more tolerant. His concern was not only to improve living conditions for the Albanian Greeks but also to bring an end to an embarrassing problem—namely, the arrival in northern Greece of impoverished refugees, whom the country could ill afford to take care of.

Mitsoakis's visit achieved little. The Albanian side vigorously denied mistreatment of the Greek minority. Albania also adamantly rejected Greek suggestions that Greek consulates be set up in the villages of southern Albania inhabited primarily by

Independence 1912	Formation of the Albanian Communist Party; Hoxha becomes the head 1941	The Albanian Communists take power with the help of Yugoslav Communists 1944	Communist leader Hoxha becomes the head of government 1945	Albanian Communists break with Yugoslav Communists 1948	Albania joins the Warsaw Pact 1955	Albanian-Soviet relations are broken; Albania strengthens ties with China 1961	Albania ends participation in the CMEA 1962	Albania withdraws from the Warsaw Pact 1968	All Chinese military and economic ties with Albania are severed 1978

1980s–1990s

Communist rule weakens and eventually collapses; Albania begins economic and political liberalization	35,000 Albanians seek refuge in Italy and are turned away; Sali Berisha, a non-Communist, is elected president; Albania seeks entry into NATO	Albania asks the West to send troops to Kosovo to prevent the spread of Serb ethnic cleansing

Greeks and that the United Nations be allowed to investigate and monitor living conditions in the Greek-inhabited areas.

Nevertheless, the Alia regime did not want difficulties with its Greek neighbor, given Albania's impoverishment and the growing anxiety over the Serb mistreatment of Albanians in Kosovo. Accordingly, while refusing to acknowledge any impropriety in its treatment of the Greek minority, Tirana agreed that Albanian Greeks had a right to live securely in their ancestral homeland in southern Albania as free citizens of Albania.

THE YUGOSLAV CIVIL WAR

Albania has been alarmed by the violent disintegration of Yugoslavia and in particular by the harsh behavior of the Serb republic government under President Slobodan Milosevic toward its Albanian minority in Kosovo. In mid-1991 Milosevic reduced Albanians to second-class citizens by abolishing their autonomy, dissolving their local parliament, and closing down Albanian-language radio, television, and newspaper publications. Following the invasion of Croatia by the Serb-dominated Federal Army, Serbia intensified its repression in Kosovo. The Albanian government responded in the summer of 1991 by accusing Serbia of planning genocide. Alia appealed for intervention to the European Community, the UN Security Council, and the European Conference on Security and Cooperation. Albania fears

not only the spread of violent civil war from Bosnia to Kosovo but also the explosion of a larger Balkan conflict in which Albania's neighbors, plus others in the region, would start fighting one another over the future of all the Albanians in Southeastern Europe.

POST-COMMUNIST POLITICAL DEVELOPMENT

In the period following the March 1992 parliamentary elections, Albania began to sink into a kind of anarchy. There was violent public disorder, largely in response to a deep and pervasive economic misery that seemed beyond remedy. Armed gangs of hungry villagers sought to augment their meager food supplies by plundering warehouses. By the fall of 1992, a reorganized police force, which had shed many who had served the Communist government, restored order, but only through draconian measures, including ad hoc execution of perceived lawbreakers.

There was also instability at the top of the Albanian political system, with the appearance of polarization among President Berisha's followers, who split over the issue of his increasingly autocratic style of leadership. Factions emerged in the parliament, complicating government decision making at a critical juncture, when the new leadership was trying to cope with the horrendous economic problems bequeathed by the Communists. One prominent faction, led by Gramoz Pashko, an economist and

cofounder with Berisha of the Democratic Party, formed a new party organization, called the Democratic Alliance, to oppose Berisha's autocratic behavior.

Since the beginning of democratic government in 1992, the Albanian economy has been in the doldrums. Agricultural production declined sharply as collective farms were disbanded and farmers were left on their own to make a go of private farming. Many lacked the skills and tools needed for profitable cultivation. Industrial production suffered from the emigration of skilled workers and the unavailability of spare parts; much equipment was either obsolete, stolen, or vandalized. By the end of 1993, Albania had become dependent on Western aid for its day-to-day economic survival.

DEVELOPMENT

Albanian economic development is at a standstill. Many plants have been dismantled by their workers, partly in anger over the continuing influence of former Communist managers and partly to get equipment for personal use. The chromium and copper mines that were Albania's main producers of foreign exchange are paralyzed. Agricultural output is so low as to cause widespread malnutrition.

FREEDOM

In free and competitive parliamentary elections in March 1992, the the opposition Democratic Party won overwhelmingly, punctuating the end of almost half a century of Communist dictatorship. In 1993 a revival of religious freedom was evident, and outdoor political rallies no longer met with the kind of fierce official opposition of past governments.

HEALTH/WELFARE

In the wake of Communist collapse, people in the countryside went on a rampage, indiscriminately destroying state property, including health stations, which have yet to be rebuilt, leaving villages without basic medical care. In other respects the material well-being of Albanians has remained at a low level when compared with other Central/Eastern European societies, never mind those in the affluent West.

ACHIEVEMENTS

In the short post-Communist era, daily life has changed radically—and for the better, despite profound economic hardship. There is a burgeoning of small-scale private entrepreneurialism. The monotony of daily life, long a hallmark of Albanian society, especially in the cities, has at last been broken, with boisterous, lighthearted pedestrians filling the public thoroughfares to an extent unimaginable in the past.

Bulgaria

GEOGRAPHY

Area in Square Kilometers (Miles):
110,994 (42,855) (slightly larger than Ohio)
Capital (Population): Sofia (1,200,000)
Climate: dry, hot summers and damp, cold winters, but with strong regional variations

PEOPLE

Population
Total: 8,832,000
Annual Growth Rate: -0.39%
Rural/Urban Population Ratio: 33/67
Ethnic Makeup of Population: 85% Bulgarian; 9% Turk; 6% Gypsy, Macedonian, Armenian, Russian, and others
Languages: Bulgarian; secondary languages closely correspond to ethnic breakdown

Health
Life Expectancy at Birth: 70 years (male), 76 years (female)
Infant Mortality Rate (Ratio): 12/1,000
Average Caloric Intake: 146% of

FAO minimum
Physicians Available (Ratio): 1/337

Religion(s)
85% Bulgarian Orthodox; 13% Muslim; 2% Jewish, Roman Catholic, Protestant, and others

Education
Adult Literacy Rate: 93% (estimate)

BULGARIA'S UNCERTAIN POLITICAL FUTURE

Post-Communist Bulgaria is a conservative country in which the transition to a new liberal political order is proceeding very slowly. Reform Communists, now known as Socialists, continue to exert a major influence over national public policy making. The country's current caretaker government of nonparty professionals, under Premier Lyuben Berov, depends upon a parliamentary coalition led by ex-Communists, who, many Bulgarians think, are coming back to rule, even though President Zhelyu Zhelev believes that they do not have the credibility needed to lead the country. The future of democracy in Bulgaria is by no means secure.

COMMUNICATION

Telephones: 2,600,000
Newspapers: 17 dailies; 2,200,000 circulation

TRANSPORTATION

Highways—Kilometers (Miles): 36,908 (22,030)
Railroads—Kilometers (Miles): 4,294 (2,662)
Usable Airfields: 380

GOVERNMENT

Type: emerging democracy
Independence Date: October 5, 1908
Head of State: President Zhelyu Zhelev
Political Parties: Union of Democratic Forces; Movement for Rights and Freedoms; Socialist Party
Suffrage: universal and compulsory at 18

MILITARY

Number of Armed Forces: 127,000
Military Expenditures (% of Central Government Expenditures): 6.0%
Current Hostilities: none

ECONOMY

Currency ($ U.S. Equivalent): 24.5 levas = $1
Per Capita Income/GDP: $3,800/$34.1 billion
Inflation Rate: over 80%
Total Foreign Debt: $12 billion
Natural Resources: bauxite; copper; lead; zinc; coal; lignite; lumber
Agriculture: grain; tobacco; fruits; vegetables; sheep; hogs; poultry; cheese; sunflower seeds
Industry: food processing; machinery; chemicals; metallurgical products; electronics; textiles; clothing

FOREIGN TRADE

Exports: $3.5 billion
Imports: $2.8 billion

BULGARIA

Bulgarian Communists were in a hurry to come to power and right the wrongs of a conservative and despotic past. During World War II, they made common cause with other anti-Fascist elements in the so-called Fatherland Front, which fought against the Bulgarian monarch and his German ally. When the war was over, the Bulgarian Communists controlled the Front and used it as a stepping-stone to power.

The first postwar leader of the Bulgarian Communist Party (BCP) was Georgi Dimitrov, who had had a long career in the world communist movement before the war. He was extremely loyal to the Soviet Union, which had obtained his release from a Bulgarian prison in the early 1920s and helped him to become secretary general of the Comintern from 1935 until 1943. His only apparent sin—but it was a major one in Soviet eyes—was his willingness to cooperate with Yugoslavia's Tito in the proposed establishment of a Balkan union of Communist parties, which the Soviets successfully blocked.

Dimitrov's successors to the leadership of the BCP, Vassil Kolarov in 1949 and Vulko Chervenkov from 1949 to 1954, followed in his footsteps. They loyally pursued Soviet-inspired policies in their transformation of Bulgaria into a socialist state. By 1953 the new People's Republic of Bulgaria, which had replaced the monarchy, was a replica of the Soviet dictatorship and a loyal Soviet ally. Chervenkov's successor, Todor Zhivkov, who led the BCP until 1989, continued the conservative and loyalist traditions of his predecessors.

Soviet-style political authoritarianism was unchallenged in Bulgarian society. In the era of Communist rule after 1946, Bulgaria had a very small intelligentsia and virtually no dissent. Bulgarian society had little experience with Western-style political liberalism, partly because of the autocratic monarchs who ruled the country from 1878 until 1946.

The economy was another dimension of Bulgaria's Soviet-inspired authoritarian socialism, but it did experience some modest yet promising reform. In the 1950s and 1960s, Bulgaria's economic organization conformed very closely to the Soviet model. Beginning in the 1970s, however, the Bulgarian Communist leadership introduced changes in industry and agriculture that, while not identical, did resemble in some respects the Hungarian reforms of that era. The Bulgarian leadership established its own "New Economic Mechanism," which provided for some decentralization of managerial decision making. In the 1970s the government created huge agro-industrial complexes that integrated the growing, processing, and marketing of food products. In addition to increasing the mechanization of agriculture, the Bulgarians expanded the amount of cultivable land to be set aside for private use.

FOREIGN POLICY

The most conspicuous aspect of Bulgarian foreign policy in the era of Communist Party rule was closeness—indeed, subservience—to the Soviet Union. This existed for several reasons. The two countries shared common cultural characteristics, such as the use of the Cyrillic alphabet and the prevalence of the Orthodox faith. Bulgarians also remembered how the Russian Czarist government helped Bulgaria to emancipate itself from Turkish rule in 1878; although the Russians were sometimes overbearing in their relations with the new monarchy in Sofia, they were not

(United Nations/Chen)

A Bulgarian patriarchate was established in 1235 by Tsar Ivan Asen II. However, Bulgaria fell to the Turks in 1393, under whose domination it remained for five centuries. During the relatively brief Bulgarian patriarchate, innovative art flourished. Pictured above is the double portrait of Sebastocrator Kaloyan and his wife painted in 1259, showing a significant departure from the rigid canonical style of medieval Byzantine art.

threatening. In addition, the Kremlin acknowledged that, unlike Hungary and Romania, Bulgaria did not participate in the German military invasion of the Soviet Union in June 1941. The Bulgarian Communist leadership also identified with the Russian revolutionary tradition. Like the Marxists in prerevolutionary Russia, Bulgarian Communists were faced with a brutal authoritarian regime and endorsed violence to overthrow it. Finally, Bulgaria was close to the Soviet Union out of gratitude. Bulgaria's relative economic well-being could be attributed largely to help given by the Soviet Union.

Bulgaria and the Balkans

Bulgaria has had much in common with other states in the Balkans—Yugoslavia, Albania, Romania, Greece, and Turkey. They have had similar economic problems: all agrarian, economically underdeveloped, and dependent upon foreign sources for manufactured necessities. They also have shared a common political past: They have all been governed at one time or another by the Turks.

At the same time, Bulgaria under the Communists saw an opportunity in the Balkans to play an important international role that gratified national sentiment. Despite their intimacy with the Soviet Union, Bulgaria's Communist leaders showed a continuing interest in cooperating with other Balkan countries, both socialist and capitalist, to solve political and socioeconomic problems that the countries of the region shared. Their shared interests included the creation of a nuclear-free zone; the establishment of a regional parliament and other devices for regular discussion of regional problems; and the acceptance of a declaration of respect for territorial integrity, noninterference in internal affairs, and renunciation of the use or threat of force.

Limits on Bulgaria's role in the Balkans have concerned problems with particular countries, such as Yugoslavia, Greece, and Turkey. These problems are historic and continue to be a source of antagonism between Bulgaria and its neighbors. They discourage development of real friendship, mutual understanding, and effective regional cooperation.

Yugoslavia and Greece

Bulgarian Communist relations with Yugoslavia and Greece were strained because of differences over Macedonia. Macedonia remained an issue in Bulgarian–Greek relations primarily because of the Sofia government's concern about the well-being of a Bulgarian-speaking minority living in the part of Macedonia ruled by Greece.

Moreover, in the nineteenth and early twentieth centuries, Bulgaria sought control of this region because of its location on the Aegean Sea. In 1941 Bulgaria temporarily annexed Macedonia in conjunction with the German invasion of Greece.

Turkey

Bulgaria's difficulties with Turkey resulted in part from alleged efforts of the Sofia regime to obliterate the ethnic identity of its Turkish minority, nearly 800,000 people. The BCP asserted that there were no Turkish people in Bulgaria, only "pure Bulgarians," some of whom were converted to Turkish culture when Bulgaria was part of the Ottoman Turkish Empire.

To the dismay of Sofia, the Turkish leadership championed the rights of people in Bulgaria said to have Turkish blood. The Turks invited their kin in Bulgaria to return "home," where they were promised a hospitable reception, but Bulgaria refused to allow emigration.

Bulgaria and the West

The Bulgarian Communists did not trade as much as they would have liked with the United States, because they had not been given most-favored-nation treatment, but their trade with Germany increased to the point that Germany has become Bulgaria's largest trading partner in the West. Out of a desire to avoid prejudicing their relations with the West, the Bulgarians maintained a careful neutrality in the growing East–West confrontation over arms control. While Czechoslovakia went out of its way to support the Soviets against the West, the Bulgarians showed restraint.

The Plot to Assassinate the Pope

In the early 1980s, Bulgaria encountered a new international problem—one of image—that compromised its relations with the West. This problem stemmed from charges that Bulgaria was complicitous in the attempted assassination of Pope John Paul II in 1981. It has been said that Bulgarian officials acted as intermediaries between Turkish gunman Mehmet Ali Agca and the Soviet Union's KGB, reputed to be the inspiration of the plot. Some have speculated that the Soviets wanted to kill the pope because of his sympathy for and encouragement of political opponents of the socialist regime of his Polish homeland and that they used their servile Bulgarian ally in this effort. It may be a long time before the truth about any Bulgarian complicity in the plot is known. But, in the 1980s, people in the West were willing to believe the worst about the Bulgarians.

BULGARIA AND PERESTROIKA

Bulgaria seemed to be embracing a form of Gorbachev's glasnost and perestroika, though with mixed success. Bulgaria's more narrow definition of glasnost was evident in the renewal of its aggressive cultural-assimilation policies toward the Turkish minority. Worried that the country might be overwhelmed in the next decade by a Turkish minority, the Bulgarian authorities seemed determined to prevent people of Islamic and Turkish culture from becoming a factor in Bulgarian society and government.

As the leadership in Sofia intensified its policies of forced assimilation of its Turkish-speaking citizens, it met resistance. In May 1989 the villagers of Razgrad and Shumen, east of Sofia, demonstrated against the government, presumably to attract the attention of the East–West Conference on Human Rights meeting at that time in Paris. The authorities responded with overwhelming force. Using helicopters and tanks against civilian protesters, they ruthlessly suppressed the demonstration and deported many of the Turkish activists. This repression provoked an unexpected exodus from Bulgaria to Turkey in June and July 1989 of about 150,000 ethnic Turks. The emigrants vacated key jobs in the Bulgarian economy, crippling factories, mines, and agriculture, in particular undercutting the production of tobacco, a cash export crop that earned desperately needed hard currency.

Nevertheless, rather than retreat from its policies of cultural homogenization, Sofia replaced the ethnic Turkish people with imported Vietnamese labor. Willing to work at very low wages, these workers, numbering about 17,000, were intensely disliked by the local population.

In the economic sphere, however, there were both logic and justification for reform. This was recognized by the leadership, some of whom called for Gorbachev-style administrative reform to correct flaws in the highly centralized Stalinist administrative mechanism, with its emphasis on heavy industrial output. They wanted to emphasize the production of consumer goods and to improve the standard of living. Incentives to undertake economic reform included the acute energy shortage in 1985, which led to darkened and unheated apartments and disrupted the manufacture and distribution of industrial goods. In 1986 there was a significant lag in the production of housing and foodstuffs.

Changes outlined by party leader Zhivkov in 1987 included the introduction of self-management throughout the Bulgarian economy. While some central planning would continue, industrial enterprises would be free to make their own adjustments to assure profitable levels of quality and quantity. Industries would raise capital through newly created investment banks, determine their own management, and use income as they wished, for wages or reinvestment and expansion.

Whether these measures will ever remedy the country's growth problems and improve its output still remains to be seen. For the moment at least, the Bulgarian economy has outgrown the reforms of the 1970s and faces a stagnation that could be a potential source of popular discontent.

THE UPHEAVAL BEGINS

Encouraged by the popular attacks on Communist Party rule in East Germany and Czechoslovakia—two conservatively ruled socialist states that in this respect had much in common with Bulgaria—large numbers of Bulgarian citizens staged antigovernment demonstrations in November 1989, calling for democratization in Sofia. Zhivkov responded in a somewhat conciliatory fashion, no doubt influenced in this regard by the fate of Honecker and Jakes. The demonstrations, however, continued. Unwilling to use force, and in the absence of any Soviet support, Zhivkov resigned as party leader on November 9. He was quickly succeeded by Petar Mladenov, a less-well-known party official with close links to Gorbachev. In April 1990 the Bulgarian Parliament elected Mladenov president of the republic. Mladenov was replaced as president in August 1990 by Zhelyu Zhelev.

The new party leadership introduced many changes. It eased media censorship and quickly rid itself of the most conservative elements in the top leadership and renewed a pledge to enact substantive political reforms that would lead to democratization of Bulgarian life. It was careful to avoid saying or doing anything that would compromise its leadership role, at least for the time being, but it did promise political pluralism and a greatly reduced party role in Bulgarian life.

Limits on how far Bulgaria would go in liberalizing its repressive political order, however, were apparent from the outset. It did little to initiate extensive political changes. Thus, in December 1990 the National Assembly delayed enactment of a constitutional amendment that would have stripped the Bulgarian Communist Party of its monopoly of power. And the readiness of Bulgarian society for democratization seemed in doubt when, as a result of the government's decision to restore some cultural privileges to Bul-

garia's large Turkish-speaking minority, there was an explosion of popular opposition, which was embarrassing to liberals advocating equality and protection of minority rights.

Political Liberalization
In early 1990 Bulgaria seemed to be following Gorbachev's perestroika model. The Bulgarian Communist Party continued to dominate both cabinet and Parliament while making changes in leadership, policies, and institutions intended to effect a thorough democratization of Bulgarian political life. At the head of the new leadership were two Gorbachev-style reformers, Mladenov and the premier, Andrei Lukanov. One suspects, however, that their commitment to democratization was partly motivated by an attempt to preserve the BCP's dominant position.

Among the changes that occurred in early 1990 were the Bulgarian Communist Party's adoption of a new name, the Bulgarian Socialist Party (BSP); the abandonment of all vestiges of Stalinism; and a call for coalition government, which the newly formed non-Communist parties ignored, because they did not want to prejudice their chances of defeating the Communists in the parliamentary elections scheduled for the spring of 1990 by cooperation with the Communists. The new Communist leadership also produced a draft constitution that contained a detailed bill of rights and provisions for a powerful legislature. Opinion polls in early April seemed to suggest that the Communists were making progress in strengthening their credibility with Bulgarian voters: their party was given a lead in public support over the opposition groups—this despite new revelations of excesses by the Zhivkov regime in its early years, when it had established Nazi-style concentration camps where prisoners were tortured and killed.

Parliamentary Elections in June 1990
Parliamentary elections in June 1990 gave the Bulgarian Socialist Party (the former Communist Party) a decisive victory. Although the Bulgarian Communists had shed their old name and eased their grip on economic and political life by abandoning their claim to a monopoly of power; by reducing their control of factories, farms, the military, and the police; and by adopting the rhetoric of liberal democracy, their victory set a precedent in Central/Eastern Europe in 1990: It was the first time that a ruling Marxist party in the region had competed in multiparty elections and won without recourse to the quasi-legal shennanigans that had enabled

them to obtain large voter majorities in the late 1940s. Moreover, the final days of the campaign passed without violence.

The success of the BSP was partly the result of a strong conservative tendency in the countryside. Farmers had a sense that Bulgaria had not done badly, even if it had not thrived, under Communist rule. Moreover, as one influential member of the Socialists explained, the party was victorious because its policies still corresponded to the interests of a majority of Bulgarian voters. Those interests remained security of work, income, and well-being, through continuation of the state-administered comprehensive welfare program, which guaranteed medical care and education. But it was also true that the former Communists had been successful because of their continued stranglehold over local political life. Finally, the BSP benefited from the fact that the Bulgarian party had its own integrity and was not viewed as a stooge of the Kremlin. In any event, anti-Soviet and anti-Russian feelings had never been as strong in Bulgaria as elsewhere in Central/Eastern Europe.

The euphoria of the Socialists, however, was short-lived. They tried to form a coalition with the opposition parties but failed, weakening their power to govern, never mind to implement controversial reform measures.

Economic Crisis
People were angry over a deepening economic crisis: sooty and crumbling facades of buildings, giant potholes in roads, tunnels closed indefinitely for repairs. They endured hours-long waits at gas stations, frequent power cuts, and rationing of such essentials as butter, cheese, sugar, eggs, and detergents. The economic structure still favored production of capital and industrial goods at the expense of consumer goods. Unfavorable weather contributed to economic hardship: A continuing drought dried out the food-producing countryside north and east of Sofia, which looked yellowish when it should have been green. Bulgarian farmers began to withhold livestock from government slaughterhouses toward the end of 1990, in anticipation of vastly higher prices when price controls should be lifted.

As in other former Soviet bloc nations, there was a downward trend in both exports and imports. Bulgaria had to stop arms shipments to the Middle East. It also had to cope with reduced oil supplies from the Soviet Union, its principal supplier of petroleum products, partly because Moscow wanted to be paid in hard currency. In other respects trade with the Soviet Union, which had been Bulgaria's largest trading partner, was disrupted as a result of production slowdowns caused by political turmoil. Moreover, Bulgarian hopes for replacement deliveries of oil from Iraq to pay back the latter's approximately $2.6 billion debt were dashed by the international trade embargo imposed after Iraq's August 2, 1990, invasion of Kuwait. In the meantime the government further depressed Bulgarian foreign trade by forbidding the export of scarce agricultural commodities and by suspending payments on its $12 billion foreign debt, thereby cutting itself off from trade credits and other forms of overseas help.

Leadership Problems

The Socialists were divided in their leadership of the country. Membership of the party in the Parliament was split between moderates, who sought rapid, radical reform, after the fashion of Poland, and conservatives, who advocated a very slow pace of change. The moderates were youthful, energetic, and outspoken in their advocacy of change, but the conservatives were more influential, because they still controlled the levers of power in the party, as evidenced by their success in reelecting Aleksandur Lilov as party leader at a Congress in the summer of 1990.

Furthermore, the BSP was distracted in its management of the country by its efforts to bring former leader Todor Zhivkov to trial on charges of corruption and the commission of illegal actions. Unfortunately for the Socialists, Zhivkov fought back and insisted that he was innocent. He defended his record by condemning the Soviet invasion of Prague in August 1968, saying that he and Bulgaria had been forced by the Kremlin to participate in "this foreign occupation" of Czechoslovakia. He also denied any responsibility for the plot to assassinate Pope John Paul II. His resistance to his party's effort to use him as a scapegoat turned out to be a time-consuming, energy-wasting exercise in futility that prevented the Socialists from focusing on the real economic problems facing the country in its new era. Worse, Zhivkov threatened that if persecution of him continued, he would make startling revelations that would implicate many influential members of the Socialist Party.

Antigovernment demonstrations erupted anew in Sofia in the latter part of 1990. The Union of Democratic Forces, which supported the demonstrations, was predicting the downfall of the Socialists. It pressed for another election for Parliament and called for a confidence vote. It also refused to back a government economic plan to turn over state enterprises to private hands, end price controls on most goods, and expand foreign trade until the resignation of the prime minister. Angry workers, especially miners, backed the Union and seemed ready to man the barricades, so to speak, to force the former Communists out of power. The frustrated Lukanov resigned on November 29, 1990, taking his 5-month-old Socialist government with him.

Leaders of the largest of the many Bulgarian parties agreed to establish a coalition in which the Socialists would participate, but without Lukanov. His successor was Dimitar Popov, a lawyer without party affiliation. Although the coalition was made up of the three largest parties plus five independents, the Socialists remained in a dominant position, by virtue of their majority in the Parliament. Ironically, this new government was very similar to what Lukanov had been seeking since the June 1990 elections: a multiparty coalition with the Socialists dominating it. But all parties agreed that the country's new leadership would last only until the next parliamentary elections.

Without waiting for new elections, Prime Minister Popov announced in January 1991 a major long-term shake-up of the Bulgarian economy. It involved substantial austerity to halt the decline in output and to reduce the country's foreign debt. It abandoned subsidies on many basic goods and utilities as part of an overall effort to create a market economy. Anticipating increases in the price of heating, public services, and many food items, the government struck a deal in advance with trade unions to allow a modest increase in wages and a hike in the minimum wage.

Popov's economic changes met with immediate opposition. In August 1991 some 21,000 Bulgarian miners in 81 of the country's 90 mines again struck, ostensibly for wage increases, better working conditions, and a government guarantee that mines would not be closed as part of the austerity program. The strike threatened to interrupt the supply of coal to plants producing more than a third of the country's electricity.

Miners are unlikely to find themselves better off very soon, despite the government's best efforts. Working against success are powerful external factors, most significantly Bulgaria's enormous foreign debt and its inability to trade with hard currency countries. Its goods lack the quality to compete on the open market. The future of Bulgarian trade, at least until the economy is successfully overhauled and made competitive with that of hard currency areas, is likely to lie in sales of computers at cut-rate prices to the soft currency countries of the Third World. And, although Bulgaria joined the International Monetary Fund and the World Bank in the fall of 1990, swift help was not forthcoming. Finally, the inefficient and dilapidated production and distribution systems remained obstacles to substantial foreign investment in the Bulgarian economy.

Renewal of Hostility toward the Turkish Minority

Complicating Popov's problems was a renewal of anti-Turk chauvinism among ultra-nationalist groups like the Fatherland Labor Party. The Socialists were annoyed that Turkish-speaking voters had elected 23 of 400 deputies to Parliament in the June 1990 elections; they were afraid that this development might cause an erosion of Slavic dominance in Bulgaria or become a secessionist movement that could compromise the country's territorial integrity. But hostility toward the Turkish minority also had a narrow economic motive: the Socialists' anxiety over the loss of jobs to small ethnic groups. Bulgarian nationalists wanted the government in Sofia to enact job quotas in areas where Bulgarians were outnumbered by ethnic Turks and at the least to guarantee a continuation of the practice, followed by the Zhivkov regime, of excluding ethnic Turks from managerial positions in state-owned enterprises. In July, in places with large concentrations of people of Turkish cultural origin, the nationalists staged protests against the Turks by blocking their access to municipal buildings, closing down factories, blocking roads, and preventing people from shopping.

THE END OF COMMUNIST RULE

The final collapse of Communist power in Bulgaria came with the parliamentary elections in October 1991. The Union of Democratic Forces (UDF) bested the BSP, though by only a hairsbreadth margin. Nevertheless, the results of the elections formally terminated 40 years of Communist Party rule.

The new government was headed by Prime Minister Filip Dimitrov. Without an absolute majority of seats in Parliament, Dimitrov needed to form a coalition but was determined not to ally with the Socialist, who had one-third of the seats. He went instead to the Movement for Rights and Freedom (MRF), which represented Bulgaria's Turkish minority and had won 7 percent of the popular vote. Ironically, this gave the Bulgarian Turks an opportunity to play a pivotal role in national politics. Here was the very situation the former Communist leadership had tried to prevent through a ruthless policy of forced assimilation.

The MRF wasted no time in advising the Union of Democratic Forces leadership that its cooperation in producing the majority needed to govern the country would come at a substantial price. The MRF wanted several ministerial posts and meaningful participation in the formation of Bulgarian foreign policy. The UDF responded cautiously, recognizing that its cabinet would need popular acceptance to function effectively and that popular acceptance might be hard to achieve, given the national prejudice toward Bulgarians of Turkish background.

The UDF pledged to privatize state-owned businesses quickly, to change laws on land ownership to encourage private entrepreneurialism in agriculture, and to stimulate foreign investment. It also promised to confiscate property illegitimately held by Communists.

But by late 1992 UDF rule had become unpopular as a result of continuing economic hardship for most Bulgarians. The UDF government was replaced in December by what was thought at the time to be a short-term caretaker government of non-party professionals to keep the country going to elections, which would produce a workable parliamentary majority. The new government of Prime Minister Lyuben Berov, however, struck a deal with the BSP and the MRF to give him a majority, enabling him to run the country throughout 1993.

Immediately there was disagreement over when parliamentary elections should be held. The Socialists preferred elections at the end of 1995, when their chances of winning an absolute majority would be better. The UDF wanted elections much earlier, before the BSP could strengthen its appeal among voters. The UDF tried to get President Zhelev to press the Parliament, which has the authority to dissolve itself (the president does not have the dissolution power), to set elections sooner, say, in 1994. Zhelev resisted and stood by Berov's regime, provoking the anger of his party and, ironically, undermining its image.

The BSP seems to have benefited from this division within the UDF. As compared to the UDF, it began to look like a calm, professional, political force worthy of popular support and national leadership. It would like to govern the country without reliance on a coalition. Its chances of doing well in the near future looked good in 1993 and early 1994.

FOREIGN POLICY

The government must keep an eye on its borders, where regional unrest threatens to slow Bulgaria's programs of change. Of most immediate importance is Bulgaria's relations with Greece; here there are currently two issues of concern. One has to do with the new political influence of Bulgaria's Turkish minority, the other with the future of Macedonia, which recently declared its independence of Yugoslavia. The new leadership of Bulgaria also wants good relations with Turkey and other Balkan neighbors and continues to look to the United States for encouragement and support of its program of reforms.

Greece

In the 1991 parliamentary elections, the MRF became Bulgaria's third-largest political force. Some Greek politicians and journalists expressed concern that Bulgarian Turks—and, indirectly, the Turkish Republic—thereby stood to gain an excessive influence in Bulgaria's internal affairs. The new government faced the delicate task of preserving a close relationship with Greece while continuing a rapprochement with Turkey; for reasons of national security and regional stability, Bulgaria cannot afford to have difficulties with either Greece or Turkey.

One cause of misunderstanding and of potential conflict between Bulgaria and Greece concerns the future of Macedonia. Bulgaria's support of Macedonia's independence of Belgrade drew criticism in Athens, where there is fear of a resurgence of Macedonian irredentism aimed at uniting Macedonians living in Greece and Bulgaria in a greater Macedonian state. There is good reason for the Greeks to worry about this possibility. In its first relatively free parliamentary elections, in November and December 1990, the Internal Macedonian Revolutionary Organization (IMRO), which supported the creation of a greater Macedonia, won a substantial minority of votes. In a referendum held several months later, Macedonians voted overwhelmingly for the complete independence of their republic. Athens feared that the speed with which Sofia and Ankara recognized the new Macedonian state would embolden the new Macedonian state to raise claims of territory in northern Greece, Greek Macedonia, inhabited by kin.

To reassure the Greek government, Bulgarian president Zhelev attended a conference with Greece about Balkan issues but insisted that if Macedonia were to be discussed, its representatives should also attend. He told Athens that while Bulgaria

accepted Macedonia's independence of Yugoslavia, it would not endorse the idea of a Macedonian nation that included territory belonging to Greece. He assured the Greeks also that Bulgaria had no claims on Macedonian territory.

Macedonians, however, are suspicious of Bulgaria's disclaimer and fear that the Bulgarian government does harbor some designs on Macedonian territory, given the interest of Bulgaria in Greek Macedonia dating back to the Treaty of San Stefano ending the Russo–Turk War of 1878. In this treaty Bulgaria, which won autonomy of the Ottoman Empire, was assigned a portion of Greek Macedonia, only to lose it years later to Greece.

Further complicating the issue of Macedonia is the question of Serbia's intent. In 1992 Serbia's forces were engaged in Croatia and Bosnia-Herzegovina, but alarming signals suggested that Macedonia might be the next object of Serbian territorial aggrandizement, the pretext being protection of the small Serb minority in Macedonia. A Serbian invasion of Macedonia might be acceptable to Greece, as a means of discouraging development of the idea of a "Macedonian nation," but such a move would threaten Bulgaria and provoke a confrontation between the two countries.

Turkey

The Dimitrov government also inherited problems in Bulgaria's relations with Turkey. When it took office in late 1991, there was a legacy of bad feelings as a result of the Communist policy of the late 1980s to "Bulgarianize" the country's Turkish minority. But relations began to improve; the Dimitrov government's commitment to democratization and in particular to alter past policy toward the Turkish minority and allow a measure of equality was seen as a willingness of the Union of Democratic Forces to work with the MRF following the 1991 parliamentary elections. Furthermore, Sofia fully appreciated the importance of good relations with Turkey, which, like Greece, was a member of NATO, for strengthening Bulgarian ties with the West. Bulgarian–Turkish relations took a slight turn for the better when Dimityr Ludzhev, an adviser to President Zhelev, visited Ankara in October 1991. Ludzhev assured the Turkish government that Bulgaria was committed to full equality for its Turkish minority. Unfortunately, Bulgarians still want to impose restrictions on and limit the political and economic influence of the Turkish minority. Good Bulgarian–Turkish relations in the future will depend on how the Bulgarian government proceeds on this issue.

| Independence 1908 | Bulgaria joins the Rome–Berlin Axis 1941 | Soviet troops enter Bulgaria; Dimitrov returns to Bulgaria from the Soviet Union to head the BCP 1945 | Dimitrov dies; "nativist" Bulgarian Communists succeed to leadership of the party 1949 | Zhivkov becomes the first secretary 1954 | The new Constitution reaffirms Bulgarian commitment to Soviet-style socialism 1971 | Bulgaria supports the Soviet invasion of Afghanistan 1979 | 1980s–1990s |

150,000 Bulgarian Turks flee to Turkey; 50,000 Bulgarians participate in the country's first mass protest in 40 years

The collapse of Communist power; the Turkish minority gains a pivotal role in national politics

Bulgarians directly elect their president for the first time

An auspicious development occurred at a Turkish-sponsored summit of 11 nations with interests in the Black Sea in Istanbul in June 1992. The Balkan states of Bulgaria, Romania, Turkey, Greece, and Albania plus Armenia, Azerbaijan, Moldova, Georgia, and Russia signed a declaration of economic cooperation with a pledge to contain regional conflicts. Turkey was especially gratified, because the summit represented a first step in the development of its idea of creating a European Community–style grouping of the Balkan–Black Sea countries. But, more importantly, the emergence of an organization of countries that traditionally had been rivals could provide the means of lessening confrontation and conflict in the region. The willingness of Bulgaria to go along with this plan was appreciated by the Turkish leadership.

Russia

The Kremlin's ties with the East bloc had been not only economic, political, and military but also psychological and emotional. As Moscow's most faithful ally, Bulgaria always had expected to be protected. But Bulgaria suffered as the Soviet state disintegrated. In particular, like other former Soviet satellites, Bulgaria had to grapple with the sudden, devastating effects, starting in 1990, of massive reductions in the quantity of inexpensive Soviet oil that Bulgaria purchased.

Nevertheless, the Dimitrov government has a positive base on which to develop friendly and cooperative relations with post-Soviet Russia, with which Bulgaria

has so much in common. President Zhelev reacted to the August 1991 anti-Gorbachev coup attempt by condemning the plotters immediately after learning about the coup and personally contacting Russian president Yeltsin. (The Bulgarian Socialists [Communists] were somewhat less discreet and took the position of neutrality that implied sympathy for the Soviet hardliners.) The fall of the Socialists from power 2 months after the failed coup in Moscow opened the way for the new relationship between Bulgaria and Russia. The Bulgarian policy has focused on regenerating trade with Russia.

The West

As an alternative to intimacy with Russia, Bulgaria has tried to ingratiate itself with the West, with which it desperately wants to strengthen economic and other links. To this end Sofia has undertaken a sweeping investigation of accusations of Bulgaria's complicity in the plot to assassinate Pope John Paul II. Despite the reticence of senior Bulgarian police and intelligence officials, who are reluctant to compromise colleagues and apparently have tried to destroy incriminating documents, the Bulgarian government released more than 127 volumes of secret police documents in May 1991. President Zhelev offered to provide whatever additional relevant documents came to light. At the very least, this gesture of candor was intended to increase the credibility of Bulgaria's stated commitment to break completely with the Communist past.

Bulgarian relations with the United States improved substantially as a result of the political changes in Sofia, notably the decisive Communist loss of power in the October 1991 parliamentary elections and the reelection of President Zhelev in January 1992. Prime Minister Dimitrov was well received in Washington in March 1992 and noted with satisfaction American appreciation of the changes taking place in Bulgaria. Whether this event will lead to stronger American–Bulgarian ties, especially in the economic sphere, remains to be seen.

PROSPECTS OF STABILITY

There are grounds for optimism in Bulgaria. The semblance of a market economy seems to be emerging, albeit with difficulty, in both the industrial and agricultural sectors. In the international sphere, Bulgaria has achieved a measure of acceptance and legitimacy, and Western countries have come forward with much needed economic assistance.

DEVELOPMENT

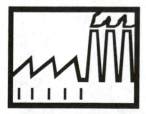

After a slow start, Bulgaria has made progress in the transition to a free market economy: Almost 80 percent of properties (houses, shops, warehouses) in the Sofia region earmarked for private ownership had been returned by the end of 1992, and reprivatization of agriculture gained momentum in 1992. Privatization of state- and municipal-owned industrial enterprises has proceeded much more slowly.

FREEDOM

Bulgaria, frequently seen by outsiders in the West during the communist era as "the 16th Republic of the former Soviet Union," where KGB colonels sat in on councils of government, is now trying democracy. But it took cautious Bulgarian voters more than 2 years of thinking things over, as well as 2 parliamentary elections, to vote Communists out of power.

HEALTH/WELFARE

Bulgaria has a serious environmental problem with nuclear-energy production. The nuclear-power plant in Kozlodui has a reputation as the most dangerous nuclear facility in the world. The transition from the slovenly safety norms practiced by former Communist administrators to a safety-conscious Western system has been an uneasy one for the 5,000 engineers, technicians, and other workers.

ACHIEVEMENTS

Bulgaria has earned a grudging respect from the West for its perceived commitment in the post-Communist era to the development of democratic government and the free market economy. The IMF and World Bank now consider Bulgaria a legitimate candidate for substantial loan money.

Czechoslovakia (The Czech Republic and Slovakia)

THE CZECH REPUBLIC

GEOGRAPHY

Area in Square Kilometers (Miles): 78,703 (30,379) (slightly smaller than South Carolina)
Capital (Population): Prague (1,200,000)

PEOPLE

Total: 10,389,000
Annual Growth Rate: 0.16%
Ethnic Makeup of Population: 94% Czech; 3% Slovak; 3% Polish, German, Gypsy, Hungarian, and others
Life Expectancy at Birth: 69 years (male); 77 years (female)
Infant Mortality Rate (Ratio): 10/1,000
Religion: 40% atheist; 40% Roman Catholic; 5% Protestant; 3% Orthodox; 12% others
Adult Literacy Rate: n/a

GOVERNMENT

Type: parliamentary democracy
Head of State: President Vaclav Havel
Political Parties: Civic Democratic Party; Christian Democratic Union; Christian Democratic Party; Czech People's Party; Czechoslovak Social Democracy; Republican Party; others

ECONOMY

Currency ($ U.S. Equivalent): 29.8 korunas = $1

IS REUNIFICATION POSSIBLE?

Czechs have accepted the "uncoupling" of the two sections of Czechoslovakia with equanimity, convinced that they will do better without close ties to the less developed and more conservative Slovaks. The Slovaks, though not yet their political leaders, have begun to have some regrets about the breakup, as they experience some of the long-term costs of having overindulged their national pride. There is unemployment, shortages of everything, and in Bratislava a drab and deprived physical environment reminiscent of the Communist era that constrasts sharply with the growing affluence of sparkling and confident Prague. Though some Slovaks think their country should reunite with the Czechs, their leadership considers independence "irrevocable."

Per Capita Income/GDP: $7,300/$75.3 billion
Inflation Rate: 12.5%

SLOVAKIA

GEOGRAPHY

Area in Square Kilometers (Miles): 48,845 (18,854) (about twice the size of New Hampshire)

Capital (Population): Bratislava (440,000)

PEOPLE

Total: 5,376,000
Annual Growth Rate: 0.51%
Ethnic Makeup of Population: 86% Slovak; 11% Hungarian; 2% Gypsy; 1% Czech
Life Expectancy at Birth: 68 years (male); 77 years (female)
Infant Mortality Rate (Ratio): 11/1,000
Religion: 60% Roman Catholic; 10% atheist; 8% Protestant; 4% Orthodox; 18% others
Adult Literacy Rate: n/a

GOVERNMENT

Type: parliamentary democracy
Head of State: President Michal Kovac
Political Parties: Hungarian Christian Democratic Movement; Christian Democratic Movement; Movement for a Democratic Slovakia; Party of the Democratic Left; Slovak National Party; others

ECONOMY

Currency ($ U.S. Equivalent): 32.92 korunas = $1
Per Capita Income/GDP: $6,100/$32.1 billion
Inflation Rate: 8.7%

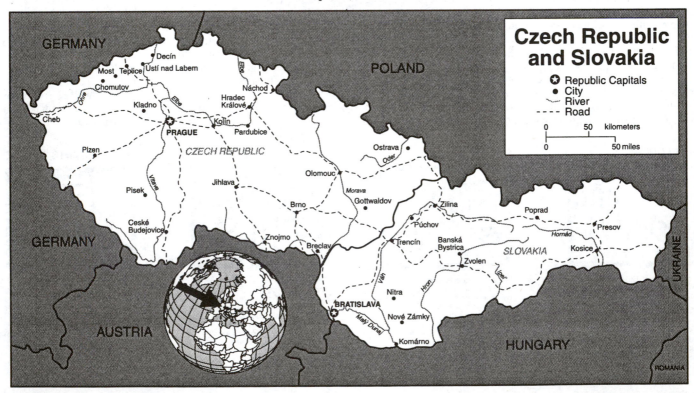

Czech Republic and Slovakia

- ✪ Republic Capitals
- • City
- ⌇ River
- --- Road

CZECHOSLOVAKIA

Already one of the most industrialized countries in Central/Eastern Europe at the time of the Communist takeover, Czechoslovakia accommodated the Communist Party's Soviet-inspired transformation to socialism with far less stress than other Central/Eastern European countries did. By the early 1950s, Czechoslovakia had become a Soviet-style socialist dictatorship and a loyal ally of the Soviet Union.

In the early years of Communist Party rule, the Czechoslovak people, unlike most other Central/Eastern European peoples, had no deep-seated hostility toward the Russians. They did not seem to blame the Soviet Union for not helping them to defend their territory against Nazi aggression in 1938 and 1939. In fact, after World War II, Czechoslovakia viewed the Soviet Union as the only country able to assure its security and survival. The Czechoslovaks had little faith in the West—even if culturally they were closer to it than to the Soviet Union—because of the way in which the great Western powers (Britain and France) had appeased the Nazis in the pre–World War II era and thereby contributed to the invasion and partition of Czechoslovakia in 1939.

When the Czechoslovak Communist Party (KSC) gained power after World War II, it enjoyed substantial popularity, in contrast to the Communist parties of other Central/Eastern European countries. The Czechoslovak Communists had participated in the parliamentary system of the 1930s, had fought the Nazi occupiers in the 1940s, and were active partners with other Czechoslovak parties in the coalition governments following the war. The KSC thus had credibility with many voters, as seen in the first national elections after the war, when the Communists won more than one-third of the popular vote.

In the years following Joseph Stalin's death in 1953, when its neighbors Poland and Hungary were experiencing political turmoil, Czechoslovakia remained the ideal Soviet satellite. It had a tight Stalin-like dictatorship under KSC leader Antonin Novotny; it slavishly imitated the Soviet model of socialist development in other ways, especially in the economic sphere; and it remained closely linked to the Soviet Union and the Warsaw Pact.

The appearance of stability belied the reality of developing problems in Czechoslovak society. In the 1960s influential people both within and without the KSC discussed the need for significant divergence from Soviet practices in order to improve economic performance and raise the standard of living. Some also favored political liberalization and an expansion of trade with the West. There was enough support for sweeping change to replace Novotny, the symbol of Czechoslovakia's subservience to the Soviet model. In January 1968 he was succeeded as general secretary of the KSC by Alexander Dubcek, the leader of the Communist Party of Slovakia.

THE PRAGUE SPRING

Dubcek began an unprecedented effort at systemic reform in Czechoslovakia to give Czechoslovak socialism "a human face." The reforms, which involved liberalization of Czechoslovakia's repressive political environment, its highly regimented economic system, and its overly centralized administrative system, which had discriminated against the large Slovak minority in the eastern part of the country, have come to be known as "the Prague Spring." But Dubcek had hardly begun the political phase of the Prague Spring, with a relaxation of censorship and a toleration of open discussion and debate of national problems, when the Kremlin became alarmed and quickly suppressed it.

The Soviet Intervention

The Soviets led a Warsaw Pact invasion of Czechoslovakia. Pact forces occupied Prague in August 1968. The Soviets ultimately forced the ouster of Dubcek. They

(Gamma-Liaison/Gilles Caron)

The Soviet invasion of Czechoslovakia in August 1968.

approved his replacement by Gustav Husak, another Slovak but a conservative willing to lead Czechoslovakia exactly as the Soviets wanted.

The Soviets imposed on the Czechoslovak state what they termed "normalization." Soviet normalization meant the reversal of Dubcek reformism, the imposition of strict political discipline throughout society, Czechoslovakia's explicit reaffirmation of its loyalty to the Warsaw Pact, and Czechoslovakia's acceptance of the supposedly temporary stationing on its soil of an unspecified number of Soviet troops.

Charter 77

While the Soviet intervention restored stability in Czechoslovak society, it also provoked an undercurrent of opposition. A major challenge to the Husak regime's political repression and servility to Moscow occurred in January 1977, when 300 Czechoslovak intellectuals from different sectors of national life signed a document called Charter 77. The charter contained a detailed condemnation of the government's political repression, accusing it of a systematic discrimination in education, in employment, and elsewhere in society against citizens critical of its policies.

The Charter 77 movement was quickly and ruthlessly suppressed. The regime continued in succeeding years to persecute and harass any who were associated with the charter. Although the signatories tried to show resilience in succeeding years by holding parties commemorating the signing of the charter, the fact remained that they had been silenced and their complaints largely ignored.

THE CATHOLIC CHURCH

A more recent challenge to the stability and conformity imposed by the Soviets was the Czechoslovak Roman Catholic Church, for a long time politically quiescent in the face of official atheism and efforts to undermine traditional religion. There was an increase in church attendance in eastern Slovakia, where people had always been deeply religious and seemingly impervious to the KSC's antireligion policies. Even more striking was a new expression of interest in religion and in the church by youth in the large urban centers. There was also substantial clandestine religious activity in the home.

Several factors helped to account for the resurgence of interest in the church. One was the resilience of the church itself. It was one of the few surviving non-Communist institutions in Czechoslovak life.

Because the socialist regime was neither willing nor able to attack the church in the same compulsive and brutal way it attacked political dissidents, the Czechoslovak people found that they could express their inner hostility toward the regime—albeit in an oblique way—by association with the church and through the pursuit of permitted religious activity. The Czechoslovak Catholic Church, like its Polish counterpart, also benefited from its ties with the Vatican and gained strength from the leadership of Pope John Paul II.

CONFORMITY TO SOVIET MODELS

In the area of foreign policy, the Husak regime displayed consistent servility to the Soviet Union. The party leadership dutifully accepted the deployment of additional Soviet SS-20 missiles on Czechoslovak territory. It strongly supported the Soviet position in East–West arms negotiations. Its official press even outdid the Soviet press in its denunciation of Western policies and in its placing blame for the collapse of the arms control dialogue on the United States. It also condemned Poland's Solidarity movement and in other ways reinforced Soviet policy toward the Polish political crisis of the early 1980s.

Czechoslovakia was supportive of Soviet policy in Poland, however, not only out of loyalty to the Kremlin but also for reasons of national self-interest. Both the Czechoslovak people and their party leadership were critical of Solidarity's confrontation with the Warsaw authorities in 1980 and 1981. Unlike the Poles, the Czechoslovaks were not given to street demonstrations and the use of violence to protest government policies. The Czechoslovaks also believed that the Poles themselves, as much as their Soviet-style system, were to blame for their country's economic and social problems. The Czechoslovaks, with their high regard for the authority of the state, also believed that the Poles were too political for their own good and too cynical and rebellious in their relations with the state.

With all that was wrong with the Soviet economic model, the Czechoslovak economy still provided its society with an adequate standard of living. The standard of living was not as high as it might have been under capitalism or with a major overhaul of the highly centralized administrative apparatus, but it was better than that of most other socialist economies. However, the regime's excessive conformity with the traditional Soviet model was a serious liability for future economic growth and political stability.

FROM HUSAK TO JAKES

Serious problems threatened Czechoslovak economic health and social stability; they disturbed the Kremlin as well as the Czechoslovak party leadership and led eventually to Husak's resignation as head of the party. Czechoslovakia's relative well-being in the Soviet bloc was not the result of positive conditions but of a serious aberration: a flourishing nonsocialist underground economy in which a very high percentage of the people produced and consumed outside the official economic structure. The official economy was doing very poorly in terms of modernizing its antiquated and inefficient industrial facilities, checking pollution, protecting health, keeping pace in science and technology, and innovating to enable its exports to gain greater access to Western markets.

Making the Czechoslovak economy and society permanently healthy, however, required doses of glasnost and perestroika, to which Husak was disinclined. He and other party officials worried that economic reform would generate political pressures like those in the Prague Spring of 1968 for a radical liberalization of society, in particular individual freedom and human rights.

Indeed, there was no let-up in the regime's emphasis on repressive political conformity. It opposed the revival of interest in religion, a growing popular interest in Western music, and the development of peace movements among the youth as well as dissident groups like Charter 77.

Mikhail Gorbachev seemed in no hurry to push the Czechoslovak party leadership toward change, but the Kremlin was concerned that Husak's conservatism could turn out to be a dangerous threat to the long-term stability of Czechoslovak socialism, which had yet to achieve the legitimization essential for its survival. In December 1987 Husak was replaced as Czechoslovak Communist Party leader by Milos Jakes—a move approved, and possibly encouraged, by the Kremlin. Husak remained as president of the republic, a far less powerful post than that of party leader.

In many respects the regime under Jakes continued the spirit, if not the letter, of its predecessor's conservative policies in the political and cultural spheres. Jakes reacted strongly to the revival of popular interest in religious activity. He asserted that while the church was legal and free, some people used it for political purposes, in the form of church-supported demonstrations. These, Jakes argued, had nothing to do with religious services and served only to undermine social stability. The Czechoslovak regime therefore moved in the direction opposite of the Soviet Union in its policy toward religion and the church.

In 1988 the government disrupted and dispersed a demonstration in favor of religious freedom in Bratislava. This use of force against the peaceful protestors provoked an angry reaction in the West, but the Czechoslovak government did not respond to this pressure, possibly because it feared the church's potential for disruption.

In the political sphere, hard-liners in the Czechoslovak political leadership increased their power when, in October 1988, Premier Lubomir Strougal was replaced by Ladislav Adamec, a pragmatic economist but also a political loyalist who was expected to support Jakes's conservative strategies. Jakes used the opportunity of Strougal's removal to warn against hurried solutions to economic difficulties and underlined his belief in centralized control.

Repression of dissent intensified. On November 11, 1988, the authorities broke up a meeting in Prague that had been called by Charter 77 to examine recent Czechoslovak history. A major confrontation between dissidents and the regime occurred in January 1989, coincidental with the government's signing of a newly strengthened Helsinki agreement on human rights. Thousands of Czech and Slovak youth held rallies in Wenceslas Square in Prague to commemorate the 1969 death of Jan Palach, a student who set fire to himself to protest the Soviet invasion. The government responded forcefully. Among other actions, it detained writer Vaclav Havel, a leading signatory of Charter 77, while he was trying to lay flowers at the place where Palach set himself on fire. This move provoked a counterresponse in the form of a petition by 1,000 people in theater, the arts, and television demanding Havel's release as well as a warning letter from Cardinal Frantisek Tomasek to Premier Adamec.

PRESSURES FOR CHANGE

Pressure mounted on the Communist regime to alter its conservative course. Much of this pressure came from within the country, but socialist neighbors, in particular the Soviet Union, Poland, and Hungary, also contributed.

The Czechoslovak crackdown on dissidents, including the imprisonment of Havel, was a burden for Soviet efforts to strengthen ties with the West through a more liberal policy toward human rights. Furthermore, the Kremlin worried that this conservatism would eventually destabilize Czechoslovak society and endanger its socialism. In November 1988 Soviet Politburo member and Gorbachev adviser Aleksandr Yacovlev journeyed to Prague to urge a more tolerant approach to political dissent. The Soviets led the Czechoslovak leadership to expect sometime in the near future a Soviet reassessment of the 1968 invasion of Prague, perhaps including an exoneration of Dubcek. Such a move would weaken the credibility and authority of conservative elements in the Czechoslovak Party and, possibly, encourage increased tolerance of political dissent. Indeed, many in the Czechoslovak opposition were confident that continuing Soviet pressure on Prague eventually would force the regime to embrace a reformism similar to, if not identical to, perestroika.

Poland and Hungary, which used to be reticent about the internal politics of their allies, also began to speak out against the repressive policies of the Prague regime. During the month between the eruption of antigovernment demonstrations in Prague in January 1989 and the trial of Havel and other leading Czechoslovak dissidents in February, the Polish and Hungarian party leaderships met with Jakes to urge leniency.

Internal pressure to liberalize the political environment came especially from the youth. The regime's agreement with the public—a sort of social contract whereby the population remained politically passive so long as there was economic stability—crumbled as a younger generation of students and workers, untainted by the fear and defeatism that followed 1968, grew increasingly impatient for the change the Gorbachev era appeared to promise. Although their organization was weak and their political strategy almost nonexistent, their aspirations for change were vocal and persistent.

THE BEGINNINGS OF REFORM

In late 1988 there was some evidence that the Jakes regime was loosening up. The conservative leadership promoted younger and more pragmatic elements to the Politburo, and conservative figures departed. The leadership also showed restraint in dealing with political dissent. For example, the government ceased jamming Radio Free Europe broadcasts and authorized the publication of the works of Franz Kafka after a 20-year ban imposed in the aftermath of the Prague Spring. And although the authorities had arrested Havel, they did not stop a public demonstration in Prague in early December commemorating the 40th anniversary of the signing of the universal declaration of human rights. Eventually, Havel's sentence was reduced to 8 months. He was released in May 1989, after he had served 4 months.

This slight shift in politics was accompanied by a gradual implementation of modest economic reforms. State companies were made more independent of central planning and accountable for their profits and losses. The government called for the setting up of workers' self-management councils in all factories, divided the state bank into several autonomous commercial banks, revised industrial pricing, and encouraged joint ventures with Western companies. Official economists suggested, however, that change would be slow; they wondered whether popular pressure for reform extended beyond the youth who thronged to demonstrations.

THE UPHEAVAL BEGINS

Events, however, had a momentum of their own. After the sudden and unexpected collapse of conservative rule in East Germany in early October 1989 and in Bulgaria in early November, as well as the subsequent relaxation of political control in Czechoslovakia itself, Czechoslovaks started to organize and demonstrate for swifter change in their own country. The Jakes regime initially tried to resist this pressure, using force to disperse demonstrators. On November 12 it warned that the party would not tolerate dissent and would not diminish control.

But public pressure on the regime intensified, and on November 24, 300,000 people demonstrated in Prague in favor of political reform, an unprecedented gesture of massive protest and dissent. This time the regime capitulated, probably because the only alternative was the use of massive force with unpredictable consequences. Jakes resigned as party leader in favor of Karel Urbanek, and power shifted to the moderate and reform-minded Premier Adamec. Subsequently, other hard-liners resigned from the party leadership or were ousted.

In December Husak resigned as president and Havel, who had the overwhelming backing of the Parliament as well as tremendous support among Western nations, became interim president. Dubcek was named presiding officer of the Parliament. Before long even Adamec was obliged to resign because of popular dissatisfaction with the slowness of his reform program—opposition leaders were angry over his hesitation to assign to them

(Reuters/Bettmann Newsphotos/Jaroslav Koran)

Vaclav Havel, the noted playwright, was arrested in January 1989 in response to his being a leading signatory of Chapter 77. By the end of 1989, the conservative hard-liners were forced to relinquish power. By December Havel had become the president of Czechoslovakia.

a substantial share of cabinet seats. He was succeeded as premier by an obscure Communist leader, Marian Calfa.

The party eventually met the demands of the newly formed coalition of opposition groups, called Civic Forum, and agreed to share power with non-Communist organizations. It also agreed to relinquish its monopoly of power by accepting the establishment of a multiparty system, and it consented to free and open parliamentary elections in 1990. In January 1990 it agreed, albeit grudgingly, to give up 100 seats it had held in the federal Assembly. It was also about this time that Premier Calfa announced his withdrawal from the Communist Party.

The Soviet Union played a neutral role that benefited and encouraged the reformers. The Kremlin refused to support the Jakes regime. The ease with which the regime fell affirmed the obvious: namely, that survival of the Communist regime had depended not on Soviet backing but on popular loyalty and support.

As the country looked forward to the parliamentary elections scheduled for the middle of 1990, a number of important events marked the progress of Czechoslovakia's decommunization and desatellization in the aftermath of the November upheaval. In response to demands by the Czechoslovak government for the departure of all Soviet troops by the end of 1990, the Soviets agreed to start the withdrawal process. The government terminated all course work and academic programs in Marxist-Leninist studies in the nation's universities and dismissed those faculty who had participated in and benefited personally from the purge of instructors and administrators carried out by the Husak regime 20 years earlier. Finally, Prague prepared to take major steps in "desocializing" the economy by expanding private entrepreneurialism.

THE COMMUNIST ERA ENDS

Czechoslovakia held its first free national parliamentary elections since the end of World War II on June 8 and 9, 1990. Twenty-two parties fielded candidates for seats in the two houses of the federal Parliament and for seats in the Czech and Slovak provincial parliaments, but only three groups had substantial popular backing. The Civic Forum and its co-movement in Slovakia, the Public Against Violence, reflecting their leading role in toppling the Communists and the popularity of their leader, President Havel, received the overwhelming majority of votes on both the federal and provincial levels. The Christian Democratic Bloc, a bloc of parties somewhat to the right of Civic Forum and less eager than the Forum to proceed with a rapid purge of Communists from the central administrative apparatus, received the next-largest number of votes. The Communists, discredited by their past leadership of the country and by recent public revelations of the degree of secrecy with which they had ruled, received 13 percent of the votes, somewhat more than the 10 percent they had been expected to win. None of the other 19 parties, many of which were committed primarily to local interests, obtained more than 4 percent of the electorate.

Following the elections Havel promptly reappointed Calfa as premier and charged him with the formation of Czechoslovakia's first democratic government in more than 40 years. On July 5, 1990, Parliament overwhelmingly elected Havel president of the republic. He became Czechoslovakia's first non-Communist president since 1948.

DEMOCRATIC DEVELOPMENT

While most of the important positions in the federal government were filled by Charter 77 activists, who were strongly committed to democratic principles, making democracy work has not been easy.

Havel's own party, the Forum, was sharply divided over the question of what to do with the old Communist elite in positions of administrative responsibility. Havel wanted to avoid a witch-hunt, if only because in many instances ex-Communists were the only people with the technical skills needed to manage the bureaucracy. Moreover, more than half the signatories of Charter 77 who founded Civic Forum were themselves former Communists, even if they were disciplined by the Husak leadership after 1969 for their reformist instincts and their involvement in the Prague Spring reforms. Havel's support for utilizing Communist experience has met opposition from many in the Forum who suffered persecution under the former regime and want to expel former Communists.

Forum leaders also disagreed on economic reforms. Finance Minister Vaclav Klaus supported rapid movement to a free market system with a minimum of restrictions on the development of capitalism and free enterprise. Havel wanted this but with safeguards to protect people from hardship. While Klaus spoke for the farmers and other entrepreneurs in the countryside, Havel spoke for the wage-earning groups in the densely populated urban centers who were worried about job security and adequacy of wages. Toward the end of 1990, Klaus started a campaign to pack the Forum with people who shared his views. In response, Havel, Foreign Minister Jiri Dienstbier, and other close supporters of the president created a dissident faction within the Forum called the Liberal Club. Havel's supporters accused Klaus and his followers of being little more than heartless technocrats, oblivious to the misery of the poor and the displaced caused by the gradual termination of the security and protection of the socialist welfare state.

The split in the Forum undermined the stability and unity of post-Communist Czechoslovakia. Despite the pledge of the newly formed Civic Democratic Party and the Civic Movement to remain together in a coalition, they became rivals, disagreeing over key issues, eventually destabilizing the national government and weakening Havel's leadership and his ability to keep the Czechoslovak state unified. Czechoslovak Democrats, never mind the rest of society, had little experience with the culture of dialogue. Even

signatories of Charter 77 now were intolerant of divergent views.

Shortly after the Civic Forum formally split in February 1992, the Communists went on the offensive, asking voter support to avoid further revolutionary upheavals. But Czechoslovak voters did not respond; the memory of Communist absues was still too strong. Communist membership in Parliament declined throughout 1991 to barely 20 percent of their original pre-revolutionary membership, with many party members at or past retirement age.

Economic Reform

Beyond Havel's caution there were other reasons why Czechoslovakia initially moved slowly toward the market economy. By the end of 1990, most industries were still state-owned, most stores still offered only a narrow, drab supply of items, and legislation providing for privatization was still stalled. Many people had little if any spare capital to purchase newly privatized industries. Czechoslovaks also lacked entrepreneurial experience.

Beginning in January 1991, however, with Klaus pushing for change, the Prague government took major steps to accelerate the desocialization of the economy. The government removed price controls on 85 percent of goods sold, initiated the closure of inefficient state-owned enterprises and the privatization of thousands of shops, and restricted the money supply and took other measures to make the Czechoslovak currency convertible.

Nevertheless, Czechoslovakia still faced serious problems in making the transition from socialism to a market-based economy. Scarce hard currency had to be spent on the purchase of oil rather than on modernization of industry. Outdated machinery was keeping costs of production high and preventing Czechoslovakia's exports from becoming competitive on the world market, stunting growth, pushing up consumer prices, and depressing the standard of living. Federal authorities tried to control the effects of high costs of food and energy production by establishing price ceilings in retail outlets.

The government tried some imaginative ways to facilitate privatization in its capital-starved society. It began auctioning state-run stores to the highest bidders, who paid much less than market value for what they were buying. But citizens were angry that those among them who had the money to take advantage of the auctions were ex-Communist officials, money changers, swindlers, and black marketeers; they also were concerned about Germans and Austrians coming into their country to exploit the cheap prices.

Another effort to facilitate privatization of large industrial enterprises involved the "coupon method." It allowed the public to obtain shares in these firms or to buy shares in something similar to mutual funds in Western countries. Once again, however, there were complaints of the unfair advantages enjoyed by former Communist Party big shots and well-heeled foreigners. Furthermore, the voucher system was criticized as little more than a giveaway program.

Special problems were involved in privatizing agriculture. There was little knowledge on how to run a private farm, as a result of the completeness of collectivization by the former Stalinist leadership of the country, as well as a lack of will to do the endless work that private farming entails. Furthermore, large cooperatives, which controlled 80 percent of Czechoslovak farmland, had proved to be more efficient than the tiny family farms they replaced. This efficiency was the result of the autonomy that farm managers had enjoyed in the recent past that had allowed them to become imaginative and innovative, plus the practice of distributing the cooperative's profits to its workers, who consequently had more incentive than workers in factories to excel in the quality and quantity of their output.

But Prague wanted to put agriculture back into private hands. In May 1991 Parliament passed a bill returning all land confiscated by the Communists to their original owners, on the assumption that clearly defined property titles are fundamental for prosperity. This law was not likely to affect the farm cooperative system adversely, because most of those people who regained land were expected, at least initially, to rent it back to the cooperatives.

The Environment

The Czech Republic and Slovakia have one of the most polluted environments in Central/Eastern Europe. More than 30 percent of their combined territories is ecologically devastated. Prague is frequently darkened during the day by a foul smog that endangers both the health and spirit of people living there and causes many of them to flee the city when the smog sets in.

The town of Most, at the edge of the Erzgebirge Mountains, is a symbol of the tragedy of the entire region. The town was literally swallowed up by pollution resulting from the use of lignite, a low-quality coal used to fuel factories throughout Central/Eastern Europe that has high sulphur and ash content. Factories and plants using lignite surround Most and caused the government literally to depopulate it, in order to prevent an epidemic of chronic pollution-caused illnesses.

Environmental protection presents government with almost insurmountable problems because of the cost and complexity of remedial policies. There is a debilitating lack of funding in the region for the environment, requiring leaderships to look outside their countries for help. Political parties lack the experienced and talented leadership and organizational unity needed to lobby effectively for environmental cleanup programs. Finally, an effective cleanup program depends on the cooperation and control of emissions of neighboring countries.

Interethnic Conflict

From the end of Communist rule in 1989, there was a renewal of Slovak demands for separation from the Czechoslovak federation. While Slovaks were more resentful than ever before of Czech dominance of the federation (Czechs constituted 65 percent of the population, controlled an equal percentage of federation territory, and exerted a dominant influence over the national economy), the Public Against Violence Party, which represented the majority of Slovak people, considered separation impractical and lobbied for autonomy. The party wanted a new federal constitution that would give Slovaks their own central bank, labor market, and, eventually, taxation rights and customs control. They also wanted to enter the European Community as an equal and independent partner of the Czechs. They sought control of railroads and the national pipeline network located in their territory.

Another cause of Slovak separatism had to do with economic conditions in Slovakia, especially unemployment and other hardships resulting from the transition to a market economy pursued by the central government in Prague. Slovakia was vulnerable to worsening economic conditions because it was home to giant smelting, chemical, and weapons industries built by the Husak regime after 1968. These were unprofitable and required huge amounts of costly energy while polluting the atmosphere and therefore were prime candidates for closure. Finally, Slovaks worried about being left out of the huge programs of Western economic and technological assistance to the Czech part of the federation; they complained that of 3,000 joint ventures with Western companies, only 600 had located in Slovakia by the fall of 1991.

President Havel adopted a conciliatory approach to Slovak nationalism. He chose as premier a Slovak, Marian Calfa; he agreed to call Czechoslovakia the "Federation of Czechs and Slovaks"; and he

began to explore ways of granting the Slovaks the substantial autonomy that they wanted. In November 1990 the federal government and the governments of the Czech and Slovak republics drew up a compromise on power sharing. But the Czechoslovak federal Parliament made changes requiring a restoration of federal control over the post office and the central bank and assumption of responsibility for the protection of minority rights, instead of placing that responsibility in the hands of the republics. In late November the Slovak Parliament in Bratislava threatened to declare its laws to be paramount over those of the federal government. Havel responded by asking the federal Parliament to grant him emergency powers to preserve the unity of the country and worked to meet Slovak demands, but Slovak anger mounted.

By the end of 1991, however, it was clear that Slovaks were not unanimously in support of secession from the Czechoslovak state. While Slovak nationalists harassed advocates of moderation and demanded secession, other Slovaks called for less radical solutions to the problem of self-determination.

Right-Wing Violence

As Czech–Slovak relations became quarrelsome, so too did the national temper. Post-Communist Czechoslovakia, which prided itself on the nonviolent character of its political transition to independence, in what has frequently been referred to as the "velvet revolution," began to experience a new and disquieting phenomenon of street violence. Right-wing gangs of young people in their late teens and early twenties, trapped by high unemployment and social dislocation, went on a rampage. They attacked migrating Gypsies and Vietnamese workers brought to Czechoslovakia by the former Communist leadership. In the industrial city of Teplice, gangs of several hundred youths on October 5, 1991, overturned a car carrying two Gypsies and beat the driver so badly that he required hospitalization. The attackers, wearing arm bands with swastikas, chanted Nazi and xenophobic slogans.

Prague authorities worried that this unrest would worsen if economic problems, in particular unemployment, did not soon abate. Moreover, they expected an increase in the population in Czechoslovakia of Gypsies, fleeing hardship in Romania (Germany and Hungary had closed their borders to them). On a deeper, psychological level, the behavior of the youth toward foreigners was disquieting. It reflected a racist-inspired intolerance incompatible with a liberal democratic political system. In Oc-

tober 1991 Havel established a commission to examine the violence and recommend ways of curbing it.

FOREIGN POLICY INITIATIVES

The Prague government wanted Czechoslovakia to be the bridge between East and West. (In this policy the government reflected the thinking of the late Eduard Benes, the last president before the Communist takeover.) To facilitate this role, President Havel and Foreign Minister Jiri Dienstbier sought a resumption of Czechoslovakia's traditional closeness to the West, to which they believed it belonged, while maintaining close relations with the rest of Europe and especially with the Soviet Union.

The United States

The government and residents in Prague enthusiastically received U.S. secretary of state James Baker when he visited in February 1990. Baker's visit offered Prague the hope of American material assistance and symbolized an end to Czechoslovakia's isolation from the West. When President Havel visited Washington at the end of that month, he received a warm welcome from the White House, a standing ovation from Congress, and promises of investment from members of the business and banking communities. In October 1991, during another visit to Washington, Havel assured Americans willing to invest in Czechoslovakia that they could return their profits to the United States and freely exchange currencies.

The Bush administration was responsive to Czechoslovakia's interest in restoring good relations with the United States and was forthcoming with praise and encouragement, but it did not offer much financial support. Washington wanted to foster, but not bankroll, economic reform and development in Czechoslovakia. Still, the United States did much to help the country through the transition from socialism to democracy. In April 1990 a trade agreement between Prague and Washington reduced tariffs on Czechoslovak imports into the United States. The Overseas Private Investment Corporation, which provides insurance for American business firms interested in foreign investment, began operation in Czechoslovakia. The U.S. government supported Czechoslovakia's request to join the International Monetary Fund, which would make Prague eligible for lending programs; and it also supported a European Development Bank location in Prague (the bank was established to aid Central/Eastern European countries in reconstruction). Washington planned to reopen the American consulate in Bratislava, which had been closed in 1948. Also proposed were the opening of American cultural centers in Bratislava and Prague, an increase in cultural and educational exchanges, the start of a Peace Corps program for English-language instruction, and a joint study of Czechoslovakia's air pollution problem, the worst in Europe.

Yet economic progress was slow. Potential U.S. investors were wary of sinking capital in Central/Eastern Europe. Havel's efforts were hampered by the possibility, however remote, that the country might experience a severe ethnic-based turmoil. Moreover, American investors were put off by the slowness of Czechoslovakia's dismantling of the state-controlled economy.

A final aspect of relations with the United States concerned American policy toward the Soviet Union and Yugoslavia. In his address to a joint House–Senate meeting of Congress during his February 1990 visit to Washington, Havel asked the United States to help the Soviet Union navigate the "immensely complicated" road to political and economic democracy. He argued that the sooner and the more peacefully the Soviet Union moved toward political pluralism and a market economy, the better for not only Czechoslovakia but also all the other new democratic governments in Central/Eastern Europe. His advice struck a very responsive chord among the American legislators.

During his visit to Washington in October 1991, Havel emphasized the negative impact on Czechoslovakia of the growing Soviet economic and political crises. He also asked for the Bush administration's intercession with the European allies to obtain their approval of Czechoslovakia's membership in NATO. The American response was very restrained. The administration was of the opinion that NATO could not at the moment give Czechoslovakia the security guarantee it wanted; instead it supported a German proposal that the Central/Eastern European democracies have a loose association with NATO, involving consultations and discussions but no binding commitments.

The Bush administration's apparent indifference during 1992 toward the growing crisis in Czech–Slovak relations and the threat of a breakup of Czechoslovakia merits criticism. The administration apparently was of little help to Havel in his efforts to preserve Czechoslovak unity. Washington could have exerted pressure behind the scenes on Czech and Slovak nationalists to encourage compromise and prevent an event that could be very costly in material terms to both sides as well as to Europe. This pressure might have taken the form

of some additional economic assistance to both Czechs and Slovaks, but especially to Slovakia, which desperately needed it.

Germany
Havel established good relations between Czechoslovakia and Germany. In late 1989, shortly after being elected president, Havel declared that Czechoslovakia must apologize to the 3.2 million Germans who were expelled from their homes in the Sudetenland when, after World War II, Czechoslovakia recovered that region, which had been annexed by Nazi Germany on October 1, 1939. To underscore the importance of good relations in the post-Communist era, Havel also chose the two Germanys, rather than the United States or the Soviet Union, for his first official visit abroad as chief executive, in January 1990. While his discussions with German leaders focused on practical matters like border crossings and protection of the environment, their real importance was in their symbolism: They punctuated the Czechoslovak state's determination to begin a new chapter in relations between the two countries and not allow the past to poison the present and the future.

At the end of February 1992, German chancellor Helmut Kohl met Havel in Prague to implement their policy of reconciliation, friendship, and cooperation. They concluded a treaty that had great symbolic importance even if it was short of specific commitments. The Czechoslovaks acknowledged their forceful expulsion of Germans after the war, while the Germans gave unqualified support for Czechoslovakia's entry into the European Community. The treaty did not address the issue of restored property rights, though, leaving open an issue that could complicate relations in the future; and right-wing pressure groups urged Bonn to hold back on economic and political concessions to Czechoslovakia.

Relations with Germany have been very profitable for the Czechs and Slovaks. German entrepreneurs, taking advantage of next-door-neighbor status and long historical and cultural ties, now account for 75 percent of all foreign investment in the Czech Republic and Slovakia. The overwhelming German economic presence by far exceeds the U.S. presence, which also lags behind that of Austria, France, and Switzerland.

German investment in the Czech Republic and Slovakia is seen as a mixed blessing. Although appreciated for its enormous contribution to economic development and reform, ordinary citizens are uncomfortable as hordes of German executives fill Prague's best restaurants and

hotels in ways that call to mind the German presence in the country during World War II. Nationalist politicians have discussed the possibility of erecting barriers to slow German investment in Bohemia and Moravia.

The Soviet Union
While seeking to develop strong links to the West, Czechoslovakia also tried to reassure the Soviet Union of its friendship and readiness for cooperation in many areas, especially trade, on which the Czechoslovaks had long depended for their material well-being. But there were problems between post-Communist Czechoslovakia and the Gorbachev Kremlin.

The most serious of these problems involved the withdrawal of about 80,000 Soviet troops stationed in Czechoslovakia since August 1968. Moscow agreed to a joint Czechoslovak–Soviet commission of military and civilian officials to examine all aspects of the Soviet military presence. But a speedy Soviet military withdrawal was problematic, if only because it had moved so slowly on previous troop withdrawals and because the Soviet leadership was distracted by so much turmoil at home. Moreover, as was the case in other Central/Eastern European countries, the Kremlin had problems with housing, feeding, and employing its returning military personnel.

The Czechoslovak Foreign Ministry publicly accused the Soviets of foot-dragging on the withdrawal issue; its spokesperson added on another occasion that the Soviet forces deployed in Czechoslovakia had broken many agreements and had violated the UN Charter. He declared that Soviet reluctance to start the troop withdrawal had provoked tension among the Czechoslovak public, as seen in demonstrations in Prague and other cities. The strong language to the Soviets may have helped to speed withdrawal, which finally was complete by the end of 1991.

Poland and Hungary
The Czech Republic and Slovakia share four key problems in common with Poland and Hungary. One is economic and concerns the difficulty in moving away from socialism to a market economy. A second has to do with security in connection with the disintegration of the Soviet state and a fear that the northern part of Central/Eastern Europe will be vulnerable to a possible resurgence of Russian influence. A third problem concerns the entry of the countries into the European Community. The fourth problem involves the Baltic states as they have emancipated themselves from Soviet control and have

tried to maintain their political, economic, and diplomatic independence. The countries recognize that their domestic stabilty as well as external security depend on their willingness to cooperate and diminish parochial rivalries.

In February 1991 Czechoslovak leader Havel met Polish president Lech Walesa and Hungarian prime minister Joszef Antall at Visegrad, Hungary, to discuss their shared interests. Expressing sympathy for Baltic peoples' efforts to emancipate themselves, they criticized the bloody Soviet military crackdown in Lithuania in response to its campaign for independence of Moscow. Havel went further than Walesa and Antall in backing the Baltic peoples, saying that Czechoslovakia would open offices of representation in Lithuania despite its continuing legal membership in the Soviet Union. The three leaders also emphasized their shared commitment to joining Western Europe, viewing this as an alternative to creating a new formal trade organization among themselves to replace the defunct Warsaw Pact and the Council for Mutual Economic Assistance.

The condition of the Hungarian minority living in southeastern Slovakia is a major problem in Slovak–Hungarian relations. The Hungarian minority constitutes about 600,000 people, or about 4 percent of the total national population and 10 percent of the Slovak population. Although it is not as badly off as either the Gypsy population in the Czech Republic and Slovakia or the small group of Slovak people living in Hungary, it is the object of some discrimination. With the Slovak movement toward independence in 1992 and the ascendancy of nationalist politicians in Bratislava, the Hungarian government worried that discrimination against kin in Slovakia would escalate.

THE SPLIT OF CZECHOSLOVAKIA

An ominous development for the future of Czechoslovak unity occurred in June 1992, when parliamentary elections produced a new federal Legislature strongly polarized between political extremes. Federal prime minister Vaclav Klaus's followers in the Civic Democratic Party won 33 percent of the ballots cast in the Czech Republic for the national Parliament. The Movement for Democratic Slovakia (MDS), a nationalist party, won about 33 percent of the ballots cast for the national Parliament as well as 37 percent of ballots cast for the republic Parliament. Newly elected Slovak deputies belonging to the MDS were strongly pro-separatist. They were led by Vladimir Meciar, who pledged pub-

licly to press ahead with plans to create a sovereign Slovak state that would split Czechoslovakia in two. The more moderate groups that had done so well earlier, the Forum and the Public Against Violence, did very poorly.

Klaus and Meciar, now leaders of their respective republic governments, tried in the early months of 1992 to reach an agreement on preserving the unity of the Czech state, but the two sides could not be reconciled. The Slovak side demanded a loose economic and defense union between two internationally recognized states, with each state having its own banking and credit system and separate membership in international organizations like the UN and the EC. Meciar insisted that this plan would not mean a breakup of Czechoslovakia. The Czech side disagreed, however, with Klaus demanding a complete break unless the Slovaks agreed to keep a federation with a strong central government capable of implementing reforms for the entire country. Meciar said also that he wanted to slow down the pace of Czechoslovakia's transformation to a market economy. Klaus's policies, Meciar said, hurt the Slovaks unfairly, with unemployment 4 times greater than in the Czech part of the country. Klaus, on the contrary, wanted to avoid a slowdown and sought a strong central government that could speed change. In Klaus's view a looser federation would be an obstacle to Czechoslovakia's transformation into a capitalist state and its eventual integration into Western Europe.

Havel's position in June 1992 was that the Czechs and Slovaks, in accordance with the Constitution, should be allowed to decide in a referendum, saying that if people wanted unity he would work for it. Klaus dismissed the idea of a referendum, arguing that even if it showed that a majority of Czechs wished to remain with the Slovaks in a common state—and this was the case, according to public opinion polls—the same problems would remain: The federation was not working and couldn't be fixed, at least to the satisfaction of the Czech side. Thus, the Czech side under Klaus showed some interest in separation, even though Havel and his followers still hoped for a compromise with the Slovaks that would hold the country together. All that was eventually decided in the Czech and Slovak talks was that the issue of separation and independence should be decided definitively by the two republic-level parliaments by September 30, clearly a rebuff to Havel's idea of a popular referendum.

Another setback for unity occurred in July 1992, when Havel failed to gain re-

election to the federal presidency in the first of two ballots in the tricameral federal Parliament. The Slovaks were largely responsible for Havel's failure, given the rules governing presidential election whereby either Slovaks or Czechs had the power to block any candidate—a 60 percent majority was needed for election. Czech deputies led by Klaus must also bear some blame for Havel's failure. They held a second ballot too soon to allow Havel to lobby for support with Slovak nationalists. One can surmise that Klaus and his followers were only mildly supportive of Havel's reelection because of their eagerness for a separation of the Czech lands from Slovakia, which Havel had been trying to avoid, as well as because of Klaus's own ambitions to replace Havel as leader of the Czechs.

After Havel's defeat events moved quickly toward the dissolution of Czechoslovakia. Later in July the Slovak parliament approved a declaration of sovereignty, prompting Havel to resign. He said he did not intend to hold power so that he could preside over the liquidation of the Czech state. On July 23, with no compromise in sight, Klaus and Meciar agreed to divide Czechoslovakia into two separate republics. Under the agreement the two republics were to ask the federal Parliament to dissolve the federation on September 30. Meanwhile Czechs and Slovaks discussed the details of separation, in particular coordination of defense and foreign policies of the new Czech and Slovak states, close trade contacts, and protection of the rights of all citizens in both countries.

On November 25 the Czechoslovak federal Parliament passed a law formally dividing the country into two separate republics, effective December 31, 1992. The law was passed despite reservations in the Parliament about the breakup; in September a national poll showed that only one-third of the population of the country favored a breakup. Czech and Slovak politicians worried that if the Parliament did not provide a legal framework for the separation of Czechs and Slovaks, there could be destabilization of the political environment, which would adversely affect foreign investment. The law was supported by Klaus, Meciar, and Havel, who by now was reconciled to the breakup of the Czechoslovak state. Havel was thinking about his own role of leadership in an independent Czech Republic. He wanted to run for president and believed he had a good chance of winning. His closest rival, Klaus, though second in popularity in Bohemia and Moravia, was still far overshadowed by Havel. The law provided for a temporary joint currency until both re-

Independence
1918

Nazi Germany conquers and partitions Czechoslovakia, annexes Bohemia
1939

Nazi Germany establishes a protectorate over Moravia and gives Slovakia its independence

Czechoslovak Communists obtain control over the national government in Prague
1948

Pro-Soviet and Stalinist Novotny becomes leader of the KSC
1953

Dubcek replaces Novotny; Soviet military intervention in Prague
1968

Husak replaces Dubcek
1969

Czechoslovak dissidents sign Charter 77
1977

Jakes replaces Husak as leader of the KSC; he later resigns in favor of Urbanek; massive public demonstrations force political liberalization
1980s–1990s

Playwright Vaclav Havel is arrested, imprisoned, and released in 1989; later he is named president of Czechoslovakia

Czechoslovakia splits into two separate and autonomous states: the Czech Republic and Slovakia

Kovac is elected president of Slovakia, Havel of the Czech Republic

publics had established their own monetary systems; for the setting up of a customs union; and for the division of the federal armed forces into two separate organizations, one for the Czech Republic and one for Slovakia.

Cost and Liabilities of the Split

The overall economic cost of an end to the Czech–Slovak marriage will be high. Jan Klacek, director of economics at the Czechoslovak Academy of Sciences, predicts a flight of foreign investment from both republics and trade barriers depriving each of its best customers. Slovakia stands to suffer more, if only because of an inevitable isolation. Slovakia is farther from Western Europe in both geography and culture than are Bohemia and Moravia. And it has tense relations with Hungary, a strong neighbor to the south. Moreover, the prospects of Slovakia profiting from links to the former Soviet republics are at the moment dim because of these republics' intense internal turmoil and poverty.

There is also a potential political cost of separation for Slovakia. The Slovak government may become authoritarian, forfeiting the democratic gains made since the fall of 1989. By the end of 1992, there was already disquieting evidence of an authoritarian style. Meciar remained as premier. Not only did his party have a majority in the Slovak Parliament, but he also had control of the Slovak National Party, giving him close to the 60 percent majority necessary to change the Constitution. At the same time, he gradually brought

institutions like Slovak television and the State Control Commission, a watchdog commission once responsible to Parliament, under the direct control of his cabinet. He replaced people in the universities, the health service, and the public administration with party loyalists.

The most persuasive evidence of Meciar's autocratic ways was his treatment of the press. The large Danubia printing company has the only equipment in Bratislava capable of handling the print run of the large dailies. Privatized by the preceding government, it has now been renationalized, on the grounds that a monopoly in private hands is more dangerous to society than a monopoly under public ownership. Furthermore, in 1991, because he felt some Slovak journalists were sullying the image of Slovakia abroad, Meciar encouraged the formation of a rival union of journalists, as he put it, "for a truthful picture of Slovakia." And while the Slovak Constitution adopted in 1992 does not permit censorship, a new press law bristled with restrictions.

Slovak voters throughout 1993 were disappointed with their newly won independence. Many regretted the split, believing that had the federation survived they would have been politically and economically better off. While they acknowledged the irreversibility of the split, they fretted over a conviction that they had been led down the garden path in 1992 by Meciar and other ultra-nationalists. Not surprisingly, Meciar's popularity declined precipitously.

In March 1994 the Slovak Parliament, reflecting popular disenchantment, voted no confidence in Meciar and forced his resignation. His successor, Josef Moravic, formed a coalition government and pledged a climbdown drom the nationalist and neo-authoritarian policies of his predecessor. But the prospects of political stability, never mind an improvement in living conditions for Slovaks, remain problematical. Moravic's coalition is made up of diverse political elements that will have difficulty achieving consensus on controversial policies like the introduction of a market economy, which Meciar stalled and perverted (in the last weeks of his premiership, he approved the privatization of about 50 Slovak firms, but they were purchased by his cronies). Moreover, Meciar is far from out of the political picture and can be expected to challenge Moravic. There is reason to worry about the future stability of the Slovak government and its ability to address pressing economic problems.

DEVELOPMENT

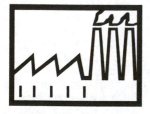

The Czech Republic has made rapid and substantial progress toward a free market system without setting off the kind of backlash that has dogged Poland and other former Soviet bloc countries. By contrast, a large part of the former Slovak economy remains under state control. It is far less well off than the Czech economy, with higher unemployment and slower annual growth.

FREEDOM

While Czechs have more personal political freedom and a leader, President Havel, who has impeccable democratic credentials, their new republic has shown a dark side in its efforts to purge and punish former Communists, including those who were considered dissidents. In Slovakia there is evidence of strong antidemocratic and illiberal thinking among politicians and citizens.

HEALTH/WELFARE

The Czech and Slovak republics have ended state subsidization of the national health care system and now require employers and employees to contribute to new national health care plans. Abortion is now considered "nonessential" treatment for which the patient must pay most or all of the cost. Private medicine has been introduced.

ACHIEVEMENTS

The end of the 75-year-old federation of Czechs and Slovaks was achieved with impressive civility, sometimes called the "velvet divorce." Czech prime minister Vaclav Klaus and Slovak prime minister Vladimir Meciar amicably settled on a division of public property, including the armed forces and its weaponry. They agreed on a customs as well as a common currency.

Hungary

GEOGRAPHY

Area in Square Kilometers (Miles):
92,980 (35,900) (slightly smaller than
Indiana)
Capital (Population): Budapest
(2,016,000)
Climate: temperate

PEOPLE

Population

Total: 10,324,000
Annual Growth Rate: –0.7%
Rural/Urban Population Ratio: 38/62
Ethnic Makeup of Population: 90%
Hungarian; 4% Gypsy; 3% German;
2% Serb; 1% others
Language: Hungarian

Health

Life Expectancy at Birth: 67 years
(male); 75 years (female)
Infant Mortality Rate (Ratio):
13/1,000
Average Caloric Intake: 134% of
FAO minimum
Physicians Available (Ratio): 1/306

Religion(s)

67% Roman Catholic; 20% Calvinist;
5% Lutheran; 8% Jewish, atheist, and
others

Education

Adult Literacy Rate: 98%

COMMUNICATION

Telephones: 858,200
Newspapers: 29

A HAZY MEMORY OR AN ANTIDEMOCRATIC TRADITION?

In September 1993 the remains of Admiral Miklos Horthy, the Hungarian
leader who embraced Adolf Hitler's policies of expansion, anti-Semitism,
and authoritarianism in the late 1930s and early 1940s, were reburied in
his hometown of Kendres. Tens of thousands of ordinary Hungarians as
well as members of the Hungarian cabinet attended the ceremony. Many
Hungarians believe that he tried to keep Hungary independent and get back
for it some of the territories lost at the end of World War I. He also gave
Hungary a long period of political and economic stability that enabled the
country's middle class to prosper. But other Hungarians worry that the current popular feeling for Horthy is more than a hazy national memory—that
it is, rather, evidence of an antidemocratic tradition with anti-Semitic un-
dertones that bodes ill for Hungary's political future.

TRANSPORTATION

Highways—Kilometers (Miles):
29,701 (18,414)
Railroads—Kilometers (Miles): 7,766
(4,815)
Usable Airfields: 92

GOVERNMENT

Type: pluralistic parliamentary
democracy
Independence Date: April 4, 1919
Chief of State: President Arpád Göncz
Political Parties: Socialist Party;
Alliance of Free Democrats;
Democratic Forum; Independent
Smallholders Party; Federation of
Young Democrats
Suffrage: universal over 18

MILITARY

Number of Armed Forces: 94,500
*Military Expenditures (% of Central
Government Expenditures):* 5%
Current Hostilities: none

ECONOMY

Currency ($ U.S. Equivalent): 84
forints = $1
Per Capita Income/GDP:
$5,380/$55.4 billion
Inflation Rate: 23%
Total Foreign Debt: $23.5 billion
Natural Resources: fertile land;
bauxite; brown coal
Agriculture: corn; wheat; potatoes;
sugar beets; wine grapes; vegetables;
fruits
Industry: precision and measuring
equipment; mining; pharmaceuticals;
textiles; food processing;
transportation equipment

FOREIGN TRADE

Exports: $10.9 billion
Imports: $11.7 billion

HUNGARY

Soviet troops liberated Hungary from Nazi control in the spring of 1945 and helped Hungarian Communists, who formed a new party called the Hungarian Socialist Workers Party (HSWP), to expand their influence in the postwar Hungarian government. There were two groups of Hungarian Communist leaders: conservatives, who were loyal to Moscow and ready to imitate Soviet policies in the development of Hungarian socialism; and pragmatists, who favored deviations from the Soviet model to make socialism fit the characteristics of the Hungarian environment. Metyas Rakosi, a conservative, was HSWP first secretary from 1945 until 1956. Under Rakosi party pragmatists and reformers like Imre Nagy were ousted from positions of power in the late 1940s. By 1953 Rakosi and the conservatives had replicated the Soviet model of socialism and had transformed Hungary into a Soviet satellite.

THE OCTOBER 1956 CRISIS

In the aftermath of Stalin's death in 1953, people from all sectors of Hungarian society—workers, farmers, students, intellectuals, and bureaucrats—wanted major reforms. Some wanted a Western-style pluralistic social democracy, others an end to collectivization of agriculture and an adjustment in investment priorities away from the emphasis on capital goods expansion. They wanted production of more consumer goods. Many would have liked to expand ties with the West.

Reformist elements in the Hungarian party leadership who had kept silent in the Stalinist years were emboldened after Stalin's death to elevate one of their own, Imre Nagy, to the premiership of the government. Rakosi stayed on as party leader.

Nagy promised reforms, but few occurred. By 1955 the conservatives, who still controlled the party and opposed reform, ousted Nagy. In the next year, intense popular pressure for change mounted, reaching a climax with antigovernment demonstrations in Budapest in October 1956. University students and dissident intellectuals, meeting in recently formed discussion clubs, demanded political liberalization. There was unrest also in the countryside, where farmers demanded a return to private ownership of farm property. The country seemed on the threshold of revolt.

In response the party leadership returned Nagy to the premiership and replaced Erno Gero, who had succeeded Rakosi in April, with Jänos Kadar as party first secretary, with a mandate to achieve some reforms in the political and eco-

nomic spheres. But when, on November 1, Nagy announced over Hungarian radio a restoration of the multiparty system, the appointment to his cabinet of members of non-Communist parties long since banned in Hungary, and Hungary's withdrawal from the Warsaw Pact, the Soviets became alarmed. On November 4, 1956, they intervened with massive military force. Soviet tanks patrolled the streets of Budapest, and Soviet armor quickly overwhelmed popular resistance. The Soviets ended Nagy's reform efforts and insisted upon his ouster from power. Nagy was executed in 1958. The Soviets obliged party leader Kadar to restore public order, to guarantee Hungary's conformity with Soviet–style socialism, and to ensure its loyalty to the Warsaw Pact alliance system.

With Soviet backing Kadar suppressed political opposition in Hungary. He rebuilt the Hungarian Communist Party, ridding it of reformers and deviants. In the 1960s he presided over a tightly disciplined, conformist, and loyal Hungary.

MODERATE SOCIALISM

Determined to avoid the extremes of his predecessors, Kadar remained a moderate. He supported neither the radical democratization that Nagy had tried to put through nor the reactionary Stalinism practiced by the conservative Rakosi. During the 1960s Hungary developed into what might be called a middle-of-the-road socialist system. And, under Kadar's leadership, Hungarian society became stable and comparatively well-off.

The hallmark of Hungarian socialism was its success in the economic sphere, achieved partly through deft reforms starting in 1968 and called the "New Economic Mechanism." The reforms were intended to correct some of the flaws of the Soviet model. They provided factory managers with much autonomy in plant operation, in particular in the setting of wages, the procurement of raw materials from foreign sources, and the renewal of equipment. Efficiency and profitability were to determine the sizes of industries. Firms unable to sell their products and make a profit were to be liquidated. The New Economic Mechanism led to a reduction in the size of enterprises, making it easier for them to adjust production to accommodate changes in demand; the establishment of a flexible pricing system; the creation of a sphere of individual activity free of state central planning; and permission for workers to organize themselves into teams and offer their labor to a factory at premium wage rates.

An important aspect of the reform program involved agriculture. There was a significant departure from Soviet-style collectivization. Farm families had fewer centrally imposed quotas to meet, more control over the use of their time and labor, and lucrative remuneration. Productive farmers were rewarded by permission to use state-owned land as if it were their own property. Farm families also were encouraged to establish cooperatives that enjoyed a substantial independence of the central planners in Budapest. The result of these reforms was an astounding increase of agricultural output during the 1970s and early 1980s, producing enough for domestic needs and also for export.

After 1956 there was very little political dissent and no mass antigovernment demonstrations in Hungary. Hungarians seemed willing to tolerate the political dictatorship of the Communist Party, partly because of what it had achieved in the economic area. Hungarians were inclined to remain silent about the regime's much-resented insistence upon political discipline. The absence of any massive unrest in Hungary must be attributed also to Kadar's willingness to tolerate some public discussion of controversial issues and to allow some criticism of regime policies.

In sum, one might characterize Kadar's behavior toward the Soviet Union as autonomous without having aroused the Kremlin's animosity. Hungary was close to the Soviet Union in terms of foreign policy. It was usually supportive of Soviet international positions. Thus, despite reservations, Hungary participated in the Soviet-led Warsaw Pact intervention in Czechoslovakia in 1968. And in the 1970s, although he echoed Eurocommunist advocacies of Communist party autonomy, Kadar carefully refrained from endorsing the Eurocommunist position on a liberal path to socialism, which the Soviets had strongly criticized. In the Afghanistan crisis, however, Hungary was only mildly supportive of the Soviet position, because of Hungarian sensitivity to Soviet interventionist behavior anywhere.

HUNGARY AND PERESTROIKA

Hungary began to embrace perestroika in the late 1980s, with plans to go beyond the scope of reforms that Gorbachev was introducing in the Soviet Union to remedy serious economic and social problems. The severity of these problems caused widespread demoralization, a sense of hopelessness about the future, and political alienation and popular distrust of the Communist Party. Eventually, there developed support everywhere in Hungarian society—including the leadership of the party—for radical and immediate change in all spheres of Hungarian life.

In the mid-1980s Hungary's buoyant economy turned sour. State-owned smokestack industries like steel and coal mining were bleeding the economy dry with their losses. The Hungarian government heavily taxed the private sector to subsidize these enterprises.

The country also had difficulties with the Council of Mutual Economic Assistance. For example, a Soviet demand for products that were already outmoded by Western standards at unreasonably low prices forced Hungary to maintain inefficient industries and discouraged production of advanced goods at world market prices. Hungary also had to invest in the Soviet infrastructure, for example in the Yamburg oil fields, or in Soviet-designed development projects inside Hungary that were not cost-efficient. Moreover, CMEA trade reportedly resulted in the conversion of dollar imports into transferable ruble exports at a rate that was highly unfavorable to Hungary.

Additionally, as a result of decisions made at the beginning of the 1980s to finance growth through Western loans and to import about one-half of Hungary's energy requirements for hard currency, the country's net foreign debt rose from $6 billion to $12 billion between 1981 and 1988. Between 65 and 70 percent of convertible export earnings was spent on debt service. Because hard currency growth had not kept pace with imports, Hungary had an increasingly difficult time repaying its debt and finding new credit.

Finally, Hungary's economic malaise was attributable to the inadequacy of existing reforms. For example, some of the reforms already on the books, such as the bankruptcy law, had not been fully enforced, because of the authorities' fear that strict application would affect about 30 percent of Hungarian industrial enterprises and cause massive unemployment.

Economic stagnation aggravated social ills. There was a frightening deterioration in the delivery of medical services, because of decreasing expenditures for public health. Approximately 90 percent of the entire population suffered from poor nutrition, smoking, alcoholism, or chronic nervous strain. Hungary's life expectancy at birth was among the lowest in 33 developed countries examined by the World Health Organization. As a result Hungary's population was no longer reproducing itself. During the second half of the 1980s, the country's net population decreased by 125,000.

A chronic housing shortage worsened people's physical and mental health. The state failed to continue redistribution of existing housing, and not enough was invested in the construction of new housing. Assistance to those who wanted to build their own residences by the offer of loans at reasonable rates benefited only the well-to-do. The vast majority of people still lived in substandard housing.

RENEWAL OF REFORM

The government's response to these problems included short- and long-term economic strategies. In June 1987 Kadar appointed Karolyi Grosz as premier. Grosz was personally committed to economic reform. He had criticized the inept handling of the economy by the Kadarists and also had publicly castigated Hungary's workers for their low productivity. When Grosz took over, he made important changes in top government and party posts to strengthen the hand of those who shared his commitment to achieving a revitalization of the Hungarian economy.

Grosz's strategy started with an austerity program, which included a reduction in deficit spending and foreign borrowing. On July 19, 1987, prices were increased by 10 to 20 percent in four categories of products: bread, gasoline, cigarettes, and household energy. The price hikes drastically reduced consumers' purchasing power, and the aged and disadvantaged, especially in rural areas, suffered. This upward adjustment of prices, however, was little more than a quick fix for the economy, because no steps were taken to expand output or to reform the deficit-ridden industrial sector.

The new program also called for further decentralization of the economy. Enterprises were allowed more independence; central control over operations was diminished. Emphasis was placed on increasing profits and exports for hard currency. Enterprises that were consistently losing money were to be liquidated. However, this policy was not aggressively implemented, for political reasons—the liquidation of all of Hungary's inefficient enterprises would have created horrendous unemployment.

The Hungarian government's long-term strategy sought to expand economic output and make Hungarian exports competitive in the world market. It involved an expansion of private entrepreneurialism in agriculture, the service industries, and retail trade; substantial wage differentiation to increase workers' incentives; and the introduction of a two-tier banking system, consisting of a central bank and a series of commercial and specialized banks.

Hungarian reformers also wanted to curtail uneconomic projects imposed on Hungary as a result of its membership in the Soviet bloc.

Some of the economic changes in 1987 were quite innovative and unique, especially those in the area of monetary and fiscal policy. The new banks made short-term loans to enterprises, issued bonds to raise capital that would make possible larger loans for longer periods to more extensive and ambitious enterprises, and gradually developed a substantial autonomy—although not complete independence—of the Hungarian national bank, which continued to be the chief source of investment capital for very large industrial enterprises and showed no sign of relinquishing its hold over the investment area.

In the fiscal area, the government introduced Western-style personal-income and value-added taxes while reducing taxes on enterprises, thus departing from the traditional socialist emphasis on collective responsibility for funding public policy. The hope was that by shifting the tax burden to the individual, there would be increased popular pressure on the bureaucracy to use public money judiciously and discreetly to improve economic efficiency, while enterprises would be encouraged with additional discretionary funds to improve production and maximize output.

The regime introduced more radical economic reform in October 1988 to diminish still further state control of the economy and expand the free market. Parliament unanimously passed a new law that opened the way for full foreign ownership of Hungarian companies and provided that joint ventures with less than 50 percent foreign participation no longer needed official registration. It also allowed Hungarians to trade shares in private companies (previously, Hungarians could own shares, but their holdings were restricted to the companies where they worked) and employ up to 500 citizens for private profit. The law created a framework for a Western-style capital market and revived types of companies not seen in Hungary since before the Communist takeover in the mid-1940s. The law also abolished a number of rules governing state and private enterprises, leaving regulation mainly to financial means.

MOVEMENT TOWARD DEMOCRACY

Pressure had been mounting both inside the Communist Party and throughout the society as a whole for a radical alteration of the political system, in the belief that economic improvement depended on political change. Much like Poland, but in contrast with the Soviet Union, the impetus for change came as much from outside the party leadership as from within it.

Beginning in 1987 there was an increase of popular interest in democratic reform. In September 1987 Hungarian intellectuals established a new umbrella-type organization of political advocacy, the Democratic Forum, which invited all Hungarians interested in solving the nation's economic, social, and political problems to join its ranks. It called for open and uncensored debates in periodicals.

In May 1988 some 200 Hungarian journalists applied to the government to establish a "glasnost club." They wanted to provide ordinary citizens with information about important issues in the reform movement neglected in the official media. They also wanted to publicize violations of citizens' rights.

Also in May 1988, workers and academics formed Hungary's first independent labor union since the Communist takeover. The Democratic Union of Scientific and Academic Workers (TDDSZ) consisted of academic and nonacademic university personnel in Budapest and pledged to protect the professional interests of its members. The creation of TDDSZ apparently inspired similar initiatives by other special interest groups.

THE END OF KADAR'S RULE

Because Grosz could not make great strides as long as the Kadarist conservatives dominated the top party and state organs, he decided to challenge the conservatives at a special party conference. To Grosz's satisfaction the party rank-and-file for the most part favored change. Apart from wanting to replace Kadar, who was personally blamed for much of what had gone wrong in the country during the 1980s, many in the party apparatus were critical of democratic centralism, which had left excessive control over decisions in the hands of the Politburo at the expense of the Central Committee. They argued that personal as well as collective responsibility for party behavior was essential to more efficient policy making and to a restoration of popular confidence in the party's leadership of the country.

In May 1988 the special party conference formally endorsed major political reforms, starting with the replacement of Kadar as party first secretary with Grosz. Imre Pozsgay, one of the founders of and the chief spokesperson for the Democratic Forum and Reszo Nyers, another prominent advocate of reform, were elevated to the Politburo. While Pozsgay sought radi-

cal political change, Nyers wanted an extension of economic reform. He was among the leaders who initiated the first phase of Hungary's economic reforms in 1968. Miklos Nemoth, an economic reformer, became prime minister.

The final conference statement, adopted on May 22, called for greater intraparty democracy, involving increased participation of local party organs in national-policy decision making; direct election of at least some of the party's national leadership by local organs, which should have the power to recall those elected; and personal political responsibility of those involved in formulating and implementing policy. The conference also endorsed an expansion of political pluralism outside the party and emphasized the exclusiveness of National Assembly jurisdiction over law making.

POLITICAL LIBERALIZATION

The Grosz regime soon came under intense pressure of reformers to move ahead with political liberalization, in particular the reinstitution of a multiparty system and free parliamentary elections. Grosz somewhat grudgingly acknowledged that this might be the only means of achieving the openness needed to facilitate economic improvement. Yet he called for sharp limits on party proliferation, insisting that the transition must be gradual to avoid destabilization. In any event, he insisted that parties allowed to compete in parliamentary elections in 1990 would have to respect the constitutional provision mandating socialism for Hungary and to accept the Communist Party's preeminence in the government.

In the spring of 1989, the party leadership reviewed the draft of a new constitution, which would retain public ownership of industry and reaffirm Hungary's existing alliances with the Soviet Union and other Warsaw Pact countries but which also would include radical changes in the governmental system. It would create a new, powerful, popularly elected president who would not simultaneously hold high office in either the Communist Party or any other party. A new, powerful constitutional tribunal would be empowered to accept or reject applications of new political parties, after examining their programs to determine if they were congruent with socialism.

Under the constitution, the party leadership would expect the opposition groups to allow a Communist to occupy the presidential office and to guarantee a certain proportion of seats in the Parliament to the Communist Party. The party also would control the ministries of foreign affairs, in-

terior, and defense during a transition period. And while new political parties would slowly build their strength and become accustomed to operating in Parliament, the Communist Party would use the transition period for a radical transformation of its role from one of security and economic administration to grass-roots electioneering.

While the proposed constitution was being reviewed, reformers in the party leadership tried to strengthen their influence. In May 1989 they ousted Kadar from the Central Committee, thus limiting even further the power of conservatives. Advocates of radical reform within the Politburo also weakened Grosz, who differed with Pozsgay and Nyers in the belief that political reform should preserve the socialist regime.

In June 1989 Pozsgay, Nyers, and other reform-minded party leaders, along with many others in the party's Central Committee, mobilized a majority in the Committee in favor of replacing Grosz as first secretary with Nyers, who assumed the new title and post of president of the party. The Central Committee also created a new leadership quartet of Nyers; Pozsgay, who was nominated to be president of the republic (a post introduced early in 1990); Nemeth; and Grosz, whose membership in the new executive body indicated some support for caution and restraint.

In October 1989 the reform-oriented leadership accelerated Hungary's move toward political democracy but also tried to safeguard the Communist Party's role in Hungarian politics in this new era, when it would have to compete for leadership with other groups. It agreed to hold free elections for Parliament in March 1990, 3 months ahead of the original date of June. The Communists also changed their name to the Socialist Party and officially abandoned orthodox Marxist ideology.

The Communists' strategy to keep power in the new decade, however, suffered a setback in November, when, under pressure from the democratic opposition, they were obliged to hold a national referendum to allow the public to decide whether elections for the presidency of the republic should be held before or after parliamentary elections. The referendum, which was the first really free electoral experience Hungarians had had in 42 years of Communist rule, was significant also because of its outcome. Hungarians voted to hold presidential elections after the parliamentary elections. Since the Communist Party was expected to lose its majority in the parliamentary elections and thus lose control of the government, it would be severely handicapped in the presidential elections.

THE END OF COMMUNIST RULE

In early 1990 Hungary made further strides toward pluralistic democracy. For example, in January Parliament passed a law establishing freedom of conscience and religion that marked a final break with past policies of atheism and repression of the churches. But the most dramatic development was the parliamentary election held on March 25 and April 7, 1990, which brought to an end almost 45 years of Communist totalitarian rule in Hungary. Not surprisingly, the former Communists suffered a decisive defeat in the election. Victory went to the parties of the center right, in particular the Democratic Forum.

Three factors explained the success of the Democratic Forum in winning more than 50 percent of the seats in the new Parliament. First was a pervasive popular aversion to the former Communists, including those who had spearheaded reform and laid the groundwork for the democratization of Hungarian politics, because of revelations about scandals in the mishandling of state property and continued abuses of the secret police and because of the memory of Communist Party repression, incompetence, and subservience to Moscow. It was impossible for the Communists to regain credibility with Hungarian voters, changes in name, program, and leadership notwithstanding. Second, the Forum offered a moderate, confidence-inspiring program that called for a careful transition from socialism to a free market economy, the creation of a convertible currency, and integration with Western Europe. The Forum also expressed concern about the treatment of Hungarian minorities abroad. Third was the weakness of other parties, in particular the Forum's nearest competitor and rival, the Alliance of Free Democrats. The Free Democrats lacked dynamic leadership. And the Independent Smallholders, a reincarnation of the farmers' party that had been suppressed by the Communists after having won 58 percent of the popular vote in parliamentary elections in 1945, was now too small and too new, although it clearly had the promise of becoming more popular in the near future.

POLITICS AFTER COMMUNISM

Hungary faced serious problems as it developed democracy. In the first place, the new democratic political system sometimes functioned more like an oligarchy. For example, following the parliamentary elections, leaders of the two large parties, the Forum and the Free Democrats, secretly agreed among themselves on a wide range of issues concerning the style and content of policy making in the new government. They did this without consulting their own party colleagues, never mind other political groups supporting them in the Parliament.

Forum and Free Democratic leaders agreed that the president of Hungary would be Arpád Göncz, the noted Free Democrat. They also decided on the staffing of the 10 permanent and 5 special committees of the Parliament. They agreed to establish an independent body to supervise radio and television and to require a two-thirds majority in Parliament for the adoption of amendments to the Constitution. They chose Josef Antall, charismatic leader of the Forum, the plurality party, as prime minister. This tendency to make deals rather than engage in debate and seek a compromise with various constituencies was unfortunate. It worked against representative and responsible government.

Hungary's democracy needs the support of its people. But the July 1990 referendum on directly electing the president of the republic brought out only 14 percent of the vote, indicative of a pervasive political apathy suggesting either disinterest in or depression over national politics. When this referendum was declared invalid because of the small turnout, conservative politicians in Budapest, who feared a popular demagogic political leader, were relieved because 85 percent of those who did vote wanted a directly elected chief executive.

There are grounds for optimism about the future of Hungarian democratic development. The parliamentary elections and the referendum signaled the arrival of pluralistic democracy in Hungary. In these elections Hungarian voters peacefully removed from power the bulk of the Communist leadership that had ruled them since the end of World War II. Moreover, the retreating Communist establishment has not presented much of a threat of a counterrevolution. Democratic groups, which have multiplied in the new pluralistic environment, have not immobilized or destabilized the political system; rather,

(AP/Wide World photo)

The dismantling of a Soviet-inspired red star in Budapest (pictured above) was symbolic of citizens' disillusionment with communism and the collapse in 1990 of Communist rule in Hungary.

democratic elites of different policy persuasions have tried to be conciliatory in the interest of preserving stability. Finally, voter turnout may increase once the democratic system is regularized.

Furthermore, there was growing popular interest in the political party known as the Alliance of Young Democrats (Fidesz). Originally, the party limited membership to Hungarians under age 35, but by 1993 the party was courting voters of all ages with a sincere interest in politics. According to Andreas Kovacs, a sociologist and Fidesz adviser, the party's original strength lay in its young membership, who carried no burden of the past. Fidesz came in fifth in the April 1990 parliamentary elections; in the local elections 6 months later, it captured mayoral seats in 9 large cities; and in the fall of 1991, the party was top in public opinion polls. The party repeatedly vowed not to make promises it could not keep. It was not embarrassed about taking unpopular positions on controversial issues. For example, in the summer of 1991, Fidesz unanimously opposed any plan to compensate former owners of nationalized property. In its role as outsider and critic, Fidesz also benefited from the weak economy; it did best in those regions hardest hit by mounting unemployment. Some of its most loyal supporters were pensioners on fixed incomes.

The results of the Parliamentary elections in May 1994, however, showed that Fidesz had lost considerable public support, a reflection of Hungary's continuing economic hardship and of voters' disillusionment with the post-Communist political order. Fidesz, as well as the Forum, had lost the confidence of voters, who seemed to be showing a new interest in the former Communists, now calling themselves Socialists in 1994. Indeed, not only disgruntled workers but also discontented entrepreneurs who deplore the huge bureaucracy and continuing budget deficit appeared to be gravitating toward the Socialists, who in the past few years had been hard at work changing their image and broadening their appeal by adopting a moderate, go-slow reformism. The Socialists in 1993 and early 1994 called for a market economy with a "human face" and had made a complete and perhaps clean break from their discredited past. On May 28–29, 1994 the Socialists solidified their political legitimacy by winning the Parliamentary elections and designating their leader, Gyula Horn, as its choice for prime minister. The vote assures that Horn will become Hungary's next prime minister after the new Parliament covenes in early July.

The new popular sympathy for the reconstructed Socialists has a dark side. Should the Socialists disappoint ordinary people in terms of their expectations of improvement in living conditions, the political pendulum might then swing away from the moderate Socialists to the extreme right. A far-right group would certainly try to cultivate popular support for neo-fascist leadership by exploiting a new popular nostalgia for the pre-Communist conservative past.

Economic Deterioration

In addition to the problems of setting up democratic government, Hungarians have to struggle with economic problems inherited from the Communist past. In 1990, the first year of post-Communist government, the country was in the third straight year of recession. The annual rate of inflation was 23 percent, and 75 percent of the money in cash or bank accounts belonged to only 25 percent of the population, while 2 million people—20 percent of the total population—lived below the poverty level. Hungary also had (and still has) the highest per capita foreign debt in Central/Eastern Europe. To complete this somber picture was the significant decline in trade with the Soviet Union, because Moscow held back the payment of almost 1 billion rubles for the buses, machinery, and other Hungarian products that it had imported in 1989.

Some of the new economic initiatives set in motion in 1990 have not worked out. For example, in 1990 the government set up a stock exchange, but it has had hardly any business, largely because most enterprises remain under state control and no one has spare cash to spend on stock in enterprises that have been privatized. Moreover, many Hungarians are suspicious of the stock exchange, which they view as little more than a capitalist gambling table. In addition, they hardly know what securities are, never mind how they are valued. After all, stock exchanges represent values and attitudes that the Communist government criticized throughout its rule.

The Hungarian government also has tried to attract foreign investment. It has offered joint ventures with tax breaks and liberal rules for foreign investors who create jobs in Hungary to repatriate their profits. It points to an efficient labor force willing to work for far less than workers in the West. This strategy has worked to some degree. Many U.S. firms see in the Hungarian market a stepping-stone to the huge Russian market and Central/Eastern European markets.

The government has undertaken an ambitious privatization program. More than 150 money-losing state-run industries are being sold. The government predicts that by 1995 private enterprises should account for more than half the economic output. But by mid-1992 only 10 percent of state-controlled industrial enterprises had been privatized. Partly this has resulted from political leaders' continuing questions about the wisdom of the state's abandonment of control over the national economy.

The transition to a free market economy is proceeding very gradually because, unlike Czechoslovakia's complex voucher scheme for mass privatization and Poland's "shock therapy" approach, Hungary has been concentrating on building a legal infrastructure to support private enterprise. The government has been working on the development of clear laws similar to those in the West regarding the incorporation of businesses, personal and corporate taxation, and bankruptcy procedures. It has also laid the groundwork for an efficient banking system.

Social Problems

Poverty is severe and much more obvious today than it was under communism. Homeless people live in the railway stations of Budapest. The situation is made worse by Budapest's chronic housing shortage and the migration of people to Hungary from Romania, where living conditions are even more intolerable. Indeed, with more than 100,000 Romanians living illegally in Hungary, almost half the homeless people sleeping in railway stations are Romanians.

In coping with the homeless, the Hungarian government has come up against problems familiar to social agencies elsewhere, including the "not in my backyard" phenomenon. When the Budapest City Council considered in late 1990 turning an empty military barracks into a shelter for the homeless, residents of the district protested, causing the city to back down temporarily. And private charity is in no position to be of much help. Both the Red Cross and the Roman Catholic Church sponsor shelters, but they are dependent on state aid, which has been modest.

By late 1992 many in the government were afraid that if pushed too far, the middle classes could set off a social explosion, forcing strikes and other protests. To forestall such an explosion, the government modified the list of goods and services to be subject to a new value-added tax of 6 percent. But middle-class disillusionment with the steady decline in living standards remains a time bomb in Hungarian society.

Another major social problem is an apparent resurgence of anti-Semitism. Sometimes anti-Semitic expressions are oblique; at other times they are obvious and blatant, as when a small weekly publication in the provincial city of Debrecen openly blamed Jews for the calamities of the Communist era, which were described as the revenge of the Jews for the Nazi horrors. The paper accused the Jews of responsibility for a range of problems, from Hungary's rising crime rate to liberal abortion policies. Hungarian Jews say that these expressions of anti-Semitism are isolated and that the vast majority of Hungarians are not anti-Semitic. But it is also true that Hungary has a tradition of anti-Semitism, which reached a climax in World War II, when the Hungarian government joined the Axis alliance and cooperated with German policy to exterminate the Jews by sending 500,000 Hungarian Jews to death camps.

Hungarians are also dissatisfied with how the democratic leadership has dealt with former Communists. Certainly the government of the late Jänos Kadar was the least inefficient of the Central/Eastern European socialist governments, but it too was guilty of abuses and excesses. Yet the country cannot afford a witch hunt, which might well divide and demoralize people just as they are being asked to show tolerance of difficult circumstances. In addition, the new democratic order has relied on former Communists to provide administrative experience.

The government, however, has agreed in many instances to a restoration of property or some kind of cash indemnification for those hurt under communism. It has also stonewalled some demands, especially when they involve searching for past records to identify guilty parties or to determine the fate of victims, some of whom disappeared without a trace. Today's officials simply do not want to open old wounds. Indeed, some members of Parliament have suggested destroying old files of the secret police. That is not likely to happen, and neither is it likely that the Hungarian government will be able to satisfy Hungarians seeking retribution. With priority given to stability, justice will be served only when it does not cause more problems than it solves.

Popular resentment toward the former Communists exists in part because many still enjoy much of the privilege they had under Communist rule. The party's political network has been broken, but its members' economic might remains formidable, as many of the Communist era elite are still in place as factory managers, bank executives, and business owners. People see this lingering Communist influence as an obstacle to the country's well-being and disagree with the government's rationale that the former Communists' talents are needed to keep the economy going.

(UN photo/Interfoto)

Margaret Bridge and Margaret Island on the Danube River in Budapest, Hungary.

REFORM AND FOREIGN POLICY

Change in both the political and economic spheres in the late 1980s depended on the external environment—in particular, Hungary's relations with the Soviet Union and with the West. Indeed, East–West détente as well as Hungary's relations with the superpowers were essential to the success of its reforms.

The Soviet Union

Mikhail Gorbachev viewed the Hungarian reform program as an experiment in socialist change important to the development of perestroika. The Kremlin valued the enthusiastic Hungarian support of perestroika and the Hungarian potential for encouraging reformism in other Soviet bloc countries that were resisting it. Thus the Kremlin accepted the removal of Kadar, the ascendancy of radical reformers like Pozsgay and Nyers, and the prospect that Hungary would adopt political pluralism and substantially reduce the role and power of the Communist Party in the foreseeable future. The Soviets did not pressure the Hungarian regime to close its frontiers to the East German citizens seeking refuge in West Germany but did privately advise the Hungarian Communists to diminish tensions with their Soviet bloc neighbors.

Finally, the Kremlin punctuated its acceptance of Hungary's rapid democratization by agreeing in January 1990 to begin discussion of a withdrawal of Soviet forces deployed in Hungary since 1956. The Kremlin accepted the argument of Premier Nemeth in talks with Soviet Premier Ryzkhov that Hungary's strategic position in Central/Eastern Europe—Hungary has no borders with NATO countries—made the Soviet withdrawal logical and risk-free. The Soviets withdrew 48,000 troops from Hungary by mid-1991.

Although the new democratic leadership was concerned about the Kremlin's anxieties over the loss of Soviet power in Central/Eastern Europe at the end of 1989, it moved also to dissolve the Warsaw Pact. In June 1990 Parliament voted unanimously to withdraw Hungary from the Warsaw Pact by the end of 1991. The democratic government in Hungary now sought to protect itself against a possible reassertion of Soviet influence and to give itself maximum diplomatic flexibility in negotiations in April 1991 over a new bilateral treaty with Moscow. Hungary resisted language that would have banned either country from joining any alliance that could be considered hostile to the other country. To prevent Hungary from prejudicing its chances of eventually joining the European Community or NATO, Prime Minister Antall said that Hungary wanted a treaty with Moscow guaranteeing Hungary's right to join groups and alliances of its own choosing.

While seeking to protect the country's independence in foreign policy, the Hungarian government tried to avoid anything in the nature of anti-Soviet rhetoric. It proceeded discreetly in cultivating relations with the republics that were declaring their independence of the Soviet center, notably Russia and Ukraine, which together accounted for 90 percent of Hungarian–Soviet trade. The Hungarians found the individual Soviet republics eager to establish bilateral trade relationships, which they as well as Hungary desperately needed. For example, Hungary's search for oil since the Soviet central government could no longer guarantee delivery led to purchases from individual Soviet oil-producing regions, such as the Bashkir and Tatar autonomous republics.

Hungary and the West
During the Communist era, Hungary's relations with the West, in particular West Germany and the United States, were good and thus an asset for reform. Since 1990 Hungary has strengthened its ties with the West. As part of its desire for stability, it particularly wants to be linked with NATO, perhaps through NATO's political consultative committees.

West Germany
The Hungarian Communist leadership in the late 1980s found in West Germany strong support of its commitment to economic reform. The leadership, especially Grosz, deftly exploited West Germany's strong interest in not wanting Hungarian reforms to flounder, because of their importance to similar reforms elsewhere in Central/Eastern Europe. Grosz visited Bonn in 1987, where he concluded five different agreements on economic, scientific and technological, and cultural matters, the most important involving a government guaranteed credit of 1 billion marks. The two leaderships also endorsed the pending Soviet–American agreement over nuclear missiles and stressed their interest in the continuation of the Helskini process. Helmut Kohl commended Hungary for the liberalization of travel restrictions, for Hungary's persistent diplomacy of dialogue with the West, and for its equitable treatment of the small German minority living within its borders, which was especially important for Bonn because of the implications for the well-being of German minorities in Poland, Romania, and the Soviet Union.

The United States
Hungary also sought good relations with the United States, for economic as well as political reasons. The Hungarians wanted American companies to participate in Hungarian enterprises, as a means of injecting new technology and investment capital into the Hungarian economy, especially the consumer sector. But Hungary's interest in developing good relations with Washington was also part of its strategy of doing its part to strengthen East–West détente and to protect Hungary's links with the West against possible difficulties between the superpowers.

In 1988 Grosz came to the United States for a meeting with then–president Ronald Reagan and a visit to several U.S. cities to promote investment in Hungarian industry. He was given a very warm reception by Reagan, who extended to him the same courtesies given to Gorbachev, to a degree that signified American recognition of Hungarian reformism as well as the expectation that it would continue to go forward.

Grosz obtained a joint venture agreement worth $115 million between Guardian Industries of Northville, Michigan, and a glassworks enterprise in southeastern Hungary that will transform it into a modern manufacturer of glass products to be sold in Western Europe. Grosz also discussed the expansion of an educational exchange program between Hungarian and American secondary and higher education institutions in which Hungarian high school and college students would study in the United States.

George Bush's visit to Hungary in July 1989 punctuated the good feelings Washington had developed toward the Hungarian reform movement. Bush announced in Budapest unlimited access to U.S. markets and a token $25 million aid package to encourage Hungary's free enterprise system.

Israel
In recent years the Hungarian regime sought ways to improve the condition of Jewish culture in the country. It was the only Soviet bloc state to have a rabbinical seminary. In 1988 the Hungarian government established a Center for Jewish Studies at Budapest University. At the same time, Hungary moved closer toward the resumption of formal diplomatic ties with Israel. In 1988 Grosz met with then–Israeli premier Yitzak Shamir in Budapest. Grosz agreed to meet an Israeli request to act as intermediary between Israel and the Soviet Union to urge on Gorbachev an improvement of the conditions of Soviet Jews, especially a lifting of restrictions on their emigration to Israel. On September 18, 1989, Hungary and Israel formally restored diplomatic ties with each other.

Austria
Hungary also improved relations with Austria, to which it is bound by centuries of cultural and political tradition. Since 1988 Hungarians have been free to travel to Austria. On June 27, 1989, Hungarian officials cut the barbed wire at the border at Sopron. There has since been a flood of citizens from each country to the other. Indeed, Austria may turn out to be a valuable lever for Hungary's eventual integration into Western Europe. Anticipating a move by Austria to join the European Community, Hungarian authorities are studying the possibility of applying for membership in the European Free Trade Association, which groups Austria with Sweden, Switzerland, and other neutral Western European countries. Such a step could give Hungary indirect access to the European market.

Hungary and Central/Eastern Europe
Hungary's reformism complicated its relations with Nicolae Ceausescu's Romania. Hungarian citizens openly called for an end to Romanian discrimination against people of Hungarian extraction living in Transylvania. In August 1988 Hungarians demonstrated at the Romanian Embassy in Budapest and persuaded the Hungarian leadership to accept an invitation from Ceausescu to discuss the nationalities issue. At the end of that month, Grosz met Ceausescu in the Romanian city of Arad, near the frontier with Hungary. Grosz wanted Ceausescu to agree to four points: 1) Romanian recognition that Hungary had a legitimate interest in the fate of its ethnic minority; 2) concessions on Romania's program of consolidating rural communities by eliminating thousands of villages historically inhabited by Hungarian-speaking peasants; 3) the reopening of the Hungarian consulate in Cluj, the capital of formerly Hungarian Transylvania, which was ordered closed by Romania in June; and 4) establishment of a Hungarian cultural center in Bucharest.

To the dismay of his party colleagues and the anger of the Hungarian population, Grosz came back from his meeting with Ceausescu virtually empty-handed. Worse, he had accepted a joint communique stressing mutual goodwill that clearly was not achieved in the talks between the two leaders.

Relations took another turn for the worse when the Hungarian government in 1989 honored Imre Nagy, by exhuming his remains from the unmarked grave into which they had been deposited by the Kadar regime in 1958 and reburying them in a public ceremony. In a statement

Independence
1919

Soviet troops
liberate Hungary
from Nazi
control; Rakosi
becomes the
leader of the
Hungarian
Communists
1945

Nagy becomes
the premier
1953

Nagy is ousted
by Rakosi
because of his
reformist
orientation of
independence
from the Soviet
Union
1955

Antigovernment
demonstrations
in Budapest;
Nagy is restored
to the premiership
1956

The Soviets
intervene
militarily to block
liberalization and
Hungarian
withdrawal from
the Warsaw Pact
1956

The Kadar
regime
announces the
New Economic
Mechanism
1968

Economic
relations with the
United States are
normalized;
Hungary receives
most-favored-
nation treatment
1978

Hungary allows
7,000 East
Germans to
emigrate to the
West; new
freedoms of
travel and
emigration

1980s–1990s

Steady economic
and political
liberalization; the
Soviets withdraw
their troops from
Hungarian soil

The Hungarian
Communist Party
changes its name
to the Socialist
Party, ousts
Kadar, and
abandons
Soviet-style
Marxist ideology

Parliament
approves liberal
abortion law;
results of
parliamentary
elections in May
1994 suggest
popular
disillusionment
with post-
Communist
political order

handed to the Hungarian ambassador in Bucharest, the Romanian government said the funeral service betrayed "anti-Socialist, anti-Romanian, nationalist-chauvinistic, and revisionist manifestations." The angry Romanian reaction had to be understood in the light of not only the dispute over the long-simmering ethnic issue. Ceausescu also disliked the political liberalization program going on in Hungary, fearing that the Romanian people would soon demand similar reforms in their country—which indeed they did in the fall of 1989, leading to Ceausescu's execution.

The honoring of Nagy also provoked the conservative Czechoslovak Communist leadership, which feared an equivalent evaluation of Alexander Dubcek and criticism of the strict orthodox dictatorship imposed by the Kremlin in 1968.

Hungary's rapid movement away from orthodox socialism also strained relations with the former East Germany. The East Berlin regime was not happy that in the summer of 1989 thousands of East German citizens, professing themselves tourists, emigrated through Hungary to West Germany. The refusal of Hungary to close its frontier to the East German refugees violated past agreements among Warsaw Pact countries not to allow one another's citizens transit rights to the West without official approval of the home country. It also contributed to an increasingly embarrassing political problem for the East Berlin regime, which was hard put to stem the flow of its citizens westward.

The Hungarian leadership faced a dilemma in its decision to allow the East Germans to travel through Hungary without visas. On the one hand, the Hungarian leaders knew that they would provoke neighboring East Germany and probably the Kremlin as well, further isolating Hungary in the Soviet bloc as the pariah of reform. At the same time, however, the leaders in Budapest wanted to strengthen their credibility with both their own people and the West and therefore were unwilling to turn back the East Germans. The Hungarian regime was also under considerable pressure from West Germany to treat the East German refugees tolerantly. Since Hungary desperately needed West German economic assistance, there was a strong practical incentive for the Hungarian leadership to accommodate Bonn.

In the post-Communist era, Hungary remains vulnerable to political instability in neighboring countries. For example, with a large Hungarian minority of some 600,000 people living in the newly independent republic of Slovakia, Hungary's government worries that the nationalist-led government in Bratislava might hurt the Hungarian minority in the pursuit of cultural homogenization policies.

Hungary also has problems with the Slovak government in Bratislava over the opening of a large hydroelectric dam and power plant at Gabrcikovo, on the Danube River. The Hungarian government vehemently opposes construction and operation of the dam, warning that it will alter the flow of the Danube and pollute one of Central/Eastern Europe's largest aquifers supplying drinking water for several million people in Hungary and Slovakia.

Also disturbing is the ethnic conflict and civil war in Yugoslavia. Hungarians feel some solicitude for the Croats, who were governed by Budapest before World War I and with whom they have familial links. And they also worry that the fighting in Croatia will cut off Hungary's access to the Adriatic oil pipeline, a problem for the strained Hungarian economy. Yugoslav federal airplanes violated Hungarian air space on several occasions and caused some minor damage to Hungarian border villages. In addition, fighting has spilled over from northern Yugoslavia into southern Hungary. With 35,000 refugees from the fighting in Yugoslavia, Hungary has to provide food and shelter from its own limited resources.

DEVELOPMENT

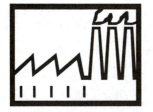

After a fast start in 1990, the pace of large-scale privatization has slowed, due to the collapse of Hungarian markets in the former Soviet Union, recession in Western Europe, and the complaints of the right wing that too much of Hungary's economic assets are being transferred to foreigners. On the positive side is the establishment of 80,000 new small businesses in Budapest. The Hungarian forint can be considered a convertible currency, and inflation has been controlled.

FREEDOM

The openness of Hungary's new political environment is evident in the reappearance of right-wing tendencies. The scope of liberalism is seen also in the 1993 ruling of the Constitutional Court allowing the formation of private television and radio broadcasting, prohibited by parliamentary decree in 1989, an event that may signal the beginning of an unfettered private broadcasting industry in Hungary.

HEALTH/WELFARE

With the market economy has come more crime and violence in the streets because of increasing social inequality. One particularly alarming aspect of crime is the increase in drug traffic. Hungary has become one of the main corridors for drug traffic along the so-called Balkan route from Turkey and Bulgaria to markets in western Europe, a radical development in a country that was virtually drug-free under the Communists.

ACHIEVEMENTS

Hungary has taken a big step forward in the controversial area of corporate support for cultural institutions: IBM agreed to sponsor the Hungarian Symphony Orchestra's 1993–1994 performance season. IBM's funding sponsorship is the first of its kind in Central/Eastern Europe and is expected to inaugurate a new trend in private funding of public cultural institutions and events.

Poland

GEOGRAPHY

Area in Square Kilometers (Miles): 312,612 (120,700) (smaller than New Mexico)
Capital (Population): Warsaw (1,649,000)
Climate: temperate

PEOPLE

Population

Total: 38,520,000
Annual Growth Rate: 0.35%
Rural/Urban Population Ratio: 38/62
Ethnic Makeup of Population: 98% Polish; 2% Ukrainian, Belarussian, and others
Language: Polish

Health

Life Expectancy at Birth: 68 years (male); 77 years (female)
Infant Mortality Rate (Ratio): 14/1,000
Average Caloric Intake: 123% of FAO minimum
Physicians Available (Ratio): 1/471

Religion(s)
95% Roman Catholic; 5% Uniate, Greek Orthodox, Protestant, and Jewish

Education

Adult Literacy Rate: 98%

COMMUNICATION

Telephones: 3,648,000
Newspapers: 99 dailies; 9,630,000 circulation

CHANGE—BUT NOT ALL FOR THE BETTER

The rapid expansion of private entrepreneurialism in Poland has brought plenty of food, clothing, and appliances to stores. People are able to buy anything they want—as long as they have the money to pay the high prices asked for these previously scarce commodities. But with their stagnant wages, most ordinary Polish people do not have the means and are experiencing extreme hardship as the country moves from the old socialist order to the free market economy. Polish people have mixed feelings about this abundance, which is beyond their grasp. A sign of the hard times is a craving, evidenced in popular support for the left in the 1993 parliamentary elections, for some of the paternalism of the Communist past.

TRANSPORTATION

Highways—Kilometers (Miles): 360,629 (223,950)
Railroads—Kilometers (Miles): 26,250 (16,301)
Usable Airfields: 163

GOVERNMENT

Type: democratic state
Independence Date: July 22, 1918
Head of State: President Lech Walesa
Political Parties: Social Democracy; Democratic Union; Democratic Alliance of the Left; Peasants' Party; Christian-National Union; Liberal-Democratic Congress; Solidarity Trade Union; Union of Labor; Christian Democratic Party; Conservative Party; others
Suffrage: universal and compulsory over 18

MILITARY

Number of Armed Forces: 312,800 including frontier and security forces
Military Expenditures (% of Central Government Expenditures): 7.7%
Current Hostilities: none

ECONOMY

Currency ($ U.S. Equivalent): 15,879 zlotys = $1
Per Capita Income/GDP: $4,400/$167.6 billion
Inflation Rate: 44%
Total Foreign Debt: $48.5 billion
Natural Resources: coal; sulfur; copper; natural gas; silver
Agriculture: grains; sugar beets; oilseed; potatoes; hogs; other livestock
Industry: machine building; iron and steel; extractive industries; chemicals; shipbuilding; food processing

FOREIGN TRADE

Exports: $14 billion
Imports: $12.9 billion

POLAND

After World War II, the Polish Communists, under the leadership of Boleslaw Bierut and Wladyslaw Gomulka, established a new party called the Polish United Workers' Party (PUWP), which acquired power in the late 1940s. But there were differences between Bierut and Gomulka over how much of the Soviet model should be replicated in the development of Polish socialism. Bierut was a conformist; he favored complete adherence to the Soviet line, whereas Gomulka wanted to make adjustments where imitation of the Soviet pattern would cause unrest in Polish society. With Soviet support, Bierut ousted Gomulka, who was subsequently brought to trial, convicted, and imprisoned for his will to deviate. In the meantime the PUWP, under Bierut's leadership, created the Polish People's Republic, a Soviet-style socialist dictatorship, and transformed Poland into a Soviet satellite.

THE OCTOBER 1956 CRISIS

The first outbreak of protest and dissent in Poland reached a climax in 1956. There were popular demands for an end to the excesses of Stalinist policies of the late 1940s and early 1950s. People wanted a higher standard of living, the establishment of political freedoms, democratization of the Polish government, and independence of the Soviet Union.

Following Stalin's death moderates in the party Politburo, having voted to oust conservatives subservient to the Kremlin, including Bierut himself, tried to accommodate popular pressures for reform. They released Gomulka from prison and returned him to power, relaxed censorship, halted persecution of the Roman Catholic Church, and allowed resumption of religious instruction in schools. They also permitted private ownership of some farms.

The Kremlin was uncomfortable over these changes, especially as they had led to the appearance in the Polish media of anti-Soviet sentiment. In October 1956, fearful of a nationalist-inspired move to weaken Poland's ties with the Soviet Union, Soviet Communist Party leader Nikita Khrushchev and other members of the Soviet Politburo paid a surprise visit to Warsaw to discuss the Polish internal situation with Gomulka. The Soviets apparently told Gomulka of their willingness to allow Poland a limited amount of autonomy in the economic sector, provided that Gomulka restore political discipline, curtail the influence of the church, suppress anti-Soviet sentiment, and assure Poland's loyalty to the Warsaw Pact.

Although Gomulka's leadership in the early 1960s provided Poland with a measure of stability, it became repressive. His efforts to assure political discipline provoked popular opposition. In 1968 there was an outbreak of strikes by students and workers. A significant aspect of the political scene at that time was the appearance of anti-Semitism. Party leaders blamed certain Jewish students and professors for stirring up criticism of the government's authoritarianism, even though at that time the influence of Jews was minimal in Polish life and almost nonexistent within the Communist hierarchy.

THE DECEMBER 1970 CRISIS

A crisis occurred in December 1970, when the government announced a decision to raise food prices. Agricultural output had not kept up with demand, and by the end of the 1960s, government subsidization of food prices was becoming an intolerable burden. When the authorities used force to suppress protests against the increased prices, the workers struck. By the end of December, antigovernment demonstrations and violent confrontations between angry citizens and the authorities were occurring throughout the country. The government now retreated and rescinded the price increases. Under great pressure from flustered colleagues, Gomulka resigned in early 1971.

The party leadership changed to Edward Gierek, who promised more food and higher wages and increased popular participation in factory management. But workers struck again in 1976, ostensibly because of another regime decision to increase food prices but also because Gierek's promises of 1971 had not been fulfilled. For the first time, dissident intellectuals showed some interest in the complaints of workers. Even the Catholic Church became vocal in the mid-1970s, demanding the regime's acknowledgment of the church's moral leadership in Poland and of its right to speak out on public policy matters.

THE AUGUST 1980 CRISIS

Once again it seemed as if the regime had learned nothing from the past. In the summer of 1980, there was another explosion of strikes and antigovernment demonstrations, more violent and more prolonged than similar events in the 1970s. Workers in shipyards of the Baltic Sea port of Gdansk struck for more food, higher wages, new fringe benefits, and a democ-ratization of Polish society, including workers' real participation in factory management and freedom for the Catholic Church.

Polish workers had lost confidence in the official, party-controlled trade union organization, which they considered unresponsive. They thus insisted upon the Polish government's acceptance of a new federation of factory unions independent of the party, called Solidarity, and the legal right to strike to obtain redress of grievances. After a month of strike actions that spread beyond Gdansk, the Polish workers, led by one of their own, Lech Walesa, obliged the Polish government to agree to approve the establishment of Solidarity, in the so-called Gdansk Agreement between the workers and the government on August 31, 1980. In this unprecedented action—no other Central/Eastern European country had allowed an independent trade union organization—the Polish workers had the support of the dissident intelligentsia and the Catholic Church.

In the latter half of 1980 and during most of 1981, prominent members of the dissident intelligentsia came out in support of the workers. They helped with the establishment of Solidarity and with the workers' efforts to get the government to accept the union. They repeated their demands for a sweeping liberalization of the political system, including foreign policy independence of the Soviet Union.

The Catholic Church also was active in this new crisis. While it avoided open confrontation with the regime, it restated its criticisms of official atheism and its condemnation of the regime's harassment of the clergy, destruction of personal freedoms, and subservience to Moscow.

ROOTS OF POLISH DISSENT

Periodic expressions of protest and dissent in Polish society since the death of Joseph Stalin, especially the crisis that began in August 1980, had many roots. The more important of them were the unrelenting and excessive political repression by the Polish Communist leadership of a traditionally politically active society; the leadership's inept management of the economy, especially in agriculture and industry; its offensive servility to the Soviet Union; and the increasing political activism of the Catholic Church, which enjoyed strong and dynamic leadership in both Poland and the Vatican.

Regime political repression involved the persecution of critics and opponents of the regime, insistence upon Poles' acceptance of Soviet-inspired norms of po-

litical discipline and ideological orthodoxy, and other offensive gestures. Poles
believed that the party treated them as
children, expecting blind obedience while
denying them a say in the management of
their affairs. There were also complaints
about corruption in the party and state bureaucracies and misuse of privileges.

Although the government retreated
from collectivization to increase incentives of farmers to expand output, the production of food did not keep pace with
demand. The government's inept economic management thus contributed to
dissent. While it is true that Polish farmers
lacked modern machinery and labor-
saving technology, especially in the area
of fertilizers, an equally important explanation of the party's failure to expand
agricultural output was its conscious discrimination against the private farmers it
had created. Polish authorities made it
very difficult for these farmers to acquire
credit and supplies, thus impoverishing
and demoralizing them; in the 1960s and
1970s, the regime apparently had ideologically inspired, and perhaps Soviet-en-
couraged, second thoughts about having
allowed the departure from collectivization.

During the 1970s the Polish Communists made serious errors in their extensive
investment in so-called turnkey industries,
in an effort to upgrade rapidly the quality
and quantity of industrial output. They
purchased entire industries from the West
and transplanted them to Poland. But
these industries, paid for by substantial ad-

vances of credit from the West, did not
function well, because Poland lacked the
proper technology. Industrial output did
not expand, and matters were made worse
by the international recession that followed the 1973 Arab oil embargo. By the
end of the 1970s, the country was deeply
in debt to the West.

The conspicuous servility of the Polish
leadership to Moscow also galled the
Poles, not only because of their historic
dislike of Russians but also because of a
belief that most of what was wrong with
Poland since World War II was attributable to the Soviet Union. Especially
provocative to Poles was the regime's insistence on including in the draft of a new
Constitution in 1975 a statement about Poland's closeness to the Soviet Union. It
caused such an uproar in the Polish Parliament (Sejm) and elsewhere in society
that the regime agreed to alter the wording. Polish intellectual and church leaders
persistently called for independence from
the Soviet Union and for closer relations
with the West. Mounting Polish hostility
toward the Soviet Union peaked in the
summer of 1981, when there was a visible
outbreak of anti-Soviet sentiment throughout the country that took such ugly forms
as the desecration of the graves of Soviet
soldiers killed in Poland in World War II.

In the 1970s the Polish Catholic Church
insisted that Polish Communists recognize
its role as the moral guardian of Polish
society and its right to speak out on Polish
national affairs. The church benefited

from the election in 1978 of the Polish-
born Pope John Paul II. The pope encouraged the church to resist Communist
atheism and Communist efforts to deny
the church's legitimate influence in Polish
life.

SOVIET RESPONSES TO THE AUGUST 1980 CRISIS

The Soviets were alarmed by the apparent
unwillingness or inability of the Polish
Communist Party to restore public order
to Polish society during the autumn of
1980. The Soviets suspected that some in
the party leadership, including First Secretary Stanislaw Kania, who succeeded
Gierek in September, favored major departures from Soviet-style socialism and
from Poland's closeness to the Warsaw
Pact and the Soviet Union.

The Soviets also were appalled by divisions within the Polish Communist
Party over how to cope with the crisis.
There were those who favored conciliat-
ing the workers and tolerating Solidarity;
others wanted a severe crackdown on opposition to the regime. These divisions
were forbidden by the rules of democratic
centralism, and the Soviets were concerned that they would weaken the party
in its confrontation with groups that were
aggressively seeking wide reforms.

Toward the end of 1980, the Soviets
considered a military intervention in Poland to help the Polish party restore order.
They ultimately decided in December

(Katalin Arkell/Spooner/Gamma)

Poland under Wojciech Jaruzelski saw the rise of the black market as commodities became scarce. These people are lined up for food at a shop in Warsaw.

against an intervention, for several reasons, not least of which was the possibility of meeting fierce popular resistance, which could have led to a full-scale war. The Soviets had to take into account the strongly expressed opposition of the West, in particular the United States, which threatened retaliation. There is also reason to believe that the Soviets were not militarily prepared for the deployment of massive military forces in Central/Eastern Europe, because of mobilization problems. Finally, a number of the Soviet Union's allies, in particular Romania and Hungary, opposed intervention.

During most of 1981, the Kremlin exerted intense political pressure on the Polish leadership, demanding that it take a firm line against the opposition. The pressure climaxed in the summer of 1981, during the PUWP's 9th Congress in Warsaw. The Soviets were disturbed by the party's decision to increase its responsiveness to popular will by democratizing its leadership-selection process and in other ways departing from democratic centralism. In the fall of 1981, the Soviets sought the replacement of Polish leader Kania. Because the Polish Communist Party's Politburo agreed that Kania had failed to restore order in the past year, thus provoking the Soviets and increasing the risk of their interfering in Poland, it removed him from the position of first secretary and elected Premier and Defense Minister Wojciech Jaruzelski in his place.

Jaruzelski's Ascendancy

Although Jaruzelski was not their first choice, partly because of his military background, the Soviets approved of his selection as PUWP first secretary and agreed to support him. Jaruzelski did not disappoint the Soviets, at least in the short term. He quickly took steps to restore order in Poland. In December 1981 he declared martial law. The following year he banned and arrested the leaders of Solidarity and other independent union organizations that had sprung up, like Rural Solidarity, which had been formed by independent farmers. Subsequently, Jaruzelski harassed, persecuted, and silenced most of the dissident intellectuals. He also denied the Catholic Church the influence over public policy making it had been seeking. The official Polish press mercilessly attacked the church, accusing it of "expanded sponsorship of underground culture" and of inculcating the youth with a hatred of socialism.

But Jaruzelski also tried to avoid excesses he knew would provoke a new outbreak of unrest and pursued his own policy of normalization. He allowed for-

mer Solidarity leader Lech Walesa to continue to express his views, which were often critical of the regime. He continued to dialogue with Cardinal Joseph Glemp, the Catholic primate of Poland, and he consented, despite the political risks, to allow the pope to visit Poland in 1983. While it is true that Jaruzelski tried to restrict the church's influence in the spring of 1984 by calling for the removal of crucifixes from public places, this was an ephemeral gesture that did not interfere with the ongoing church–state dialogue. Jaruzelski also tried to increase worker participation in management of factories and to address the complaints about unresponsive trade unionism by the creation of new union organizations (which were, however, still under party control). And in 1985 he encouraged independent candidates in parliamentary elections.

ECONOMIC DECLINE

The Polish economy steadily deteriorated during the 1980s. Economic underperformance, which caused shortages of everything—especially consumer necessities—was partly the result of public apathy, inspired by pervasive hostility toward the Communist regime and by pessimism about the prospects of economic improvement. But the Polish economy also still suffered from outdated industrial practices and obsolete machinery.

Polish agriculture in particular was badly off; it was unable to feed the population. Output was inadequate because of the low priority the Polish government assigned to the agricultural sector, which received about one-fifth of total investment capital. Also, the regime still discriminated against the private farms, which nonetheless now produced 80 percent of all foodstuffs and were 13 percent more productive than state farms.

The regime attempted to improve output in industry as well as in agriculture, in three ways. The first, a reform program initiated in 1981, guaranteed self-management and some autonomy of central control to state enterprises to set wage rates and reinvest profits. It failed because the party leadership imposed restrictions on certain heavy industries, amounting to a recentralization of government control and effectively depriving workers of independent action, initiative, and responsibility in their operation.

The second Jaruzelski scheme was to allow the Catholic Church to channel funds from the West into the private sector of Polish agriculture in order to purchase badly needed machinery, spare parts, and

fertilizers. This scheme led nowhere, as a result of party opposition to an increase of church influence.

The third Jaruzelski plan involved Poland's readmission to the International Monetary Fund, enabling Poland to obtain new sources of Western credit for economic rehabilitation, provided it pursued austerity measures to curtail consumption and limit inflation. It was hoped that access to new credit and the economic belt-tightening program mandated by the IMF would facilitate Poland's economic recovery.

The Polish government tried to improve the country's economic health also by reducing the gap between the real value of goods and what was charged for them. In 1987 the regime announced a 40 percent increase in food prices and asked for popular backing of this move. But in a referendum held to approve the price increase, Polish voters responded with a resounding "No!" Jaruzelski thereupon had to retreat: the government announced a scaled-down price increase to be introduced gradually.

THE FRAGILITY OF COMMUNIST RULE IN POLAND

The Jaruzelski regime itself admitted—albeit in secret—its chief weaknesses. A confidential report, issued in numbered copies to the Polish Council of Ministers in March 1984, described the perceived threats to the regime's efforts to expand its influence over Polish society. The document, which was surprisingly candid, singled out credibility as the Jaruzelski government's major problem, a problem that persisted because the conditions that gave rise to the unrest in the summer of 1980 remained unresolved.

The regime tried to bolster its credibility with the Polish public in 1986–1987 by several conciliatory actions designed to curry popular support. For example, the official media acknowledged the pluralistic character of Polish society and the permissability of a diversity of popular views. The media recognized that the system could be questioned, though they rejected the concept of pluralism advocated by Solidarity and continued to insist that there were limits on tolerable debate of national questions.

Jaruzelski tried to increase popular acceptance of his regime by strengthening ties with the Catholic Church. He met twice with Pope John Paul II in 1987 to normalize relations with the Vatican. But on both occasions, the pope put pressure on Jaruzelski to liberalize, saying that normalization of church–state relations must await the end of the regime's interference with the work of his bishops in promoting Polish political freedom.

The pope used Jaruzelski's eagerness for normalization of relations to encourage his departure from Soviet-inspired policies of atheism and repression. In June 1987, in the most direct attack on Poland's socialist system he had yet made, Pope John Paul called upon Polish Catholics "to rethink communism" and to consider major changes in the country's political, socioeconomic, and cultural life.

POLAND AND PERESTROIKA

In the late 1980s, Poland was faced with an enormous economic and political crisis, which ultimately forced the Communist leadership to adopt many of the reforms Soviet leader Mikhail Gorbachev had addressed in speeches on perestroika. During these years the Polish economy became bankrupt. There were shortages of everything, especially the daily necessities of life, including food and clothing. Coupled with the repressive policies of the Jaruzelski regime, the economic hardship became intolerable.

In the spring of 1988, when workers in the steel mills and coal mines of the highly industrialized Silesian region of southern Poland called for strikes for higher wages to offset galloping inflation, strike actions quickly spread to other industries. By the end of the summer, workers were calling not only for higher wages but also for the legalization of Solidarity. Church leaders stated that the principal cause of the social disorder was the regime's violation of the rights and dignity of working people.

Newly appointed Premier Miezyslaw Rakowski called for limited pluralism, the legalization of some non-Communist clubs and organizations, the broadening of ministerial leadership to include non-Communists, and negotiation with the outlawed Solidarity to obtain the trade union's help in resolving the economic crisis, especially the paralytic strikes. Solidarity demanded legalization and political democratization involving a reduction of Communist Party control of the government. The regime at first refused to accommodate these demands, hoping for Solidarity's cooperation with minimum concessions required of the government. The Communist authorities were betting that older Polish workers would soon weary of the strikes. They also thought that most workers would not support the radical changes that would be required if economic reform were to take place. These would include wage differentiation, factory closings, and other hardships.

The authorities tried to undermine Solidarity's bargaining position. For example, in November 1988 the government decided to close the Lenin Shipyards in Gdansk—Solidarity's home, the symbol of its defiance, and the focal point of popular loyalty to it. The government defended the decision on economic grounds—namely, that the yard had been losing money, that it was a drain on precious economic resources, and that foreign demand for Polish ships had declined, all of which were true.

But the continuation of strikes and political protests through December and January, despite the government's repressive measures, ultimately proved that its assumptions about dealing with Solidarity on the cheap, so to speak, were counterproductive. Its refusal to agree to the legalization of the trade union enhanced Lech Walesa's already substantial popular charisma and contributed to the soaring percentage of Poles who favored Solidarity's legalization.

In early January 1989, Jaruzelski sought, with several concessions, to break a deadlock in the talks with Solidarity. He decided to approve Solidarity's legalization and to introduce democratic changes in the Polish political system. The dialogue between the union and the government resumed in earnest and in April produced an agreement that satisfied both sides. In return for a government pledge to legalize Solidarity, Walesa agreed to certain conditions: Solidarity renounced strikes for 2 years, accepted the Communist system, and rejected links with groups calling for the abandonment of communism.

The agreement provided for the creation of a second chamber for the national Parliament, to be called the Senate. Members of the Senate were to be elected in a free and open way with no restrictions on who could run for seats or who could be elected. The agreement also said that in the other, lower house of the national Parliament, the Sejm, independent groups not under the control of the Communist Party could compete for seats, provided that Communist Party candidates and candidates of parties in alliance with the Communist Party held a majority. The two houses would elect a head of state, called the president of the republic, who would have substantial policy-making authority in both domestic and international affairs. The president would be commander-in-chief of the nation's military forces and would have the authority to select a premier who, in consultation with the president, would appoint a cabinet. The choice of premier and the cabinet would need the approval of Parliament. Both sides also agreed that implementation of the

agreement would be immediate, starting with the legalization of Solidarity, to be followed by the holding of elections for the Sejm and the Senate, which would then elect a president and ratify a new government.

Under the new arrangements, the Communists would still maintain their grip on the administration of the country, through understandings that provided for party control of a majority in the Sejm, for party leadership of the defense and police establishments, and for the election of Jaruzelski as the first president. But Solidarity and other non-Communist groups gained substantial political advantages, and the way was now open for a progressive weakening of communism in Poland. Political events moved very quickly following the agreement. In fact, the scope and pace of change far exceeded the expectations of either the party or Solidarity.

Elections
Elections for a new bicameral Parliament began on June 3, 1989. Despite the complexity of the balloting, which was designed to assure a Communist majority, the elections resulted in Solidarity's winning 99 of the 100 seats in the Senate and every possible seat in the Sejm. Polish voters had used every opportunity to express their opposition to the party's candidates. Solidarity now had more political strength than ever.

The next step in the implementation of the April agreement was the new Parliament's election of the president. Although Jaruzelski had been ready to run as the Communist Party's candidate, there was now a chance that he might not get elected. Many Solidarity-affiliated members of both houses of Parliament opposed him. The two small parties that had loyally worked with Communists over the past 40 years wavered in their support as well, no doubt due to the prospect that Solidarity might someday rule Poland and because they feared being shut out of power because of their close association with the Communists.

However, Jaruzelski decided to run when the small parties agreed to back him and when Walesa also indicated his support. He was elected president on July 19, 1989, by the slimmest of majorities. It was clear that his election was by no means a strong mandate or a statement of popular preference for him.

Appointment of a Non-Communist Premier
President Jaruzelski initially ruled out the possibility of a non-Communist premier,

saying that Poland's socialist neighbors, East Germany and Czechoslovakia, would oppose such an unprecedented move. His first appointment, however, was vehemently rejected by Solidarity deputies in Parliament. Eventually, Jaruzelski turned to Solidarity to propose a premier. Although many wanted Walesa, the Solidarity leader demurred, pleading the priority of his interest in dealing with large organizational and policy problems confronting the trade union. There was speculation that he preferred to run for the presidency in the 1990s and thought it best to remain aloof from the premiership.

The Solidarity leadership, in consultation with leaders of the Peasants' and Democratic parties and Jaruzelski, put forward Tadeusz Mazowiecki, a less politically prominent but a politically active member of Solidarity's leadership with close connections to the church. On August 19 Parliament formally endorsed, by majority vote, Mazowiecki's appointment by the president.

Formation of a Cabinet
Solidarity assumed policy-making responsibility, but the Communist Party still held police power of the state and controlled the economy. Moreover, hard-liners in the Politburo were reeling over the new situation of non-Communist control of the cabinet. On August 20, 1989, the party's Central Committee announced in militant tones that membership of the cabinet that Premier Mazowiecki was now forming "must correspond to [the Communist party's] political and state potential." In other words, the Communists should have the lion's share of ministerial posts, including the Ministry of Foreign Affairs.

But the party quickly backed down, not only because the Solidarity leadership had no intention of accepting a Communist monopoly of the cabinet but also because the trade union was willing to allow the party four ministries, including defense and interior. It accepted this concession and gave up claims to the Foreign Affairs Ministry. Gorbachev's personal intervention may have been instrumental in the party's retreat. He called Jaruzelski to urge the new party leader to pursue a conciliatory approach.

POLITICAL DEMOCRATIZATION

The Polish leadership also took important steps in moving the country closer toward political democracy. In December 1989 the Polish Legislature formally amended the national Constitution to eliminate reference to the leading role of the Communist Party, thereby officially ending its

historic monopoly of power and legalizing the already extensive political pluralism. The cabinet also sought to schedule local elections in the spring of 1990 rather than later in the year, to give voters an opportunity to vote Communists out of power on the municipal level, where they were able to block reforms lessening state control and expanding private entrepreneurialism.

As a practical matter, the Poles were steadily moving toward a return to political pluralism as individuals and groups became increasingly active in public criticism of government policies. Solidarity deputies in the Parliament no longer showed the same unity they had in the summer and were faction-ridden over the issue of how far and how fast to go in dismantling Communist rule.

At the end of January 1990, the Polish Communist Party, at a Congress in Warsaw, formally dissolved itself and created a new organization called the Social Democracy of the Republic of Poland. By trying to distance themselves from those discredited, the Polish Communist elite acknowledged the former party's loss of popularity and its failure to lead. The new organization, which seemed to be using the Socialist parties of France, Spain, and Italy as models, presumably was trying to offer itself as an alternative to Solidarity. Miezyslaw Rakowski, the head of the old Communist Party, became the new party's leader.

Jaruzelski's Resignation
In December 1990 President Jaruzelski resigned, with 4 years remaining in his term of office. He was the last of Europe's old-guard Communist leaders to relinquish power and, quite unlike any of them, he did so with some grace. People probably will be arguing for a long time about what kind of leader he was—Soviet puppet or national patriot. As the instrument of martial law and brutal repression in the 1980s, he clearly followed the Brezhnevian Kremlin; but it also is true that he helped along the radical political reform that restored democracy to Poland.

The 1990 Presidential Elections
The presidential elections on November 25 and December 9, 1990, brought about a further reduction in Communist influence. The three candidates were quite different from one another. Prime Minister Mazowiecki, representing the intelligentsia and professional groups, advocated gradualism in the movement, away from socialism to a market-based economy; good working relations with the Soviet Union; and the avoidance of an anti-Communist witch-hunt. Solidarity leader Lech

Walesa favored rapid acceleration of economic reform accompanied by policies to ease the hardships of ordinary Polish citizens, the immediate removal of Communists from whatever authority they still had, and restrictions on Communists' acquisition of newly privatized enterprises. Joseph Tyminski, a Canadian citizen of Polish origin, promised to apply the economic principles that had led to his own business success. Tyminski, a somewhat bizarre candidate, given that he was a foreigner with no political experience in Poland, appealed to disaffected workers whose industries were hardest hit by Mazowiecki's reforms. He was especially popular with young workers, who were willing to overlook his political inexperience, his abusive criticism of opponents, and the inconsistencies of his arguments. His appeal to Polish frustrations and phobias struck a responsive cord throughout Polish society, and the fact that he was a self-made millionaire gave him a lot of credibility with ordinary Polish citizens, who have always admired successful emigrants. Tyminski also was a beneficiary of public disillusionment over the bribery, fraud, and corruption that accompanied the transition away from socialism. He capitalized on public anger over the continued influence of former Communists.

In the first ballot, on November 25, none of the candidates obtained the 50 percent–plus of popular votes needed to win: Walesa won a 40 percent plurality, Tyminski came in second, and Mazowiecki was a weak third. Mazowiecki, shocked by the lack of popular support for his leadership and by the vote for Tyminski, withdrew from the race and resigned the premiership. In the run-off election, on December 9, Walesa ran against Tyminski and won by a 3-to-1 margin.

New Political Cleavages and Conflicts
The elections showed how fractured Poland's post-Communist political leadership had become. The intelligentsia, including former dissident Adam Michnik, editor of *Gazeta Wyborcza,* the Solidarity daily, questioned Walesa's fitness for national leadership, viewing him as a radical populist and would-be strong leader who might sacrifice democratic principles for the sake of policy-making expediency. They thought that Walesa lacked the education and intellectual sophistication needed to manage power effectively and humanely; they also were envious of Czechoslovakia's sophisticated, cosmopolitan political leadership. Walesa, backed by industrial workers, was convinced that the Mazowiecki group was insufficiently sensitive to the hardships endured by ordinary

Polish people in the move toward a market-based economy.

Finally, farmers, who constituted 35 percent of the population, represented a relatively homogeneous economic and social constituency and were bound by their shared sense of historical oppression under the Communists. They were dissatisfied with attempts of the post-Communist leadership to foster a market economy by streamlining the distribution system. This system increased the food supply and brought an end to long lines and hoarding but left farmers with a surplus that they could not sell and had to destroy; Polish farmers had lost the Soviet market.

Governmental Stalemate

In December 1990 President Walesa appointed as prime minister an economist with a background in private business, Jan Krzysztof Bielecki, charging him to expedite the move toward a free market economy. Both he and Walesa wanted the fastest possible privatization of the economy. Walesa also asked for new parliamentary elections, hoping to rid the government of the Communist hangers-on who had been guaranteed a majority in the Sejm by the terms of the agreement between the Solidarity and Communist leaderships in April 1989. These Communists wanted to prolong their privileged economic situation. They had obstructed implementation of a sweeping privatization bill, passed in July 1990, designed to privatize 7,600 state enterprises making up 80 percent of the economy. The slowness of this process was politically and socially damaging; it also jeopardized the government's effort to obtain debt relief from Western creditors. In June 1991 Walesa asked the Polish Parliament to empower the cabinet to rewrite the nation's economic laws—he wanted Prime Minister Bielecki to be able to issue decrees with the force of law to break the logjam. But the Legislature eventually refused to accommodate the president: On September 14 the Sejm rejected the government's request for extraordinary powers.

The 1991 Parliamentary Elections

The parliamentary elections of October 1991 confused rather than clarified the political situation. Only 40 percent of eligible voters participated in the elections; the rest abstained to show their dissatisfaction with politics as well as, perhaps, their disinterest. No single party win a majority of the votes, which were distributed among more than 25 parties, with many holding no more than 1 percent of the total vote. The Democratic Union, led by Mazowiecki, and the former Polish Communists, who now called themselves the Democratic Alliance of the Left, each won about 12 percent of the popular vote, and each received 24 out of 460 seats. But Mazowiecki wanted nothing to do with the Communists, and the Communists had no enthusiasm for cooperating with Mazowiecki.

Walesa had to form a coalition from these divergent groups, recognizing that any such coalition would be extremely fragile, compromising his ability to continue implementation of controversial reforms. His response to this confusing political situation was immediate, striking, and, in character with himself and with Polish history: He offered to serve as his own prime minister. This move would have greatly strengthened his personal political power and called to mind the behavior of Josef Pilsudski, the Polish president of the 1920s who emasculated democracy and became an autocratic leader for the sake of assuring discipline and stability in the conflict-ridden society of that era. Poles wondered whether Walesa's offer reflected the beginnings of autocracy or whether Walesa was simply trying to goad the different factions to find some common ground that would allow a prompt resumption of policy making.

In any event Walesa continued the search for a new prime minister capable of forming a coalition cabinet. In November 1991 he selected Jan Olszewski, a former Solidarity lawyer who had the support of a center-right coalition of parties, including the Christian National Union, the Center Alliance, the Confederation for an Independent Poland, the Peasants' Party, and the Liberal Democratic Congress. Olszewski was critical of the rapid pace of free-market reforms and, therefore, at odds with Walesa, but he was the only political figure of stature who could muster a near majority of support in the Sejm.

Olszewski lasted only 5 months. Without an absolute majority of the 460 seats in the Sejm, he could not be a strong leader. His supporters were fragmented, and their agreement to cooperate was extremely fragile. They differed on such key issues as the size of the 1992 budget deficit, foreign investment, and the stabilization program required by the International Monetary Fund as the price for loans. Olszewski also angered many in the Parliament by allowing the Interior Ministry to release the names of alleged collaborators with the Communists. Many of those who allegedly had worked with the Communists were still in the Legislature, in danger of being politically discredited, and enraged at the prime minister for attempting to intimidate them into refraining from

(Reuters/Bettmann/Gary Cameron)

Under Lech Walesa the Polish presidency has become a strong element in post-Communist politics. In the early 1990s, Walesa viewed the presidency as the dominant institution within the national government that set the tone and character of Poland's political development.

engaging in a no-confidence vote over other issues.

On June 4, 1992, the Parliament voted to dismiss Olszewski and his government. Walesa started searching for a new prime minister. He nominated Waldemar Pawlak, head of the Peasants' Party, a politician of little political controversy who Walesa thought would loyally support presidential policy. Pawlak, however, could not form a government precisely because he was thought to be no more than a spokesperson for Walesa.

The Democratic Union proposed Hanna Suchocka, a lawyer and supporter of aggressive economic reform. Seven parties made a coalition to support her leadership, and she was formally approved by the Parliament in mid-June 1992. Suchocka became Poland's fifth prime minister in less than 3 years of non-Communist leadership.

The Polish Presidency under Walesa

Perhaps the answer to Poland's search for stability with democracy lies in the presidency. Walesa seems to think so. He sees the presidency, despite limits on its authority, as the dominant institution within the national government, affecting not only the operations of the state's administrative and legislative bodies but also the style and character of the country's politics. The general public as well has come to regard the presidency as the center of government decision making.

The sources of the Polish president's growing authority are historical, constitutional, political, and personal. Historically, Polish society has always admired strong leaders, no doubt a result of the somewhat anarchic character of the Polish people, who deeply cherish their freedom and independence, if only because they have been deprived of it so often in the recent past. The president, elected by direct popular vote, has an institutional authority that cannot be matched by any other political figure in the country. In contrast, other state institutions, particularly the national Parliament, show weakness and fragility and are often divided by internal differences or rendered ineffective by a lack of public support.

Walesa must be given credit for trying to build a strong presidency in the post-Communist era. As the incumbent in the early 1990s, he tried to place the presidency above politics, to make it the leader of all the Polish people, not simply of those who voted for the incumbent. He tried to keep the presidency above narrow political conflicts, avoiding identification with nascent political parties or direct involvement in their organizational affairs. Furthermore, Walesa has sought to assert his decision-making authority by expanding his influence over the executive branch of the government. He has provided members of his staff with power to influence government operations in the areas of national defense, foreign affairs, local government, and the economy. He also has played an active role in selecting members of the Council of Ministers.

ECONOMIC REFORMS

Former premier Mazowiecki announced in September 1989 his intention to introduce capitalist practices to revive Polish economic life. He found the going tough, for at least two reasons. First, he had to reduce party control over economic enterprises. Second, as state control ended and private entrepreneurialism was introduced, ordinary Polish people were going to suffer even more: Prices based on supply and demand would remain prohibitively high for most, and production would not increase substantially right away.

The success of domestic reforms depended partly on debt relief. Poland needed outside help in easing its enormous debt burden. In the summer of 1989, it owed Western creditors about $39 billion and the Soviet Union $6.5 billion. The new government sought help in the form of a major rescheduling of debt payments, new loans, and increased foreign investment. It looked for help to the IMF and the World Bank as well as to West Germany and the United States. By the end of 1989, both the Sejm and the Senate had approved a program of radical reform that put Poland in the forefront of the movement toward capitalism in Central/Eastern Europe. In addition to ending price subsidies, this new law terminated price controls, transferred many state-owned companies to private ownership, and allowed employers to dismiss redundant employees to cut costs and increase efficiency. The law also provided for bankruptcy proceedings in the case of firms unable to make a profit. This program made Polish currency convertible, was supposed to promote financial accountability in industrial management, and laid the groundwork for an expansion of both industrial and agricultural output.

Problems Promoting Privatization

Privatization has proceeded very slowly. People do not have the resources to buy the large industries that the government wants to sell. Most Poles, with an average per capita income of $2,000, have barely enough cash to buy food, never mind stock. The government also has difficulty assessing the real value of the enterprises to be sold, often overvaluing them—or, more often, undervaluing them, thereby encouraging the people who do have spare capital, namely former Communists, to buy them at bargain prices. Poland also lacks an effective banking system to provide the credit to finance purchases and operate enterprises. Poland lacks computer systems, so it often takes banks weeks, not hours or days, to cash checks and transfer funds from one geographic location to another. Privatization is hamstrung also because of the lack of an adequate communications infrastructure, essential for a complex capitalist economy. Poland also lacks people with managerial skills capable of running the large, complex enterprises that it wants to privatize. Nor does Poland have business schools and other educational institutions to provide a reservoir of trained executives for the management of private firms. Finally, many of the large enterprises that the government wants to unload are so inefficient that no one wants them.

In June 1991 the Polish government introduced an imaginative program to increase the reservoir of potential buyers of state concerns. All of Poland's 27 million adults will receive vouchers in the form of what is called National Wealth Management Funds. These are to be the Polish equivalent of U.S.-style mutual funds, with each citizen owning about $9,000 worth of shares. Under the plan 60 percent of each enterprise's shares will go to the Funds for distribution to the general public, while the remaining 40 percent will go to the employees of the enterprise and to the central government in Warsaw. A lead shareholding of 33 percent should go to one fund, with the remaining 27 percent distributed equally among other funds, with the idea that one investment group will take primary responsibility for overhauling a particular enterprise. Fund managers are not to be allowed to own shares, except to the extent that fees paid to them may be in shares as opposed to cash. The Polish government hopes that this program not only will allow privatization of about 7,000 enterprises by the end of 1994 but also will have some positive political fallout, in the sense of involving as many people as possible in the ongoing process of economic transformation.

The High Economic Cost of Rapid Change

Other reforms to move the country toward a free market capitalist economy included slashing inflation to 40 percent, a far cry from the 2,000 percent rate, or hyperinflation, that the country had at the end of 1989; making food lines a thing of the past—it was now possible to buy anything in Warsaw for a price; and stabilizing the Polish currency, which at long last was made convertible. Its value against Western hard currencies steadily rose in the 2-year period of intensive reform, and the black market in currency virtually faded away.

But these reforms caused enormous hardship for Polish citizens, who could not afford to buy even simple necessities. To make matters worse, production plunged by more than 25 percent in 1990, partly because of economic turmoil in the Soviet Union. Poland also needed to pay for expensive energy imports at world market prices. Finally, the disruption of old patterns of trade within the region, which had been run by the now inoperative Council for Mutual Economic Assistance, had not yet been replaced by new ones, and so the government had little capital to soften the blow of economic dislocation.

A possibility of renewed social turmoil threatened Polish economic reform in early 1992. The country had suffered a 10 percent decline in industrial outlook and a sharp rise in unemployment throughout 1991. Making matters worse was a Russian decision to interrupt deliveries of natural gas to Poland to allow Russian producers to sell more of their output to buyers with hard currency. The Russian action, which violated a previously signed trade agreement, caused the shutdown of Polish industry and paralyzed the already enfeebled national economy.

Prime Minister Olszewski wanted to ease the hardships of ordinary Polish citizens by guaranteeing prices for farmers, providing financial help to potentially profitable state enterprises as an alternative to privatizing, lowering interest rates, and printing more money. But President Walesa opposed this conservative approach, insisting that Poland should stay the course in its rapid transition to the free market and echoed the IMF demand that Poland accept a harsh stabilization program as the prerequisite for receiving Fund credits and the forgiveness of half of Poland's enormous foreign debt. Eventually, Olszewski opted for a continuation of the "shock therapy" approach, despite its political risks.

By the end of the first quarter of 1992, one could point to significant, if modest, achievements of reform: Real wages had risen in 1991 by 3 percent and a private-sector boom had occurred that promised more and better jobs and an eventual easing of inflation. Furthermore, large Western investment was coming to Poland: In February 1992, General Motors Europe

agreed to a $75 million joint venture, in one of the largest external investment deals in Poland since the collapse of Communist rule.

Olszewski's successor, Prime Minister Suchocka, continued progress toward free enterprise. Determined to brook no opposition to privatizing the country's remaining state-controlled enterprises, she told angry workers and frustrated managers in September 1992 to decide how to terminate state control: They could try to survive by trimming the work force and pursuing other cost-cutting procedures, or they could accept closure. Suchocka took the unprecedented step of firing workers who refused to end strikes at factories on the verge of collapse. The IMF acknowledged the progress Poland had made, and was trying to make, under Olszewski and Suchocka. In November 1992 the IMF allowed Poland to draw on about $700 million. This paved the way for additional debt relief from Western creditors who had promised to forgive 50 percent of Poland's indebtedness provided it could reach an agreement with the IMF.

The High Political Cost of Rapid Change

But Suchocka's success in the economic sphere cost her dearly in politics. She lasted in power less than a year. Although public opinion polls showed her to be immensely popular with the public and although she had successfully steered Poland further toward a market economy, she had alienated important groups in the Parliament, notably deputies associated with Solidarity. They and others, including some of her own supporters, dealt her a serious blow in March 1993, when Parliament rejected a government bill to accelerate the move toward capitalism by privatizing 600 state-owned enterprises, fearing additional unemployment and increased misery for already hard-pressed wage earners. Although Parliament reversed itself and passed the privatization bill on April 30, 1993, it was still worried about moving too far too fast toward the market economy and uneasy over Suchocka's aggressive approach to the introduction of free enterprise. Many in Parliament also resented Suchocka's refusal to grant pay raises to striking health workers and teachers and increases in pensions, as there was no money to pay for them. She was determined not to rekindle inflation. She also had difficulty with President Walesa, who favored a softening of her austerity policies to ease the hardships of workers. The prime minister had been pulled in one direction by free market reformers responding to pressures

from the international financial community, which tied the granting of much-needed credit to Poland to pursuit of an anti-inflationary austerity. She was pulled simultaneously in the opposite direction by Polish society and its representatives in Parliament who wanted relief from the hardship caused by the rapid pace of Poland's move toward the free market economy.

Suchocka's position by the end of May 1993 was untenable. Walesa decided against a cabinet reshuffle. He preferred to ask the public for its opinion, no doubt hoping that Poles would support the moderate groups that had done so much to move the country away from the old socialist order. He dissolved Parliament, and elections were scheduled for the end of September.

The parliamentary elections in September 1993 gave the parties on the left a plurality. The Democratic Alliance of the Left, made up of former Communists, won 20 percent of the popular vote, the left-wing Peasants' Party won 15 percent, and a grouping made up of the left wing of Solidarity won 7 percent. Suchocka's Democratic Union won 12 percent. The most plausible explanation for the success of the left was voter anger over economic hardships, especially inflation and unemployment. Farmers were especially infuriated over the failure of the Suchocka government to give them relief from the flood of subsidized agricultural imports from the European Community and the EC's barriers against Poland's products. Indeed, 51 percent of the electorate voted, a rather high turnout for Poles and a sign of their unhappiness. At the same time, people were annoyed by the sustained efforts of the Catholic Church to expand its political influence over post-Communist Poland, as seen in its aggressive lobbying for a strict ban on abortion, which does not have the support of most Polish voters, despite their loyalty to the church. Many educated young people, especially women, who were not particularly sympathetic to the Democratic Alliance, voted for it because it had promised to overturn recent anti-abortion legislation. Finally, the left won because of Suchocka's perceived failure to empathize with the plight of the workers. She either did not know how badly off many workers were—and this is hard to believe—or she did know but decided to stay the course for the sake of completing the transition to capitalism in the short term and of assuring continued financial support by the West.

The shift to the left should not be dangerous to Poland's reform program, which already is well established and would be difficult, if not impossible, to reverse.

Left-wing leaders, including Democratic Alliance leader Alexander Kwasniewski, have reassured both the Polish public and the international community that they have no intention of backtracking on reform and fully intend to continue the transition to a free market economy, though somewhat more slowly than Suchocka because of their concern to avoid the buildup of social tensions. However, the new prime minister, Waldemar Pawlak, still the leader of the Peasants' Party, which cooperated with the Democratic Alliance in the early 1990s, tried to appoint ministers to key economic posts who wanted to preserve a large amount to state control over the economy. But Pawlak had to back off. Fearful of antagonizing the West, the Democratic Alliance insisted that Pawlak select ministers who favored privatization and continued movement toward the free market economy.

CONTROVERSIES SURROUNDING THE CHURCH

The Polish Catholic Church has long had enormous credibility with the Polish people because of its outspoken opposition to the Communists. It has tried to expand its influence with the help of the Vatican. The church is working to make Poland a role model for Catholicism in post-Communist Central/Eastern Europe. In 1990 Poland's bishops won a big victory, with Parliament's approval of a return of religious education to the schools.

Behind this ambitious agenda is the church's worry that it might lose the loyalty of the young people as a democratic and capitalist society opens itself up to materialistic values and attitudes. Sure enough, the new education policy has sparked controversy, with the Protestant minority complaining that the return of religion to the classroom will foster division among students and even encourage intolerance and acts of discrimination.

With the pope's aggressive advocacy, the Polish church has supported restrictions on abortion. But most Polish people oppose restrictions. In 1990 the Sejm refused to pass a restrictive abortion bill endorsed by the pope.

The Polish government, and in particular President Walesa, who is very loyal to the church, are in a quandary. While the Warsaw government does not want to antagonize the Vatican, it also cannot ignore popular misgivings about the church's effort to influence how Poles live. Leading politicians have responded with silence to demands from the church for the rewriting of the Polish Constitution to omit clauses that guarantee the separation of church and state. Parliament also has not supported the church's desire to limit the number of divorce courts. Despite evidence that its political efforts are losing popular support, the church still tries to strengthen its political influence by urging the faithful to vote for candidates, in particular those of the Catholic Action Committee, who espouse Christian values and oppose abortion.

Muddying the situation is an oblique linkage of the church to a resurgence of anti-Semitism in Poland. Anti-Semitism is bizarre in Poland because most Polish Jews died in the Holocaust. Of those Jews remaining after the war, most emigrated when the Communists took power. But the church aroused anti-Semitic feelings when, in 1990, Cardinal Glemp entered a dispute over the location in 1984 of a convent at the site of the Auschwitz death camp. Jews had objected to this convent dedicated to Catholic values, in the light of the special significance of Auschwitz for Jews. In fact, the church had signed an agreement to remove the convent. But Glemp angrily declared that Jews were attacking Polish feelings and national sovereignty and were using the "Jewish controlled" Western media to promote their views. Glemp provoked an angry outcry from Jewish groups in the West and embarrassed the new non-Communist government, which wanted the friendship and support of Western countries. The government considered Glemp's remarks very damaging to the world prestige of Poland as well as to the harmony, unity, and peace of an already deeply conflict-ridden Polish society. Nudged by an embarrassed Vatican to take a more conciliatory stand on the issue, Glemp eventually retreated, saying that Catholics in Poland knew too little of the sentiments of the Jews and the wounds that remained from the Holocaust.

FOREIGN POLICY

Reform in the domestic sphere in the late 1980s influenced Polish foreign policy because the Polish political leadership looked to both East and West for support of its version of perestroika. But there were problems that caused tensions in Polish–Soviet relations; and while relations with the West, in particular West Germany and the United States, steadily improved, there were difficulties with these countries, too.

The Soviet Union
Polish relations with the Soviet Union were very good in the late 1980s. Jaruzelski looked to Gorbachev for friendship and support in his efforts—ultimately futile, of course—to stabilize and legitimize socialist rule in Poland in the face of mounting popular opposition to it. Jaruzelski scored points with Gorbachev in 1988 and 1989 for having enthusiastically supported Soviet perestroika, in contrast to the stubborn resistance to it of the East German, Czechoslovak, and Romanian leaderships. Jaruzelski was thought well of in the Kremlin also for having taken care in the transition to non-Communist government in the summer of 1989 to protect the instruments of Communist Party power in Poland and to guarantee Poland's continuing commitment to the Warsaw Pact, the CMEA, and Moscow.

Gorbachev reciprocated by backing all Jaruzelski's decisions to loosen Communist Party control of Poland in 1989. The Soviet leader approved, albeit reluctantly, the April 1989 agreement between the Warsaw authorities and Solidarity that legalized the union and provided for radical changes in electoral rules for June 1989, which allowed Solidarity to obtain control of the Senate. He also raised no objection to Jaruzelski's appointment of a non-Communist prime minister in August 1989. Thus, Soviet policy toward Poland had significantly changed from what it had been under Brèzhnev, who would have fiercely resisted the weakening of Communist influence in Poland that Gorbachev was willing to accept in the expectation that liberalization would strengthen, not weaken, the chances for survival of the socialist system.

The Soviets also accommodated the Poles on a more difficult issue: the Kremlin's candor in Polish–Soviet relations. Reform-minded Polish leaders wanted the Soviet Union to acknowledge responsibility for its actions during World War II, which were suppressed by the Communists in the past but which most of Polish society knew about. Warsaw wanted the Soviets to speak frankly about the Soviet–German Non-Aggression Pact of August 1939, which led to the invasion of Poland; the mass deportation of Poles from Soviet-occupied Poland between 1939 and 1941; and the Katyn Forest massacre in 1940, when the Soviets killed about 10,000 interned Polish officers and enlisted men.

In early 1989 the Polish government issued a formal charge of Soviet responsibility for the massacre, specifically indicting Stalin's secret-police establishment, the NKVD. The Kremlin initially refused to acknowledge responsibility for Katyn. A Polish–Soviet commission formed in 1987 had investigated the massacre for more than 2 years but had not issued a formal report, despite intense pressure from the Polish side. All that the Kremlin had been willing to allow, because of its acute sensitivity to the Katyn issue, was discussion. For more than 40 years successive Soviet leaderships had blamed the Nazis for the killings. But in April 1990 the Kremlin finally stopped lying about Katyn and acknowledged Soviet responsibility for the tragedy. Gorbachev personally delivered to Jaruzelski, during a meeting in Moscow, documents that made clear that the NKVD, Stalin's secret-police apparatus, had killed thousands of Polish officers in the Katyn forest. TASS immediately published an official Soviet expression of regret for the tragedy.

The Kremlin was also forthcoming in regard to the Soviet–German Non-Aggression Pact. It acknowledged that there were secret protocols that provided for the partition of Poland and which led very shortly afterward on September 1, 1939, to the German invasion of western Poland. This Soviet gesture provided Warsaw with at least a moral if not a legal basis for demanding of the Soviet Union at some future time the return of deported Poles scattered throughout the Soviet Union and for making other claims, such as for war reparations.

There were several reasons for this Soviet candor. First was Gorbachev's sympathy for Jaruzelski and his interest in doing what he could to strengthen the Polish leader's political situation. Second was his commitment to glasnost, which extended to foreign as well as domestic Soviet behavior. Finally, there was a strategic consideration. Gorbachev wanted to strengthen Polish–Soviet relations in an era when Poland might be under non-Communist rule and both countries will need to cooperate to meet the challenge of a powerful united German state.

The number-one issue in post-Communist Poland's relations with the Soviet Union was the withdrawal of 50,000 Soviet troops from Polish territory. The continued presence of Soviet troops heightened Poland's sense of vulnerability to the Soviets. Moreover, with guarantees of its western border from Germany, it no longer considered itself mortgaged to the Soviet Union for defense.

The Soviets were slow to leave. The reason was partly logistical. The Soviet military's links to its much larger contingent of troops in what was formerly East Germany ran through Poland, and Moscow said that it would take at least through 1993 to complete the Soviet military withdrawal from Eastern Germany. But it was also true that the Soviet military was dragging its feet for reasons of pride and prestige. Legal, financial, and property issues also had to be settled: Moscow wanted compensation from the Polish government for military housing built in Poland, and Warsaw filed a counterclaim demanding that the Kremlin pay for the damage done to its environment by the long Soviet military presence. Behind this rhetoric was the Soviet military leadership's general discomfort over the way in which it had to curtail Soviet military strength in an area of historic importance for Soviet security.

However, after the failed August 1991 coup attempt in the Soviet Union, troop withdrawals accelerated. In October 1991 the Kremlin agreed to withdraw the remaining 45,000 Soviet troops by the end of 1992. The Kremlin had apparently abandoned efforts to use a definitive agreement on troop withdrawal as leverage to get the Poles to accept a bilateral political agreement with a provision barring Poland from joining NATO or any other alliance regarded as hostile. The Poles had balked at making such a deal, rightly seeing it as an attempt on the part of the Soviet Union to recoup some of the influence it had lost with the demise of the regime in Warsaw in 1989.

Russia finally completed the withdrawal of all ex-Soviet troops from Poland in September 1993, but Warsaw remains uneasy about the future of relations with the Russian Republic. Polish leaders worry about the growing influence over Russian domestic and foreign policies of a large constituency of conservative and ultra-nationalistic politicians, especially their chief spokesperson, Vladimir Zhirinovsky.

President Walesa's efforts to obtain full membership for Poland in NATO to strengthen its security vis-à-vis Russia antagonized the Kremlin and provoked a stern Russian warning against NATO membership for any of the ex-Soviet Union's allies in Central/Eastern Europe. In early 1994, to the dismay of Russian leaders, Walesa barely concealed his disappointment over an American proposal, the so-called partnership for peace, to admit Poland and its neighbors only as junior members of NATO, without the security guarantee that full members have and Poland desperately wants. While there were no serious issues dividing Poland and Russia in early 1994, nor could it be said that their relations were good and getting better. Warsaw is watching with some anxiety political developments in Moscow and continues to be concerned about the relationship between the two countries as moderate and conciliatory elements lose influence within the Russian leadership establishment.

The West

Poland desperately needed Western economic, technological, and financial assistance. In the short term, it needed help to relieve immediate emergencies like the scarcity of food. Jaruzelski asked the Western powers at their summit in Paris in July 1989 for a multibillion-dollar emergency aid package over the next 2 years, with $1 billion allocated for food, $2 billion to support the economy through 1992, a rescheduling of the Polish debt by Poland's Western creditors, and a series of measures to enhance Poland's export capabilities. Jaruzelski also sought assistance in Poland's privatization of the economy. He wanted help with several projects in fields such as mining, telecommunications, and banking; with private foreign investment in Poland; and with the modernization of the agricultural infrastructure.

The Polish regime's high expectations of the West were not unreasonable. For years the West had let it be understood that any serious help for Poland's devastated economy and $39 billion of debt to the West was contingent on the regime's agreeing to legalize Solidarity and move toward democracy. Now that that had happened, the Polish government expected help.

The two Western countries to which the Poles now looked were the United States and Germany. While Bonn and Washington expressed satisfaction over the extensive political changes about to take place in Poland, they reacted with caution and restraint.

The United States

Since coming to power in August 1989, the non-Communist leadership has looked to the United States for support. The United States, after all, had urged Poland to stand up to the Soviet Union. The Poles have sought an American aid program of Marshall Plan dimensions. Poland, moreover, needs and wants close ties with the United States to counterbalance the vast, if somewhat benign, economic influence of Germany.

But so far the United States has provided limited help, nowhere near the scope sought by President Walesa. The Bush administration, taken by surprise when Communist party rule in Central/Eastern Europe abruptly collapsed in 1989, was reluctant to give large amounts of financial assistance without a planned program of aid that clearly defined goals and methods. U.S. officials also wished to be sure that Poland really wanted a free market economy. Aware of the slowness of privatization in Poland and the continued power, by whatever label, of Communists in top managerial positions, the Bush administration was determined to wait before considering large grants of aid. In addition, it preferred to have the Central/Eastern Europeans help themselves rather than provide massive support. It was also true that in light of its own economic recession, the United States had "more will than wallet," as Bush said. Nevertheless, partly in response to support in Congress and among the voters, especially those of Polish-American origin, the Bush administration made several, if modest, gestures of financial support to Poland. It supported loans to Poland by the IMF and the World Bank. And in March 1991, during Walesa's visit to Washington, the Bush administration agreed to erase 70 percent of Poland's $3.8 billion debt to the United States. Then, in June, the United States agreed to allocate $15 million to help develop Polish business, agriculture, and health services.

The Bush administration also began to pressure Japan to be more forthcoming with aid to the developing democracies in Central/Eastern Europe. The Japanese had not been sympathetic to the debt-forgiveness policy toward Poland. They were critical of American readiness to allow politics to influence, even prejudice normal business relationships, arguing that debt forgiveness was bad economics, encouraging irresponsibility among poor but spendthrift nations. Japan was especially annoyed by the American policy because it contradicted past U.S. behavior, which was very conservative on the issue of debt repayment—from Tokyo's point of view, a correct policy.

Poland and Germany
The Mazowiecki government watched with anxiety the unexpected progress that West Germany and the newly emancipated East Germany made toward reunification in 1990. The Polish people and their new leadership worried about Poland's strategic vulnerability to a united Germany with the political unity, economic power, and diplomatic will to lead and influence Europe in the next century. This worry was rooted, of course, in the brutal German treatment of Poland during World War II, when the Hitler regime attempted to go beyond mere conquest of Poland to achieve the systematic destruction of the country's national identity.

Contributing to Polish anxiety was the border question. One part of this question concerned the region known as western Pomerania, which consists of territory in northwestern Poland including Szcezin (in German, Stettin) and along the Baltic

coast. Poland acquired this territory from a defeated Germany after World War II as compensation for the loss of the eastern part of Poland, including the city of Lvov, to the Soviet Union. The Polish leadership was afraid that a powerful unified Germany someday would demand the return of the lost territory, because many of its inhabitants are ethnic Germans and some at least would prefer German to Polish rule.

In early 1990 Premier Mazowiecki asked West German chancellor Helmut Kohl, an ardent champion and facilitator of German reunification, to guarantee Poland's western frontier with Germany. Eventually, Kohl offered a compromise: West Germany would guarantee the Polish border if Poland agreed to give up any claims to reparations from Germany for the damage done to Poland during World War II and if it pledged fair, equitable, and tolerant treatment of the German-speaking minorities in Poland. Kohl's plan was met with suspicion about the real German intent with regard to the border. The Bush administration, as well as the Kremlin, put tremendous pressure on Kohl to back down, and in March Kohl agreed to propose that both German parliaments adopt matching pledges on the sanctity of the frontier. On March 8, 1990, the West German Parliament agreed that a united Germany should honor Poland's current boundary.

There was also a potential problem for Warsaw in Silesia, a highly industrialized coal-rich area in southwestern Poland that borders Germany and Slovakia. This region, inhabited by 600,000 to 800,000 people of ethnic German origin, was part of Germany before World War II. Among the Silesians of German origin there seemed to be a certain nostalgia for German rule, when life was easier and better than under Polish Communist rule. Contributing to this nostalgia was resentment among the German-speaking Silesians over Polish policy after the war, when Warsaw forced them to adopt Polish culture or be deported, and subsequently encouraged the migration of Polish citizens from other parts of the country to settle in Silesia and facilitate the imposition of Polish ways on the region. Especially disturbing was an apparent resurgence of Naziism in Silesia among some of the residents of the area whose only memory of German rule was the Hitlerian state. The Polish leadership, therefore, had good reason to worry about the future of Silesia and about its relationship to a powerful unified Germany.

The border question led the Mazowiecki government, which was not completely sat-

isfied with matching pledges from the two Germanys on Poland's western boundary, to demand a role for Poland in the international discussions of German reunification among the Four Great Allies (the Soviet Union, France, Britain, and the United States) begun in Ottawa in March 1990. In Ottawa the Allies agreed on the two-plus-four formula, which involved discussions by the two Germanys on technical details of reunification and discussions by the four wartime Allies on the acceptability of these details to all of Europe. Poland demanded that the constitution of a united German state should contain a provision guaranteeing the existing Polish–German frontier in perpetuity. At the opening of reunification discussions among representatives of the two Germanys and the four World War II Allies, an agreement was reached to include Poland in discussions about borders of the new state.

On November 14, 1990, the border issue was formally put to rest with the signing of a Polish–German agreement, which recognized the Oder–Neisse line as the permanent border between Poland and Germany. In addition, Foreign Minister Hans Dietrich Genscher pledged that Germany would help Poland and other Central/Eastern European countries to rebuild their economies to assure, as he put it, that "the frontier [between Germany and Poland] does not become a watershed between rich and poor." Genscher also announced Germany's intention to lift visa requirements for Polish citizens, allowing them for the first time since World War II to have easy access to a country within the European Community.

In June 1991, the issue of German reparations to Poland was settled in a manner somewhat favorable to Poland. Bowing to intense Polish pressure on Bonn to make restitution to Poles forced to work in Nazi labor camps during World War II, Chancellor Kohl announced that a new German–Polish friendship treaty, designed to mend the wounds caused by Germany's invasion and occupation of Poland beginning in 1939, contained a provision for German compensation. This treaty, which also pledged German financial help for Poland's economic reforms and assistance to Poland in gaining entry into the EC trading bloc, reaffirmed the German commitment before and after reunification to develop strong, close German–Polish relations.

Poland and Lithuania
Poland has always had close cultural and political links to Lithuania, which had been united with Poland in a confedera-

tion from 1386 until 1569. Lithuania remained an integral part of Poland until the partitions at the end of the eighteenth century. Conflict broke out between the two peoples in the late nineteenth century and persisted with increasing intensity in the period between the two world wars. A Lithuanian national movement arose in opposition to Polish culture in the late nineteenth century and in the immediate aftermath of World War I, when Lithuania became independent, along with Poland. The two countries fought over possession of Vilnius, which ended up as part of Poland in the interwar period. Many Poles regard Vilnius, originally called Vilna, as a Polish city and remember Vilnius as the home of some of their nation's greatest poets and politicians; some would like to see Vilnius returned to Poland.

Poland and Lithuanian Independence

In any event, Poland did try to encourage and help Lithuania toward emancipation of the Soviet Union at the risk of straining relations with Moscow; at one point the Soviets complained that Poland was interfering in the internal affairs of the Soviet Union.

Despite popular sentiment in favor of an early Polish recognition of Lithuania's independence, the Warsaw government was inclined to proceed cautiously in 1990. While Poland had a lot at stake in avoiding actions that might antagonize Moscow and provoke retaliation, say, in the form of foot-dragging on the issue of the Soviet troop withdrawal, it was also true that an independent Lithuania posed special problems for Poland. One had to do with the Polish minority of 300,000 people living in the countryside surrounding Vilnius. The other had to do with the uncertainties surrounding Poland's boundary with Lithuania.

The Polish Minority in Lithuania

The Polish leadership remained uneasy over the excessive chauvinism of the government of Vytautas Landsbergis, afraid that it would try to homogenize Lithuanian society at the expense of its minorities. Poles in Lithuania felt discriminated against by the Lithuanian government, especially since the surge of Lithuanian nationalism at the end of the 1980s. Polish regions reportedly received 50 percent less funding from the Vilnius government than Lithuanian ones, and ethnic Poles claimed that their region had the lowest per capita number of doctors, hospitals, schools, and telephones in Lithuania. Adding to interethnic antagonism were class-based distinctions between Poles and Lithuanians:

Poles in Lithuania were mainly workers and peasants without a local intelligentsia that could act as intermediaries for the Polish community with the Lithuanian leadership. Lithuanian nationalists were annoyed by the preference of Poles, who entered higher education, for the study of Russian, which was close to their own language, rather than Lithuanian, on the assumption that fluency in Russian would be more useful than fluency in a language spoken by only a very small minority in the Soviet system. The Polish minority strongly resented Lithuanian language laws of 1988 and 1989 that established Lithuanian as the official state language and made no concession to districts in Lithuania that were predominantly Polish. Finally, more than half of the Polish minority, fearful of its status under a nationalist leadership, opposed Lithuania's independence and supported preservation of the Union to which Lithuania technically still belonged until the independence decrees of Moscow following the abortive anti-Gorbachev coup in August 1991.

While Warsaw was concerned about the fate of the Polish-speaking minority in Lithuania, it did little to encourage its achievement of increased autonomy of Vilnius. The Polish government did not want to antagonize the government in Vilnius, which certainly would have taken umbrage over any Polish effort to champion the cause of autonomy for the Poles living permanently in Lithuania. Nor did Poland want to raise the hopes for autonomy of the small Polish minorities living in Byelorussia and Ukraine or, worse, arouse fear in the governments of these republics of the prospect of Polish territorial claims against them in the future. Also, the post-Communist Mazowiecki leadership had a bit less sympathy for the Polish minority in Lithuania than one might have expected, because Polish government officials with roots in the Polish intelligentsia were more interested in contacts with their Lithuanian counterparts in the Vilnius administration than they were with Polish-speaking Lithuanians, who had little in common with them intellectually. In sum, there was some mistrust between Poles in Poland and the Polish minority in Lithuania. The government in Warsaw hoped that the government in Vilnius would take care to avoid blatant acts of discrimination that might force a reluctant Warsaw to champion the rights of Lithuanian Poles.

Nevertheless, the Polish government did speak out strongly against the Vilnius government decision on September 4, 1991, to dissolve the two self-governing

Polish regional councils and to impose direct rule on the areas inhabited primarily by people of Polish culture. According to the Lithuanian side, the action was the result of the alleged support by Polish Lithuanian citizens of the failed anti-Gorbachev coup as well as their boycott of the 1990 referendum on independence, which had been approved overwhelmingly by ethnic Lithuanian voters.

The Polish Boundary with Lithuania

Another major issue in Polish–Lithuanian relations concerns the border between the two countries. As a consequence of the August 1939 Molotov-Ribbentrop Pact and related agreements, Lithuania gained territories that had belonged to Poland in the interwar period. According to the secret protocols of the pact, Lithuania and eastern Poland were to fall within the Soviet sphere of influence. After the Soviet Union's conquest of eastern Poland in September 1939, Stalin gave Vilnius to Lithuania. In the fall of 1940, after Lithuania was annexed by the Soviet Union, Lithuania received additional Polish territories which Stalin had originally given to Byelorussia. The postwar Polish–Soviet border, which was imposed on Poland by Stalin, was confirmed in an August 16, 1945, Polish–Soviet treaty. In declaring their independence in March 1990, the Lithuanians repudiated the Molotov-Ribbentrop Pact once and for all, but they did not reject the territorial changes brought about by the pact—changes that worked to Lithuania's advantage. The Lithuanians feared that Poland might in the future attempt to reclaim territories, especially Vilnius.

Poland, however, is unlikely to make border claims against Lithuania or any other of its eastern neighbors, because any such demands would encourage German groups, if not the German government itself, to call for a reassessment of the November 1990 German–Polish treaty of guarantee confirming Poland's post–World War II western border. Moreover, any territorial claims by Poland would impede its progress back to Europe. Polish leaders have given oral assurances of their country's disinterest in reclaiming lost land and have acknowledged that Vilnius is now a Lithuanian city. But, just as oral assurances by German leaders on the permanence of the German–Polish frontier had not been sufficient for Poles, so Polish oral assurances on the Polish–Lithuanian border will not be sufficient to quiet Lithuanian anxieties. The border remains a hidden issue in Poland's relations with the new Lithuania.

Independence
1918
●

Poland is
invaded,
partitioned, and
occupied by Nazi
Germany and the
Soviet Union
1939
●

Polish
Communists and
like-minded
political groups
coalesce to form
the Polish United
Workers' Party
1947
●

Polish industrial
workers strike in
Poznan for
economic and
political
concessions
1956
●

Students' and
workers' strikes
in Warsaw
against regime
repressiveness
1968
●

The regime's
announcement of
increased food
prices provokes
industrial strikes
and
demonstrations
1970
●

Another
announcement
of increased food
prices provokes
a wave of
industrial strikes
1976
●

Industrial unrest
spreads quickly; the
establishment of
Solidarity; martial law;
Solidarity is banned

1980s–1990s

Martial law is
lifted; political,
economic, and
social liberal-
ization move
briskly forward;
Walesa becomes
president

The last Russian
combat troops
are withdrawn
from Poland

Constitutional
Tribunal upholds
the legality of
compulsory
religious
teaching in public
schools; parties
on the left win a
plurality in
parliamentary
elections

Relations with Hungarians, Czechs, and Slovaks

While its relations with the former Soviet republics continue to be problematic, Poland has sought the friendship and co-operation of the new democratic governments in Hungary, the Czech Republic, and Slovakia. All four countries have much in common: a shared colonial past, an interest in limiting Soviet and Russian influence in Central/Eastern Europe while continuing to maintain good relations with Moscow, the need to cooperate in solving regional problems such as environmental pollution, and a concern about German economic expansion.

Working together, however, will be difficult. In the Communist era, Poles, Czechoslovakians, and Hungarians often found it more difficult to meet one another than Westerners: Borders were difficult to cross, and barriers of language and of diverse ethnic and historical conditions were steep. In recent years there have been personality clashes: Polish president Walesa does not especially like Czech president Vaclav Havel, with whom he has had some difficulty getting along because each comes from different backgrounds: Havel is an intellectual, while Walesa lacks advanced educational training and comes from the working class. Finally, there is an economic diversity that reinforces differences among the countries: They all have different levels of economic well-being. They are introducing economic reform at different rates of speed, with the Poles moving fastest toward free enterprise and a market-based economy.

Nevertheless, the impetus for working together seems to outweigh the obstacles to cooperation. Several international events tended to push the four states closer: the erosion and subsequent dissolution of the Warsaw Pact and CMEA; the emergence of the U.S.–led Gulf alliance against Iraq, which jeopardized an important source of energy for Central/Eastern Europe; and the destabilization of the Soviet Union after the August 1991 anti-Gorbachev coup and the collapse of the Soviet state in December 1991. Moreover, there is the possibility, however remote, of an attempt by the Russian republic to regain lost influence in Central/Eastern Europe. In the spring of 1991, some conservative Soviet foreign policy strategists publicly advocated the use of energy supplies and the manipulation of exports to exercise leverage over the foreign policies of the Central/Eastern European countries. And between February and late April 1991, the Kremlin tried to get the new post-Communist governments in Warsaw, Prague, and Budapest to sign a basic treaty with the Soviet Union stipulating that they would refrain from joining an alliance (i.e., NATO) directed against the Soviet Union. (Such a treaty could also have applied to membership in the European Community.) Poland, Hungary, and Czechoslovakia opposed this move.

Polish, Czechoslovakian, and Hungarian diplomats conferred intermittently on problems of regional concern, notably at Bratislava in April 1990, at Visegrad in February 1991, and at Krakow in October 1991. At Bratislava, they merely agreed to meet again to discuss matters of common interest. At Visegrad they agreed to endorse several statements of principle to guide future discussions, in particular their shared commitment to making their countries part of the EC. President Walesa also suggested the importance for Poland, Hungary, and Czechoslovakia of approaching the EC not in competition but in cooperation with one another. At Krakow the three leaderships discussed their relationship with NATO. They suggested the establishment of more than political links, namely, links similar to those existing among NATO members. The Poles joined their Hungarian and Czechoslovakian colleagues in expressing concern over the expanding civil war in Yugoslavia and insisting on the inviolability of the country's pre-war internal boundaries.

DEVELOPMENT

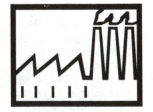

An overwhelming public consensus in favor of radical change, an explosion of pent-up entrepreneurial spirit, and a relatively productive agricultural sector account for the success in 1993 of Poland's "shock therapy," or rapidly paced introduction of the free market economy. The Polish economy today is much healthier than it was in 1989 but still has severe problems.

FREEDOM

In the 1993 parliamentary elections, voters freely and with some enthusiasm returned the left to power. The Democratic Alliance of the Left of ex-Communists made the largest gain. Voter support for the left appeared rooted not in any nostalgia for the old Communist regime but in concerns of workers threatened by the rapid pace of economic change. The success of the left was a reflection of strong popular interest in the old social security system.

HEALTH/WELFARE

Underneath the new wealth in Poland is a current of concern over those who are being left behind. Nobody knows exactly how many people are really poor, but President Lech Walesa has said that about one-third of the population, mainly entrepreneurs, are doing better; one-third, mainly urban wage earners, are the same as under communism; and one-third, mainly the unemployed and the elderly, are worse off.

ACHIEVEMENTS

Poland is the first Central/Eastern European country to show economic growth after the fall of communism. By September 1993 the annual growth rate was 4%. In 1992 the private sector contributed a minimum of 45% of Poland's gross domestic product, up from 10% in 1989. Poland's exports abroad have soared, from $8 billion in 1988 to $14 billion in 1993, with 80% of 1993 sales headed to the West.

Romania

GEOGRAPHY

Area in Square Kilometers (Miles):
237,499 (91,699) (slightly smaller than Oregon)
Capital (Population): Bucharest
(2,064,000)
Climate: moderate

PEOPLE

Population
Total: 23,172,000
Annual Growth Rate: 0.02%
Rural/Urban Population Ratio: 45/55
Ethnic Makeup of Population: 89%
Romanian; 9% Hungarian; 2%
German, Ukrainian, Serb, Croat,
Russian, Turk, and Gypsy
Languages: Romanian; Hungarian;
German

Health
Life Expectancy at Birth: 68 years
(male); 74 years (female)
Infant Mortality Rate (Ratio):
21/1,000
Average Caloric Intake: 126% of
FAO minimum
Physicians Available (Ratio): 1/472

Religion(s)
70% Romanian Orthodox; 6%
Roman Catholic; 6% Protestant;
Jews, others, or unaffiliated

Education
Adult Literacy Rate: 98%

COMMUNICATION

Telephones: 1,960,000
Newspapers: 60

A LONG ROAD TO DEMOCRACY

Old habits die hard in Romania. Under the Communist regime, which was the most repressive in Central/Eastern Europe, Romanians were forbidden to own typewriters without police permission. That rule no longer exists, but the mentality that inspired it still prevails, and any journalist whose writing is disliked by the authorities is subject to punishment. Under Ceausescu the Romanian Legislature was a "rubber stamp" for regime policies. In today's Romania the national Legislature is not much better: The public is denied information and even access to it, draft bills cannot be scrutinized, and the influence on policy making of newly formed interest groups is severely limited. Post-Communist Romania still has a long way to go before it achieves a Western-style liberal democratic political system.

TRANSPORTATION

Highways—Kilometers (Miles):
72,799 (45,208)
Railroads—Kilometers (Miles):
11,275 (7,002)
Usable Airfields: 158

GOVERNMENT

Type: democratic republic
Independence Date: August 23, 1878
Head of State: President Ion Iliescu
Political Parties: National Salvation
Front; Democratic National Salvation
Front; National Unity Party; Magyar
Democratic Union; National Liberal
Party; Civic Alliance; Agrarian
Democratic Party; Democratic
Convention; National Peasants'
Christian and Democratic Party; others
Suffrage: universal and compulsory
over 18

MILITARY

Number of Armed Forces: 163,000
*Military Expenditures (% of Central
Government Expenditures):* 2.6%
Current Hostilities: none

ECONOMY

Currency ($ U.S. Equivalent): 470 lei
= $1
Per Capita Income/GDP:
$2,700/$63.4 billion
Inflation Rate: 200%
Total Foreign Debt: $3.0 billion
Natural Resources: oil; timber;
natural gas; coal
Agriculture: corn; wheat; oilseed;
potatoes; livestock
Industry: mining; forestry;
construction materials; metal
production and processing; chemicals;
machine building; food processing

FOREIGN TRADE

Exports: $3.5 billion
Imports: $5.1 billion

ROMANIA

Romania paid a heavy price for its support of the Nazi invasion of the Soviet Union in June 1941. When World War II was over, the Romanians had to cede Bessarabia to the Soviet Union; pay reparations to the Soviets and other Central/Eastern European countries invaded by the Nazis; and, worst of all from the point of view of Romania's King Michael, allow Communists to participate in the national government. And that was only the beginning. With Soviet support the Romanian Communists, who formed with other reformist elements the Romanian Workers' Party (RWP) in 1947, expanded their influence throughout Romanian society and ultimately forced the king's abdication in December 1947. The RWP converted Romania into a republic and in 1948 proceeded to eliminate political opposition and to establish state control over industry, agriculture, and foreign trade.

In the late 1940s, the RWP leadership was divided into so-called nativist and Muscovite groupings, the former having spent the war years in Romania, and the latter having stayed in the Soviet Union in continuous contact with the Soviet leadership. But the RWP leadership was in agreement on fundamentals: It was committed to imposing the Soviet socialist model on Romania and to remaining loyal to Soviet foreign policy. By 1953 Romania had become a Soviet satellite.

MONARCHICAL SOCIALISM

Under the leadership of Gheorghe Gheorghiu-Dej and his successor, Nicolae Ceausescu, who became RWP first secretary in 1965 and president of the republic in 1974, Romania remained faithful to the Soviet model. Gheorghiu-Dej and Ceausescu tolerated no challenges to democratic centralism inside the party and no expression of political criticism among the Romanian people. They were also very sensitive to the slightest expression of hostility toward the Soviet Union.

Another dimension of the regime's repressiveness was the personality cult around Ceausescu to compensate for the regime's waning popular support, legitimacy, and authority. Ceausescu's birthday was a national event in which journalists and public figures tried to outdo one another in praising him. His home village of Cornicesti contained a memorial house and a museum and became a national pilgrimage site with almost religious overtones.

The Ceausescu personality cult included a vicious nepotism. He gave close relatives enormous political influence. His wife, Elena, for example, was a full member of the Political Executive Committee (PEC), equivalent to the Soviet Politburo. She was also first deputy prime minister and head of the party's cadre commission, which oversaw all personnel matters. Ceausescu also continued the practice of rotating individuals in and out of party and government positions to prevent party officials from establishing a solid geographic or organizational base from which to challenge him.

For the most part, the RWP's political authoritarianism was acceptable to the Romanian people. Liberal and democratic ideas never took deep root in Romanian society. Even when Romania had parliamentary institutions in the 1920s and 1930s, the political system was democratic only in appearance. The Romanian people historically have admired charismatic leadership. Economic conditions also made authoritarian government expedient. To strengthen and modernize the Romanian economy, the Communists insisted upon social discipline and absolute obedience to party rule.

The RWP leadership showed some independence in foreign policy, inspired by a nationalism born of a strong and long-standing hostility toward the Russians. Since Romania's political independence in 1878, the Czarist government and its Soviet successor had threatened Romanian territorial integrity. Romanians rightly feared the Russians and believed that they intended someday to dismember and annex Romanian territory.

The groundwork for Romania's independence of the Soviet Union in foreign policy was laid shrewdly by Gheorghiu-Dej in the late 1940s and early 1950s. By convincing Moscow of his own personal loyalty, he was able to obtain its approval of changes in the RWP leadership, in which he gradually removed Muscovites.

The Soviets hardly noticed, until it was too late, their loss of influence over RWP decision making. The Kremlin's influence was further eroded when, in 1958, it removed Soviet troops from Romania. The Sino–Soviet dispute in the 1960s also diminished Soviet influence over the Romanians by demonstrating to them the limits of Soviet capability to oppose the independence of other socialist countries with which it had disagreements. The first expression of Romanian independence of the Soviet Union was Gheorghiu-Dej's 1957 announcement of a decision to accelerate industrialization. This decision ran counter to a Soviet-inspired policy of the Council for Mutual Economic Assistance, which sought to have Romania concentrate on agricultural expansion and to export primary products to the already industrialized socialist countries in the north.

In the 1960s and 1970s, the Romanians differed with the Soviets on many international issues. They maintained party and state ties with China despite its dispute with the Soviet Union. Romania also insisted on Soviet respect for the principles of Communist party autonomy and noninterference in the internal affairs of other parties. The Romanians thus opposed the Soviet intervention in Czechoslovakia in August 1968, despite a dislike of Czechoslovak leader Dubcek's liberalization policies, and endorsed the advocacies of autonomy by the Eurocommunist parties in the 1970s, despite opposition to their liberal ideas.

Romania also proceeded independently of the Soviets in its relations with the West. It was the first Central/Eastern European country to respond to West Germany's Ostpolitik (the policy of good relations with socialist countries in the Soviet bloc) and to restore relations with Bonn in 1968. Romania also sought an expansion of trade with the West.

Romania gave special attention to relations with the United States, a source of desperately needed industrial technology. Ceausescu paid several visits to Washington, seeking more trade and the credit needed to finance Romanian industrial expansion. This policy paid off; Ceausescu was more successful than some other East bloc leaders in obtaining American trade concessions, including most-favored-nation status.

Another example of Romania's foreign policy independence was opposition to a Warsaw Pact proposal to increase defense spending. Ceausescu instead reduced Romanian defense expenditures, to allow increases in spending on social welfare. He supported multilateral nuclear disarmament in Europe and called for the withdrawal of Soviet troops from Afghanistan. He also defied the Soviet boycott of the 1984 Summer Olympics in Los Angeles. The Romanians also reaffirmed their misgivings about membership in CMEA and the Warsaw Pact.

Soviet Toleration

The Kremlin tolerated Romanian independence in foreign policy mainly because of its conformity in domestic policy. The Soviets understood how Ceausescu's challenges, the result of nationalism, strengthened his control over the country and its commitment to socialism. Romania also had not threatened Soviet regional power nor compromised Soviet or Soviet bloc security.

Romania's independence of the Soviet Union in foreign policy eroded somewhat in the late 1980s. By turning to the Soviets for oil, Ceausescu weakened Romania's unique influence in the Arab world. Furthermore, when Poland upgraded its ties with Israel in 1986, Romania's relations with Israel became less strategically significant for the United States. And with the visits of East German and Polish Communist leaders to China in 1986, the significance of Romania's having been the only Warsaw Pact member to maintain links with China during its long dispute with the Soviet Union diminished.

ETHNIC PROBLEMS

Although Romanian society is made up principally of ethnic Romanians, there are several minority groups. Of these, Hungarians and Jews have attracted attention in the West, because of their complaints of official discrimination. The egalitarian principles of Marxist socialism did not seem to have applied to these peoples, despite special provisions for minority groups in the Constitution.

Discrimination against Hungarians and Jews

Approximately 1.7 million Hungarian-speaking people live in the Transylvanian region of Romania, which was part of Hungary before World War I. Romania's Hungarian-speaking citizens complained of discrimination in education and employment and accused the authorities in Bucharest of trying to Romanianize them by making fluency in the Romanian language obligatory for jobs and even to obtain food in state stores. These complaints were taken up by the Hungarian government; but when protests were made to Bucharest, the official response was that Hungarian-speaking citizens received the same treatment as Romanians. Therefore, there was "no discrimination."

Hungarian-speaking citizens tried to emigrate to Hungary. But when they did, they confronted obstacles in the form of overelaborate bureaucratic procedures for getting exit visas and the payment of an obligatory tax (although eventually this was lifted in response to complaints and threats of retaliation from the United States). The Hungarian minority living in Romania was virtually marooned; and there was little prospect of change, because of the hypernationalism of the leadership and a historic ill will toward Hungary, due to its alleged mistreatment of Romanians living in Transylvania prior to World War I.

Tensions between the two countries reached an all-time high in the spring of 1987. The Hungarians charged that Romania was steadily diminishing the rights of the Hungarian-speaking population in Transylvania and was destroying their cultural identity by preventing the circulation of Hungarian newspapers and confiscating Hungarian-language books. The Romanians countered with accusations of Hungarian atrocities against Romanian-speaking people in the region when it was under Hungarian control during World War II. Hungarian officials did not deny the Romanian revelations, but they did condemn them as a propaganda maneuver.

Both sides were warned by the Soviets to keep a lid on this dispute and to work to resolve it by themselves. During his visit to Romania in May 1987, Soviet party leader Mikhail Gorbachev pointedly reminded his hosts of Vladimir Lenin's view that issues like the treatment of national minorities in a socialist society must be handled with "delicacy and care."

Romania came under substantial pressure from outside the socialist community to alter its policy toward its Hungarian-speaking citizens. A Helsinki Watch Group report encouraged the UN Human Rights Commission to investigate accusations of widespread human rights abuses in Romania.

Another minority problem involved Romania's Jews, who were convinced that the historic anti-Semitism of Romanian society persisted and that there was discrimination against them everywhere. The Jewish population of Romania, drastically reduced as a result of official persecution during World War II, when Romania was an ally of Nazi Germany, had diminished even further in recent times.

Romanian Jews began to speak out against their government's perceived discrimination in the 1970s. People with Jewish names, they said, did not get the same treatment as others. There were few Jews in the upper echelons of the Romanian Communist Party, and none was in the top leadership close to President Ceausescu. And when Jews tried to emigrate, they encountered difficulties.

The Ceausescu regime pleaded innocent to charges of discrimination. Romanian officials pointed to the existence of synagogues and kosher butchers to prove their point. They reminded others that Romania was the only country in Central/Eastern Europe to maintain relations with Israel after the 1967 Six-Day War.

Only outside pressure, in particular from the United States, seemed to make a difference for the Jews, albeit a modest one. When the Romanian government cur-

tailed Jewish emigration in the 1970s and imposed an emigration tax at the end of 1982, the United States warned that Romania would lose the newly acquired trade advantages that it had been seeking for so long. This warning caused the Romanians to relent. They allowed a substantial number of Jews to emigrate and in 1983 rescinded the emigration tax.

The regime, however, continued to mistreat members of other religions, such as Evangelical Christians, Seventh-Day Adventists, and Baptists. As a result relations between Romania and the United States deteriorated steadily. In 1987 the U.S. government removed Romania from the duty-generalized system of preferences—an action that may have cost Romania about $150 million in exports to the United States in 1988. A second setback was the bipartisan action of the U.S. Congress to suspend most-favored-nation status for 6 months or longer because of Romanian human rights violations. Yet the Ceausescu regime still did not curtail its repressive policies. Indeed, in an act of defiance, in 1988 it renounced most-favored-nation privileges with the United States.

ECONOMIC PROBLEMS

Romania continued throughout the 1980s to have one of the lowest standards of living in Central/Eastern Europe. There were chronic shortages of everything the consumer needed or wanted—especially food, much of which was exported to offset the country's indebtedness to the West incurred for the sake of industrial development. But food shortages were also the result of poor labor productivity, attributable in part to the absence of incentives, as Romanian agriculture still followed the Soviet model of collectivization. The country also lacked modern agricultural machinery. A shortage of energy was especially painful to Romanians: It increased their dependence on Soviet oil and imposed an unpleasant austerity.

The harshness of daily life provoked a renewal of social unrest in November 1987. Thousands of workers in Brazov, a model industrial city whose work force was supposed to be the elite of the Romanian proletariat, demonstrated in the streets, an event that was indicative of the depth of popular discontent.

Dismissing the country's shortages and other economic hardships as inconveniences that did not justify further reform along Soviet lines, the Ceausescu regime exhorted workers to expand productivity, threatened them with further wage cuts if they did not fulfill quotas, and called for "increased revolutionary awareness" among the people. It blamed the country's economic woes on inadequate loyalty and reliability of party leaders. And instead of looking to systemic reform to resolve these problems, Ceausescu opted for a diversion of resources from the military to the civilian sector.

POLITICAL PROBLEMS

Prospects of change in Romania in the late 1980s seemed slim, despite changes taking place almost everywhere in Central/Eastern Europe. Egoism or stupidity, or both, made Ceausescu stubbornly oblivious to the flaws and failures of his Stalinist-inspired policies. He was determined to transform Romania from a backward agricultural society into a socialist industrial nation, much like the one Stalin had tried to build in the Soviet Union.

Dissatisfaction with Ceausescu's leadership had been growing not only among hard-pressed workers but also among former high-ranking party officials, like George Apostol, Alexandru Birladeanu, and Constantin Pirvulescu, who had been disgraced for having revealed their disillusionment and disagreement with Ceausescu. In March 1989 they and others had sent a letter to the Romanian leader attacking his hardline policies, accusing him of violating human rights agreements, and condemning him for a gross mismanagement of Romania's economy. The letter called for the abandonment of Ceausescu's plan to eliminate villages and move peasants to new urban centers, and it took issue with an unpublished but widely feared law banning Romanians from talking to foreigners. This criticism was a significant challenge to Ceausescu's leadership, but it had little impact on his offending policies, which remained intact.

As late as November 1989, after the ouster of conservative leaders in East Germany, Czechoslovakia, and Bulgaria, the likelihood of change seemed slight. People feared the extraordinarily efficient and ubiquitous state security police, the Securitate. They lacked organization and had nothing comparable to Czechoslovakia's Charter 77 group. Also, leaders at the top of the party hierarchy seemed unified; there appeared to be no faction within the inner core of the party leadership willing to exploit the popular dissatisfaction with Ceausescu.

In addition, the Soviets were reluctant to do anything about Ceausescu, despite their intense dislike of his policies, especially his opposition to perestroika. Gorbachev was determined to refrain from interfering in Romanian internal affairs. He may have expected the Romanian

leader, who was in his early seventies and reputed to be ill, to resign and be succeeded by more flexible and pragmatic leadership. This is not to say that the Kremlin lacked leverage with the Romanians—the Soviet Union remained Romania's largest supplier of energy and chief trade partner. Still, Gorbachev was unwilling to exert economic pressure on the Romanian regime to induce a change in policy.

THE 1989 REVOLUTION

Thus, the sudden collapse of the Ceausescu regime in December 1989 came as a shock to everybody, including the Romanian people themselves, who were surprised by the spontaneity and success of their sudden explosion of resistance.

The beginning of the end of Ceausescu's rule occurred in Timosoara, in west-central Romania, where in early December security forces were carrying out orders to deport a dissident cleric of Hungarian background, Laszlo Toekes of the Reform Church, who was being protected by local citizens. With massive and brutal military force, killing hundreds of people, the Securitate attacked these people and others who were demonstrating in support of the beleaguered priest. To the shock of the police, the demonstrations not only continued but spread to other Romanian cities as news of the brutality spread.

By the third week in December, elements of the national army joined the insurgents in what was fast becoming a national insurgency against the regime, spontaneous in its origins but furious in its opposition to the old order. The army hated the regime because of its establishment and lavish support of the Securitate, a rival military organization favored by Ceausescu over the army, as well as because of its policies of reducing investment in the conventional military establishment and channeling these funds to the police. Eventually, with the help of the army, the insurgents captured Ceausescu and his wife and executed them on December 25. The trial and punishment occurred more quickly than most had expected because it was necessary to undercut the morale of the Securitate forces to discourage their continued fighting.

With Ceausescu gone, power passed into the hands of the Council of National Salvation, which consisted of a variety of Ceausescu's political opponents, including members of the Romanian Communist Party. The new administration quickly took steps in early 1990 to introduce political relaxation. There was a deluge of new policies. These included the lifting of

censorship; the acceptance of new, non-Communist political organizations demanding a share of power in the government of Romania; the formal abolition of the Communist Party's political monopoly; and the toleration of new freedoms of speech, assembly, and travel. Romanians were no longer required to register their typewriters, to address one another as "Comrade," and to submit to laws against abortion and the use of birth control devices. The new government also announced the immediate cancellation of Ceausescu's rural modernization program, which involved the destruction of many villages and the annihilation of much of the country's traditional village life. The regime abruptly ended Ceausescu's intolerable program of economic austerity and made available food that had been destined for export.

In the aftermath of this revolution, there seemed to be three sources of political power. One was the insurgency, a mixture of dissident elements with different ideas about what to do next, ranging from the complete destruction of the old socialist and authoritarian order to less extreme alternatives, which included a role for the Communist Party, albeit a totally reformed one under a pragmatic leadership sympathetic to a thorough, perestroika-like overhaul of the Romanian system.

A second source of political power was the Communist Party, or what was left of it following the removal of a large number of officials closely associated with Ceausescu. The party was totally discredited in the eyes of most Romanians. They began calling for its dissolution because of the excesses of its former leader. These calls intensified as a result of new revelations of the shocking personal corruption of the Ceausescu family, who apparently lived in a grotesque luxury while the rest of the country suffered miserably from acute and persistent shortages of everything. The party nevertheless angled to preserve some role in the future governance of Romania. It had a reasonable chance of achieving this goal because of its experience and the lack of any real alternative to it.

Third, there was the army, now the most powerful physical force in the country. It supported the Council of National Salvation and a program of radical reform of the Ceausescu order. However, it would not stand idly by if law and order broke down and the country sank into anarchy because of the Council's lack of authority. A military dictatorship that might lead eventually to a monarchical restoration still is not inconceivable—King Michael, the last sovereign of Romania, who left the county in 1948, offered to return home to lead his people.

Ceausescu's collapse was partly the result of Gorbachev's policy of noninterference. But other, equally important, determinants of the rapidity of change in Romania in December 1989 concerned the internal situation. In no other Soviet bloc country was the socialist regime more irrationally oppressive than in Romania. As a result of the excesses of the Ceausescu regime, there was a latent popular desperation, perhaps unequaled in its depth and severity elsewhere in Central/Eastern Europe. Consequently, the regime had almost no margin for error: One slip was all that was needed to provoke an explosion of popular wrath capable of destroying the system, despite its impressive defense mechanisms. Finally, there was the logical but unanticipated role of the Romanian Army, bent on retribution for the discriminatory policies of the Ceausescu regime; it called to mind the efforts of German officers in July 1944 to get rid of Adolf Hitler because of a pent-up desperation over his irrational policies and of the favoritism he showed the SS, the Nazi equivalent of the Securitate.

GROPING FOR DEMOCRACY

Many Romanians distrusted and disliked the National Salvation Front (NSF) and its chief executive, President Ion Iliescu. In mid-January 1990 Bucharest crowds demanded the resignation of both Iliescu and the prime minister, Petre Roman, as well as the immediate banning of the Romanian Communist Party. The NSF Council voted to ban the party but spoke of a Romanian "brand" of democratic development different from that of "outmoded Western democracies." Maintaining a strong grip over the mass media, the NSF obstructed political criticism. Independent newspapers and magazines had difficulty in getting newsprint supplies and making distribution arrangements. Opposition parties also had problems: they could not get office equipment or space. Some opposition politicians complained of harassment by security forces.

But in the face of the almost daily antigovernment demonstrations in Bucharest, the Iliescu leadership consented to share power with other opposition groups in a coalition. The NSF Council of 145 members was replaced by a new Council for National Unity of 180, representing the NSF and the 30-odd opposition groups. The NSF itself split into two sections, one concerned with administration and made up of the Council leaders governing the country, another concerned

with developing a new political party with candidates in the parliamentary elections scheduled for the spring of 1990.

The May 1990 Parliamentary Elections

Popular hostility to the Iliescu regime did not abate. At the end of April, some 40,000 people in Timosoara, the cradle of the anti-Ceausescu revolution, demanded Iliescu's resignation, accusing him of seeking to reestablish some form of communism in Romania. As the election drew near, the mood became bitter and divisive. The central issue in the elections—the first free elections in 40 years—was the credibility of the NSF and its leadership. Romanian voters were split between those who supported the Front (mainly industrial workers, miners, and other wage-earning groups) and those who opposed the Front (notably the intelligentsia).

The outcome of the elections was a disappointment for reformers. The Front won about two-thirds of the vote, a strong showing, even allowing for some high-handed, quasi-legal pressure tactics by the NSF to get out the vote in support of it. Perhaps the vote also reflected a greater popular concern for stability than for democracy and the success of the Front as well as Iliescu in exploiting a strong anti-intellectual bias among working-class Romanians. Ordinary people, Iliescu said, should keep the intelligentsia from power, because these privileged city people were rich and educated and unjustly looked down on them. This rhetoric called up the kind of radical-populist appeal made by Fascists in Romania in the pre–World War II period. Many wondered if Romania, despite its Marxist interlude, had ever lost its Fascist orientation.

Explosions of popular wrath continued after the elections. Many Romanians were furious over what appeared to many to have been an ill-conceived manipulation of the new political system by Communists. It was now common knowledge that the Front's list of parliamentary candidates for the recent election had included many of the former regime's regional Communist Party bosses and several former close associates of the late Ceausescu. In what was perhaps the worst episode of repression since taking office, the Iliescu regime called miners in northern Romania to Bucharest to help the government put down the demonstrations. About 7,000 miners, among the most hard-pressed of economic groups in Romanian society and the most supportive of Iliescu, whom they hoped would do something to improve their lot, mercilessly beat down and bloodied the demonstrators, bringing what

seemed to be an incipient coup d'etat against Iliescu to an end.

New Political Opposition

Opposition groups in Romania eventually began to grasp the weakness of their situation: They had been continually bested in their confrontation with Iliescu, especially in the elections, because of deep internal divisions which deprived them of leadership, cohesion, and unity. The opposition seemed willing to compromise and unify around one party, the Civic Alliance (PCA), which, in July 1991, pledged to transform itself into a national political party to challenge the Front in the next parliamentary elections, tentatively slated for June 1992.

The Alliance claims several million backers and is supported by the largest-selling antigovernment daily, *Romana Libera*. The Alliance in fact may signal a watershed in the political development of post-Communist Romania. Its leadership is drawn from the intelligentsia and consists of university rectors, medical doctors, trade-union leaders, lawyers, student activists, and artists. The young age of the leadership is indicative of the PCA's determination to represent young Romanians. And party leader Nicolae Manolescu seems to have no links with the discredited Communist past. Furthermore, the Alliance supports ties to the Western democracies and the protection of minorities and thus rejects the racist nationalism that seems to inspire other Romanian political groups, including the Front. The Alliance favors an independent media and strict control over the secret police. It champions a free market economy and substantial investment in the service industries.

Meanwhile, popular opposition to the NSF government persisted throughout 1991. In September 1991 aggrieved miners were back in Bucharest. This time they opposed the regime, blaming President Iliescu and Prime Minister Roman for the persistence of inflation, food shortages, and unemployment. Despite sharp social differences between the miners and the residents of Bucharest, there was an apparent solidarity between the two constituencies. This time the din was so loud, the demands so compelling, and the violence so threatening of anarchy—thousands of protesters of all persuasions and backgrounds penetrated the Parliament and firebombed the main television center—that Roman agreed to step down. He was succeeded by Theodor Stolojan, a former finance minister who announced in October 1991 that he intended to continue Roman's economic reform program but would try to make adjustments to quiet social discontent. He indicated his determination to stay with his predecessor's price hikes but said that he would allow some wage increments.

The September 1992 Elections

Iliescu and Stolojan managed to contain public discontent up to the parliamentary and presidential elections of September 1992, when the opposition had at last some chance to take its policies to the voters. The Democratic National Salvation Front, led by Iliescu, won 28 percent of the seats, the Democratic Convention won 20 percent, and former prime minister Roman's party, the National Salvation Front, won 10 percent with the rest of the seats divided among 5 other parties. In the presidential contest, 2 ballots were needed because none of the candidates won an absolute majority in the first instance: Iliescu won 48 percent of the popular vote versus 31 percent for Emil Constantinescu, the rector of Bucharest University, and 11 percent for Gheorghe Funar, a rabid nationalist who advocated suppression of minority rights and a return to a centralized economy. When the runoff was held 2 weeks after the first ballot, Iliescu obtained a clear victory, with 60.5 percent versus Constantinescu's 39.5 percent.

The results of the parliamentary and presidential elections signified popular acceptance, at least for the time being, of Iliescu's conservatism. Iliescu stood for retention of many former Communists in positions of political influence and for proceeding only very gradually toward reduction of state control over the economic life of the country. On the other hand, Iliescu did not do as well in 1992 as he had in 1990, when he won 85 percent of the popular vote. This decline in popularity undoubtedly was the result of worsening economic problems and the further pluralization of Romanian politics, which permitted the electorate some alternative choices. For example, Constantinescu advocated rapid movement toward a market economy and removal of Communists from government. He did well in the large urban centers but was unable to counter Iliescu's support in conservative rural areas.

Several factors influenced Romanian voting behavior in September 1992. There was a disquieting popular nostalgia for Ceausescu. Many voters still thought of him as a patriot and made daily pilgrimages to put flowers and candles at his grave. Underlying this nostalgia were terrible economic conditions. Daily necessities were scarce, inflation was rampant, and 1 million jobs had disappeared.

According to one Romanian pollster, people were taking a second look at the Communists, considering both the positive as well as negative aspects of their rule and judging that there was much good, such as full employment and price stability, under Communist rule. For many Romanians Iliescu seemed to express association with what was good. Rural voters were strongly supportive of Iliescu because he had returned land and awarded them pensions. Finally, the conservative outcome of the elections could be traced to a pervasive fear of the future: Romanians, especially in the countryside, craved political stability and had tired of the party conflicts in Bucharest that had been magnified in the campaign.

Having said all of the above, it is still possible to find some positive aspects of the September 1992 elections in regard to the prospects for future democratic development. Constantinescu's ability to obtain the support of almost 40 percent of the electorate suggests the willingness of an increasing number of Romanians to support an alternative to the Iliescu regime. And Iliescu indicated sensitivity to the evident decline in popular support when he said that he would always bear in mind the views of the many people who voted for his opponent. Whether he will be more tolerant of opposition and responsive to alternative points of view remains to be seen; skepticism about his intent is not unreasonable, given his past behavior. Moreover, he has support in Parliament of his conservative policies. His government relies on a parliamentary coalition made up of his own party and other groups that share his conservative approach in the political and economic spheres.

A wild card in future Romanian political development is the miners, who have now become a visible political force in the country. They seem to have little understanding of or interest in democracy. Indeed, they see the myriad of political parties that Romania adopted after Ceausescu as little more than anarchy. The miners want relief from the austerity policies that accompanied the introduction of a market-driven economy; some frankly acknowledge that all they had demonstrated for was some additional pay to improve their living standard, rather than the fall of the regime. Not surprisingly, therefore, economics as much as politics continues to destabilize post-Communist Romania.

ECONOMIC REFORM

The Romanian economy remains in desperate straits. Ordinary Romanian citizens live in hardship. Food and fuel are scarce. Prices are sky-high, making many necessities of daily life unaffordable for many wage earners.

The Iliescu regime reluctantly decided to introduce market forces and private enterprise, changes that in the short term have tended to worsen rather than improve living conditions. In February 1990 the regime allowed private businesses with up to 20 employees. Then it opted for a completely free economic system, on the assumption that a centralized sector could not coexist with a free sector and that economic life had to be in one camp or another. But privatization led to an increase of prices without an adequate expansion of supply; private enterprise in Romania has remained small.

There have been other problems. There was much opposition to NSF market reforms. Managers of economic enterprises, many of whom had been appointed by the Ceausescu government, were reluctant to implement changes leading to a market economy because they would lose their jobs and relative personal comfort. Members of the Parliament had reservations about undoing the social order too quickly. They were concerned with the social consequences of privatization, in particular price increases and unemployment. They did not want Romania to imitate Poland's "shock therapy" approach to the development of a market economy. The top leadership of the NSF, including Iliescu, sympathized with this conservative position.

After freeing up business, the regime did not go forward with other reforms. For example, Iliescu postponed for several months into 1993 a cut in state subsidies to certain enterprises. In early November 1992 he replaced Prime Minister Stolojan with Nicolae Vacaroiu, a technocrat with no ties to the Communist past. Vacaroiu's lack of political identity suggested that Iliescu may have wanted to invigorate the free market and regain some leadership in setting national economic strategy.

Private enterprise in agriculture promised initially to be more successful than in the manufacture and retailing of durable goods. In 1990 the regime distributed leaseholds to farmers amounting to almost one-third of the country's arable land, a stunning departure from the nearly 100 percent collectivized agricultural system left by Ceausescu. Romanian farmers showed some initiative and persistence and managed to increase the supply of meat and fresh produce in the unregulated farmers' markets. But prices of commodities in private markets were much higher than in state stores, which remain almost empty because of pent-up demand. Indeed, the sharp increase in prices for staples like bread, eggs, and meat led the regime, beginning in April 1991, to provide compensatory cash handouts and to allow wage increases. By the beginning of 1992, a year after the reform law redistributing land had been in effect, however, there were serious problems in Romanian agriculture. Although agricultural cooperatives ceased to exist as of January 1, 1992, the overwhelming part of Romanian agriculture was unaffected, with most farmers still landless, still only employees of the former collective farms, now called agricultural associations, and still under management that consisted primarily of ex-Communists who were enriching themselves at everybody else's expense. The government had failed to provide the farmers with the wherewithal not only to buy but also to cultivate the land they were supposed to obtain. There was no farm machinery for them—what there was belonged to the associations—and no gasoline to run the machinery, even if the would-be free farmers had had such machinery. In sum, the reform turned out to be only a beginning of private farming, with little of the follow-up needed to develop an efficient farm sector capable of feeding the country.

SOCIAL PROBLEMS

Romania confronts serious social problems inherited from the Ceausescu era, when they were all but swept under the rug by a socialist society that said it was perfect, or, at least, superior to the societies of the capitalist world. The primary problems have to do with ethnic minorities and AIDS.

Conflict between Hungarians and Romanians

Romanians in Transylvania distrust the Hungarian majority there. In the immediate aftermath of the December 1989 Revolution, the Romanians in Transylvania mobilized for resistance to demands of the region's Hungarian population for cultural autonomy. They set up an organization, called Romanian Hearth, committed to the perpetuation of Romanian cultural hegemony in Transylvania. The organization is highly nationalistic, somewhat right wing in its political thinking, and reminiscent of the chauvinistic and Fascist groups that sprang up in Romania on the eve of World War II. The danger in this organization lies in its ability to encourage and support physical violence by ethnic Romanians against their Hungarian neighbors. Evidence of their disruptive power occurred in March 1990 in Tirgu Mures. Crowds of

angry Romanian peasants attacked Hungarians with clubs and sticks, sending many to the hospital, and shattered the windows of stores owned by people with Hungarian names. The conflict shows no signs of abating, and many Hungarians hope for an eventual union of their region with Hungary.

Hostility toward Jews and Gypsies

Anti-Semitism is also on the rise. A gutter press spews hatred against all minorities, especially Jews. When, in what should have been a redemptive gesture, Romania dedicated in the summer of 1991 a memorial in Bucharest to the 400,000 Jews who fell victim to the local Fascist regime during World War II, people commenced with an ugly taunting of Elie Wiesel, a Nobel laureate who had survived the pogroms in Transylvania. Meanwhile, the Romanian Parliament "rehabilitated" Ion Antonescu, the Romanian ally of the Nazis who initiated the mass killings of Romanian Jews in the World War II era.

Worse off than the Jews in Romania today is the very small minority of Gypsies. Romanians have accused the Gypsies of black marketeering, saying that this is causing the shortages and high prices in Bucharest. Anti-Gypsy sentiment has erupted in pogroms, characterized by collective attacks by ethnic Romanians on rural communities inhabited by Gypsies. Local administrative authorities do little to punish the aggressors, thereby encouraging them. The failure to provide security of life and property to the Gypsy population may have a sinister motive: to make living in the country as uncomfortable as possible, thereby to encourage the emigration of Gypsies to other countries and to preserve "racial purity."

The AIDS Epidemic

Of all the legacies of the Ceausescu era, the epidemic of AIDS among newly born Romanian children may be the most grim. According to statistics gathered by Romanian virologists and confirmed by French doctors, Romania has an epidemic of AIDS, concentrated in crowded orphanages and clinics, which was spread by an old-fashioned practice of giving blood transfusions to newborn infants. This was compounded by poor equipment, bad medical practices, and large numbers of abandoned children born as a consequence of the prohibition of birth control devices and of abortion by the Ceausescu regime, which had been eager to swell the population of Romania. Hard evidence about AIDS among Romanian children was first reported only in June 1989, as a result of random testing for other viruses. When the

investigating doctors reported their findings to the central Ministry of Health in Bucharest, they were told bluntly to stop testing. They ignored this instruction and continued their investigation at different hospitals in the country; they discovered that children with untreatable AIDS-related infections were everywhere in the hospital system. The post-Communist leadership of Romania, hampered by a continuing shortage of equipment and a sluggish bureaucracy, never mind chronic instability and severe economic stagnation, has made scant progress in fighting AIDS.

FOREIGN RELATIONS

The post-Ceausescu leadership has had to make adjustments in foreign relations. Although its first concern was the Soviet Union and, following its collapse, the Russian republic and other former Soviet republics that border Romania, the Iliescu government has also been eager to improve relations with the West, especially the United States.

Russia and the Eurasian Republics

The new Romanian leadership looked to the Soviet Union for security and stability. Although relations with the Soviets had been poor, they improved as soon as the Ceausescu leadership, long an object of Soviet contempt and embarrassment, was deposed. In January 1990 then–Soviet foreign minister Eduard Shevardnadze said that he found the new atmosphere in Bucharest "absolutely purifying," and he pledged Moscow's support of any political system that the Romanians should choose. "Whatever political groups lead Romania is the business of Romanians themselves," he said. Nothing has changed since this declaration: the republics of the former Soviet Union have shown no interest in resuming Soviet-era influence over Bucharest and seem to want a normal relationship with Romania based on mutual trust and advantage.

But there are problems. One concerns the republic of Moldova. Largely inhabited by people of Romanian culture, Moldova was known historically as Bessarabia and was a part of Romania before 1878, and from 1918 until 1940, when it was ceded under duress to the Soviet Union. The future of Soviet Moldova became an issue with the advent of glasnost and a gradual opening of Moldova's frontier with Romania after Ceausescu's overthrow. For the moment, the open border, which has led to free movement of peoples between Moldova and Romania, has been peaceful. In August 1991, following the abortive anti-Gorbachev coup in Mos-

| Independence 1878 | Romania joins the Nazi invasion of the Soviet Union and recovers Bessarabia 1941 | Romania loses Bessarabia to the Soviet Union and pays war reparations 1944 | Soviet troops enter Bucharest to force King Michael to include Communists in his government 1945 | The Soviets withdraw their occupation forces from Romania 1958 | Gheorghiu-Dej dies; Ceausescu succeeds 1965 | The Ceausescu regime is deposed; Ceausescu and his wife are executed 1980s–1990s |

| Romania embarks on a new, hopefully better, economic, social, and political path | Iliescu and his NSF win parliamentary elections; a non-Communist economist, Nicolae Vacaroiu, is named prime minister | Romania agrees to accept Gypsy deportees from Germany; the United States gives Romanian trade most-favored-nation status |

cow, Moldova declared its independence of the Soviet Union, but it has not yet raised the issue of a possible transfer of Moldova to Romania, perhaps because of the hardship and misery in Romania. While emotional ties to the Romanian motherland are strong, and while their visits to Romania have been welcome, Moldovans are not yet ready to seek annexation to Romania. Ordinary Moldovans criticize the Romanian government for its communist tendencies, its antidemocratic policies, and its delay in reform. Moldovan Jews are wary of calls for Moldova's reunification with Romania.

Romania and the West

In 1990–1991 Romanian relations with the West, especially with the United States, were strained as a result of the Iliescu government's repressive policies, of its evident Communist background, and of its slowness in moving toward pluralistic democracy and free enterprise capitalism. The Western powers suspended major aid and cooperation with Romania, and the United States shunned the inauguration of President Iliescu in 1990 to protest his use of the miners to break up an antigovernment demonstration in Bucharest. Nevertheless, in 1991 Western Europe and the United States brought Romania into an aid program, set up a year earlier, which provided a total of $38 billion in assistance to Romania.

The United States, however, remained reluctant to replicate for Bucharest the assistance programs that it had formulated for Poland, Hungary, and Czechoslovakia. Indeed, the apparent shift in Washington's attitude toward Romania in early 1991 may have been merely a one-time reciprocation of Romania's support of the Allies in the Gulf War. While the United States would have liked to have helped Romania develop and maintain independence, Washington declined to offer Bucharest large assistance programs until it made more progress toward democracy, free enterprise, and equitable treatment of its ethnocultural minorities.

In 1992, however, the official American position on Romania seemed to soften somewhat, partly as a result of local elections held at the end of February. These were the first free local elections since the Communist takeover after World War II; they resulted in a setback for the ruling NSF. Although NSF candidates won most of the 1,340 mayoral races, candidates of democratic opposition parties won local government posts in the major Romanian cities, including Bucharest, confirming the extensive popular disillusionment with the NSF national leadership, which, to the surprise of Washington and other Western capitals, had done little to prevent the democratic ascendancy. The only negative feature of the elections, from the U.S. point of view, was the success of the extreme right-wing Romanian National Unity Party (RNUP) in the Transylvanian city of Cluj, which is inhabited by a large Hungarian ethnic minority. The RNUP favors a tough national response to the Hungarian minority's demands for increased cultural autonomy. Furthermore, Washington was still concerned about lingering vestiges of the old authoritarian order. These were the government's monopoly over television; the absence of parliamentary control over the intelligence service, which had replaced Ceausescu's Securitate, had reported directly to President Iliescu, and had been suspected of maintaining a domestic political surveillance program; and continuing violations of human rights, in particular a perceived official tolerance of anti-Semitism.

The new Clinton administration initially was concerned about the Iliescu government's reported discrimination against the Hungarian minority in Transylvania and mistreatment of the country's Gypsy population. Relations between Bucharest and Washington in early 1993 were cool, but by October the administration was ready to acknowledge the Romanian government's efforts to move the country toward a free market and restored most-favored-nation treatment to Romanian trade with the United States.

DEVELOPMENT

Romania continues to move slowly in the transition to a free market economy. The transfer of agricultural property to private ownership has barely begun. The expansion of industry is still hampered by a lack of management skills. The Iliescu regime has rejected a swift transition to a free market economy not only to avoid the kind of disruption caused by "shock therapy" in Poland but also to preserve as much as possible centralized power and state control.

FREEDOM

The peaceful parliamentary and presidential elections in 1992 showed Romania has made progress in its often clumsy march toward democracy. Nevertheless, in light of his authoritarian political style, Iliescu's electoral victory suggests that Romania is still far from having achieved a truly Western-style democractic political system. In addition, Gypsies continue to suffer from discrimination and occasional violence by ethnic Romanians.

HEALTH/WELFARE

Romania is afflicted with some of the worst pollution in the countries of the former Soviet bloc. An estimated 80% of Romania's rivers are polluted and 4,500 water purification plants ineffective. In the famous "black town" of Copsa Mica, for example, houses, trees, and grass are so coated with soot from a nearby chemical factory that the town looks like it has been soaked in ink.

ACHIEVEMENTS

In 1993 Romania regained most-favored-nation status for its trade with the United States. Although the commercial benefits of MFN are likely to be small in the short run because of the small amount of Romanian trade with the United States, the U.S. gesture had great symbolic importance for the Romanian government, helping to strengthen its legitimacy at home as well as abroad.

The Republics of the Former Yugoslavia*

BOSNIA-HERZEGOVINA

GEOGRAPHY

Area in Square Kilometers (Miles): 51,233 (19,776) (slightly larger than Tennessee)
Capital (Population): Sarajevo (n/a)

PEOPLE

Population
Total: 4,618,800 (data subject to considerable error due to military action and ethnic cleansing)
Annual Growth Rate: 0.72%
Ethnic Makeup of Population: 44% Muslim; 31% Serb; 17% Croat; 8% others
Major Language: Serbo-Croatian

Health
Life Expectancy at Birth: 72 years (male); 73 years (female)
Infant Mortality Rate (Ratio): 13/1,000

*NOTE: Maps in this volume weigh Kosovo and Vojvodina as separate republics. The lack of separate statistics for Kosovo and Vojvodina reflects the fact that, at this writing, they have not been internationally recognized as autonomous republics but, rather, are still legally categorized as provinces of Serbia.

THE DISINTEGRATION OF YUGOSLAVIA

The Yugoslav Civil War, which started in the summer of 1991 with federal military action to suppress separatist movements in Slovenia, Croatia, and, in the spring of 1992, Bosnia-Herzegovina, has killed thousands of soldiers and civilians, wrecked one of Central/Eastern Europe's most promising economies, created a half-million refugees, and stirred enough interethnic hatred to incite generations of future conflict.

Virtually no one in Yugoslavia believes that Yugoslavia still exists. Citizens, soldiers, and officials everywhere describe national disintegration as complete. Separate transportation, financial, and communication systems are beginning to rise from the ruins of the old Yugoslav state. Citizens and officials alike now frequently refer to "the former Yugoslavia" in their discussions.

Religion(s)
40% Muslim; 31% Orthodox; 15% Catholic; 4% Protestant; 10% others

Education
Adult Literacy Rate: n/a

GOVERNMENT

Type: emerging democracy
Head of State: President Alija Izetbegovic
Political Parties: Party of Democratic Action; Croatian Democratic Union of Bosnia and Herzegovina; Serbian Democratic Party of Bosnia and Herzegovina; Muslim-Bosnian Organization; Democratic Party of Socialists; Party of Democratic Changes; Serbian Movement for Renewal; Alliance of Reform Forces of Yugoslavia for Bosnia and Herzegovina; Democratic League of Greens; Liberal Party

ECONOMY

Currency ($ U.S. Equivalent): Croatian dinar or Yugoslav dinar
Per Capita Income/GDP: $3,200/$14 billion (estimates)
Inflation Rate: 80%

CROATIA

GEOGRAPHY

Area in Square Kilometers (Miles): 56,538 (21,824) (slightly smaller than West Virginia)
Capital (Population): Zagreb (n/a)

PEOPLE

Population
Total: 4,694,400
Annual Growth Rate: 0.07%
Ethnic Makeup of Population: 78% Croat; 12% Serb; 10% Muslim, Hungarian, Slovenian, and others
Major Language: Serbo-Croatian

Health
Life Expectancy at Birth: 70 years (male); 77 years (female)
Infant Mortality Rate (Ratio): 9/1,000

Religion(s)
77% Catholic; 11% Orthodox; 1% Slavic Muslim; 1% Protestant; 10% others or unknown

Education
Adult Literacy Rate: n/a

Republics of Former Yugoslavia
⊛ Republic Capitals
● City
〜 River
- - - Road
── Republic Boundary

0   100 kilometers
0   100 miles

GOVERNMENT

Type: parliamentary democracy
Head of State: President Franjo Tudjman
Political Parties: Croatian Democratic Union; Croatian People's Party; Croatian Christian Democratic Party; Croatian Party of Rights; Liberal Party; Croatian Peasant Party; Istrian Democratic Assembly; Social Democratic Party; Croatian National Party

ECONOMY

Currency ($ U.S. Equivalent): 60 Croatian dinars = $1
Per Capita Income/GDP: $5,600/$26.3 billion (estimates)
Inflation Rate: 50%

MACEDONIA

GEOGRAPHY

Area in Square Kilometers (Miles): 25,333 (9,778) (slightly larger than Vermont)
Capital (Population): Skopje (563,000)

PEOPLE

Population
Total: 2,194,000
Annual Growth Rate: 0.91%
Ethnic Makeup of Population: 67% Macedonian; 21% Albanian; 4% Turkish; 2% Serb; 6% others
Major Languages: Macedonian; Albanian; Turkish; Serbo-Croatian; others

Health
Life Expectancy at Birth: 71 years (male); 75 years (female)
Infant Mortality Rate (Ratio): 30/1,000

Religion(s)
59% Eastern Orthodox; 26% Muslim; 4% Catholic; 1% Protestant; 10% others

Education
Adult Literacy Rate: n/a

GOVERNMENT

Type: emerging democracy
Head of State: President Kiro Gligorov
Political Parties: Social-Democratic League of Macedonia; Party for Democratic Prosperity in Macedonia; National Democratic Party; Alliance of Reform Forces of Macedonia; Socialist Party of Macedonia; Internal

Macedonian Revolutionary Organization; Party of Yugoslavs in Macedonia

ECONOMY

Currency ($ U.S. Equivalent): 240 dinars = $1
Per Capita Income/GDP: $3,110/$7.1 billion (estimates)
Inflation Rate: 114.9%

FEDERATION OF SERBIA AND MONTENEGRO

GEOGRAPHY

Area in Square Kilometers (Miles): 102,350 (39,507) (slightly larger than Kentucky)
Capital (Population): Belgrade, Serbia (n/a); Titograd, Montenegro (n/a)

PEOPLE

Population
Total: 10,700,000
Annual Growth Rate: n/a
Ethnic Makeup of Population: 63% Serb; 14% Albanian; 6% Montenegrin; 4% Hungarian; 13% others
Major Languages: Serbo-Croatian; Albanian

Health
Life Expectancy at Birth: n/a
Infant Mortality Rate (Ratio): n/a

Religion(s)
65% Orthodox; 19% Muslim; 4% Catholic; 1% Protestant; 11% others

Education
Adult Literacy Rate: n/a

GOVERNMENT

Type: republic
Head of State: President Slobodan Milosevic (Serbia); President Zoran Lilic (Montenegro)
Political Parties: Serbian Socialist Party; Serbian Radical Party; Serbian Renewal Party; Democratic Party; Democratic Party of Serbia; Democratic Party of Socialists; People's Party of Montenegro; Liberal Alliance of Montenegro; Democratic Community of Vojvodina Hungarians; League of Communist-Movement for Yugoslavia

ECONOMY

Currency ($ U.S. Equivalent): 28.23 Yugoslav new dinars = $1

Per Capita Income/GDP: $2,500–$3,500/$27–$37 billion (estimates)
Inflation Rate: 81%

SLOVENIA

GEOGRAPHY

Area in Square Kilometers (Miles): 20,296 (7,834) (slightly larger than New Jersey)
Capital (Population): Ljubljana (323,000)

PEOPLE

Population
Total: 1,967,700
Annual Growth Rate: 0.23%
Ethnic Makeup of Population: 91% Slovene; 3% Croat; 2% Serb; 1% Muslim; 3% others
Major Languages: Slovenian; Serbo-Croatian; others

Health
Life Expectancy at Birth: 70 years (male); 78 years (female)
Infant Mortality Rate (Ratio): 8/1,000

Religion(s)
96% Roman Catholic; 1% Muslim; 3% others

Education
Adult Literacy Rate: n/a

GOVERNMENT

Type: emerging democracy
Head of State: President Milan Kucan
Political Parties: Slovene Christian Democratic; Liberal Democratic; Social-Democratic Party of Slovenia; Socialist Party of Slovenia; Greens of Slovenia; National Democratic; Democratic Peoples Party; Reformed Socialists; United List; Slovene National Party; Slovene People's Party

ECONOMY

Currency ($ U.S. Equivalent): 112 tolars = $1
Per Capita Income/GDP: $10,700/$21 billion (estimates)
Inflation Rate: 2.7%

YUGOSLAVIA

Yugoslavia, a federation of the south Slavic peoples created in 1918, was invaded and occupied by German and Italian forces during World War II. The Yugoslav monarch went into exile, never to return to his country. When the war was over, the Yugoslav Communists, under the leadership of Joseph Broz Tito, had achieved military and political dominance. Tito refused to allow a monarchical restoration. Yugoslavia became a republic in 1946.

Unlike most other Central/Eastern European Communist parties, the Yugoslav Communists were a popular political force because of their resistance to the Fascist enemy during the war. This popularity helped them to sweep the monarch aside, eliminate political opposition, and establish a Soviet-style dictatorship by 1947.

Tito's biggest problem in the immediate postwar period—a problem that still characterizes the republics of the former Yugoslavia—was assuring the loyalty of the different ethnic groups that comprised Yugoslavia's multinational society. In the early years of Communist rule, however, Tito's personal popularity, which had been reinforced by his successful resistance to Soviet pressures, was sufficient to guarantee a national unity needed to begin the transformation of the country to socialism. By 1953 Yugoslavia was a socialist dictatorship that in many ways resembled, but was in no way subservient to, the Soviet Union; it was not a Soviet satellite.

Yugoslav socialism tried to achieve three objectives: to foster societal harmony and national unity; to expand agricultural and industrial output in order to raise the standard of living of Yugoslav society; and to maintain ties with, but independence of, the Soviet and Western blocs. The achievement of these objectives was essential to the long-term stability and legitimacy of socialist regimes in Yugoslavia.

INTERETHNIC TENSIONS

The Yugoslav Communists inherited from their conservative monarchical predecessor a deeply divided, conflict-ridden multinational society. The dimensions of this ethnocultural and linguistic diversity were impressive. In the northern part of Yugoslavia were Croats and Slovenes, who belonged to the old Austro-Hungarian Empire, which had collapsed in World War I. They were the most economically developed of all the Yugoslav peoples and were predominantly Catholic. In the center of the country were Serbs, the first Balkan people to emancipate themselves from

Turkish rule (in 1828). The Serbs were the largest ethnic group in Yugoslavia, the most politically experienced of the Yugoslav peoples, and nominally of the Eastern Orthodox faith. In the south were other, smaller ethnic groups—Bosnians, Macedonians, Montenegrins, and Albanians—who were among the last to achieve independence of the Turks and who were less economically developed than the peoples in the north.

Conflict among these groups was historic and continued through World War II. It seemed to subside in the early years of Tito's leadership, because of his national popularity. But in the 1960s and 1970s, there was a distinct resurgence of interethnic hostility. This was largely in consequence of the sharp disparity in levels of material well-being among the different national groups. In the north the Croats and Slovenes and some Serbs were (and remain) much better off than the peoples in the south, many of whom were dreadfully poor.

Kosovo

Albanians living in Kosovo, a self-governing province in the Serbian republic, were another source of interethnic tension. The Albanians, 75 percent of Kosovo's population, lobbied aggressively for the status of self-governing republic, like that of the Serbs. The Albanians also resented other, smaller ethnic groups in Kosovo, a resentment fueled by economic poverty—Kosovo had the highest unemployment rate, the lowest per capita income, and the highest birth rate of all the regions in Yugoslavia.

Albanians used violence against Serb and Montenegrin minorities living in Kosovo, who in turn carried out their own counterprotests and demanded additional protection by the local authorities, who were predominantly Albanian. The Albanians seemed bent on forcing the Serbs and other non-Albanian groups to leave the province and to get republic status within the Yugoslav federation. While they did not appear interested in joining their cousins in the neighboring Albanian republic, which covertly encouraged the ferment in Kosovo, Yugoslavia's Albanian minority shared much in common with the independent Albanian state, in its political conservatism, economic backwardness, and cultural parochialism.

Yugoslav authorities in Belgrade worried that the bitter ethnic feuding in Kosovo would eventually lead to the emigration of all non-Albanian peoples from the province. Since 1981 more than 10 percent of the Serb population of Kosovo have emigrated. In 1988 and 1989, there were new outbreaks of ethnocultural con-

flict between Albanians and Serbs in Kosovo because of a depressed standard of living and because of a campaign by the Albanian majority to harass Serb residents by acts of terrorism. The Albanian authorities in Kosovo did little to protect the Serbs, and Serb republic authorities in Belgrade could not interfere with the province's autonomy.

Serb resentment of the Albanians in Kosovo steadily mounted. The Serb minority looked for help to the Serb party and state authorities and to their charismatic leader, Slobodan Milosevic, an aggressive exponent of Serb nationalism. He expressed concern over the plight of Serbs living among the Albanian population in Kosovo and encouraged huge pro-Serb, anti-Albanian rallies throughout the Serb republic. He supported a change in the Serb Constitution to increase the republic government's authority over the autonomous provinces of Kosovo and Vojvodina, and he replaced local political leaders in Kosovo and elsewhere in Serbia opposed to his policies. He wanted to establish Serb control of the police, court system, and civil defense of both Kosovo and Vojvodina, thereby lessening their autonomy; and, in the case of Kosovo, to prevent the provincial Albanian authorities from condoning the violence against the Serb minority.

In March 1989, in response to these efforts, there was an explosion of Albanian wrath. Tens of thousands of Albanians struck in Pristina, the capital of Kosovo, and other Albanians went on a rampage against Serbs, wreaking havoc by murder, rape, theft, and wanton vandalism. This episode turned out to be a personal political boon for Milosevic, increasing his popularity and the appeal of his calls for reform. By the summer of 1989, he had become the most powerful republic-level politician in Yugoslavia and an obvious candidate for national leadership.

Slovenia

Still another dimension of the nationalities problem in Yugoslavia involved the wealthy republic of Slovenia, which had the highest standard of living in the country and resented having to share its wealth with the much less developed southern republics, notably Bosnia-Herzegovina, Macedonia, and Montenegro. Slovenes made up only 8 percent of the Yugoslav population, but their republic produced 18 percent of Yugoslav gross national product and 25 percent of the country's exports.

While they did not immediately advocate separatism, the Slovenes wanted more independence of the central authorities in Belgrade, less official interference in the economic life of the country, and the opportunity to keep within Slovenia the wealth it generated—in short, a Yugoslav version of Soviet perestroika. These Slovenian ambitions illustrated in still another way how the rich-poor split of republics in Yugoslavia not only undermined its fragile national unity but also challenged its orthodox socialist system.

EFFORTS TO ENSURE UNITY

To maintain the loyalty of Yugoslavia's ethnic groups to the socialist system and thereby ensure political stability and administrative unity once he was gone, Tito and his successors modified the central government in Belgrade in the 1970s and early 1980s. The objectives were to provide equitable representation of the major ethnic groups and adequate means of reconciling policy differences among them.

The changes included a new head of state consisting of 9 persons, 1 from each of the country's 6 constituent republics and the 2 autonomous provinces, and 1 *ex-officio* member. A chairperson of this executive was to be elected annually on a rotational basis.

Ministerial leadership continued to be in the hands of the Federal Executive Council, or cabinet. This body was the real source of day-to-day governmental administration of the country, rather than the presidency, which was concerned primarily with ceremonial responsibilities. The Council was constructed to ensure equitable representation of the different ethnic groups. The Yugoslav national Legislature as well was organized to provide equitable representation of the national groups. Its upper house, called the Chamber of the Republics, consisted of members of the legislatures of the various republics and autonomous provinces.

Tito also made changes in the Yugoslav Communist Party. In 1952 the party was renamed the League of Yugoslav Communists, to stress its federative and collective character and to assure members of different ethnic backgrounds that the party would not try to destroy their cultural identities. Along with the change in name was a decentralization of authority. Leaders of republic-level party agencies dominated the central organs of the party in Belgrade. Representation in those central organs was apportioned equitably among the ethnic groups of Yugoslavia.

While these changes contributed to the development of some interethnic harmony in state and party agencies at the center, at the same time they contributed to divisiveness and conflict, especially within the party. The diffusion of power worked against cohesiveness in the party and encouraged competitiveness between republic-level party leaders, thereby weakening the party's leadership role in Yugoslav society.

ATTEMPTS AT PARTICIPATORY DEMOCRACY

The post-Tito leadership tried in the 1980s to increase participatory democracy in Yugoslavia without inducing pluralism and a threat to the Communist Party's monopoly of power. A new and complex process of electing members of the federal Assembly in Belgrade was supposed to stimulate popular interest in self-government. The process started with ordinary voters nominating delegates to communal assemblies, who nominated members of republic-level assemblies, who in turn selected the membership of the federal Assembly.

Yugoslav voters showed little interest in this cumbersome procedure. Candidates continued to be hand-picked and approved by Communist authorities. At the same time, the Assembly lacked the kind of authority in policy making enjoyed by legislatures in Western democracies and therefore did not inspire much popular interest.

The Yugoslav national leadership continued to insist on political conformity and severely limited expression of criticism, protest, and dissent. Milovan Djilas, an eminent and perennial regime critic, was still in some ways treated as a nonperson (he did, however, receive a passport in 1987), and the leadership still feared the ideas he had presented in his *New Class* more than 30 years before. Indeed, the establishment of Western-style political freedoms and of a multiparty system were forbidden topics of public discussion in the late 1980s, even in places like Slovenia, which was more politically tolerant than the other republics.

The elevation to the federal prime ministership in 1987 of Branko Mikulic, a hard-liner known for his criticism of internal dissidence, affirmed the Communist Party's determination to enforce a somewhat neo-Stalinistic political conformity throughout Yugoslav society. The conservatism of past Yugoslav leaders on the issue of political expression—which was at odds with their efforts to generate popular interest in government elections—was a result of the country's ethnic diversity, of a fear that toleration of pluralism would encourage ethnic particularism and national disunity, and of the problem of containing pressures for political liberalization that could challenge the Communist Party's control of the country.

ECONOMIC REFORMS

Starting in the 1950s, Tito introduced substantial decentralization and democratization of the Yugoslav economy in order to increase productivity. The Communist leadership returned some farms to private ownership. Private farms eventually had 83 percent of the country's cultivable land and 88 percent of its livestock.

In the 1960s the Yugoslav leadership reformed industrial management by increasing the autonomy of plant-level managers and diminishing the power of central administrators and planners. Yugoslav industrial production also took into account market forces, and prices were responsive to supply and demand. While there was a state planning agency in Belgrade that continued to draw up a national plan, production goals were determined by republic-level planning agencies, with the national agency serving primarily as a coordinator. These changes had a drastic impact on Yugoslav economic and social life. Enterprises produced what would sell and improved the quality of their output, and the economy became more consumer-oriented.

The establishment of "workers' councils" was the most controversial of Yugoslav economic reforms. The councils gave workers an opportunity to participate in managerial decision making and to share responsibility for running factories. In theory, at least, workers were entitled to help determine wages, plant renewal, and production rules.

A growing indebtedness to the West, however, beginning in the 1970s, and the appearance of recession in the early 1980s made it difficult to judge the effectiveness of the economic reforms. There were no startling increases in Yugoslav agricultural and industrial output. At the same time, unemployment climbed and prices rose, partly because of low labor productivity and the increase in energy costs.

While the concept of the workers' councils was very attractive, because it derived from Marxist ideas of direct worker ownership of the means of production, it remained controversial. It was criticized inside Yugoslavia on the grounds that it fostered individualism, competed with and undermined party rule, and increased anarchy in an already conflict-ridden society. Worse, it contributed to the development of a privileged class in a society that was supposed to be working to eliminate such distinctions.

Moreover, it became clear that self-managed enterprises had not worked as they were supposed to. They were unable to cut wages to the minimum to increase profit and had difficulty liquidating themselves, as required by law, when they were on the verge of bankruptcy. It would appear also that some workers in managerial positions often were not good decision makers.

By the late 1980s, inflation had become the country's number-one problem. In 1987 the Yugoslav economy had $21 billion of debt to the West; inflation was running at more than 200 percent; and 1 million, or 15 percent, of Yugoslav working people, were unemployed. Yugoslavia was suffering from the same kind of slowdown that afflicted almost all other Soviet bloc countries in the 1980s. It was attributable to a stagnant economy that desperately needed restructuring of the kind started by the Soviet Union, Poland, and Hungary in the late 1980s.

The galloping inflation seemed to defy economic solutions and forced the conclusion among party officials that the cause lay in the system of Yugoslav socialism itself. In this system workers' councils voted wage increases at the expense of investment. In addition, the monopoly status of many firms enabled them to fix prices at artificially high levels to justify the wage hikes voted by workers. Finally, cost-cutting measures to increase profitability, such as layoffs of unneeded and uneconomical labor, were unacceptable, because Yugoslav socialism was committed to full employment. A draconian program of quick-fix wage and price controls in November 1987 hardly made a dent in the inflationary spiral.

In May 1988 the central authorities in Belgrade adopted another austerity plan, on the prodding of the International Monetary Fund as a precondition for a $430 million loan. They imposed new wage ceilings and spending cuts while allowing prices to float upward. Living conditions for many Yugoslav citizens sharply deteriorated as earning capacity declined. Food shortages became so severe by October that the Belgrade government finally eased the austerity program and agreed to import emergency food.

While official economists, political leaders, and Yugoslavia's Western creditors all agreed that it was necessary to expand output by reliance on market forces, to close many unprofitable concerns, and to reduce substantially state control over the economic life of the country, the central leadership of the Communist Party, despite much discussion in 1988 and early 1989, was unable to agree on any decisive action. It could not depart from traditional orthodox socialist practices and was unable to goad the conservative bureaucracy to implement changes that inevitably would lead to a loss of jobs and a lessen-

(UN photo/Philip Teuscher)

These farmers selling their produce at a market in Sarajevo typify the movement to stimulate personal initiative as a means of increasing republic-level productivity.

ing of its influence and power over the country's economic life. The country's leaders also feared the destabilizing effects of strict application of laws providing for bankruptcy and the closing of unprofitable enterprises.

The new Yugoslav premier, Ante Markovic, in a televised address in January 1989, acknowledged the failure of socialism in its approach to the market and promised substantial curtailment of state interference in business. He promised to allow currency, prices, wages, and interest rates to move freely. And he spoke about opening the Yugoslav market to competition from imports and of inviting new foreign investment. Even Serb leader Milosevic supported the application of market forces to Yugoslavia, allying him with many of his detractors, including the Slovene leadership.

But by the end of 1989, the Yugoslav economy confronted four major problems that hampered growth and the achievement of improved living conditions: 1) the need to spend 44 percent of precious foreign currency to service a staggering foreign debt; 2) rising inflation and declining

exports, which complicated debt repayment; 3) a 14 percent unemployment rate; and 4) the continuing and unequitable division of the country into two economic spheres—one developed and relatively well off (in the north), the other underdeveloped and poor (in the south). Having reached the outer limits of change in the Yugoslav socialist economy, some officials wondered whether the time had come to introduce substantial private enterprise and lessen party and state control of the economy in order to stimulate personal initiative as a means of increasing national productivity.

FOREIGN POLICY

Perhaps the most important foreign policy objective of the Yugoslav state under Tito was independence of the Soviet Union. Throughout his period of leadership, Tito successfully resisted Soviet efforts to limit his independent foreign policy. A conflict with Stalin in 1948 merely strengthened Tito's resolve to go his own way in domestic and foreign policy. He opposed Soviet efforts in the early 1960s to isolate

China and to force other socialist countries, notably Czechoslovakia in 1968, to follow the Soviet line. Tito steadfastly refused to bring Yugoslavia into the Warsaw Pact and the CMEA, although in 1964 he sought and received for Yugoslavia affiliated status with the CMEA in order to facilitate trade with its members.

In the 1970s Yugoslavia diverged sharply from the Soviets on several matters. Following Mao Zedong's death in 1976, Tito undertook an improvement in relations with China. The Yugoslav leadership condemned the Soviet invasion of Afghanistan in 1979 and opposed the Soviets intervening in Poland in 1980 and 1981.

Yugoslav relations with the Soviet Union improved substantially in the late 1980s, however, mainly because Mikhail Gorbachev favored the autonomy of socialist countries. In March 1988 Gorbachev went to Dubrovnik, on Yugoslavia's Adriatic coast, to conclude a joint declaration in effect ruling out future Soviet interventions in Central/Eastern Europe. The declaration, intended to reaffirm Soviet adherence to agreements concluded in 1955 and 1956 establishing Yugoslavia's independence of Moscow, said that the two countries had no intentions of imposing their concepts of socialist development on anyone.

Although the Yugoslavs had not sought this declaration, which was the result of Soviet initiative, they did benefit from accommodating Gorbachev's request for it. By specifically acknowledging and thereby endorsing Yugoslav self-management policies—which, incidentally, the Soviets were beginning to copy—the declaration removed from the sphere of interstate relations an aspect of the Yugoslav reform program of which the Kremlin had been skeptical. The declaration seemed to imply that henceforth the Kremlin would not make an issue in diplomatic relations with Belgrade of advanced Yugoslav domestic reforms or radical foreign policy initiatives.

Yugoslavia also pursued a separate and independent policy toward the Third World. While sharing Soviet sympathy for revolutionary movements and left-leaning governments, it supported the policies of neutralism and nonalignment of Third World countries.

The Yugoslavs, however, began to reassess their leadership role in the nonaligned movement with the decline of the East-West rivalry. At the meeting of the nonaligned countries in Belgrade in September 1989, the Yugoslav delegates were somewhat embarrassed over the West-bashing by delegates from Libya and Cuba. Yugoslavia had increasingly looked to the West for stronger economic and political ties

and therefore was no longer as interested in occupying a middle position.

Yugoslavia also wanted to improve ties with Israel as a means of broadening its influence in the Middle East. Yugoslav and Israeli officials met in 1986, and Belgrade reportedly hosted secret Palestine Liberation Organization–Israeli meetings. Perhaps Yugoslavia planned to assume the role of peacemaker in the Middle East and in that way strengthen its influence with wealthy Arab states, which could provide some economic assistance.

Yugoslavia avoided the harsh and often belligerent anti-West rhetoric of the Soviet Union and its Warsaw Pact allies and, rather, worked to improve political and economic ties with Western countries. The Belgrade government showed an interest in joining the European Community. Major issues in the late 1980s in Yugoslavia's relations with the West were a rescheduling of the country's huge debt and an expansion of joint ventures.

Yugoslavia and the United States
The Yugoslav leadership went out of its way to cultivate good relations with the United States. Yugoslav leaders saw political ties with the United States as a counterweight to Soviet efforts to move Yugoslavia into the Warsaw Pact. An equally important objective of Yugoslav policy toward the United States was American economic assistance.

In recent years Yugoslav leaders had found Washington sympathetic to their requests for help and willing to make generous offers of financial aid, despite ideological differences between the two countries. The United States wanted to encourage Yugoslav independence, not only because of its importance to the security of Yugoslavia's non-Communist neighbors, Italy and Greece, but also because it contributed to the peace and tranquillity of the entire Mediterranean region. Moreover, a weakening and ultimate subversion of Yugoslavia by the Kremlin, never mind the disintegration of the Yugoslav state in consequence of civil war or economic collapse, would upset the strategic balance in Europe, to the detriment of NATO and American security.

The Impact of the Central/Eastern European Upheavals in 1989
The collapse of Communist party rule elsewhere in Central/Eastern Europe, as well as Lithuania's movement toward independence of the Soviet Union in late 1989, 1990, and 1991, contributed to a restiveness in Yugoslavia's northern republics of Croatia and Slovenia, where there had been much internal pressure for liberalization

and independence. The Slovenes in particular were more eager than ever before to abandon communism; to achieve sovereignty over their national life; and to strengthen political, economic, and cultural ties with Western Europe. Slovenes complained that their wealth was being drained by the demands of the impoverished south of the country. (In 1989 the annual per capita income in Slovenia was the equivalent of $5,700, vs. $2,500 for Yugoslavia as a whole and $750 for the province of Kosovo.) They resented the loss of 11 percent of their total earnings to the central government in Belgrade.

Slovenia, always more tolerant than the other republics of political discussion and criticism, allowed in February 1989 the establishment of two new political organizations that contested the Communist Party's monopoly of power in Slovenia. In December 1989 Croatia expressed support of a pluralist system. Addressing the Croat party Congress in Zagreb, party leader Stanko Stojecevic called for freedom of expression and association and early elections for a new federal Parliament. There was a strong Slovene–Croat entente in support of democratization of the Yugoslav national government in Belgrade as the only real way of ensuring the continued unity of the country.

Serbia, too, showed some interest in political liberalization. In 1987 a Serb presidential commission, under the direction of Milosevic, proposed changes in the Yugoslav Constitution limiting the Communist Party's monopoly of power, although not providing for the establishment of opposition parties. The proposals called for a transformation of the Communist Party-dominated socialist alliance into a pluralistic entity that would welcome all shades of opinion, for an end to party control of nominations of candidates in elections to legislative bodies, and for the institution of direct and secret elections. The commission also urged abolition of restrictions on speech and on political criticism throughout Yugoslavia as well as guarantees of freedom of thought and association.

The Serb proposals, however, were less radical than they appeared. The commission did not recommend a multiparty system; it reaffirmed the country's commitment to socialism; and it supported Communist Party rule. The commission insisted that the Communist Party play a necessary integrative role in what were described as the conditions of political and economic disintegration of society existing in Yugoslavia.

In early 1990 Croatia and Slovenia accused the conservative Serb leadership of seeking to destroy Yugoslavia by its perceived political conservatism, which was running against the tide of change elsewhere in Central/Eastern Europe—the Serbs wanted to preserve the Communist Party's leadership monopoly to control the federation. In response the Serb republic government broke off all economic relations with Slovenia. However, it was unable to block the national party leadership's approval of a recommendation in January 1990 to the upcoming national party Congress to allow other political parties to compete in parliamentary elections.

On January 20, 1990, the Yugoslav League of Communists met for the 14th Congress in Belgrade to address the new shape of Yugoslav government. Trouble began when the Congress opposed a transition from the old Yugoslav federal and socialist system to a federative, pluralistic, and democratic version. Serbia wanted to preserve the old Union of the Tito era; Slovenia and Croatia preferred a loose confederation, with the constituent republics and provinces largely autonomous in fiscal, monetary, and defense matters. In addition, liberals from Slovenia wanted the establishment of political pluralism and democracy in both the federal government and in party organizations; while conservatives, led by Milosevic, opposed liberalization. Milosevic believed that centralism could revitalize the party. He also had in mind his own elevation to the party leadership, with the support of the Serb republic delegation and the delegations from Vojvodina, Kosovo, and Montenegro to unify the country and restore a measure of discipline to Yugoslav society. This bid to preserve Communist power failed, and the Congress rejected Milosevic's schemes for an internal strengthening of the party under his leadership. Indeed, the Congress voted to end the party's monopoly of power. Nothing else was resolved because, when it failed to get an agreement on the confederative type of union or democratization, the Slovene delegation walked out of the Congress, forcing its adjournment and destroying any chances the Yugoslav Communists might have of reforming the Yugoslav political system.

Slovenia and Croatia Move toward Autonomy and Independence

On the eve of the republic-level presidential and parliamentary elections held in April 1990, Slovene voters and politicians were comparing themselves to Lithuanians, saying the Slovenes shared the feelings Lithuanians had of being a foreign element in their own country.

Although a conservative separatist-oriented coalition of political groups, known as Demos, won a majority in the lower house of the Slovene Parliament, there

was no evidence of a Slovene intention to adopt a Lithuanian-style unilateral declaration of independence. Unlike Lithuania, which was annexed by the Soviet Union, Slovenia joined the Yugoslav federation in 1918 voluntarily. Moreover, while Lithuania could exert little economic influence on the Soviet Union, that was not the case with Slovenia, which was critical to the economic well-being of the Yugoslav state and provided the republic with some leverage in dealing with Belgrade. It was possible that the Slovenes might now work more arduously for a substantial loosening of the federation to allow the republics maximum control over their internal affairs and to look to secession only as a last resort.

On the other hand, the defeat of the Communist Party in the Slovenian parliamentary elections (a Communist Party reformer won the republic's presidency), despite the party's reformist orientation and despite its role in sponsoring democratic reforms in Slovenia, including the republic's right to secede, confirmed the electorate's unequivocal hostility to Marxist-Leninism. It also confirmed Slovenia's eagerness to embrace Western-style political and economic institutions.

The results of the Slovenian elections troubled federal Premier Markovic, who was trying to unite the Yugoslav peoples in support of his belt-tightening economic policies. For example, the new Slovene government refused to support his proposal to amend the federal Constitution to give the national government in Belgrade taxation and monetary powers at the expense of the republics.

The anti-Communist and pro-independence movement in Slovenia also affected Croatia, which shared Slovenia's yearning for democratization and increased autonomy. On May 6, 1990, Croatia held republic-wide elections for a new Parliament. The Croatian Democratic Union, led by Franjo Tudjman, won two-thirds of the seats in the Zagreb Legislature, while the Communists won only 18 seats. The results showed that there was strong public sympathy for a transformation of the Yugoslav state into a confederation of autonomous republics.

But, unlike Slovenia, Croatia had a problem in the pursuit of autonomy—namely, the aspirations of the Serb minority of about 600,000 people in the southern parts of Croatia bordering the Serb republic in the east and along the Adriatic in the west. Leaders of the Serb minority demanded cultural, political, and territorial autonomy within Croatia. Intimidated by the new forceful expression of Croat nationalism in the April 1990

elections and the subsequent Croat declaration of sovereignty in July, the Serbs were afraid that if Yugoslavia became a confederation, an independent Croat republic, inspired by old prejudices dating back at least to World War II, when Croats fought Serbs, would try to obliterate Serb cultural distinctions for the sake of homogeneity-inducing unity.

The new democratic Croat government was sympathetic to the demands of its Serb minority for cultural autonomy. But it firmly rejected any kind of administrative autonomy. It called a demand of the Serb minority for a referendum on administrative autonomy unconstitutional, insisting that the republic's Constitution protected the rights of minorities in the republic. The leadership in Zagreb accused Serbia's President Milosevic of stirring up the Serb population in Croatia with a view to encouraging its union with Serbia. In any event, the referendum was held in August 1990, and 99 percent of Serb voters endorsed their political autonomy of Zagreb. On October 1, 1990, the Serb National Council, a local political party speaking for all Serbs living in Croatia, declared the territory inhabited predominantly by Serbs autonomous of the Croat republic government. In the following weeks and months, extreme Serb nationalists in Croatia formed parmilitary organizations, their weapons and ammunition seized from local police stations and from depots belonging to Yugoslav federal forces stationed within Croatia. Croat authorities responded by sending police to Serb-inhabited areas to seize weapons.

Meanwhile, in a plebiscite held in Slovenia on December 23, 1990, 88 percent of voters opted for an independent and sovereign Slovenia. The Slovenian government in Ljubljana said that a confederation pact modeled on the European Community must be formed in 6 months or Slovenia would secede from Yugoslavia. To emphasize its independence, Slovenia occupied federal posts on the republic's frontier with Austria and began collecting customs duties. In June 1991 both the Slovene and Croat parliaments declared the formal independence of their republics of Yugoslavia, although they would agree to remain in a very loosely structured Yugoslav federation. These declarations of independence by Slovenia and Croatia brought the old Yugoslav system a step closer to disintegration.

THE BEGINNINGS OF CIVIL WAR

The federal government tried to reverse Slovenia's control over the frontier posts and the collection of customs duties in the spring of 1991, but it could not evict Slovenian forces. Despite their overall numerical and weapons superiority, federal forces could not prevail against the united Slovenian republic. In Croatia, by contrast, the Serb minority was in a position to cooperate with and strengthen the federal military should it try to force a change in Croat policy.

Not surprisingly, the federal army turned to Croatia, where the conflict between Croats and Serbs had been escalating in the spring of 1991. In July federal army forces crossed the Serb frontier into Croatia and, with the help of armed Serb guerrillas living in Croatia, fought Croat paramilitary forces in Glina. Within several weeks fighting between federal and Serb groups and Croat forces spread to Vukovar and Vinkovici along the Sava River, in a northerly and westerly direction toward the Kraijina region and the Croat capital of Zagreb. This effectively removed about 20 percent of Croat territory from Zagreb's control.

What were the federal army's objectives in Croatia? Was the army fighting for Yugoslavia and under the authority of the federal presidency, or was it fighting for the interests of the Serb republic and following instructions from the Serb president, Milosevic? Or, given the predominance of Serbs in the army's officer corps and the fact that the army seemed to be seeking control over those parts of Croat territory inhabited by Serbs, did the army have its own agenda?

Although the army leadership insisted that it would not act without authorization of the federal presidency, eventually the army on its own expanded into Croatia and extended the civil war. The federal presidency was paralyzed. Four republics opposed the use of force in Croatia (Slovenia, Croatia, Bosnia-Herzegovina, and Macedonia). Two republics (Serbia and Montenegro) and two autonomous provinces of Serbia (Kosovo and Vojvodina) favored force. President Stipe Mesic, a Croat and the chairperson of the collective presidency, had legal control over the Yugoslav armed forces. He ordered federal forces in Croatia to return to barracks to avoid violence in dealing with Croat independence moves. The army ignored him.

In this response, the army was protecting its own interests. The army wanted the kind of Yugoslav state bequeathed by Tito. In Tito's unified country, the army had enjoyed a special place of honor and had been amply rewarded for its loyalty with very high wages and generous pensions. Were the Yugoslav state to disintegrate or to lose control over the two wealthy northern republics, the army's privileged economic situation would have been severely compromised.

Of significance was the fact that the army's officer corps was composed largely of Serbs; it was more sensitive to the aspirations of the Serb republic and its president, and of Serbs living in Croatia, than it was to Yugoslav national interests. Its relentless efforts to control Croat territory inhabited by Serb minorities left little doubt that it was under the influence of Milosevic and that it shared his commitment to the creation of "greater Serbia," a term that meant an extension of the Serb republic's jurisdiction over Croat areas with Serb minorities.

Role of Serbia

Apart from its dedication to preserving the old Yugoslav union, the Milosevic leadership was fighting to preserve the old Communist system. Serbia still had a centrally controlled economy and a monolithic political system. In January 1991 Milosevic arrested a number of opposition politicians, while authorities in other republics were moving their societies toward pluralistic democracy. The Milosevic regime's crackdown provoked turmoil in Belgrade, especially after the arrest of the popular and charismatic Vuk Draskovic, head of the anti-Communist Serbian Renewal Movement. Furthermore, in September 1991 the Communist-dominated Serb Parliament adopted a new Constitution that greatly strengthened the presidency. Despite more liberal provisions, such as the legalization of political pluralism and the acceptance of a mixed economy involving private ownership, the Constitution indirectly strengthened Communist influence by taking almost all autonomy from the Serb provinces of Vojvodina and Kosovo.

Serbia still repressed its Albanian minority in Kosovo, which further deepened the crisis in Yugoslavia. Popular demonstrations against Serb control took place in Pristina, the capital of Kosovo; and an Albanian antigovernment opposition group developed called the League of Democrats of Kosovo, under Ibrahim Rugova, an Albanian intellectual. A major political association, with 300,000 supporters, including former members of the Kosovo branch of the Yugoslav Communist Party, the League called for a multiparty system and an independent judiciary. Most Serbs in Kosovo as well as the republic government in Belgrade were suspicious of the League, viewing it as a camouflage for a nationalist grouping with separatist tendencies.

Milosevic fought back. He encouraged the formation of vigilante groups, made up of radical Serb nationalists, to go into Kosovo and engage in hand-to-hand combat with the Albanians. He also financed the return to Kosovo of Serb citizens who, in past years, had left when Albanians trying to achieve ethnic homogenization of their province had discriminated against Serbs.

This conflict between Serbs and Albanians, along with the Serb–Croat conflict, polarized the country as different ethnic groups chose to be pro- or anti-Serb. The efforts of Serb republic authorities to centralize administrative control aroused fears in other republics of Serb nationalism, affirming deeply held suspicions of Croats and Slovenes—for example, of Milosevic's ambition to build a greater Serbia out of the Yugoslav state. Indeed, Kosovo became a code word for Serb aggrandizement at the expense of non-Serb minorities; and Croats and Slovenes, who never had had a high regard for their Albanian compatriots, were now very sympathetic.

The situation in Kosovo became explosive in 1992 and 1993. Albanians accused local Serb authorities of throwing Albanian teachers and students out of schools and universities, of closing hospitals to Albanians, and of firing more than 100,000 Albanians from state jobs. Serbs answered that the Albanian community had caused these changes when it established separate institutions in pursuit of independence. In fact, the Albanians had built up their own institutions, creating their own schools in private homes (with teachers who worked without pay) and electing their own Kosovan Parliament in May 1992, selecting Ibrahim Rugova as "President of Kosovo." As Serbia escalated its support of the Bosnian Serbs against the Muslim government in Sarajevo during 1992 and 1993, the Albanian population, which was Muslim, talked about secesson from the Serb republic. On May 24, 1992, Albanians in Kosovo voted overwhelmingly in favor of independence. Angry Serb authorities declared this vote illegal and reasserted a pledge to keep Kosov a part of Serbia forever because of its historic significance for the Serb nation in its war with the Turks centuries ago.

In the spring of 1993, Zeljko Raznatovic, a Serb militia leader who had fought in Bosnia (and a thug identified as a war criminal by the United States and wanted for armed robbery in Sweden) arrived in Kosovo. Known as Arkan, he was suspected of atrocities against Muslims during the Serb takeover of Zvornik, Bjeljina, and other Bosnian towns. Much to the anger of the Albanians, he was elected in December 1992 to the Serb Parliament as a representative from Pristina.

With this development Kosovo became a new Balkan tinderbox. If Serbs and Albanians in Kosovo started fighting, the Albanian state and the large Albanian minority in the newly independent Republic of Macedonia might feel the need to protect the Albanian minority there. If that happened Serbia might invade Macedonia, which it has called "South Serbia." In turn Greece and Bulgaria might well enter this conflict to take shares of Macedonian territory. Turkey might eventually join on behalf of the Muslim Albanians against Serbia, its age-old enemy, and against Greece, its current antagonist in Cyprus. Russia might ultimately become involved, should it feel the need to protect Serb territory.

ECONOMIC DETERIORATION

Economic chaos accompanied civil war in Yugoslavia. The central banking system collapsed, with republic banks issuing money through credits and promissory notes independently of the Yugoslav national bank in Belgrade. A debilitating trade war developed between Slovenia and Serbia. Belgrade stores refused to sell consumer appliances manufactured in Slovenia; Slovenes were depicted as clever exploiters taking the artificially low-priced energy, food, and minerals from Serbia and other regions and selling manufactured goods at inflated prices.

Wage earners suffered. With industry at a standstill and the movement toward a market economy erratic, hundreds of thousands of Yugoslav workers were out of work or had not been paid for several months. Many more received only minimum wages. Also, because of the economic and political turmoil in the country, Yugoslav workers abroad were reluctant to send money home. The Yugoslav tourist industry, which had always been a lucrative source of foreign hard currency, disappeared as the war intensified.

In 1990 then–Yugoslav federal prime minister Markovic put in place a belt-tightening reform program, starting with a devaluation of the Yugoslav dinar. He opened the country to almost unlimited foreign investment by permitting 100 percent foreign ownership of business, 99 percent foreign ownership of banks, and liberalization of rules for imports and the repatriation of profits. He also sought but had to abandon wage controls and currency convertibility to stimulate Yugoslav exports to hard currency countries.

Impeding his efforts to stimulate output and expand exports were not only the persistence of inefficient management inherited from the Communist past but also the unwillingness of the republics to cooperate with the federal reform program. Thus, the leaderships of Croatia and Slovenia,

the two most well-off republics, raised wages to gain political popularity with workers, although in so doing they contributed to an expansion of inflation, which the federal prime minister had successfully controlled since coming to power. Serb president Milosevic opposed a market-based economy in Yugoslavia, for ideological reasons: He was skeptical about the efficacy of privatization and preferred policies that would keep people at work. Finally, making matters worse for Markovic was the failure of the republics to pay federal taxes while helping themselves, without authorization, to money from the national banking system. In 1990 Serbia took $1.8 billion, by far the largest amount.

FOREIGN RELATIONS

Fearful that a breakup of Yugoslavia in 1991 could lead to violence and spread instability throughout the Balkans, the 12-nation European Community and the 34-nation Conference on Security and Cooperation in Europe initially opposed moves of Slovenia and Croatia toward independence. But there were serious disagreements among Western countries. For example, Germany and Austria, with strong historical and cultural links to Slovenia and Croatia, adopted a more flexible attitude, suggesting that these republics conceivably might receive recognition if they could demonstrate effective control over their territories. In the late summer of 1991, the Germans warned federal army leaders against the conquest of Croatia, saying that they should respect the right of republics to self-determination and threatening economic sanctions if the army did not show restraint. At the same time, France and Spain tended to favor preservation of a united Yugoslav state, if only to avoid setting a precedent. With regional identities strong in these and other countries of Western Europe, there was evidence of growing regional particularism, which conceivably could be strengthened by a successful separatism in Yugoslavia.

The West responded to the civil war by escalating its protests against Serbia's behavior. It proposed conferences and cease-fires and, when these led nowhere, the EC countries made recourse to sanctions. They froze arm sales and financial aid to Yugoslavia, in the hope that the combatants would stop fighting once they ran out of ammunition. One official observed that the combatants intended to fight each other indefinitely; and once they had run out of guns and bullets, they would use knives to kill each other; and if they had no knives, they would use their teeth!

Fourteen cease-fire agreements between Croat and Yugoslav federal forces in 6

months of war preceded the UN-sponsored cease-fire, concluded in Sarajevo on January 2, 1992. Former U.S. secretary of state Cyrus R. Vance, the UN special envoy to Yugoslavia, used shuttle diplomacy between Zagreb and Belgrade to get the Serb-led Yugoslav Army 'and Croat military forces to lay down their arms and make way for the deployment of a UN peacekeeping force in the Krajina and other disputed areas of Croatia. The UN presence was intended to lay the groundwork for a permanent political settlement. By the end of 1991, according to Vance, both Croat and Serb republic leaders welcomed the prospect of a winding-down of the war. Both sides were worn out. There had been more than 10,000 casualties, a terrible toll on the physical environment, and the refugee problem had burgeoned. The Western trade embargo on Serbia had contributed to shortages, especially of gasoline; and the Serb government's fevered printing of money to pay for the war had ignited debilitating hyperinflation. An economist at Belgrade University estimated that the civil war had cost the Serb republic $6.5 billion in lost trade and production. Many ordinary Serb citizens also were beginning to criticize the conflict with Croatia, saying that Serbs living outside of Serbia were dragging the republic into a dangerous war. At the same time, the Croats, who originally preferred European mediation because of the sympathy of the EC for the independence policies of the republics, now welcomed the prospect of a UN intercession. This, they hoped, would eventually restore Croat authority to areas of the republic seized and controlled by the Yugoslav Army.

But many in Western Europe as well as in the war zone were skeptical of the cease-fire. Serbs in Croatia feared the evacuation of Yugoslav forces, who were protecting them from Croat retaliation. In February and March 1992, local Serb extremists blew up some Croat homes. Croats retaliated, destroying vacant Serb homes. Eventually, however, Serb moderates in Croatia accepted the UN presence in their territory. Croat leaders agreed that rebel Serb governments set up in the disputed areas overrun by Yugoslav forces could remain until a general political solution was worked out. The Croat leaders, however, were determined to prevent the Serb minority from cemeting its control over disputed areas and discouraging the return of Croat refugees who had fled to Zagreb months earlier.

In April 1992 UN peacekeeping forces finally arrived. But the obstacles to a peaceful settlement in Serb-dominated areas in Crotia such as the Krajina were enormous. UN officials feared that extremists on both sides were opposed to a negotiated settlement and wanted to wreck the peacekeeping operation. While Serbia's Milosevic and Croatia's Tudjman still supported a negotiated political settlement, it was by no means clear that the Serb minorities in Croatia would accept anything less than their complete independence of Zagreb or their annexation to Serbia.

MACEDONIA MOVES TOWARD INDEPENDENCE

Macedonia also was moving toward independence, although with its ethnically diverse population it seemed to have more to gain than other republics in the preservation of a unified Yugoslav state, which could provide much-needed economic help to improve its poor living conditions. Macedonian Communists and the Reform Party of former federal prime minister Markovic shared a common interest in keeping Macedonia within a unified Yugoslavia; they had the support of Macedonian intellectuals, business executives, and others. Markovic saw the Yugoslav federal union as the only means of restoring economic health and improving living conditions in the less well-off central and southern republics. Futhermore, as an independent state, Macedonia might well become prey to ethnic-based territorial ambitions of its neighbors Bulgaria and Greece. These two countries had their own Macedonian minorities and might in the future claim the allegiance of Yugoslav Macedonians. Indeed, the dominant language of Yugoslav Macedonia remains a dialect of Bulgarian, while the northern part of Greece, from Thessaloniki to the Turkish frontier, is inhabited by people of Macedonian extraction who trace their history back to the pre-Christian era of the Macedonian empire-building King Alexander the Great.

But there were also strong reasons in favor of Macedonian independence. Many people in Yugoslavia's Macedonia cherished the hope of a reunification of Macedonians throughout the southern Balkan region in a "greater Macedonia." A referendum on the issue of independence, on September 9, 1991, showed voters overwhelmingly in favor of separation unless the Yugoslav state could be transformed into a loose confederation.

In early 1992 Macedonia tried to get Western recognition of its independence. Greece opposed its independence, on the grounds that an independent Macedonia would eventually lay claim to Greek territory on the frontier with Bulgaria that

was also known as Macedonia. Greek fears were based upon alleged efforts of Macedonian Communist leaders to undermine the sovereignty of Greece over *its* Macedonia, which they called "Aegean Macedonia" and characterized as "occupied" territory.

The NATO allies, including the United States, decided to accommodate Greece on this issue, at least temporarily. No doubt they considered the vulnerability of an independent Macedonia to the territorial pretensions of its Balkan neighbors and the possibility that it could become a new object of contention among these countries. They might also have wanted to protect the Albanian minority in Macedonia, which constituted about 40 percent of Macedonia's population and had been systematically underrepresented in the republic's Parliament. The two political parties committed to Albanian interests urged the EC not to recognize Macedonia's independence because of its perceived failure to meet the Community's human- and civil-rights standards for recognition. The Macedonians worried that their Albanian minority might someday seek to join their kin in the Kosovo province of Serbia and ultimately become part of a greater Albanian state on the Adriatic.

BOSNIA-HERZEGOVINA ACHIEVES INDEPENDENCE

Fear of domination by the Serb republic led President Alija Izetbegovic to press for the independence of Bosnia-Herzegovina. Having failed to obtain the Serb republic's support for the transformation of Titoist Yugoslavia into a loose federation of semisovereign republics, Izetbegovic felt that he had no other choice. Serb republic president Milosevic wanted to retain a strong central administration that the Serb republic government could influence and control. When, in early January 1992, General Blagoje Adzic, a pro-Serb hardliner, became Yugoslavia's defense minister, Izetbegovic made up his mind to take Bosnia out of Yugoslavia and put the issue of independence to the Bosnian people in a referendum. In February 1992 the Bosnian Muslims and Croats, who constituted a majority of the population, voted overwhelmingly in support of independence. Izetbegovic then appealed to the West for recognition of the republic's independence. The Serb minority boycotted the referendum. Izetbegovic wanted not only to legitimize the new government but also to strengthen it vis-à-vis Croatia and Serbia, which were suspected of wanting to partition Bosnia along ethnic lines. In early April 1992, the United States and the

European Community recognized the independence of Bosnia-Herzegovina.

SERBIA AND MONTENEGRO FORM A SMALL YUGOSLAV STATE

After international recognition of the independence of Bosnia-Herzegovina, the two republics of Serbia and Montenegro formed a new small Yugoslav federation in April 1992, preserving most of the federal administrative apparatus of the former Yugoslav state, including the president, the prime minister, the cabinet, and an Assembly. In the Constitution for the new Yugoslavia, which had a population of 10.5 million people, most of whom lived in the Serb republic, its leaders said that it had no claims on the territory of its neighbors; it appeared that they had no territorial ambitions. The Yugoslav leaders declared as well that their new state would be a democracy based on respect for human rights and on the principles of a market economy. The government pledged to avoid force and to use diplomacy in the settlement of any outstanding differences with neighboring republics.

But this new Serb-dominated Yugoslav state was anything but what its leaders said it was. From the outset the new "Yugoslavia" was heavily influenced by Serb president Milosevic, who made sure that the federal Yugoslav government was led by people congenial to Serb interests. Indeed, the new Yugoslavia was little more than an enlarged Serbia. Montenegro's small population was, for all intents and purposes, without influence.

CIVIL WAR IN BOSNIA-HERZEGOVINA

Once the Bosnian republic became independent under the Muslim-led government in Sarajevo in early 1992, Bosnian Serbs, who made up about 31 percent of the republic's population, went into opposition. They wanted their own independent state, which someday would join the neighboring republic of Serbia. In their drive for separation, the Bosnian Serbs recalled the Muslim Turkish conquest of their land in the fifteenth century. That conflict ended with the establishment of Sarajevo as a predominantly Muslim city, with the Christians a persecuted community. Christian Serb fears of the same kind of repression by Muslims was fed by fanatical Bosnian Serb nationalists. The Bosnian Serb political leader Radovan Karadzic pushed the idea that the Muslims, who made up about 44 percent of Bosnia's population, had a higher birth rate and someday soon would be an absolute majority in Bosnia-Herzegovina's 4.4 million people. The Muslims would then establish an Iran-like fundamentalist state, despite repeated assurances by Muslim leaders of their commitment to a "citizens' state with equal rights for all." Indeed, despite the cultural reality of Muslim Slav secularism—most Muslims in Sarajevo, for example, were insistently "un-Islamic" in their personal behavior—the Serbs chose to believe the worst. They ignored the long experience of peaceful living with the Muslims, who in fact were very Western in their lifestyle. They ate pork, drank alcohol, and spoke disparagingly of Islamic theocracies like the one in Iran. And there had been a common belief among Bosnian Serbs that the Muslims were really just Serbs who had adopted Islam only as a means to survive the Turkish overlordship.

When the international community formally recognized Bosnian independence, leaders of the Serb community in Bosnia responded by declaring their own independence. They called themselves the "Serb Republic of Bosnia." Following the example of what Serbs in the Krajina region of Croatia had done soon after that republic had seceded from Yugoslavia, Bosnian Serb leaders claimed the right to associate their lands with Milosevic's new state of Yugoslavia.

Serb militias, armed with weapons from the old Yugoslav state, set out from the villages and towns of Bosnia-Herzegovina to liberate Serbs from the control of the Muslim-dominated government in Sarajevo. They wanted the territory that Bosnian Serbs inhabited, but they also went after other territory belonging to Muslims. It was a land-grabbing campaign carried out with a ruthlessness and cruelty that had not been seen since World War II. In the 18 months following their assertion of independence, local Serb military forces, backed by contingents of the Serb-led Yugoslav federal army, went on the offensive, capturing villages, towns, and cities along the Bosnian frontier with Croatia, from Kupres to Bosanzki Brod, and in the east along Bosnia's border with the Serb republic. Before long Serb forces had removed approximately 70 percent of the Bosnian republic's territory from the authority of the government in Sarajevo. By the fall of 1993, the Bosnian government controlled only a few pockets of territory in the northwest, the southeast, and in Sarajevo, the capital.

While they expanded their military control of much of the Bosnian countryside from April 1992 onward, the Serb nationalists also began an 18-month bombardment of Sarajevo. They destroyed much of the city and tried to starve it into submission. Although Bosnian government forces occasionally counterattacked, they never completely silenced the Serb heavy artillery firing from the mountains on the outskirts of the city. Serbian snipers inside the city kept its citizens continuously on edge, killing civilians at will. They destroyed the electrical generators, the water-pumping stations and pipes that delivered water to city streets and homes, and the city's telephone system, cutting off all but top government and military leaders from communication with the outside world.

Ethnic Cleansing

In their war against the population, the Serb nationalists pursued what came to be known as "ethnic cleansing": ridding communities of Muslims. This policy, which included forcing Muslims from their homes and villages and frequently imprisoning or killing them, aroused international concern and anger. Human rights groups, using information from interviews with victims of the Serb onslaught, told of the frequent use of torture in the fighting in Bosnia-Herzegovina. This was mainly, though not exclusively, the work of Serb nationalist groups and included the rape and abuse of women; the killing of captives, including in many cases small children; and the burning of people in barns, houses, and other buildings. Although the scale of the killings was far smaller than in World War II, the violence affected cities, towns, and villages everywhere in Bosnia. Allegedly, more than 20,000 Muslim women were raped, suggesting a deliberate pattern of abuse to demoralize and humiliate Muslim Slavs and drive them from Bosnia. By the late summer of 1992, there were reports of Nazi-like detention camps that Serb nationalist forces had set up throughout Bosnia-Herzegovina and into which they herded thousands of innocent civilians, mostly Muslims. Conditions in many of these camps were brutal. At one camp in Omarska, prisoners were beaten like abused animals, according to one prisoner who survived the ordeal.

Serb ethnic cleansing caused a horrendous refugee problem, the worst since the end of World War II, and certainly equal in scope to, if not greater than, the Palestinian diaspora. By July 1992 roughly 2.3 million people had fled from towns and villages of the former Yugoslavia. Another 850,000 were trapped in their homes in 4 Bosnian towns being attacked by the Serbs: Sarajevo, Bihac, Tuzla, and Gorazde. Of the 2.3 million refugees, more than 400,000 fled to countries outside the former Yugoslavia's borders, while the rest were living precariously within parts of the former Yugoslavia. Croatia had the largest number of refugees, 630,000, while Serbia had 375,000 and Bosnia 598,000, a figure that had escalated to 1.3 million by November 1992.

Serbia and the Bosnian Civil War

The Serb republic government of President Slobodan Milosevic in Belgrade supported the Bosnian Serb insurgency and its "ethnic cleansing." He wanted all Serbs living in other former Yugoslav republics eventually to be under the control of Belgrade. The Yugoslav Army—100,000 federal troops were deployed in Bosnia when the war began in April 1992—delivered weapons to Bosnian Serbs and did not interfere with either the bombardment of Sarajevo or Serb ethnic cleansing. Subsequently, the republic became a funnel for weapons and other supplies that enabled the Bosnian Serb insurgents to maintain a successful offensive strategy against the Muslims.

Milosevic imposed his policy of expansion in Bosnia as a skeptical Serbian society becoming increasingly fatigued and demoralized by the heavy economic cost of the war and the diplomatic isolation imposed on Serbia by an angry international community. But Milosevic forced public acceptance of his policy in Bosnia despite much opposition from the Serb middle class, especially people living in Belgrade, and from the Orthodox Church. He appealed to the patriotism of Serbs, pledging, for example, to defend the rights of the Serb minority in Kosovo. It was difficult for opponents to criticize him because of his control of the mass media as well as of funds that kept afloat bankrupt enterprises, the bureaucracy, and the military.

Milosevic himself was under pressure to support the Bosnian Serbs because he did not want to be outdone as Serbia's first patriot by Vojislav Seselj, leader of the Serbian Radical Party (and an ultra-nationalist whose hero was the Serbian conservative World War II general Draza Mihailovic). Seselj advocated all-out Serb support of kin in Bosnia, hoping someday to have their territory a part of "greater Serbia." Seselj was a potentially dangerous nuisance. Milosevic tried to limit Seselj's influence. In the early months of 1993, the Serb chief withdrew support from Seselj and prevented him and his party from gaining access to Serb television. But when Seselj told Milosevic that he should continue to support the Bosnian Serbs despite mounting U.S. and European opposition, and when he supported Milosevic's removal in June 1993 of Yugoslav president Dobre Cosic, who Milosevic thought was too eager for peace in Bosnia, Milosevic welcomed Seselj back as an ally.

Perhaps the most dramatic threat to Milosevic's support of the Bosnian Serb insurgency was Milan Panic, a Belgrade-born American businessperson whom Yugoslav president Cosic had invited in June 1992 to become prime minister. Milosevic initially thought that Panic's U.S. citizenship would be helpful in restoring Yugoslav relations with the United States, frozen since the breakup of the old Yugoslavia in April 1992. But to the chagrin of the Serb leader, Panic challenged both Milosevic's policy in Bosnia and his dictatorship of Serbia. Panic wanted to democratize Yugoslavia through the establishment of a free press, of open and competitive parliamentary elections, and of a free-market economy. He wanted peace in Bosnia even if the Bosnian Serbs had to give back some captured territory.

Panic challenged Milosevic in Serbia's December 20, 1992, presidential elections. He appealed to the so-called silent Serb majority suffering from Milosevic's policies of dictatorship at home and aggression abroad. Working to Panic's advantage was the enfeebled Serb economy. By the end of 1992, the economy was in a shambles, with more than 60 percent of the Serb work force unemployed and an annual inflation rate of 1,000 percent. Indeed, Panic had a fair chance of besting Milosevic in the presidential elections: Many Serbs liked him because he was an American and thought that, if elected, he could and would improve living conditions.

But Panic failed to gain the Serb presidency. His campaign was undermined by Milosevic, who tried to get Panic disqualified as a candidate before the election on the grounds that he failed to meet a hastily enacted 1-year residency requirement. This ploy failed; Serbia's Supreme Court gave Panic the right to run. Then Milosevic blocked Panic's access to national television, which was controlled by the state. Panic had other difficulties. Many Serb voters believed that however good he might be, Panic could never defeat Milosevic or be allowed to take office if he did. Therefore, they did not bother to vote for him. When the Bush administration, which was rooting for Panic, labeled Milosevic a war criminal for his role in fostering ethnic cleansing in Bosnia, Milosevic's argument that Serbs were victims of Western aggressiveness and that he was the only one capable of "standing up to the Americans" gained credibility.

Although Panic won 90 percent of Belgrade's votes, Milosevic ran strongly in the countryside, where the rural population liked his willingness to stand up to the outside world. Milosevic eventually won the presidency, with 55 percent of the national vote to Panic's 33 percent.

Milosevic's electoral triumph in December 1992 was a bad omen for peace and stability in Bosnia: The Serb president now was free to continue his backing of the Serb insurgency. Although his people were getting tired of the conflict, Milosevic continued throughout 1993 to provide material and moral support to the Bosnian Serbs. Indeed, as long as he remained in power, there was little chance of Serbia reversing its policy in Bosnia.

Weaknesses of the Bosnian Government
The war went badly for the Muslims almost from the beginning. The Bosnian government was physically and psychologically weak. The Muslim administration in Sarajevo was chaotic. Decisions were made on the spur of the moment, without benefit of careful discussion and deliberation. Most Serb members of the government had left and not been replaced, leaving huge gaps in chains of responsibility. Serb police set up parallel police forces, driving out the legitimate law-enforcement authorities over most of the republic. The Bosnian government's so-called army was a popular defense force made up of Muslim Slavs, Croats, and some Serbs, hastily thrown together without even uniforms to draw them together. There were many criminals in the military ranks, and many people used their weapons to fight private wars. A weapons shortage soon became apparent, especially when an international embargo on weapons shipments to either side in the fighting was declared by the UN in mid-1992. The Serb nationalists, however, were much better off, because they had earlier taken possession of the weapons, including tanks and multiple rocket launchers, left behind by federal Yugoslav forces when they withdrew from Bosnia in May 1992.

The Sarajevo government was handicapped in other ways. Serbs soon barricaded Sarajevo and blocked normal food and medicine deliveries to the city. Serbs disrupted communications facilities, forcing government leaders as well as EC and UN personnel to negotiate with representatives of the Serb Army over television or radio, with amateur radio operators providing the government's only communication links with most of the republic. Banks had no money. The eventual failure of the payment system obliged practically everyone to work voluntarily.

Further weakening and demoralizing the Muslim government was the defection throughout 1993 of Bosnian Croats. In the early months of the war, especially in Sarajevo, Bosnian Croats had fought side by side with the Muslims against the common Serb enemy. But this comaraderie had its limitations. From the outset of the war in Bosnia, the Croats had been closely linked to the Croat republic, from which they received most of their weapons. The Zagreb government also had its own game plan for Bosnia. Croat president Franjo Tudjman, despite his hostility to the Milosevic regime in Belgrade because of its vigorous support of the Serb insurgency in the Krajina region of Croatia, shared the Serbian leader's desire to partition Bosnia. Tudjman wanted to annex territory in northwestern Bosnia inhabited by Croats. In addition, Tudjman and most Croats in Croatia and in Bosnia believed they were defenders of Croatian–Catholic civilization against the Muslims and that Croatia had a historical right to much of the territory in Bosnia-Herzegovina.

Tudjman had other incentives to make common cause with Milosevic. He did not believe that the Muslims would win. Western governments had consistently rejected his many requests for intervention in Bosnia to stop the Serb onslaught. In December 1992, partly in response to U.S. president-elect Bill Clinton's statement that the time had come "to turn the heat up a little in Bosnia," Tudjman made a desperate request to the West, saying that intervention was essential to keeping the conflict in Bosnia from spreading south to Macedonia as well as to Kosovo. The West did not act. As the Serbs continued to score victories over the Muslims and take more of their land with impunity, Tudjman looked to Croatia's interests.

The Croats in Bosnia had their own reasons for defecting from the Muslim side. They wanted to control the southeastern part of Bosnia, including Mostar. Like the Serbs of Bosnia, the Croats took steps to assert their independence of the Muslim government shortly after the West had recognized Croatia's independence by proclaiming a Croatian state within the Republic of Bosnia. By the spring of 1993, Bosnian Croat military forces, with the encouragement and support of Zagreb, had turned on the Muslims in the southeast and were fighting to obtain control of Mostar and other Bosnian territory southward to Dalmatia and the Adriatic. At the end of April 1993, Bosnian president Izetbegovic complained about growing "collusion" between Croats and Serbs, with Croats viciously attacking Muslims in Sarajevo itself and Muslims retaliating equally viciously against Croat civilians in predominantly Muslim towns. Croat battles with the Muslims were so fierce because of the steady stream of weapons into Bosnia from Croatia. Germany, Croatia's closest ally, began insisting that Tudjman rein in the ethnic Croats in Bosnia. The Croats had now become as much of an enemy to the Muslims as were the Serbs.

Reconciliation between Croats and Muslims

By early 1994, however, the Croatian leadership adjusted course in the Bosnian Civil War. International pressure had been mounting on Zagreb to withdraw its "invisible army" of regular Croatian forces in Bosnia that was supporting the efforts of the Croat minority to stall Muslim advances and secure more territory from the Muslim government. Zagreb feared UN sanctions and a deterioration of relations with its chief European patron, Germany. A possible setback for Croatian policy in Bosnia, when considered with the loss of one-third of Croatian territory, the Krajina, to its rebellious Serb minority by the end of 1991, would have been an intolerable embarrassment for the Tudjman government. Furthermore, removal of forces from Bosnia would allow Zagreb to focus its energy on recovering administrative control over the Krajina, which, surprisingly, Milosevic seemed willing to allow it to do. In late January 1994, Croatia and Serbia signed an agreement of friendship providing for the establishment of representative offices for each country in Belgrade and Zagreb. Although the Krajina was not mentioned in this agreement, the implication was that Milosevic was no longer willing to support the independence of the Krajina Serbs to the same extent as the Serbs in Bosnia, if it involved confrontation with Croatia. The leadership of the Krajina Serbs declared that "the treaty does not infringe on the integrity and sovereignty of the Republic of Serb Krajina."

Tudjman may have anticipated a confederation between Croatia and Bosnia-Herzegovina that would better serve the interests of the Croatian minority in Bosnia than trying to seize more Muslim land as well as strengthen Croatia's ties with the West, which supported any gesture that might reduce the fighting. Finally, the Croatian-Bosnian agreement would isolate the Serbs and possibly help to induce them to negotiate a peace with the new Muslim-Croat alignment that could bring the fighting in Bosnia-Herzegovina to an end.

The West was very interested in the possibility of a confederation. The United States, in particular, took the initiative in February 1994 to further a confederation as part of its contribution to Western peacemaking in Bosnia-Herzegovina. Working behind the diplomatic scene, U.S. special envoy Charles E. Redman successfully brokered a truce between Bosnian Muslims and Croats at the end of February and, eventually, an agreement to bring Bosnia-Herzegovina and Croatia into a confederation. Talks between Croat and Bosnian diplomats began in Washington and continued intermittently for several months. While the two sides remained committed to confederation, the talks stalled primarily on how territory in Bosnia-Herzegovina would be administratively subdivided between Croats and Muslims. By mid-May 1994 all sides—Bosnians, Croats, and Americans—were optimistic about the eventual materialization of an agreement on confederation that would be an important step toward a final wind down of the Civil War in Bosnia-Herzegovina.

In the short term, however, the reconciliation between Bosnian Muslims, Bosnian Croats, and their patrons in Zagreb did not look promising for peace in Bosnia-Herzegovina. Rather, it coincided with an escalation of Serb nationalist efforts to expand military control over Muslim land, which included UN-designated "safe havens" like the cities of Sarajevo and Gorazde. In January 1994 the Serb leadership called for a total mobilization that involved a redirection of the entire economy of Bosnian-held territory toward military purposes in an effort to win the war. The Serb nationalists apparently wanted to induce Muslim acceptance of the European plan to partition Bosnia into three ethnic cantons, of which the Croatian and Serb cantons would eventually be annexed by the Republics of Croatia and Serbia. In February and March 1994, the Serbs mounted unrelenting artillery offensives against Sarajevo and Gorazde, causing enormous casualties among civilians.

The United Nations threatened NATO bombardment of Serb artillery deployed outside Sarajevo unless the shelling ceased and heavy weapons were turned over to UN officials. At this point the Russians suddenly intervened diplomatically to avert a NATO bombing maneuver. They persuaded the Serb nationalist leadership, which considered Russia its only friend abroad, to meet UN demands. But, just as the Russians were beginning to celebrate a great diplomatic victory that seemed to symbolize a resurgence of their international political influence, and just as they were beginning to insist publicly on being included in any Western decision making regarding the Civil War in Bosnia, the Serbs intensified bombardment of Gorazde. The Serb action triggered an explosion of Western anger and new threats of NATO military action against them. This time the embarrassed Russians, furious over their apparent betrayal by the Bosnian Serb military leadership, accepted, albeit grudgingly, a limited NATO air action against the Serbs.

By mid-May 1994 hopes in the West that a lull in the Serb offensive against Sarajevo might have been the prelude to a wind-down of the civil war there and elsewhere in Bosnia and Herzegovina were dashed. The Bosnian Serb military forces seemed to be determined to continue their war for control of Muslim territory, including the safe havens, indefinitely. As of early June 1994, the Civil War in Bosnia was still raging.

International Involvement

The Muslims suffered without the help of the international community. The UN Security Council, the NATO allies, and the United States, despite their acceptance of Bosnia's independence in early 1992 and their condemnation of Serb aggression, generally did not offer any real military assistance to the Muslim side. The international community was willing to send relief to besieged areas and to mediate an end to the war, but its unwillingness to provide the Muslims with weapons and troops to offset the extraordinary military superiority of the Serb side seemed to assure the Serbs of eventual victory in their land-grabbing war against the Bosnian Muslims.

Unfortunately for the Muslims, their positions during negotiations were based on some expectations of Western support. Hence, the Muslims consistently demanded as the prerequisite of a cease-fire Serb evacuation of captured territory. On their side, the Bosnian Serbs insisted that the Muslims accept the permanent loss of territory and recognize their so-called Serbian Republic of Bosnia-Herzegovina. In most instances the Bosnian Serbs broke cease-fire agreements because they knew that the Serb government in Belgrade would send support despite fears of provoking European retaliation. Indeed, the Serb fighters knew from experience that their disregard of UN- and EC-sponsored cease-fires carried little threat of retribution. They could continue to break their pledges to stop fighting with impunity.

The United Nations

One ambitious effort of the United Nations to stop the bloodshed in Bosnia was a peace plan drawn up by its chief Balkans mediator, Cyrus Vance, and Lord David Owen, the chief European Union representative in Yugoslavia. The Vance–Owen Plan would have loosely preserved, but divided, Bosnia-Herzegovina into 10 largely autonomous, ethnic-based provinces under a confederated central government in Sarajevo.

Problems with the Vance-Owen Plan. Bosnian president Izetbegovic said that acceptance of the plan was tantamount to an endorsement of Bosnian Serb ethnic-cleansing policies and that the plan in effect would result in the dissolution of his country. Many citizens of Sarajevo, from Muslim, Croat, and Serb backgrounds, criticized the plan. They said that it divided power on the basis of nationality and creed, effectively destroying Bosnia's unique multicultural ethnic mix of population. They noted that these peoples of different nationalities and cultural origins had lived together in peace and harmony for centuries.

Western leaders had some doubts as well. Former British prime minister Margaret Thatcher opposed the Vance–Owen Plan, convinced that it would leave the Muslims powerless; they would become an irredentist refugee population who eventually would become radicalized and, like Palestinians who had lost their homeland, resort to terrorism in Europe to get back what they had lost. Finally, the new Clinton administration objected to the plan because it accepted Serb seizures of territory by force and insisted that the plan would never work because the Serbs could not be trusted to make peace, given their dismal past record. U.S. secretary of state Warren Christopher believed that the plan failed to address the causes of the conflict, such as the intense interethnic hatred among the belligerents, and would soon be violated by one or more of the signatories. The most serious obstacle to implementation of the plan was Bosnian Serb opposition, because the plan preserved the original Bosnian state, denied their own declaration of independence, and precluded the possibility of annexation of their territory to the Serb republic. In a referendum in May 1993, Bosnian Serbs voted overwhelmingly against acceptance of the Vance–Owen Plan.

In their rejection of the plan, the Bosnian Serbs defied Milosevic. In the early months of 1993, Milosevic had become concerned about the impact of the international trade embargo on the enfeebled Serb economy. He was convinced that the Bosnian Serbs had probably got as much of Muslim territory as the international community would let them get away with. He advised Bosnian Serb political leader Radovan Karadzic to make peace.

But by this time the Bosnian Serbs were quite independent of Milosevic. Their military successes against the Muslim forces throughout 1992 and the first half of 1993 had emboldened Karadzic and his military chief, General Ratko Mladic to pursue their own road to victory. In addition, many Serb militia leaders in Bosnia were out of anyone's control by this time. Militia commanders familiar with the local terrain were unable to resist the temptation to use their military power to settle old scores with people in nearby villages. The influence of Milosevic over Karadzic and Mladic diminished. But even at his most concerned, Milosevic was not altogether unhappy with the independence of fellow Serbs in Bosnia since they were winning their war against the Muslims and their gains seemed irreversible.

The Owen–Stoltenberg Plan. In June 1993 former Norwegian foreign minister Thorwald Stoltenberg, Vance's successor as chief UN mediator in Yugoslavia, and Lord David Owen came up with a new peace plan. This plan provided for the partition of Bosnia-Herzegovina into three ethnic-based mini-states. Recognizing some of the Serb gains, the plan gave the Bosnian Serbs up to 50 percent of the republic's territory, the Croats about 30 percent, and the Muslims 20 percent. The Croat and Serb mini-states could eventually link up with the Croatian and Serb republics that they bordered. This new plan, which obviously discriminated against the Muslims while grotesquely advantaging the Serbs, had been favored all along by Croatia's president Tudjman and Serbia's president Milosevic.

Bosnian president Izetbegovich denounced the Owen–Stoltenberg Plan as tantamount to genocide for the Muslims. Indeed, it represented a step toward the creation of the "greater Serbia" and the "greater Croatia" long sought by the nationalist leaders of those republics and seemed to contradict numerous UN Security Council resolutions pledging to reverse the acquisition of territory by force and intimidation. Furthermore, the plan required large population transfers and raised the prospect of renewed fighting. Finally, the plan made no provision for the hundreds of thousands of people of mixed ancestry or mixed marriage—Which state would they call home?

Enforcement of the Owen–Stoltenberg Plan required a large UN peacekeeping force. Although the Clinton administration had said that it would contribute American ground forces in connection with its enforcement, in September 1993, the administration now said that it would send no American troops to support this plan without explicit authorization of Congress. In any event the United States would insist that the command of peacekeeping forces be entrusted to NATO, which was under U.S. leadership, rather than to the UN secretary general. While the details of the plan were being discussed, with the Muslims demanding more territory than had been assigned to them, fighting continued; by the end of the fall of 1993, none of the combatants had formally accepted it.

Safe Havens. Meanwhile people continued to suffer. The United Nations tried to ease the plight of refugees in Bosnia through the establishment of safe havens in Sarajevo, Tuzla, Zeppa, Gorazde, Bihac, and Srebrenica, where more than 1 million Muslims were located. The Security Council had said that these places should be free from armed attacks and from any other hostile act, but no mention was made of how the UN would obtain compliance. Indeed, the Serbs attacked these "safe havens" anyway. The Security Council had authorized the NATO allies to use air strikes against Serb forces and to double the 9,000 UN peacekeeping force protecting the Muslims and the delivery of food and medicine. But Western European countries had been reluctant to commit more ground troops to UN peacekeeping forces, insisting that others contribute, namely the United States, which tried very hard to evade such activity despite promises and pledges to help the United Nations enforce its resolutions.

Sanctions. Finally, the United Nations imposed or threatened to impose penalties on the Bosnian Serbs and the Yugoslav and Serb republic governments in Belgrade. They imposed sanctions on trade of all kinds; established a ban on military flights over Bosnia-Herzegovina; authorized air strikes against Bosnian Serb artillery; and undertook investigation of alleged Serb and Croat atrocities, with the idea of holding trials for those charged with war crimes comparable to the Nuremberg trials following World War II.

The sanctions were tough, but not as tough as they could be. All commercial and financial links with Yugoslavia were severed, and assets abroad were frozen. Food and medicines were exempted. All air traffic to Yugoslavia was suspended, and repair or replacement of aircraft was strictly forbidden. The sanctions required all countries to suspend cultural, scientific, and technical contacts with Belgrade and to reduce the size of foreign diplomatic missions. The sanctions were to remain in place until the Serb republic ceased all forms of interference in Bosnia-Herzegovina and used its influence to promote a general cease-fire.

The sanctions severely hurt the weakened Serb economy, but they did not cripple it. The Serb republic, which had been preparing for a trade blockade for several months, leased additional oil-tanker river barges from Czechoslovakia and Ukraine and used its own and Romanian vessels to bring oil up the Danube River from Romanian ports to refineries near Belgrade. So the Serb republic economy avoided the kind of collapse that would have required it to stop helping the Bosnian Serbs. Indeed, the Bosnian Serbs actually benefited from the arms embargo because they were able to obtain the weapons of the Yugoslav army. By contrast, the sanctions disadvantaged the Muslims, who had virtually no alternative source of weapons beyond what they were able to steal and capture from the Bosnian Serbs. While they did receive some financial assistance from oil-producing Islamic countries, it was not enough to help them offset the Serb advantages. Consequently, the embargo's main accomplishment may have been to prevent the Bosnians from getting what they needed to turn the tide on the battlefield.

No-Fly Zones. In addition, in response to an increase of Bosnian Serb air attacks on defenseless Muslim population centers in eastern Bosnia in the fall of 1992 and Serb use of air power to harass UN flights carrying food and medicine into Sarajevo, the Security Council voted overwhelmingly on October 9, 1992, to ban all military flights over Bosnia-Herzegovina, asking the United States and other countries with advanced intelligence capabilities to monitor Bosnian air space and report any breaches and promising further measures to enforce the ban if violations were detected. The UN action, however, was weaker than it should have been, since it lacked explicit enforcement procedures. The Western Europeans favored postponement of enforcement until it was actually needed to discourage direct UN involvement against one of the sides in the war. UN officials were in contact with the military commanders of all sides and were hopeful—though with little reason—that the Serbs would comply with the ban.

The Bosnian Serbs all but ignored the no-fly zone. Angry UN leaders might have increased pressure on the Serbs, but the Russian government, under President Boris Yeltsin, responding to demands of conservative nationalists to stand by Serbia,

on the basis of historic and religious ties between the two countries, did not want further pressure applied. Instead, the UN Security Council voted to give the Serbs 15 days from March 31 to accept the Vance–Owen Plan or risk a tightening of sanctions, including the use of force against Serb planes violating the no-fly zone. The Bosnian Serbs ignored this ultimatum.

War Crime Trials. Meanwhile world outrage at Serb atrocities was increasing. In response the United Nations decided in early October 1992 to set up a war crimes commission to investigate atrocities, including the policy of ethnic cleansing. Modeled loosely on the World War II Allied War Crimes Commission, the current commission would look for breaches of the 1949 Geneva Conventions, which define the rights of prisoners of war and civilians caught in war zones. It would also look for violations of principles of international law recognized in the Charter of the Nuremberg Tribunal. These principles define three sets of international crimes: crimes against peace, which include planning or waging a war of aggression; war crimes, which include mistreatment of civilians or prisoners of war; and crimes against humanity, which include murder, extermination, enslavement, deportation, and other inhuman acts done against any civilian population. By February 1993, with endless reports of atrocities by all belligerents—Serbs, Croats, and Muslims—against civilians, the UN decided to convene a war crimes trial. The support for such a move was strong among Western European nations and the United States. They saw Milosevic, as the chief culprit in the ethnic cleansing policies pursued by the Bosnian Serbs.

U.S. Policy

On a rhetorical level, both the Bush and Clinton administrations severely condemned the Serb insurgency and its atrocities, which called to mind the horrors of World War II. The rhetoric seemed to reflect an hostility to the excesses of the conflict. But on a practical policy level, both administrations were unwilling to use force against the Serbs or to help the beleaguered Muslims. Rather, both Bush and Clinton opted for support of UN initiatives and avoided direct military intervention. Although Clinton had criticized Bush's refusal to act decisively in Bosnia during the 1992 presidential campaign, his administration did little to change Bush's policy.

The logic behind U.S. restraint was compelling. Joint Chiefs of Staff general Colin L. Powell argued against force in

places like Bosnia where there were no clearly defined goals that assured efficient use of power and that were consistent with U.S. objectives and interests. Because of the deep interethnic animosities driving the war between the Muslims and the Serbs, Powell declared, only a political solution was viable. Moreover, there was virtually no mandate from the American people to send American soldiers to resolve ancient blood feuds in Bosnia-Herzegovina; they mostly believed that trying to make peace in Bosnia was the job of the Europeans, not the Americans. The United States also did not identify vital American strategic and economic interests in Bosnia-Herzegovina. Worse, Milosevic might have become a hero in his defiance of the United States and the West should the U.S. take him on. Americans, the U.S. administration concluded, had more serious foreign issues, like the political instability in Russia, to worry about.

Both Bush and Clinton were tempted at times to consider and even to threaten to intervene militarily in Bosnia-Herzegovina. For example, Bush half believed that his refusal to use force against Serb aggression undermined the credibility of his commitment to a new world order cited to justify the war against Iraq in 1991. Also, the refusal to take a strong stand against Bosnian Serb land grabbing risked setting an example for aggressive ethnic groups elsewhere in the world in areas that were of strategic importance to the United States.

The Western European allies certainly did not favor force. Although they professed sympathy for the fate of Bosnia's Muslims and a distaste for seeming to appease the Serbs in the same way that Europe had once appeased Adolf Hitler, European leaders firmly opposed military intervention in Bosnia. Although the British and the French contributed 5,000 troops to UN peacekeeping forces in Yugoslavia, they worried that their lives could be endangered if the West attacked the Serbs. The allies were also aware that there was no popular support in Europe for a direct military intervention in the Balkans that risked casualties.

Bush Administration Initiatives. During 1992 the Bush administration firmly rejected repeated requests by Bosnian president Alija Izetbegovic for American military help. Bush rejected a request to use U.S. air power against Bosnian Serb artillery trained on Sarajevo and bombarding it relentlessly. The administration preferred to pressure the Milosevic regime to stop giving weapons to the Bosnian Serbs. Bush assigned a senior diplomat, Ralph R.

Johnson, deputy assistant secretary of state for European affairs, as a special envoy to Bosnia to signal both the Bosnian Serbs and the Serb republic of U.S. concern about the plight of the Muslims. In this spirit the administration withheld recognition of the newly established "rump Yugoslavia" consisting of Serbia and Montenegro and recalled Ambassador Warren Zimmerman to Washington, indicating that it was unlikely he would return to Belgrade. The administration announced new American sanctions against the Yugoslav rump government, notably the closure of Yugoslav consulates in New York and San Francisco and the expulsion of Yugoslav military attachés in Washington. Finally, the Bush administration tried to isolate and ostracize Serbia by proposing to the Conference on Security and Cooperation in Europe meeting at Helsinki a suspension of Serbia from membership unless its forces withdrew from Bosnia within a 2-week period. The Americans also began to question Serbia's claim to represent Yugoslavia.

Finally, the Bush administration tried to undermine Milosevic's political position inside of Serbia during the presidential elections in December 1992 by obliquely favoring the candidacy of Milan Panic, the Yugoslav prime minister. For example, the administration asked the Security Council to exempt from sanctions the export of communications equipment to be used by an independent television station in Belgrade to counterbalance Milosevic's control of the state television service. Deputy Secretary of State Lawrence Eagleberger called upon voters to change their leaders. He accused Milosevic and other Serb nationalists of being war criminals who should be prosecuted. Unfortunately, this interference backfired, and Milosevic appeared as a nationalist hero able to stand up to the overbearing Americans.

The Clinton Administration's Approaches. For all his criticism of Bush, Clinton changed very little of Bush's policy. Clinton's objectives in Bosnia were the same as Bush's: Ease suffering and curtail fighting. And although at times his sympathies for the brutalized Muslim population and his exasperation over Serb intransigence led him to consider using military force, he avoided getting the United States militarily involved and emphasized cooperation with the United Nations. Moreover, like Bush, when he contemplated military involvement, it was strictly limited and dependent on the willingness of the European allies to support U.S. policy.

The Clinton administration considered three military options. One was air strikes to knock out Serb artillery bombarding Sarajevo and other Muslim population centers. A second was lifting the UN arms embargo imposed on the Yugoslav republics in the fall of 1991 in order to arm the Bosnians. A third was the deployment of U.S. ground combat troops to help enforce the Vance–Owen and Owen–Stoltenberg peace plans.

There were problems with all three options. For example, while air strikes were attractive because they seemed most likely to influence Serb behavior and entailed the least risk to American personnel, air strikes might have strengthened the Serb siege mentality and driven the Serbs to escalate the war. Even with laser-guided weapons, bombs could fall in densely populated areas, something the U.S. public would not tolerate. Finally, in early 1993, congressional representatives from both parties warned the president that he simply did not have the votes in Congress for armed action in Bosnia. In addition, the Europeans opposed air strikes as being too little to do the job. And although the Yeltsin government had given the Americans assurances that it would support an anti-Serb military action, the Russian Supreme Soviet had voted at the end of April for Russia to use its Security Council veto against any UN military action targeting the Serbs.

Arming the Muslims also was a possibility for the Clinton administration. But American experts were skeptical about how much the Bosnians could do even if they had a full complement of weapons. It could have taken weeks, maybe months, to train government troops to use antitank weapons. At the same time, there were logistical problems. Bosnia is landlocked, the only nearby ports in Croatia, which would demand compensation for allowing the transit of the weapons through Croat territory, greatly increasing its military strength and the temptation to turn on the Muslims and make common cause with the Serbs. Moreover, the British, French, and Russians opposed arming the Muslims as much as they opposed air strikes against the Serbs. The British and the French believed that the introduction of more weapons into Bosnia would simply escalate the killings and increase the risk of casualties for peacekeepers.

In the spring of 1993, the Clinton administration raised the issue of deploying American combat troops in Bosnia to help enforce the Vance–Owen peace plan. Urging the European allies in early March to start preparing an international force of more than 50,000 troops, up to a limit of 150,000, the

administration seemed willing to contribute up to 20,000 U.S. ground troops. But Clinton was uncomfortable over his promise and hedged on it. For example, he insisted that he would not send U.S. troops to Bosnia without assurances that Serb military forces would abide by the plan—they had violated almost every cease-fire they had pledged to respect.

The issue of deploying U.S. troops in Bosnia was raised again in connection with the negotiation during the summer of 1993 of the Owen–Stoltenberg Plan dividing Bosnia into three autonomous republics. But, once again, the administration came forward with qualifications that complicated and reduced the likelihood of an actual U.S. troop deployment in Bosnia. For example, Clinton emphasized the need to obtain congressional approval for deployment of U.S. troops abroad. Since all sides were dissatisfied with the Owen–Stoltenberg division of territory, the plan in all likelihood would fail. Thus, the balance of opinion inside and outside the U.S. government continued to tilt in favor of restraint, especially as U.S. troops deployed in Somalia began to incur casualties in late September and early October 1993. The administration could not possibly put American troops into Bosnia without serious political risk at home.

By the fall of 1993, the Clinton administration, convinced, as the European allies had been, that force against the Serbs would simply prolong the war rather than shorten it, hardened its attitude toward Muslims' demands for military help, sympathy for their plight notwithstanding. Clinton told Bosnian president Izetbegovic that his people should cut their own best deal with the militarily superior Serbs and Croats at the peace table; Washington and its allies could not and would not commit military resources to change the balance of power. Indeed, in early fall 1993, the Clinton administration seemed more determined than ever to focus on domestic problems and not to allow itself to be distracted by events in Bosnia-Herzegovina.

The administration, however, wanted to ease the suffering of several hundred thousand Muslim civilians stranded in eastern Bosnia. Serb military forces were blocking the arrival of UN truck convoys into Muslim enclaves. In March 1993 Clinton proposed to the allies and the United Nations an airlift of emergency food and medicine. The administration had other motives: It wanted to highlight for the world the insufficient amount of aid that the Serbs were allowing into Bosnia overland and to increase pressure on them to stop pilfering much of the humanitarian assistance earmarked for refugees (a State

Independence
1918

Nazi Germany
invades
Yugoslavia
1941

Yugoslav
Communists
acquire control of
the government
1946

Tito's
independence of
the Soviet Union
is condemned
1948

Yugoslavia
begins
decollectivization
of agriculture
1953

Tito calls for the
dissolution of
NATO
1957

Yugoslavia
condemns the
Soviet
intervention in
Czechoslovakia
1968

Yugoslavia
condemns the
Soviet invasion of
Afghanistan
1979

The Yugoslav
party Central
Committee
endorses political
pluralism;
Slovenia and
Croatia end
Communist Party
rule; Tito dies

1980s–1990s

Civil war begins;
Slovenia,
Croatia, and
Bosnia-
Herzegovina
receive
international
recognition as
independent
states

Macedonia seeks
recognition as an
independent
state; Serbia and
Montenegro
establish a new
"rump" state of
Yugoslavia

Central
Yugoslavia is
devastated by
the Civil War
while the West
debates how to
respond

Department report had indicated that about 25 percent of all aid to Sarajevo had been diverted by the Serbs). Moreover, the airlift would give Clinton a chance to redeem at least part of the promises of U.S. involvement he had made during his campaign and demonstrate that in making these promises he had not been simply trying to badger and embarrass the Bush administration in the eyes of American voters during the recent presidential campaign.

While a 3-day U.S. airlift in early March 1993 dropped about 58 tons of food and medicine, very little of the aid reached Muslim towns under siege, like Cerska, which fell into Serb hands only hours after American planes had dropped supplies for the town. The airlift did, however, send a message of American concern and of a strong will to do something to ease the suffering of war victims. It was also an implicit criticism of the Western European nations for not doing more to help the Muslims. Subsequently, there were more U.S. airlifts to central Bosnia in cooperation with the UN, which welcomed the American gesture. The allies criticized it as diplomatic grandstanding. There was little else of a humanitarian dimension that the Clinton administration did to help the Muslims. The United States, like many other countries, refused to admit more than a very limited number of refugees, though it did support the UN safe havens and no-fly zone. Certainly, the administration's humanitarian actions could not make up for what was *not* done in the military sphere.

All in all the U.S. involvement in Bosnia contributed little or nothing to ending the conflict that its rhetoric so frequently denounced. To that extent it is possible to argue that U.S. policy toward Bosnia paradoxically and tragically weakened the Muslim side, for which there was so much sympathy both in and out of government, and strengthened the Serb side, for which there was so much contempt. U.S. policy not only helped to prolong the conflict but also increased the likelihood of the partition and possible extinction of Bosnia-Herzegovina.

THE END OF YUGOSLAVIA

From its creation in 1918, the Yugoslav national idea was artificial, contrived for reasons of expediency by the victorious great powers in World War I. Neither the Yugoslav constitutional monarchy of the interwar period nor the post–World War II Communist state under Tito succeeded in homogenizing Yugoslav society. Indeed, some of their policies intended to strengthen the unity of the country by centralizing administrative power in Belgrade actually accentuated local nationalisms and increased the prospect of interethnic conflict. Perhaps the kind of societal homogenization and national unity found in the United States eluded Yugoslavia because historical cultural identities remained too strong to be modified, even by Tito's powerful regime. Although some citizens of Yugoslavia considered themselves Yugoslav because of intermarriage or other circumstances, especially in urban centers like Sarajevo and Belgrade, most people in the former Yugo-

slavia, especially in Croatia, Slovenia, and Serbia, always seemed to identify themselves first by their regional culture and secondarily, if at all, by their citizenship in the Yugoslav state. At the moment the political future of the peoples that made up the now-defunct Yugoslav state is not at all clear, and the prognosis for a transition to a peaceful coexistence of peoples in this ethnically diverse area is poor.

The cost of the Civil War is now incalculable. It has devastated what was Central/Eastern Europe's most prosperous economy, severely damaging the economic future of central Yugoslavia for decades to come. The human suffering, too, has been enormous, including more than 50,000 dead and 1.3 million persons homeless. The most hard hit of the former Yugoslav republics has been Bosnia-Herzegovina and the Adriatic portion of western Croatia, where the physical landscape has been ravaged beyond repair. The beautiful and historic cities of Sarajevo, Mostar, and Dubrovnik will never be the same, with the demolition of priceless cultural buildings, monuments, and bridges.

DEVELOPMENT

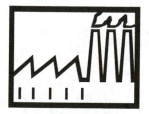

"All investment has ceased, meaning no development," according to Radoje Kontic, and today's Yugoslavia has "reached the level of an underdeveloped country of the Third World." The war in Bosnia, international sanctions, and the stubborn determination of Serb president Slobodan Milosevic to preserve the old socialist command economic structure have wrecked the Yugoslav economy.

FREEDOM

The Serb republic has degenerated into a neo-Communist authoritarian dictatorship under President Milosevic. His regime has nearly doubled the size of Serbia's police force; has harassed rivals and critics; controls the flow of information; has severely restricted political parties; and has denied the Albanian majority in Kosovo the administrative autonomy granted under the Serb Constitution.

HEALTH/WELFARE

Public health in the new rump Yugoslavia has sharply deteriorated because of the Civil War in Bosnia-Herzegovina. While medicines are allowed into the country under the international embargo, the raw materials to manufacture them are not, and few medical facilities have the money to purchase what is needed.

ACHIEVEMENTS

The demise of the Yugo, the cheap car from Yugoslavia marketed in the 1980s, is emblematic of what has happened to the Yugoslav state in the early 1990s. The car was the paramount representative of the economic and technological power of Tito's unified Yugoslavia, but the breakup of the country inevitably crippled and destroyed the Yugo.

Articles from the World Press

Russia

1. **Why the Soviet Economy Failed,** H. Brand, *Dissent,* Spring 1992. The reason for the disintegration of the Soviet empire can be simply stated as economic decline. To analyze the problem further, one must consider how this erosion occurred in a country that prided itself on 60 years of economic planning. How this command economy stymied the progress it was meant to foster is the subject of this article.   212

2. **Russia: Yeltsin's Kingdom or Parliament's Playground?** Stephen White, *Current History,* October 1993. For the three years following Boris Yeltsin's takeover of the chairmanship of the Russian parliament, it was unclear what kind of society would replace the Soviet system of the late Communist period.   222

3. **No Reason to Cheer,** Jill Smolowe, *Time,* December 27, 1993. When Vladimir Zhirinovsky's neo-fascist party won a surprising success in Russian parliamentary elections, political and even economic reform seemed to be imperiled. President Boris Yeltsin had to rethink his relationship with Parliament and seek a degree of conciliation to isolate the radical Zhirinovsky.   227

4. **Privatization in the Former Soviet Empire,** Stephen S. Cohen and Andrew Schwartz, *The American Prospect,* Spring 1993. When Communism collapsed in the Soviet empire, the resultant vacuum caused enormous repercussions in the "command economy." In a rush to solve economic stagnation and move the country to a "market economy," rapid privatization of industry was attempted. This article reviews how well this plan is working and considers alternatives that are much more pragmatic.   229

5. **Social Problems in Russia,** David E. Powell, *Current History,* October 1993. Communism gave rise to many kinds of social problems, and it was anticipated that with the resultant move toward democracy and a market economy many of these problems would disappear. However, with the dissolution of communism, social problems have gotten much worse; crime and juvenile delinquency, public health, and the spread of drug abuse have become of increasing concern.   235

6. **Will Russia Disintegrate into Bantustans?** Bogdan Szajkowski, *The World Today,* August/September 1993. As Russia continues to experience significant internal unrest, the possibility of the once-powerful federation disintegrating into smaller units is a real and present problem. Russia is a mosaic of cultural and ethnic groups, and the potential of these factions gaining autonomy would splinter Russia into a community of small nations.   241

7. **Sacrificed to the Superpower,** Michael Dobbs, *Washington Post National Weekly Edition,* September 20–26, 1993. Under Communist rule, the Soviet Union launched a program of industrialization and military expansion that attempted to rival the United States. However, this combination of totalitarian rule and socialist economics has so damaged the environment and the economy that it will almost certainly take generations to heal.   248

Eurasian Republics

8. **Active Leadership: Russia's Role in Central Asia,** Vitaly Naumkin, *Harvard International Review,* Spring 1993. In the Soviet Union's final years, the republics of Central Asia had exceptionally close ties to the Russian Republic. As the Soviet dissolution accelerated, these ties dramatically weakened. What role Russia will play in future relationships is in question.   252

9. **On Its Own: Islam in Post-Soviet Central Asia,** Shirin Akiner, *Harvard International Review,* Spring 1993. Under Soviet rule, the state waged an all-out campaign to destroy the Islamic identity of republics in Central Asia. After the collapse of the Soviet Union, Islam has become a significant political force in the newly independent republics of Kazakhstan, Kyrgyzstan, Tajikistan, Turkmenistan, and Uzbekistan.   255

10. **Russia and the Caucasus: Empire in Transition,** Daniel Sneider, *Christian Science Monitor,* December 13, 1993. The Abkhazian separatist movement in Georgia was initially backed by the Russian military. Georgian leader Eduard Shevardnadze appealed to Moscow and agreed to join the loose confederation of former Soviet republics in return for Russian military presence and help in suppressing the civil uprising. How this will affect the future of the Russian empire is discussed in this article.   259

11. **Estonia Leads Baltic States into New Era,** Daniel Sneider, *Christian Science Monitor,* January 25, 1993. Of the three Baltic states (Latvia, Lithuania, and Estonia), Estonia has experienced the most significant changes since the breakup of the Soviet Union. In many ways, Estonia can claim to be the first truly post-Soviet economy. It has issued its own currency, the kroon, which is freely exchangeable for any Western monies.   263

Central/Eastern Europe

12. **Nationalism Redux: Through the Glass of the Post-Communist States Darkly,** Steven L. Burg, *Current History,* April 1993. The violence taking place in eastern Europe has risen to a scale not seen since the end of World War II. Ethnic hatreds and historical incompatibility have been allowed to intensify since the fall of Soviet Communism. Traditionally, the Soviet Union was able to establish a political stability, however artificial, in the Balkans and the Caucasus (Armenia, Azerbaijan, and Georgia).   265

13. **Albania's Road to Democracy,** Elez Biberaj, *Current History,* November 1993. Albania was the last East European state to free itself from Communist rule. However, they have survived an extremely difficult post-Communist period and seem to have settled down to a painful but astonishingly smooth transformation into a pluralistic democracy and a market economy.   270

14. **Bulgaria: Stable Ground in the Balkans?** Luan Troxel, *Current History,* November 1993. Over the last several years Bulgaria has demonstrated a consistent commitment to maintaining democracy. It has also shown that it is serious about economic change by adopting privatization legislation and implementing austerity measures. One question remains, and that is why the West has not tried to exploit Bulgaria as a political ally and cultivate it as an island of democratic stability in the Balkans.   275

15. **After the Uncoupling, Slovakia Seems Unnerved,** Jane Perlez, *New York Times,* July 30, 1993. Czechoslovakia was divided against the wishes of a majority of Czechs and Slovaks. The split came at the instigation of Vladimir Meciar, who became the prime minister of Slovakia, and the Czech prime minister, Vaclav Klaus. After the division was formalized by a vote of the Czechoslovak Parliament, nobody thinks it is reversible.   280

16. **Hungary: Counting the Social Cost of Change,** Rudolf Andorka, *The World Today,* April 1993. The movement of Hungary toward a developed market economy and a stable democratic society will not come easily. The fundamental shifts in the social and political institutions that are necessary for development may cause significant disruption of the current structure.   281

17. **Poland Turns the Corner,** Francine S. Kiefer, *Christian Science Monitor,* May 26, 1993. Poland has begun to experience positive economic growth and appears to be the first country in Eastern Europe to emerge from the severe post-Communist recession. This has been done without the help of foreign investors.   285

18. **Communism's Staying Power in Romania,** Mike Maturo, *The World & I,* May 1993. After the overthrow of the Communist dictator Nicolae Ceausescu in 1989, Romania still has not felt any significant or positive reform. The citizens' inexperience with electoral politics and a market economy has allowed former communists to retain control by default. If Romania is to advance they will have to institute reforms that reflect a more realistic sense of people's needs.   287

19. **Why Yugoslavia Fell Apart,** Steven L. Burg, *Current History,* November 1993. The disintegration of the Yugoslav federation cannot be attributed to any single factor. The cohesion of the country's regional Communist leaderships was weakened by the fall of Soviet Communism, and violent civil eruptions were fueled by repressed ethnic identity and historical national allegiances.   291

Topic Guide to Articles

TOPIC AREA	TREATED IN	TOPIC AREA	TREATED IN
Civil Unrest		*C/E Europe*	13. Albania's Road to Democracy 14. Bulgaria: Stable Ground in the Balkans? 16. Hungary: Counting the Social Cost of Change 17. Poland Turns the Corner 18. Communism's Staying Power in Romania
Russia	5. Social Problems in Russia		
Eurasia	10. Russia and the Caucasus		
C/E Europe	12. Nationalism Redux		
Caucasus		**Environment**	
Eurasia	10. Russia and the Caucasus	*Russia*	7. Sacrificed to the Superpower
Current Leaders		**Foreign Investment**	
Russia	2. Russia: Yeltsin's Kingdom 3. No Reason to Cheer	*Eurasia*	9. On Its Own: Islam in Post-Soviet Central Asia
Eurasia	10. Russia and the Caucasus	*C/E Europe*	17. Poland Turns the Corner 18. Communism's Staying Power in Romania
C/E Europe	14. Bulgaria: Stable Ground in the Balkans? 15. After the Uncoupling 18. Communism's Staying Power in Romania	**Foreign Relations**	
		Eurasia	9. On Its Own: Islam in Post-Soviet Central Asia 10. Russia and the Caucasus
Democracy		*C/E Europe*	14. Bulgaria: Stable Ground in the Balkans?
Russia	2. Russia: Yeltsin's Kingdom	**Health and Welfare**	
C/E Europe	13. Albania's Road to Democracy 14. Bulgaria: Stable Ground in the Balkans?	*Russia*	5. Social Problems in Russia 7. Sacrificed to the Superpower
Development		*C/E Europe*	16. Hungary: Counting the Social Cost of Change
Russia	1. Why the Soviet Economy Failed 4. Privatization in the Former Soviet Empire 7. Sacrificed to the Superpower	**History**	
		Russia	1. Why the Soviet Economy Failed
Eurasia	9. On Its Own: Islam in Post-Soviet Central Asia 11. Estonia Leads Baltic States into New Era	*Eurasia*	9. On Its Own: Islam in Post-Soviet Central Asia
C/E Europe	13. Albania's Road to Democracy 14. Bulgaria: Stable Ground in the Balkans? 16. Hungary: Counting the Social Cost of Change 17. Poland Turns the Corner	**Independence**	
		C/E Europe	12. Nationalism Redux 13. Albania's Road to Democracy
Disintegration		**Industry**	
Russia	5. Social Problems in Russia 6. Will Russia Disintegrate into Bantustans?	*Russia*	4. Privatization in the Former Soviet Empire 7. Sacrificed to the Superpower
Dissolution		**Islamics**	
Russia	5. Social Problems in Russia	*Russia*	6. Will Russia Disintegrate into Bantustans?
Eurasia	8. Active Leadership: Russia's Role in Central Asia 9. On Its Own: Islam in Post-Soviet Central Asia	*Eurasia*	8. Active Leadership: Russia's Role in Central Asia 9. On Its Own: Islam in Post-Soviet Central Asia
C/E Europe	15. After the Uncoupling		
Economic Reform		**Leadership**	
Russia	1. Why the Soviet Economy Failed 4. Privatization in the Former Soviet Empire 7. Sacrificed to the Superpower	*Russia*	1. Why the Soviet Economy Failed 2. Russia: Yeltsin's Kingdom 3. No Reason to Cheer 7. Sacrificed to the Superpower
Eurasia	11. Estonia Leads Baltic States into New Era	*Eurasia*	8. Active Leadership: Russia's Role in Central Asia

TOPIC AREA	TREATED IN	TOPIC AREA	TREATED IN
C/E Europe	13. Albania's Road to Democracy 15. After the Uncoupling 16. Hungary: Counting the Social Cost of Change 18. Communism's Staying Power in Romania	**Religion** *Eurasia*	9. On Its Own: Islam in Post-Soviet Central Asia
		C/E Europe	12. Nationalism Redux
Military		**Revolution**	
Russia	7. Sacrificed to the Superpower	*C/E Europe*	12. Nationalism Redux 19. Why Yugoslavia Fell Apart
Minorities		**Roots**	
Russia	6. Will Russia Disintegrate into Bantustans?	*Russia*	6. Will Russia Disintegrate into Bantustans?
Nationalism		*Eurasia*	9. On Its Own: Islam in Post-Soviet Central Asia
Russia	6. Will Russia Disintegrate into Bantustans?	*C/E Europe*	12. Nationalism Redux
Eurasia	8. Active Leadership: Russia's Role in Central Asia 9. On Its Own: Islam in Post-Soviet Central Asia 10. Russia and the Caucasus 11. Estonia Leads Baltic States into New Era	**Social Reform** *C/E Europe*	17. Poland Turns the Corner 18. Communism's Staying Power in Romania
C/E Europe	13. Albania's Road to Democracy 14. Bulgaria: Stable Ground in the Balkans? 15. After the Uncoupling 17. Poland Turns the Corner	**Social Unrest** *Russia*	5. Social Problems in Russia
		Eurasia	10. Russia and the Caucasus
Politics		*C/E Europe*	12. Nationalism Redux
Russia	1. Why the Soviet Economy Failed 2. Russia: Yeltsin's Kingdom 3. No Reason to Cheer 6. Will Russia Disintegrate into Bantustans?	**Standard of Living** *Russia*	1. Why the Soviet Economy Failed
		C/E Europe	16. Hungary: Counting the Social Cost of Change 17. Poland Turns the Corner
Eurasia	8. Active Leadership: Russia's Role in Central Asia 10. Russia and the Caucasus 11. Estonia Leads Baltic States into New Era	**Trade** *Russia*	8. Active Leadership: Russia's Role in Central Asia
C/E Europe	12. Nationalism Redux 13. Albania's Road to Democracy 15. After the Uncoupling 18. Communism's Staying Power in Romania	*C/E Europe*	17. Poland Turns the Corner
		Yeltsin, Boris *Russia*	2. Russia: Yeltsin's Kingdom 3. No Reason to Cheer
Privatization		**Zhirinovsky, Vladimir**	
Russia	4. Privatization in the Former Soviet Empire	*Russia*	3. No Reason to Cheer

Article 1   *Dissent*, Spring 1992

WHY THE SOVIET ECONOMY FAILED

Consequences of Dictatorship and Dogma

H. Brand

H. Brand writes frequently in these pages on economic issues.

The disintegration of the Soviet Union stemmed largely from the long decline of its economy. This decline undermined the role of the Communist party, which had been the central force in the country's political and economic structures. The legitimacy of the party derived from its promise of social progress. But the command economy that Stalin had built in the name of the party stymied the very progress, the very "forces of production" that were to be promoted. How did this come about?

The decline of the Soviet economy cannot be reliably documented; statistical data are in dispute. Until recently, the official statistics indicated falling rates of economic growth rather than actual contraction. Industrial production was reported to have risen at an average annual rate of 8.5 percent during the five-year plan of 1966–70, but to have receded to 3.7 percent a year for 1981–85. The rates for agricultural output and labor productivity show similar trends for the two decades that ended in 1985.[1]

Reported Soviet growth rates have been widely judged to be partly fictitious. Enterprises often overreported their output. The value of total Soviet output was not, or was not appropriately, adjusted for changes in prices; it also included much double counting. Aside from these reliability problems, the decline is puzzling in view of the pervasive shortages of goods and services. Since declining growth rates imply more and more idle capacity, the shortages should have been overcome and the earlier, more rapid rates sustained. So careful a student as Alec Nove early raised the question of Soviet economic growth's having stopped; Soviet sources put the growth rate for the early 1980s at less than zero per capita. For the late eighties, a downward trend has been confirmed by official Soviet sources as well as by CIA estimates.[2]

In a study of the East European economies the CIA stated, "The region's poor performance can be attributed to a number of traditional factors—... declining labor and capital productivity, crumbling infrastructures, excessive bureaucratization, technological stagnation, and distorted incentives."[3] This statement also largely fits the Soviet Union—largely, but not wholly: for there bureaucratization was not so much "excessive" as integral to the economic structure. Nor can the factors of decline be understood simply as "traditional." For the study raises the question: how could sixty years of economic planning (the first five-year plan was introduced in 1929)—years that included a great war against an industrially superior foe, the creation of great industries and the deployment of a vast labor force, and the urbanization of what had been an overwhelmingly rural population—how could such achievements end in failure?

The question, as well as whatever answers one finds, addresses the fate of an entire people; beyond this, it involves the idea of socialism. The Soviet Union was until recently a totalitarian state, yet it sought to link its legitimacy with the socialist idea. The history of the Soviet Union renders these claims baseless, but they retain a powerful ideological influence—in an increasingly negative way.

Perhaps no socialist idea was more profoundly subverted by the Soviet regime than that of planning. For democratic socialists, planning historically has been thought of as dealing rationally with the blind forces of the market and of reconciling, to the extent possible, public and private interests. Planning historically embodied reason—reason as a moral value—and the ends for which it strove were inseparable from this value. That the attainment of these ends would depend on the participation of those affected by them was a key premise of socialist advocates of planning. To approach problems in the spirit of reason has always been at the core of socialist thought.

Although planning in the Soviet Union had some roots in a few undeveloped statements by Marx and Engels, its early model was the authoritarian wartime planning in Germany during World War I. Soviet planning was to be implemented by directives having the force of law. There was never any thought of allowing participation by those affected by the planned targets, although enterprise management could attempt to bargain with the authorities. In a sense, the administrative bureaucracy replaced what should have been the work of collective participants. Furthermore, planning in the Soviet Union entirely disregarded the social and environmental costs of industry. That is evident from even such crude indicators as life expectancy and infant mortality, the one being much lower in the Soviet Union than in the OECD (Organization for Economic Cooperation and Development) countries, the other much higher.[4] And it is even more strikingly evident from consumption standards, which were deliberately kept low so as to gain resources for capital investment. It appears never to have occurred to the policymakers that repressing the sphere of consumption would in time result in the deterioration of productivity and thus constrict production, making the breakdown of the economy inevitable.

The Effects of Perestroika

Before examining the Soviet economy's long-term decline, let us consider the crisis into which it led or, better, the crisis created by the reform efforts—perestroika. First of all, supply shortages worsened; consumer and producer goods had always been scarce, now their scarcity intensified. If general availability of foodstuffs in the Soviet Union was measured on a scale from 100 percent to zero, then in 1983 it stood at 90; by 1989, it had fallen to about 20, by 1990 to 10.[5] The intensification of shortages has been attributed by some scholars to greater pull of demand arising from large earnings increases granted in the mid-eighties as part of a reform designed to enhance work incentives and raise productivity. Moreover, after 1987, enterprises were permitted to retain a large part of their profits, all or most of which had been previously appropriated by the state (in line with its command over the allocation of capital investments). Self-financing was now to be encouraged and reliance on (often) nonrepayable credits lessened—the beginnings of a "hard-budget constraint." However, this policy fueled inflation; retained profits swelled by a factor of eight between 1985 and 1989, giving the enterprises great spending power. Enterprise profit retention and lower taxation reduced state revenues, adding to the state deficit. In earlier decades, deficits had been minor—or were so reported—relative to the national income; now they soared to unprecedented levels. Because they were financed in effect by printing more rubles, they added to liquidity, hence inflation.

Perhaps the most important reason for inflation was that state prices remained fixed while prices on the black or gray markets, for exports, or for hard currency circulating domestically, were far higher.[6] This led to empty shelves in state stores. It disrupted supplies to intermediate or end users, causing production to drop, thus further disrupting the flow of distribution, now less easily bridged (if at all) by middlemen acting against or outside the law.

Underlying these crisis manifestations was the failure of perestroika as an *economic* reform. Unlike earlier reforms, which also failed but did not lead to crisis, perestroika occurred in the context of a political liberalization that, with all its unquestionable benefits, fatally weakened the center's authority. The center's command over the economy lost effectiveness—not least because Gorbachev's "restrictions on ministerial powers were accompanied by an extraordinary cut in personnel," by close to one half.[7]

The rise to prominence of the "shadow economy"—the black and gray markets—can only be explained in terms of the political demoralization of the center, a factor that deepened the crisis of the economy. Although the shadow economy was not a new phenomenon, "under Gorbachev (it) . . . increased markedly despite measures to suppress or to legalize it."[8] The enormous overhang of money since the late 1980s provided the incentive not only to illegally produce consumer goods that were scarce but to steal them from state enterprises.[9] In fact, enterprise management frequently steered its products to dealers in the shadow economy rather than into official channels. Gorbachev has stated that when "salt, sugar, flour, and many other goods that are not in short supply are continuously vanishing from the trade network . . . one automatically gets the idea that someone has a stake in maintaining shortages."[10] It was not someone but "millions who steal and embezzle from the state or defraud it. . . . The crucial importance of theft from the state for the Soviet underground cannot be overstated."[11]

Gorbachev's Aims

Some scholars have reproached Gorbachev with lacking the boldness to break radically with the command economy and institute a market. However, Gorbachev viewed perestroika as a way to advance rather than to surrender his concept of socialism.

Perestroika was meant to restructure the economy along the following lines: to encourage cooperatives in services, distribution, and small manufacturing and to promote farm leaseholds (the letting of farmland to farmers for up to fifteen years; leasing was to avoid the ticklish question of land ownership). It sought to substitute economic norms (that is, costs, prices, profits) for the physical quantities that had been assigned by Gosplan (the centralized planning agency) as output targets to state enterprises and to shift to them certain responsibilities from the industry-branch ministries. And it began to realign investment priorities in favor of consumer goods. In general, perestroika aimed to diffuse the system of centralized economic power, but it could not overcome the resistance of the bureaucratic-hierarchical structure.

Although the number of cooperatives grew, the local economic directorates and Communist party organs interposed all manner of difficulties, often outlawing them altogether. Needed raw materials or equipment or access to technologies were often unobtainable for them; their requirements were usually not considered by the planning agencies. Where they obtained them outside the law, their bribes made them even more dependent upon the arbitrariness of the authorities.[12] As regards leaseholders, they remained subject to the directives of the state or collective farm from which they held their lease and to which they had to sell the larger part of their produce. Whether leaseholds would be economically viable has been widely questioned; but evidently, they were meant to get around the stiffly bureaucratic agricultural directorates, which resisted yielding autonomy to the farms under their control. The rural infrastructure (storage and refrigeration facilities, paved rural roads, and so on) remains profoundly deficient. The wastage attributed to these and related deficiencies has been estimated at 25 percent of total agricultural output in the former Soviet Union, roughly equivalent to the amount of imported foodstuffs. However, leaseholds as conceived under perestroika would be unlikely even to begin to overcome, and might worsen, the low productivity in Soviet agriculture. They would more or less perpetuate the farming of small inefficient plots conceded by Stalin in 1934 to a peasantry that had been beaten by collectivization in the early 1930s, and which subsequently cared little about the efficient operation of collectivized agriculture.

Perestroika was an attempt to open Soviet institutions to the codetermination of the public and revitalized representative institutions. It was undertaken by leaders who had a more generous view of social possibilities than their predecessors; some of them even believed in *The Second Socialist Revolution*, the title of Tatyana Zaslavskaya's passionately argued work. Perestroika meant to ease the dead weight of bureaucracy and expand the reach of autonomous decisions.

Costs of the Command Structure

Nor could perestroika bring about a fundamental change in the command structure of industry. The reform attempts have probably been rendered moot by the disappearance of the Soviet Union. We broach the subject because it will help us to examine the dysfunction of the centralized planning system.

The Law on State Enterprise, passed by the Supreme Soviet in mid-1987, exemplifies in its ambiguity the institutional obstacles to reform. Reform in the context of the law meant the granting of autonomy to the state enterprise—the work collective was to decide all questions concerning the "development of production."[13] Enterprises could now devise their own annual and five-year plans. They were to operate within the ambit of economic controls, such as value of production, profit (or sales revenue), and so on. But these controls were not to be "directives." However, the law also provided that enterprise activity be based upon the state plan; the control numbers were viewed as guides to the (essentially continued) relationship between enterprise and central plan. More important in ensuring continuity of that relationship was the system of state orders also initiated under the new law, which captured virtually all the output of the state enterprises and in fact did not differ from the plans earlier imposed upon them.[14] Finally, the enterprises remained subject to allocations of investment capital and material supplies—matters that belonged "entirely to the sphere of the command economy."[15] The carrying out of the reforms was assigned to the various branch ministries, although Soviet commentators had offered devastating criticisms of their past work and attitudes.[16] In brief, the practice of central guidance endured although its scope was reduced somewhat.

The nub of the problem was the continued suppression of horizontal, that is, inter-enterprise, direct supplier-customer linkages. Enterprise autonomy in this regard implies freedom to choose among suppliers on the basis of quality, promptness of service, and price. But that is the essence of market relations. Direct links between customer and supplier would have derogated the center's powers to allocate resources. The intent of perestroika was to shift an increasing proportion of supply functions to wholesalers, but for this no substantial work force with the requisite training and service orientation was available. The monopoly of the centralized supply agency (Gossnab) in allocating materials and equipment persisted.

The nodal point of centralized command structure was Gosplan; and the coherence of such planning primarily derived—or was meant to derive—from the material balance system, consisting, for every major item of production, of estimates of supply needs balanced against estimated requirements, all in terms of physical (or volume) units, with allowances being made for underlying production technologies, composition of materials, etc.[17] These allowances, however, could not take account of myriad changes in technologies, work organization, production procedures, details in the composition of materials, and so on, which are normal where enterprises are autonomous.

In a market economy, the coherence and function of the division of labor are achieved socially by those networks, and economically by prices based on costs and validated by demand. The validity (or acceptance) of price relationships is premised on a monetary standard of value (or of account) whose stability, and whose reliability as medium of exchange, is ensured by appropriate financial policies. In the Soviet Union, the central planning system as such existed *above* any monetary nexus, the ruble being used as a mere accounting device. Thus, money was not a measure of value independent of administrative pricing decisions. True, since the mid-1960s, attempts were made to make prices more responsive to efficiency in resource use, but the relevant reforms " . . . consisted in administrative manipulation and rules," that is, the inclusion in prices of markups for fixed and working capital, with only "limited results" achieved.[18]

The theory underlying centralized nonmarket planning and of the material balance system arose from the assumption that the disproportionalities inherent in the business cycles of capitalist economies could be overcome by applying "the principle of proportional functioning of the economy," which (according to Gosplan officials) central planning ensures.[19] In fact, the material balance system was "an administrative-operational tool, designed to reshuffle resources between particular users in the light of priorities and bottlenecks"; and because users could not link up with suppliers other than those to which Gosplan and the ministries tied them, disequilibria became endemic to the system.[20] Reforms to move away from the imperative of physical balances and toward the use of economic levers (such as the ascription of value to physical inputs) essentially failed; the values were not determined by the feedback that characterizes markets but were based on the very physical quantities they were supposed to replace, and which in effect continued to underlie the planning targets imposed upon the state enterprises.[21]

We note three features of centralized planning and its material-balance method that contributed to the Soviet economy's decline.

1. *The exclusion of a stable monetary standard obscured true costs and in part accounted for the ultimately unsustainable rise in inputs of capital, materials, and energy per unit of output.* In addition to the administrative-institutional reasons for excluding an objective standard of account and value from the planning system, there was the avoidance of consumer choice that true pricing would spell. "The ruble is an instrument for the influence of the population upon economic plans, beginning with the quantity and quality of the objects of consumption," Leon Trotsky wrote in the mid-1930s.[22] But it was precisely such influence the planners sought to bar and the party never allowed.

2. *A more immediate cause for this authoritarian system's becoming a barrier to the development of the Soviet economy was its growing inability to absorb the information load that the innumerable input-output linkages of modern industry would impose on it.* Among the limits imposed by the information load was the system's difficulty or inability to deal with changes (normally small and step-by-step) that occur at the factory level. Soviet enterprise management was left little initiative to do so; it was constrained not only by output targets but also by detailed specification of material use, product characteristics, and so on. Alec Nove cites a central regulation stipulating the norms for utilizing wire to bale hay on farms.[23] Although some of the detailed rules were abandoned, the list of material utilization rules became longer over time, the aim being the reduction of waste inasmuch as in this setup economic incentives "in no way penalize waste and sometimes even reward it."[24]

3. *The system bred not only indifference to change and improvements but resistance as well.* The following example illustrates this: output of pipe was always measured in tons produced. A lighter, less material-consuming pipe was then developed, but it would have reduced output so measured. Changing the output target measure to length and diameter was approved only after much wrangling with the bureaucracy. But then the new measure was objected to by the customers using the pipe, whose own output was gauged by the weight of the installed materials.[25]

The system thus condemned itself to a kind of stasis with a gradual institutional and doctrinal disintegration.

Bureaucracy and Monopoly

The Soviet bureaucracy has usually been regarded as the chief impediment to the economy's progress. That is too simple a formulation. Bureaucracies exist in all modern states and industries without necessarily becoming insurmountable obstacles to progress. The Soviet bureaucracy's class interest was tied to a rapid buildup of industry and military strength and to securing a stable social order. Also, the Soviet bureaucracy (along with its surviving republican counterparts) was more than just the parasitical power elite that Trotsky condemned; large parts of it performed vital economic and administrative functions.

Its economic functions might be grouped into three categories. One was the routinization of the tasks believed necessary to achieve economic growth. Another was to implement the planning targets set by the central authorities. The third was to ensure the full utilization of the labor force. This meant that deployment of the labor force was subject to the directives of the center just as material resources were. Leaving aside the question of forced labor, which disappeared after Stalin's death in 1953, Soviet workers seemed to enjoy full employment. But there was a dark side here: full employment was possible largely because mechanization of manual labor was neglected in industry, where such labor accounted for 40 percent of the work force; in construction, where 60 percent performed manual labor; and in agriculture, 70 percent.[26] Such tasks as loading and unloading, shelving, feeding parts to machinery, long mechanized in Western industry, continued to be done by hand in the Soviet Union.

The Soviet bureaucracy's inability to carry out intensive economic development was caused in part by monopolistic industrial structures and by the destruction and subsequent intolerance of the horizontal relationships between autonomous business establishments, so basic to the spontaneous evolution of the social division of labor elsewhere. True, bureaucracies and monopolies in capitalist economies may retard that evolution—the know-how, innovation, spirit of initiative, diffusion of techniques that have marked the growth of modern economies. But bureaucracies and monopolies have not ordinarily prevailed for an entire era of economic history. Schumpeter has argued the *impermanence* of capitalist monopolies, their breachability. Here, his idea applies, but negatively: the Soviet bureaucracy and the monopolistic structures it composed were *unbreachable*.

Alec Nove has written, "Most of the deformations of Soviet planning could be observed in the war economies of the Western states" (during World War II), and quotes Oskar Lange, the Polish economist, as describing the Stalinist economic system as a "war economy *sui generis*."[27] But the war economies of the Western states were superimposed upon economic structures that reasserted themselves once the war was over. By contrast, in the Soviet Union, the "war economy" *created* the structures it required and gave them their permanence. A "war economy" is tantamount to mobilization; the Soviet economy found itself in a permanent state of mobilization. It is characteristic of mobilizations that they draw mostly on existing technologies, exhaust resources, are heedless of long-term needs and social costs, and exact great human sacrifice. This underlay the ultimate ruin of the Soviet economy and the exhaustion of its working people.

To trace the roots of the Soviet bureaucracy's monopoly power, we must turn back to E. Preobrazhensky's *The New Economy* (1926). In this book, Preobrazhensky outlines the model of the industrial system that he called "socialist." It is of interest because together with Nicolai Bukharin, he was one of the two outstanding Soviet economists.

The "state economy of the proletariat," Preobrazhensky wrote, has arisen in the global context of monopoly capitalism. Among lessons this economy can learn from monopoly capitalism is monopoly pricing, which the proletarian state could use as a form of taxation, charging dear for manufactures while buying cheap from the peasantry. That would facilitate capital accumulation in a capital-poor economy. A monopolistic pricing policy was also necessary because the capital gains available to early capitalism, which provided an important source of capital accumulation, were not available now. The development of an efficient agriculture, based on functional cooperatives (that is, selling, purchasing, credit), was seen as taking decades, and "in step with the preparation of the material and cultural conditions for it . . ."[28] Hence, the exploitation of peasantry by way of the state's price policy had to be moderate. And there was an added pressure upon the "proletarian state" to pursue monopolization, which was that today's capitalist economy "stands arrayed in the full panoply of its fundamental advantages, which . . . make it impossible . . . for the socialist form to compete with it on a footing of equality."[29]

The way to overcome these drawbacks—that is, the paucity of internal sources of capital and the competitive external pressures from superior levels of technology—was to construe the individual Soviet enterprise as part of "the unified complex of the state economy," whose combined strength would back it up. Here, he held up the example of the German economy during World War I, which succeeded in supplying a large army and population in conditions of a two-front war. Preobrazhensky explained this success as being due to the fusion between the capitalist state and the capitalist economy.

For Preobrazhensky, Bukharin, and Lenin, monopoly capitalism was no mere academic category. They conceived it to be immediately relevant to the formative phase of the Soviet economy. Monopoly capitalism, moreover, was conceived as a function of modern technology, which, so Lenin held, required the concentration of industrial and much agricultural production in a few giant establishments.[30]

All this was a misestimation of the capitalist economy as an *industrial* organization. Eduard Bernstein, an intellectual leader of German social democracy, basing himself on extensive data covering many countries, had already in 1899 argued the prevalence of smaller businesses, whose existence ran counter to the old Marxist theory of the inevitable concentration of capitalist production.[31] The continued viability of smaller firms, he wrote, arose from the following factors: the division of labor between them and larger, less flexible firms; the smaller firms' ease of accessibility to consumers; the declining costs of materials and equipment that the very operation of large-scale industry brought about; the availability of labor displaced from large industry; and the often ample availability of capital.[32] The Bolsheviks, however, scorned such "revisionist" arguments.

Notwithstanding Bernstein and much other evidence, the closure or consolidation of smaller enterprises was in the Soviet Union pursued "ruthlessly" (the term is Trotsky's) after about 1924. Deep into the 1920s consumer goods output had depended vitally upon peasant households and handicrafts, but by the mid-1930s, "the Soviet Union became the only country in the world where the small independent producer of goods and services represented an insignificant segment of the economy."[33] Nor was efficiency the only reason for closing or consolidating small enterprises. Their suppression facilitated central planning and the political control that went with it. It also spelled the virtual elimination of inter-enterprise linkages unsupervised by the center.

The Weight of Dogma

It is undeniable, nevertheless, that industrialization in the Soviet Union achieved a limited measure of success. The question remains why success could not be sustained. Alec Nove notes the great sacrifices that marked the Soviet industrialization drive; the terrible violence against the peasantry that accompanied forced collectivization of agriculture; the forced labor used to construct key infrastructure projects; the purges of the 1930s, which, according to a Soviet source, "caused an immense loss of economic cadres and disorganized the normal work of industry."[34] "Yet," Nove writes, "a great industry was built," and "the success of the Soviet Union, albeit by totalitarian and economically inefficient methods, in making itself the world's second industrial and military power is indisputable."[35] Like no one else, Nove has analyzed the numerous deficiencies of the command economy, yet that these deficiencies would crystallize into large-scale failure he could not foresee. The force with which the essential *political* ingredient of this crystallization would assert itself was unpredictable.[36]

The Soviet bureaucracy abhorred all structural change as a threat to its position and privileges. It sought to repress it by the controls inherent in the centralized planning system, by economic and political pressure, or by police measures. It resisted decentralization. It left intact the disincentives to innovation that inhered in the quantitative target planning system. And it prescribed ever more detailed planning targets.[37] The more detailed the instructions or indicators, the less likely any deviation from the prescribed course of economic activity and the lower the "risk" of "spontaneity." "Spontaneity has long been regarded as a bad thing in Soviet history; it is the opposite of control, and planning requires control," wrote Joseph Berliner.[38]

Furthermore, the economic thinking that evidently guided much of economic policy in the Soviet Union was often mistaken or wrong-headed. We saw this in the adoption of "monopoly capitalism" as a kind of model for the Soviet economy. Equally important, Soviet economic thinking adhered to a notion of "productiveness" that was confined to the production of means of production and capital investment projects. This was by no means a mere theoretical proposition; the dogmatism that informed Soviet economic policy led to dire consequences. The neglect of the Soviet transportation network, for example, is attributable largely to its not having been seen as directly "productive." More strikingly, the defining of trade as "unproductive" in an economy where the household had long ago ceased to be self-sufficient led to a totally inadequate distribution system, which contributed to consumer goods shortages and low productivity. The relegation of health and educational services to "unproductive" status tended to justify, in the eyes of Soviet policy makers, their notorious underfinancing.[39] Finally, the Soviet bias toward heavy industry and extensive (resource-using rather than -saving) investment, the utter lack of balance between heavy and light industries, with the former allocated up to 90 percent of total manufacturing investment funds and the latter the pitiful remainder, again exemplifies Soviet conceptions of "productiveness."[40]

The Stalinist Model: Gigantomania

Industrial expansion in the Soviet Union followed what has been termed the Stalinist model. This model was defended as ideologically and materially appropriate well into the 1980s. It gave priority to the construction and expansion of heavy industry—steel, coal, electrical generation and distribution, machinery, trucks, tractors, construction equipment. The defense of this model reflects both the material interest of the party and its academic allies and their inflexible attachment to the dogma of "productiveness," by which perhaps the more conscientious among them rationalized their interests. That goes also for Gorbachev: he viewed as central the re-creation of Soviet industry on the basis of science and electronics and the upgrading of machinery and equipment to world standards." The greater emphasis he wanted to give to consumer goods output was a concession without a commitment.[41]

The priority of heavy industry in Soviet planning was not (so far as I know) originally justified as a foundation of military power. Like the notion of monopoly capitalism, it derived from a simplistic perception of capitalist industrialism in the early twentieth century. It was adopted largely out of ideological motivations: Soviet industry was to overtake American capitalism, and thus demonstrate its superiority over the anarchy of the free market.

Heavy industry was built in a manner profoundly wasteful. Waste and inefficiency have been ascribed to the "backwardness" of the labor resources available in the early days of Stalinist industrialization; but they persisted long after such backwardness had become a thing of the past. The pattern set in the 1930s has been termed "gigantomania," and the term was still used by Gorbachev in a speech he delivered in 1985.[42]

In the 1930s and after, Soviet industries were created on a scale often far beyond the point of the lowest (most economical) cost per unit of output. The "giantism" associated with scale had political and quasi-technical reasons. It was part of the effort to outclass the United States; it was also to impress the world with Soviet industrial muscle. Furthermore, it seemed easier to plan for a small number of larger plants than for large numbers of smaller plants. At any rate, the source of the much admired American efficiency was seen in America's "big" plants. Yet, in reality these efficiencies often stemmed from standardization, specialization, and from the linkages to suppliers and wholesalers with their own access to know-how and customer needs. Efficiencies could be attained—as American consultants to the Soviet regime advised—in smaller plants and by means of subcontracting.[43] But Soviet planners eschewed the horizontal linkages that smaller plants and subcontractors imply, since that would have meant the economy was escaping their control.

In the United States—and this bears on the dated view the Soviets had of American industry—plant size had actually been decreasing. Between 1914 and 1937 when, according to John Blair, "the large plant was capturing the imagination of observers everywhere," average plant size measured in terms of employment declined in one third of the 204 industries for which comparable data were available. Between 1947 and 1963, a period of strong economic expansion, the number of manufacturing plants with 2,500 employees or more declined by 13 percent.[44] American enterprises in the machine building and metal-working industries averaged seventy-four workers in 1958; the comparable enterprise in the Soviet Union averaged 2,608 in 1963. Such Soviet giantism was inimical to the adoption of decentralizing technologies, such as are to be found in electronics, plastics products, computer-controlled manufacturing processes, and so on.[45] The creation of overly large projects was essentially an outcome of the command economy. But their productivity probably began to decline as early as thirty years ago; that is, output per unit of input of labor, materials, and capital lessened steadily. It is true that declines in the rate of productivity advance also occurred in the United States and elsewhere after about 1970. But here, stringent

capacity cutbacks of the least efficient operations as well as technological and organizational innovations (often to the detriment of the affected workers) in time reversed the trend. No such reversal took place in the Soviet Union. The required enterprise autonomy and the learning processes such autonomy affords were lacking.

An Incoherent Economy

Among the functions of the Soviet bureaucracy we listed the routinization of tasks necessary to promote the expansion of output—"year after year . . . from 5-year plan to 5-year plan," as one observer put it.[46] The statement needs amending. Economic growth refers to the measured expansion in a nation's total output. Inasmuch as the rate of output growth in the Soviet Union was steadily diminishing, what the bureaucracy truly routinized was not output growth so much as a steady buildup of inputs, especially of capital equipment and construction projects, energy, and materials. These inputs have been rising relative to the output they produce for a quarter century, perhaps more.

Striking examples of declining capital productivity are given by Soviet economists N. Shmelev and V. Popov in The Turning Point.[47] Output per unit of capital input in Soviet industry dropped by more than one-third between 1960 and 1985; by three-fifths in construction; and by seven-tenths in agriculture. In construction, "one fifth of the construction equipment stands idle, and for many years, 70 to 90 percent of the capital investment in construction has remained unfinished. It takes 11 to 12 years . . . to carry out a construction project, in contrast to 1½ to 2 years everywhere else in the world."[48]

Where, then, is the coherence one expects from economic planning? We might reply with Gorbachev that "life" gave the answer: there was no coherence. Users, say, of tractors had no choice but to accept delivery, even though this meant that the excess tractors would stand idle. The supplier cared only to fulfill the planning target. Costs were not a constraint for either the supplier or the user, enterprise budgets being "soft," that is, deficits could be covered by frequently nonrepayable credits. The system led ultimately to ruinous waste of resources and neglect of quality.

Here, a brief explanation concerning productivity. Growth in the real national product or income hinges upon two kinds of increases: one consists of tangible or physical inputs, such as employment and hours worked; the capital services rendered by the stock of machinery, equipment, and structures; and materials and fuel. These inputs are readily calculable. The other variant is productivity—the efficiency with which physical inputs are transformed into output. Efficiency subsumes intangible ways of saving labor, capital services, materials, and fuel per unit of output. Efficiency is achieved to an extent by instituting economies: for example, by compelling fewer workers to produce the same output. But gains in efficiency arise mostly from new or improved technologies, or from new ways of organizing work, plant layout, or delivery systems. These factors, mostly due to advances in knowledge, are not calculable; their magnitude, however, is indicated by the difference in real value over time between physical inputs and outputs. Thus, in the United States, the real national product rose at an average annual rate of 2.9 percent between 1929 and 1982; two-thirds of the rise originated in increased physical inputs mainly employment; the remaining third was attributable to an improvement in productivity, with advances in knowledge judged to have been the most important factor.[49]

In the Soviet Union, even in years of vigorous economic growth (prior to about 1965), mainly "traditional" inputs fueled such growth. The intangible factors that composed productivity are estimated to have come to one-half or less the amount calculated for the American economy.[50] The material balance system and the command hierarchy that had created it stood as a barrier.

The technological backwardness of Soviet industry has been widely documented; a few examples will suffice.[51] Military technologies and innovations were often on a par with those of the West. The development of military technology is linked to well-defined objectives whose effectiveness can be pretested. But the objectives of the development of *industrial* technologies are as varied as the industries and production processes to which they are directed, and the markets their outputs serve. They cannot be subjected to the commands of the planning bureaucracies because these bureaucracies are unable to master the necessary knowledge. Furthermore, industrial innovations, unless specific to the establishment adopting them, cannot usually be pretested. They require links to suppliers to make sure of relevant delivery capacities; to customers, to ascertain that *their* needs are more readily met than before; and the availability and proper array of skills and know-how internal to the innovating enterprise. We need hardly repeat that the precondition for all this—namely enterprise autonomy—was lacking in the Soviet Union.

It is true that the Soviet Union boasted more than four times as many degree engineers as the United States. But observers have reported that the Soviet engineer's training and experience is narrower and levels of skill lower than his or her U.S. counterpart's, at times even lower than those of a master mechanic.[52] Yet, while weakness in industrial engineering is a proximate cause of a lack in innovation, it is the *institutional* impediments that prevented the Soviet engineer's native abilities from flourishing.

An indication of technological backwardness is the low rate of retirement of obsolete industrial machinery, equipment, and structures that prevailed in the Soviet Union. These rates have been estimated to run to only about half of those in the United States. Alec Nove writes that in the 1970s, "it was hoped that greater effectiveness would be achieved by spending more on re-equipping existing factories than spending on totally new ones. . . . This did not happen to the desired extent, and we saw a decline in the already grossly inadequate rate of retirement of obsolete machinery." That rate in fact had been falling over the previous twenty years, such that the service life of the Soviet stock of industrial capital averaged an estimated forty-seven years, compared to seventeen years for the United States.[53]

Operating with obsolete equipment is generally more wasteful of human labor, materials, and fuel than operating with its modernized replacement. For example, between 30 and 70 percent of the metal used in machine-tool manufacture in the Soviet Union was wasted as filings because of obsolete technology. Insufficient production of plastics compels the use of fourteen to sixteen million tons more metal than would otherwise be called for.[54]

Innovations, the embodiment of technological and organizational changes, complicate planning, even vitiate it, because their effects elude prediction and depend on know-how the central planner can't assimilate. Planning is facilitated, the enterprise's targets are more readily met and bonuses for "overfulfillment" of assigned targets more easily earned if long runs of standard products are ground out. Innovations may well cause slowdowns in production, owing to complications in dealing with the new learning curve. Moreover, management cannot be assured of receiving the appropriate supplies that innovations may require; it has no choice of supplier, which is made by its supervisory agency. Finally, no benefit may accrue to the enterprise if, as was likely, the increment in production that the innovation enables is incorporated in future production targets, without any change in allowed compensation. In sum, innovative managers as well as workers risked partial nonfulfillment of the plan, and hence income loss and penalties. They often stood to lose rather than to gain from innovation.[55]

There was also a *disrupted* tradition of innovation in Russia. Pre-revolutionary Russia had a record of significant innovations in a number of key industries, and by 1916 technology in many of these was on a par with world standards.[56] Although many managers, technicians, and skilled workers emigrated after the Bolshevik revolution, many stayed, with the encouragement of Lenin. However, beginning in the late 1920s, there began purges of technical experts and denunciation of engineering personnel as "wreckers." "This had an inhibiting effect on technological innovation. . . . One can trace at least some of the most serious problems of the Soviet economy, including lags in agricultural output, lags in automation of industrial processes and the use of computers, to the negative atmosphere created by the political authorities during the thirties."[57]

Joseph Berliner writes that "new combinations" must emerge to suit the requirements of new technological processes—new organizational setups, formed either by independent entrepreneurs or corporations. (The recent split-up of IBM into several autonomous design, production, and marketing divisions is a striking example of the "Schumpeterian" organizational behavior Berliner has in mind.) "Central planning, however, leans toward uniform structures. Once a certain organizational structure is decided upon for a certain enterprise, a statute is issued that requires all enterprises of that type to employ that structure."[58]

Diversity of structure and smallness of enterprise size have clearly fostered innovation. " . . . [S]mall businesses are efficient performers of innovation . . . [and] contribute a disproportionately greater share of product innovation and bring these products to market faster than large business. . . . Small firms produce 2.5 times as many innovations as large firms, relative to the number of people employed."[59] In the United States small firms contributed one half of the "salient" innovations in machine manufacturing; plant maintenance, sanitation, and design; and instrument and control manufacturing.

It is remarkable that recent developments in the Soviet Union's industrial structure ran directly counter to those in the United States and elsewhere. Industrial reorganization in the Soviet Union since 1973 "was an attempt to concentrate power in the center of the decision-making hierarchy," resulting in a "massive merger movement." By contrast, in the OECD countries, the employment share of smaller manufacturing firms has been rising, even as manufacturing employment as a whole has receded.

The planning bureaucracy was averse to all diversity that threatened slippage of its control; but technological change, of which innovations are the vehicle, compels diversity of structure and introduces incalculable elements into the centralized planning on which the command structure of the Soviet economy depended.

A Summary

In the former Soviet Union, all economic agents were controlled by the political center, closely identified with the Communist party of the Soviet Union (CPSU). The political center swiftly lost authority as democratic forces, opened up by glasnost and perestroika, asserted themselves. The integrative organs of the economy, articulated by the economic command hierarchy and the planning system they imposed, largely fell apart—albeit not the industrial enterprises on which they were based. The causes of the Soviet economy's failure are rooted in policies, institutions, and dogmas tracing back sixty to seventy years. They include the following:

- a steady decline in productivity—that is, output per unit of input of labor, capital, materials, and fuel has kept shrinking over the past quarter century;
- an inability to adopt, or adapt to, technologies and innovations that would make for more intensive uses of inputs, that is, that would save rather than expend inputs per unit of output;
- the perpetuation of a planning system that mandated physical quantities and volume as planning targets upon industry, construction, and agriculture, and proved unable to enforce norms of quality, unmanageable in a central planning system;
- a system predicated upon a rigid monopolistic structure of industry, consisting of mostly overlarge enterprises, all hierarchically tied to the center, unable to develop licit inter-enterprise ties and unable, furthermore, to rely on overlapping (nonexistent) networks of smaller firms as suppliers of goods, services, information, and spare capacity;
- an unwillingness to adopt a monetary nexus embodying a stable standard of account as a parameter of the planning system thus preventing any true judgment of relative values on the part of consumers and foreclosing rational calculation of input costs, thereby contributing to waste and excess of inputs and capital investment;
- jealous control of the economic planning monopoly and intolerance of autonomous actions by enterprise management; as well as insistence on the priority of heavy industry and an inability to diversify, and thus to modernize, Soviet industry, and with it the occupational structure of employment;
- the constriction of industries supplying consumer goods and services, largely owing to an outmoded "productiveness" dogma that implied the priority of producing means of production, narrowly defined; that could be enforced chiefly by suppressing the protest movements of working people and their advocates; and that was in large part responsible for the persistently low productivity levels of the Soviet work force.

The social conflicts that beset the Soviet Union manifested themselves in a degree of corruption that infected perhaps all strata of Soviet society, and that was associated chiefly with the never-ending shortages that the central planning system bred. It was the deep revulsion against such pervasive corruption that moved people like Zaslavskaya to ally themselves with Gorbachev and his unsuccessful effort at restoring what they conceived to be socialism.

Asked why he would promote the failed British general whose troops had been defeated by the Japanese in Burma during World War II, Winston Churchill replied that it was not the failure but the quality of the effort that counted. Gorbachev's did have grandness of quality.

Notes

1. Hansgeorg Conert, *Die Oekonomie des unmoeglichen Sozialismus.* (The Economics of Infeasible Socialism); *Krise und Reform der sowjetischen Wirtschaft unter Gorbatschow* (Crisis and Reform of the Soviet Economy under Gorbachev) (Muenster, Germany: Westfaelisches Dampfboot, 1990), 127.

2. Alec Nove, *An Economic History of the U.S.S.R.* (London: Penguin, 1989), 394. Central Intelligence Agency and Defense Intelligence Agency, *The Soviet Economy Stumbles Badly in 1989.* Presented to the Technology and National Security Subcommittee, Joint Economic Committee of Congress, 20 April 1990, Table C-4.

3. Central Intelligence Agency, *Eastern Europe: Long Road Ahead to Economic Wellbeing.* Presented to, as in n. 2, May 16, 1990, p. 4.

4. Male and female life expectancy in the USSR: 64.2 and 73.3; in OECD countries: 71.6 and 78.0. Infant mortality in the USSR: 25.1 per 1,000 live births; in OECD countries: 8.4. Sources: International Monetary Fund, World Bank, and others. *The Economy of the USSR. Summary and Recommendations* (Washington: The World Bank), Appendix Table III.

5. Anders Aslund, *Gorbachev's Struggle for Economic Reform* (Ithaca: Cornell University Press, 1991), 183.

6. ibid., p. 186.

7. ibid., p. 196.

8. Gregory Grossman, "Sub-Rosa Privatization and Marketization in the USSR." *The Annals* (January 1990), 44.

9. ibid., p. 47. "[G]oods are massively stolen."

10. Nicolas Spulber, *Restructuring the Soviet Economy: In Search of the Market* (Ann Arbor: The University of Michigan Press, 1991), p. 220.

11. Grossman, op. cit., p. 48.

12. Conert, op. cit., pp. 190–1.

13. ibid., p. 148; see also Aslund, op. cit., p. 126 ff.

14. Aslund, op. cit., p. 127.

15. ibid., p. 126.

16. Conert, op. cit., pp. 143, 148 ff.

17. Alec Nove, *The Soviet Economic System*, third edition (Boston: Unwin, Hyman, 1988), 23.

18. Spulber, op. cit., p. 65.

19. Quoted in Aslund, op. cit., p. 125.

20. Nove, *System,* op. cit., p. 24.

21. Spulber, op. cit., p. 61.

22. Leon Trotsky, *The Revolution Betrayed* (New York: Pioneer Publishers, 1936), 76.

23. Nove, *System,* op. cit., p. 28.

24. ibid.

25. ibid., p. 88.

26. Ed A. Hewett, *Reforming the Soviet Economy* (Washington D.C.: The Brookings Institution, 1988), 91. See also, Guy Standing, ed., *In Search of Flexibility: The New Soviet Labour Market* (Geneva: International Labour Organisation, 1991), essays by Y. Antosenkov, especially p. 64, and by A. Samorodov, especially p. 145.

27. Alec Nove, *History*, op. cit., p. 387.

28. Leon Trotsky, op. cit., p. 73.

29. E. Preobrazhensky, *The New Economy* (reprinted by Clarendon Press, Oxford, 1965), 127.

30. Quoted in L. Slomonski, "The Scale of Soviet Industrial Establishment, 1928–1958: A Study in the Theory and Practice of Economic Planning" (Ph.D. diss., Columbia University, 1960), 71.

31. Eduard Bernstein, *Evolutionary Socialism* (New York: Schocken Books), p. 59 ff.

32. ibid.

33. Adam Kaufman, "Small-scale Industry in the Soviet Union," Occasional Paper 80 (New York: National Bureau of Economic Research, 1962), 5.

34. Alex Nove, op. cit., p. 228.

35. ibid., p. 387.

36. See Alec Nove, *The Soviet Economic System*, third edition (Boston: Unwin, Hyman, 1988).

37. Ota Sik, *Plan und Markt im Sozialismus* (Vienna: Fritz Molden, 1967), 90. Nove, *System,* op. cit., pp. 28, 83.

38. Joseph Berliner, "Entrepreneurship in the Soviet Period: An Overview," in G. Guroff and F. V. Carstensen, eds. *Entrepreneurship in Imperial Russia and the Soviet Union* (Princeton: Princeton University Press, 1983), 197.

39. Ota Sik, op. cit. There are many references to this problem.

40. Nicolas Spulber, *Restructuring the Soviet Economy: In Search of the Market* (Ann Arbor: The University of Michigan Press, 1991), 56.

41. ibid., p. 83.

42. ibid., p. 76.

43. L. Slomonski, op. cit., p. 158.

44. John M. Blair, *Economic Concentration, Structure, Behavior, and Public Policy* (New York: Harcourt, Brace, 1972), 99.

45. ibid., p. 682.

46. Gregory Grossman, "Soviet Growth: Routine, Inertia, and Pressure," *American Economic Review*, vol. 50, #2, p. 65.

47. N. Shmelev and V. Popov, *The Turning Point* (New York: Doubleday, 1989) 138–141.

48. ibid., p. 142.

49. Edward F. Denison, *Trends in American Economic Growth, 1929–1982* (Washington: The Brookings Institution, 1985), 111.

50. See the discussion and references in Ed A. Hewett, *Reforming the Soviet Economy*, op. cit., n. 44, p. 71.

51. See Ronald Amann and Julian Cooper, *Technical Progress and Soviet Economic Development* (Oxford: Basil Blackwell, 1986); and Antony C. Sutton, *Western Technology and Soviet Economic Development, 1945 to 1965* (Stanford: Hoover Institution Press, Stanford University, 1973).

52. A. C. Sutton, op. cit., p. 405.

53. Shmelev and Popov, op. cit. n. 27, p. 145.

54. ibid., p. 130.

55. Joseph Berliner, *The Innovation Decision in Soviet Industry* (Cambridge: The MIT Press, 1976), 518.

56. A. S. Sutton, op. cit., p. 409.

57. Kendell E. Bailes, *Technology and Society under Lenin and Stalin.* (Princeton: Princeton University Press, 1978), 420.

58. Joseph S. Berliner, "Entrepreneurship in the Soviet Period . . . ," op. cit., p. 197.

59. Ed A. Hewett, op. cit., pp. 247–249; Zoltan J. Acs and David B. Audretsch, *"Small Firms and Entrepreneurship: A Comparison Between West and East Countries"* (Discussion Papers, University of Baltimore, August 1990), 32.

Article 2

Current History, October 1993

Russia: Yeltsin's Kingdom or Parliament's Playground?

The cacophony that passes for political discourse in Russia continues as Yeltsin and parliament trade edicts and laws in a test of wills that has left most Russians indifferent— and confused. "Who does rule Russia then? According to surveys from late last year, resondents said it might be the mafia (21.8 percent) or no one at all (9.3 percent); 9.7 percent thought President Yeltsin was in charge, but only 3.9 percent believed the government was, and just 0.2 percent thought parliament governed Russia— the same proportion that said the country was being run by alcoholics."

Stephen White

Stephen White is a professor of politics at the University of Glasgow. His recent publications include After Gorbachev *(Cambridge: Cambridge University Press, 1993) and, with Graeme Gill and Darrell Slider,* The Politics of Transition *(Cambridge: Cambridge University Press, 1993).*

The resignation of President Mikhail Gorbachev and the end of Communist rule in late 1991 appeared at first sight to open the way to a new and democratic politics in what had been the Soviet Union. No longer was there any need to reconcile the competing claims of the Communist party and an elected parliament with the party consigned to the "dustbin of history" to which it had tried to send its opponents more than 70 years earlier. The search for a "socialist market" was replaced by a commitment to private ownership, and the rights of citizens did not have to be understood within the context of "socialist pluralism," as first the Soviet Union and then the Russian Federation pledged themselves to a wide range of liberal freedoms. The Soviet parliament had already adopted a "Declaration of the Rights and Freedoms of the Individual" in September 1991. Two months later the Russian parliament made a similar commitment, and in April 1992 the declaration—with its guarantees of equality before the law, freedom of speech and worship, the right to own property and engage in "entrepreneurial activities"—was written into the Russian constitution. The "natural, inviolate and inviolable rights" of the Russian citizen seemed by these actions to have been secured in law for the first time in Russian, and not just Soviet, history.

The man who was now leader of the largest of the former Soviet republics was still something of an enigma. Boris Yeltsin, a month older than Gorbachev, had been a party member since 1961, and was first secretary of the party's regional organization in his native Sverdlovsk from 1976 to 1985, when he joined the central leadership. A hastily written autobiography—published in English as *Against the Grain*—made it clear he had been lucky to rise at all: he was nearly drowned by a priest while being baptized, lost two fingers in an accident during his schooldays, and later contracted typhoid fever.

When he took over as chairman of the Russian parliament in 1990, Yeltsin was asked if he was a socialist. What, he responded, could this mean? There had been "developed socialism," "finally and irrevocably established" socialism, Pol Pot socialism, even National Socialism. Were terms of this kind any longer of real value? In speeches and interviews during the campaign for the June 1991 Russian presidential election, Yeltsin was scarcely more forthcoming. He was in favor of "radical reform," a transition to the market, and the preservation of peace and stability—but so was Gorbachev. Once a month, Yeltsin told interviewers last year, he attended a religious service, but in general he was happy to rely on his intuition. A close analysis of his speeches by three academics that appeared in the June 10, 1991, *Pravda* found Yeltsin was "predictable in only one respect—his unpredictability."

After three years or more of Yeltsin's leadership, it is still unclear what kind of society has replaced the Soviet system of the late Communist period. The Russian parliament was elected in March 1990 and Yeltsin himself was voted in as president of Russia with a Communist running mate when the party was still the dominant political force. Some of the largest former republics of the Soviet Union, such as Ukraine and Kazakhstan, are headed by men who held prominent party positions during the late Communist years. Local officials were often party secretaries in the latter years of Communist rule. The Communist party, banned after the failed coup of August 1991, was allowed to reconstitute itself this year and has become the largest of the new parties, with a substantial popular following. And popular values are still highly supportive of traditional socialist objectives, such as full employment and the comprehensive provision of housing and social welfare. Indeed, an October 1992 poll showed that most Russians were still in favor of the Soviet Union a year after its official demise. The old system, it has to be remembered, had collapsed—it was not overthrown—and the mix of people and institutions that have succeeded it show a substantial degree of continuity at least in Russia and the other former Soviet republics that remain inside the Commonwealth of Independent States.

PRESIDENT AND PARLIAMENT FACE OFF

Political developments after the aborted coup centered around the Russian Congress of People's Deputies, the 1,068-member "super-parliament." Led by its increasingly influential speaker, Ruslan Khasbulatov, the congress included a sizeable bloc of former Communists and directors of state enterprises, and it showed little sympathy for the market-oriented reforms promoted by president and government. At the sixth session of the congress last April—the first since the demise of the Soviet Union—a bid for debate on a motion of no confidence in the government was narrowly defeated, and a resolution was adopted that called for "basic changes" in the economic reform program, including large increases in public spending.

The seventh session in December saw a still more open cleavage between the president and his parliamentary opponents. Khasbulatov, in a warmly received speech, attacked the "Americanization" of the Russian economy and called instead for a "socially oriented market" like the one that operated successfully in Europe, Canada, and China. In the end, despite Yeltsin's support, his nominee for prime minister, Yegor Gaidar, was forced to step down as acting prime minister. Gaidar's place was taken by Viktor Chernomyrdin, a former member of the Communist party Central Committee who had previously served as deputy prime minister in charge of energy; Chernomyrdin told parliament he was in favor of reforms, but "without deepening the impoverishment of the people."

The seventh congress agreed to hold a referendum on April 11, 1993, in which the basic principles of a new constitution would be placed before the Russian people. An extraordinary eighth session of the congress, however, unfolded in March. Parliament stripped Yeltsin of the emergency powers he had been granted in November 1991 and ordered him to act in accordance with the Russian constitution, under which the congress is designated the "supreme body of state power" and the president merely the "chief official and head of executive authority." At the closing of the session, the parliament issued an appeal to the Russian people in which it described all of Yeltsin's initiatives as aimed at the "preservation of special powers for himself that are not in conformity with the constitution." It also reversed the earlier decision to hold a referendum April 11, earmarking the money that would be saved for housing for servicemen returning from eastern Europe.

The Russian Constitution: The Rival Drafts Compared

THE PARLIAMENTARY DRAFT	THE PRESIDENTIAL DRAFT
The State System	
"a sovereign, legal, democratic, federal and social state"	"a democratic, legal, secular, federal state"
Civil and Political Rights	
Based on the Russian constitution and "the generally recognized principles and norms of international law"	Based on the Universal Declaration of Human Rights and the "generally accepted principles and norms of international law"
Separation of Powers	
Separation of legislative, executive, and legal functions	Same
President	
The "highest official of the Russian Federation" heads the executive, and represents the Russian Federation internally and abroad; directly elected for a five-year term; "directs the activity" of the government and appoints "with the agreement of the Supreme Soviet" the prime minister and other ministers; commander in chief; cannot suspend parliament; can be impeached	The "head of state" and "highest official"; represents the Russian Federation internally and abroad; elected for a five-year term; nominates candidates for prime minister to the Federal Assembly and can propose the resignation of government; appoints and dismisses ministers on nomination of prime minister after "consultation" with Council of the Federation; appoints and dismisses heads of administration and representatives of the president in the regions; calls elections and dissolves parliament after "consultations"; commander in chief; declares emergencies; may he impeached for violation of constitution
Vice President	
Elected together with the president	None
Government	
Conducts foreign and domestic policy under the direction of the president and coordination of the prime minister; reports annually to and can be dismissed by Supreme Soviet	Determines the "main directions of the policy and activity of the government"; responsible for budget and finance, education and culture, defense, and law enforcement
Legislature	
Supreme Soviet of the Russian Federation; two chambers: the State Duma, elected on a population basis, and the Federal Assembly elected by republics and regions; amends constitution and adopts federal laws; approves the government on nomination of president and decides on members' dismissal; can impeach president, vice president and others; can override presidential veto on legislation	The Federal Assembly is the "highest representative federal organ"; two chambers: Council of the Federation, elected by republics and regions, and the State Duma, elected on a population basis; amends constitution and adopts federal laws; Council of Federation on nomination of president appoints prime minister and decides on dismissal of government; Council of Federation can declare emergency or impeach president
Referendum	
Called by Supreme Soviet	Called by president
Constitutional Court	
The "highest organ of legal authority for the defense of the constitutional order of the Russian Federation"; 15 members, individually appointed	Considers the constitutionality of laws, presidential and other decrees and decisions

Sources: Based on the draft constitution approved by the Sixth Congress of People's Deputies in April 1992 (Proekt konstitutsii Rossiiskoi Federatsii, Moscow: Republika, 1992), and the presidential draft published in Izvestia, April 30, 1993.

Yeltsin's personal response to this challenge emerged on the evening of March 20, when in a nationally televised address he called for the introduction of a "special form of administration." Parliament would not be suspended, and the ordinary rights of citizens would be unaffected, but the legislature would be unable to overrule the decrees that the president or the government might choose to issue. In the meantime, Yeltsin promised, there would be a popular vote April 25, in which the president and vice president would ask for an expression of voters' support and a new constitution and electoral law would be submitted for their approval.

The address was supported by the Russian government, but it was swiftly condemned by the chairman of the Constitutional Court as an "attempted coup" and deplored by Vice President Aleksandr Rutskoi, the prosecutor general, and parliamentary representatives. When the text of Yeltsin's decree was finally published a few days later, it did not contain a reference to a "special form of administration" and called for no more than a vote of confidence in the president and an expression of opinion on the draft constitution and electoral law.

The Congress of People's Deputies was hurriedly convened to consider this new challenge to its authority. When members met on March 26, an attempt to impeach Yeltsin was narrowly defeated. In the end, a referendum was set for April 25, but it was agreed that this would consider different questions from those—including the establishment of a "presidential republic" and private ownership of land—that Yeltsin had originally suggested.

The referendum did little to resolve the continuing impasse. The ballot contained four questions: (i) "Do you have confidence in the president of the Russian Federation B. N. Yeltsin?"; (ii) "Do you approve the socioeconomic policy that the president and government of the Russian Federation have been conducting since 1992?"; (iii) "Do you think it necessary to hold early elections for the presidency of the Russian Federation?"; and (iv) "Do you think it necessary to hold early parliamentary elections?"

The outcome, in most respects, was a victory for Yeltsin, although a less dramatic one than early exit polls had seemed to promise. Turnout nationwide was a respectable 64.6 percent (voting took place everywhere except the Chechen republic; in Tatarstan the turnout of just 22 percent was not high enough to produce a valid result). Of those who voted, 58.1 percent supported the president and 52.9 percent backed his socioeconomic policies. The other two questions, according to the Constitutional Court, required a majority of the total electorate, not just of those who voted in the referendum. Counting this way only 32.4 percent had called for an early election for president, and 41.4 percent for early parliamentary elections.

For Yeltsin and his supporters this was a verdict that justified pressing ahead with a constitution that provided for a presidential republic with a much more limited legislature, and this was the basis on which a constitutional convention began to function from May onward. For Yeltsin's opponents it was a result that owed a great deal to media pressure and in any case exposed the limits of the president's support, particularly outside the large cities and in non-Russian areas.

THE TEST OF WILLS

Several elements were involved in the deepening political stalemate that by the early 1990s had begun to threaten the exercise of government itself in Russia. One was certainly the continuing competition for authority between president and parliament. As Yeltsin saw it, without a strong executive there would be "no reforms, no order and no statehood worthy of Russia, its history and traditions." Reducing the presidency to a figurehead, he told the congress in April 1992, would lead to chaos and regional separatism; only a strong executive could preserve the integrity of Russia and with it, the continuation of reform. He had received his authority directly from the Russian people, Yeltsin made clear early this year, and he did not necessarily consider himself bound by a constitution that had been repeatedly amended since he had sworn to abide by its provisions as Russian president.

The congress, the president complained in December 1992, tended "just to reject, just to destroy." Too many deputies engaged in "cheap populism and open demagoguery . . . and, in the final analysis, [worked toward] the restoration of a totalitarian Soviet-Communist system." The only way forward was a direct appeal to the voters who had elected him and resolution of the basic question—who rules Russia, president or congress?

For parliamentarians and their speaker, Ruslan Khasbulatov, the issue was a rather different one: whether government should be accountable to elected representatives, and whether a broadly representative parliament should be allowed to act as a counterbalance to what would otherwise be an overwhelmingly powerful executive. For Khasbulatov, Russian history before the revolution and then Marxism-Leninism had combined to exaggerate the power of a single "czar." Thus it was crucial to establish a secure division of powers and to develop the role of parliament as a representative organ of the whole society. Parliament in particular could serve as a counterweight to the executive, exercising its influence over public spending, legislation, and the composition of government as parliaments did in other countries.

Khabulatov, an economics professor in his early fifties, had become acting speaker in July 1991 with Yeltsin's support and had taken part in the defense of the Russian White House in the August attempted coup, but had subsequently emerged as the president's most effective opponent. Opening the Russian parliament last March, Khasbulatov accused the government of an "attack on democracy." He also insisted, in the confrontation between parliament and presidency, that the Cabinet of Ministers be accountable to the congress and not to the "collective Rasputin" that surrounded the president. Whatever the merits of these views, Khasbulatov had less public support than Yeltsin; he was, after all, a Chechen, not a Russian, and his main quality (according to opinion polls discussed in the March 27, 1993, *Izvestia*) was "cunning" rather than statesmanship. He was less important as an individual than as a symbol of the principle of representative rather than presidential government.

UNINVITING PARTIES

Other political systems, the French and American among them, have managed to operate effectively despite the separate election of an executive president and a working legislature. What has rendered the Russian system peculiarly immobile is the absence of a party system that could bind together a president and a parliamentary majority. Yeltsin spoke last November of attempting to establish a party or movement that would support him, but the proposal made little progress.

Nor were other parties strong. The Communist party, suspended in August and banned entirely in November 1991, was allowed to reconstitute itself after the Constitutional Court ruled the ban illegal (although the court also found the suppression of the party's central institutions legitimate, since these had usurped the state). The party was duly revived in February claiming more than half a million members; this made it the largest of the new parties, although still far smaller than the Communist party of the Soviet Union it had succeeded.

Altogether, by the summer of 1992 there were at least 1,200 parties or movements in operation across Russia, and 28 of them had been formally registered with the Justice Ministry by early 1993. Surveys conducted earlier this year suggested popular support was most widespread for Nikolai Travkin's Democratic party (17.8 percent viewed it "positively" and 16.8 percent would vote for its candidates). But Communist groupings came in second and third, with about 23 percent between them, followed by the All-Russian Union of Cossacks, the Democratic Reform Movement, and the Peasant Party of Russia.

This still falls short of a party system that could sustain effective government, much less a pluralist democracy. Party membership, for a start, was very low and active memberships at only about 30,000 for all parties combined, according to an estimate published in the April 20, 1992, *Izvestia*. Levels of knowledge and identification were little better. A survey conducted in late 1991, for instance, found that more than half those asked "knew nothing" about Travkin's Democratic party and that a further 39 percent "knew only the name." Although the Democratic party is one of the largest of the new crop, the survey could find no members or supporters whatsoever; more generally between 70 percent and 80 percent of those asked were outside political life altogether, and only 5 percent had some regular involvement. Levels of knowledge were lower still in many localities: in the Vladimir region, for example, almost two-thirds of respondents "had not the slightest idea" about any of the parties they were questioned on. And there was a clear distinction, as in other countries, between verbal support and willingness to attend meetings, carry out party activities, or even vote for the party for which one expressed a nominal preference.

There was, in fact, some hostility to the very idea of a political party. "Why have two parties?" it had been remarked during the decades of Communist monopoly; "wasn't one bad enough?" Surveys conducted in late 1992 and early this year found that more than half those asked thought all the new parties had been founded by people who were simply "greedy for power," and 12 percent thought party activists were "misfits who had nothing better to do." Almost 40 percent believed party activities had "no bearing upon the life of ordinary people," and one-fifth felt the new parties played no substantial role in politics. An overwhelming 78 percent said there were no parties anywhere in Russia with which they could identify.

The very word "party" was deeply compromised after the many years in which it had been a synonym for single-party dictatorship. And what was a party anyway? As a 45-year-old woman, formerly a member of the Soviet Communist party, explained in *Augumenty i fakty*, "I don't believe in any of the parties anymore. . . . All the ones we have at the moment are only interested in getting into power, and no one is concerned about ordinary people. Not even the Communists."

If there are organized forces in Russian politics, they are parliamentary factions rather than political parties. The most influential of these is the Civic Union, a broad coalition established last summer by a newly formed association calling itself Renewal, together with the People's Party of Free Russia led by Vice President Rutskoi and Travkin's Democratic party. Renewal had been created in April 1992 by figures grouped around the Russian Union of Industrialists and Entrepreneurs, led by Arkadii Volsky, a former member of the Soviet Communist party Secretariat. Volsky, the most influential exponent of the new bloc's views, called for "radical reform and strong government" and expressed some interest in the "experience of the Chinese reforms."

The selection of Chernomyrdin as prime minister, and Yeltsin's own increasing emphasis on the need for socially oriented policies without any further shock therapy, suggest that Civic Union—despite the defection of the Democratic party—has become the dominant voice in policymaking. But it has more developing to do before it becomes the kind of stable parliamentary party on which governments in liberal democracies can normally rely.

QUESTIONED AUTHORITY

Relations between the president and the parliament played themselves out against the background of a deepening crisis of governance. Chernomyrdin, addressing the Congress of People's Deputies this March, spoke of a "catastrophic loss of manageability." Laws were being adopted but largely ignored. Taxes were being levied but not paid; the city of Moscow was collecting only about half of what it was due, and the Russian government was itself collecting only two-thirds. At least four republics were making no contribution.

The authority of the Russian government was directly called into question by the 20 autonomous units located within its borders: only 18 of them agreed to sign a federal treaty in March 1992, and by this summer at least 8 had declared sovereignty over their own territory. The Chechen republic in the northern Caucasus Mountains went still further and (according to its constitution) became an entirely independent state outside the Russian Federation.

Who does rule Russia then? According to surveys from late last year, respondents said it might be the mafia (21.8 percent) or no one at all (9.3 percent); 9.7 percent thought President Yeltsin was in charge, but only 3.9 percent believed the government was, and just 0.2 percent thought parliament governed Russia—the same proportion that said the country was being run by alcoholics.

Confronted by these depressing developments, Russian citizens are tending to opt out of political life completely. There is great disappointment with the course of developments since the attempted coup in 1991, and a great deal of disillusionment with the parties and parliaments that have succeeded the Communist order. A representative group was asked in December 1992 who had benefited from the system that has been established in post-Communist Russia. The largest number of respondents thought the system operated "for its own benefit"; 6 percent said it operated "for the rich and entrepreneurs"; 5 percent "for the mafia"; and a further 5 percent said it operated for "nobody at all." When in fact

had there ever been a government in Russia that took account of the needs of ordinary people? For most of those responding to a poll late last year, it had been during the Brezhnev era (21 percent) or under the czars at the start of the century (14 percent); but 44 percent had no idea when there had been such a government. In these circumstances, many Russians were transferring their energies outside the political system: particularly to religion and the supernatural, but also to business, pornography, bodybuilding, organized crime, and rock music.

Values of this kind have left the Russian system in an uncertain state. There are few who wish to see the Communists return to power; at the same time, the unreformed Communist system is generally seen as preferable to both the economic and political turmoil that succeeded it and to the system likely to exist in five years' time. There is strong support for the reimposition of public order and morality; at the same time there is widespread commitment to glasnost and the division of political power from the center to the regions and republics. This leaves considerable scope for political leadership, which is often crucial to the establishment and consolidation of democratic politics. Yet the elites are divided, their institutions discredited, and none of them can count on the firm support of a major political party.

Other countries have made the transition to democracy, yet there are few that have done so in a time of falling living standards and lacking a developed civil society of groups and institutions or an extended experience of democratic self-government. Russia, it was argued in the late 1980s, needed to "learn democracy." The evidence of the first years after communism has been that the educational process will be a difficult and extended one, with no guarantee of success.

Article 3   *Time*, December 27, 1993

No Reason to Cheer

The surprise success of Vladimir Zhirinovsky's neofascist party in the parliamentary elections imperils reform at home and sets off alarm bells abroad.

Jill Smolowe

In 1917 it took Russia 10 days to shake the world. Last week it took just one. Although the latest revolution unfolded peacefully at the ballot box, the aftershocks were no less unsettling than those triggered by the Bolshevik coup. Ultranationalist Vladimir Zhirinovsky, a golden-tongued demagogue who has been compared with Adolf Hitler, looked to have swept enough votes to establish a powerful bloc for his neofascist party in the State Duma, the lower house of the new Russian parliament.

Although Moscow watchers in the West played down the possibility of a revanchist Russia, panicky East Europeans renewed their entreaties for prompt entry into NATO. Zhirinovsky's past pledge to reincorporate Latvia, Estonia and Lithuania into Russia had leaders of the three Baltic republics huddling to shore up international support for their independence. As editorialists in the capitals of Western Europe and Asia warned of "dangerous fascism," Vice President Al Gore cast Zhirinovsky's views as "reprehensible and anathema to all freedom-loving people."

The squalls stirred by Russia's first real multiparty elections in 76 years may yet prove overblown. In reality, there were no decisive winners—only losers. Of the eight parties that ran strongly enough in the 13-party free-for-all to secure seats in the Duma, none will enjoy anything near a majority. Zhirinovsky's misleadingly named Liberal Democratic Party stands to claim fewer than 80 seats in the 450-seat lower house of the new bicameral legislature, while reformers will occupy roughly twice that number. A preliminary count suggests that the lower house will be divided almost evenly among democrats, nationalists, Communists and independents—thus assuring a future of gridlocked misery for the Deputies. Voters also found little cause to celebrate their grand experiment in democracy: nearly as many people stayed home as came out to vote.

As for President Boris Yeltsin, who called the elections last September before crushing a hard-line revolt in a bloody showdown with the former parliament, he is reaping precisely what he sowed. Having chosen to stand above the electoral frenzy and endorse no party, Yeltsin threw his energies into only one contest—the referendum on a new draft constitution. Yeltsin's popular clout brought in a 58% vote of support for the constitution, which grants him sweeping powers, among them the right to disband the parliament. But the legislative races failed to produce a new guard of professionals who would put constitutional rule and economic reform back on a fast track. Instead he now faces a parliament that promises to be as belligerent as the one he dissolved—only this time legislators enjoy the same electoral legitimacy that Yeltsin once claimed as uniquely his own.

In the U.S. Zhirinovsky's appeal was read much like the maverick presidential challenge mounted by Ross Perot in 1992. Zhirinovsky, too, campaigned skillfully as an outsider. He slung verbal Molotov cocktails at a system tainted by gridlock and inefficiency. And he aimed right at Russians' pocketbooks, denouncing the economic reforms that have hiked the price of metro tickets from five kopeks to 30 rubles, pushed middle-income households toward the poverty level and withheld wages from such key constituencies as the coal miners. But like the U.S. billionaire, Zhirinovsky had far more to offer in the way of fire-brand bombast than coherent policy. "Zhirinovsky has no program and offers no alternatives," says Marie Mendras, a Russia specialist with the National Foundation of Political Science in Paris. "He simply reflects the mood of the population today, which does not want to see the continued deterioration of daily life."

Europeans, who are reminded daily by events in former Yugoslavia just how porous borders can be, were more inclined to see the parallels between Russia and Weimar Germany: vast economic dislocations, hyperinflation, national humiliation and a disaffected officer class. Of course, there are notable differences too. For all its economic troubles, Russia does not suffer the massive unemployment that plagued Germany just after World War I. And rather than being slapped with steep reparations, Russia is receiving aid from abroad.

While reform candidates shrank from direct contact with the people, offering only boring TV speeches and glum-faced round-table discussions on esoteric subjects during the election campaign, Zhirinovsky held regular Saturday-afternoon street-corner rallies drawing crowds that numbered in the thousands. For every constituency, he designed a tailor-made message. The military received pledges of a resurrected and expanded Russian Empire. Fixed-income pensioners and students were promised a decent standard of living. Crime-weary citizens were assured that gang leaders would be executed. Meanwhile, foreigners were offered up as scapegoats, and Jews were blamed for provoking anti-Semitism.

For those watching from beyond Russia's borders, Zhirinovsky's improbable but disquieting suggestions of "new Hiroshimas" and "Chernobyls" were enough to force a swift rethink of strategy. Last week Germans modified their enthusiastic calls for an eastward expansion of NATO, pushing instead for a "gradual and controlled" opening in order to assuage Russia's paranoid generals. In Washington the dominant refrain was to urge the U.S. Administration both to reduce its personal identification with Yeltsin and to broaden its contacts within Russia. And Westerners everywhere read the returns as proof positive that Yeltsin's personal popularity did not translate into broad-based support for Western-style, free-market economy.

Despite the global shudder, the betting is that Yeltsin will lurch forward with his economic and social agenda, his hand strengthened by new constitutional powers. Now, when legislators balk three times at his choice of a Prime Minister, he can call new elections. He can also select his government in sole consultation with the Prime Minister. That makes it unlikely that Yeltsin will offer a post to anyone in Zhirinovsky's camp. If Yeltsin doesn't like a piece of legislation, Deputies will have to corral a two-thirds vote in both chambers to override his veto.

While there was loose talk last week of coalition building, especially between the Communists and Zhirinovsky's followers—a so-called Red-Brown coalition—Russia's once daunting mastery of party discipline has gone the way of the honor guard at Lenin's tomb. Any alliances forged in coming days are likely to founder shortly after the Duma convenes in Moscow next month and Deputies get their first real taste of lawmaking. Despite the surprising showing by the Liberal Democrats, Zhirinovsky's power will be much diluted once the Duma gets down to business.

Chastened reformers have been swift to heed the electoral message that when Yeltsin does not offer his coattails, they risk a ride into oblivion. While Yeltsin remained silent after the electoral returns, his confidant Mikhail Poltoranin warned, "Fascism is creeping in the door opened by our divisions and our ambitions." Yegor Gaidar, who heads Russia's Choice, the largest reformist party, and is architect of Yeltsin's economic reforms, was more blunt, calling upon the three reformist parties to "lay aside all ambitions and disagreements" to forge a "united front."

Yeltsin will also have to rethink his strategy. The President can no longer afford to dissipate his energies by constantly squabbling with the parliament. A new posture of conciliation was hinted at last week when Kremlin spokesman Vyacheslav Kostikov publicly allowed that parts of the Liberal Democratic and Communist programs "quite correspond to the social aspects of the President's policies—that is, the social policy of the state, patriotism, making Russia great."

The biggest clue as to whether Yeltsin is ready to move closer to the political center will come in his dealings with such radical reformers as Gaidar, Finance Minister Boris Fyodorov and Foreign Minister Andrei Kozyrev. The President may decide that the time has come to jettison all or some of them from his team in the interest of building a consensus for reforms that proceed at a slower pace and demand less exacting social sacrifices. Last week he signalled his anger at the nationalists' strong showing by firing his chief legal adviser

and the chairman of a television company that broadcasts to most of the former Soviet states.

The West is already girding for a more aggressive Russian line in foreign policy. In recent weeks Moscow has toughened its expressions of concern about the shabby treatment of ethnic Russians in former republics. It has also signalled a vague willingness to retaliate if NATO decides to open its membership to the former Warsaw Pact states. That may mean the parliament balking at the provisions of the Treaty on Conventional Forces in Europe and SALT II. U.S. analysts warn that under the new parliament, Russia's arms sales abroad will rise, as will the budgets of the security and military services.

Perhaps most worrisome to Westerners is how military loyalties will divide if Yeltsin and Zhirinovsky bump heads. "Until now the army has proved itself to be very mature," says German Foreign Minister Klaus Kinkel. "But after the latest events, we can only hope it stays that way." Strange as it may seem, Zhirinovsky's elevation to a Duma seat may be the best thing for Yeltsin: better to have "Vladimir the Terrible" spouting off in the parliament than rabble rousing in the streets. Then again, Zhirinovsky is now well poised to use his seat in parliament as a launching pad for his presidential ambitions.

—Reported by John Kohan/Moscow, J. F. O. McAllister/Washington, with other bureaus

---

Article 4

The American Prospect, Spring 1993

Privatization in the Former Soviet Empire

The Tunnel at the End of the Light

Stephen S. Cohen and Andrew Schwartz

Stephen S. Cohen is co-director and Andrew Schwartz is a research associate at the Berkeley Roundtable on the International Economy at the University of California at Berkeley.

In the former Soviet empire, the collapse of Communism created an opportunity for the victims of one failed utopian ideology to find another. The evaporating Soviet system left an ideological vacuum that was quickly filled as legions of Western advisers arrived to help translate the goals of political democracy and a market economy into an action agenda: "democracy" translated quickly into elections; a "market economy" into privatization.

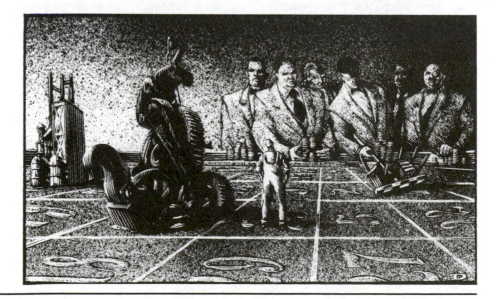

As in many hurried translations, the bare essentials were grasped, but much was missed. Elections are essential to democracy, but functioning democracies are built on much more than just elections. And private ownership is only one element of a modern market economy. But it was fundamentalist capitalism that poured in—the simple, universal program that all could understand: free prices, free trade, and, above all, privatize.

The fate of small enterprises like shops, restaurants, or farms was never at issue. Everyone agreed that rapid small-scale privatization was the best way to energize private sector growth and to develop a capitalist ethic and an entrepreneurial class.

The thornier question was how, and how fast, to privatize the clunking state enterprises that employed thousands and thousands. Supposedly, only an abrupt and ruthless privatization could clear the stage of the remnants of a command economy—the perverse incentives, the incompetent and corrupt apparatchiks, the endless subsidies, the mindless production of the wrong goods. Delay risked permitting those who stood to lose the most from privatization—the old-line bureaucrats and the managers and workers of the giant state enterprises—to undermine the privatization process, thereby jeopardizing the transition to a market economy. According to Harvard University economist Jeffrey Sachs:

The need to accelerate privatization in Eastern Europe is the paramount economic policy issue facing the region. If there is no breakthrough in privatization in large enterprises in the near future, the entire process could be stalled for political and social reasons for years to come, with dire consequences for the reforming economies of the region.

The *Economist* agreed, calling "the growing acceptance of . . . gradualism . . . the greatest peril now facing the countries of Eastern Europe."

But there is an alternative to radical privatization, and it is not just a smokescreen put forward by nostalgics for the old system. It is rather the safest and sanest approach to building a market economy and democratic society.

Rapid privatization will backfire, for few of the newly privatized big companies can survive in a competitive market environment. The structures of both supply and demand for these giant firms

have been shattered; the industrial linkages among Eastern Europe and the former Soviet republics are severed. The abrupt political change separated enterprises from their traditional customers the way the movement of rivers into new channels left medieval entrepots high and dry on silted streams. The economic collapse resulting from sudden privatization would result in extensive layoffs, massive bankruptcies, and social unrest. In a climate of chaos, the state would eventually have to support the failing enterprises, one way or another.

Markets can't regulate monopolies. A heritage of monopolies implies active regulation. Who shall regulate monopoly and oligopoly industries? Who shall oversee the liquidation of the losers, the temporary subsidy of restructurings, and the re-employment of workers? For a prolonged period, newly privatized firms won't be able to compete in their home markets against superior imported goods. Who shall oversee international trade and ration foreign exchange, as West European governments had to do after World War II? Further, such essential preconditions for modern capitalist economies as an established legal system or tax code, financial institutions, and effective capital markets do not exist. These shortcomings increase the odds that a "big bang" privatization will turn into a "big bust."

This essay develops the argument for a pragmatic approach to privatization. It boils down to three basic contentions.

First, the creation of capitalist institutions takes time. Privatizing ownership will not by itself make large, uncompetitive enterprises operate efficiently. Nor will distributing ownership of shares create a market system or a capitalist culture. Giant corporations need internal capabilities in organization, pricing, labor relations, accounting, and marketing in addition to productive incentives. The repair of severed domestic and international linkages—among existing plants, between suppliers and users, between firms and their traditional markets—will also take time.

Second, private ownership, even in the Western context, makes sense only in the context of embedded socioeconomic institutions. Big companies don't exist in an institutional vacuum. Nor do markets. Both require external structures of law, finance, and regulation. Erecting a system of domestic finance with efficient capital markets is but one important example of such needed institutions.

Third, the state will inevitably play the major role in industrial development

in most of the countries of the former Soviet empire, especially Russia, for a long interim. It will help create and regulate markets; it will control imports and oversee the flow of capital; and, irrespective of the chosen privatization strategy, it will effectively control substantial portions of major industrial assets. The competitive vulnerability of existing industry allows no other alternative for the near future. The creation of an honest and effective public administration—not the broad distribution of shares in uncompetitive giant firms—is the key step toward the creation of a successful capitalistic market system and a functioning democracy.

Varieties of Capitalism, or Who Owns Mitsubishi?

Radical capitalists ignore the great differences in the institutions of private ownership of big firms in such successful capitalist countries as the U.S., Japan, Germany, France, and Italy, as well as the other enormous institutional differences that distinguish the competing capitalisms. They strip away the complex variety and reduce private ownership to the simple model of textbook economics. They neglect history, they discard experience. Any remotely appropriate historical experience—such as Europe after World Wars I and II—points in a quite different direction.

Radical capitalists insist that only a system of privately owned firms linked together by markets provides the right incentives and the right constraints, a set of signals that promotes social dynamism and optimal allocation. Moreover, market signals are prompt and unrelenting. Adaptation is fast and permanent. One of the impressive aesthetics of capitalism is the perfect match between efficiency in capital formation and efficiency in production. Moreover, newly privatized industries are likely to attract foreign investors—the main sources of modern technology and management skills—more readily than state counterparts. Finally, competition will relentlessly downsize the old industrial monsters into more productively sized companies.

At first glance, the radical capitalist argument is appealing. The problem, of course, is that the textbook caricatures of the institutions of modern capitalism obscures an understanding of how the different systems actually function. Take the two critical institutions—price-driven, "free" capital markets and private ownership of giant corporations.

Neither is simple in practice; and neither is universal in form.

In France, as in Japan, Germany, and Korea, for more than a generation after World War II, capital markets were neither "free" nor price-driven. To a critical extent, especially where giant corporations were concerned, capital was allocated less by price (as in the proposed capital markets for Eastern Europe) than by administrative systems of priorities.

Nor does the pragmatic experience of forms of ownership correspond to the simplistic radical capitalist model. In Japan, the most successful case ever of rapid development, ownership is "private," but only if one defines private as not owned by the state. Interlocking shareholding and finance within the industrial groups known as *keiretsu* created something far removed from the simple ownership model of the radical capitalists. Keiretsu have no obvious analogy in the rest of the First World, and no place whatsoever in Econ 101 textbooks. Who owns Mitsubishi? Perhaps the most accurate functional answer is "Mitsubishi owns Mitsubishi."

The form of ownership is an important element in modern capitalism, but it is less a unifying than a differentiating characteristic; and it takes its real world meaning only within the complex institutional context that defines a particular capitalist system. There is more than one variety of successful capitalism.

Structural Constraints and Realistic Choices

Just as it is dangerous to apply narrowly naive concepts of capitalist institutions to the different countries of the former Soviet realm, so it is dangerous to generalize about this region. The several countries have different political systems, legal traditions, ownership patterns, educational levels, industrial structures, languages, ethnic cleavages, religions, and, of course, sizes. It is little wonder that of the countries most actively engaged in privatization—the Czech Republic, Slovakia, Poland, Hungary, Slovenia, and Russia—each has a different privatization strategy. Nonetheless, the Communist system left a shared legacy that constrains the prospects for rapid privatization. At least seven of these troubling legacies will shape the results of privatization.

1. Shortage of entrepreneurial experience; surplus of criminal experience. More than 40 years of Communism have produced a managerial class ill-equipped to function in a capitalist market. The best of the technical-managerial leadership is lodged in the military-industrial complex, a declining market. Most of the market experience comes from the "second economy," and it is dubious that such experience will translate into competent large company ownership or management.

Besides petty black marketeers, the other likely new ownership stratum is those who made money illegally—big-time black marketeers or corrupt bureaucrats—or both working together, as they always have. They are best positioned to cash in on abrupt privatizations. They can split enterprises into valuable and potentially negative parts, shift labor across those parts, maintain control of the good bits, and reap a capital gain at the moment of privatization—millionaires in one quick shot. They can reap a windfall gain no matter how the enterprise performs. Even where assets are auctioned to the highest bidder, these networks of officials and plant managers, with their underground allies (most often called, locally, "the Mafia"), typically have the cash and insider knowledge to bid. This potential was not lost on sophisticated foreign advisers: bars in foreigners-only hotels are filled with International Monetary Fund and World Bank officials explaining how the late medieval capitalists in Europe were considered, in their time, to be criminal elements. Likewise, the winners of the American bootlegging wars have now become solid, corporate capitalists. Privatization ideally would transform the criminal mafia into normal organizations—unless, of course, the Southern Italian model were to prevail.

2. Shortage of companies ready for a market economy. Most of the giant enterprises are burdened with obsolete product and process technology and mountains of debt. The debt will be written off by the state one way or another. But even with newly cleaned balance sheets, they are poor candidates for market viability. Finding real private owners to run them, without permanent subsidy and protection, will be difficult. Even the German privatization agency the *Treuhandanstalt*, despite an infusion of about $100 billion, had only privatized about half of the eastern German industries by 1992, representing the best of Communist enterprise. Some 1.6 million workers remain under Treuhand jurisdiction. Despite its ferocious determination to the contrary, it would not be surprising if the Treuhand found itself slowly transformed into a new German version of Italy's much maligned I.R.I. (the giant state holding company).

3. Poor work habits. This report from the *New York Times* is typical: "Managers of new private companies say they must dismiss dozens of people to find one not afflicted by the lackadaisical work ethic fostered by the Communist system. Private hotels in Warsaw do not even accept applications from former state employees." In addition, a hierarchical mentality still pervades enterprises. In the past, incentive structures in Communist enterprises discouraged managers from acting with initiative. In most cases, managers were better off playing along with the system than risking their position by exercising discretion.

4. Shortage of domestic and international capital. The previous regimes left the economies virtually without savings. The rebuilding of the industrial capacity in the region cannot rely on small contributions from the accumulated savings of the domestic population. Newly privatized firms will need debt financing from domestic banks or from institutions based abroad. Yet none of the governments has yet established a banking system ready to make the loans. Moreover, real and/or nominal rates are high, and credit is generally very tight throughout the region. The major source of capital is likely to remain the state, or in very selected circumstances, foreigners.

The newly privatized firms, striving to become competitive, will not be the only large claimants on the small capital pool. Indeed, they will most likely find themselves at the end of the queue. The best candidates for privatization, and for capital infusions, are the classic infrastructural industries: telecommunications, road building, railways, airlines, and the like, not to mention electric power generation—the handling of those dangerous nuclear power plants on West Europe's doorstep. The Western Europeans want those stations rebuilt for safety, and their nuclear power industry is hurting from a lack of orders. They will provide massive investment to the newly privatizing electric utilities, thus combining safety and capitalist development in the East along with safety and the generation of business for state-supported industry in the West.

Privatizing infrastructural industries would also have the advantage of producing tradable shares with which to generate capital markets. Moreover, they would be acceptable vehicles for international aid and investment institutions that are obligated to make a substantial portion of their financing to private firms. All in all, such industries present an ideal set of financeable and potentially privatizeable activities, protected from the vicissitudes of markets and competition. They are not, however, very likely, to be particularly generative of a new capitalist culture.

Those who expect a major capital injection from the West are likely to be disappointed. A "Marshall Plan" for the former Soviet empire is not in the cards. For one thing, recession and high government deficits have drained public coffers in the West. For another, there are alternative targets for scarce Western and Japanese capital, in Asia and Latin America. To date, inbound private investment has been quite small. For instance, in 1990 and 1991, Poland received $1.3 billion, Czechoslovakia $800 million, and Hungary $2.3 billion. World Bank commitments to the region for 1991 amounted only to a little over $3 billion. The EBRD (European Bank for Reconstruction and Development) put in only about $800 million, about half for telecommunications loans. Over the same period, as noted, East Germany, a territory of some 17 million souls, received almost $100 billion. Multiply that amount by ten to get a comparable infusion for Russia alone, and one can see that the German experience, a new intra-German Marshall Plan, is not a model for the region. Finally, there will be dramatic differences among the host nations in the role of foreign capital. Foreign capital and foreign markets will be major shapers of the Czech economy; they will necessarily have only a small impact on the Russian economy.

5. Risky business conditions. Marko Simonetti, director of privatization for Slovenia, argues that the challenge of privatization is to find active owners willing to lead companies through the transition period. But why should new owners restructure their enterprises when there may be an immediate payoff if they simply liquidate the assets? Domestic producers won't be able to compete effectively in open markets, at home or through exports. A quick taste of what lies ahead is the case of large state enterprises in eastern Germany. Unable to compete abroad, these firms lost their home market when products and companies from the western part of the country moved in.

The temptation to liquidate rather than to invest is heightened by the asset value of many companies. The company's land, buildings, and the right to do business may be worth more in the marketplace than its productive poten-

tial, lying in often dubious and difficult assets like machinery or the labor force. A common story is that of CKD Tatra—until recently the world's largest maker of tram cars, but last year the manufacturer of only 300—which has attracted investment interest mostly because its factory sits on valuable land in central Prague. This is simple rent-seeking, not entrepreneurship.

6. Weak links between labor, suppliers, manufacturers, and consumers. First World countries like Japan and Germany were able to get back on their feet quickly after World War II partly because reconstruction meant the reconstitution of forms of economic organization established years earlier rather than the creation of completely new relationships. For instance, keiretsu, the centralized forms of ownership in Japan, were antedated by *zaibatsu* which originated a century ago in the Meiji era. German business and unions reached durable working arrangements long before the postwar German miracle. Eastern Europe won't be able to manufacture those relationships overnight.

7. Fragmented markets; broken international linkages; ethnic hostility. The countries emerging from the former Soviet empire are fractured by unresolved differences in ethnicity, language, and religion. In many cases these differences have not been politically or economically resolved. Divisions between Czechs and Slovaks, Hungarians and Romanians, Armenians and Asseris, Russians and Ukranians, to name a few, are likely to stymie economic rationalization. Perhaps the most poignant example is most of Yugoslavia, where civil war has halted economic reform.

The long-run economic choices of Eastern European countries will be restricted by the poverty and small size of most of the national markets in the region. To be competitive, industries in small countries must be active participants in foreign markets. Ideally, industries in small countries operate in a very open international market, buy where value is best, and sell internationally in niches. They must be outward looking and dynamic: exactly the opposite of Eastern European large enterprises.

The industrial structures of Eastern Europe did not develop according to classic economic logic; they were defined by planned linkages within the regions of the ex-Soviet empire. Isolated from world markets, large firms produced goods made better and cheaper abroad. They operated in captive markets and exported on a large scale to

similarly noncompetitive markets. They learned to operate with constant output and input prices and virtually unlimited access to credit. Sooner or later, many of those companies must be eliminated as national resources are channelled into products where the Eastern European countries are likely to have a competitive advantage, not just compared with one another but compared with the entire world. As one big firm in the region tries to improve itself by buying quality components from the world market, it dries up the markets for the other large firms, its traditional suppliers. When local consumers get a little real money and the chance to buy coveted imported goods rather than generally lower quality local products, the entire system collapses.

These old networks are now completely severed. As a result, Eastern European companies have lost the only conceivable buyers for much of what they produce. The problem is not simply one of price efficiency: it is one of political borders and disruption. Even a substantial increase in efficiency will not make up for the tattered regional industrial structure. It takes years to build a new structure, and a new structure cannot be built until the political uncertainty is overcome. Private investment—obtained in a real capital market—won't be readily forthcoming in newly privatized companies that are unsure of where their markets lie, where their sources of supply are located, or who their competitors are.

These seven obstacles would deter the most ardent reformers from attempting a program of drastic and potentially all-or-nothing industrial change. But the radical capitalists argue that it is essential to privatize quickly precisely because of such problems. That prescription might be tenable given a stable institutional setting with stable national boundaries and political systems, functioning tax codes, financial and legal systems, and broad-based capital markets, as well as plausible networks of international markets and industrial linkages. But there are few credible tested institutions. Without them, rapid privatization won't provide a solid base for prosperity, nor will it aid the development of independent entrepreneurs.

The Crucial Role of Capital Markets

Capital markets, just one of the absent institutions, invite particular attention. Price-driven capital markets are dear to the hearts of privatizers. Capital markets remove power, in giant dollops, from the hands of entrenched bureaucracies. They are fast, powerful, and provide invisibility for the market movers. It is difficult for a public bureaucracy to close down the only industry in a midwestern American town; that now-familiar objective is more easily achieved by a twitch on the Tokyo or New York stock exchange.

In capitalist economies, broad-based equity markets serve both investors and corporations in several ways. First, equity markets signal the underlying value of securities. Theoretically, this facilitates the proper allocation of resources by providing both investors and companies opportunities to raise cash as well as to spread resources among businesses that vary by product line and investment risk. Accurate share valuations provide stockholders with a de facto evaluation of management, which may sometimes precipitate corrective action. Second, equity markets provide avenues for companies to raise capital (equity or debt) from a wide net of investors. By the same token, equity markets enable investors to control risk in their portfolio more easily. Finally, equity markets ease the costs of investment and corporate restructuring by providing liquidity to both investors and corporations.

Because they are so powerful, capital markets are dangerous, especially when they lack proper safeguards and depth. In the lands of the ex-Soviet empire, the hazards are particularly acute because of the complete lack of experience in using these markets. Additionally, capital markets are likely to attract more attention than usual because of their novelty in the region and their significance as a capitalist symbol. Radical capitalists assume, correctly in our view, that capital markets will arise concurrently with privatization and the issuance of shares. Despite few viable companies, public stock markets are being organized in most of the countries.

Unfortunately, in spite of good intentions, these equity markets probably won't be able to perform efficiently—and just may perform with delegitimating perversity. It will be virtually impossible to establish fair market value for the exchange's listed companies given the shortage of capital in the region and the unstable business conditions. The lack of well-established, highly capitalized market participants implies that there will be a lack of liquidity in the equity markets. This will produce thin equity markets and wild price swings. The inexperience of the traders

may also increase the likelihood of price gyrations.

Corruption is sure to become a big problem. Inexperienced market regulators will not be able to police markets that are moving quickly and without apparent reason. Market rigging and stock manipulation are inevitable. As most experienced traders will attest, financial market operations are very complex and enforcing fair rules can be nearly impossible. The first rounds of stock market activity are sure to see managers and their invisible partners in the administration cash in big. A crop of instant millionaires—whom everyone knew as the old *nomenklatura*—will become conspicuous symbols to be manipulated by potential demagogues.

If the resentment against black marketeers in Russia is any indication, there will be a groundswell against the "excessive" greed and corruption in the equity markets. Legitimate operators could get caught up in the popular outrage; so might the whole reform movement, especially in the context of large-scale economic misery and uncertainty experienced "by honest, hard working, native people."

Until a viable equity market is operational, companies will go elsewhere to raise capital or sell assets—by privately placing equity or raising capital through debt rather than equity. However, whereas in the West, market valuations can be made quickly due to the relatively free flow of information and the efficiency of markets, in the East, market valuations will be much more problematic. The lack of accepted accounting standards and a credible tax system will exacerbate the problem. These added uncertainties will make it much tougher to raise capital. Under these conditions, big firms will have no choice but to rely on the state, or in special cases private banks or foreigners, for their capital requirements. The investment policy of the newly privatized enterprise is likely to become dependent on the state. Independent active ownership may become an illusion, despite rapid privatization.

Public Enterprises Reconsidered

Radical capitalists insist that state ownership and capitalism don't mix, nor do state ownership and rapid development. In their view, the Communist economic malaise is just another failure of state ownership. Throughout the world, and in the Third World in particular, they argue, stated-owned industries are notoriously inefficient and corrupt. Little

wonder that many poor nations, as diverse as India, Turkey, and Mexico, have embarked quite successfully on massive privatization programs in recent years.

Yet state ownership makes sense at certain times under certain conditions. For instance, when markets are imperfect and capital scarce, institutional malfunctions may channel investment away from industries that are key to long-term development. In several countries, a sudden implosion of whole sectors, sometimes whole sets of sectors, has resulted in the state finding itself forced to step in and nationalize the losers. Hence the typical state sector, with its portfolio of coal mines, steel mills, railways, and shipbuilding docks. Italy and Spain have lavish government portfolios so acquired. This history of nationalizing dying industries in response to political pressures or more simply of managing the difficult task of restructuring and downsizing as painlessly as possible has given state-owned enterprises their bad name. They are, most often, collections of basket cases that no one else would take. This is what makes their experience particularly relevant to the former Communist realm.

There are, however, other examples of state-owned companies, nationalized for one reason or another, that were not already dying. France provides the best examples, and the history has been anything but negative. As late as 30 years after World War II, the French state still owned all or major firms in steel, coal, oil distribution, transportation, automobiles, cigarettes, electronics, ocean shipping, aircraft, skyscraper office development, radio and television broadcasting, telephone services, gas, electricity, plus, horrid as it may seem, most big banks and insurance companies. This is a partial list. The postwar modernization, restructuring, and growth of the French economy has been, by anyone's standards (except Japan's) extraordinarily successful. What is more, state-owned firms played a leading role, not simply a shock-absorbing role, in that transformation and modernization.

In Japan and Korea, the giant industrial groupings that dominate the economy defy simple classification as private or public. Nor is there any compelling reason to make the distinction. Surely the great Japanese keiretsu are not public firms; the government does not own them. But it is extremely difficult to assimilate the Sumitomo or Mitsubishi groups into the traditional category of a private firm. The market is not the opposite of the government; the firm is not in opposition to the state. There are many varieties of institutional arrangements, and they change with time and circumstance. The all-or-nothing dichotomy of public bureaucracy or private (capital market based) firm is dangerously simplistic—especially as a guide for Eastern Europe, where capitalism does not yet exist. It pops out of textbook economics, not out of the history of successful economic development, especially "catch-up" development. That is the relevant genre: the people of Eastern Europe do not have to invent their positive future—just catch up with it.

What determines the success of state-owned enterprises? State-operated industries can be operated efficiently or inefficiently, using technologically advanced production techniques or backward ones. Empirically, the answer is clear. Good performance is a function of the domestic political economy and its institutions, not just of the nature of ownership. Drawing from a cross-national collection of case studies of privatization, Raymond Vernon *in The Promise of Privatization* concluded:

"Where governments have been reasonably competent and responsible, and where comparisons between private enterprises and state-owned enterprises have been possible, the technical performance of state-owned enterprises has not appeared much different from that of private enterprises. Here and there a strikingly efficient performance by a state-owned enterprise has cast doubt on the simple stereotypes of the public enterprise as a perennial wastrel."

In certain circumstances, reliance on the public sector and public ownership, in particular, may actually be good strategy. State ownership is certainly not to be sought as an end in itself; nor for the matter is private ownership of large enterprises. It all depends on the context in which choices must be made. Where private ownership seems doomed to fail—as in the case of many large enterprises in the ex-Soviet empire—the failure will result in a sudden implosion of the economy and society. In these cases, alternatives to simple privatization should be sought.

Further, the recent surge of privatization throughout Europe, Japan, and the Third World indicates that state ownership need not be permanent. Those trying to design new systems might profitably sift the rich varieties of institutional experience of other countries to see what made for better or worse performance: from state-owned, state-regulated, state-controlled, or state-in-cahoots-with. Ownership is a complex concept, contingent on embedded institutions. Given current conditions for big industry in the former Communist realms, some state ownership may be more desirable than simple "private ownership." Indeed, the logic of privatization in those lands does not ensure a dynamic market economy dominated by private firms. More likely, rapid privatization would precipitate state re-intervention sooner or later.

The Faulty Institutional Logic of Rapid Privatization

The focus on privatization, especially rapid privatization, diverts attention from implementation of policies and creation of market firms and institutions that encourage the development of competitive industries and an effective state bureaucracy to ensure viable democratic societies.

More than increasing efficiency expected from privatization, these troubled nations need the benefit of rebuilding the networks of industrial linkages and trade within the region. They need outlets for goods—such as steel, ships, coal, and especially agriculture—to Western Europe; this will not be easy to obtain. They will need import controls so all savings won't wash out quickly in a wave of consumer buying, and most likely controls on capital outflows too. More than anything, they need a competent and honest public administration to recreate those international linkages, administer those controls, negotiate those trade agreements, regulate the new and wildly imperfect markets, and buffer the shocks of industrial restructuring.

To the radical capitalists, rapid privatization is a shortcut. Eliminate the state, and voila, economic growth. But this is myth, ideology. The state will not whither away despite the dreams of radical capitalists any more than it did despite the dreams of Karl Marx. The state will run things for a long time, if not as owner, then as regulator.

Ironically, the logic of rapid privatization does not make the dependence of industry on the state any less likely. The state is destined to be the key economic player for the foreseeable future, whether privatization be rapid or gradual. Newly privatized giant enterprises will depend on the state for financing and for establishing rules and regulations. The state will also maintain a heavy hand in the industrial core of the economy because the inherited industrial structure provides most industries with too few firms for successful self-regulation by competition. And regulation by foreign competition may prove fatal.

Just as the state will necessarily be interventionist, given rapid privatization, so it will be protectionist. Assisted by their new armies of shareholders, the newly privatized enterprises, unfit to meet foreign competition, are likely to press for protectionist measures, especially since competing in an open economy would be suicidal. Free competition would open the field for Japan, the newly industrialized countries, and other low-cost, high-quality producers and leave little chance for inefficient domestic producers. They are inefficient now, and by world standards, they will be inefficient and uncompetitive for the near term. One must recall that Japan, Korea, France, and Germany never exposed their "infant industries" to the rigors of foreign competition; nor will most of the struggling new nations of the ex-Communist bloc.

Finally, rapid privatization plans aren't necessarily conducive to narrow, active, and independent ownership. Some rapid privatization plans envision ownership through mutual funds or through national distribution of share vouchers. In either case, there is no guarantee that active, independent ownership pressing for dynamic restructuring will emerge. Mutual funds owning shares in many firms, as in the Czech plan, may react to poor performance by selling shares, not necessarily by restructuring industry. If they don't, or are not allowed to, they become more like Italy's I.R.I. than a Wall Street fund. More important, the mutual funds (even with foreign advisers) are likely to advocate conservative measures for change due to the dependence of enterprises on the state and perhaps ultimately on the workers.

Grand designs are associated with great risk. So it was with Communism, so it will be with capitalism. The radical capitalists' fallacy is that pragmatism will ultimately result in the loss of discipline as local interests forestall change. Their concern is valid, but their prescription is not. The risks associated with rapid privatization skew the odds toward failure and ultimately toward disenchantment with capitalism and a democratic, more liberal state.

The big, inefficient state enterprises will not succeed as private enterprises. But they cannot simply be abolished. Building the structures of capitalism, the institutions of a functioning market system, will take time and breathing room.

Radically pure markets won't build them; they will destroy those structures and risk ending the capitalist experiment before it has had a chance to develop into something worthwhile. It was no less than Joseph Schumpeter, the great advocate of entrepreneurial capitalism, in his brilliant case for maintaining less-than-perfect markets, who remarked: "You put brakes on a car so that it can go faster, not slower."

An uncut version of this article, with 72 footnotes, is available from BME, University of California, Berkeley, California 94720.

Article 5

Current History, October 1993

Social Problems in Russia

"If communism gave rise to many kinds of social problems, the attempts by Gorbachev and Yeltsin to move toward democracy and a market economy have only made those problems worse. And their efforts to transform the system into something that Gorbachev used to call 'normal' and 'civilized' have actually given rise to new sources of discontent, new forms of deviant, or illegal, behavior, and ever greater travails for the Russian people."

David E. Powell

David E. Powell is a fellow of the Russian Research Center at Harvard University, where his research focuses on Russian society.

Shortly after the collapse of the attempted coup against Soviet President Mikhail Gorbachev, a journalist wrote mournfully in the September 14, 1991, Pravda that "Social disorder, a lack of confidence in the future, and the gulf dividing the truths proclaimed on lofty platforms from real life—all these things have led to people's alienation." For him, economic disarray was at least as much to blame as political instability for the plunge in morale. "The market," he wrote, "with its frightening uncertainty, has confronted everyone with the need to save his own skin." Even the armed forces, which for years had been depicted as a model of social solidarity and discipline, were now revealed as organizations where bullying is rampant and "thefts and robberies, sales of weapons and bribe-taking, and drug addiction and drunkenness are flourishing."

All these problems, and others as well, pervade Russian society and have begun to undermine it. Crime and juvenile delinquency, public health, and the spread of drug abuse are three areas that are of special concern to the people and the government of Russia.

THE NEW VIOLENCE

NOVOROSSIK—A 13-year-old boy tries to rape his 9-year-old brother and 10-year-old sister. When his plan fails, he hangs both of them.

MOSCOW—in a robbery attempt, teenagers strangle an 11-year-old girl with her own tights.

KOSTROMA—Deciding to make a little money, a 14-year-old schoolboy brutally murders an 8-year-old boy and demands a ransom from the parents for the body.

MOSCOW—A 14-year-old girl who had been receiving excellent grades in school gives birth and, with a friend's help, kills the baby and dismembers the body.

These episodes all occurred recently in Russia, and for obvious reasons have elicited feelings of horror and fear among the people. Such behavior was literally unheard of when the Communist party ruled by terror, the threat of terror, or—in the final years—a combination of pressure, intimidation, and manipulation. Whether crimes like these were unheard of because the censorship agencies did their work well or because they seldom occurred remains unclear. Violent crimes did occur during the Soviet period; perhaps the most terrifying were those of the serial killer Andrei Chikatilo, who was found guilty of murdering, mutilating, and cannibalizing at least 53 young men and women between 1978 and 1990. But the evidence suggests that perestroika brought with it political, economic, and social chaos that has contributed to a dramatic upsurge in reported crimes, and a radical change in their character.

In 1992 the number of "registered" crimes in Russia rose to 2.76 million and the crime rate to 1,857 per 100,000 people—a 27 percent increase in both categories over 1991 figures. Indeed, the crime rate almost doubled between 1985 and 1992. A high-ranking official in the Ministry of Internal Affairs (MVD) predicted in March that the current calendar year would see 3.4 million crimes recorded, a figure that he expected to climb to 4 million in 1994. Theft, burglary and other property offenses account for two-thirds of all crime in Russia, but what disturbs most people is the extremely rapid growth in violent crime. In 1989 the death rate from homicide in Russia was 12.5 per 100,000 people—a level higher than the rate of 9.2 in the United States. The disparity today is even greater. When asked by pollsters in May 1992 for their reaction to the statement, "No one feels safe any more," 74 percent in European Russia agreed. And crime is generally lower in European than in non-European Russia, particularly the easternmost reaches of the country. (Some of this east-west differential has been attributed to the movement of "criminal elements" from the Caucasus to Siberia and the Far East.)

Cities have also seen an increase in crime. The November 16, 1992, edition of *Rossiikaia gazeta* said Moscow is "one of the most crime-ridden cities in Russia," noting that approximately 145 crimes had been recorded by the Moscow police on November 14; on the same day a year before, the figure was 100. The result has been a growing fear. Victor Yarin, head of the MVD, has denied that people are afraid to go out at night in the capital: "I myself live in Moscow and walk the streets," but the minister acknowledged that ordinary citizens were reluctant to walk about, and with good reason.

The period since Mikhail Gorbachev assumed power in 1985 has also witnessed a dramatic upswing in organized crime (some 4,000 organized crime groupings, 150 of them with international links, currently operate in Russia), assaults against foreigners (who have foreign goods or the hard currency with which to purchase them), weapons theft (especially from military and police barracks), economic crimes involving businesses and banks operating outside state control (especially those involved with convertible-currency transactions), and the integration of Russia into the international drug production and distribution network.

SPIRALING DELINQUENCY

Crime among minors, the MVD chief asserts, "has assumed the character of an epidemic." Last year, minors (those under the age of 16, except in cases of especially serious crimes) committed almost 200,000 crimes, one-sixth of which were classified as "grave." One-third of all participants in group crimes are minors, and of the more than 20,000 "criminal groups" known to police, 85 percent include minors. Almost 100,000 lawbreakers in 1992 were under the age of 14, and over the last five years the number of criminals aged 14 or 15 has jumped by more than 50 percent. More than one-fourth of extortionists are teenagers, and drug-related thefts, beatings, and other criminal acts by teens have skyrocketed.

A prominent legal scholar, I. Antonian of the MVD's Research Institute, asserted earlier this year that "murders for no apparent reason have now become especially common among teenagers." When questioned about their motives, he found that the youths often just shrugged their shoulders; their violent acts seem to have been random, and "as if [they] had nothing else to do."

There is a desperate shortage of institutions that could help rehabilitate wayward youngsters, and there are none whatsoever for teenage lawbreakers who are mentally ill. In fact, to some extent the existing centers are a breeding ground for juvenile delinquency. Children who have committed relatively petty offenses (stealing or "hooliganism" in 60 percent of the cases) are incarcerated along with those found guilty of extremely serious crimes (10 percent are there for murder or rape). In addition, the authorities place in these same facilities children diagnosed as suffering from "feeblemindedness with mild derangement"—that is to say, mentally retarded boys and girls who have found it impossible to cope with a school curriculum. Once they enter these institutions, the March 31 *Nezavisimaia gazeta* reports, "these children are, as a rule, victimized by their crueler and more mentally developed contemporaries, and in the end lose any chance of returning to a normal life." Some fall into depression, while others become aggressive; either way they become lost souls.

But most cities—Moscow included—do not have even facilities for youths found guilty of criminal behavior. Some are sent to other parts of Russia (under police escort, of course), but the overwhelming majority are simply given a warning and left to their own devices. Recent educational reforms have authorized school officials to expel pupils 14 years of age and older who are failing their courses. By the end of last year some 200,000 schoolchildren had been expelled in Russia, and the number who had dropped out was two to three times that. Of the 400,000 pupils held back to repeat a grade during the 1991–1992 academic year, one-third did not resume their education; another 70,000 were expected to wind up in the same situation this year. And it is precisely these two groups of youths—those who are expelled and those who drop out of school—from which the great majority of juvenile delinquents come.

In view of the continuing disruptions and instability afflicting the country, there is little room for optimism. Indeed, Yarin said late last year that a ministry forecast for crime rates through 1995 made for "depressing" reading. The latest statistics, released June 2, indicate that the number of people arrested in the first quarter of 1993 was 12 percent higher than during the corresponding period a year earlier. Only someone who is convinced that this demonstrates improved police work could react favorably to such information.

FAILING PUBLIC HEALTH

Between 1980 and 1988 the population of the Russian republic rose annually by approximately 1 million. In 1989 the figure fell to 600,000, and by 1991 it was a mere 200,000; this year the population actually fell by some 190,000. (As of January 1, 1993, Russia's population was about 148.5 million.) The decline in growth rates, and then the absolute decrease in population, can be attributed to a combination of significantly lower birth rates and somewhat higher mortality rates.

Why are birth rates declining so rapidly? According to Valentma Matsko, the chief physician at St. Petersburg's Maternity Hospital No. 1, economic hardships and fears dominate women's thinking on the question of having children. As she explained in the June 27, 1991, *Pravda*:

> Society is literally filled with fear—of possible unemployment, of inflation, of the long lines in stores. . . . Add to that the jumps in prices, wages that buy less and less, and the threat of losing the housing one already has or the prospect of never getting out of a communal apartment. . . . Naturally the social climate has been reflected in nature. The "health coefficient" of women is falling, so not everyone wants to risk becoming a mother. The number of infertile women has increased sharply. . . . At the heart off it all is this general social neurosis.

Women are simply refusing to have babies or, for health reasons, are finding it extremely difficult to conceive.

Health care for women, and maternal care especially, ranges from poor to horrendous in Russia. According to a comprehensive survey by the Ministry of Health and other government agencies, only 25.8 percent of all pregnant women were "healthy" and another 20.8 percent "practically healthy." Similarly, less than half of women who give birth experience no complications during labor.

But these figures actually understate the problem. The officials who cite them acknowledge that in reality a mere 25 percent of all pregnant women should be classified as "healthy" or "practically healthy"—which means that three-quarters experience some sort of medical difficulty during pregnancy. This contributes to birth defects and infant mortality and morbidity as well as to maternal mortality.

Another statistic indicating that health care and health education for women in Russia leave much to be desired is the number of abortions performed every year. (What one journalist called "the quiet suicide of a nation" is a sign of other problems in society as well.) Estimates range from 3.5 million to 7 million annually, with the latter probably closer to the truth. In 1991 one out of every ten women in the Soviet Union aged 15 to 49 underwent an abortion; there were 137 abortions for every 100 live births that year. Between 1985 and 1991 the number of abortions performed rose by 200,000 a year.

It is not only uninformed young girls who resort to abortion as a major (if not the major) method of birth control. One study found that 14 percent of women with 16 or more years of schooling had had 8 to 10 abortions.

The conditions under which abortions are performed in Russia have traditionally been gruesome. To quote one former patient: "Abortions are carried out on two, even on six women simultaneously in the same theater. The tables are placed so that a woman can see everything that goes on opposite her: the face distorted in pain, the bloody mess extracted from the womb. In the theater, there are two doctors and one nurse. . . . Sometimes [the doctor] gives her an injection, but it has no effect because so little Novocain is used, and he doesn't wait for it to work anyway. As she isn't anesthetized, the woman suffers terrible pain. Some lose consciousness."[1]

Slightly more than one-quarter of abortions are classified as "early"—presumably performed during the first trimester—which means that almost three-quarters are carried out at a time when the woman is at greater risk. Furthermore, more than 300,000 abortions each year are undergone by women under the age of 17, and 16 percent are not performed in hospitals—again, two factors that carry considerable risk for the patient. It is not surprising, therefore, that 276 women died during abortions in 1991. (These are official figures; reality, as usual, is probably a good deal worse.)

As for the other side of the fall in population, despite considerable fluctuation over the short term, life expectancy for both men and women in Russia is about the same as it was three decades ago. Male babies born in 1990 could expect to live 63.8 years. For the past 35 years women have outlived men by about a decade; in 1990 female life expectancy was 74.3 years.[2]

By the standards of the industrialized world, these figures, especially those for males, are exceedingly low. As Murray Feshbach and Alfred Friendly, Jr., observed in their 1992 book *Ecocide in the USSR*, "By failing to invest effectively in health care and environmental protection, the rulers of the USSR brought the average life expectancy of its citizens down to the average life expectancy in Paraguay. . . . Fifty-year old males could expect in 1985 to die earlier than men who reached the half-century mark in 1939."

As for infant mortality, officials statistics put it at 24.9 per 1,000 in 1976 and 17 last year. But it is important to note that Russian public health authorities use a highly idiosyncratic definition of the term: the number of deaths within the first year of life, per 1,000 live births. They now suggest that if international standards were applied the figure would rise by 15 to 30 percent, and perhaps even as much as 50 percent. Feshbach and Friendly have estimated that the true infant mortality rate *in the Soviet Union* in 1989 was as high as 33 per 1,000, a level comparable to that in China and Sri Lanka. (Statistics for the United States show infant mortality of 9.2 per 1,000—far better than in Russia, but only good enough to put America in twentieth place worldwide.)

Morbidity levels among newborns have risen dramatically over the past decade: between 1980 and 1991 the figure went from 82 to 174 cases per 1,0000 live births. The share of newborns officially classified as "healthy" is expected to decline to only 15 to 20 percent by the year 2015, while that of newborns suffering from congenital or acquired chronic diseases is expected to rise to 25 percent.

A study carried out in the city of Lipetsk on a cohort of children born in 1979 found morbidity levels during the first year of life to be 4,736 per 10,000 children of that age; during the youngsters' second year the figure rose to 5,391 (primarily because most were enrolled in preschool institutions), while in the third it fell to 4,500. Still, this means that on average, each child was sick four or five times a year during each of his or her first three years of life. (No information was given on the length of these illnesses, but that the youngsters experienced so many bouts of poor health is extraordinary, and must have proved debilitating.)

A number of factors are at work here. First, more than half of all new mothers in Russia are unable to breastfeed, mainly because of poor diet. Second, large numbers of younger women—many still just girls—become pregnant and have babies. These mothers tend to be less mature, physically as well as psychologically, than women in their twenties and thirties who give birth. In addition, there is a higher incidence among the youngest mothers of premature births, low birth weight, and other major risk factors that inevitably contribute to higher infant mortality and morbidity. Third, since virtually all women of child-bearing age in Russia work, children almost always have to be placed in day care centers, where they are exposed to infectious diseases and, more often than not, inadequate care and feeding.

Diseases that have been all but eradicated in other advanced industrial societies—cholera, typhoid fever, diphtheria, whooping cough, and polio, among others—continue to plague the children of Russia. Precisely how many cases occur there is unclear, due to the breakdown in statistical reporting, but the number unquestionably is far higher than that prevailing in Western Europe, North America, and Japan.

A DECAYED HEALTH CARE SYSTEM

The public health delivery system in Russia is in crisis. Doctors and paramedics, though relatively numerous, are notoriously poorly trained, lack modern equipment, and are badly paid. While figures for their wages in rubles are all but meaningless, owing to the collapse of the ruble, it is noteworthy that in 1991 the average salary in the sphere of health care was only 68.2 percent of the average for the national economy as a whole. This helps to explain the corruption rampant among medical personnel—bribes are generally required for everything from a change of bed linen to obtaining the services of the "right" surgeon.

Concerned about the growing disparity between their pay and the cost of living, the All-Russian Medical Workers Union last year went on strike for higher wages and improved state financing of medical institutions. Not all health care personnel joined in, however; in some places emergency services were provided, while in others a decision was taken not to strike at all, so as not to make things even worse for patients.

Hospital and polyclinic buildings in Russia are in dubious shape. Approximately 15 percent of these were built before 1940, and only about the same percentage were constructed between 1981 and 1990. Nine or 10 percent are said to require "emergency" repairs; they should in fact be torn down and replaced. At the same time, 46 percent of the former and 31 percent of the latter are in need of a major, though not complete, overhaul. Roughly 12 percent of the country's hospitals and 7 percent of its polyclinics lack running water; 42 percent and 30 percent, respectively, are not supplied with hot water; 18 percent and 15 percent, respectively, are not connected to a sewage system; and a mere 12 percent of both have central heating.

As if all of this were not bad enough, there is no space for almost 60 percent of the currently occupied beds in hospital wards or 14 percent of the beds in polyclinic rooms. (Many beds are simply placed in hallways, and patients often wind up staying there for days on end.) Children's medical units and maternity hospitals are in especially neglected condition; more than one-tenth of all children's hospitals and children's units in general hospitals and polyclinics, it is said, should be demolished, and others need major repairs. Of 38 obstetric in-patient departments in Moscow—presumably the country's best—only 9 meet modern standards.

Among the most widely discussed aspects of Russia's health care problem is the shortage of medicines—termed "catastrophic" by a correspondent in the December 31, 1991, *Pravda*. Between 1985 and 1991, supplies of pharmaceuticals fell from 82 percent to 70 percent of the country's needs. Since 1985, domestic production of pharmaceuticals has gone from supplying 52 percent to 34 percent of demand; imported drugs come primarily from eastern Europe, and the "newly emerging democracies" there now demand hard currency for their products.

Not all the blame should be assigned to Gorbachev—or now to Russian President Boris Yeltsin. The newest pharmaceutical manufacturing plant in Russia is at least 15 years old, while a combination of poor maintenance, low rates of investment, and raised popular consciousness on ecological issues has led to the closing each year of between 10 percent and 30 percent of remaining facilities. Of course, foreign countries like the United States, the European Community nations, Japan, and even India, Israel, and Turkey have provided emergency subsidies. But donors, faced with the theft of medicines once they reach Russia, are wary about providing too much without adequate supervision. As a German television commentator pointed out in 1990, German companies are prepared to send "valuable medical equipment and medical supplies, just so long as they do not spoil in the open air or vanish in a bureaucratic 'Bermuda Triangle.'"[3]

This spring Yeltsin signed a decree entitled "On Immediate Measures to Provide Health Care for the People of the Russian Federation." In it, he instructed the government to submit to parliament by October 1 programs for 1994–1995 for lowering the rate of premature death, for prenatal care for women, and for improving emergency services. By August the govenment was to approve a state system that would assure pregnant women, nursing mothers, and children under the age of seven adequate supplies of nutritional foods, with benefits to be extended to other "socially vulnerable groups" in 1994–1995. Whether any of these reforms will become reality must remain in doubt, given the severe financial disruption in Russia today. Indeed, the president's decree is probably just another cri de coeur in the face of a public health system in danger of falling apart.

DRUG ABUSE

Before glasnost, authorities routinely denied the existence of a drug problem in the Soviet Union. Today denial has all but disappeared, but the difficulties of dealing with the medical, social, and law enforcement aspects of the problem remain.

Estimates for the number of drug users, abusers, and addicts vary widely, but it is clear that the figures in each category are growing every year. In 1985 an April 4 broadcast of Radio Moscow put the number of addicts in the Soviet Union at between 2,500 and 3,000, and said that most had developed their addiction as a result of improper medical treatment. By the beginning of 1990 there were said to be 130,000 addicts, and police announced that they had registered 32,000 people "who had used narcotic substances for non-medical purposes" in the previous year alone.

Using a figure of 121,000 (rather than 130,000), the head of the MVD declared in mid-1990 that the true number of addicts was actually five times higher. Professor Anzor Gabiani, a Georgian expert on drug abuse who carried out extensive classified research during the 1960s and 1970s, said a more accurate estimate would be 10–12 addicts for each one registered—that is, a total of 1.2–1.4 million.[4] At the same time, another high-ranking law enforcement official said that "there are approximately 1.5 million people who have tried or are using drugs." (These individuals need not be addicts, of course; indeed, the same source speaks of 130,000 individuals engaging in "the non-medical use of narcotic substance," including "over 60,000 drug addicts." But he too says the "real" figures are roughly 10 times higher than those he cites.)[5]

Suddenly, on April 24 this year, *Komsomolskaia pravda* asserted that there were between 5.5 million and 5.7 million "drug users" living in the territory of the former Soviet Union, as well as a million and a half "addicts" in Russia alone. At first glance these numbers may seem absurdly inflated, but in fact the true dimensions of the problem are not known. Observers know it is getting worse, and at a rapid rate—but how much worse, and how rapidly remain something of a mystery.

What kinds of people abuse drugs? According to Gabiani, who researched the subject in Georgia in 1984 and 1985, far more men than women are involved (92 percent versus 8 percent), and most are in their twenties or early thirties. The overwhelming majority (86 percent) of addicts and other users are under the age of 35, and nearly one-third are under 25. Their average educational level is quite high, far higher than is typical in Georgia—or Russia. Less than 3 percent have no more than an elementary education, and 84 percent graduated from high school; of these graduates, 9 percent went on for more schooling and a further 8 percent received a diploma from an institution of higher education. Almost half had criminal records, nearly three-quarters of these having been convicted of drug-related crimes.

Perhaps 80 percent of users tried drugs for the first time before they reached age 25, and some have suggested that 60 percent of users began before they turned 19. When asked why they started with drugs, more than two-thirds cited "a desire to experience a feeling of euphoria, a high [kaif]"; one-quarter attributed their decision to a desire "to imitate others"; and 10 percent to dissatisfaction with or a desire to forget about their lives, even briefly.

To a large extent, drug use in Russia and the other successor countries resembles what takes place in the United States, although the incidence is much lower. The most popular drugs are marijuana and hashish, used by 84 percent of the people Gabiani studied; morphine, used by 47 percent; and opium, close behind at 44 percent. In the former Soviet Union, as in the United States, drugs tend to be ingested in a social setting, when groups gather—or perhaps groups gather in order to ingest drugs. "At gatherings of hedonistic youths, the use of drugs, especially the smoking of hashish, is [regarded as] prestigious and fashionable," *Zaria vostoka* reported on February 20, 1987. With underground laboratories and synthetic drugs beginning to become significant factors on the drug scene in Russia, preferences and patterns of use may change.

How do users obtain their drugs? One group of researchers says the most common method is purchase on the black market from professional traffickers organized as a kind of mafia, with a network of "pushers" and "runners"—some of whom are the buyer's friends. Other people go directly to the vast regions of the former Soviet Union (especially in Central Asia) where hemp and poppies grow wild, or grow their own, consuming a portion and selling the rest. Pharmacies, hospitals, and other medical institutions are yet another rich source of drugs for illicit use. Indeed, they are said to provide between 30 percent and 40 percent of all drugs used illegally in Moscow, St. Petersburg, and the Baltic states. (People either steal the drugs, use fraudulent prescriptions, or purchase drugs stolen by doctors, nurses, and other public health workers.)

A final, and increasingly important, source is smugglers, both amateur and professional; some are foreign students or tourists, while others are professionals operating out of Afghanistan or southern and southeast Asia. There is also considerable evidence suggesting that the Italian Mafia, in collaboration with organized crime in the former Soviet Union—including, but not only in, Russia—has established production facilities in Russia and several other successor states. The Italians have also helped launder drug money for Russian criminal groups.

Yeltsin has expressed great concern about the drug problem in Russia, focusing especially on ties with organized crime and the international narcotics trade. At the All-Russian Conference on Problems of the Fight Against Organized Crime and Corruption, held earlier this year in Moscow, he spoke of the growth of organized crime as "particularly dangerous," in part because it lends so much support to the drug trade. "Organized crime," he asserted, "has become a direct threat to Russia's strategic interests and national security.... The criminal milieu is becoming more insolent and aggressive."

Vice President Aleksandr Rutskoi, addressing the same conference, also spoke of the need "to stop the importation and sales of narcotic substances in Russia." (He made no mention of drug exports or of the fact that Russia has been serving as a conduit for drugs destined for other countries.) Like Yeltsin, he focused on the links between organized crime and "corrupt elements in Russian administrative bodies." Corruption, he declared, "corrodes the state apparatus and society like rust.... Rampant crime and corruption are a bomb under our political and economic reforms."

Similarly the April 24 *Komsomolskaia pravda* referred facetiously to Russians "our Narcostan" and asked whether the Commonwealth of Independent States would be transformed into the Commonwealth of Drug-Producing States. Certainly the newspaper is pessimistic on the subject, saying, "the prospects for stopping the emergence of a powerful drug mafia on the territory of the former USSR are virtually non-existent."

The government's response to the drug problem has involved elements of police work, customs control, medical treatment, and education. As far back as 1972, a decree issued by the Russian Republic Supreme Soviet stipulated that drug addicts be subject to "compulsory treatment and labor reeducation" in special institutions. More recently, some teachers have begun to discuss drug-related issues in class and have made antidrug literature available to pupils. In addition, hotlines have been established in Moscow, St. Petersburg, and other major cities, and walk-in clinics where an individual can seek advice or be treated anonymously have appeared in a few places. Unfortunately, however, the consensus among Russian experts is that none of this has much of an effect; the problem is expanding, not contracting.

DISCONTENT AND DEVIANCE

The situation in Russia today resembles—but is even less healthy than—that of a decade ago. If communism gave rise to many kinds of social problems, the attempts by Gorbachev and Yeltsin to move toward democracy and a market economy have only made those problems worse. And their efforts to transform the system into something that Gorbachev used to call "normal" and "civilized" have actually given rise to new sources of discontent, new forms of deviant, or illegal, behavior, and ever greater travails for the Russian people.

NOTES

1. V. N. Golubeva, "The Other Side of the Medal" in *Women and Russia (First Feminist Samizdat)* (London: Sheba Feminist Publishers, 1980), p. 56. Cited in Shalvia Ben-Barak, "Abortion in the Soviet Union: Why It Is So Widely Practiced," in Peter J. Potichnyj, ed., *The Soviet Union: Party and Society* (Cambridge: Cambridge University Press, 1988), p. 211. I have made several minor changes in spelling and word usage to conform to American practices.

2. See also David E. Powell, "Aging and the Elderly," in Anthony James et al., eds., *soviet Social Problems* (Boulder, Colo.: Westview, 1991), pp. 173–175.

3. Quoted in *Izvestia*, November 30, 1990.

4. *Moscow News*, no. 24 (1990).

5. *Izvestia*, August 29, 1990.

Article 6   *The World Today*, August–September 1993

Will Russia Disintegrate into Bantustans?

Bogdan Szajkowski

Bogdan Szajkowski is a Senior Lecturer in Politics at the University of Exeter specialising in social and political conflicts and in ethnic and nationality issues in the former Soviet Union and Central and Eastern Europe. He is the author of numerous books and articles on the former Communist countries. His most recent book, Encyclopedia of Conflicts and Flashpoints in the Former Soviet Union and Central and Eastern Europe, *will be published by Longman in December 1993.*

Will the Soviet Union Survive until 1984? was the title of a somewhat prophetic book by Andrei Amalrik, published in 1970. Had he lived until 1991, he would have witnessed the final disintegration of the Soviet Union. Today, only two years later, paraphrasing Amalrik we must ask: Will Russia be fragmented into numerous smaller units, the equivalent of South Africa's old Bantustans? The signs are that the processes are set for the 'Bantustanisation' of the once-powerful Federation.

The past four years have seen the emergence of a multitude of conflicts and flashpoints in the former Soviet Union. A map prepared by the Office of the Geographer of the United States at the beginning of 1990 listed some 40 ethno-territorial conflicts in the Soviet Union. By March 1991, some 80 conflicts had been identified by a Russian academic, Vladimir A. Kolossov. By February 1992, Kolossov had listed 164 conflicts affecting 70 per cent of the territory of the former Soviet Union.[1] Today both publications are already substantially out of date. My own research suggests over 204 ethno-territorial conflicts in the former Soviet Union.[2]

The Soviet Union officially ceased to exist on 8 December 1991, when the leaders of Russia, Ukraine and Belarus unilaterally abrogated the Union Treaty of 1922 and created the amorphous Commonwealth of Independent States (CIS). This was the first stage in the disintegration of the Bolshevik empire.

Thereafter trends were set for the second stage—the disintegration of the former constituent republics. It is worth bearing in mind that, while the first stage of disintegration proceeded along the lines of existing borders and the titular majority of a particular republic, the second and subsequent stages are delineated along ethnic lines without clearly defined or indeed previously acknowledged (identifiable) borders.

The demands for independence of the so-called Transdniestr Republic and the Gagauz Republic fractured the territorial and political cohesion of the Moldovan Republic and set a precedent for future divisions accompanied by civil wars and militarisation of a number of areas. The disintegration of Georgia and, more recently, of Tajikistan, followed this route. To this list can also be added Karakalpakia, an autonomous republic on the territory of Uzbekistan, whose Supreme Soviet on 10 April 1993 approved a new Constitution under which

MAP OF THE RUSSIAN FEDERATION

the territory will become a sovereign parliamentary republic within Uzbekistan.

The third stage is the disintegration of the Russian Federation. The trend for the forth stage of further disintegration of the Federation's components into even smaller entities is already clearly detectable.

Ethno-territorial conflicts

Although the Soviet Union was a multinational state, only 67 nations out of the 103 recorded in the 1989 census had their own autonomous areas. As early as 1918, Lenin set out the framework for the ethno-territorial division of the Soviet state. According to him, there could be no norm which would ensure the right of all ethnic groups to their own autonomous territories. Rather, autonomous and ordinary districts should be united for economic purposes in large autonomous regions (krays). Consequently, internal divisions of the former Soviet Union were purely administrative; ethnic demarcations seldom corresponded to the ethnic composition of a particular area. Frequent changes in the political-territorial organisation were used mainly for the centralised control and direction of the economy and society. The residues of this Leninist policy are still with us today.[3]

Between 1941 and 1957 repeated changes in the national-territorial organisation of the Soviet Union were made. In 1941–44, seven peoples accused of collaborating with the German occupiers were deprived of their autonomous status and deported to Siberia, Kazakhstan and Kyrgyzstan. The claims of the deported peoples (14 altogether) for the restoration of the boundaries of their states now have a legal basis in addition to their historical and moral foundations. In 1990, the Supreme Soviet of the Russian Federation adopted a special resolution on justice for deported peoples. One of the main points envisages the reconstitution of their national-territorial units with the boundaries which existed on the day of their deportation. But how, in practical terms, is that to be implemented, and what would be the political consequences? What rights do the titular peoples have to their designated territories if their boundaries are legitimised only by Soviet power, which no longer exists?[4]

The catastrophic decline of the Russian economy has had substantial negative consequences for Russia's state sovereignty. The recently published data on the socio-economic situation during the first quarter of 1993 make grim reading indeed.[5] The 19 per cent drop in industrial production during the first quarter, compared with the same period in 1992, has been accompanied by a 193 per cent inflation rate, compared with December last year. The percentage of unprofitable enterprises in all sectors of the national economy rose to 21, compared with 17 per cent last December. The highest proportional share of unprofitable enterprises (between 41–47 per cent) was recorded in the republics of Tuva and Sakha (Yakutia), the Magadan *oblast* and the Chukotka *okrug*. By the end of March 1993, one per cent (1.1m persons) of the total labour force of Russia had been registered as unemployed. Some 38 per cent of the unemployed are young people under 30 years of age. One in every three residents of Russia now has a per capita income below the minimum subsistence level. At the same time there has been a sharp increase in crime—12 per cent up on the first quarter of 1992—with only 45 per cent of reported crimes solved.

Communist collectivism and ethnicity

The common denominator for potentially the most explosive conflicts is the intertwining between Communist collectivism and ethnicity. One of the most important aspects of the operation of Communism was the collective nature of the system. Individual rights (including human, civil and property rights) were subjugated to the collective and controlled by the Communist party-state. The system not only negated the individual but, more important, used the oppressive apparatus in order to enforce compliance with collective (party-state) values, structures and procedures. Communist collectivism reinforced group rather than individual identity, but at the same time offered a comfortable net of social and political arrangements. There were few if any choices to be made, the answers were all but supplied, little if any exercise of individual responsibility was required. The persistence of the political culture of collectivism remains one of the main obstacles to the effective transformation of the former Communist societies. It is also the main factor in the re-emergence of the ethnic conflicts.

There are both objective and subjective elements in the concept of ethnicity.[6] The objective elements cover characteristics which are actually held in common—kinship, physical appearance, culture, language, religion and so on. Some combination of these characteristics, but not necessarily all, would have to be present for a group of people to qualify as an ethnic grouping. The subjective elements rest on the feeling of community. What is important here is the representations which a group has of itself—regardless of whether those representations are actually correct or not. 'The myth can be potent, and it is the group's representations of itself that are important.'[7]

I should like to stress the importance of the subjective elements. Ethnic groups can only be understood in terms of boundary creation and maintenance. In such cases a common culture is not a defining characteristic of an ethnic grouping; it may, in fact, come into existence as a result of a particular grouping asserting its own position. Cultural features are used by ethnic groupings to mark the groupings' boundaries. Similarly, notions of kinship can be projected and/or constructed so as to give greater

body to the feelings of commonality within the grouping. The retreat into ethnic socio-political boundaries and values offers safety at turbulent times. In post-Communist Russia, as elsewhere in the former Communist countries, it has become one of the most poignant socio-political forms of organisations and threats.

The decline of presidential authority

The continuous power struggle in the centre and, in particular, the confrontation between the Russian President on the one hand and the Supreme Soviet and the Congress of the People's Deputies on the other, has already had a very adverse effect on the regions.

One of the more recent examples comes from the Rostov *oblast*, where the local soviet abolished on 30 April 1993 the post of the representative of the Russian President. The representative and his staff were told to vacate their offices within a week and stop their activities. A serious conflict between the Supreme Soviet of Moldova and President Yeltsin (and thus the Russian Federation) erupted in April 1993 over the right of the Federation's President to interfere in the republic's power structure. On 2 April the republic's Supreme Soviet voted (by 116 votes to 37) to abolish the position of President of the Moldovan Soviet Socialist Republic. The deputies blamed the incumbent, Vasiliy Guslyannikov, for current economic hardships and accused him of abusing his position and attempting to create one-man rule. In turn, Boris Yeltsin on 8 April issued a decree confirming the powers of Guslyannikov. The decree has been seen in Moldova as a violation of Article 78 of the Constitution of the Russian Federation and Article 3 of the Federation Treaty which state that federal power may not intervene in the organisation of the republics' power structures. On 20 April Moldova's Supreme Soviet, ignoring the presidential decree, dismissed the government and created a new Council of Ministers.[8]

The growing disenchantment of the regions with the Russian Federation and President Yeltsin's policies were also reflected in the voting figures during the referendum of 25 April 1993.[9] In 10 of the 19 republics—Adygeya, Bashkortostan, Altay, Dagestan, Ingushetia, Kabarda-Balkaria, Karachay-Cherkessia, Mari-El, Moldova and Chuvashia—Yeltsin failed to win a vote of confidence from the majority of voters.[10] It is interesting to note that several major *oblasts* and *okrugs* voted against the President. In the European part of Russia, voters in Belgorod, Bryansk, Kursk, Lipetsk, Orel, Penza, Pskov, Ryazan, Saratov, Smolensk, Tambov and Ulyanov *oblasts* expressed lack of confidence in Yeltsin. Beyond the Urals, voters in Altay *kray*, Admur and Chita *oblasts* and the Aga-Buryat and Ust-Orda Buryat autonomous *okrugs* also failed to deliver a vote of confidence.[11]

Crisis of statehood

The population's confidence in the authority of the state is extremely low. Laws that have been adopted are inoperative. There is increasingly evidence of a crisis of authority and of deepening antagonism between the executive and representative bodies.

As a consequence of the Russian Federation's inability to develop its own concept of state formation and bringing the federal mechanisms into operation, authorities in some of the republics and in *krays* and *oblasts* have been quite successful in building up their power structures based on the efficient interaction of local sources of power. Against the backdrop of the constant weakening of presidential and federal powers and the increasing turmoil in Moscow, local administrations have become guarantors of stability and formed the nuclei of state formation. There has been growing evidence that local soviets are slowly paralysing presidential power and breaking down the unity of executive power.

By now, many of Russia's regions have elected their own heads of administration. Previously, these had been appointed by President Yeltsin. The new heads have become responsible to the local electorate and are primarily influenced by local factors and conditions. Their legitimacy is based mainly on local constituencies rather than on central, federal authorities. If they are to survive in their posts they must above all respond to local demands for greater economic and political autonomy. The resolution of the local agenda—social/ethnical problems, border adjustments and so on—are often at variance with the interests of the Federation and its structures. The elected heads of local administration are unlikely to support the federal authorities (including the President) for long.

In many respects we are seeing the repetition of the 'Gorbachev delusion'. Here was a man confident that he was running *perestroika,* but his *perestroika* operated only in the centre and was executed through presidential decrees. Meanwhile, the peripheries and local party bosses strengthened their own powers and developed and slowly put into operation their own ideas reflecting local needs and aspirations.

The inoperability of the Federation Treaty

The Russian Federation technically consists of 18 union republics and 69 other subjects of the Federation (6 *krays,* 51 *oblasts,* 1 autonomous *oblast* and 11 autonomous *okrugs*). Eighteen of the 20 republics identified in the Federation Treaty[12] and invited to sign the Treaty did, in fact, put their signatures on the document on 31 March 1992.[13] Tatarstan and Checheno-Ingushetia refused to sign. Subsequently, Checheno-Ingushetia split into two separate entities. The Ingush Republic, created by the decision of the Russian Parliament on 4 June 1992, has so far not signed.

The Federation Treaty offered, at least in principle, the opportunity to conclude additional agreements on the re-allocation and mutual delegation of powers. More than a year after its signing, hardly any of the Treaty's provisions have been implemented.[14] The proclamation of norms has not been followed by appropriate additional legal provisions which would allow the exercise of rights granted in the Treaty. According to the Chairman of the Soviet of Nationalities of the Supreme Soviet, Ramazan Abdulatipov, a majority of the subjects of the Federation are dissatisfied with the way the Treaty is being executed.

The central and most contentious issue is that of the status of the components of the Federation and consequently the rights and obligations of the Union republics vis-à-vis the Federation, and similarly the rights of *krays, oblasts* and *okrugs* vis-à-vis the republics and the Federation.

The Treaty appears to hold the prospect for all the 87 subjects of the Federation to be given the rights and status of Union republics. Many of the *krays* and *oblasts* and several autonomous *okrugs* have been demanding political and economic rights equal to those of the republics. However, neither the federal nor the republican authorities are willing to accede to these demands, increasingly afraid of the loss of economic and political control and the possibility of demands for a greater degree of political independence.

After a year of confusion over the precise rights and obligations of the subjects of the Federation, President Yeltsin has only recently indicated his opposition to *krays* and *oblasts* acquiring the constitutional right to issue their own laws.[15] He has also spoken against the equality of all the subjects of the Federation as regards political rights. Not only do his pronouncements contradict the spirit of the Federation Treaty, but in many cases they come too late since many of the subjects of the Federation have already adopted a variety of their own legal provisions, which they see as being within their sphere of competence.

In the absence of any effective execution of the Treaty provisions, the republics and regions want to replace the federal authority, a demand which is fiercely opposed by the centre. The absence of a clear demarcation of powers between the centre and the regions is contributing to the weakening of state authority and the integrity of the Federation. For as long as the shape of the new federal structure and the prerogatives of its constituent parts remain unclear, problems of constitutional authority and delineation of prerogatives will, more likely than not, lead to a series of escalating conflicts.

The republics of Tatarstan and Yakutia-Sakha have drafted their own Constitutions. That of Tatarstan ignores the existence of the Russian Federation, while the Yakut version allots only defence and boundary protection to the federal level. There are numerous claims for the partition of 'double republics'. Given the incredibly complex pattern of ethnic distributions, no national and/or linguistic boundary can be wholly satisfactory to all parties. The Yakuts, for example, refer to the boundary of Yakutia as it was in the early nineteenth century, Tatarstan to that before 1552. They also express concern for their 'blood brothers living abroad', claiming the right to annex their settlement areas or at least to establish autonomous territories for them.[16]

On 30 April 1993, **Kalmykia** became a presidential republic within the Russian Federation, when deputies voted by an overwhelming majority to dissolve the Supreme Soviet and replace it with a 25-member 'professional' Parliament. They also abolished the local soviets throughout the country. The decision followed the election, on 11 April, of Kirsan Ilyumzhinov, a 30-year-old multimillionaire, as President of the republic. Subsequently, Ilyumzhinov imposed direct rule through a system of personal representatives in whom he vested special powers. The new President has emphasised the need for economic autonomy from Russia. It is, however, hard to imagine that such an autonomy can be achieved without the loosening and eventual severance of federal links with Russia.

The **Tuva** Supreme Soviet defied the Russian Federation on 11 May 1993 and amended the republican constitution to include the right to self-determination and the right to secede from Russia.[17] It was decided that a new constitution would be debated by the Parliament in June. Nationalists in the republic have long argued that Tuva's incorporation into the Soviet Union was no more legal than that of the Baltic states. Given that two-thirds of the population is Tuvin, secession has become an achievable option.

Bashkortostan has been in serious dispute with the Russian Federation for over 18 months now. In the spring of 1992, the republic's Supreme Soviet demanded of the Russian leadership that 30 per cent of Bashkortostan's industrial output should remain in the republic. The republic signed, albeit with serious reservations, the Federation Treaty establishing the Russian Federation. Bashkortostan insisted that a special appendix should be added to the Treaty. In it, the republic proclaimed that land minerals, natural and other resources (including oil, of which Bashkortostan is a major producer) on its territory are the property of its population and not of the Federation. It declared that issues related to the utilisation of its resources will be regulated by Bashkir law and agreements with the federal government. The republic

has also proclaimed itself an 'independent participant in international law and foreign economic relations, except areas it has voluntarily delegated to the Russian Federation'.

In April 1993, Bashkortostan's Parliament approved a question to be put to a republic-wide referendum: 'Do you agree that the Republic of Bashkortostan must have economic independence and treaty-based relations with the Russian Federation and Appendix to it, in the interests of all the peoples of the Republic of Bashkortostan?' The wording of the question predetermines the outcome of the voting—few if any of the voters in the republic are likely to object to greater economic independence. In practice it means the freedom to export its products and maintain its own tax system, whereby Bashkortostan remits fixed payments to the Russian Federation budget, keeping the rest for itself. What is more significant, however, is that the republic's authorities intend to place any agreement with Russia on 'treaty-based relations', i.e., relations between states. By asserting at the referendum the need for treaty-based relations, the Bashkir authorities have put pressure on Moscow to admit that Bashkortostan has a special status within the Federation. That precedent can now be followed by any of the Federation's units.

Tatarstan declared its sovereignty on 30 August 1990. On 21 February 1992 the Parliament of Tatarstan decided to hold a referendum on the status of the republic. Four million voters were asked: 'Do you agree that the Republic of Tatarstan is a sovereign state, a subject of international law, building its relations with the Russian Federation and other republics (states) on the basis of fair treaties?' The referendum took place on 21 March 1992, despite the ruling of Russia's Constitutional Court that it was unlawful. The results confirmed the earlier decision on the declaration of sovereignty of the Tatar state.

In November 1992, the Parliament of Tatarstan adopted a new Constitution which clearly defined the powers, sovereignty and independence of the republic. At the same time the deputies insisted on associated membership for Tatarstan of the Russian Federation—something that is not envisaged by the Federation Treaty. After the adoption of the Constitution, Moscow faced the dilemma of whether to sign a treaty with Tatarstan as an equal partner, thus creating a political precedent, or whether to treat the republic as an integral part of Russia, which Tatarstan refused to acknowledge. The second option could have far-reaching economic, military and political repercussions.

The nationalist and secessionist movement in Tatarstan continues to grow in strength. Eleven organisations and movements in the republic advocate the complete independence of Tatarstan. In an appeal issued on 13 April 1993 they called for a boycott of the all-Russia referendum on 25 April, arguing that Tatarstan had never voluntarily been a part of Russia and that the people of Tatarstan did not need a referendum into which the imperial forces wanted to drag them.[18]

On 11 May 1993, during President Mintimer Shaimiev's visit to Budapest, Tatarstan, in pursuit of its independent foreign and economic policy, signed an economic cooperation agreement with Hungary for 1993–98. Under the agreement Tatarstan will deliver 1.5m tons of crude oil per year to Hungary and in return receive industrial and agricultural products. It was the first such agreement negotiated between Tatarstan and a foreign country. In 1992 trade turnover between the two countries exceeded $235m.

The **Tyumen** region, rich in oil and natural gas, refused to sign the Federation Treaty in March 1992 and is now threatened with the secession of two of its autonomous *okrugs:* Khanty-Mansi and Yamalo-Nenets, both of which want to acquire the status of separate republics. Secession of the two *okrugs* would reduce the area of the Tyumen region from 1.4m sq km to a mere 161.000 sq km and deprive it of much of its resources and industry.

The division of the Magadan *oblast* and the creation of the **Chukot** Republic became a reality when, on 11 May 1993, the Constitutional Court of the Russian Federation decided that the separation of the Chukchee autonomous *okrug* from the Magadan *oblast* was in accordance with the Russian Constitution. In 1989 the Chukchee accounted for only 7.3 per cent of the *okrug*'s population, while Russians and Ukrainians made up 83 per cent. In September 1990, the *okrug*'s soviet proclaimed itself an autonomous republic, and in March 1991 it decided to separate from the *oblast*. Magadan's authorities contended that such a decision could be taken after a referendum had been held. The Court's decision opens the way for the secession of numerous other *okrugs* throughout the Russian Federation.

Conclusions

The argument in this article is based on two broad assumptions. The first is that the residues of Communism will remain for a long time to come. It has proved relatively easy to carry out structural transformation in the former Soviet Union in order to achieve the edifices of liberal democracy. However, their functioning is more often than not at variance with liberal democratic principles and values. These will be able to take root only with generational change. The symbiotic relationship between Communist collectivism and ethnicity will continue to dominate the wider political agenda. It is the most difficult aspect to tackle because it reflects the basic, and in some sense perhaps irrational, feelings of individual and group insecurity.

At the same time, however, it has in political and strategic terms become the avenue for the expression of political, economic and social aspirations which had been denied so far. The substantial credibility gap which exists between the old structural (federal) arrangements and the demands of an essentially new post-Communist situation can only be bridged by drastic action: either by the dismantling of the old structure or through their fundamental modification. So far there has been little, if any, evidence of either.

Russia still wants to remain a federation rather than, for example, a confederation, a commonwealth or a community of nations. The old Tsarist slogan 'Russia is indivisible' is used as a rallying point by new democrats and old Communists alike. In one important respect the new Federation Treaty is even more reactionary than the 1922 Union Treaty, which contained at least a token provision for secession from the Union. The new Treaty does not. According to it, the territory of the Federation is integral and inalienable. The spectre of the disintegration of Russia is indeed threatening, but it is a progressive reality. The way this reality is dealt with in the long term will determine the stability of international relations.

The second assumption is that there are two incompatible processes taking place in Western Europe, on the one hand, and the former Soviet Union and Central and Eastern Europe, on the other. For four decades now the West European agenda has been dominated by integration in political, economic and strategic terms. This has been a long and arduous process based, first, on the clear identification of separate interests and, second, on the development of common strategies and goals. The East is now only at the stage of identifying separate interests. Integration may follow in due course, but if it is forced or artificially accelerated it will inevitably be full of cracks and consequent instabilities.

Perhaps one of the most important lessons to be learned from the historical experience of the former Soviet Union, and from the tragic events in former Yugoslavia, is that the federal organisation of the state and the multinational structure of its population are quite different things. There is an urgent need to re-examine our well-accepted analytical and methodological tools such as the concept of the nation-state, sovereignty, self-determination, nation and borders.

Notes

1. Vladimir A. Kolossov, *Ethno-Territorial Conflicts and Boundaries in the Former Soviet Union* (University of Durham, International Boundaries Research Unit, 1992), p. 3.
2. Bogdan Szajkowski, *Encyclopedia of Conflicts and Flashpoints in the Former Soviet Union and Central and Eastern Europe* (London: Longman, December 1993).

3. Vladimir A. Kolossov, *op. cit.*, p. 10.

4. *Ibid.*, p. 12.

5. For details, see 'The socio-economic situation and the development of economic reforms in the Russian Federation in the first quarter of 1993', *Ekonomika i Zhizn*, No 17, May 1993.

6. Bogdan Szajkowski and Tim Niblock, 'Islam and Ethnicity in Eastern Europe'. Paper presented to the International Conference on Moslem Minorities/Communities in Post-bipolar Europe' at the Saints Cyril and Metodij University, Skopje, Macedonia. April 1993, pp. 2–3.

7. Eliezer Ben-Rafael and Stephen Sharot, *Ethnicity, Religion and Class in Israeli Society* (Cambridge: Cambridge University Press, 1991), p. 6.

8. BBC SWB, SU/1676 B/5, 30 April 1993.

9. Of the 107.3m eligible voters in the Russian Federation, 69.2m participated in the referendum. Of them, 58.7 per cent had confidence in President Yeltsin: 53 per cent approved of his economic reforms; 31.7 per cent wanted early presidential elections; and 43.1 per cent favoured early parliamentary elections. Under the conditions set out by the Congress of People's Deputies and the Constitutional Court, the last two questions were not passed since they attracted less than half of the potential votes.

10. Only 2.7 per cent of voters in Ingushetia, 14.3 per cent in Dagestan, 25.9 per cent in Karachay-Cherkessia and 35.8 per cent in Kabarda-Balkaria voted 'yes' in answer to the question: 'Do you trust the President?'. BBC SWB, SU/1675 B/2, 29 April 1993; and BBC SWB, SU/1680 B/3, 5 May 1993.

11. BBC SWB, SU/1675 B/2, 29 April 1993. Interestingly, the referendum also showed considerable dissatisfaction with Yeltsin and his policies among the Russians living outside the Russian Federation. For example, of the eligible Russian citizens residing in Estonia, only 27.9 per cent of those voting expressed confidence in the President, with 71.3 per cent voting against. 72.6 per cent rejected the reforms; some 70.3 per cent supported early presidential elections, with 28.3 per cent against; and 50.3 per cent backed early parliamentary elections, with 48.7 per cent against. Of the 4,525 Russian citizens in Latvia who participated in the referendum, 21 per cent voted 'yes' and 78 per cent 'no' on the question of confidence in the President; 19.5 per cent voted 'yes' and 80 per cent 'no' in support of reform policy; 79 per cent voted 'yes' and 19 per cent 'no' on presidential elections; and 40 per cent voted 'yes' and 59 per cent 'no' on the question of fresh elections to the Russian Parliament. BBC SWB, SU/1674 C/5. 28 April 1993.

12. The Federation Treaty replaced the Union Treaty of 29 December 1922, which was abrogated by Russia, Belarus and Ukraine on 8 December 1991 when the three countries created the Commonwealth of Independent States (CIS).

13. The Treaty was signed by the Russian Federation, the Soviet Socialist Republic of Adygeva, the Republic of Bashkortostan, the Buryat Soviet Socialist Republic, the Republic of Gornyy Altay, the Republic of Dagestan, the Kabardin-Balkar Republic, the Republic of Kalmykia-Khalmg Tangch, the Republic of Karachay-Cherkessia, the Republic of Karelia, the Komi Soviet Socialist Republic, the Republic of Mari El, the Mordova Soviet Socialist Republic, the North Ossetian Soviet Socialist Republic, the Republic of Sakha (Yakutia), the Republic of Tuva, the Udmurt Republic, the Republic of Khakassia and the Chuvash Republic.

14. See, for example, an interview with the Chairman of the Soviet of Nationalities of the Supreme Soviet, Ramazan Abdulatipov. BBC SWB, SU/1656 B/5. 6 April 1993.

15. See Yeltsin's address to the Council of Heads of Administration of *Krays, Oblasts* and Autonomous *Okrugs* within Russia on 28 May 1993. BBC SWB, SU/1701 B/1, 29 May 1993.

16. Even in Kazakhstan, with its extremely mixed population and relative tolerance, the legislators wish to extend citizenship to all Kazakhs living 'abroad'.

17. Tuva enjoyed at least nominal independence between 12 August 1921 and 11 October 1944, when it was incorporated into the Soviet Union.

18. *Izvestia*, 13 April 1993.

Map supplied by Bogdan Szajkowski.

Article 7   *The Washington Post National Weekly Edition*, September 20–26, 1993

Sacrificed to the Superpower

The Soviet drive to achieve nuclear dominance left lives and the land in ruins.

Michael Dobbs

Washington Post Foreign Service

SEMIPALATINSK, Kazakhstan
It was the happiest day of Sergei Davydov's life: Aug. 29, 1949. The retired engineer still remembers the blinding flash and his "feverish joy" at the sight of a huge, mushroom-shaped cloud erupting over the desert of northern Kazakhstan. The Soviet Union, the world's first Communist state, had become a nuclear superpower—and he had pressed the button.

In a squalid wooden hut 600 miles away in southern Russia, by the bank of the Techa River, Mavzhida Valeyeva remembers 1949 for a different reason. It was the year her health began to deteriorate dramatically.

Along with practically all her neighbors, she now suffers from violent headaches and constant nosebleeds. Her blood is anemic. Her four children and five surviving grandchildren are all invalids.

It took Valeyeva more than four decades to make a connection between her family's devastating health problems and the Soviet Union's nuclear bomb project. In 1990, the Soviet government finally acknowledged that millions of tons of highly toxic radioactive waste had been secretly dumped in the Techa by a plutonium plant 49 miles upstream from Valeyeva's village, Muslyumovo. The river the villagers saw as a source of life was in fact a source of death.

"It would be better if they had never discovered this nuclear energy," says Valeyeva, who visited the river daily to collect drinking water and wash her family's

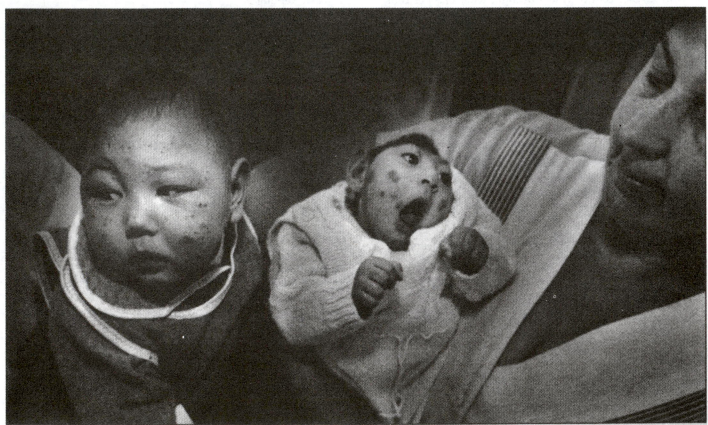

PHOTOS BY LUCIAN PERKINS—THE WASHINGTON POST

Deformed babies, ages 10 months and 9 months, are among many at an orphanage in Semipalatinsk, a former nuclear test site.

clothes. "It would be better to be poorer, but at least to be healthy and give our children and grandchildren a chance of living a normal life."

The Communist politicians who launched the Soviet Union on a program of breakneck industrialization and transformed the country into a military and political rival of the United States, believed that the natural resources under their control were inexhaustible. Yet future generations of Russians and Tatars, Balts and Ukrainians, Czechs and Poles will pay a heavy price for the hubris of their leaders. There came a point when nature simply rebelled.

A two-month journey from the center of Europe to the Russian Far East to review the legacy of Marx, Engels, Lenin and Stalin revealed the destructive impact that communism had on the environment in Russia—one of the scars left by the combination of totalitarian rule and socialist economics that will almost certainly take generations to heal.

The environmental catastrophe left behind by 70 years of Communist rule is visible in poisoned rivers, devastated forests, dried-up lakes and smog-polluted cities. Some of these disasters, such as the evaporation of the Aral Sea after the diversion of rivers for an irrigation project, have permanently changed the contours of the vast Eurasian landmass. But, according to Russian scientists and ecologists, the most lasting physical damage will probably have been caused by the unleashing of nuclear power.

"Radioactive contamination is the number one environmental problem in this country. Air and water pollution come next," says Alexei Yablokov, a biologist who serves as President Boris Yeltsin's chief adviser on environmental matters. "The way we have dealt with the whole issue of nuclear power, and particularly the problem of nuclear waste, was irresponsible and immoral."

The scale of nuclear contamination in the former Soviet Union has only become clear over the last few years, with the advent of free speech and the lifting of censorship restrictions. In the wake of the 1986 Chernobyl catastrophe, Russians learned about other disasters, including a series of accidents at a plutonium-producing plant near the southern Urals city of Chelyabinsk between 1948 and 1967. They also learned about dozens of ad hoc nuclear dumps, some of which could begin seeping radioactivity at any moment. The seas around Russia—from the Baltic to the Pacific—are littered with decaying hulks of nuclear submarines and rusting metal containers with tens of millions of tons of nuclear waste. Russia itself is dotted with dozens of once secret cities with names like Chelyabinsk-70, Tomsk-7 and Krasnoyarsk-26, where nuclear materials have been stock-

Mavzhida Valeyeva's health has been broken by the radioactive drinking water in her village.

piled. Unmarked on any map, they hit the headlines only when there is an accident. Vast areas of the country have been treated as a nuclear dump, the result of four decades of testing.

"We were turned into human guinea pigs for these experiments," says Bakhit Tumyenova, a senior health official in the Semipalatinsk region, the main Soviet nuclear test site until 1989. "They kept on telling us that it was for the good of the people, the Communist Party, the future. The individual never counted for anything in this system."

The testing of the Soviet Union's first atomic bomb in 1949 represented a huge achievement for a backward, semi-Asiatic country. It had mobilized vast economic and human resources, from the team of elite

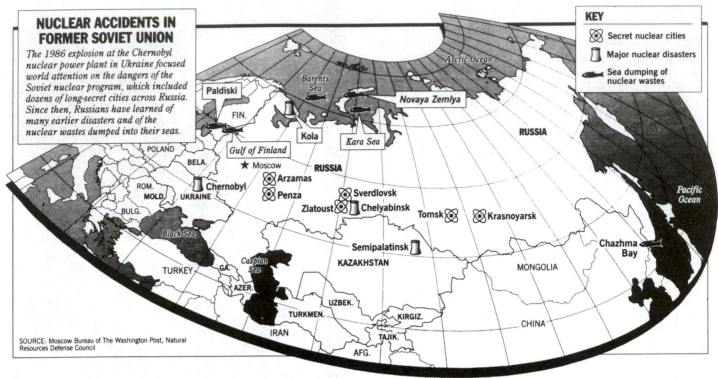

NUCLEAR ACCIDENTS IN FORMER SOVIET UNION

The 1986 explosion at the Chernobyl nuclear power plant in Ukraine focused world attention on the dangers of the Soviet nuclear program, which included dozens of long-secret cities across Russia. Since then, Russians have learned of many earlier disasters and of the nuclear wastes dumped into their seas.

KEY
- Secret nuclear cities
- Major nuclear disasters
- Sea dumping of nuclear wastes

SOURCE: Moscow Bureau of The Washington Post, Natural Resources Defense Council

BY RICHARD FURNO—THE WASHINGTON POST

scientists who designed the bomb to the army of slave laborers who mined the uranium and disposed of the nuclear waste.

The two sides of the Soviet nuclear project—the epic achievements and the disregard for human life—are symbolized by the man initially in charge of it. Lavrenti Beria, the chief of Stalin's secret police, was a great organizer. But he was also a great destroyer, willing to obliterate any obstacle to achieve his goal.

"It was a heroic epoch," recalls Igor Golovin, a leading scientist and biographer of Igor Kurchatov, the head of the nuclear project. "We worked days and nights and really believed in what we were doing. The propaganda instilled the idea that the United States had the bomb and wanted to enslave us, so it was vital that we acquired our own nuclear weapons as soon as possible, whatever the cost."

Few of the scientists and engineers working on the project gave much thought to the dangers of radioactive fallout. After pushing the button that triggered the first nuclear device, Davydov rushed to the site of the explosion without any protective clothing or gas mask. He was later sick with leukemia for about 20 years.

"They gave me special injections, and it somehow stabilized. Now I feel all right," says the 76-year-old pensioner, proudly displaying a chestful of medals. "Personally, I think that all those people who demand privileges from the government because their health suffered as a result of these tests are just crooks and swindlers."

The idea that any sacrifice was justified in the effort to turn the Soviet Union into a superpower was a fundamental part of the Communist ethos. ("You can't make an omelette without cracking eggs," Lenin liked to remark.) It permeated the nuclear project right from the start, and still exists to some extent among older people. The system elevated the state above ordinary individuals—and this was its basic flaw.

"The postwar generation was brought up with the idea that they should be ready to sacrifice themselves for the state. This was the philosophy of the time. It was a pernicious philosophy because it prevented any thought being given to ecological problems," says Natalya Mironova, an environmental activist in Chelyabinsk. "For many years we were unable even to discuss such matters."

Little attention was paid to such issues as nuclear safety and the training of responsible personnel. The manager of the Chernobyl plant at the time of the 1986 disaster had previously been in charge of a heating plant. According to officials, roughly 50 percent of the accidents in nuclear power stations and 75 percent of accidents on nuclear submarines are due to "human error."

This year alone, there have been at least three accidents at nuclear facilities in Russia involving the release of radioactivity. The government has been inundated with dozens of letters from scientists at both military and civilian nuclear facilities warning of "further Chernobyls" because of rapidly deteriorating working conditions and the departure of many highly qualified workers.

For the 1,000 inhabitants of Muslyumovo in the southern Urals, the Soviet Union's experiments with the atom are a curse that will blight the lives of many generations. According to the local doctor, Gulfarida Galimova, four of every five villagers are "chronically sick." She says the effects of radiation have altered the genetic code of the local Tatar population, with the result that babies are often sick from birth.

"We do not have a future," says Galimova. "We have been so genetically harmed that our descendants will not be able to escape this curse. Patients come to me, and I know I can never cure them. Radiation has entered the food chain. Our cows eat radiated grass. The potatoes we grow in our back yards are poisoned. The only solution is to close this entire region off—and not let anyone come here for 3,000 years. But they won't do that, because there isn't enough money."

The 2.75 million curies of radioactive waste flushed into the shallow Techa was equivalent to half the fallout from the bomb that fell on Hiroshima, but nobody bothered to inform local inhabitants. In the late 1950s, signs were posted along the Techa warning people not to bathe in the river. The nature of the danger was never explained, so most villagers paid little attention.

In the early 1980s, Galimova first started noticing that something was terribly amiss with the health of Muslyumova residents. Nearly 10 percent of births in the village were premature. Many of her patients were anemic. There was a high incidence of cancer. When she reported her findings to her superiors in Chelyabinsk, the problems were blamed on bad food and a lack of hemoglobin. She was accused of being a bad doctor.

What local people refer to as "the river illness" is now affecting the third and even fourth generation of Muslyumovo residents. Valeyeva's eldest son, Ural, 33, is mentally retarded. His three children—aged 6, 4 and 18 months—can barely summon up the energy to get out of bed. Another daughter, Sazhida, 29, has a chronic craving for chalk that has destroyed all her teeth. Her oldest son, Vadim, 11, has been sick from birth. Timur, 6, has chronic bronchitis and anemia.

It was not until April 1986 that Galimova finally guessed what was the matter. Chernobyl played a crucial role in convincing Mikhail Gorbachev and other Soviet leaders that the country's problems could not be solved without *glasnost*, openness. Discussion of ecological problems was no longer taboo.

When they finally came clean about the contamination of the Techa, the authorities also admitted two disasters involving the Mayak plutonium-producing plant at Kyshtym, about 60 miles northwest of Chelyabinsk. In 1957, a waste storage tank exploded at the plant, releasing 20 million curies of radiation. A decade later, a drought dried up nearby Lake Karachai, which had been used as a storage tank for 120 million curies of waste products from Mayak. High winds scattered radioactive dust over a wide area.

According to an official Russian government report released earlier this year, the three disasters at Mayak affected 450,000 people living in a contaminated region roughly the size of Maryland. The amount of radioactivity still stored at Mayak—much of it in insecure conditions—is equivalent to the fallout from 20 Chernobyl disasters.

Nearly 20,000 residents of the Chelyabinsk region were evacuated from their homes. By a tragic twist of fate, some of these people were moved from one high-risk region to another.

Valentina Lazareva, for example, was evacuated from a village near Mayak in 1957 as a 9-year-old orphan. There were rumors of an "explosion" at the plant, but nobody knew anything for sure. She spent the rest of her childhood in an orphanage in Brodokalmak, a village a few miles downriver from Muslyumovo. The children crossed the Techa every day on their way to school and drank water from a nearby well. In the summer, they would swim in the village.

"Now we are all sick," says Lazareva, who is 46 but looks much older. "There were 32 people in my class. We have already buried five of my classmates. Another 10 are dying. But all are invalids, in one way or another."

Today, there is no shortage of glasnost about the man-made environmental disaster confronting the former Soviet Union. But there is a desperate shortage of resources to do much about it. The amount of money the government has earmarked to clean up the Chelyabinsk region—roughly $20 million—is minuscule compared to the $40 billion to $60 billion cost the United States has projected for the cleanup of its main plutonium-producing facility, the Hanford nuclear reservation in Washington state.

In Kazakhstan, which declared itself an independent state in December 1991 after the breakup of the Soviet Union, health officials say they are unable to provide even basic medical care to villages exposed to four decades of nuclear tests. The lack of basic health services has encouraged many people to turn to charlatans and faith healers for help. In Semipalatinsk—the site of 470 nuclear explosions, including 116 in the atmosphere, between 1949 and 1989—a Muslim preacher named Sary-Aulie has been attracting crowds of 10,000 with his promise to cure aches and pains through "vibrations."

"We can't do much for these people, so it's not surprising that they put their trust in charlatans," says Tumyenova, the regional health administrator. "The Semipalatinsk test site served the entire Soviet Union. Now the other republics have gone their own way—and we have been left alone, sitting on top of a gigantic nuclear rubbish heap."

Article 8   *Harvard International Review,* Spring 1993

Active Leadership

Russia's Role in Central Asia

Vitaly Naumkin

Vitaly Naumkin is President of the Russian Center for Strategic Research and International Studies in Moscow and Deputy Director of the Institute of Oriental Studies at the Russian Academy of Sciences.

The five central Asian republics of the former Soviet Union—Kazakhstan, Uzbekistan, Tajikistan, Turkmenistan, and Kyrgyzstan—became independent states after the demise of the Soviet Union. In contrast to most of the republics in the USSR, these five did not express any desire to leave the Union; they were quite prepared to sign the Treaty of the Union. Events since then, however, have revealed that trends toward independence in the Central Asian societies were developing for years. The sudden break-up, however, produced an avalanche of problems, many of which are still unsolved. One of the consequences has been a dramatic weakening of the traditional ties between these states and Russia.

Crisis of Linked Economies

In the Soviet Union's final years, the republics of Central Asia had exceptionally close links to the Russian Republic. Even today, the Russian share of Kazakhstan's imports amounts to 65 percent, and the figures are only slightly lower for Uzbekistan (58 percent), Kyrgyzstan (51 percent) and Tajikistan and Turkmenistan (48 percent each). Russia receives 61 percent of Uzbekistan's exports, while its share of exports amounts to 54 percent for Turkmenistan, 53 percent for Kazakhstan, 51 percent for Tajikistan and 39 percent for Kyrgyzstan.

The disruption of previously existing economic ties has been the main cause of the deepening crisis in the Central Asian economies. Gross national income fell 25 percent in Kyrgyzstan during the first seven months of 1992; even for the relatively comfortable republic of Turkmenistan, the drop was 18 percent. Predictably, this has diminished industrial production. Retail trade has also suffered: during this period, trade fell by 43 percent in Uzbekistan.

Among the republics, prospects are most favorable in Kazakhstan, with its natural resources and agricultural potential, followed by Turkmenistan, with its oil and gas, and Uzbekistan, which has retained state control of the economy and natural resources. The situation is worst in Kyrgyzstan and Tajikistan, where the new costs of importing energy from Russia have been traumatic.

After independence, the establishment of trade and economic links by these five states with their neighbors, chiefly Turkey, and hopes of obtaining large-scale economic assistance produced an initial state of euphoria that was quickly followed by disillusionment. Strict limits appeared on both the ability of neighboring states to help and the capability of the Central Asian republics to rapidly restructure their economies.

Considering the present conditions, one can confidently predict that for three or four years at the very least, the Central Asian republics will remain closely tied to Russia. During this transitional period, barring unexpected development, there will probably be no dramatic change in relations between these states and Russia. If the Central Asian states can develop a new system of external trade links and attract large-scale foreign investments, the situation will improve. True economic independence for these states seems to be in the interests of the world community, since further economic breakdown would invite a new wave of instability and strife in the region. However, economic independence should be established through gradual involvement of the republics in a system of international and regional economic ties in which Russia plays a role. Autarchy would only hamper development and lead to new conflicts.

An ideal solution to the problems facing the republics would be to preserve the existing economic ties with Russia and to take advantage of the Russian experience with economic restructuring. The preservation of ties with Russia, given its stabilizing influence upon the Central Asian economies, would also strengthen the position of Central Asian reformers—as long as reformers retain power in Russia. This should, however, coincide with the establishment of new external links along with a gradual transition to independence in the world economy. Fundamental restructuring of economies that have been too closely bound to Russia for too long seems necessary and unavoidable, but this process will require a massive infusion of foreign capital.

An alliance with fundamentalist and authoritarian regimes may lead to regional destabilization. As the Russian economist Leonid Fridman puts it, "There remains a possibility of some of these newly independent states becoming—for a certain period—something like a sediment-collector of archaic political and religious structures with relatively high—more precisely, with not too low—standards of life, in local terms; they will be based on incomes from trade in energy and other valuable mineral resources in the world market." Naturally, Russia's influence will be significant in determining the strength of the various political forces in the Central Asian nations.

Does Russia Want to Stay?

Russian interests would be best served by an active policy toward Central Asia. This view has been embraced by the present Russian leadership, although at first its stance toward Central Asia could have been interpreted as isolationist. At present, even the most active backers of Russia's pro-Western position realize that Russia has lost initiative and the chance to develop renewed relations with the states of the southern half of the Commonwealth of Independent States (CIS). It will be extremely difficult to re-establish what seems to have been lost. A document presented by the Russian Ministry of Foreign Affairs at the end of 1992, entitled "A Concept of Russia's Foreign Policy," stressed the need to actively develop relations between Russia and the Central Asian states. At a conference of Russian experts in December, the former deputy Foreign Minister F. Shelov-Kovedyayev stated, "In order not to lose its position, the Russian Federation should have changed its tactics by July or August (not later than September); it should have made active use of various means of influence upon the situation in the 'new foreign states,' including differentiated approaches to the development of economic relations."

Russia needs to preserve its links to the Central Asian market. Bowing to the demands of the situation, Russia has downgraded its partnership with the Central Asian states, but it should not allow other countries to oust it completely from the region. This would threaten both the regional political balance and the security of Russia.

Recently, Russia has taken several steps toward developing greater economic cooperation with the Central Asian republics, mainly on a bilateral basis. It has intensified contacts, leading to a number of important agreements. For instance, Russia has established special economic relations with Kazakhstan, giving it priority status, and has given Tajikistan substantial credit for grain purchases.

According to the Russian government, the retention of a common currency by Russia and these republics should have been an important stabilizing factor in preserving the existing trade links. Another important step in the financial sphere was the establishment of the CIS Interstate Bank at the Minsk meeting in January 1993. But, in practice, Russia adopted world-market prices in its trade and economic accounts with the other republics, and some of the republics, after signing the Minsk agreements, declared their intention to introduce their own currency in response to Russia's position. Russia's strict financial policy has resulted in additional obstacles for these states. Some of the more sensible Russian politicians believe that it is worth the financial sacrifice to secure stability around the southern borders of the country. The Central Asians, too, need stable monetary conditions, both to support normal development and to overcome dangerous economic crises.

Ethnic and National Conflicts

Conflicts originating from the ethnic tensions that have surfaced in various parts of Central Asia threaten the region's stability. Until now, the conflict in Tajikistan, which can be defined as "quasi-ethnic," i.e., as a conflict between different factions of a single ethnic group, has produced the biggest shock. However, its latest stage has acquired some characteristics of an inter-ethnic conflict in a narrower sense. The division is between the Tajiks proper and the various groups of Upper Badakhshan related to the Tajiks. Despite their internal divisions, all the Farsi-speaking peoples of Tajikistan find themselves united in opposition to the Turkish peoples, primarily the Uzbeks. Although this conflict still remains below the surface, it is capable of exploding Central Asia from within.

The Tajik conflict has cooled to a certain degree, although a solution is still a distant dream. External help has relieved some of the tension. In this sense, the role played by Russia may be summarized as follows: (1) protection of the border between Tajikistan and Afghanistan in order to stop the flow of arms into the republic; (2) a limited peace mission—protecting communication lines, separating the opposing factions and assisting noncombatants—carried out by

Russian troops in the republic; (3) diplomatic efforts to find a way out of the crisis including active support before and during the assembly of the Supreme Soviet and in the election of a new leadership, cooperation with other states in creating special peace-forces and mediation missions in the republic.

This particular episode shows that today's Russia prefers to act in accord with other Central Asian states and tries to legitimize its actions through bilateral and collective agreements. In this case, the efforts to find a solution to the Tajik conflict were made in November, 1992, by Kazakhstan, Kyrgyzstan, Russia and Uzbekistan. Turkmenistan refused to take part in such efforts, considering the conflict an internal matter of Tajikistan.

The Tajikistan experience has also shown that the Central Asian states still have confidence in Russia's role as a mediator and are willing to ask for both military and economic assistance. The prevailing attitudes in this region stand in sharp contrast to those of Transcaucasia, where the opposing sides prefer to make appeals to the United Nations, the North Atlantic Treaty Organization (NATO), the Council on Security and Cooperation in Europe and various Western countries. Russia's behavior has served as an indicator that it will be fairly active in the Central Asian republics. While attempting to leave the "Afghan syndrome" behind, Russia has shown itself able to intervene effectively, collaborating with other states of the region to reestablish law and order. This policy has been motivated largely by the threat to Russia's own security originating south of the CIS borders. The constant struggle of warring factions in Afghanistan could spread armed conflict into the other CIS member-states and into Russia itself. The situation appears even more ominous if one considers the Islamic dimension of the Tajik conflict, as well as the attempts by Islamic forces in Iran, Saudi Arabia and Pakistan to gain a foothold inside the CIS by backing Islamic propaganda campaigns.

The threat of Afghan influence, which is strong in Central Asia, appears more serious when we take into account the fact that internal strife in Afghanistan also has an ethno-national dimension. The combatants are various ethnic groups that are also present in Tajikistan and Uzbekistan. The Tajik conflict has also forced a large number of refugees to seek asylum in Afghanistan, many of them ethnic Kyrgyz. Fortunately, organizations such as the National Islamic

Movement of Afghanistan with its Uzbek leader, General Dostum, and the Observer Council of Field Commanders, composed mainly of Tajiks led by Minister of Defense Masud, can play an important part in maintaining stability in the border region. There is some evidence of regular cooperation between the Russian frontier guards in Tajikistan and General Dostum, who has control of some parts of the border region and is considered by Russia to be working in a constructive manner during this conflict.

Borders and Ethnic Groups

In this context, border problems have acquired a special importance for Russia. In the first half of 1992, Russia was forced to define its border policy. In one sense, Russia felt that it could continue to keep its borders with the other CIS states "transparent." To do this, though, Russia would have to maintain a high level of security on the frontier between the southern republics of the former Soviet Union and their neighbors to the south. Turkmenistan and Azerbaijan increased tensions by opening their borders with Iran. The "transparency" of the CIS borders was preserved, though, and the Minsk meeting on January 22, 1993, of the state and government leaders of the CIS member states produced an agreement on joint protection of the borders, though not all the member-states have signed it. They decided to send five border-guard battalions to Tajikistan from all the signatory states as additional support for the Russian frontier guards.

The Central Asian states are quite concerned about border security because they fear the spread of intra-ethnic tensions and Islamic extremism. This is very important in the case of Uzbekistan, where centers of ethnic tensions exist alongside Islamic fundamentalist movements. Turkmenistan is an exception for several reasons. First, it is richer in natural resources than the other countries. Second, there are no centers of intra-ethnic tensions, and third, there is no Islamic fundamentalist movement, nor is there any political opposition. For these reasons, Turkmenistan tries to distance itself from its Central Asian neighbors. It does not shun closer contacts with Iran and prefers to sign bilateral, not collective, agreements taking a stance toward the CIS similar to that of Ukraine. Nevertheless, Turkmenistan participated in the meeting of the Central Asian leaders in Tashkent on January 4, 1993, at which the establishment

of a commonwealth was proclaimed. Its membership in other international associations, such as the Economic Cooperation Organization and the Organization of the Caspian Sea States, lends a touch of dynamism to Turkmenistan's foreign policy.

The most potentially dangerous hotbeds of internecine strife in Central Asia are well-known: the Osh Valley (between the Kyrgyz and Uzbek populations), the districts of Samarkand and Bukhara (between the Tajiks and Uzbeks), and the Ferghana Valley (mixed populations with a growing level of Islamic influence). At any moment the region may witness a conflict between the northern and southern factions of the Kyrgyz people. But the gravest crisis, which could endanger not only this particular region but could also acquire global dimensions, is the worsening relations between the Turkish and Slavic populations in Kazakhstan, where both are densely settled. Russia recognizes the status of Kazakhstan as a nuclear power. The Kazakhstan leadership is fully aware of its responsibility and is working hand in hand with the Russian government, establishing very close relations between the two countries. This alliance with Kazakhstan, as well as its stability, could have a decisive influence upon Russia's future.

A possible source of tension among the states of Central Asia can be found in border disputes concerning arable land and other natural resources, since borders were drawn arbitrarily during the process of ethnic and national demarcation in the 1920s. Until now, it has been possible to contain these disputes at the earliest stages, and Russia's role in maintaining the status quo in this respect seems indispensable.

Russia also faces a moral dilemma in its relations with the Central Asian republics: should it back those regimes that can guarantee their nations' internal stability, or should it support the forces that declare "democracy" as their aim but are undermining political stability? Russia's choice has been in favor of stability and acceptance of legitimate governments—even those that do not share the liberal and democratic principles of the present Russian leadership. This choice was influenced by events in Tajikistan, where Islamic forces were prepared to use democracy the way the Islamic fundamentalists did in Algeria; in the latter case the West did nothing to stop the interruption of the democratization process. The Tajikistan experience has helped the President of

Uzbekistan in his efforts to weaken the Islamic forces in the republic and to tighten his control over the opposition as a whole.

The developing geopolitical situation will dictate the means that should be used to guarantee regional stability. In what direction is the CIS evolving? What will be the interrelationships among the Central Asian states? Outside the region, what form will their relations with the countries of the Near East or Russia take? In what direction will the formation of their national armies take them? What will be the military doctrines of the Central Asian states? Who will be their partners? What is the fate of the Russian military still remaining in the region?

Russia and the Central Asian states are still looking for the solution to these problems. Some of them are prepared to develop a system of collective security in the region. Thus, Kazakhstan, Tajikistan and Uzbekistan, at the meeting of their leaders in Tashkent on May 15, 1992, signed a collective security treaty with Armenia, Belarus and Russia. Moscow is quite interested in this system and naturally would like to have Kyrgyzstan and, if possible, Turkmenistan, join, but the latter state still prefers to develop bilateral relationships with Russia. Kazakhstan has expressed its desire that NATO should support it in preparing its military cadres.

Treaties signed by these states have created an observer corps and peace-keeping forces. A special council of collective security has been created, and the foundations for peaceful solution of conflicts were laid out at a joint meeting of the Council of the Ministers of Foreign Affairs and the Council of the Ministers of Defense of the CIS in Tashkent on July 16, 1992.

One of the most important factors influencing Russian policy in Central Asia is the large number of Russian residents in the region. Moscow is fully aware of the limits of its ability to influence their fate. Nevertheless, any threat to the Russian population could draw a response from Moscow. Guaranteeing the security of this population will serve as an argument for the Russian authorities to push forward their peace-keeping activities in Central Asia.

At the Alma Ata meeting in November 1992, the "foursome" decided to send to Tajikistan a peace-making force containing Russian military detachments. The fulfillment of the decision was delayed because the Kyrgyz Supreme Soviet would not sanction the action; Uzbekistan also did not completely support the move. Action was finally taken in January 1993, when Russia decided to send 500 military personnel to Tajikistan as part of the peace-force.

The main problem is whether or not Russia will still be able to play an active part in solving any future conflicts in this region. The answer seems to be "yes" as far as the near future is concerned. The West and the world community ought to be interested in Russia's restraining influence, since any destabilization in this region could have an adverse influence upon the whole Middle East. Nor can the West tolerate drastic changes in the overall situation that may lead to a deepening crisis. If destructive or extremist forces come to power, they will endanger the process of gradual introduction of reforms in the new states—a process that will bring Central Asia closer to the world community.

Article 9

Harvard International Review, Spring 1993

On Its Own

Islam in Post-Soviet Central Asia

Shirin Akiner

Shirin Akiner is the Director of the Central Asia Research Forum at the School of Oriental and African Studies of the University of London.

The territory of the formerly Soviet regions of Central Asia, which lies at the heart of the Eurasian land mass, encompasses an area of some four million square kilometers. The strategic importance of this region, together with its world-class reserves of minerals and hydrocarbons, makes it the focus of considerable international interest. It has a population of approximately 50 million, of whom 35 million are Muslims. With the exception of a few thousand Pamiri Ismailis in the Southeast, almost all are Sunnis of the Hanafi School.

Islam was introduced into the southern tier in the second half of the seventh century, when Transoxania was incorporated into the Arab Caliphate. The new religion spread fairly rapidly among the settled peoples, but took far longer to reach the nomads of the steppe region in the North. The cities of the South became centers of Islamic orthodoxy, but elsewhere, especially in the North, adherence to Islam was more perfunctory. Nevertheless, throughout the region the impact of the religion was such that Islam became one of the chief elements of self-definition for nomads and settled peoples alike.

Under Soviet rule, the state waged an all-out campaign to destroy this sense of Islamic identity and to replace it with a secular identity that was partly "national" in character (i.e., with a territorial base in a given republic), and partly "international" (i.e., Union-based). Ten years ago, after some six decades of oppression, harassment and relentless anti-religious propaganda, knowledge of Islam had been undermined to such an extent that for the great mass of the population it survived only in the form of a few rites of passage and of the awareness (though not always the observance) of dietary laws prohibiting the consumption of pork and alcohol. Yet today, a year after the collapse of the Soviet Union, Islam has already become a significant political force in the newly independent republics of Kazakhstan, Kyrgyzstan, Tajikistan, Turkmenistan and Uzbekistan.

Islamic Revival

There were two developments in the second half of the 1980s that prepared the ground for this Islamic revival. The first was a small-scale, personal reaction against the moral and spiritual bankruptcy of Marxist-Leninist materialism. Individuals, singly or in groups, began to seek instruction on Islam and to try to live according to its precepts. The movement was strongest in the Ferghana Valley, where it gained momentum fairly rapidly. According to local estimates, by 1989 it had some 8,000 to 10,000 adherents. The press described them as *Wahhabis*, implying that they were both fanatics and traitors employed by a foreign power—presumably Saudi Arabia. The believers did not use the term themselves, however, and there is no evidence to suggest that this was anything but an indigenous impulse, similar in character to the religious revivals that took place elsewhere in the Soviet Union at the time. The movement, too weak and uncoordinated to have much direct influence on society, did arouse the admiration of some intellectuals in the republican capitals, especially in Tashkent, and thus indirectly acquired a wider significance than the actual number of its supporters would suggest.

The second development occurred at the state level. In the early years of *perestroika*, government officials, including Mikhail Gorbachev himself, had often placed the blame for the social and economic shortcomings of the region on Islam. In 1989, however, the state experienced an abrupt change of policy. This coincided with the election in March of that year of a new Chairman of the Muslim Spiritual Board of Central Asia and Kazakhstan. Ostensibly, the Muslim community "spontaneously" took the unprecedented step of insisting that the then-incumbent, Mufti Shamsuddinkhan Babakhanov, be removed from office because of his immoral lifestyle. A more probable reason was that Babakhanov, a product of the Brezhnev era, had become an embarrassment to policy-planners in Moscow. A new figurehead was needed, and was found in Muhammad Sadyk Muhammad Yusuf Khodzha-ogli, the 36-year-old rector of the Tashkent *madrassah* (the senior of the only two Soviet *madrassahs*). Forthright about his desire to see a return to Islamic orthodoxy, he nevertheless understood clearly the need to work with the gov-

Islam has been revived after years of restriction within the Soviet system.

ernment. Within weeks, he was given a prominent role in public life, which included invitations to participate in state ceremonies and to mediate in civil disorders such as those between Uzbeks and Meskhetian Turks in the Ferghana Valley in June, 1989. The official justification for this role was his position as a Deputy of the All-Union Congress of Peoples' Deputies (his election to this office had been secured by ensuring that he was the sole candidate in his ward). The people treated him and other Muslim clerics with the deference usually reserved for government representatives, which was, in effect, what they were.

The government rewarded Mufti Muhammad Sadyk's cooperation with a number of concessions to the Muslim community. More mosques were opened in that one year than in the whole of the previous decade. Copies of the Koran and records of Koranic recitations appeared in state-run kiosks in increasing quantities, while the number of pilgrims allowed to go on the *hajj* rose from some 30 in 1989 to 1,500 the following year. Senior government officials began to express positive sentiments about Islam in public, and the celebration of Islamic feast days (and even pre-Islamic feast-days such as Now Ruz, the Zoroastrian New Year, mistakenly ascribed to Islam) received official encouragement.

A number of general reasons explain the government's *volte-face* toward Islam. One was the greater religious toler-

ance that was becoming prevalent throughout the Soviet Union; another was the feeling that religion could help to revive a sense of personal accountability and stop the moral disintegration of society. However, a more specific reason was Moscow's fear of imported Islamic fundamentalism. The central government had neither the means nor the will to use force to combat this threat (more imagined than real) and chose instead to promote indigenous orthodoxy as a defense against extremist influences from abroad. Mufti Muhammad Sadyk played a key role in propagating the message that Central Asian Islam was a uniquely authentic tradition and that Soviet Muslims had no cause to look elsewhere for guidance. On the contrary, he suggested, a revitalized Islamic community in Central Asia, faithful to its roots, could act as a beacon of inspiration for the whole Islamic world.

Islam in Central Asian Politics

These two currents—the grassroots activities of the *Wahhabis,* together with the state's approbation of Islam—brought about a perceptible change in society. Although there was no mass return to active observance of the religion, by 1991 the fears and inhibitions that the years of Soviet rule had inculcated had been largely overcome, and Islamic symbols and references were becoming an accepted feature of public discourse. This

turnaround was particularly evident in Uzbekistan, the republic with the strongest Islamic heritage, but similar tendencies began to emerge even in Kazakhstan and Kyrgyzstan, where allegiance to Islam had traditionally been weaker.

The trend toward the Islamicization (or more accurately, re-Islamicization) of the social environment became more pronounced after independence. Central Asia, partly because of its physical remoteness and partly because of the uneven economic development to which it had been subjected, remained more dependent on the "center" than did other regions of the Union. The senses of Soviet and national identity were more closely intertwined, and for the vast majority of the population, an existence outside the Union was inconceivable. Consequently, the sudden dissolution of the Union in December, 1991 produced a psychological trauma that devastated the population as much as the economic collapse. Islam filled, to some extent, the ideological vacuum that ensued. It became a surrogate for the liberation struggle that had never occurred, providing the basis for the fashioning of new, post-Soviet identities. This would probably have happened of its own accord, albeit slowly and more hesitantly, had not the ruling elites given added impetus to the process by adopting Islam as the mechanism whereby they effected their own transformation from Communist Party functionaries to national patriots. By transferring their support from the discredited Soviet system to Islam, these functionaries established an alternate form of legitimization. The Uzbek and Turkmen leaders have carried this to the greatest lengths through such gestures as performing the pilgrimage to Mecca. Other leaders have also placed similar, though less dramatic, emphasis on their Islamic heritage.

The fact that Islam has been co-opted by the nascent state nationalisms has made it vulnerable to fragmentation by inter-republican rivalries. The formal unraveling began with the dismemberment of the unified Muslim administration that had previously served all five Central Asian republics. It was replaced by autonomous national organizations that are effectively extensions of their respective republican governments (just as the unified administration had formerly reflected official Soviet policies). Within the republics, Islam has become a political tool, or, more cynically, merely a label to be appropriated by ever-increasing numbers of mutually hostile factions. Secular movements, such as *Birlik* in Uzbekistan or some of the human rights organizations in Kazakhstan, have been compelled to adopt a more Islamic stance to conform to the new environment.

> *Having recently escaped from the embrace of one "elder brother," the Central Asians remain sensitive to any suggestion that they should again assume the role of "junior partner." Consequently, many regard Turkey's generous . . . offer to act as an interim representative for these new countries in international organizations as a slur on their competence and an affront to their sovereignty.*

Ironically, the politicization of Islam has largely defused its religious impact. Knowledge of Islamic precepts today remains slight, and interest in the religion is still passive rather than active. The only formally constituted Muslim party, the Islamic Revival Party (IRP), draws its support mainly from the Ferghana Valley and some areas of Tajikistan, the stronghold of the so-called *Wahhabis*. Many who live elsewhere in Central Asia, even those who profess themselves to be Muslims, regard it with deep suspicion. The IRP's leaders insist that they espouse a moderate form of Islam and do not seek the introduction of *sharia* (canonical law), but it is a gauge of the deep distrust that most Central Asians still feel toward religion—a legacy of the Soviet period—that, although they welcome a re-introduction of the cultural symbols of Islam, they are firmly opposed to any attempt to give it a more regulatory role in society.

Effects on Foreign Policy

A new element that has been introduced into Central Asian society over the past year is the presence of a considerable number of foreigners. In the past, the Soviet Union virtually sealed off Central Asia from the outside world. Now, the republican governments have become acutely aware of the need to attract foreign aid in order to help resolve the formidable economic, social and environmental problems of the region. Similarly, many foreign countries are interested in developing links with the Central Asian republics because of their rich natural resources, their strategic importance and their large, but as yet uncommitted, markets. The Central Asian leaders are shrewd enough to exploit the "Islamic card" in their efforts to secure investment, training and technical assistance from Muslim countries in the Middle East and Southeast Asia. This does not, however, prevent them from being extremely active in their pursuit of aid from other sources. Many other countries, most noticeably Israel and South Korea, have become heavily involved in the region.

The external influences are therefore by no means exclusively Islamic. Indeed, they go some way toward counteracting the creation of a specifically Muslim-oriented foreign policy in these newly emergent states. Nevertheless, the relationship with the Muslim world does have a special significance. Many Muslims abroad are eager to establish a sphere of influence in Central Asia and are willing to expend substantial funds to promote their particular brand of Islam. On a governmental level, Iran, Pakistan, Turkey and Saudi Arabia play the most active role. Libya and Egypt provided advanced training in Islamic studies for senior clerics during the Soviet period and continue to expand this relationship with the independent states. India and Malaysia are newer contenders who offer the experience of Islam in a multi-cultural context. A number of nongovernmental organizations continue to make energetic efforts to win support. Chief among them are the *Ahmaddiya* (regarded as heretical by some Muslims) and smaller fundamentalist groups such as the Turkish *Zaman* movement. These various Islamic influences counterbalance one another on both the popular and the administrative levels. Consequently, no single strand of Islam has to date acquired greater support than the others. From a Western perspective, the choice now facing Central Asian republics is between secular democracy, as exemplified in Turkey, or Islamic fundamentalism, as in Iran. In reality, such a choice does not exist. An Islamic state of any type is based upon an interpretation of *sharia* law; in Central Asia, however, a mere handful of clerics, all of whom were trained and governed under Soviet rule, have more than a rudimentary knowledge of Islamic precepts. The recent proliferation of training and proselytizing activities initiated by Muslims from abroad has undoubtedly heightened awareness of the religion, but such work has not yet had a profound impact, given the almost total lack of an indigenous Islamic infrastructure. Secularism, a result of the policies of the past 70-odd years, is now firmly entrenched and will be difficult to dislodge.

This does not mean that it will be easy to introduce democratic ideals. The traditional power structures, characterized by strict hierarchies of deference, have survived the Soviet period almost unchanged. Questioning the actions of those in authority is still seen as an unforgivable breach of the communal ethic. Consequently, not only have would-be democratic groups received very little popular support, but current leaders have been able to introduce regimes that are in many ways more repressive than those of the recent past. It is likely to be a very long time before those republics initiate any genuine moves toward multiparty systems.

Western Misconceptions

Concern about the possible threat of Islamic fundamentalism has led the West to strongly endorse Turkey as the preferred model for regional development. Such an approach might seem to be logical in the capitals of the West, but is perceived very differently in Central Asia. Having recently escaped from the embrace of one "elder brother," the Central Asians remain sensitive to any suggestion that they should again assume the role of "junior partner." Many regard Turkey's generous, and indeed sensible, offer to act as an interim representative for these new countries in international organizations as a slur on their competence and an affront to their sovereignty. The more that the West presses Turkey's merits as a model, the more that the Central Asian leaders insist that they intend to follow their own models. In their determination to demonstrate their countries' independence, Central Asian leaders have in fact placed greater stress on developing good relations with Iran than might otherwise have been the case.

Central Asians have accepted the need to secure Western aid. It does not, however, follow that the West will be loved for the assistance it provides. A mounting wave of anti-Western sentiment has been compounded in part by a reaction against the humiliations of the colonial-type experience of Soviet/Russian rule, which Central Asians now equate with general white, Christian oppression. In part, this is a remnant of old-style Soviet anti-Western demonology, and, in part, anger at what is perceived as grudging Western support for the region. The popularity of Saddam Hussein has proven to be the most potent expression of this anti-Western trend. Neither Turkey nor Iran can compete with the power of this man's appeal as the "champion" who dared to oppose the West.

Westerners have a facile tendency to equate "political Islam" exclusively with fundamentalism. However, in Iraq, as in a number of other countries, religion has been used as an adjunct of extreme nationalism—the cloak for a dictatorial, one-party system that is Islamic in name alone. This form of political Islam, not fundamentalism, is taking root in Central Asia. The West has been inadvertently aiding the process: its obsessive preoccupation with the supposed threat of fundamentalism has effectively given the regional governments *carte blanche* to silence all opposition, since whatever a party's orientation, these governments can claim that it is "fundamentalist." Such iron control will no doubt enable the present leaders to remain in power for some time. Individuals may be toppled, but there is unlikely to be a major institutional change in the near future.

The manipulation of Islam for political purposes is a risky undertaking. The poorer, mainly rural, sectors of the population for whom independence has brought little more than increased hardship already feel angry and frustrated. Abandoned and marginalized by the affluent urban classes, they have begun to turn increasingly to Islam, both as a source of hope as well as a vehicle for the expression of their alienation. If the economic deterioration continues and the abuse of human rights grows unchecked, the two conditions could well combine to produce an Algerian-style Islamic opposition. This opposition will not be the result of foreign intervention (though this might well give added impetus to the movement), but rather a reaction against a situation that has become intolerable. This reaction has already been experienced in Tajikistan, and similar developments may eventually occur in Uzbekistan. These two republics have historically had the strongest Islamic base. In the less Islamic republics, such an extreme reaction is less likely. The possibility cannot be entirely excluded, however, particularly in the regions of Kazakhstan and Kyrgyzstan that border Uzbekistan.

The West's desire to encourage the development of open, pluralistic societies in Central Asia is understandable. The temptation to adopt a proactive policy, however, must be resisted. Democracy cannot be imposed either by force or by paternalism. It must develop of its own accord and be based on conviction and experience, not on the desire to acquire rapid access to foreign capital. Given the complexities of the situation—the internal tensions as well as the already explicit disaffection from the West—the only effective course of action will be the least dramatic: the gradual integration of these new republics into the international community. The more that they are exposed to the outside world, the easier that it will be for them to develop the foundation for a tolerant, self-confident society in which a multiplicity of views can be accommodated. An exaggeration of the threat of Islamic fundamentalism and ill-considered attempts to combat it could lead to a polarization of positions and possibly bring about the very fundamentalist uprising that the West fears. Russia, partly out of ignorance of the actual state of affairs in Central Asia and partly in the hope of attracting more sympathy and support from the West, actively engages itself in sensationalizing the supposed danger of Islamic revolution in the region. One can only hope that in the West, more sober counsel will prevail.

Article 10   *The Christian Science Monitor*, December 13, 1993

Russia and the Caucasus: Empire in Transition

Daniel Sneider

Staff writer of The Christian Science Monitor

TBILISI, GEORGIA

At dawn on Nov. 4, warships of the Russian Black Sea fleet, their holds crammed with armor and marines, sailed into the Georgian harbor of Poti. It had to be a bittersweet moment for Georgian leader Eduard Shevardnadze, who was on hand to greet the arriving troops.

Little more than a month earlier, he was forced to flee the resort city of Sukhumi up the Black Sea coast to the north in the region of Abkhazia. As Mr. Shevardnadze left, he cursed the Russians for militarily and politically backing the Abkhazian separatists in pursuit of reestablishing their imperial dominance.

But as he returned to the capital, Shevardnadze faced yet another revolt from supporters of former President Zviad Gamsakhurdia in western Georgia. His back to the wall, the man who served long in the Soviet empire as

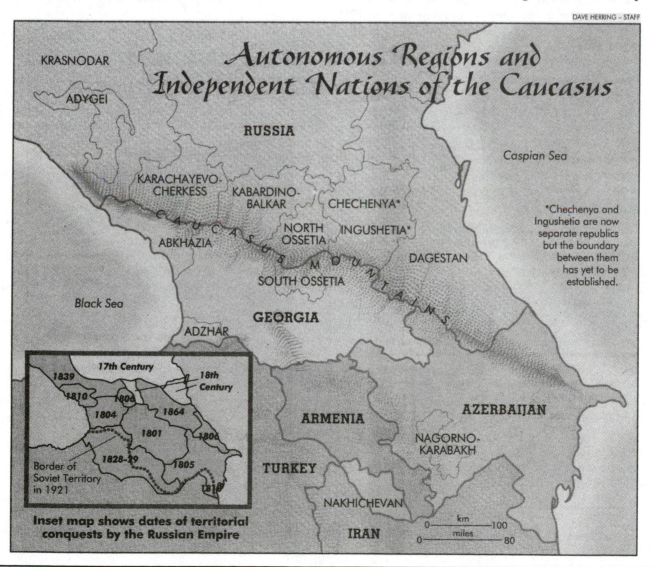

DAVE HERRING – STAFF

Autonomous Regions and Independent Nations of the Caucasus

KRASNODAR
ADYGEI
RUSSIA
Caspian Sea
KARACHAYEVO-CHERKESS
KABARDINO-BALKAR
CHECHENYA*
NORTH OSSETIA
INGUSHETIA*
ABKHAZIA
DAGESTAN
SOUTH OSSETIA
Black Sea
GEORGIA
ADZHAR
ARMENIA
AZERBAIJAN
NAGORNO-KARABAKH
TURKEY
NAKHICHEVAN
IRAN

*Chechenya and Ingushetia are now separate republics but the boundary between them has yet to be established.

CAUCASUS MOUNTAINS

Inset map:
17th Century
1839
18th Century
1810
1806
1804
1864
1801
1804
1828-29
1805
Border of Soviet Territory in 1921

Inset map shows dates of territorial conquests by the Russian Empire

km 0 — 100
miles 0 — 80

head of the Georgian Communist Party, and later as Soviet foreign minister, bowed to reality.

Called to Moscow, Shevardnadze agreed on Oct. 8 to join the Commonwealth of Independent States, the loose confederation of former Soviet republics, satisfying one of Moscow's long-standing desires.

The next day, the Georgian military signed an agreement legalizing the presence of Russian bases on Georgian soil and Russian troops along the border with Turkey.

Shevardnadze's reward was not long in coming. Covertly, though it was a poorly kept secret, Russian T-72 tanks driven by Russian crews drove back the Gamsakhurdia rebels. And the Black Sea marines arrived to establish control over the rail lines that link Russia to the Trans-Caucasus, through Georgia, down to Azerbaijan and Armenia.

All this was just another familiar moment in the Great Game, as the struggle for empire in the Caucasus and Central Asia has long been known. The empire of the czars collapsed in 1917 but was reestablished by the Bolsheviks in a new form. The Soviet Empire itself fell apart in 1991 as the nations captive within it regained long-lost freedom.

Will another Russian Empire emerge? The answer can best be sought here in the Caucasus, a region once celebrated by a Russian general as "the greatest fortress in the world."

From the days of Ivan the Terrible in the 16th century, Russia has sought and won control over this mountainous bridge between Europe and Asia. Its principal enemies were the Persian and Turkish empires, which at various times held sway here. And the tools of battle were often a combination of military force and subterfuge, playing off the various nationalities of the Caucasus in a complex game of divide and conquer.

"The Trans-Caucasus have been part of the Russian Empire for over 200 years now," says Gela Charkviani, Shevardnadze's foreign policy adviser. "It wants to retain the territory, now not as part of its empire but as a sphere of influence. The Trans-Caucasus is the key to the Middle East and the Middle East has been and always will be a strategic part of the world."

In the new Russia, diplomats and generals brush aside charges of imperial ambition with a smile. They talk more gently of "interests," of negotiation, of the dispatch of "peace-keeping forces" to end the civil wars and ethnic conflicts that have burst into the open since the Soviet Union's demise. The officials refer, sometimes only obliquely, to the threat of Muslim neighbors in Turkey and Iran who seek to expand into the space of the collapsed empire by "internationalizing" conflicts there.

"This is an area of special interest, of special responsibility for Russia," Foreign Minister Andrei Kozryev told reporters last month. "We have historical ties to the region, including a history of agreements and treaties that are still in force."

> *'If Russia tries to reconstruct the empire, it will be destroyed. That is why the fate of Georgia is associated with Russian democracy. . . .'*
> —*Eduard Shevardnadze*

Russia wants stability

Deputy Foreign Minister Boris Pastukhov, a soft-spoken former leader of the Komsomol, the Communist Party youth organization, is Moscow's point man for Georgia. Like other Russian officials, he vehemently denies any Russian military involvement in the Abkhazia conflict. Pointing to the two ethnic wars that have torn apart Georgia and to the bloody war between Armenians and Azerbaijanis, he talks of Russia's desire for stability in that region.

"Our main interest is that calm and peace should prevail in the Caucasus, in the North Caucasus, in the Trans-Caucasus, a very explosive region," Mr. Pastukhov explains during an interview in his Moscow office. "We don't have any intent to keep our armed forces there forever. We are interested in having our military presence in the Caucasus but in accordance with international law, on bases with states that sign agreements with us."

Russians sometimes compare their role in the Caucasus to that of the United States in Central America, their bases to US bases in Panama or Cuba. Russia's desire to play the role of peacekeeper in what was once its empire is a Russian version of the Monroe Doctrine, some say. But in moments of candor, Russians acknowledge, though with some discomfort, that old imperial games are still being played according to old imperial rules. Air Marshal Yevgeny Shaposhnikov, the genial soldier who served as the last Soviet minister of defense and the commonwealth's first commander in chief told a group of security experts last month that Russia is enduring its second imperial transition.

The first, from October 1917 to December 1922, resulted in the creation of the Soviet Union. The second, going on now, is no less bloody and violent as nations seek self-determination. The Soviet leadership of Mikhail Gorbachev tried in its final years to halt the tide of nationalism by triggering separatist struggles within the republics, such as Georgia, he said.

Now, the air marshal continued, the same thing is happening. "In principle, Russia is a mighty state and she should carry out her policy not secretly but openly," Shaposhnikov said. "We should not resort to lies and cunning tricks. How come Abkhazia all of sudden had heavy tanks and aircraft? What is this? Again resorting to the principle of divide and rule."

The intrigues and battles under way in the Caucasus are deeply rooted in centuries of Russian history, says Sergei Arutyunov, head of the Caucasian department of the Institute of Ethnology and Anthropology in Moscow. Mr. Arutyunov's biography gives a hint of the complex interactions of this region: He is a Russified Armenian, born and brought up in the Georgian capital of Tbilisi.

The North Caucasus mountain chain is a wall stretching from the Black Sea to the Caspian Sea, pierced by only two passes, the ethnographer explains. It is the stronghold of a string of mountain peoples, mostly Turkic or Persian in origin and Muslim in religion, but also of ancient pagan tribes turned Christian, such as the Ossetians.

Beyond the wall lies the Trans-Caucasus, inhabited mainly by three peoples—the Christian nations of Georgia and Armenia, whose languages and cultures date to before the Christian era, and the Azerbaijani Turks, who inhabit an area that includes the northeastern part of modern Iran. Until the 17th century, Persian dynasties held most of the region. But they were challenged by Ottoman Turkey, which by the mid-18th century controlled most of eastern Caucasia.

Russia, driven in large part by its rivalry with Turkey for control of the Black Sea, sought allies among the Christian Georgians and Armenians, who themselves saw Russia as a protector against their Muslim overlords. By the first quarter of the 19th century, Georgia was annexed, and the Armenian-populated khanates (areas ruled by khans) were seized from Persia.

The conquest of the North Caucasus Muslim tribes of Chechen, Dagestan, and Circassia, celebrated in the works of Russia's greatest writers, including Alexander Pushkin, Mikhail Lermontov, and Leo Tolstoy, took even longer.

"In Russian eyes, the Caucasus was a country of romance, of militant tribes, of alien Islamic ways of life, and of brotherly islands of Christian civilization and Christian mentality," Arutyunov says. "The Muslim nations were considered potential allies of Turkey that had to be pacified. . . . When it was not possible to pacify them, they had to be conquered, subjugated, or destroyed completely."

Modern nationalist movements in Armenia, Georgia, and Azerbaijan quickly seized the opportunity provided by the 1917 revolution to restore independence. In the midst of Russia's civil-war turmoil, they sought new allies from among the Western powers warring in Europe—the Georgians among the Germans, the Armenians among the British, and the Azeris, in Turkey and Britain.

*'The only way for the world to solve the acute problem of luring Russia to a democratic way is to bar all roads to restoring Russia's empire.'
—Nodar Notadze, Georgian Popular Front leader*

But independence was short lived. By 1922, the Bolsheviks had marched back in under the banner of world revolution. The Western powers were unwilling to fight for the Caucasus, despite the lure of Azeri oil; Turkey was sated with a treaty ceding significant parts of Armenian territory to its control.

Despite the Bolshevik pledge of self-determination for all nationalities, Soviet rule was even more ruthless in imposing Russian colonial control. Yet national yearnings persisted, even grew, exploding in the late 1980s as Moscow's grip began to weaken. The collapse of the Soviet Union in December 1991 ended Moscow's formal control over the Trans-Caucasus for the first time in nearly 70 years.

But Russian involvement remained largely intact. Economically, all the former Soviet republics remain tightly bound into the vertically integrated industrial structure created by Soviet central planners. Militarily, Soviet—now Russian—troops still sat on the borders with Turkey and Iran and manned radar stations, air force units, and bases within all three Trans-Caucasus republics.

Each newly independent country took a different stance towards its former colonial master. Armenians were angry over Moscow's failure to restore the Armenian-populated enclave of Nagorno-Karabakh, put under

Azeri control by the Bolsheviks. But as they did in the past, the Armenians have generally embraced Russia as a strategic ally against their historic enemies, the Turks, who virtually surround them.

"We proceed from the assumption that in this unstable situation, this transitional period, Armenia could not risk its security, could not leave a security system created over decades," Armenian President Levon Ter-Petrosyan told this reporter in an interview in his Yerevan office.

"The Russian presence in the Caucasus is a factor for stability," the Armenian leader, a former nationalist dissident, continued. "If Russia left completely, a very serious vacuum would be created and other forces would try to fill this vacuum—Turkey and Iran."

A different stance

Azerbaijan's attitude toward Moscow has swung widely, shaped by the largely unfavorable course of the war over Karabakh and the resulting political turmoil. The first post-independence government of former Communist leader Ayaz Mutalibov sought Moscow's aid, but military setbacks led to a takeover by the nationalist Azerbaijan Popular Front in the summer of 1992.

Then nationalist President Abulfaz Elchibey adopted a strongly pro-Turkish stance, looking to the Azeris' ethnic brethren for aid and political support. He ousted all Russian troops from Azeri soil, moved to develop rich oil reserves with Western help, and withdrew from the commonwealth.

But the fortunes of war led to a military coup, aided, many say, by Moscow, and the eventual ascension to power this past summer of former Communist leader Heidar Aliyev. The one-time member of the Soviet Communist Party Politburo quickly moved to gain Moscow's goodwill, rejoining the commonwealth in September and allowing Moscow a piece of the Caspian oil project. But the Azeri leader has balked at allowing a full return of Russian troops, insisting Moscow first deliver a retreat by the Karabakh Armenians from captured Azeri territory.

Nationalist resistance

Georgia elected fiery nationalist dissident Zviad Gamsakhurdia, who joined the three Baltic states in refusing to join the commonwealth. He pursued a tough policy as well toward the breakaway aspirations of the Ossetians and the Abkhaz, both of whom looked to Russia for help.

"A considerable part of the troops that fought against Georgia were composed of North Caucasians—Ossetians, Chechens, Kabardins, Adygeis, and Cos-

sacks," says Fyodor Starcevic, a Bosnian Serb who serves as the United Nations representative in Georgia. "Those people were promised land and property in Abkhazia once the Georgians were chased out."

But Moscow also faced rebellions from its own Caucasian minorities—the Chechens have virtually seceded from the Russian Federation and separatist tendencies abound elsewhere in the mountains. "The rational goal is to ensure the territorial integrity of Russia itself," comments Ghia Nodia, the head of the Caucasian Institute for Peace, Democracy and Development in Tbilisi. From this strategic point of view, "Georgia is the rear of the North Caucasus," he says.

Indeed Moscow's actions—whether in the Karabakh war or in Georgia—are often incoherent and contradictory. Georgian leader Shevardnadze seeks to explain this as a conflict between "democrats" and "reactionary forces," the latter term a blanket reference to everyone from the deposed Russian parliament to elements of the military.

"If Russia tries to reconstruct the empire, it will be destroyed," Shevardnadze told this reporter in Tbilisi. "That is why the fate of Georgia is associated with Russian democracy. . . . Democratic Russia is not a threat to Georgia."

The military is often the chosen culprit on which to blame Russian imperial impulses. "There are feelings of humiliation among the Russian military who were kicked out of many countries and regions," Mr. Nodia says. "They need some satisfaction of some place where the Russian military presence is extended."

But even those who share this schematic view of division in Russian ranks agree things are not quite so neat. "Some of the lines are blurred," foreign policy advisor Charkviani says. "You cannot see where one Russia ends and the other Russia begins."

Nodar Notadze, the leader of the Georgian Popular Front, offers a darker picture of the Russian mind. Whatever the opinion of any individual Russian leader, "the average Russian thinks and feels imperially and he is sure to go on thinking this for decades," he says. "The only way for the world to solve the acute problem of luring Russia to a democratic way is to bar all roads to restoring Russia's empire."

But the view shared by both the Georgian and Armenian leaders, men who have long experience of interaction with the highest levels of Soviet and Russian leaders, is more nuanced and optimistic.

For Shevardnadze, the key to changing Russia is to foster the nation's desire for prosperity, a condition antithetical to once again taking on the burdens of empire. "When the economy of Russia transfers completely into a free market economy, I think that will change the point of view and perspective of people alot," he says.

Ter-Petrosyan also sees Russia struggling with the tension between its desire to spread its political influence and its economic future. "Of course, there are serious forces in Russia that would like to restore the empire and the Soviet Union," he says. "But as concerns official forces of Russia, they haven't made up their mind. They haven't determined their strategic interests.... Russia is trying to make a choice between both political and economic interests, achieving prosperity."

For now, Russia seeks only to prevent others from invading its sphere of influence, waiting for better days to decide its ultimate policy.

"Russia is in a period of transition," says Ter-Petrosyan. "If it can't strengthen its position, it feels it should at least not lose those positions and give them away to others.... Today Russia would like to keep its presence in its previous domain, waiting for better days for itself."

Article 11   *The Christian Science Monitor*, January 25, 1993

Estonia Leads Baltic States into New Era

The Monitor looks at the progress of economic reforms after a year of Baltic independence.

Daniel Sneider

Staff writer of The Christian Science Monitor

TALLINN, ESTONIA
Like the other capitals of the three former Baltic republics of the Soviet Union, Tallinn has always been relatively prosperous and Western in appearance. But the changes here in Estonia since the breakup of the Soviet Union have far

SHIRLEY HORN – STAFF

outstripped even those of fellow Baltic states, and certainly those brought by reforms in Russia. In many ways, Estonia can claim to be the first truly post-Soviet economy.

A visitor from Moscow to this lovely medieval Baltic capital experiences future-shock from the first moment of his journey. A Tupolev-154, the workhorse of the vast Aeroflot fleet, has been repainted with the clean blue and white colors of Air Estonia.

The plane's interior is glistening, years of accumulated dirt scraped off, the carpets pristine and tacked securely down.

The welcoming stewardesses wheel a drinks trolley down the aisle, followed by a well-presented in-flight snack. It is a startling experience for the traveler accustomed to the filthy cabins and surly crews for which the Soviet state airline was notorious.

The gap widens on the ground. Neon signs illuminate downtown streets, brightening the winter gloom. The shelves of the main department store, bare as recently as last April, are filled with attractively displayed Western consumer goods. The narrow cobblestone pathways of the old city offer charming boutiques and coffee shops.

The most dramatic evidence of Estonia's new status is the crisp, new Estonian kroon notes that have circulated since last June. Not only is this the first former Soviet republic to issue its own

currency, but the kroon is still the only fully convertible currency, pegged in value to the German mark and freely exchangeable for any Western monies.

The dual economy of full dollar stores and empty ruble shops that is so visible these days in Moscow has disappeared here. All goods, from Westinghouse refrigerators to milk, are sold for kroons. At a small kiosk inside the department store, typical of ones found all over town, a man plunks down $940 and gets kroons back, no questions asked and no forms filled out. A purchase of dollars with kroons is equally easy.

Trade pattern shifts

Both Estonian officials and Western economic advisers here express some surprise at the rapid success of the new currency. The most notable sign has been the growth of Estonia's foreign-exchange reserves, which have almost quadrupled from about $50 million in June to $195 million at the beginning of December.

Exports doubled by August, as an export drive took hold. Trade patterns have already shifted, with Finland replacing Russia as Estonia's No. 1 trading partner and dependence on trade with the former Soviet republics going from more than 90 percent to about a third of total trade.

"Today's success has been larger than we expected," admits Estonian Central

Bank spokesman Kauto Pollisinski. "We succeeded in making the Estonian kroon legal tender in only three to four days. The growth of central bank reserves was very fast. Monetary reform and a stable kroon have forced our economy to turn to Western markets."

The establishment of a hard currency has forced a variety of changes, including compelling all enterprises—private or state-owned—to live within their means, on the basis of real costs and incomes. This is due to the strict control, set by law, over the amount of new money that can be issued. The money supply is managed by a currency board with the requirement that any new money be backed by an influx of foreign-exchange reserves.

"It imposes a tremendous discipline," comments a Western economic adviser. "Under the former system, an enterprise could finance its operating deficits by going to the banking system or the government to make up the difference. Under this system, the central bank has no way of pumping money into the system without foreign exchange from abroad. It has taken some time to sink in. Enterprises keep asking for money but they aren't getting it."

Estonia is the first former Soviet state to actually let enterprises go under. This was demonstrated dramatically in December when the government closed down a large bank, the Tartu Commercial Bank, and forced the merger of two others. All three had been found to be in de facto bankruptcy, a condition that most experts believe could apply to most Russian commercial banks as well.

"The government wanted to shed some blood to show that there are risks involved in doing business," the Western expert says. "The prime minister [Mart Laar] told me—'this is going to be a lesson in the behavior of the market economy.'"

Living standards fall

But critics say this tough-minded devotion to the market has come at tremendous cost. Production levels fell almost 40 percent after the currency change as enterprises lost both markets and sources of raw materials in the former Soviet Union. Estonians have seen their living standards plummet, in part due to the decision to keep the kroon's value low to promote exports. Despite the positive impact of recent monetary controls, inflation remains very high.

Many factories are operating only by giving workers unpaid leave and not paying bills. Official unemployment is about 14,000 or around 2 percent, but officials admit that understates reality. They predict the number of unemployed will hit 100,000 in 1993.

The government has recommended wage increases of 20 to 30 percent at state-run enterprises and institutions but even that will not stop a further decline in real incomes, officials admit. Pension levels and the minimum wage are being held to 260 kroons a month (about $22) to keep the budget under control.

"Of course it is very difficult," says the central bank's Pollisinski, "but I haven't met a person who lives on the minimum wage. Pensioners are being helped by their families. There is no other way today."

Estonian officials are hopeful that if they can get through this winter, including an energy shortage that followed the end of the supply of cheap energy from the former Soviet Union, the worst will be behind them.

Ties with the West

Much of Estonia's relative success is due to its close links to the West and especially Finland. The Finns not only are a short boat ride away across the Baltic, close enough for Finnish TV broadcasts to be easily viewed, but they also share a common linguistic and ethnic heritage with Estonians.

"Whole generations of Estonians were brought up in front of Finnish television screens," says foreign minister Trivimi Velliste. "You could watch the ads and you see an image of everyday life in the West."

This accounts in large part for what the Western adviser sees as the difference between Estonia and its former Soviet neighbors. "The ability to adopt new thinking, new technology, is ahead of their neighbors to the south," he observes.

Indeed, the Estonian desire to see itself as part of the West is so strong that they balk even at favorable comparisons between their progress and that of Russia or Ukraine.

"People don't want to see themselves in the old context anymore," says Tarmu Tammerk, the editor of the Baltic Independent weekly. "It doesn't mean anything anymore."

Article 12

Current History, April 1993

Nationalism Redux: Through the Glass of the Post-Communist States Darkly

The murderous intensity of newly fanned ethnic hatreds in the post-Soviet sphere surprised most, who considered such antagonisms confined to history textbooks. As Steven Burg points out, however, nationalism in all its forms is very much alive and, ironically, in some instances catalyzed by elements of the democratic forces that have swept the region.

Steven L. Burg

Steven L. Burg is an associate professor of politics at Brandeis University. This article is based on the forthcoming Nationalism and Democracy in Post-Communist Europe: Challenges to American Foreign Policy, *which was supported by the Twentieth Century Fund.*

The wanton violence of the fighting taking place in the Balkans and the Caucasus (Armenia, Azerbaijan, and Georgia) has brought death and destruction to Europe on a scale not seen since the end of World War II; it threatens to destabilize not only the continent but other international communities. Because political boundaries rarely match ethnic boundaries, conflicts based on calls for ethnic self-determination inevitably threaten to involve neighboring states. And, as has been seen in the Balkans and Caucasus, once initiated, the violence of ethnic-based conflicts is easily escalated by individual acts of brutality into widespread death and destruction.

Failure to contain the conflicts that have already broken out, forestall future ones, and secure the democratization of the successor states of the former Soviet bloc would have a negative effect on the direct economic, political, and security interests of the West. Left unattended, the rise of nationalist regimes in eastern Europe, and the consequently increasing political appeal of nationalism in western Europe, may stimulate further violence by neo-Nazi and other ethnocentric groups in the West. The strong reactions such developments would bring from responsible governments, if sustained for long periods, might themselves become real threats to the foundations of liberal democracy. The military issues raised by continuing conflicts in the East, and intra-alliance differences over them, may stall the deeper development of the

European Community and perhaps even erode the basic cohesiveness of NATO. It would almost certainly deal a powerful setback to the process of establishing a security framework among the North American, western European, and post-Communist states to replace the obsolete security architecture of the cold war.

The appeals of nationalist-separatist groups to the principle of national self-determination challenge the principles of state sovereignty, territorial integrity, inviolability of borders, and noninterference that have been central to the post–World War II international system. This challenge must be addressed if peaceful mechanisms for the resolution of ethnic conflicts are to be established, and the stability of the international system is to be preserved. This will inevitably require the careful redefinition of these postwar principles and the obligations arising out of them. The conflict between nationalism and democracy in the post-Communist states also presents a direct challenge to the ability of the United States to make human rights principles central to the international system.

FROM CONTAINMENT TO INVOLVEMENT

As long as the Communist leadership in Moscow exercised hegemony over the states of eastern Europe, the United States and its allies had only limited involvement in the region. The artificial stability the Soviet Union imposed on the domestic and international relations of eastern Europe was also found in states outside direct Soviet control, where independent Communist regimes created domestic stability by force and refrained from upsetting the political balance between East and West. Although ideologically opposed to communism, the West accepted the apparent certainties of Soviet domination of the region and refrained from direct attempts to undermine it.

Although the United States adopted a strategy of "containment," it consistently refrained from becoming directly involved in the internal affairs of the Soviet bloc countries. Even when faced with outbreaks of popular unrest or mass opposition to Communist rule (as was the case in Hungary in 1956, in Czechoslovakia in 1968, and in Poland in 1979 and 1980), the West refrained from intervening directly. Paradoxically, it was the onset of détente and the collaborative Soviet-American effort to ratify the status quo that created new opportunities for change in eastern Europe.

In 1975, 35 countries—including those from the Soviet bloc, western Europe, and the United States—concluded the Helsinki Final Act. Although the Helsinki agreement ratified the international status quo, it also provided the basis on which the West and, more important, domestic groups in the Communist states, could pursue political changes in eastern Europe. The Helsinki Final Act included 10 basic principles that were to be used to evaluate the actions of the signatory countries. These included some that ratified the postwar configuration of states in Europe by establishing their sovereignty and territorial integrity, affirming the inviolability of their borders, and mandating nonintervention in their internal affairs. Other principles committed the signatories to peaceful relations by disavowing the threat or use of force and calling for the peaceful settlement of disputes; the principles also committed them to respect "human rights and fundamental freedoms" and "the equal rights of peoples and their right to self-determination." The act further established the right of peoples to determine their political status. In effect, the Helsinki principles made Western concepts of individual liberty and collective democracy the political standard, and applied that standard to all the signatory states, from the countries of North America to the Soviet Union.

One consequence of the Helsinki agreement, certainly unanticipated in the East and perhaps in the West as well, was the formation in the Communist countries of small but active dissident grass-roots political organizations to uphold these political standards. The increase in cultural contacts between East and West that followed the act also reinforced a process already under way among the broader, nondissident social elites in the East: the development of increasingly liberal political values and growing national consciousness. This liberalization of values and new emphasis on national identity contributed—once Soviet President Mikhail Gorbachev's attempt to reform the Soviet system had introduced new opportunities for grass-roots political activity—to the reemergence of national movements aimed at the estab-

lishment of independent states; in the end it also contributed to the collapse of communism.

The apparent marriage of liberalism and nationalism in the Communist states in the 1970s and 1980s echoed a similar marriage between these forces in Central Europe in the mid-nineteenth century. That alliance led to the devolution of power to nationalist leaderships, but failed to produce democracy. The implosion of the Soviet domestic political order, the emergence of independent states in the former territory of the Soviet Union, and the emergence of new regimes in eastern Europe has produced an analogous devolution of power to the state. As a result, nationalism has again become a powerful legitimating force for new governments with uncertain bases of popular support. It remains to be seen whether these post-Communist regimes will be able to transform the bases of their legitimacy from nationalist to democratic principles. The increased salience of nationality has rekindled many of the ethnic issues of the late nineteenth and early twentieth centuries. And these, as they have in the past, may yet lead some of these states to more authoritarian arrangements.

A BAD FIT: NATIONALISM AND DEMOCRACY

The commitment and ability of a government to guarantee individual rights is a necessary element in solving any ethnic conflict. As the scholars Larry Diamond and Juan Linz have pointed out, "for all their procedural messiness and sluggishness, [democracies] nevertheless protect the integrity of the person and the freedoms of conscience and expression."[1] Such protection is essential to ending the threat felt by individuals in situations of intergroup conflict and establishing interethnic peace. But the establishment of stable democratic regimes in the post-Communist states is also strategically important to Western security; democratic regimes are the strongest social foundations on which to build an international security framework.

The development of democratic regimes in eastern Europe and the former Soviet Union, and the construction of a new framework for Euro-Atlantic security, are best served by linking Western aid to local efforts to establish democracy. It cannot be taken for granted that, because Communist authoritarianism has given way to more open electoral processes and governments, the new regimes are "democratic." The loosening and even abandonment of state censorship and state-imposed limits on individual expression have indeed permitted the emergence of a multitude of citizens organizations of varying size and interests. And the introduction of competitive electoral politics has stimulated the formation of independent political parties. These expanded freedoms of expression, participation, and organization are essential to the democratization process. But the degree to which government institutions are becoming instruments for the representation of social interests and can impose accountability on the national leadership, not to mention the extent to which individual rights are protected, varies greatly from state to state.

It is not clear that democratic regimes will be consolidated even where elements of democracy have already been established. In some cases greater openness has accelerated political and cultural polarization: witness the open expression of extreme nationalist, ethnocentric, and anti-Semitic sentiments, the organization of political movements based on these sentiments, and the eruption of violent ethnic conflict across the region. Local political leaders need to address this explosion of ethnic tensions, and Western assistance must support their efforts to do so in ways that help moderate conflict and ensure the effectiveness of democratic institutions.

Nationalism is distinguished from social movements that arise among other aggrieved groups by the powerful emotions associated with it. In extreme cases, nationalist movements evoke a willingness to fight and die on behalf of the cause. This derives from the notion that what is at issue is group "survival." Nationalist movements, however, cannot be understood as solely "primordial" in nature. They are most often also organizational vehicles for the articulation of arguments over rights, goods, status, power, and other material and political issues. Hence, the conflicts between Serbs and other groups in the former Yugoslavia, and between Armenians and Azerbaijanis in Nagorno-Karabakh may be exceptional cases by virtue of the disproportionately powerful role primordial hatred has played and the extreme violence that has taken place. Their ultimate solution, however, must involve the redress of grievances over rights, status, and power that also motivate and mobilize the populations—and especially their leaders—in these conflicts.

The strength of nationalist political movements, the popular appeal of avenging long-held ethnic grievances, and the resultant escalation of ethnic conflict impede the transition from authoritarianism to democracy. Democratization involves the creation of stable political institutions and processes "that make conflict, change, and conciliation possible without institutional collapse."[2] Nationalist conflict suppresses the importance and, in some cases, even the emergence of multiple issues, demands, and interests as nationalist leaders try to subordinate all other issues. Nationalist movements usually demand autonomy and seek a separate existence, denying the reality of commonalities, shared interests, or even mutual dependence. Ethnically based claims to autonomy thus strike at the heart of the process of democratization, since

they compete with individual rights-based legitimation of a liberal democratic order.

The political organizations characteristic of nationalist movements, and the state institutions and processes they spawn are therefore ill-suited to the conciliation of competing demands. They tend to adopt exclusivist rather than inclusivist policies, and tend to extremism rather than moderation. In this way the politics of nationalism are contrary to the essence of the liberal democratic process.

The enormous hardships that have been imposed on the people of eastern Europe and the former Soviet Union by the transition from central planning and state ownership to market-based economies make it difficult, if not impossible, for governments to win popular support on the basis of the material benefits they can deliver. This heightens the effectiveness of a government's appeals to national sentiments. The declaration of "sovereignty," the establishment of cultural supremacy, or even the threat of military action are promises more easily delivered than an improvement in the standard of living. Moreover, such acts strengthen the state's power and secure the positions of political incumbents far more effectively than efforts to institutionalize civil liberties, which would facilitate criticism of the government and the activities of an opposition.

Attempts to legitimate even democratically elected governments through appeals to nationalism may unsettle relations between neighboring states. Expressions of concern for minority communities of ethnic brethren in neighboring countries, no matter how carefully constructed, may raise the specter of irredentist claims and stimulate nationalist responses among the neighboring ethnic majority. Given the changing historical/political status of territories throughout eastern Europe and the former Soviet Union, real and imagined irredentist issues claims represent sources of potentially serious interstate conflict.

Nationalist legitimation of new states may also lead to actions that impede the development of internal democracy. Several post-Communist governments have attempted to redress the ethnic grievances of the majority or eponymous population through legislation that effectively discriminates against minorities. Already, new citizenship laws, laws on language rights, voting rights laws, and other legislation have heightened tensions between dominant and minority groups. The popular support these measures evoke suggests how difficult it is to establish a broad social and political commitment to the pluralistic concept of civil society that underlies Western liberal democracy. The prospect of successfully establishing the political culture of tolerance for differences that underlies American democracy, for example, appears to be especially limited.

The post-Communist regimes are experiencing a broad, multidimensional transition from the enforced integration, artificial homogeneity, and stability of communism to the more open and pluralistic patterns of public discourse and behavior associated with incipient democracy. The rapid multiplication of political groups and organizations, the narrowness of support for most of them, and in some cases the obviously satirical if not cynical intention behind their formation suggest that the eastern European and post-Soviet states are undergoing processes of social and political fragmentation. With only a few notable exceptions, political organizations and institutions in these states have yet to bring together diverse groups and reconcile their conflicting interests. Their inability to do so may reflect the absence of interests that bind their populations together. At the very least it suggests that such interests are now far less important to the population than those that divide them.

Even where common economic interests, for example, might provide a pragmatic basis for linking constituencies to a common administrative and political center, the power of nationalist-separatist sentiments among the populace makes it difficult for local leaders to act on them. Indeed, even the distribution of economic interests and resources themselves may be in dispute, held to be illegitimate legacies of the old regime for which contemporary compensation is due. In competitive elections, greater support—and therefore greater political power—may be gathered by exploiting the coincidence of regional economic differences and inclinations toward ethnic self-assertion than by advocating economic compromise and political unity. The perception of material conflicts in ethnic terms by the mass populace, the acceptance or exploitation of such ethnic definitions by elites, and the frequency with which conflicts defined this way produce violence, make the resolution of differences over the distribution of government functions and over economic and other issues much more difficult to achieve. If liberal democracy depends on the mastery by political leaders of the art of compromise, then a successful transition to democracy is made more difficult in eastern Europe because the new countries' leaders, facing populations whose nationalist aspirations are unconstrained by other competing interests and aspirations, enjoy little leeway in which to develop this art.

THE TIES THAT DIDN'T BIND

In the post-Soviet states, the former Yugoslav states, and in Czechoslovakia, the transition from authoritarianism was turned into a simultaneous "end of empire" process. Once seen this way, intellectual, economic, and other groups who might otherwise have been inclined to support a transition to democracy were drawn toward more nationally determined positions. The Slovenian and Croatian challenges to rule from Belgrade, for example, stimulated a conservative and even reactionary response among some Serbs, whose earlier support for democratization proved less powerful than the appeal of Serbian nationalism. Similarly, the opportunity to establish an independent state proved more appealing to democratic activists in Slovenia than the task of democratizing a common Yugoslav state. In Czechoslovakia, the alliance of Czechs and Slovaks opposed to communism soon disintegrated and electoral support in both Slovakia and the Czech Republic shifted to leaders and parties intent on pursuing regional interests at the expense of continued federation.

The rush to redress long-suppressed national grievances has also led in some cases to the partial legitimation, or re-legitimation of the antidemocratic aspects of national political history. The Fascist and Nazi collaborationist regimes established in Hungary, Slovakia, and Croatia during World War II have been the object of public, and in some instances de facto official re-valuation by nationalist leaders. New governments in Lithuania and Slovenia have pardoned Nazi collaborators. These actions are one dimension of the reaffirmation of collective identities, and a reflection of the powerful urge to reject any negative judgments of them. They also reflect, however, how weak concerns are for individual and human rights in the contemporary politics of the region. The still overwhelming strength of collective identities makes efforts to distinguish between national-cultural communities and the actions of individuals, especially when they are government officials, very difficult. And such distinctions are essential to the success of a transition from nationalist to democratic bases of legitimation.

The supporters of democratization in the region thus confront a vexing dilemma: the collapse of authoritarianism has unleashed forces that make the establishment of liberal democracy difficult. Yet to suppress these forces would require actions that might make democracy impossible. Some accommodation of the national aspirations of local populations is essential in order to avoid violence, to strengthen the legitimacy of new democratic institutions, to motivate these populations to endure the sacrifices associated with transition and, not least of all, because of the moral virtue of doing so.

Democratically inclined leaderships in the region are, therefore, confronted with the task of establishing an enforceable boundary between democratically acceptable and unacceptable political behavior. This is an immensely difficult political challenge. Debate over this issue continues in the United States even after 200 years of institutionalized democratic experience. It should not be surprising, therefore, that this is so difficult to achieve in the post-Communist states. It is clear that these states cannot depend on either a mass civic culture or on their own accumulated legitimacy to insulate them from popular discontent; moreover, they do not have the resources to deliver sufficient benefits to their people to counterbalance the social, economic, and political hardships that confront them.

THE NEED FOR INTERNATIONAL ATTENTION

The fate of democracy in the successor states of eastern Europe and the former Soviet Union depends on both internal conditions and the international environment. On the international level, the wars in the former Yugoslavia and rising ethnic tensions elsewhere have stimulated efforts to find a new framework for international peace and security and the collective mechanisms to enforce it. The conflict in Yugoslavia has revealed the weaknesses of the Conference on Security and Cooperation in Europe (CSCE), or the "Helsinki process." They have contributed to concerns about the need to strengthen the peacemaking and peacekeeping capabilities of the UN. And they have underscored the importance of direct bilateral and multilateral negotiations among the post-Communist successor states to address and eliminate potential sources of conflict between them.

Despite the differences that have arisen, negotiations among the democratically elected governments of eastern Europe and their active engagement in the CSCE and other international organizations have contributed to peaceful relations among them. Their behavior reflects, in part, the powerful norms of negotiation, compromise, and peaceful behavior that prevail among democratic governments. Their behavior also stands in sharp contrast to that of authoritarian states, governments, and organizations in the region, which have resorted to force to achieve their goals. Events in the former Yugoslav states, in the Caucasus, and in Moldova make it clear that the use of force in pursuit of nationalistic goals threatens the stability of neighboring states and raises the prospect of direct military involvement by outside actors, including the West. The costs and controversy such involvement would create place a premium on preventing and resolving these conflicts before they turn violent. The peaceful character of dispute resolution between democratically elected governments, therefore, gives the United States and its allies a strategic interest in the consolidation of democracy in the post-Communist states that parallels their interest in establishing an international security framework.

Post-Communist Europe thus presents the United States and its European allies with important and difficult foreign policy challenges. More direct involvement in the region seems essential. This requires coordination with European allies, whose own interests in the region may, in some cases, differ from or even conflict with those of the United States. The task of meeting these challenges must be met in ways that contribute to the further integration of the Euro-Atlantic community, and especially to the institutionalization of mechanisms for the prevention and peaceful resolution of conflict.

American policy must support the development of democratic governments in the region. It can do so directly and through multilateral arrangements. American efforts must be multidimensional, addressing the social and political dimensions of democratic development, as well as providing direct economic assistance. Policies toward individual states must reflect the nature of the threat to democracy in that state. And where democracy is threatened by interethnic conflict, special efforts must be devoted to building counterweights to the appeals of nationalism.

Clearly, any external power—European or American—that attempts to impose solutions in these conflicts will find it difficult to achieve success. The challenge to the United States and its allies, therefore, is to find ways to structure conditions in such a way that the conflicting parties themselves recognize incentives to resolve their disputes and become willing to initiate and sustain efforts to defuse ethnic tensions. The Yugoslav crisis demonstrates the importance of concerted international action to prevent and resolve conflicts before they turn violent.

American policy must support the development of an international framework for the prevention and peaceful settlement of conflict in the Euro-Atlantic community. This will require a multilateral effort to reconcile the conflicting principles of sovereignty, territorial integrity, noninterference, human rights, and self-determination on which conflicting claims in specific cases are based. This effort, while difficult, can be coordinated with and reinforce efforts to promote the democratic development of new governments. Because no framework for peace can prevent all conflicts, the United States must also consider ways to strengthen, through the UN and regional organizations, the peacekeeping and peacemaking resources of the international community, both as a means of encouraging parties to accept negotiated solutions and in case enforcement action becomes necessary.

Although the dramatic events of recent years heighten the temptation to resort to political hyperbole, the West *does* confront a historic opportunity to encourage the democratic development of the formerly Communist regimes and aid in the emergence of a new framework for maintaining peace in the expanded Euro-Atlantic community. The collapse of communism by itself does not guarantee this will happen. The strength of nationalisms throughout the region provides a powerful instrument for the construction of new authoritarian regimes. The prospect of a nationalist authoritarian government in

Russia, for example, offers dangers many orders of magnitude greater than those already created by such a government in Serbia. Ameliorating the nationalist threat to democracy in the post-Communist states, therefore, must be seen as a strategic goal of American foreign policy, one to which an appropriate level of American attention and resources need to be devoted.

NOTES

1. Larry Diamond, Juan Linz, and Seymour Martin Lipset, "Preface," in Diamond et al., eds., *Democracy in Developing Countries, Vol. 4: Latin America* (Boulder, Colo.: Lynne Rienner, 1989).
2. Ibid., pp. 385–386.

Article 13   *Current History*, November 1993

Albania's Road to Democracy

"Albanians have survived an extremely difficult first year after communism, and seem to have settled down to a painful but astonishingly smooth transformation into a pluralistic democracy and a market economy." But, hemmed in by threatening neighbors and ethnically involved in regional conflicts, will Albania remain unaffected by the passions sweeping the Balkans?

Elez Biberaj

Elez Biberaj is chief of the Albanian Service at Voice of America in Washington. He is the author of Albania: A Socialist Maverick *(Boulder, Colo.: Westview Press, 1990) and* Albania and China: A Study of an Unequal Alliance *(Boulder, Colo.: Westview Press, 1986). The views expressed here are the author's and do not necessarily represent the official position of Voice of America or the United States government.*

Albania was the last Eastern European state to free itself from Communist rule, and its prospects of democratization seemed incomparably less promising than those of the others. Enver Hoxha's regime, among the most repressive in the world, had effectively prevented the emergence of democratic leaders and thinkers. The Democratic party, which came to power in a stunning victory in elections held March 22, 1992, inherited a polity on the verge of disintegration. The economy had all but collapsed, and Albania had become totally dependent on humanitarian aid from abroad to feed its people. Most observers were predicting the country would either descend into anarchy or slide back into dictatorship.

While many hurdle remain, Sali Berisha, whom parliament elected Albania's first post-Communist president in April 1992, has initiated major reforms aimed at establishing a genuine pluralistic democracy and a free market economy. A man of keen intellect and formidable political skills, Berisha has handled his job with insight and confidence.

Having received a clear popular mandate for radical change (it captured 92 seats in the 140-seat parliament), Berisha's Democratic party has proceeded with remarkable speed to dismantle the Communist system and lay the groundwork for a society based on the rule of law. The Law on Constitutional Provisions, which superseded the country's Communist-era constitution, endorses the principle of separation of powers, guarantees human rights, and protects private property. A special commission, assisted by experts from abroad, is drafting a new constitution.

In the midst of an intense debate between proponents of executive power and those who favor a larger role for the legislative branch, Berisha came out on the side of a parliamentary system and championed the development of political institutions that would maintain sufficient checks on the chief executive. Democracy in Albania, he has insisted, depends on the establishment of a parliamentary tradition. But even some of Berisha's persistent critics have said that the nation needs a strong presidency during the transition—and indeed, the law on Constitutional Provisions gives the president broad powers.

The media in Albania are making progress toward becoming a potent force. While radio and television are government controlled, more than 200 newspapers are published throughout the country (most of these, however, have so far been dominated by former Communist propagandists). A free and objective press has yet to be firmly established.

STICK WITH REFORM, AND HOPE FOREIGN INVESTMENT FOLLOWS

Albania has been quicker than perhaps any other former Communist country in implementing radical economic reforms. Under the Berisha government spending has been slashed, the Albanian currency (the lek) has been made fully convertible, and barriers to foreign trade have been eliminated. The government swiftly tackled perhaps the most explosive economic and social problem facing the country: it ended most subsidies and liberalized prices, with the exception of those on staple consumer goods such as bread and milk, for which ceilings were set.

An important element of the government's economic plan has been the development of the new private sector. Some 90 percent of the land has been distributed to private farmers. About half the state farms have been privatized, and the government hopes to put the rest in the hands of private owners by year's end. Agriculture has responded favorably to price reform and privatization: production this year is expected to grow between 10 percent and 15 percent. Privatization has progressed rapidly in retailing and services, transportation, and housing. Some 100,000 of Albania's 3.2 million people have found employment in private enterprises.

But in the vital industrial sector the process has been very slow. Given the lack of domestic capital and the resources required for restructuring, privatization of large industrial concerns will probably be impossible without substantial foreign investment. For the foreseeable future the government is likely to continue operating unprofitable large enterprises, fearing that support for reform cannot be sustained if there are massive liquidations and layoffs.

Privatization has also been hindered by uncertainties regarding settlement of the claims of those whose land and property were confiscated without compensation under communism. Both ex-owners and emerging entrepreneurs, most of the latter former members of the nomenklatura who bought shops and small businesses for token payments during the last year of Communist rule, have criticized a new law that provides for compensation but not full restitution.

The government has also moved rapidly to create the legal framework for a market economy. Legislation concerning taxes, legal accounting, bankruptcy, and the banking system has been adopted. Parliament is in the process of amending the law on foreign investment, and officials say the new version will be among the most lib-

eral in the region. Nevertheless, hoped-for major foreign investments have not yet materialized because of Albania's poor—or in some cases, nonexistent—infrastructure, and because of instability in the region.

By this summer the government claimed that the precipitous fall in production that began in 1990 had been arrested, the currency had been stabilized, and inflation had dropped to zero. But despite these encouraging signs the economy still faces serious problems. Enormous institutional obstacles remain in the conversion of a centrally planned economy to a market economy. Foreign debt has climbed to $625 million. Some 450,000 Albanians are unemployed, of whom 350,000 receive government assistance.

The crisis has been mitigated by substantial humanitarian and economic assistance from Italy, the EC, the United States, and Turkey. Albanian refugees in Greece, Italy, and other Western countries have also played an important role: remittances from abroad are estimated at $400 million annually.

The prospects for a quick economic recovery are good. Albania is relatively rich in minerals and petroleum, and with assistance from other countries it will be in a position to efficiently tap its natural resources. But the keys are foreign investment, the government's perseverance with the reform, and continued political stability.

DEMOCRACY: MORE EXPERIENCE NECESSARY

As the concept of a market economy is a new one for Albania, so is that of democracy. Although the country briefly experimented with multiparty politics in the 1920s, it did not develop a genuine pluralistic democracy, and then communism descended; the majority of Albanians have had no direct experience with a democratic system. In the present formative stage of political pluralism, Albania has seen a volatile party system come into being. While political participation is concentrated almost exclusively within the realm of the parties, citizens' identification with parties remains relatively weak as these groups seek to develop their positions on the issues amid shifting political allegiances. Despite the rise of numerous parties covering the spectrum from extreme left to extreme right, there are striking similarities among the programs of the country's most important parties. It will take some time for Albanian parties to become viable political entities.

The ruling center-right Democratic party has from the beginning been the country's most important, with a wide base of support that cuts across all segments of society. Founded as the first non-Communist political force in Albania in December 1990, the party attracted individuals with diverse interests, which led to acrimonious in-fighting over the pace and extent of the dismantling of the Communist system. Initially, a leftist faction led by economist Gramoz Pashko controlled top positions and influenced the tone of debate within the party. This faction was gradually shunned after the Democrats joined with the Communists in a coalition government in June 1991, Pashko becoming deputy prime minister. Strong anti-Communists advocating the rapid eradication of communism gained influence. Berisha maintained a centrist position, juggling and usually managing to balance contending forces within the party.

But after its triumph in the 1992 election the Democratic party was unable to preserve its unity, and within months the leadership split. This split derived less from differences over policy than from personality clashes and competition for power. Opinion within the party having shifted significantly to the right, Berisha and his mainstream faction saw no reason to placate the left wing. Pashko and his supporters had been kept out of the new government, and Berisha further upset his rivals by endorsing as his successor for party leader the 32-year-old intellectual, party secretary Eduard Selami. Naturally some in the leadership, particularly deputy chairmen Azem Hajdari and Arben Imami, believed themselves to be more qualified than Selami. The leftists precipitated an open division by publicly proclaiming that rightist forces had usurped power within the party. Berisha and his men responded by expelling from the party Pashko, Imami, and several other founding members, but—significantly—not Hajdari, who at the last minute switched sides. The disgruntled politicians formed their own party, the Democratic Alliance.

Although rightists seemed to have gained the upper hand, Selami has been careful to keep the extremists at bay, pursuing policies that attempt to reconcile conflicting interests among the party's constituency. This August right-wingers suffered a severe blow with the dismissal of Agriculture Minister Petrit Kalakula, who had called for an aggressive approach in wiping out the Communist legacy. Kalakula's departure was a clear indication the party will stay its moderate course.

Other forces will no doubt strive to become the beneficiaries of popular discontent caused by economic hardship. So far, however, no one else has come up with a credible alternate plan, and the Democratic party is likely to remain the country's main political force. If party unity begins to disintegrate, however, this will open the door for others, perhaps undermining Berisha's ability to keep to the path of radical economic reform.

The Socialist party, the second largest in parliament, with 38 seats, adopted its current name and western European social-democratic labels at the tenth congress of the Albanian Party of Labor in June 1991. Its membership consists mainly of the most militant elements of Hoxha's old party, but its leaders maintain it is a new grouping, not burdened by the Party of Labor's past. The party has refused to express remorse or apologize for Communist crimes, and its criticism of Hoxha has been halfhearted. Focusing on giving voice to the egalitarian and anti-capitalist sentiment of workers who have suddenly found themselves in a free market society, the Socialists have taken every opportunity to undermine the government.

The party was shaken in July by the arrest of its leader, Fatos Nano, who was accused of having misappropriated $8 million during his short stint as prime minister in 1991. Going beyond their usual practice of attacking Berisha and his party with harsh invective, leading Socialists called for the use of "all democratic means" to get the present government out of office. In an attempt to provoke mass protests the Socialists organized rallies throughout the country, but this strategy backfired when large numbers of demonstrators failed to turn out.

The authorities, increasingly confident of their strength and of popular support for the anti-corruption drive, moved against corrupt former Communists even at the cost of heightening tension between parties. Former President Ramiz Alia (who had already been under house arrest for almost a year), and several former Politburo members and senior government officials were arrested on charges of corruption and abuse of power.

Berisha has denied Socialist charges that the anti-corruption drive was politically motivated, saying corruption is an evil that must be rooted out if Albania's fledgling democracy is to have credibility. But despite the highly publicized crackdown, there have been allegations of corruption within the Democratic government, including ones touching members of the cabinet. Minister of Economy and Finances Genc Ruli has faced persistent charges of corruption going back to 1991, when he served in the coalition government; he has consistently denied the accusations.

While the Socialist party will probably continue to represent a formidable challenge to the Democrats, it will gradually be marginalized unless it makes a clean break with its Communist past and selects a new, uncompromised leadership.

The Social Democratic party, led by former senior Albanian Party of Labor members, is the third-largest bloc in parliament, holding seven seats. Although ostensibly allied with the Democratic party, it has been highly critical of the government. In June the Social Democrats joined the Socialists in boycotting parliamentary sessions because of the delay in adopting a new constitution, but after Nano's arrest they sought to revive their coalition with the Democratic party. With the Social Democrats apparently concerned by the public's negative reaction to their seeming alliance with the Socialists, both the dissenting parties returned to parliament in September.

The Republican party has operated largely in the shadow of the Democratic party. In the 1992 elections it received less than 4 percent of the national vote, winning only one seat in parliament. The party's poor performance is attributed to the lack of a clear program and leadership problems.

On the right, several parties have emerged, but they have been unable to build viable nationwide organizations and attract a substantial following.

THE END OF ISOLATION

Berisha has been heavily engaged in formulating and implementing foreign policy, and has put Albania back on the international map after years of isolation. His main objectives have been to assure continued economic assistance for the reform program, to persuade the world community to take action to prevent war in the former Yugoslavia from spreading to Kosovo province in Serbia, and full integration with the rest of Europe. Cognizant of Albania's domination in the past by its allies (Italy in the 1930s, Yugoslavia in the 1940s, and the Soviet Union in the 1950s), Berisha has pursued an open door policy, attempting to lead his country away from dependence on a single foreign patron by diversifying Tiranë's ties.

Since mid-1991 Albania has received an estimated $1 billion in humanitarian and economic assistance, most of it from the EC. Italy has been in the forefront here, and Albania is increasingly orienting itself toward its western neighbor. Berisha has forged especially close relations with the United States. In addition to financial and technical assistance, the Albanians are evidently looking to Washington for support in modernizing their armed forces.

Last December Albania became the first former Warsaw Pact country to request membership in NATO. Fearing a possible conflict with Serbia, Albania is desperately seeking a security arrangement with the alliance. While the request for membership has been rejected, Albania's cooperation with NATO has steadily increased.

Foreign policy remains among the most divisive issues in Albania today. While there is general agreement on the opening to the world, foreign policy options are heatedly debated. Leftist forces, particularly the Socialist party and the Democratic Alliance, have charged that Berisha's foreign policy is slavishly pro-American; the Socialists, ever more virulently anti-American in posture, have launched a campaign against United States diplomats in Tiranë, particularly the highly popular ambassador, William Ryerson. Berisha is accused of emphasizing Tiranë's relationship with Washington at the expense of closer ties with Europe.

No event has more starkly illustrated differences over foreign policy than the controversy late last year over Albania's membership in the Islamic Conference. Critics expressed concern that Tiranë's close identification with the Islamic world would lead Western Europe to reassess its policy toward Albania, whose population is predominantly Muslim. Berisha took pains to counter domestic criticism by stressing the advantages of potential assistance from the Islamic nations, and expressed confidence that Albania's membership in the conference would not adversely affect its ties with the West. But despite increasing links with the Muslim world, there is no truth to reports of Islamic fundamentalism in Albania.

DISGRUNTLED NEIGHBORS

Whereas Berisha's foreign policy has in general been successful, his efforts to begin a new chapter in relations with Albania's neighbors just across its borders have had mixed results.

After a year of promising cooperation, Albanian-Greek relations took a turn for the worse in July, when Albania expelled a Greek Orthodox priest whom it said had fanned separatist feeling among Albania's small ethnic Greek community. Athens retaliated by deporting some 30,000 illegal Albanian economic refugees and canceling several scheduled ministerial meetings. Moreover, Greece raised the specter of territorial claims on southern Albania by insisting that Albania should be willing to grant ethnic Greeks (who are concentrated in the south) the same rights it demands for the 2 million ethnic Albanians in the rump Yugoslavia. (Albania has supported demands for Kosovo's separation from Serbia put forward by the ethnic Albanians who make up 90 percent of the province's population.)

By its vitriolic reaction Greece apparently hoped to weaken Berisha's position and extract concessions on a special status for the Greek minority in Albania. But Greece's newly threatening stance had the opposite effect, resulting in an upsurge of support for Berisha and calls to halt the "Hellenization" of southern Albania. There was anger among Albanians over the deportations and, more generally, over the parallel Athens had drawn between ethnic Greeks and the Kosovars. Wary of its southern neighbor's long-term intentions, Tiranë expressed concern that Greece, despite its assertion of neutrality in the Yugoslav war, had tilted toward Serbia; the Albanian media has alleged a "secret deal" between Greece and Serbia on southern Albania, Kosovo, and Macedonia. The Albanians also appear extremely apprehensive about Greece's assumption of the EC presidency in January 1994. For its part, Greece has vehemently rejected the notion of Kosovo's separation from Serbia, claiming this would radically upset the status quo in the Balkans. It has also called Albania's increasingly close ties with Turkey worrisome.

It remains to be seen whether the recent crisis was a passing storm in Albanian-Greek relations or whether the relationship is in danger of succumbing to the powerful nationalist impulses sweeping the Balkans. Suspicions linger on both sides, and will probably prevent rapprochement in the near future.

To the east, Albania has strongly supported the independence of the former Yugoslav republic of Macedonia, and was among the first countries to recognize the Skopje government. Economic cooperation between the two nations has grown steadily and the prospects for further cooperation are good. But relations continue to be marred by disagreement regarding the status of ethnic Albanians in Macedonia, who represent between 30 percent and 40 percent of the population. The Albanians have demanded equality with Slav Macedonians, and while Skopje has promised to take steps to improve their political and social status, Macedonian extremists fear an "Albanianization" of their country. Although Tiranë has discouraged separatist tendencies among the ethnic Albanians, maintaining that an independent Macedonia is vital to Albania's national interest, there are increasing calls for the establishment of an autonomous ethnic Albanian entity in western Macedonia, and even for outright union with Albania. Unless Slav Macedonians and Albanians find an arrangement acceptable to both, Macedonia could very well face ethnic strife that could threaten its existence as an independent state.

In the most dramatic demonstration of Albania's new approach to foreign policy, Berisha has offered an olive branch to Montenegro, the junior partner in the rump Yugoslavia. Taking advantage of the different stances of the two new Yugoslav republics on a number of issues, including Kosovo, Berisha has suggested Montenegro be treated differently from Serbia. He has called for international sanctions against Yugoslavia to be lifted for Montenegro. In September Montenegro's president, Miomir Bulatovic, visited Tiranë. While the new tack is likely to be unpopular domestically as well as in Kosovo, Berisha apparently hopes to drive a wedge between Serbia and Montenegro at a time when Albania confronts the growing likelihood of a bloody conflict with Serbia over Kosovo.

Serbia, which imposed direct rule on the formerly autonomous province of Kosovo in 1989, has violated the human rights of ethnic Albanians on a massive scale, marginalizing them as a group politically and economically. With the exception of war-torn Bosnia, no ethnic group in Europe has endured more state repression than the Albanians in Serbia. Ethnic Albanians have proclaimed Kosovo's independence and have assumed some aspects of self-rule, setting up parallel institutions. President Ibrahim Rugova—who was elected in a democratic election in Kosovo but is not recognized by Belgrade—advocates the establishment of an independent Kosovo with close ties to both Serbia and Albania. He has offered guarantees for the protection of the rights of the ethnic Serbian minority in Kosovo. Serbia, however, has not only resolutely rejected the idea of independence for Kosovo but has also refused to consider restoring the autonomy the region enjoyed before 1989. Amid more onerous Serbian repression, growing numbers of Albanians are challenging Rugova's leadership, questioning his counsel of peaceful resistance.

With Bosnia divided up between Serb and Croat militias and the Bosnian army, and probably soon to be officially dismembered, many believe that Serbia's strongman, Slobodan Milosevic, will be tempted to extend his horrendous policy of "ethnic cleansing" to Kosovo. Albania has declared that in such an event it will come to the assistance of Kosovo's 2 million ethnic Albanians. Yet the Albanian army is no match for Serbia's, and if war breaks out in Kosovo Albania will ace a deluge of refugees that would severely tax its weak economy and fledgling democracy.

For Albanians on both sides of the border, the key issue is preventing war—the majority apparently having deferred for the present their unification in a single state. Berisha has suggested that Kosovo be placed under United Nations control until the final status of the region is determined through negotiations. He has also demanded that the lifting of international sanctions against Serbia be linked to the peaceful solution of the Kosovo question.

Both Berisha and Rugova have pinned their hopes on the international community's taking measures to prevent the war in other parts of what was once Yugoslavia from spreading to Kosovo. United States President Bill Clinton has reaffirmed his predecessor George Bush's warning to Milosevic that Serbian aggression in Kosovo would prompt an American military response. It is not clear, however, what specific Serbian action would trigger it. The Albanians of Kosovo are subjected almost daily to brutal acts of military and police violence. Moreover, ethnic cleansing is reportedly well underway, with some 300,000 Albanians forced to flee the province to western Europe and the United States since 1989. The Albanians fear that Milosevic, continuing with his current repressive measures and low-intensity conflict, will succeed—without triggering foreign military intervention—in drastically changing the ethnic composition of Kosovo, to the Albanians' detriment. Thousands of Serb refugees from Croatia and Bosnia are already being settled in Kosovo.

The reward of Serbian aggression in Bosnia has accentuated Albanian anxieties that the international community might remain aloof if war broke out in Kosovo. But conflict in Kosovo is not peripheral to Western interests; strategic concerns are involved. An armed conflict in Kosovo would represent the first truly ethnic war in the former Yugoslavia, pitting Slavs against non-Slav, predominantly Muslim, Albanians. It would very likely dwarf atrocities in Bosnia and precipitate an all-out Balkan war involving Albania, Macedonia, Greece, Bulgaria, and Turkey. Taking strong preventive action now and forcing Serbia into direct negotiations with Albanian representatives on a new relationship between Kosovo and Serbia will save the world from further bloodshed and instability later.

FOR THE SECOND YEAR . . .

Albanians have survived an extremely difficult first year after communism and seem to have settled down to a painful but astonishingly smooth transformation into a pluralistic democracy and a market economy. Albania's charismatic president, an optimist by nature, has an extraordinary capacity not to give in to despair and disillusionment. He has demonstrated an ability to build and sustain the coalitions necessary to ensure adequate political support for economic transition and to weather the enormous social dislocations such a transition is bound to cause. Despite the increasing nastiness of political discourse in Albania, Berisha has continued to operate within a democratic framework, and opponents' persistent warnings about his dictatorial tendencies have proved unfounded.

For half a century Albania had simply dropped off the world's radar screen. With political and economic support from the international community, under Berisha's able leadership Albania could successfully make the transition to full-fledged democracy and become a beachhead of stability in the turbulent Balkans.

Article 14

Current History, November 1993

Bulgaria: Stable Ground in the Balkans?

Considering Bulgaria's progress toward democracy and economic reform "in a region rocked by war and ethnic violence and marked by the intransigence of old elites, [it is] strange . . . that the West has not tried to exploit Bulgaria as a political ally—to cultivate it as an island of democratic stability in the Balkans."

Luan Troxel

Luan Troxel is an assistant professor of government at Smith College. Her current research concerns right-wing politics and national divisions in Europe.

Among the Balkan countries Bulgaria is a bright light in a very dark place. Over the last several years it has demonstrated a consistent commitment to maintaining democracy. Although it has not entirely integrated its sizable minority population (primarily Turkish) into the political realm, it has made strides toward greater participation by and representation of minorities in politics at the national level. It has shown that it is serious about economic change, adopting privatization legislation and implementing austerity measures, and staying the course despite severe economic shocks from without.

These trends stand out in a region rocked by war and ethnic violence and marked by the intransigence of old elites. It is all the more strange, then, that the West has not tried to exploit Bulgaria as a political ally—to cultivate it as an island of democratic stability in the Balkans.

KEEPING UP DEMOCRACY

Bulgaria's longtime Communist party boss, Todor Zhivkov, was ousted in November 1989, as other Communist leaders throughout Eastern Europe were falling.

The difference was that Zhivkov was pushed out by the party, which retained power. The agreement to open up the system to competitive elections came later, in 1990, and the winner of the first free elections held that summer for a Grand National Assembly—a constituent assembly charged with dissolving itself after writing a constitution—was the reformed Communist party, calling itself the Bulgarian Socialist party.

This led some to believe that Bulgaria was not fully democratizing, that the totalitarian system had not really broken down, or that the election had been a fraud. But most international observers asserted that the balloting had been free and fair—as they did for the country's second election, which took place in October 1991. In fact, while many Bulgarians have continued to back the Socialists, both leaders and ordinary citizens have also consistently supported democracy.

First, elections have been fair. Second, despite the severe disillusionment caused by the economic crisis of 1990–1991, citizens did not give up on the democratic process; although turnout for the 1991 election might have been expected to be far lower than for the previous year's balloting, it was actually above 90 percent. Finally, Bulgarians are still actively reading newspapers, following the proceedings of the National Assembly, signing petitions, writing open letters, and mounting demonstrations. While such activities do not always make for the most stable democracy (Bulgaria has had five prime ministers since Zhivkov), they are important elements of a free democratic society.

Moreover, while national leaders elsewhere in the Balkans have taken advantage of their popularity and ethnic divisions to indulge their authoritarian tendencies, those who govern Bulgaria have maintained democratic practices. This is not to say they are not interested in amassing power—of course they are. But leaders like President Zhelyu Zhelev, who remains among the most popular politicians in Bulgaria, have neither called out the army (which also enjoys substantial popularity) nor stirred up ethnic hostilities as President Slobodan Milosevic has done in Serbia, nor called on a group within society, as President Ion Iliescu has done with the miners in Romania, to bolster their authority and power.

Instead, when Zhelev wanted more control, he attempted to expand the power of the presidency through institutional means—as evidenced in his struggle with the government over which institution should control the national intelligence service. The strength of democracy in Bulgaria can be gauged by what happened next: the media expressed outrage, the government fell, and there were demonstrations against Zhelev, which the authorities made no attempt to hinder. Elsewhere in the Balkans this kind of response to political leaders is seldom seen.

MAKING THE TURKS AT HOME

Bulgaria's Turkish minority makes up approximately 10 percent of the population. They are Muslim, mostly agrarian, have citizenship, and have lived in Bulgaria since the Ottoman Empire. Ethnic Bulgarians and Turks lived together with relatively little friction for most of the postwar period. But problems flared up in 1984 when Zhivkov's Communist regime implemented a "Bulgarization" campaign aimed at the Turks, banning the Turkish language and traditional garb, closing mosques, and forcing Turks to take Bulgarian names. The Turks appeared to have been reined in, and the campaign seemed to have fizzled out by 1988, but problems flared up again the following spring and summer with the exodus of many of the remaining Turks and the forced expulsion of others. The combination of a resurgence of Bulgarization and greater freedom of travel resulted in some being thrown out of the country, some intimidated into leaving, and others leaving voluntarily. The timing of the exodus was crucial, since many of the Turks were agricultural workers and they left just when many fruits and other crops had to be planted or were ready for harvesting; the "Turkish problem" thus exacerbated already poor economic conditions by creating shortages of common food products. University students and other Bulgarians from the cities were organized into work brigades and sent on mandatory tours of duty to labor in the countryside.

Not surprisingly, when Zhivkov was overthrown and the transition to a new society began, one of the main problems confronting leaders and ordinary citizens was ethnic tension. A great number of people were full of resentment against the Turks (many of whom had by then returned from Turkey), feeling they had contributed to the past summer's economic crunch. The Turks had taken a little vacation in Turkey, these Bulgarians said, while they had had to report to their jobs on Saturdays and serve in work brigades to make up for it.

There was a wave of demonstrations at which protesters insisted that Turks not be given full civil rights. (Ironically, these demonstrations coincided with the ones calling for a multiparty system and full democracy.) The run-up to the first free elections was marked by ethnic hostilities, as the Socialist party ran a nationalist campaign. Before the election, the Socialists—who were the majority party in the National Assembly—managed to incorporate nationalist language into the constitution and attempted to have the predominantly Turkish party, the Movement for Rights and Freedoms (MRF), declared illegal.

Given these events, it might be difficult to believe the Turks have been incorporated into the political life of the country. Nonetheless, they have been, for two reasons:

their party's powerful and consistent base of support, and its strategic maneuvering in parliament. In both elections the MRF received the third-most seats in parliament. While this did not give the party much power in the first post-Communist legislature, it occupies an important position in the second one, as it can make or break the majority and has done so.

When the Union of Democratic Forces (UDF, a coalition of the other main opposition groups) won the second election, it took only a few more seats than the Socialists and slightly less than a majority. Since the only other party to gain representation in parliament was the Movement for Rights and Freedoms, the UDF was forced into an informal coalition with the Turkish party to assure passage of legislation. Although the MRF agreed to become a low-profile coalition partner, it was soon at loggerheads with the union's leadership, and effectively demanded a more prominent position by joining together with the Socialist party in a vote of no confidence against the UDF-government of Filip Dimitrov.

Thus the Movement for Rights and Freedoms now officially participates in the government, is accepted as a powerful player in parliament—one that neither of the other two parties can ignore, especially now they are both splitting into factions—and is recognized as a legitimate political force in the country. While there are still tensions between Bulgarians and Turks on a personal level, many of the nation's ethnic difficulties are being worked out through government committees and other parliamentary groups rather than through civil disorder or even war. This is a truly positive sign in the Balkans.

THE END OF MUTUAL ECONOMIC ASSISTANCE

Bulgaria has been remaking its economy along the lines demanded by the international community, despite severe strains imposed from the outside. The economic transition has been difficult for all the former Communist states of eastern Europe, but Bulgaria has suffered disproportionately from the effects of the collapse of the Council for Mutual Economic Assistance (CMEA), the Persian Gulf War of 1991, and the ongoing war in the former Yugoslavia.

Before 1990, the countries of Eastern Europe concentrated on trading within the Soviet bloc through the organizational mechanism of the 10-member CMEA. For instance, in 1987 Poland sent almost one-quarter of its exports to the Soviet Union, and another 19 percent to other nations in Eastern Europe. In 1988, 34 percent of Czechoslovakia's and 20 percent of Hungary's exports went to the Soviet Union, while approximately 27 percent of exports from both countries were shipped to destinations elsewhere in Eastern Europe. For Bulgaria, the concentration of trade was even more pronounced: 85

percent of 1988 exports went to CMEA members—63 percent to the Soviet Union alone. When the CMEA collapsed in 1990–1991, Bulgaria lost its primary trading partners, largely due to the lack of an organizational mechanism for trade, confusion about currency, and vague economic logic. It had not found new partners to take up the slack. Even the ideological links that had been the foundation of trade relations no longer existed.

In addition to losing its markets, Bulgaria also effectively lost the Soviet Union as its main supplier when President Mikhail Gorbachev began demanding hard currency payments for Soviet exports. Although the CMEA's collapse and the new trade relationship with the Soviet Union affected all the council's members, Bulgaria was hurt the most, insofar as it had the highest concentration of trade with the CMEA states and was the most dependent on energy imports from the Soviet Union.

When the economic and energy crises hit Eastern Europe simultaneously in late 1990, the Bulgarian economy nearly collapsed. Not caught entirely off guard, Bulgaria's leaders had arranged for oil imports from Iraq as repayment for Iraq's hard currency debt to Bulgaria, which amounted to more than $1 billion (Iraq, Libya, and Syria together owed Bulgaria $2.36 billion). But when Bulgaria upheld UN sanctions against Iraq, it was forced to forgo the energy imports, along with any hope of repayment from Iraq. Thus Bulgaria was in poor shape economically when it began implementing its structural adjustment program. And the war in what was once Yugoslavia, said to have cost Bulgaria between $1.2 billion and $2 billion so far, has exacerbated matters.

Sustaining these blows, Bulgaria has made a valiant effort to initiate and maintain an International Monetary Fund–sponsored adjustment program, despite the severe negative impact on the economy. Even before Bulgaria was admitted into the IMF in 1990, Prime Minister Andrei Lukanov's Socialist government had attempted to show good faith by implementing IMF economic reform programs before the IMF required them. In early 1990 the government announced price increases on 40 percent of goods and 60 percent of services (although prices were frozen on certain staple items such as bread, meat, dairy goods, sugar, cooking oil, and baby food). In addition, the lev (Bulgaria's currency) was formally devalued in March 1990. After the elections that year, Lukanov announced another reform plan, this one formulated in consultation with the IMF, calling for internal convertibility of the lev, price increases, wage controls, and demonopolization and privatization.

Despite the bold reform efforts, there was no substantial improvement in the economy in 1990. Production in the first three quarters declined 13 percent against the same period in 1989, and between May and October inflation increased 30 percent. By the end of the year Bulgaria had a budget deficit approaching 13 percent of gross domestic product, a $750-million trade deficit, and a balance of payments deficit of $1.15 billion; gross fixed investment had fallen 18.5 percent. In addition, Bulgaria's foreign debt crisis ($10 billion in foreign debt, with only $125 million in foreign exchange reserves) had deepened throughout the year after Lukanov suspended debt servicing.

As 1990 drew to a close, Bulgaria was experiencing political upheaval, largely for economic reasons. A general strike was called and this, in conjunction with a series of demonstrations and protests, toppled the Lukanov government.

By early 1991 the political climate was dramatically different. A new independent prime minister, Dimiter Popov, had formed a coalition government with the Union of Democratic Forces and the Socialist party. Many now believed economic reforms could take root and major changes could be effected. Indeed, the year brought even more dramatic change in the economy, when in February the lev was made internally convertible and retail prices leaped 123 percent. In March the new government approved an economic reform program that was to begin privatization but which would result in a 35 percent drop in real wages.

Nonetheless, 1991 also provided some hopeful signs for economic recovery. In March the IMF announced it would disburse more than $550 million in loans for Bulgaria, $109 million of which were intended to offset the oil crisis. Following that, the Paris Club (an informal grouping of the world's largest creditor nations) agreed to reschedule its $2-billion share of Bulgaria's foreign debt over the next 10 years. Anup Singh, the IMF representative monitoring Bulgaria, pronounced the reforms "sound," the country's first commodity exchange opened its doors, and the World Bank came through with a $250-million structural adjustment loan.

Still Bulgaria did not seem to be on track. Although the new government had undertaken many initiatives to transform the economic system, and especially to open up opportunities for its most entrepreneurial citizens, the economy was still imploding. Output had fallen 8 percent and real gross domestic product 23 percent in 1991; unemployment was at 10 percent and inflation exceeded 330 percent. Despite new elections in the fall, which the Union of Democratic Forces managed to win outright, the euphoria of the "revolution" was missing. The nation's economic woes weighed heavily on most Bulgarians, and there seemed to be no end in sight.

ECONOMIC NOSTALGIA

Of course, from an economist's point of view, what was going on was not all discouraging. Bulgaria managed to avoid hyperinflation, and if the number of jobless workers increased this could simply mean that uncompetitive firms were failing. Likewise, the decline in production in the short run could be taken as a natural outcome of structural change, because unprofitable firms curtail production and others might be reluctant to expand investment.

But from the standpoint of average Bulgarians who had become accustomed to the state providing for their primary needs, the process did not appear at all natural. Unfortunately for all these citizens, the situation did not improve in 1992 either. There was another 20 percent drop in overall production—a trend that continued in 1993—and unemployment climbed to 15 percent. The World Bank warned that if large-scale privatization did not get under way, its second disbursement of the previously granted $250 million would not be forthcoming. The National Assembly responded with a general law on privatization, but by mid-1993 only one large enterprise had been sold. Although by 1992 about 180,000 private firms had been registered in Bulgaria, half were one-person operations.

IMF officials continued to be supportive of the reform. In September 1992 Anup Singh once again praised Bulgaria for meeting IMF standards—and particularly for avoiding high inflation—keeping the lev fairly stable, and maintaining exports at a higher level than expected. Indeed, the situation had apparently improved, as Bulgaria began repaying 25 percent of the overdue interest on its foreign debt. In addition, Bulgaria ended the year with a $452-million balance of payments surplus.

People were still not happy with the government or parliament, however, and opinion polls revealed a lack of support for the government's determination to work through the crisis. According to polls conducted in September 1992, 69 percent of respondents were dissatisfied with their present "economic situation" and 65 percent with their standard of living; moreover, more than one-quarter expected their standard of living to further decline in the next 12 months. Unsurprisingly, then, many Bulgarians continued to support certain aspects of state welfarism antithetical to reforms: 87 percent agreed it was important to maintain a state welfare system while Bulgaria moved toward a market economy; 83 percent supported full employment; and 76 percent wanted the government to keep food prices down or to subsidize them. Nor were many surprised when the Union of Democratic Forces government fell last autumn.

When the government of Lyuben Berov took over early this year, Bulgaria's relations with the IMF entered a new phase. This phase seemed to be marked more by hostility than cooperation, as demonstrated by the finance minister's threat to suspend cooperation with the fund if he was not allowed to maintain a budget deficit equal to between 8 percent and 10 percent of GNP, and ultimately by the failure to reach a new stand-by agreement with the IMF.

The apparent disagreement between the Bulgarian government and the IMF is understandable. Both political leaders and citizens in Bulgaria felt that they had tried to follow the economic dictates of the international community but that there had simply been too few positive results. In addition, when Bulgaria had followed the letter and spirit of international demands, it was not rewarded.

Bulgarians felt the economic situation in their country was not in their hands, and so found it difficult to see why they should suffer through further austerity measures. In short, they felt they were damned if they did and damned if they didn't.

NOT OUR WAR

A similar dilemma has emerged with the war that began in Yugoslavia in 1991. Bulgaria has already lost a great deal of money and stands to lose much more by upholding UN sanctions against the rump Yugoslavia (Serbia and Montenegro), as well as because of the disruption of trade caused by the war. However, it would lose all respect internationally if it did not uphold the sanctions. Many Bulgarians believe some sort of compensation for their trouble is in order, and the UN has technically agreed in principle. Recognition of Bulgaria's plight and financial help to allay its losses must now come from the world community. This, then, leads to consideration of how Bulgaria's future might look.

The country is in a precarious position. It must uphold UN sanctions and endure the ensuing hardships to retain the world's respect. But it must at the same time play a careful diplomatic game with the Serbian leadership in the rump Yugoslavia, to forestall later military or (at the end of the war) economic retaliation. For a country that is expecting unemployment to reach 17 percent, in which 61 percent of people live below the official "social minimum," and that is faced with a hostile Serbian press, these are not simple tasks.

Although to outside observers it might appear unlikely that Bulgaria could be pulled into the Yugoslav war, the probability does not appear so remote to Bulgarians. When asked in a February poll what most concerned them about their future, the highest percentage of Bulgarians (41 percent) said "war."

Given the economic crisis, the perceived danger of the Yugoslav war, and the fact that Bulgaria has made a genuine effort to maintain democratic practices, ethnic participation, and economic change, it seems that strong international support for the country should be forthcoming. Positive reinforcement for what Bulgaria has achieved, rather than punishment or lack of attention to the areas in which so far it has not had success, would make sense. This is especially true because Bulgaria is not merely a country struggling to transform its economy; it is a country that has gone to great lengths and endured significant financial hardship in order to be part of the Western community of nations. With outside support, it could become an important ally in an unstable region.

Article 15

The New York Times, July 30, 1993

After the Uncoupling, Slovakia Seems Unnerved

Jane Perlez

Special to The New York Times

BANSKA STIAVNICA, Slovakia—Alena Daubnerova, whose forebears stretch back generations in this traditional area of strong Slovak nationalism, represents the ambivalent streak of many Slovaks as they confront life in their new country.

Persuaded by the charisma of the man who promised both sovereignty and prosperity, she voted for Vladimir Meciar, who became Prime Minister and led Slovakia to independence on Jan. 1.

But now that her husband is to be laid off from a faltering textile plant and she is struggling to keep her low-paying, 14-hour-a-day job as a hotel receptionist, Mrs. Daubnerova says Slovak independence was a bad idea.

"I'm unhappy with the split," she said, tears welling in her eyes as she expressed frustration at the early fruits of nationhood. "The factories here would have hung on longer if we were still part of Czechoslovakia. The Czechs, they're bigger than we are. We would be better off with them."

She No Longer Believes

Mr. Meciar had pledged that the transition from Communism to capitalism would be painless, even in an independent Slovakia, but Mrs. Daubnerova said she no longer believed him.

Much of the Slovak national pride, which simmered through centuries of rule under the Hungarians to the south and then under the domination of the Czechs to the west, has subsided into sullenness as the first half year of independence has brought increasing economic uncertainty and a rocky image abroad.

Two new countries, Slovakia with 5.5 million people and the Czech Republic with 10 million, were created in January without war but also without a referendum. Opinion polls showed that a majority of Czechs and most Slovaks were against the split, which was initiated by Mr. Meciar, agreed to by the Czech

Prime Minister, Vaclav Klaus, and formalized by a vote of the Czechoslovak Parliament.

While there is tremendous grumbling about the split, most Slovaks recognize it as a fait accompli, and nobody in the capital, Bratislava, thinks it is reversible.

The poorer, smaller and more industrialized part of Czechoslovakia, Slovakia faced a tough economic ride in the post-Communist era even if it had remained part of the Czechoslovak federation. But these vulnerabilities have been aggravated by the separation, economists and politicians here say.

Industries Inefficient

The arms industry made up a larger part of the economy in Slovakia than in the Czech Republic, and its other industries were and remain inefficient and heavily subsidized by the Government.

Foreign investment, which was much smaller in the Slovak part of the federation, has slowed sharply, with foreign businesses hesitant to pump money into an uncertain political climate.

Mr. Meciar, a 50-year-old former Communist whose newborn populism appealed to workers like Mrs. Daubnerova in

Some residents of Banska Stiavnica are regretting their support for Slovakia's independence.

last year's campaign, has curbed privatization, particularly in the energy sector. He campaigned on a platform of slow privatization, saying the methods of selling off industries used by the Czechs put too many assets into private hands.

He has yet to find a viable solution to converting the arms industries to alternative production. Unemployment stands at 11.5 percent and has reached 20 percent in some industrial centers, a slight rise since the separation. In the Czech Republic, unemployment is under 3 percent.

Officials of the Meciar Government said they expected joblessness to grow to an average of 18 percent as inefficient factories like those in this mining and textile town are shuttered. Leaders of the opposition Christian Democratic Party said they expected 30 percent unemployment in the next year or so.

Popularity Falls to 20 Percent

With prices rising and the new country lacking the federal money it used to get from Prague, Mr. Meciar's popularity has fallen from a high last year of more than 80 percent to just above 20 percent, opinion polls show.

One of the aims of a separate Slovakia was to project its interests abroad rather than remain the forgotten junior partner of Czechoslovakia.

But Mr. Meciar has turned out to be an erratic salesman for Slovakia. His comments about turning off the oil that flows to the Czech Republic through Slovakia incensed the leaders in Prague. His assertions that Hungarian military exercises threatened Slovak sovereignty annoyed politicians in Budapest, as well as the 600,000 Hungarians who live in the southern swath of Slovakia.

Indeed, Mr. Meciar conceded that he was not happy with Slovakia's image, but he blamed others for the problem. "We are very little known abroad," he said. "The information that has a seed in Budapest or Prague is not objective. The reality of the country is better than the picture."

Even many of those who would be most expected to welcome the new independence are hesitant, putting the blame for the economic difficulties on the rush to be separate.

Karol Javorka, an 82-year-old pensioner who guards the tomb of one of Slovakia's most famous nationalists, Andrej Hlinka, in the northern town of Ruzomberok, lamented: "The majority of the citizens are not happy. There's too much unemployment. For hundreds of years we were under the boot of the Hungarians. Then the Germans came.

We should be a republic together with the Czechs."

He drew an analogy with the United States. "Fifty states make one strong whole," he said. "It is the same here. We should have one government and one army. We would be stronger together."

Article 16   *The World Today,* April 1993

Hungary: counting the social cost of change

Rudolf Andorka

'Creative destruction' is what Janos Kornai, echoing Joseph Schumpeter several years ago, called the processes which have been taking place in Hungary in the past few years in the wake of the change of regime. The expression is very apt. On the one hand it is obvious that the dismantling of the remnants of centralised economic planning, the radical reduction of the state ownership of the means of production, the restructuring of the economy, the reorganisation of the structure of foreign trade, a fundamental change in our social and political institutions and the transformation of our entire culture are needed for development of the Hungarian economy to begin. The end-result of these processes will be the creation of a developed market economy and a stable democratic society. On the other hand, it is obvious that this process of destruction has economic and social costs. This article discusses the social costs of the process of change. It will focus on the question of what volume of burdens and costs Hungarian society can tolerate without the transition to a market economy, economic growth and the democratic political system being threatened, and in what way those burdens can be eased and managed by social policy instruments in the coming years. How great, then, are these social costs, and what social strata and demographic groups of Hungarian society do they affect?

Who is poorer now?

The most clearly visible social cost of the change of regime is the decline in the income level. Because of its visibility it is in the spotlight of public interest and even more of media attention. However, it must be pointed out that we know relatively little about the extent of the decline in income, at all events far less than is believed to be true or claimed by those who refer to it.

Statistics show a decline of a few percentage points. The new household income census—being held earlier than originally planned—is now under way; the previous such census showed

1987 incomes. A relatively small-scale survey by the Social Sciences Research Institute (TARKI) in April 1991 produced the perhaps seemingly surprising result that monthly average net real incomes did not decline, or more precisely, they rose by approximately the same extent as the inflation rate (that is, by around 74 per cent over a period of two years). The establishment of this fact was of special note since, according to some other surveys, 80 per cent of the population consider that their financial situation is worse than it was a year ago.

It must be added that real wages have declined since 1978 and real income has largely stagnated since the mid-1980s—that is, the unfavourable trend which began earlier has grown stronger since the change of regime in 1989–90. We also know that the decline in real wages has not led to a sharp fall in the standard of living, only because the greater part of the population has been able to counterbalance this by increasing their various supplementary incomes, principally through participation in the second economy. It can also be added that earlier data surveys by the Central Office of Statistics which asked about the subjective opinions formed on the change of income over the previous year showed that these opinions give a somewhat less favourable picture than the actual change in income.

Taking all this into consideration, I draw the conclusion that the decline in per capita real income since 1990 has been relatively slight, at all events less than the decline in per capita national income or, more precisely, gross domestic product (gdp). Thus the claim that the process of impoverishment extends to the entire Hungarian society—or its overwhelming majority—in my opinion simply does not correspond to the reality.

In contrast, the TARKI survey mentioned above found an increase in the inequality of incomes. But it must be noted that the growth in the inequality of incomes had already begun after the household income census of 1982 and that this process merely accelerated following the change of regime. It must also be added that the growth in inequality of incomes was not unexpected. In fact, Hungarian economists and sociologists had foreseen it. The majority of them agreed that for the Hungarian economy to recover from the stagnation or even recession, the market would have to be given a greater role and private enterprise would have to expand considerably. It was expected that these two processes would inevitably be accompanied by an increase in income differences. (The growth of incomes in companies successful in the market economy and in the successful private sector is not only a consequence of but also a precondition for rapid market-oriented restructuring and the growth of the private sector.)

The TARKI survey also gives a picture of the evolution of income inequalities. The inequality in the net incomes of the adults interviewed can be measured as the ratio of the highest and lowest decile incomes: the value of this ratio in an earlier data survey made in 1982 was 5.1; in 1989 it was 5.03; and in 1991, 6.01. The increase in the inequality of per capita household income was less than this: in 1989 it was 5.8 and in 1990, 6.0. The explanation for this is that the ratio of dependants to earners declined over the two years in the low-income households. We can therefore draw the conclusion that the inequality has increased, but not to a very great extent.

In my opinion, the key to understanding the objective and subjective sides of the income situation is to be found in the data of the TARKI survey which show what proportion of the subjects had an increase or a decline in personal real income in the period between 1989 and spring 1991. These data show that there was a decline in nominal income in 7 per cent of cases; real income declined in 42 per cent of cases, stagnated in 13 per cent, improved slightly in 18 per cent, improved strongly in 15 per cent and increased at least two-fold in 5 per cent of cases (total: 100 per cent). In other words, real income declined for half of the population, that is, half of the society became poorer, but at the same time there was a strong increase in real income for one fifth. This explains why the majority of those questioned in the course of other surveys feel that their financial situation has deteriorated, and it also explains why such signs of impoverishment as collecting from rubbish bins have become visible, simultaneously with the signs of an increase in prosperity (for example, the increase in the number of Western cars).

How many people can be regarded as poor and how far have their numbers increased? Of course, all definitions of poverty or the minimum subsistence level contain subjective elements, depending on the attitude prevailing in the given society. In Hungary, the Central Statistical Office has since 1982 calculated the minimum subsistence level and a so-called socially acceptable minimum (the latter is around 15–20 per cent higher than the minimum subsistence level). However, there is also an earlier minimum calculation made for 1968 which is not fully comparable with the calculations made in the 1980s. On the basis of these it can be estimated very approximately that in 1962 there must have been at least 3m persons living on an income less than the minimum subsistence level. That figure probably fell to around 1m by 1972, then declined only slowly. In 1987 it was probably around 1m again and—according to a calculation made by Tamas Kolosi—rose to 1.5m in 1991. By the summer of 1992 the percentage of the population having an income lower than the minimum of existence increased to about 2m.

The proportion of those living on an income less than the socially acceptable minimum is, of course, greater than this and the total may be above 3m. In short, there are many poor people in Hungarian society and their numbers have increased considerably in the past two years, but any claims that classify half or even more of Hungarian society among the poor seem to be exaggerated. I consider it necessary to emphasise this because the wider the definition made of poverty, the greater the number of persons and families among whom we recommend distributing the limited resources at the disposal of social policy, and consequently the less support provided per poor person.

Inflation and unemployment

There are two important direct causes of poverty and impoverishment today: inflation and unemployment. It is the consequence of inflation that all those who live on fixed earnings find themselves in a worse income situation from year to year since for the most part they are incapable of achieving an increase in their fixed earnings—wages, pensions or other social incomes—proportionate to the price increases.

Among these, the old-age pensioners are the focus of attention. The poverty of the elderly, and of pensioners in general, has been one of the main themes in sociology literature and in the mass media ever since the first household income surveys were made in Hungary in the early 1960s. However, it must be added that, whereas in 1962 it was in fact the elderly who were the stratum or social group in the country 'over-represented' among those living below the subsistence level, by 1987 the situation had fundamentally changed: the per capita income in pensioner households was 90 per cent of the national average, while it was 81 per cent for unskilled workers, 88 per cent for semi-skilled workers and 90 per cent in the households of agricultural manual workers. Paradoxically, at the same time the overwhelming majority of pensioners were justified in complaining of impoverishment since pensions were not indexed, which meant that—with the exception of the lowest pensions—the increase in their nominal value lagged behind the rise in prices.

While the proportion of those living below the subsistence level now barely exceeds the national average among those over 60, it has grown steadily among children where the proportion of those living below the minimum subsistence level far exceeds that of the elderly. This means that it is families with children—above all those with several children—who represent the demographic group most at risk of poverty today. It is true of course that in contrast with pensioners, these families have a good chance of rising above the minimum subsistence level with time—in 10 to 15 years; and it is also obvious that the family can avoid this poverty of young adulthood by having fewer children or no children at all. However, this leads to the well known long-term demographic problem—the rapid ageing of the population.

The unemployment rate attained 13 per cent in February 1993. This is unquestionably a very great shock for Hungarian society, since this problem was unknown or hardly known in the socialist period and sociological surveys conducted in the recent past have shown that the great majority thought that full employment should be maintained and that many people regarded this as the state's task. The problem is made more serious by the fact that unemployment affects principally the poorer, less educated, unskilled part of society, and in particular the gypsies. However, it must be noted that we have very little reliable sociological information on the new phenomenon of unemployment. We do not know precisely the sociological characteristics of the unemployed, how long the unemployment lasts, how the families affected try to cope with the loss of income caused by unemployment. Especially we do not know what proportion of the unemployed earn incomes in the 'grey economy' while receiving unemployment aid.

Other social costs of the change of regime are less visible but more serious and more difficult to manage than impoverishment. The housing question is to the fore here. Housing construction has declined to less than half the volume of the peak year 1975. This decline began in the second half of the 1970s and at the most it has only slightly accelerated after the change of regime. The cause is principally that state-rented housing construction has almost completely stopped. At the same time, the costs of private housing construction have grown considerably more rapidly than the inflation rate. This is causing very serious problems for young families who cannot solve them without help from their parents.

Sociological studies since the 1970s have shown that the population, and particularly the poorer strata, has responded to the stagnation of the socialist economy since 1978 and the resulting decline in real wages by taking advantage of the possibility offered by the economic reform (or, more precisely, tolerated in connection with it) of earning supplementary incomes, the 'second economy' in addition to the work done in their 'official' jobs.

In the 1980s, 70–80 per cent of the population participated in the second economy in one form or another. They devoted one third of all the time spent on income-earning work to the second economy, and at least 20 per cent of all disposable household income was derived from it. The duration of the work performed in the second economy was divided very unevenly among the various strata of society. The poorer people spent much more time on it and thus had far less time left for rest. It is thanks to this extremely heavy load of extra-work that the Hungarian economy coped with the crisis which affected all the socialist countries in the mid-1970s far better than any of the others. But there was a price to be paid. The harmful effects of this very heavy work input were seen in the deterioration of the state of health—particularly in the alarming rise in mortality among the adult population. According to the comprehensive and detailed reports and analyses of the Central Statistical Office, there are great social differences in the mortality rate: that of the better-off in Hungary is comparable to the mortality rate of the West Germans, while that of the poorest strata resembles the figures for the Syrians.

Finally, there are the social costs in the field of deviant behaviour. We know that the suicide rate has risen close to three-fold over the temporary low point of 1954, and that the rate of cirrhosis of the liver, generally used to measure the spread of alcoholism, has risen more than ten-fold since the immediate post-war years. According to investigations carried out and published in 1992, 34 per cent of the population over 16 complained of neurotic symptoms; of these, 16 per cent were serious neurotics in need of treatment, 24 per cent complained of symptoms of depression; of these, 5 per cent suffered from moderately serious and 3 per cent from serious depression. All these phenomena are more frequent in the poorer strata. Not surprisingly, widespread alienation accompanies all these phenomena. It is true that there has been a slight decline in the suicide rate in the last few years, and the spread of alcoholism seems to have halted. However, it would be premature to draw very optimistic conclusions from this.

What kind of social policy?

We can, therefore, draw the conclusion that the change of regime has serious social costs and that they are weighing disproportionately on the poorer strata of society. The question arises of whether it is necessary and possible to use social pol-

icy instruments to reduce these costs, and if so, what concrete social policy instruments can be recommended.

The following points should be taken into account:
• It would be a serious error to oppose the market-oriented economic reforms and social policy to each other in Hungary. The proponents of the economic reforms and the proponents of the reform of social policy should not argue against each other but combine their efforts because they can only attain their goals together.
• In Hungary in the socialist period the sums devoted to social expenditure were substantial, but it would be an error to claim that they were greater than in the Western European capitalist societies in general. It cannot be claimed that some form of special 'socialist model' was created in Hungary as regards the volume of social expenditure. In contrast, in many respects the use made of these sums was basically irrational, not least because many forms of the supports given through social policy did not even reach those most in need of them.

The basic principle of social policy which can be applied most effectively to moderate the social costs of the change of regime, and also numerous social problems inherited from the socialist system, should be this: it is the poorest part of Hungarian society, the roughly 1.5m persons mentioned earlier, who must be protected as far as possible from further impoverishment. Accordingly, social policy must be shaped in such a way that the funds available are distributed with the greatest efficiency and principally to this poorest stratum.

This view is not at all obvious to all Hungarian citizens or even to all Hungarian social scientists. There are very strong arguments in favour of spreading social welfare more widely and providing protection against the falling living standards for a considerably greater part of society. It has already been mentioned that in the past few years about a half of Hungarian society has experienced a decline in real income. It is these people who are frequently described as the 'increasingly impoverished middle class' or the 'lower middle class'. The majority of old-age pensioners can be classified here.

I must give a brief justification of why I consider that it would not be a good decision in the present situation to extend strong social policy support to this far larger group of about 5m. This would require devoting a greater sum than at present to social spending. While I would not be in favour of a reduction in social spending in the present economic situation—when the principal goal must be creating the conditions for economic recovery—it would be a mistake to secure the funds needed for increased social expenditure either by increasing the budget deficit or by imposing heavier taxes on the active earners or companies. But if the present social expenditure is divided among a greater number of persons, then there is a smaller amount available per person and per family, including the poorest.

In conclusion, here are a few thoughts on possible reforms of social policy which could promote the implementation of the general principles and conclusions formulated above. An analysis carried out by the International Monetary Fund very aptly characterises the faults of the old-age pension system as too many people receiving their pensions—which are too low—too early. The situation is aggravated by the fact that the pension system is already balancing on the brink of bankruptcy. If the present system is maintained it will, as a result of the ageing population, definitely become bankrupt in 10–15 years' time—that is, the pensions to be paid out will exceed the sum of the pension contributions paid in.

Over the short term, the most serious social problem in the area of pensions is that pensions are not automatically indexed to price increases; so far each government has raised only the lowest pensions largely parallel with the price rises. However, this has produced the situation—extremely unfavourable from the social psychological point of view—in which the great majority of elderly people can face the prospect that by the end of their lives their pensions will drop to, or very close to, the minimum subsistence level.

Over the very short term, the sums available for this purpose should be concentrated on ensuring that nobody's pension sinks below the minimum subsistence level, that is, priority should be given to regularly raising the lowest pensions. This proposal may appear evident, but at the time of the most recent increase in pensions the proposal to this effect made by the Ministry of Welfare was eventually amended by Parliament to increase the lowest pensions by somewhat less than was proposed, and to increase the higher pensions by a somewhat greater extent. This was hailed by some sections of the press as a victory for social justice.

A time-bomb under the system?

Since the pension contribution, and, in general, the social insurance contribution, can hardly be increased without seriously endangering the world market competitiveness of Hungarian companies, over the medium term there does not appear to be any other solution than raising the retirement age for both sexes to the 65 years which is quite general in countries more developed than Hungary, and changing the formula for calculating the pension so that the initial pension is lower but preservation of its value can be ensured.

The truth must be faced, though, that a time bomb set to go off in a few decades' time is ticking away beneath the entire pension insurance system as a consequence of the fact that with the ageing of the population, the active population paying pension contributions is declining and the population of retirement age is growing. We can draw little comfort from the fact that the same bomb is ticking under the pensions systems of practically every developed country. A few years ago in West Germany the bankruptcy of the social insurance system was predicted for the year 2020. In Hungary this will happen earlier because here the number of births fell below the level required for simple reproduction 15 years earlier. Over the long term, two instruments of social policy are available to avert a crisis: (a) a substantial increase in immigration from abroad, principally of young adults, and (b) the application of a demographic policy or family policy which makes it possible for families to have more children.

One argument for a demographic policy supporting families with children by financial means, besides this long-term goal, is the fact—already mentioned—that a not insignificant proportion of children in Hungary spend a part of their childhood under conditions of poverty. (In 1987, 21 per cent of the children aged up to two years belonged in the lowest income group, i.e., the 1m persons who can be considered as poor.) It can be debated whether it is expedient to pay a uniform family allowance for all children (in this case all children and families are treated strictly equally), or whether families with more children should be preferred through a higher family allowance (in this case, a greater part of the total sum spent on family allowances goes to those with lower incomes). The institution of child-care aid and child-care allowance has been criticised from a number of angles. At the same time it is obvious that they are of great assistance to young mothers in reconciling the

raising of children with a professional career. It is worth observing that similar supports have been introduced recently in other countries, such as Germany and Sweden.

Since the socialist system maintained full employment as a value and goal of economic policy almost to the end, open unemployment 'outside the factory gates' hardly occurred at all, so there did not appear to be a need for unemployment benefit, either. However, the transition to the market economy or, more precisely, the replacement of the so-called 'soft budget constraint'—state subsidies for loss-making enterprises—with a 'hard' constraint, put the earlier inside-the-factory unemployment 'outside the factory gates' within a very short time. The last socialist government in Hungary and then the coalition government formed after the 1990 elections reacted to this first with the introduction and then with the extension of unemployment aid.

Undoubtedly, the most acute social policy need today is in this area. Nevertheless, foreign examples serve as a warning that, if it is not applied with sufficient circumspection, unemployment aid can have undesirable influences. In particular, it can (a) keep the unemployed from seeking employment, and (b) create the opportunity for cheating through unregistered employment in the 'grey' economy. For this reason there is a need for continuous and very thorough scientific studies.

Under the socialist system emergency welfare aid was given to a very limited circle (in the 1980s about 80,000 persons received regular welfare aid), presumably as a consequence of the ideological tenet that poverty does not occur in the socialist society, and the 'large social policy systems' (such as pensions, etc.) are capable of managing the danger of poverty.

There is no need to prove here once again that for decades sociological surveys in Hungary showed the existence of poverty. After the change of regime there was a fundamental change of attitude in this area: the government recognises the fact of poverty and—for want of a better solution—attempts to ease it by extending aid on an individual basis to poor families. The aid system, based on the individual assessment and decision of the institution paying out the aid—local government, family guidance centres, social security departments and so on—is widely criticised on many counts, ranging from the possibility of arbitrary decisions through the humiliating procedures to the high costs. However, over the short term there does not appear to be a better solution for dealing with emergency situations and providing aid for those in acute poverty.

Last but not least, it must be mentioned that—whether intended or not—the entire taxation system has social effects, which means that when elaborating the reform of social policy as a whole, consideration must necessarily be given to such questions as the floor from which progressive personal income tax begins, the alternative of individual or family income tax, or whether the number of dependants should be taken into consideration when determining the taxable income or the actual tax to be paid.

Finally, there are three areas of the social costs of the change of regime listed at the beginning which do not belong in the field of social policy in the strict sense of the term but can be considered as borderline areas. Under the present circumstances, it is almost impossible to get a state-owned rented apartment and building, while buying an apartment of a size needed to set up a family costs the equivalent of 10–15 years' average wages. On the other hand, rents still lag behind what they presumably would be if set by the market. All that points to a need for a fundamental change in housing policy.

While health care is in theory free of charge, in reality quite substantial 'gratitude money' has to be paid for certain services. In other words, a part of the overall social costs of health care is passed on to the population. As a consequence, the officially recorded health spending is very low, but if we add to this the actual spending by the population we find that the real costs are far from being so low.

At the same time it is a fact—unequivocally demonstrated by sociological investigations—that the standard of health care is very poor. The weakness of the system is thus obvious, and it must definitely be changed. This could also contribute to reversing the deterioration in the mortality figures, although in my opinion the fundamental causes of this deterioration are to be found in the national life-style.

There is no need either for a detailed demonstration of the very neglected state of mental health in Hungary, and of the urgent need those struggling with psychological problems have for help. Although mental health care is unable to remedy the roots of alienation, it can provide help in resolving the most serious individual crises arising from them.

Who pays?

But where are the budget and other funds required for the social policy outlined here to come from? This question is particularly justified in view of the need to reduce the size of the Hungarian state budget as a whole compared to the national revenue. I believe that very large savings can be achieved in two areas of spending which do not belong within social policy in the strict sense, but where the spendings were justified in the past by social policy considerations. These two areas are:

(a) price subsidies for certain consumer goods; and (b) the subsidies extended to state enterprises operating at a loss.

In many cases the price subsidies were justified—openly or tacitly—on the grounds that this would bring the goods within the reach of the poorer strata of the population. This argument was not sound because the more prosperous strata naturally purchased more of the subsidised goods and thus benefited more from the subsidies than did the poorer strata. The subsidies for the loss-making enterprises, the so-called 'soft budget constraint', were justified on the grounds that this preserved jobs and ensured full employment. This argument is not sound either because the state budget funds used to balance the losses were diverted from areas where they would have served the welfare of the population directly.

This was the cause of the 'remainder'-type financing of health, education and social care, and thereby of the prolonged neglect of these areas. If these two items of expenditure—allegedly also serving social purposes but in reality not contributing to their attainment—ceased to burden the budget or were steadily reduced, it could be anticipated that more funds would be available for those forms of social spending which really improve the situation of those most in need, thus most efficiently reducing the social costs of the change of regime. In this way it would be possible to achieve a social policy 'compatible with the market' which could, on the one hand, help the Hungarian economy to enter the stage of recovery as soon as possible and, on the other, contribute towards making the social costs of the change of regime as low and tolerable as possible, without endangering the development of the modern market economy and the consolidation of the democratic political system.

Article 17   *The Christian Science Monitor*, May 26, 1993

Poland Turns the Corner

Poles Try the Free Market, and It Fits

*But perils persist: Economic growth has been uneven and
the political situation remains 'delicate'.*

Francine S. Kiefer

Staff writer of The Christian Science Monitor

WARSAW

Consider the Polish potato chip.

Available in barbecue, bacon, or plain salted flavor, and packaged in a shiny red and yellow cellophane bag, it could easily be mistaken for a Western import.

The same could be said about the Polish television set, which contestants can win on Poland's own version of "Wheel of Fortune," the American game show. Sleek, compact, and equipped with remote control and stereo sound, it could be a Sony. But—surprise!—it's produced by Elemis, a state-owned company in Warsaw on its way to privatization.

Polish entrepreneurs—and even state-run businesses—have shown an uncanny ability to adjust quickly to free-market conditions and give consumers products they want. It's this flexibility, and the government's adherence to economic reforms, that make Poland the first country in Eastern Europe to emerge from severe post-communist recession.

Largely without the help of foreign investors, the Poles last year boosted industrial production by 4 percent (it plummeted 24 percent in 1990). Inflation is on a downward trend. Still high at a targeted 32 percent for this year, it is a lot better than three years ago, when it galloped along at nearly 600 percent.

The private sector, meanwhile, has advanced beyond the stage of sidewalk kiosks and hot dog stands, although there are still plenty of those. More than half of working Poles now have jobs in the private sector, a strong incentive for them to make sure capitalism succeeds.

As far as private enterprise goes, "this country is more advanced than any in the region," says Henryk Szlajfer of the Polish Institute of International Affairs.

But like everyday life in Poland, in which BMWs speed past fields still plowed by horses, the economic and political scene is a dichotomy of positive and negative trends.

Reformers trying to move the country forward are often undermined by those who yearn for the way things were.

As one longtime observer of the country remarks, "Poland is striding boldly forward on a banana peel."

Economic growth, for instance, is highly uneven. Blossoming cities like Warsaw, Poznan, and Krakow are blessed with unemployment rates of 5 percent to 9 percent, while agricultural regions and one-industry towns suffer jobless rates of 20 percent and higher. A severe housing shortage prevents movement of labor from depressed areas to prosperous ones.

The story of contrasts repeats itself in the political arena. For the first time since the demise of communism four years ago, Poland has enjoyed a small degree of political stability, personified in Prime Minister Hanna Suchocka (pronounced Su-HOTS-ka).

Appointed last July, she enjoys the confidence of more than 75 percent of the population, according to opinion polls.

But her job is not easy. She's juggling a minority, multiparty coalition government and is up against a fractious Sejm (parliament) consisting of more than 20 parties. Still, Prime Minister Suchocka has been able to withstand two severe labor strikes, and by relying on compromise, has pushed through the Sejm a much-needed "small constitution" that defines the balance of power in government, an austerity budget, and a long-awaited mass privatization plan.

In a Monitor interview this month, Suchocka said that Poland has turned the corner, but described the overall situation as "very delicate." Populist pressure is being exerted on the government, she warned, and "one false move may make us roll back."

That "false move" may be the Solidarity trade union's push for a vote of no confidence in the government, set to be debated in the Sejm May 27. The union is demanding higher wages for teachers and health workers, but the government says there is simply no money in the budget for such increases.

Anything could happen in the Sejm. The prime minister could fall, be asked to lead a caretaker government until early elections are called, or survive the test. Although observers rule out a return to communist days, they warn that a new government could turn protectionist or pursue an inflationary monetary policy to meet higher wage demands.

Attacking budget cuts

The federal budget—set under an agreement with the International Monetary Fund—has been a favorite target for legislators. In April, the Sejm protected an increase in benefits for pensioners, undermining the budget. The farmer parties, meanwhile, are clamoring for minimum prices for agriculture goods. One recently quit the ruling coalition over the issue.

In Poland, however, "one has to make a distinction between daily events and the fundamentals," comments Ian Hume, director of the World Bank in Warsaw. Day-to-day politics is a very rough-and-tumble affair, but "the fundamentals are strong in Poland," Mr. Hume says with conviction. "The reforms are working."

Hume praises the Poles for "broadly maintaining" the painful macroeconomic reforms launched by then Finance Minister Leszek Balcerowicz in January 1990. These policies called for fiscal, monetary, and wage discipline, a task made slightly easier by the decision of the Paris Club of creditor nations to write off 50 percent of Poland's $32 billion debt.

The country is meanwhile introducing Western taxation methods, including a personal income tax and a value-added tax. Free trade, pricing, and market forces also have solid footing in Poland, with about 80 percent of the economy running on market prices.

Although Warsaw dragged its feet in setting up a plan for mass privatization of state industry, other methods have enabled 1,500 state enterprises to be privatized since 1989. Including new business start-ups, the private sector accounts for nearly half of the country's gross domestic product, which grew by an estimated 0.5 percent to 2 percent last year.

A staggering number of state concerns, more than 6,000, remain to be privatized. But because much of the state sector appears to be restructuring, improving products, and redirecting exports westward, economists are not as discouraged about this as they could be.

Meanwhile, Poland has been able to reorient its trade so 80 percent now flows to Western Europe.

But all of this restructuring and reorientation has caused massive upheaval in Polish society. In March, 2.6 million Poles were unemployed (14.2 percent) and the forecast is for 3 million by year's end. According to an April poll by the CBOS Public Opinion Research Center, about one-third of Poles consider themselves near or below the poverty line.

The gap between rich and poor is still growing in Poland and wages are not keeping up with inflation. "It's very tough on people in the working ranks," Hume admits. Most observers expect more protests and strikes this year, although they do not believe it will come to violent unrest.

'Little patience'

The prime minister sees hardship experienced by many Poles as the most likely threat to economic reform.

"People don't have enough patience and they still have this old way of thinking from the communist era, namely, that the state provides for social security and provides the right to employment," she says. "Certain parties are inspired by this old way of thinking and they want to play this card" by calling for early elections—which Suchocka says would be a diversion from economic reforms.

The Suchocka government has tried to address popular frustrations by concentrating the state's limited funds on especially depressed areas, setting up tax havens there, and allowing unemployment benefits to run longer in those regions. Medical care is still government-funded, although patients must partially pay for medicine. Meanwhile, the mass privatization plan is intended to share some of the assets left over from communist rule with the population.

Andrzej Wroblewski, editor of the banking journal Gazeta Bankowa, worries the government may go too far in trying to satisfy Poland's newly poor. The government, he warns, cannot afford to be a "good uncle" to everyone. "However cruel it may be, you must reward those who are pulling our economy ahead more than those who are pulling out."

Article 18   *The World & I*, May 1993

Communism's Staying Power in Romania

Mike Maturo

Free-lance writer Mike Maturo became interested in eastern Europe while teaching English in Hungary in 1989–1990. His most recent trip to Romania was during the winter of 1992–93.

In the old days we had money, bad politics, and nothing to buy," mused a pensioner. "We still have bad politics and each day less money to live. My vote was for nothing," he added.

Optimism, Romanian-style, challenges the accepted definition. Annual inflation, at 200 percent, erodes incomes and confidence. Sharp ethnic tensions, regional disunity, and falling industrial production provide Romanians a skewed view of the future. Since the bloody overthrow of communist dictator Nicolae Ceausescu in December 1989, demand for reform continues to threaten the old communist bosses. Yet inexperience in electoral politics and ineffective oppositions provide former communists a win by default, highlighted by the 1992 presidential reelection of Ion Iliescu. Romania remains stuck in transition, despite an economic tailspin and the democratic means to chart a new course.

Fiery campaign speeches regarding the return of former Romanian lands led many to vote with a nationalist spirit. Glorifying the image of a greater Romania, nationalists charged emotions about Russian Moldava and the Bukovina region of the Ukraine, seized during World War II. Two ultranationalist parties launched virulent attacks against the Hungarian minority in Transylvania, fanning old hatreds to split the electorate along ethnic lines. Some parties warned of the consequences of selling out to the West—portrayed as an economic occupation—through privatization of the major industries.

Incumbent candidate Iliescu—former communist and member of the National Salvation Front (NSF)—equated quick economic reforms with chaos. The Democratic Convention's candidate,

Emil Constantinescu—an outsider with no communist ties—proposed sweeping economic changes. The Iliescu victory proved the country's fear to speed up the pace of economic reform.

Yet peasant loyalty was the main force behind the Iliescu victory. During his first two years as president, from 1990–92, Iliescu deeded land to the peasants—40 percent of the population—appealing to their historic concern. That, along with promises to slow the pace of reform, secured him 64 percent of the final presidential vote and the NSF 28 percent of the seats in Parliament. An alliance with the nationalist parties in Parliament gives the political Right control.

Oppositionists accuse the state-run television of running a propaganda campaign. According to Petru Litiu of the opposition Democratic Convention Party (DCP), "The apparatus of the communist regime is still very much alive. The ultranationalists and the NSF preside over a professional system of disinformation."

A 31-year-old psychiatrist from the southwest Banat region, disappointed but not surprised at the election outcome, echoed similar comments about the influence of television, explaining, "As long as the mass media and TV are state controlled, the majority will continue to vote in the old communists. A newspaper is an expensive luxury and due to lack of transportation, often difficult to receive. Objective thinking exists only for those with access and money to afford it. Besides, in 1990 the government gave the peasants the only thing they care for, land."

Romania's struggle for political identity comes after a history of control in varying degrees by the Turks, Austrians, Hungarians, and Germans. The departure of the Turks in the 1880s led to a monarchy until the Second World War.

From 1945 until 1989, a hard-line communist regime ruled, persecuting any who dared to criticize, the end result being a country without national, political, or social cohesion. The 85 parties involved in the last election underscore the fragmen-

tation within Romania. Consensus thinking, involving compromise, never materialized between enough of the parties to form an effective opposition.

POINTS OF VIEW

Timisoara, surrounded by farmland on the country's warm southwest plains, symbolizes and lends its name to a continuing anticommunist movement. Memorials to protesters killed in the 1989 revolt and a large Romanian Orthodox church stand at one end of the broad pedestrian boulevard, while at the other stands the Hotel Timisoara, regional headquarters for Iliescu's party. A proposed amendment to the constitution, called "Optimisoara," which would have banned all former communists from participating in politics, including Ion Iliescu, enjoys the support of those who have not forgotten the communist legacy.

The first open demonstrations against communist dictatorship began in Timisoara on December 22, 1989. Iliescu, then the deputy of this southwest region, the Banat, gave the orders to kill the demonstrators. Supporters of Optimisoara view Iliescu as a murderer. The recent pardons by Iliescu for those security force members involved in the 1989 deaths of the Timisoara demonstrators only exacerbated their feelings.

One university student, a supporter of Optimisoara, commented, "The former communists play the nationalist theme, focusing attention on hatreds toward Hungarians, Germans, Jews, and even Americans. The real issue is the economy. I can't stand the thought of four more years of Iliescu."

While most Romanians bristle at references to past subjugation by Germans or Hungarians, Timisoarans acknowledge the positive imprints they left. Citizens of Timisoara pride themselves on their progressive attitudes, clean streets, sound infrastructure, and university—often crediting their former rulers for the school.

Yet Timisoara strains to maintain order during these times of economic du-

PHOTOGRAPHS BY MIKE MATURO

■ *Bucharest student:* One of many who feels that Iliescu bought the election by giving land to the peasants—some 40 percent of the population.

ress. Outside the train station men urinate on the street and fistfights occasionally break out among drunks. Lines of black-market money changers form every day outside Timisoara's Intercontinental Hotel, seeking Westerners for hard currency exchanges. Unseen a few years ago, this behavior gains acceptance as unemployment and inflation take their toll.

Several hundred kilometers east of Timisoara lies Romania's second-largest city, Brasov. Large, gray blockhouses set against towering snow-covered mountains create a paradoxical backdrop. A 25-year-old woman working as a crane operator in a state factory commutes 30 kilometers from the Hungarian village of Apatca to her job. "My take-home pay is 22,000 Lei a month, not enough these days when a pair of shoes costs about 10,000 Lei and a train pass 3,000 Lei a month." Appalling conditions in the factory only add to her frustration. "We have shortages of raw materials and contracts these days. Complaints are not allowed by the *nomenklatura* [old communist apparatchiks], who just sit all day." Her ethnicity, however, swayed her vote. "But my vote went to Emil Constantinescu because he represented the coalition made up in part by the Hungarian minority. Iliescu doesn't like the Hungarian minority and fears Transylvania's return to Hungary."

Lagging industrial production, only 40–60 percent of capacity, allows Brasov's citizens the convenience of electricity all day. But should industrial production increase to a nominal capacity of 80 percent, priority would be given to the factories. Woefully mismanaged, the important industrial sector remains firmly controlled by the nomenklatura.

Romania's inexperience with electoral politics and ineffective oppositions provided former communists a win by default.

Another 25-year-old Brasov factory employee, a mechanic, voiced similar remarks. "There are no orders for work, no materials for production. While others become unemployed, the bureaucrats keep their jobs. Iliescu won due to support from Moldavia, the military, and the nomenklatura."

On his way to the university at Bucharest, a 22-year-old student explained his political views. "The Iliescu victory was due in large part to the peasant support. Romania's inexperience in voting and engaging in politics led to the results. We need new people, not those from the past like Iliescu. The ultranationalist parties are embarrassments, nothing more than barking dogs." His views on a market economy held a twist. "Many Romanians now travel to Turkey to buy products cheaply and they sell them at higher prices here. Rumor has it the majority of prostitutes in Istanbul these days are Romanians."

At the Bessarabia End station in Bucharest, rickety mass transportation picks up the passengers. Old buses, newly painted with Pepsi ads, belch out clouds of diesel fumes. Dented trolley cars, many sporting American cigarette logos, squeak and sway down the tracks.

In the center, the enormous palace begun during the Ceausescu years stands at the head of a broad boulevard lined on both sides by government ministry offices and apartments, some still under various stages of construction. Mazes of block housing, separated by garbage-strewn streets, surround the palace. Bullet-scarred buildings mark the areas of intense fighting during the 1989 revolt.

Near the university, two memorials pay tribute to those killed during the December '89 revolt and also during the miners' riots. Following his first May 1990 nomination, Iliescu brought the country's coal miners here four times to violently quell demonstrations and sack the opposition headquarters, once publicly thanking them on television.

Along the sidewalk, close to the Bucharest Intercontinental Hotel, black-market money changers mutter "dollars, deutsche marks," to all foreign-looking pedestrians. Black-market rates for the dollar of 700Lei:$1 are nearly double the bank rate of 446Lei:$1. Taxi drivers quote fares in Western currencies at the black-market rates, preferring strong Western money. Foreigners purchasing train tickets to destinations outside Romania must pay in dollars or deutsche marks. State-run hotels charge Westerners four times the normal rate, often quoting the price in dollars and refusing to accept Romanian currency.

Throughout the city, hundreds of small private shops have sprung up, like Romanian-style 7-11s, selling anything from shampoo to beer. What the government won't encourage, the black market will finance. About 30,000 privately owned businesses now operate in Romania, both foreign and domestic, employing about three million people. Products from Turkey, relatively inexpensive, earn

PHOTOGRAPHS BY MIKE MATURO

■ *Riot memorial:* **Remembering those killed when Iliescu brought miners to Bucharest to quell demonstrations against him.**

pathetic with communist principles. Though many Hungarians voted for the opposition Democratic Convention, it was not due to their politics. Most Hungarians can't accept Iliescu's deeds [and] personality, and still remember the 1990 ethnic riots in Tirgu Mures. They didn't vote against his programs but against the man himself."

> *Retaining former communists in high political positions ensures no reforms in the infrastructure.*

In the Transylvanian city of Cluj-Napoca, the mayoral election of Gheorge Funar, leader of the ultranationalist Party of Romanian Unity, further divided the ethnic communities. Another former communist who has been riding the nationalist wave, Funar made the most of old ethnic hatreds and secured 10 percent of the initial national vote for president as well. Taking aim at the Hungarian minority in Transylvania, he fanned fears of a plot to return the region to Hungary. Two sisters, students at the university at Cluj-Napoca, condemned the stirring of hatred. "Funar has changed the names of some streets, from Hungarian to Romanian, and has placed an insulting tablet under the statue of the Hungarian King Matthias, provoking demonstrations by Hungarians and Romanians alike."

A cooperative farmer from Mara Mures, a northern town, spoke strongly against all former communists, but in support of Funar, apparently unaware of his past. "The Democratic Convention would have given back the land to King Michael and sold off the country. Funar promised to clean up the country. Iliescu, a communist, will do nothing." About the Hungarians, he replied, "They are good neighbors—never make problems and have rights in Romania."

Still, most of the Hungarians speak bitterly of Funar and Iliescu. Amid the rising tide of nationalism, many Hungarians see their existence in a more precarious state. Rather than cower, some Hungarian villages have reasserted their ethnic alliances. In the small village of Belin/Bolon, the Hungarians there recently erected a memorial to their World War II liberation from Romania (from

a modest profit after a markup. Bucharest residents, still resentful of their occupation by the Turks for centuries, now nonetheless travel to Turkey on such business.

TRANSYLVANIA'S MINORITY

Some 250 kilometers to the northwest of Bucharest, beside the foothills of the Carpathian Mountains, lies the town of Tirgu Secuiesc. About 95 percent ethnic Hungarian, it typifies many towns in eastern Transylvania, an isolated area some 400 kilometers east of the Hungarian border. Like all Hungarian villages in Romania, the town's signpost features the Hungarian name, Kezdivarsehely, underneath Tirgu Secuiesc. A statue of Gabor Aron, a Hungarian hero of the 1848 uprising against the Austrians, stands in the center. Private shops and

kiosks feature a variety of expensive Western products, and a Hungarian newspaper, the *Szekely Press*, operates in defiance of the existing government. Easy targets for the Romanian ultranationalist parties, communities like these bore the brunt of vicious speeches during the September campaigns.

In a housing project just outside the center, a 47-year-old ethnic Hungarian lawyer explained his vote for Iliescu. "Iliescu has as much experience in politics as everyone in the opposition put together and has a social program for the whole country, whereas the opposition had no realistic ideas. Though Iliescu surely wants a return to communism, the next four years aren't enough time." Discussing the ethnic problems of Transylvania, he replied, "The vast majority of the Hungarian minority are left-wing or at least sym-

PHOTOGRAPHS BY MIKE MATURO

■ *Bullet-scarred building:* **The disposal of the last dictator is a hot topic of discussion these days among Romanians weary of a corrupt and ineffectual government.**

1941–45, when Hungary seized Transylvania), placing it in front of their church.

Romanians, generally quite sensitive about the territorial questions both past and present, view Transylvania's status prudently. Fought over for centuries by the Hungarians and Romanians, Transylvania's contested history keeps the ethnic tensions simmering, especially after changing hands three times this century. The many Romanians resettled there during the Ceausescu years as part of an effort to dilute the Hungarian population remain particularly uneasy.

Fears of losing Transylvania to Hungary have been justified by calls for autonomy by the ethnic Hungarians in Romania and by Hungarian politicians in Budapest. The Budapest government recently promoted autonomy status for its minorities outside the country's borders, the bulk of whom (some 2.2 million) reside in Transylvania. Prime Minister Jozsef Antall of Hungary proclaims himself leader of all Hungarians. Another right-wing Hungarian politician, Istvan Csurka, advocates expanding Hungarian living space. These comments not only incense the Romanians, but also draw more negative attention to Transylvania's Hungarian minority.

> *Because of a recent misappropriated $1.46 billion loan, the IMF has halted further financing to Romania.*

The Romanian government, for its part, mandates special requirements for those Hungarians wishing to visit their families in Transylvania. At the Romanian consulate in Budapest a notice stipulates special conditions for Hungarians traveling to Transylvania. Effective October 11, 1991, Hungarians must spend $15 U.S. per day and have the bank receipts to prove it. Clinging to an old communist custom, Romania still charges $35 U.S. for a visa, payable only in dollars.

RULE BY CORRUPTION

Romania has joined the ranks of former communist nations that have voted party members into power. Yet Romania's future hinges partly on the noncommunist international community. Part of a recent $1.46 billion loan from the IMF to stimulate private ownership within industry supposedly went to some failing factories. Where most of the loan has gone remains a mystery, prompting the IMF to halt further financing.

Rejection by the United States of most favored nation status related directly to the reelection of Ion Iliescu. Conditions laid prior to the September elections for MFN stated that Romania would only have to reduce its federal budget by $11 million to receive favored status. But the U.S. Congress, expecting an opposition victory, changed its mind following Romania's election results.

Western organizations and governments unwittingly treat Romanian leaders as statesmen. Like the IMF, which witnessed the disappearance of $1.46 billion, many Westerners cannot fathom the depth of corruption and ignorance in Romania. The country's present leaders—communist thugs in the past—still practice the same policies that brought them to prominence during communist times, hence their success. Retaining former communists in high political positions ensures no reforms in the infrastructure. Democracy in an economically backward, peasant-based country does not produce logical results, as proven by the last election.

Until Romania focuses on reforming the economy, it will remain another backward nation, plagued by historical Balkan problems. As the country sinks to new lows, the Iliescu government faces an increasingly unhappy population and a suspicious West. Romania's disposal of its last dictator remains a hot topic of discussion these days, both as a memory and a viable alternative to elections. Should living standards continue deteriorating at their present pace, the next four years will be too long for some to wait.

Article 19   *Current History*, November 1993

Why Yugoslavia Fell Apart

The disintegration of Yugoslavia has led to a reevaluation of the idea that a multi-ethnic state is a viable entity. The factors that led to the dismantling of such a state in Yugoslavia are many and are open to revision, but one of the lessons that can be drawn from the process is clear: "The wars in the former Yugoslavia [show] that the principles and practices that provided a stable framework for international security in the era of the cold war are no longer sufficient to preserve the peace."

Steven L. Burg

Steven L. Burg is associate professor of politics at Brandeis University. This article is part of a larger project, National- ism and Democracy in Post-Communist Europe: Challenges to American Foreign Policy, *supported by The Twentieth Century Fund.*

The disintegration of the Yugoslav fed- eration and its descent into atavistic in- terethnic violence cannot be attributed to any single factor. Internal political con- flicts in the 1980s, and the effort by Ser- bian leader Slobodan Milosevic to mobilize Serb nationalism on behalf of a strengthened federation, destroyed the cohesion of the country's regional Com- munist leaderships and weakened their control over society. Deteriorating eco- nomic conditions—especially plummet- ing living standards—eroded the benefits of sustaining the Yugoslav state and stimulated the rise of mass nation- alisms and interethnic hostilities. The conflicting nationalist aspirations of the Yugoslav peoples and their leaders' ef- forts to maximize power, led to conflict over the control of disputed territories.

The end of the cold war left both So- viet and Western policymakers believing that Yugoslavia no longer held the stra- tegic significance, or merited the atten- tion, it had enjoyed in a world divided between East and West. This mistaken belief, as well as the attention com- manded by the Persian Gulf War, led to neglect of the brewing crisis in Yugosla- via until the cost of meaningful action had risen beyond the point acceptable to Western policymakers and their publics. Even when less costly but still effective action remained possible, Western poli- cymakers were deterred from acting by the fear that the dissolution of Yugosla- via, even if achieved through peaceful

negotiation, would hasten the disinte- gration of the Soviet Union.

The fall of Yugoslavia thus can be at- tributed to internal conflict and the in- ternational community's failure to respond to the crisis effectively. How- ever, forceful action by either Yugoslav leaders or American and European ad- ministrations would have required inno- vative thinking about some of the most basic principles of the international sys- tem and the post–cold war security framework in the Euro-Atlantic commu- nity. No political leadership—Yugoslav, American, or European—was then ready to confront these tasks. The only positive outcome of the Yugoslav debacle, there- fore, may be the stimulus it has provided for such new thinking.

THE DOMESTIC CONTEXT OF DISINTEGRATION

By the mid-1970s, Yugoslavia had be- come a highly decentralized federation in which the constituent republics domi- nated the central government. Regional leaderships carefully protected the inter- ests of their territorial constituencies at the expense of other regions and the fed- eration. The regional leaders shared a common interest in preserving the Com- munist political order that shielded them from responsibility and popular ac- countability but little else. Ethnic and political integration processes had only modest impact. The proportion of the population that declared itself to be "Yu- goslav" rather than an ethnic identity in the national census, for example, in- creased from 1.3 percent in 1971 to 5.4 percent in 1981. For the vast majority of the population, distinct ethnic or na- tional identities continued to command emotional loyalties and provide the most powerful bases for political mobiliza- tion.

The ethnically defined territorial structures of the Yugoslav system rein- forced the political strength of ethnic identities and intensified political divi- sions in the leadership. Federal political bodies, including the collective state presidency and the Communist party leadership, were composed of repre- sentatives of the republics and prov- inces, selected by the regional leaderships. Individual positions in these bodies, including the country's prime ministership and presidency, ro- tated among the regions according to an explicit agreement. Only the army re- mained a unified, all-Yugoslav, organiza- tion.

While the political regions of Yugosla- via were defined in ethnic terms, in most cases they were not ethnically homoge- neous. With the exception of Slovenia, their leaderships could not mobilize eth- nic nationalism in support of political ambition or fulfill the nationalist aspira- tions of their ethnic majorities without alienating substantial minority popula- tions and raising the prospect of severe ethnic conflict. The vast majority of eth- nic Slovenes were concentrated in Slovenia and made up the majority of the population. Efforts by ethnically Slo- vene regional leaders to advance Slo- vene national-cultural interests and to strengthen Slovenian autonomy effec- tively encompassed all Slovenes. At the same time, these efforts neither threat- ened the status of a large minority inside Slovenia nor challenged the power of any other group over its own republic by encouraging a large Slovene minority population outside the republic to de- mand autonomy.

In Croatia, however, Serbs constituted a large minority or even a majority of the population in several areas of the re- public. Croat leaders thus could not pur- sue exclusionary nationalist ambitions inside the Croatian state without risking the alienation of a large and territorially compact Serb minority that enjoyed strong links to Serbs outside the republic's borders. At the same time, a nationalistic Croatian government would stimulate unrest among the large, territorially compact population of ethnic Croats in adjacent areas of neighboring Bosnia and Herzegovina.

No single group could claim the overall majority in Bosnia and Herzegovina. While Muslims constituted the largest group (about 44 percent of the population in the 1991 census), they did not represent a majority. Serbs (over 31 percent) and Croats (more than 17 percent) constituted large minorities in the republic's population. In many areas of Bosnia there was no single ethnic majority. In the larger cities, those who took the nonethnic "Yugoslav" identity constituted from 20 to 25 percent of the population. Thus the pattern of ethnic settlement in Bosnia was highly complex. No ethnic leadership could advance exclusionary nationalist ambitions on behalf of its ethnic constituency without alienating vast portions of the popu-

lation—including substantial numbers of its own group who had adopted the multiethnic civic culture associated with "Yugoslavism."

By the mid-1980s, the collective leaderships of the country were divided between those who supported a looser association among the regions and those who continued to support a strengthened federal government. This division was reinforced by differences over the scope and pace of further economic and political reform. The Yugoslav economy had gone into sharp decline in the 1980s. Living standards fell and regional economic differences widened. In the 1960s and 1970s, for example, per capita national income in Slovenia had been about six times that in Kosovo province and about three times that in Macedonia and Bosnia and Herzegovina. Income in Croatia had been about four times that in Kosovo and about twice that in Macedonia and Bosnia. By 1988, income in Slovenia was more than eight times that in Kosovo and income in Croatia was approximately five times higher. The frictions introduced by these growing inequalities were intensified by the ethnic

differences between the regions, and especially by the increasingly violent conflict between Serbs and ethnic Albanians in Kosovo.

KOSOVO AND MILOSEVIC

The 1980s began with the outbreak of nationalist demonstrations by the Albanian people in Kosovo. Kosovo is viewed by Serbs as the "cradle" of their nation, but is populated by a demographically robust majority (over 80 percent in 1991) of ethnic Albanians. The demonstrations were initially suppressed by military force. But the decade saw almost continuous and often violent confrontations in the province between Serbs and Albanians. The Serbian leadership in Belgrade responded with increasingly repressive measures against the Albanians and their indigenous leaders.

Violence against Serbs in Kosovo contributed to the growth of nationalist sentiment among Serbs in Serbia and the other regions of Yugoslavia. But the movement received its most important support from Serbian Communist party President Slobodan Milosevic. Motivated at least in part by genuine personal outrage over the treatment of Serbs in Kosovo and by the failure of other Serbian leaders to defend them, Milosevic ousted a key proponent of interethnic accommodation with the Albanians of Kosovo and seized control of the Serbian leadership in September 1987. He then escalated his public defense of Serbian ethnic and political interests. He exploited the situation in Kosovo to further stimulate popular nationalism among Serbs all across Yugoslavia, and used that nationalism as leverage against the leaders of other republics and provinces. The intensity of popular emotions among Serbs was demonstrated by a series of large-scale, openly nationalist demonstrations across Vojvodina, Serbia, and Montenegro in the fall of 1988, and by a mass gathering of Serbs in Kosovo in June 1989.

The growing force of Serbian nationalism allowed Milosevic to oust independent leaders in Vojvodina and Montenegro, replacing them with more subservient ones, and to intensify repressive measures against the Albanians of Kosovo while placing that province, heretofore a relatively autonomous territory within the Serbian republic, under direct rule from Belgrade. These changes gave Milosevic effective control over four of the eight regional leaderships represented in the collective state presidency, the most authoritative executive

THE NEW BALKAN STATES

- ✪ National capitals
- ✪ Yugoslav republic capitals
- ◉ Yugoslav autonomous regions capitals
- • Other cities

0   25   50   75   100 Miles

© Current History, Inc.

body in the country. However, the disproportionate Serbian influence contributed to the de-legitimation of central authority and accelerated the political dissolution of the country.

Milosevic represented a powerful synthesis of Serbian nationalism, political conservatism, support for centralism, and resistance to meaningful economic reform. Developments in Serbia under his leadership stood in stark contrast to those in Slovenia, where the growth of popular nationalism took the form of demands for political democracy and rapid economic reform, the pluralization of group activity in the republic, and support for further confederalization of the Yugoslav regime. In Serbia the republic remained under the control of the unreformed Communist party. The Serbian Communists renamed themselves the Socialist party and co-opted some formerly dissident intellectuals into their leadership, but remained under Milosevic's control. The Slovenian Communist leadership, in contrast, cooperated with emergent social and political forces in their republic to move rapidly toward a more pluralistic order. The Slovenian leadership, rather than seeing organized popular pressure only as a threat, also viewed it as an important and necessary asset in its struggle for economic and political reform in Belgrade.

THE DISINTEGRATION BEGINS

Relations between Serbia and Slovenia began to grow tense at both the elite and mass levels. In October 1988 the Slovenian representative to the central party presidium resigned because of increasingly acrimonious relations with Milosevic. In February 1989 the use of federal militia to suppress a general strike in Kosovo raised widespread concern among Slovenes that, if such force could be used against more than 1 million Albanians, it could also be used against the 2 million Slovenes. This fear was not entirely unfounded. A year earlier an independent Slovenian journal, *Mladina*, revealed that federal Yugoslav military leaders had met to discuss emergency plans for the takeover of the republic.

After the suppression of the strike, the president of the Slovenian Communist party, Milan Kucan, publicly condemned the repression in Kosovo. This marked the beginning of open conflict between the Ljubljana and Belgrade leaderships—the former having embarked on a secessionist strategy calling for internal democratization, and the latter having begun an effort to recentralize power and authority in the entire country while constructing a new, nationalist authoritarian regime in Serbia.

The escalation of conflict in Yugoslavia reached crisis proportions in the fall of 1989. The Slovenian leadership adopted constitutional amendments in September asserting the economic and political sovereignty of the republic, denying the right of the federation to intervene, and claiming the right to secede. In December it blocked an attempt by Serbian nationalists supported by Milosevic to pressure the Slovenian government into abandoning its strategy by bringing Serbs to Ljubljana for a mass demonstration. Milosevic responded to Slovene resistance by breaking off economic relations between the two republics. Democratic activist groups in Slovenia pressed for a complete break with Serbia. That move came the following month, at the January 1990 extraordinary congress of the ruling League of Communists of Yugoslavia.

Originally conceived by Milosevic and the Serbian leadership as a means of imposing greater central authority, the congress instead became the occasion for the collapse of the old regime. Unwilling and politically unable to support a draft platform calling for greater party unity, the Slovenian delegation walked out of the congress. The military and other regional party delegations, unwilling to surrender their own independence, refused to continue the congress. The congress then adjourned indefinitely, marking the de facto breakup of the nationwide party organization. This left each of the republic party organizations to respond independently to conditions in its own region. It also left the military (the Yugoslav People's Army, or JNA) the only organization still committed to, and dependent on, the continued survival of the federation.

The electoral victories of independence-oriented coalitions in Slovenia and Croatia in the spring of 1990, and the former Communists' victory in Serbia in December of that year, deepened political divisions among the regional leaderships of the Yugoslav federation. At the same time, political support for maintaining the federation evaporated almost completely. Federal Prime Minister Ante Markovic's attempt to create a countrywide political party committed to preserving the federation, for example, generated little support. And his effort to accelerate the holding of free elections for the federal parliament as a means of democratizing and legitimizing the federation failed completely.

In August 1990, Serbs in the central Dalmatian region of Croatia began an open insurrection against the Zagreb government. Already fearful of the nationalist campaign themes of the governing Croatian Democratic Community, and mindful of the violently anti-Serb character of the most recent episodes of extreme Croatian nationalism, the Serbs of Dalmatia viewed the government's effort to disarm ethnically Serb local police forces and replace them with special Croatian police units as a portent of further repression to come.

The Dalmatian Serbs declared their intention to remain part of a common Yugoslav state or, alternatively, to become an independent Serb republic. Their uprising should have been a clear warning to all concerned: the republic borders established by the Communist regime in the postwar period were extremely vulnerable to challenges from ethnic communities that did not share the identity on which new, nationalist post-Communist governments sought to legitimate themselves. Such communities were alienated or even threatened by the nationalistic legitimation of these new governments. If existing borders were to be preserved, substantial political guarantees had to be provided for the ethnic minority enclaves in the republics.

The overwhelming declaration of support for a sovereign and independent state by 88 percent of the Slovenian electorate in a December 23, 1990, referendum made the republic's secession look inevitable. The decision by Yugoslav leaders in February 1991 to begin determining how to divide the country's assets among the regions suggested still more clearly that the breakup of the country was at hand. But the threat by the Yugoslav minister of defense in December to use force to prevent Slovenia or Croatia from seceding signaled the possibility that a breakup of Yugoslavia would not be peaceful.

The most explosive conflict in Yugoslavia has been between the political aspirations of Croats and Serbs, whose historical and imagined national homelands and claims to sovereignty overlap. This is the conflict that destabilized the interwar regime and threatened to destabilize the Communist government in 1971. In December of that year, the Yugoslav leader, Josip Broz Tito, used the military to suppress the mass nationalist movement and to purge the leadership in Croatia. As a result, in the 1980s Croatian Communist leaders remained more

The Breakup of Yugoslavia

1990

Jan. 22—The Communist party votes to allow other parties to compete in a new system of "political pluralism."

Feb. 5—Slobodan Milosevic, president of the republic of Serbia, says he will send troops to take control of Kosovo, a province where ethnic violence has entered its 2d week.

April 8—The republic of Slovenia holds parliamentary elections—the 1st free elections since World War II.

April 22—The 1st free elections in more than 50 years are held in the republic of Croatia.

July 5—The parliament of the Serbian republic suspends the autonomous government of the Kosovo region. On July 2, ethnic Albanian members of the Kosovo legislature declared the region a separate territory within the Yugoslav federation.

July 6—The state president orders Slovenia's parliament to rescind its July 2 declaration that the republic's laws take precedence over those of the Yugoslav federation.

Sept. 3—In Kosovo, more than 100,000 ethnic Albanians strike, closing factories, offices, stores, and schools to protest Serbian takeovers of formerly Albanian-controlled enterprises and the dismissal of Albanian workers.

Sept. 13—The Yugoslav press agency reports that ethnic Albanian members of the dissolved parliament of Kosovo have adopted an alternative constitution and have voted to extend the mandate of parliament until new elections are held. The Serbian government has called the alternative constitution illegal.

Nov. 11—The republic of Macedonia holds its 1st free elections since 1945.

Nov. 18—Parliamentary elections are held in the republic of Bosnia and Herzegovina.

Dec. 9—The 1st free parliamentary elections in Serbia since 1938 are held.

1991

Feb. 20—The Slovenian parliament approves laws allowing the republic to take over defense, banking, and other government functions from the central Yugoslav government; the parliament also approves a resolution to divide Yugoslavia into two separate states; Slovenia has warned that it will secede if the other republics do not approve the plan.

Feb. 21—The Croatian parliament adopts measures giving the republic government veto power over central government laws it considers threatening to the republic's sovereignty; the parliament also adopts resolutions that support the dissolution of the Yugoslav federation.

March 2—After reports of violent clashes between Serb villagers and Croatian security forces, Borisav Jovic, the leader of the collective presidency, orders federal army troops to the Croatian village of Pakrac.

March 16—Milosevic declares that he is refusing to recognize the authority of the collective presidency; with this act he effectively declares Serbia's secession from Yugoslavia.

March 17—Milosevic proclaims Krajina, an area in Croatia where 200,000 ethnic Serbs live, a "Serbian autonomous region."

June 25—The parliaments of Slovenia and Croatia pass declarations of independence. The federal parliament in Belgrade—the capital of Serbia as well as of Yugoslavia—asks the army to intervene to prevent the secessions.

June 27—Slovenian Defense Minister Janez Jansa says, "Slovenia is at war" with the federal government.

July 18—The federal presidency announces that it is ordering all federal army units to withdraw from Slovenia.

conservative than their Slovenian counterparts. More important, because Croatian leaders traced their origins to the anti-nationalist purges of the early 1970s, they enjoyed little popular legitimacy. With the breakup of the Yugoslav Communist party in January 1990 and the onset of competitive elections in the republics, they were decisively defeated by the Croatian Democratic Union, a nationalist coalition led by Franjo Tudjman. The CDU's electoral victory polarized relations between Croats and Serbs in that republic and set the stage for a renewed confrontation between Croat and Serb nationalisms.

THE BATTLE OVER THE ETHNIC MAP

By 1990, definition of the emerging post-Communist order became the object of open conflict among several competing, and even mutually contradictory, nationalist visions. The Serbian vision allowed for two fundamentally different outcomes: either the federation would be sufficiently strengthened to assure the protection of Serb populations everywhere in the country, or the dissolution of the federation would be accompanied by the redrawing of boundaries to incorporate Serb populations in a single, in-

Sept. 8—Results of yesterday's referendum in Macedonia show that about 75% of voters favor independence; ethnic Albanians boycotted the referendum.

Oct. 1—Heavy fighting in Croatia between Croatian militia and rebel Serbs (aided by the federal army) continues near the Adriatic port city of Dubrovnik.

1992

March 1—A majority of voters approve a referendum on independence in Bosnia; Serb citizens, who comprise 32% of Bosnia's population but control 60% of the territory, have threatened to secede if the referendum is passed.

March 25—Fighting between Serb militias—backed by the federal army—and Bosnian government troops begins.

April 5—After the Bosnian government refuses to rescind a call-up of the national guard, Serb guerrillas shell Sarajevo, the Bosnian capital.

April 27—Serbia and Montenegro announce the establishment of a new Yugoslavia composed of the 2 republics.

May 19—At a news conference in Washington, D.C., Haris Silajdzic, the foreign minister of Bosnia, says his country is being subjected to "ethnic cleansing" by Serb forces.

May 24—In an election in Kosovo termed illegal by Belgrade, ethnic Albanians vote overwhelmingly to secede from the rump Yugoslav state.

July 2—Croat nationalists living in Bosnia declare an independent state that includes almost one-third of the territory of Bosnia; Mate Boban, head of the 30,000-strong Croatian Defense Council militia, says the name of the new republic is Herzeg-Bosna.

Nov. 3—*The New York Times* reports the Serbian-dominated Yugoslav army has quit the siege of Dubrovnik,

Croatia, and has withdrawn its forces from the surrounding area.

1993

Jan. 22—Croatian army units attack Serb-held positions in Maslenica and the port city of Zadar; Ivan Milas, a Croatian vice president, says the attacks came after Serbs delayed returning the areas to Croatian control as called for in the January 1992 UN-sponsored cease-fire agreement; state radio in Belgrade says the self-declared Serbian Krajina Republic has declared war on Croatia.

April 7—The Security Council approves UN membership for Macedonia under the provisional name "the Former Yugoslav Republic of Macedonia" as a compromise with the Greek government; Greece has objected to the new country using the same name as Greece's northernmost province.

May 16—In the Bosnian town of Pale, Bosnian Serb leader Radovan Karadzic announces that in a 2-day referendum, at least 90% of Serb voters rejected the provisional peace plan put forward by UN mediator Cyrus Vance and EC mediatory Lord Owen; the plan called for a UN-monitored cease-fire; the establishment of a central government composed of 3 Muslims, 3 Croats, and 3 Serbs; the creation of 10 partially autonomous provinces with proportional representation of ethnic groups in the provincial governments; and the return of forcibly transferred property. Karadzic says the world should now recognize that a new state—Republika Srpska—exists in the Serb-controlled territory in Bosnia.

Aug. 28—The mainly Muslim Bosnian parliament votes 65 to 0 to reject a peace plan devised by the UN and the EC that would divide the country into 3 separate republics based on ethnicity; in the mountain town of Grude, the parliament of the self-declared Croat state approves the plan and officially declares the Croat republic of Herzeg-Bosna; the self-declared Bosnian Serb parliament also accepts the plan.

---

dependent Serb state. This did not preclude the accommodation of the Slovenian vision of an entirely independent Slovenian state, but it did contradict Croatian aspirations for an independent state defined by the borders inherited from the old regime.

Serb and Croat nationalist aspirations might both still have been accommodated by creating independent states that exercised sovereignty over their re-

spective ethnic territories. But such a solution would have required the redrawing of existing borders that would call into question the continued existence of Bosnia as a multinational state of Muslims, Serbs, and Croats. Moreover, any agreement openly negotiated by Serbia that legitimated claims to self-determination based on the current ethnic composition of local populations would strengthen the Albanian case for an in-

dependent Kosovo, and raise the prospect for Serbia of either giving up that province peacefully or having to escalate the level of repression.

The increasing autonomy of the republics and the growing interregional conflict stimulated fears among Serb nationalists that large portions of the Yugoslav Serb community might be "cut off" from Serbia. The repeated use of military force to suppress Albanian demonstrations in Kosovo in the 1980s, and changes in the Serbian constitution that revoked provincial autonomy, suggested that Milosevic and other Serb nationalists might take similar actions in retaliation for any effort to separate the Serb populations of either Croatia or Bosnia from Serbia. At the very least it suggested that any claim by Croats or Muslims to the right of national self-determination would lead to Serb demands for self-determination, and for the redrawing of internal borders to permit the consolidation of Serb-populated territories under the authority of a single Serbian national state.

Serbs, however, were not the only ethnic group in the former Yugoslavia that might exploit the redrawing of borders. Albanians in Kosovo had already declared their independence and adopted their own constitution in the summer and fall of 1990. Redrawing borders might lead them to claim several western counties of Macedonia where ethnic Albanians constituted the majority or a plurality of the local population. They might even lay claim to the bordering Serbian county of Presevo, where ethnic Albanians also constituted the majority. Radical nationalist elements in Kosovo had already called for the unification of all ethnically Albanian territories. Similarly, Muslim nationalists in Bosnia might lay claim to the several counties of the Sandzak region that lie across the Serbian-Montenegrin border in which Muslims make up the majority.

AN INEPT INTERNATIONAL RESPONSE

A narrow window of opportunity to negotiate a peaceful solution to the growing dispute among the republics and to address the demands raised by ethnic communities appeared to remain open until March 1991. The West's inaction in late 1990 and early 1991 can be partly attributed to preoccupation on the part of western European leaders with negotiations over European integration. Collective action through the European Community was further stymied by clear differences in perspective among the British, French, and Germans. United States policymakers, on the other hand, consciously chose to distance themselves from the issue. United States inaction may even have been due to a cynical calculation on the part of Secretary of State James Baker that this conflict should be left for the Europeans to handle, precisely because the difficulty of the issues and the internal divisions among them

assured that they would fail, thus reaffirming the need for American leadership in Europe.

As noted earlier, the attention of Western policymakers was also diverted by two other issues: the military effort to reverse the Iraqi invasion of Kuwait, and the continuing political crisis in the Soviet Union. Any effort to facilitate the breakup of Yugoslavia appeared to have been precluded by fear that it might create an undesirable precedent for the Soviet Union. As a result, the political responses of the United States and other Western states to events in both the Soviet Union and Yugoslavia ignored the fundamental commitments to human rights for which they had pressed in meetings of the Commission on Security and Cooperation in Europe (CSCE) for more than a decade. Yugoslav policy was shaped almost entirely by the desire to preserve the territorial integrity of the Soviet Union.

Western states remained firmly committed to the status quo in Yugoslavia. No effort was made to encourage Yugoslav leaders to hold the federation together by devising new political arrangements that addressed the special interests and concerns of the territorially compact communities of ethnic minorities in the republics. Even more important, in an unprecedented and ill-advised extension of the Helsinki principles of territorial integrity and the inviolability of state borders, the West extended its political support to the borders between the republics of the Yugoslav federation. Neither the United States nor its European partners acknowledged that the growing nationalism of the various peoples of Yugoslavia not only called into question the survival of the federation—they also raised doubts about the political viability of multiethnic republics. The same principle of self-determination that the Slovenes and Croats might use to justify their independence could also be used to justify Dalmatian Serbs' demands for separation from Croatia. Moreover, any reference to the principles of sovereignty and territorial integrity to defend the Croats' claims to Croatia could be used just as easily by Serbs in Belgrade to justify defending the integrity of the former Yugoslavia. International actors made no attempt, however, to confront these issues. They failed to address the growing probability that the Serbian leadership in Belgrade and its Serb allies in the military would use the JNA either to prevent the secession of Slovenia and Croatia or to detach Serb-populated territories of

Croatia and Bosnia and annex them to Serbia.

By taking a more comprehensive approach, the international community might have been able to mediate among the several contradictory values and goals of local actors. Extreme demands for the right to self-determination on the part of Serbs in Croatia and Bosnia might have been counterbalanced, for example, by Serbian concerns that adoption of the principle of the right to self-determination might lead to the loss of Kosovo. Croatian ambitions with respect to western Herzegovina might similarly have been moderated by the desire to hold on to the Krajina region.

Under these circumstances, it might have been possible to achieve an overall settlement based on trade-offs among the parties involved. But such an approach would have required the international community to place the peaceful settlement of conflicting demands for self-determination above the principle of territorial integrity of states. At the very least, it would have required the United States and the European Community to abandon their support for the borders of the republics as the basis for establishing new states within the boundaries of the former Yugoslavia. However, this approach stood the best chance of success before the cycle of interethnic violence had set in. By mid-1991 it already was too late.

THE LESSONS OF YUGOSLAVIA

The wars in the former Yugoslavia have made it clear that the principles and practices that provided a stable framework for international security in the era of the cold war are no longer sufficient to preserve the peace. The principles of state sovereignty, territorial integrity, human rights, and self-determination embedded in the United Nations Charter and other United Nations documents, and developed in detail in the documents of the CSCE, have proved contradictory, or at least subject to contradictory interpretation. Moreover, the mounting human tragedy in Bosnia has revealed the inadequacies of the decision-making principles, operational guidelines, and conflict-management capabilities of Euro-Atlantic institutions such as the CSCE, NATO, and the European Community, as well as the UN.

New diplomatic and political mechanisms must be developed to cope with demands for self-determination in ways that do not undermine the basic foundation of international stability—the system of sovereign states. The development of such mechanisms requires reconsideration of the meaning of self-determination in the contemporary era and the careful reconsideration of the indivisibility of state sovereignty. At the very least, it requires limiting the ability of states to use their claim to sovereignty to shield abuses from international inquiry. For any mechanisms to be effective, however, individual states and international organizations alike must become more proactive, undertaking preventive diplomatic and political efforts to solve interethnic and other conflicts before they threaten international peace.

International engagement in the Yugoslav crisis as early as 1990 would have remained futile if the Western states had continued to refuse to support the redrawing of borders as a possible path to a peacefully negotiated solution to the crisis. The declaration of independence by a territorially compact ethnic community, such as that of the Serbs in Croatia or any other group in Yugoslavia, could have been recognized as a legitimate demand for self-determination. By recognizing the equal rights of all peoples in the country to self-determination, international mediators might have been able to lead local actors toward mutual concessions. The key to such negotiations, however, lay in the recognition that international principles, and the rights derived from them, were equally applicable to all parties, as well as in a willingness to undertake the renegotiation of borders. This the international community failed to do.

Early insistence by outside powers on the democratic legitimation of existing borders might have encouraged greater concern for the protection of human rights and avoided the escalation of ethnic tensions in Croatia and Bosnia. The Communist order that held Yugoslavia together began to disintegrate as early as 1986. It entered into crisis in December 1989. This left sufficient opportunity for international actors to influence events. The importance in such a situation of clearly and forcefully articulating and enforcing the human rights standards to which states seeking recognition will be held cannot be overemphasized. By doing so international actors may affect popular perceptions and politics. In Yugoslavia, for example, the regional elections held in 1990 might have produced more moderate governments if the human rights standards of potential ruling parties had been at issue.

The existence of competing claims to territory complicated the Yugoslav crisis. But it does not by itself account for the magnitude of human destruction that has occurred. The extreme violence in Yugoslavia must also be attributed to the establishment of ethnically defined governments that failed to provide democratic safeguards for the human rights of minority communities. This reinforces the conclusion that if the international community is to facilitate the peaceful settlement of such conflicts elsewhere, it must devise the means to prevent ethnic domination and safeguard human rights. In short, the principles of sovereignty, territorial integrity, and national self-determination must be integrated into a single framework for determining the legitimacy of claims to political authority. And that framework must be based on the superiority of principles of human rights and democracy.

Credits

RUSSIA

Page 212 Article 1. © 1992 by Dissent.

Page 222 Article 2. Reprinted with permission from *Current History* magazine, October 1993. © 1993, Current History, Inc.

Page 227 Article 3. © 1993, Time Inc. Reprinted by permission.

Page 229 Article 4. © 1993, New Prospect. Reprinted by permission from The American Prospect, Spring 1993.

Page 235 Article 5. Reprinted with permission from Current History magazine, October 1993. © 1993, Current History, Inc.

Page 241 Article 6. From The World Today, August/September 1993. © 1993 by the Royal Institute of International Affairs.

Page 248 Article 7. © 1993, The Washington Post. Reprinted with permission.

EURASIAN REPUBLICS

Page 252 Article 8. Reprinted from the Harvard International Review, Spring 1993.

Page 255 Article 9. Reprinted from the Harvard International Review, Spring 1993.

Page 259 Article 10. Reprinted by permission from the Christian Science Monitor. © 1993 by The Christian Science Publishing Society. All rights reserved.

Page 263 Article 11. Reprinted by permission from the *Christian Science Monitor.* © 1993 by The Christian Science Publishing Society. All rights reserved.

CENTRAL AND EASTERN EUROPE

Page 265 Article 12. Reprinted with permission from *Current History* magazine, April 1993. © 1993, Current History, Inc.

Page 270 Article 13. Reprinted with permission from *Current History* magazine, November 1993. © 1993, Current History, Inc.

Page 275 Article 14. Reprinted with permission from *Current History* magazine, November 1993. © 1993, Current History, Inc.

Page 280 Article 15. © 1993 by The New York Times Company. Reprinted by permission.

Page 281 Article 16. From *The World Today,* April 1993. © 1993 by the Royal Institute of International Affairs.

Page 285 Article 17. Reprinted by permission from the *Christian Science Monitor.* © 1993 by The Christian Science Publishing Society. All rights reserved.

Page 287 Article 18. Reprinted from *The World & I,* August 1993, a publication of The Washington Times Corporation. © 1993.

Page 291 Article 19. Reprinted with permission from *Current History* magazine, November 1993. © 1993, Current History, Inc.

Glossary of Terms and Abbreviations

Anti-Party Group Nikita Khrushchev's opponents in the Soviet Communist Party's Politburo/Presidium who tried but failed to force his resignation as first secretary in June 1957.

Apparat The bureaucracy of the Soviet Communist Party. Workers in the bureaucracy were called *apparatchiki*.

Baltic Republics Estonia, Latvia, and Lithuania received independence recognition from the Soviet Union in September 1991.

Bolshevik The left wing of the Russian Social Democratic Party (RSDP); Bolshevik members of the RSDP believed in the necessity of the violent overthrow of the Czarist order to achieve change.

Bosnia-Herzegovina Civil War Following the 1992 independence of Bosnia-Herzegovina under the Muslim-led government in Sarajevo, the militia of the Bosnian-Serb minority attacked Sarajevo because they wanted their own independent state. The Serb forces succeeded in gaining about 70 percent of the Bosnian republic's territory from the government in Sarajevo. In an effort to end the conflict, in 1993 the UN proposed the Vance-Owen Peace Plan and later the Owen-Stoltenberg Plan—however, both plans were deemed unacceptable to the combatants and other countries that would have been involved in the implementation of either plan.

Brezhnev Doctrine A set of ideas attributed to Leonid Brezhnev, calling for collective intervention of Socialist countries to prevent counterrevolution and justifying the Soviet-led Warsaw Pact intervention in Czechoslovakia in August 1968.

Charter 77 Movement A group of Czechoslovak dissidents who criticized the human rights violations by the government in Prague in a document (charter) in January 1977 and who continued their criticism despite regime harassment and punishment of its members.

C.I.S. Commonwealth of Independent States, a name used to define the 11 republics that formed a loose confederation from the former Soviet Union. Four of the original 15 Soviet republics elected not to join the C.I.S.: Estonia, Latvia, Lithuania, and Georgia.

CMEA Council for Mutual Economic Assistance, established in January 1949 and consisted of Bulgaria, Czechoslovakia, East Germany, Hungary, Poland, Romania, and the Soviet Union. Its long-term objective was the economic integration of Soviet bloc countries. CMEA was dissolved in the early 1990s.

Cold War A sharp deterioration of Soviet–American relations immediately following the end of World War II because of a worldwide ideological and political rivalry that occasionally threatened armed conflict.

Collectivization The forced amalgamation under collective communal management of farms formerly owned privately.

Collegialism Collective decision making in which no single person dominates the process by which agreement is reached.

Cominform The Communist Information Bureau established in September 1947 to disseminate Soviet ideological principles among the European Communist parties.

Comintern The Third (Communist) International established in March 1919 to unify the world's Communist parties in their combat of capitalism. Unlike the Cominform, the Comintern required abject loyalty of its members to directives issued from its headquarters in Moscow. The Comintern was dissolved in World War II.

Committee for Social Self Defense The new (1977) name of the Committee for the Defense of the Workers set up in 1976 by Polish intellectuals to help Polish workers arrested by the Warsaw regime for involvement in the 1976 strikes against increases in food prices.

Communism The ideal classless and stateless communal societies that workers in Socialist countries are striving to create in accordance with the teachings of Karl Marx and Vladimir Lenin.

CPSU Communist Party of the Soviet Union, the successor of the Bolshevik Party that seized power in Russia in November 1917.

Cultural Autonomy The right of an ethnic group in a multinational society to speak its own language, preserve other aspects of its cultural identity, and enjoy a measure of self-administration.

Czarism The theory and practice of government under the Russian czars, notably those of the Romanov dynasty from 1614 to 1917.

Democratic Centralism The principles authored by Vladimir Lenin on which the organizational structure and behavior of Communist parties are supposed to be based.

Democratization A broadening of popular participation in electoral processes within the party, government, and the workplace.

Détente Relaxation of tensions between the Soviet Union and its allies and the Western countries.

Duma The national legislature of imperial Russia established for the first time in 1906; after the Bolshevik Revolution of 1917, it was succeeded by a new national legislature called the Supreme Soviet, established in the 1922 Soviet Constitution.

East Bloc Another name for the Soviet bloc, which consisted of the Soviet Union and its Warsaw Pact allies in Central/Eastern Europe.

Eurocommunism A set of ideas and practices embraced in different ways at different times and with different consequences by the Italian, French, and Spanish Communist parties beginning in the late 1960s that brought them into ideological and policy conflict with the Soviet Communist Party.

Fascism A set of ideas and practices calling for the establishment of an authoritarian political system to preserve the societal status quo against challenges from the "left"; for example, in Italy and Spain in the 1920s and the 1930s.

Fatherland Front A loose coalition of antifascist groups, dominated by the Bulgarian Communists, that facilitated the expansion of their political influence in Bulgaria during and immediately following World War II.

Glasnost In the Soviet Union, referred in the Gorbachev phase to a new openness or candor of political and ordinary citizens on national issues and problems.

Gosizdat Literally "published by the government" and meaning publications officially approved for public circulation, and thus the opposite of Samizdat.

Gosplan A national state planning agency in the Soviet Union that was responsible for drafting the so-called 5-year national plans of the Soviet state.

Great Purge The arrest, conviction, and punishment by death or imprisonment of high-ranking Soviet Communist Party and government officials by Joseph Stalin's regime in the mid-1930s.

Institutional Pluralism A term used to describe the appearance of interest groups and a broadening of the channels of political communication in a monolithic and authoritarian political system.

Interlocking Directorate A term used to characterize a situation in Socialist countries in which officials occupy simultaneously at least two administrative posts, one in the Communist Party and the other in the government.

KGB Committee of State Security, in the Soviet Council of Ministers, a secret investigatory agency of the former Soviet government responsible for, among other things, internal and external security and both strategic and counterintelligence work.

Komsomol The national youth organization or "Communist Youth League" of the former Soviet state. Its members ranged in age from 15 to 27 years.

Kulak Tough and resourceful Russian peasants who became wealthy and offered violent resistance to the collectivization policies of the Stalinist regime in the early 1930s.

Narodniki The "Populists," a movement of teachers, students, lawyers, physicians, and some aristocrats who tried to arouse the Russian peasantry against the Czarist regime in the early 1870s.

NATO The North Atlantic Treaty Organization, established at the height of the cold war in 1949 to defend Western countries against a threat to their security.

NEM New Economic Mechanism, established in Hungary in 1968. NEM introduced elements of a market economy with pricing and other techniques reminiscent of a capitalist economy involving a decentralization of planning and emphasis on managerial expertise and competitiveness in production. Bulgaria and Romania subsequently introduced versions of the Hungarian NEM, calling their changes by the same name even though they were not identical to those made in Hungary.

NEP The New Economic Policy under Vladimir Lenin. The development of the mixed Soviet economy in which some private ownership of the means of production continued, especially in agriculture, but other sectors of the economy, notably industry, were nationalized.

Nomenklatura The lists of positions in the party and state heirarchies to be filled only with the approval of the appropriate party officials.

Ostpolitik The policy of reconciliation and the maintenance of good relations with Socialist countries in the Soviet bloc pursued by West Germany starting in the late 1960s.

Owen-Stoltenberg Plan Following the unsuccessful Vance-Owen Plan, another UN peace plan was proposed (by European Community representative Lord David Owen and UN Yugoslavia mediator Thorwald Stoltenberg) to end the Civil War in Bosnia-Herzegovina. By late 1993 none of the combatants had formally accepted the plan.

Parallelism The existence of party organization that parallels and at the same time monitors the organization of government on all levels of administration from the top at the center of the country to the bottom or grass-roots level.

People's Democracy A term used to designate the establishment of a Communist Party dictatorship in Eastern Europe in the late 1940s and to distinguish the new and therefore less developed socialism of the Eastern European countries from the older and more developed socialism of the Soviet Union.

Perestroika A restructuring of the Soviet economy involving decentralization of business and production, producing a limited expansion of entrepreneurism in the retail sector of the economy and the introduction of profit and loss in the management of economic enterprises.

Personality Cult Popular worship of the individual, encouraged by a political leader to increase his power.

RSDP Russian Social Democratic Party, a Marxist party established in 1898 to work for the improvement of the conditions of the Russian proletariat and divided initially between evolutionists and revolutionaries, from which developed the Bolshevik Party.

Russia The largest, most populous, most ethnically diverse, and most influential of the 11 constituent union-republics of the former Soviet Union.

Samizdat Literally "self-published" and meaning publications produced clandestinely because their content is forbidden by the state.

Serfdom The system of economic and political servitude prevalent in Czarist Russia until its abolition in 1861 by Czar Alexander II.

Socialism A set of ideas and practices that call for community management and control of the scarce factors of production to achieve equality of well-being. Different kinds of socialism (Marxian socialism, Arab socialism, Indian socialism, etc.) in different national settings at different periods of national development determine the precise degree of political power assigned to the community to achieve social justice.

Soviet (local governing body) A legislative organ of government consisting of representatives of an administratively defined community and endowed with limited authority that is at all times subject to the review of higher government bodies.

Soviet (person) A citizen of the former Soviet Union.

Soviet Bloc A term used to describe the Soviet Union and its Warsaw Pact allies in Eastern Europe.

Soviet Federalism The federal type of intergovernmental relations established in the Soviet Union in 1922 wherein the bulk of administrative decision making is concentrated in the central government in Moscow, and constituent units, in particular the largest and most populous, are based on the ethnic principle but enjoy little autonomy in contrast with the constituent units of federal systems in the West, where there is more equitable balance of power between central and local government.

U.S.S.R. The Union of Soviet Socialist Republics, or Soviet Union, successor in 1922 of the Russian Soviet Federated Socialist Republic founded originally in 1917. On December 26, 1992, the Supreme Soviet passed a resolution acknowledging the demise of the U.S.S.R.

Vance-Owen Plan A UN-proposed peace plan to stop the bloodshed in Bosnia (drawn up by Balkans' mediator Cyrus Vance and European Community representative Lord David Owen). The plan, which would have divided Bosnia-Herzegovina into 10 largely autonomous, ethnic-based provinces, was overwhelmingly rejected by the Bosnian Serbs.

War Communism Sometimes called "militant communism," this term refers to efforts of the Bolsheviks between 1917 and 1921 to respond to emergency conditions resulting from World War I and the Revolution of 1917, such as acute shortages of food, and simultaneously to inaugurate the Socialist transition to communism, for example, by nationalizing industries, redistributing land, and replacing money as a medium of exchange with a barter system. War communism, along with the Civil War and the allied blockade of Russia, caused the near total collapse of the Russian economy and was superseded by the New Economic Policy starting in 1921.

Warsaw Pact An alliance of six Eastern European countries and the Soviet Union, linking them closely together in matters of defense. Established in 1955, ostensibly in response to West Germany's entry into NATO, the alliance, which was dominated by the Soviet Union, by far its most militarily powerful member, became another instrument of Soviet influence and control in Eastern Europe. With the dissolution of the U.S.S.R., the Warsaw Pact ceased to be a viable alliance.

Young Pioneers A Soviet state organization for children between the ages of 10 and 15 years that provided extensive recreational activities with strong political overtones. Membership in the Young Pioneers was a prerequisite for joining the more advanced youth group known as the Komsomol.

Zemstvos The local legislative bodies established by Czar Alexander II in a law of 1864 in which nobility, townspeople, and peasantry were to be represented and which were endowed with power to levy taxes for local economic and social needs such as roads, bridges, schools, and hospitals.

Bibliography

The following books and articles are of particular value to readers seeking more detailed coverage of a topic, country, or region.

RUSSIA AND THE EURASIAN REPUBLICS

Jonathan R. Adelman, *The Dynamics of Soviet Foreign Policy* (New York: Harper & Row, 1989).

Georgi Arbatov, *The System: An Insider's Life in Soviet Politics* (New York: Random House, 1991).

Seweryn Bialer, ed., *Politics, Society, and Nationality Inside Gorbachev's Russia* (Boulder: Westview Press, 1988).

___, *The Soviet Paradox: External Expansion, Internal Decline* (New York: Vintage, 1986).

James H. Billington, *Russia Transformed: Breakthrough to Hope, Moscow, August 1991* (New York: The Free Press, 1992).

Zbigniew K. Brzezinski, *The Grand Failure: The Birth and Death of Communism in the Twentieth Century* (New York: Scribners, 1988).

Mary Buckley, ed., *Perestroika and Soviet Women* (New York: Cambridge University Press, 1993).

Fedor Burlatsky, *Khrushchev and the First Russian Spring: The Era of Khrushchev Through the Eyes of His Adviser* (New York: Scribners, 1991).

Stephen F. Cohen, *Rethinking the Soviet Experience: Politics and History Since 1917* (New York: Oxford University Press, 1985).

Viktor Danilov, *Rural Russia Under the New Regime* (Bloomington: Indiana University Press, 1988).

Karen Dawisha and Bruce Parrott, *Russia and the New States of Eurasia: The Politics of Upheaval* (New York: Cambridge University Press, 1994).

Dale F. Eickelman, ed., *Russia's Muslim Frontiers: New Directions in Cross-Cultural Analysis* (Bloomington: Indiana University Press, 1993).

Murray Feshbach and Alfred Friendly Jr., *Ecocide in the USSR: Health and Nature Under Siege* (New York: Basic Books, 1991).

Robert O. Freedman, *Soviet Policy Since the Invasion of Afghanistan* (New York: Cambridge University Press, 1991).

Raymond L. Garthoff, *Détente and Confrontation: American-Soviet Relations From Nixon to Reagan* (Washington, D.C.: Brookings Institution, 1985).

Mikhail Gorbachev, *Perestroika: New Thinking for Our Country and the World* (New York: Harper & Row, 1987).

Philip Hanson, *From Stagnation to Catastroika: Commentaries on the Soviet Economy 1983–1991* (Westport: Praeger, 1992).

Anthony Jones, Walter Connor, and David E. Powell, eds., *Soviet Social Problems* (Boulder: Westview Press, 1991).

Anthony Jones and William Moskoff, *Ko-Ops: The Rebirth of Entrepreneurship in the Soviet Union* (Bloomington: Indiana University Press, 1991).

Amy W. Knight, *The KGB: Police and Politics in the Soviet Union* (Winchester, Allen and Unwin Hyman, 1988).

Walter Z. Laquer, *The Long Road to Freedom: Russia and Glasnost* (New York: Scribners, 1988).

Anatole Lieven, *The Baltic Revolution: Estonia, Latvia, and Lithuania and the Path to Independence* (New Haven: Yale University Press, 1993).

Yegor Ligachev, *Inside Gorbachev's Kremlin: The Memoirs of Yegor Ligachev* (New York: Pantheon Books, 1992).

David R. Marples, *The Social Impact of the Chernobyl Disaster* (New York: St. Martin's Press, 1988).

Michael McGwire, *Perestroika and Soviet National Security* (Washington, D.C.: The Brookings Institution, 1991).

Roy Medvedev, *Let History Judge: The Origins and Consequences of Stalinism* (New York: Columbia University Press, 1989).

Jim Riordan and Sue Bridger, eds., *Dear Comrade Editor: Readers' Letters to the Soviet Press Under Perestroika* (Bloomington: Indiana University Press, 1991).

Cameron Ross, *Local Government in the Soviet Union* (New York: St. Martin's Press, 1987).

Michael Ryan, *Doctors in the Soviet Union* (New York: St. Martin's Press, 1990).

Karl W. Ryavec, *United States–Soviet Relations* (New York: Longman, 1988).

Richard Sakwa, *Gorbachev and His Reforms 1985–1990* (Englewood Cliffs, Prentice-Hall, 1990).

Dora Shturtman, *The Soviet Secondary School* (New York: Routledge, Chapman and Hall, 1988).

Gordon B. Smith, *Soviet Politics: Struggling With Change* (New York: St. Martin's Press, 1992).

Graham Smith, ed., *The Nationalities Question in the Soviet Union* (New York: Longman, 1990).

Hedrick Smith, *The New Russians* (New York: Random House, 1990).

Isaac J. Tarasulo, ed., *Perils of Perestroika: Viewpoints From the Soviet Press 1989–1991* (Wilmington: Scholarly Resources, 1992).

Lev Timofeyev, *Russia's Secret Rulers* (New York: Alfred A. Knopf, 1992).

Vera Toltz, *The USSR's Emerging Multiparty System* (Westport: Praeger, 1991).

Stephen White, Graeme Gill, and Darrell Slider, *The Politics of Transition: Shaping a Post-Soviet Future* (New York: Cambridge University Press, 1993).

Boris Yeltsin, *Against the Grain: An Autobiography* (New York: Summit Books, 1990).

CENTRAL/EASTERN EUROPE

"After the Collapse of Communism in Eastern Europe," *Political Quarterly* (January–March 1991), Vol. 62, pp. 5–74.

Anders Aslund, "The East European Experiment Phase II: Four Key Reforms," *The American Enterprise* (July–August 1990), pp. 50–55.

Judy Batt, *East Central Europe From Reform to Transformation* (New York: Council on Foreign Relations, 1991).

Stephen R. Bowers, "The East European Revolution," *East European Quarterly,* Vol. XXV, No. 2 (Summer 1991), pp. 129–143.

J. F. Brown, *Eastern Europe After Communism* (Durham: Duke University Press, 1994).

____, *Surge to Freedom: The End of Communist Rule in Eastern Europe* (Durham: Duke University Press, 1991).

"East Central Europe After the Revolution," *Journal of International Affairs,* Vol. 45 (Summer 1991), pp. 1–269.

Hillary French, "Eastern Europe's Clean Break With the Past," *World Watch* (March–April 1991), pp. 21–27.

Charles Gati, *The Bloc That Failed* (Bloomington: Indiana University Press, 1988).

Todoritchka Gotovska-Popova, "Nationalism in Post-Communist Eastern Europe," *East European Quarterly,* Vol. XXVII, No. 2 (Summer 1992), pp. 171–186.

Stephen R. Graubard, ed., *Eastern Europe/Central Europe* (Boulder: Westview Press, 1991).

Bernard Gwertzman and Michael T. Kaufman, eds., *The Collapse of Communism,* 2nd ed. (New York: Random House, 1992).

Deszo Kovacs and Sally Ward Maggard, "The Human Face of Political, Economic, and Social Change in Eastern Europe," *East European Quarterly,* Vol. XXVII, No. 3 (Fall 1993), pp. 317–345.

Monty G. Marshall, "States at Risk: Ethnopolitics in the Multinational States of Eastern Europe," in Ted Robert Gurr, ed., *Minorities at Risk: A Global View of Ethnopolitical Conflicts* (Washington, D.C.: United States Institute of Peace Press, 1993).

Jan S. Prybyla, "The Road From Socialism," *Problems of Communism* (January–April 1991), pp. 1–17.

Michael G. Roskin, "The Emerging Party Systems of Central and Eastern Europe," *East European Quarterly,* Vol. XXVII, No. 1 (Spring 1992), pp. 47–63.

George Schopflin, "Post-Communism: Constructing New Democracies in Central Europe," *International Affairs* (London) (April 1991), pp. 235–250.

David Shumaker, "The Origins and Development of Central European Cooperation," *East European Quarterly,* Vol. XXVII, No. 3 (Fall 1993), pp. 351–373.

Gale Stokes, "Lessons of the East European Revolution," *Problems of Communism* (September–October 1991), pp. 17–23.

H. Jorg Thieme and Henning Echerman, "Eastern Europe: Long and Winding Road to the Market Economy," *Ausenpolitik,* Vol. 42, 2 (1991), pp. 183–193.

ALBANIA

Elez Biberaj, "Albania at the Crossroads," *Problems of Communism* (September–October 1991), pp. 1–16.

____, *Albania: A Socialist Maverick* (Boulder: Westview Press, 1990).

Bogdan Szakowski, "The Albanian Election of 1991," *Electoral Studies* (June 1992), Vol. 11, pp. 157–161.

Louise Zanga, "Albania's Local Election (July 26, 1992)," *Radio Free Europe/Radio Liberty Research Report* (September 18, 1991).

BULGARIA

Phillip Moore and Thomas Richard, "Bulgaria," *Trade Finance* (March 1992), pp. 22–25.

Luan Troxel, "Socialist Persistence in the Bulgarian Elections of 1990 and 1991," *East European Quarterly,* Vol. XXVI, No. 4 (Winter 1992), pp. 407–430.

Victor Valkov, "Partnership Between Bulgaria and NATO: A Promising Development," *NATO Review* (October 1991), pp. 13–17.

CZECHOSLOVAKIA (THE CZECH REPUBLIC AND SLOVAKIA)

Josef Burger, "Politics of Restitution in Czechoslovakia," *East European Quarterly,* Vol. XXVI, No. 4 (Winter 1992), pp. 485–498.

____, "Privatization Politics in Czechoslovakia," *Journal of Social Political and Economic Studies* (Fall 1991), pp. 259–272.

Martin Kupka, "Transformation of Ownership in Czechoslovakia," *Soviet Studies,* Vol. 44, No. 2 (1992), pp. 297–311.

Arnost Lustig, "The New Czechoslovakia: Continuing the Revolution," *The World and I* (March 1990), pp. 50–102.

Miroslav Polreich, "The Czechoslovak Revolution: Origins and Future Prospects," *International Relations* (London), Vol. 10 (November 1990), pp. 129–136.

Bernard Wheaton and Zdenek Kavan, *The Velvet Revolution: Czechoslovakia 1988–1991* (Boulder: Westview Press, 1992).

Sharon Wolchik, *Czechoslovakia in Transition: Politics, Economics, and Society* (New York: Pinter, 1991).

HUNGARY

Sandor Agocs, "The Collapse of the Communist Ideology in Hungary," *East European Quarterly,* Vol. XXVII, No. 2 (Summer 1992), pp. 187–211.

Robert M. Bigler, "From Communism to Democracy: Hungary's Transition Thirty-Five Years After the Revolution," *East European Quarterly,* Vol. XXVI, No. 4 (Winter 1991), pp. 437–461.

"Economic and Social Consequences of Restructuring in Hungary," *Soviet Studies,* Vol. 44, No. 6, pp. 947–1043.

John R. Hibbing and Samuel Patterson, "A Democratic Legislature in the Making: The Historic Hungarian Elections of 1990," *Comparative Political Studies,* Vol. 24 (January 1992), pp. 430–454.

Agnes Horvath and Arpad Szakolczai, *The Dissolution of Communist Power: The Case of Hungary* (London: Routledge, 1992).

Janos Kornai, "The Hungarian Reform Process: Visions, Hopes, and Reality," in Victor Nee and David Stark, eds., *Remaking the Economic Institutions of Socialism: China and Eastern Europe* (Stanford: Stanford University Press, 1989), pp. 32–94.

George Schopflin, "Conservatism and Hungary's Transition," *Problems of Communism* (January–April 1991), pp. 60–68.

Rudolph L. Tokes, "Hungary's New Political Elites: Adaptation and Change 1989–1990," *Problems of Communism* (November–December 1990), pp. 44–65.

POLAND

Henrik Bering-Jensen, "Poles Apart in New Era," *Insight* (September 23, 1991), pp. 11–17.

Brian N. Brown, "Poland's Leap to Democracy," *The World and I* (January 1992), pp. 180–187.

Werner G. Hahn, *Democracy in a Communist Party: Poland's Experience Since 1980* (New York: Columbia University Press, 1987).

Bogdan Mroz, "Poland's Economy in Transition to Private Ownership," *Soviet Studies,* Vol. 43, No. 4 (1991), pp. 667–668.

Janusz L. Mucha, "Democratization and Cultural Minorities: The Polish Case of the 1980's/1990's," *East European Quarterly,* Vol. XXV, No. 4 (Winter 1991), pp. 463–482.

"Poland—*Quo Vadis,*" *Military Review,* Vol. 76 (December 1990), pp. 63–79.

George Sanford, ed., *Democratization in Poland 1988–1990: Polish Voices* (London: Macmillan, 1992).

Voytek Zubeck, "Walesa's Leadership and Poland's Transition," *Problems of Communism* (January–April 1991), pp. 69–83.

ROMANIA

Mark Almond, "Romania Since the Revolution," *Government and Opposition* (Autumn 1990), Vol. 25, pp. 484–496.

Edward Behr, *Kiss the Hand You Cannot Bite: The Rise and Fall of the Ceausescus* (New York: Random House, 1991).

Matei Calinescu and Vladimir Tismaneanu, "The 1989 Revolution and Romania's Future," *Problems of Communism* (January–April 1991), pp. 42–59.

Juliana Geran Pilon, "Post-Communist Nationalism: The Case of Romania," *The World and I* (February 1992), pp. 110–115.

Nestor Ratesh, *Romania: The Entangled Revolution* (New York: Praeger, 1991).

Michael Shafir, "Romania's New Electoral Law," *Radio Free Europe/Radio Liberty Research Report* (September 11, 1992), pp. 24–48.

____, "Transylvania Shadows," *Radio Free Europe/Radio Liberty Research Report* (June 26, 1992), pp. 28–33.

Katherine Verdery, "Nationalism in Romania," *Slavic Review* (Summer 1993), pp. 179–203.

THE REPUBLICS OF THE FORMER YUGOSLAVIA

Steven L. Burg, "Nationalism and Democratization in Yugoslavia," *Washington Quarterly,* Vol. 14 (Autumn 1991), pp. 5–19.

Leonard Cohen, "The Disintegration of Yugoslavia" (Boulder: Westview, 1993).

Alex Dragnich, *Serbs and Croats: The Struggle in Yugoslavia* (New York: Harcourt, 1992).

Misha Glenny, *The Fall of Yugoslavia* (New York: Penguin, 1992).

Robert M. Hayden, "Nationalism in Formerly Yugoslav Republics," *Slavic Review* (Winter 1992), pp. 654–673.

Sabrina P. Ramet, *Nationalism and Federalism in Yugoslavia* (Bloomington: Indiana University Press, 1992).

Robin Alison Remington, "The Federal Dilemma in Yugoslavia," *Current History* (December 1990), pp. 405–408, 429–431.

Carole Rogel, "Slovenia's Independence: A Reversal of History," *Problems of Communism* (July–August 1991), pp. 31–40.

Predrag Simic, "The West and the Yugoslav Crisis," *Review of International Affairs,* Vol. 42 (April 20, 1991), pp. 1–5.

"Yugoslavia: Trying to End the Violence," *Foreign Policy Bulletin* (November–December 1991), pp. 39–46.

Sources for Statistical Reports

U.S. State Department, *Background Notes* (1990–1993).

The World Factbook (1993).

World Statistics in Brief (1993).

World Almanac (1994).

The Statesman's Yearbook (1993–1994).

Demographic Yearbook (1992).

Statistical Yearbook (1993).

World Bank, World Development Report (1993).

Ayers Directory of Publications (1993).

— Country Review Form —

Student Name _____ **Date** _____

Country _____ **pp.** _____ - _____

1. List 3 *significant* historical facts. (Be prepared to discuss the historical significance of the facts you have chosen.)

    A. _____

    B. _____

    C. _____

2. Explain the interdependence between religion and culture as they relate to the total society of the country.

    _____

    _____

    _____

3. Compare and contrast the country's educational system with that of the United States.

    _____

    _____

    _____

4. On what is the economy of the country based?

    _____

    _____

    _____

5. Briefly describe the current political system of the country.

    _____

    _____

    _____

6. Describe the country's hope for the future.

    _____

    _____

    _____

7. What is the greatest threat to the country's future?

    _____

    _____

    _____

8. Describe fully one important historical or contemporary figure and his or her importance to the country.

    _____

    _____

    _____

Your instructor may require you to use this Country Review Form in any number of ways: to report on readings that have been assigned, for extra credit, as a tool to assist in developing papers, or simply for your own reference. We encourage you to photocopy this page and use it. You'll find that reflecting on the information you have read will enhance your comprehension.

Index

Abkhazia, 69, 94, 95, 260, 261, 262
Afghanistan, 98, 107, 109, 253–254; Soviet
 Union and, 33, 37, 59, 60, 61, 63, 64, 72,
 76, 112, 128, 184, 196, 207; Tajikistan and,
 98, 99
Agca, Mehmet Ali, 145
agriculture, 119, 155, 161, 172, 185, 271;
 Soviet, 29, 41–42, 43, 47, 64–65, 84, 86,
 100, 111, 214, 217
AIDS epidemic, in Romania, 189
Albania, 32; Eastern Europe and, 114–136, 148;
 democracy in, 270–275; overview of,
 137–142; and Yugoslavia, 193, 197, 198
alcoholism, in the Soviet Union, 36, 37–38, 48
Alexander III, Czar, 11, 37
Alia, Ramiz, 138, 139–141, 142, 272
Aliyev, Geidar, 97, 262
All-Union Party Congress, Soviet, 21, 23, 34
Andropov, Yuri, 15, 19, 27, 41, 112, 128
Angola, Soviet Union and, 33, 61, 63
Antall, Joszef, 158, 164, 166, 290
anti-Semitism. See Judaism
Argentina, 63
Armenia, 5, 35, 41, 48, 50, 54–55, 68, 74, 82,
 87, 90, 96–98, 101, 111, 112, 148, 260,
 261, 262, 265, 267
arms control, 229; Soviet Union and, 61, 64,
 93, 106, 129
atheism, in the Soviet Union, 36, 49
attorneys, Soviet, 27
Austria, 114, 156, 167, 287
authoritarian government, in Central Asia,
 121–122
Azerbaijan, 5, 54–55, 68, 74, 87, 90, 96–98,
 112, 148, 260, 261, 262, 265, 267

Badakshan, 98, 253
Bakatin, Vadim, 71, 73
Baker, James, 52, 109, 141, 156, 157
Baklanov, Oleg, 71, 72
"Bantustanization," of the C.I.S., 241–247
barter, in the Soviet Union, 43, 65, 66
Bashkir, 68, 167
Bashkortostan, 245
Belarus, 6, 64, 74, 93, 101, 106, 111, 181, 241
Benavides, Pablo, 134–135
Berisha, Saul, 140, 142, 270, 271, 272, 273, 276
Berliner, Joseph, 217, 219
Bernstein, Eduard, 216, 217
Berov, Lyuben, 143, 148, 278
Bessarabia, 54, 117, 184, 189, 190
Bill of Rights, Russian, 83
Black Berets, 71
Bohemia, 158–159
Bolshevik Revolution, 10, 34, 54, 110, 117, 219
Bolshevism, in Russia, 12–14, 16, 70, 110, 217
Bosnia-Herzegovina, 76, 96, 104, 105, 134,
 274. See also Yugoslavia
Brazil, 63
Brezhnev Doctrine, 32, 61, 127, 131
Brezhnev, Leonid, 15, 18–19, 22, 24, 27, 28,
 31, 40, 43, 44, 49, 52, 60, 62, 68, 112, 121,
 128, 178
bribery, Soviet bureaucracy and, 28
Britain, 44, 61, 105, 117, 180, 205, 206
Bukharin, Nikolai, 16, 49, 216
Bulgaria, 63, 112, 186, 274; and Eastern
 Europe, 114–136; overview of, 143–149;
 and Yugoslavia, 199, 200
bureaucracy, 11, 16; Soviet, 23, 24–25, 28–29,
 48, 57, 59, 65, 75, 215–217

Bush administration: Czechoslovakia and, 157,
 158; Poland and, 179–180; Russia and, 105,
 106; Soviet Union and, 52, 61, 66;
 Yugoslavia and, 202, 205–207

Calfa, Marian, 154, 156
Cambodia, 63
Canada, 138
capitalism, vs. communism, 14
capital markets, privatization and, 232–233
Carter administration, Soviet Union and, 31
Caucasus, 96, 96, 101, 106, 108, 110; Russia
 and, 259–263
Ceausescu, Nicolae, 130, 131, 167–168,
 183–190, 287, 288
Central Committee, Soviet, 22, 23, 25, 34, 43,
 56, 71, 72, 73
Central Europe, definition of, 136
Charter 77 movement, 40, 77, 152, 153, 155,
 159, 186
Chechen-Ingushetia, 68, 91–92, 225, 227, 243,
 244–245, 261, 262
Chernenko, Konstantin, 15, 19, 27, 112, 128
Chernobyl, nuclear disaster at, 43–44, 53, 110,
 251
Chernomyrdin, Viktor, 76, 82, 84, 87, 223
China, 106, 196; Eastern Europe and, 110, 125,
 126, 130, 138; Soviet Union and, 4, 17, 24,
 32–33, 60, 63–64, 75
Christopher, Warren, 109, 110, 204
Chukotka, 243, 246
Circassia, 261
Clinton administration: Eastern Europe and,
 110, 135, 190, 204; Russia and, 77, 80,
 103, 106, 107, 108; Yugoslavia and,
 205–207, 274
CMEA (Council for Mutual Economic
 Assistance), 32, 111, 120, 123, 126, 129,
 133, 135, 136, 142, 158, 162, 177, 178,
 182, 184, 196, 277
cold war, 4, 123
collective farms, 17, 18, 29, 65, 86, 111, 118,
 185, 217, 243
Cominform, 119, 135
Comintern, 110, 135, 144
command economies, in Central Asia, 122, 123
Committee for State Security. See KGB
Commonwealth of Independent States (C.I.S.),
 10, 73–74, 112; ethnic issues in, 91–100.
 See also individual countries; Russia; Soviet
 Union
communism, 114; in Romania, 287–290; in
 Russia, 10, 13, 14–15, 21, 33, 48
Communist Party: of Albania, 138, 139–140; of
 Bulgaria, 144, 147–148; of Czechoslovakia,
 151–154; of Eastern Europe, 114, 117–118,
 120–121, 124, 129, 130, 131; of Poland,
 170, 172–173, 175; of Romania, 186, 190;
 of Russia, 16, 80; of Soviet Union, 17, 18,
 19, 20, 21–24, 26, 27, 34, 41, 46, 55–56,
 57, 58, 61, 64, 70–71, 72, 75, 212, 220,
 222, 226, 227, 235, 243; of Tajikistan, 98,
 99; of Yugoslavia, 193, 194, 293
Congress of People's Deputies: C.I.S., 243;
 Russian, 82, 85, 86, 94, 104, 107, 136, 223,
 225; Soviet, 57, 58, 69, 70, 71, 73, 74, 76,
 77, 78, 102
Constantinescu, Emil, 188, 287, 288
constitution: Russian, 81, 82–84, 224; Soviet,
 51, 53, 68, 75, 77, 78, 79
consumers, Soviet, 41–42
cooperatives, Soviet, 46

Council of Ministers, Soviet, 25, 26, 43
Council of Nationalities of the Supreme Soviet,
 24, 25, 34
Council of the Union, of the Supreme Soviet,
 25
coup attempt, 1991 Soviet, 72, 75, 81–82, 136,
 148, 182, 189, 235
coupon method, Czechoslovakia's, 155
crime: in Russia, 87–88, 235–237; in the Soviet
 Union, 36, 38
Crimea, 53, 92, 93
Croatia, 104, 134, 142, 168, 268, 274. See also
 Yugoslavia
CSCE (Conference on Security and
 Cooperation in Europe), 141, 142, 199, 206,
 253, 269, 296
Cuba, Soviet Union and, 4, 17, 24, 33, 63
cultural autonomy, Soviet federalism and, 24, 34
Cyprus, 199
Czarism, in the Soviet Union, 11–14, 16, 19
Czechoslovakia: Bulgaria and, 145, 148, 277;
 division of, 280–281; Eastern Europe and,
 114–136; overview of, 150–195; Poland
 and, 174, 178, 182; Romania and, 184, 186,
 190; Yugoslavia and, 196, 205, 207

Dagestan, 261
Dalmatia, 293, 296
decentralization, of the Soviet economy, 45–46
Democratic Union (DU), Soviet, 56
democratization: in Albania, 270–275; in
 Bulgaria, 275–279; in Czechoslovakia,
 155–157; in Eastern Europe, 132, 143, 148,
 254; in Hungary, 162–163; in Poland,
 174–176; in Romania, 187–188; in the
 Soviet Union, 45, 51, 56–57, 69–70, 75, 76,
 239–240, 266–268
détente, 31, 129
deviance, in Russia, 240
Dienstbier, Jiri, 155, 156
Dimitrov, Filip, 147, 277
Dimitrov, Georgi, 144, 148, 149
discontent, in Russia, 239–240
domestic reform, in Albania, 139
drug abuse, in Russia, 239
Dubcek, Alexander, 151, 153, 159, 168, 184
Duma, Russian, 12, 80

earthquake, Armenian, 48, 54–55
Eastern Europe, definition of, 136
Economic Cooperation Organization, 254
economic crime, Soviet, 38
economy: of Albania, 138, 141; of Bulgaria,
 144, 147–148, 275–279; of Central Asia,
 252–253; of Czechoslovakia, 155, 158; of
 Eastern Europe, 123–124, 128–129; of
 Estonia, 263–264; of Hungary, 165,
 281–285; of Poland, 170–171, 172, 175,
 176–178, 179, 182, 285–286; of Romania,
 185–186, 188–189; of Soviet Union, 29,
 41–43, 45–48, 212–221
Egypt, 63, 257
Estonia, 9, 35–36, 50–51, 52, 64, 68, 73, 101,
 102, 103, 228; economy of, 263–264
Ethiopia, 33
ethnic issues: in Czechoslovakia, 155, 158; in
 Eastern Europe, 127, 134, 168; in Romania,
 185, 287, 289; in Russia, 110–111, 115–116,
 253–255; in the Soviet Union, 34–36,
 50–55, 64, 66–69, 91–100, 232, 241–247,
 265–270
Eurocommunism, 125, 161

European Community, 134, 136, 142, 158, 166, 167, 177, 196, 199, 239, 271, 296
European Development Bank, 157
Eisenhower administration, Hungary and, 52
Elchibey, Abulfez, 97, 262
entrepreneurs: Polish, 169, 176, 285; Russian, 87; Soviet, 45, 46–47
environmental issues, 179; in Czechoslovakia, 155–156; in Eastern Europe, 133, 148; in the Soviet Union, 43–44, 65, 87, 238, 248–252
Eurasian Economic Community, 111
executive branch, of Soviet government, 24–25

federalism, Soviet, 24, 122
Federation Council, Russia's, 80, 82
Finland, Russia and, 101
500 Day Plan, 66
5-Year Plan, Stalin's, 16–17
foreign policy: of Bulgaria, 144–145, 147–148; of Czechoslovakia, 156–157; of Eastern Europe, 123, 124, 134–136; of Hungary, 166–168; of Poland, 178–182; of Romania, 185, 189–190; of Russia, 252–255; of Yugoslavia, 195–197, 199–200
France: Eastern Europe and, 125, 134, 157, 180, 199, 205, 206; Soviet Union and, 40, 44, 61, 63, 81, 230, 233, 234
Funar, Georghe, 188, 289
Fyodorov, Boris, 84, 87, 88, 104, 229

Gagauz Republic, 69, 241
Gaidar, Yegor, 80, 81, 84, 87, 88, 104, 223, 229
Gamsakhurdia, Zviad, 68, 69, 73, 94, 95, 259, 262
Gdansk Agreement, 170
Geg people, 138, 140
general secretary, Soviet, 23
Genscher, Hans Dietrich, 135, 180
Georgia, 6, 18, 41, 50, 53–54, 67, 68, 69, 72, 73, 74, 76, 82, 90, 93–94, 98, 112, 259–260, 261, 265
Gerashchenko, Viktor, 82, 87
Germany: Bulgaria and, 145, 147; Czechoslovakia and, 157, 159, 281; Eastern Europe and, 114, 117, 119, 123, 125, 127, 128, 129, 130; Hungary and, 167, 168; Poland and, 173, 176, 178–180; Romania and, 186, 287; Russia and, 101, 103, 105, 228; Soviet Union and, 17, 31, 50, 51, 61, 62–63, 91, 111, 212, 216, 230, 231, 232, 234
Gheorghiu-Dej, Gheorghe, 184, 190
gigantomania, Soviet economy and, 217–220
glasnost, 45, 48–56, 60, 69, 146, 163, 189, 220, 251
Gomulka, Wladyslaw, 119, 170
Gorbachev, Mikhail, 4, 19, 20, 27, 28, 32, 37, 38, 96, 101, 103, 106, 111, 196, 222, 223, 235, 236, 239, 240, 241, 251, 255, 261, 266, 277; and collapse of Soviet Union, 64–75, 81–82; and Eastern Europe, 127, 128, 129, 130, 131, 136, 146, 147, 148, 152, 157; Hungary and, 161–162, 166, 167; perestroika and, 44–64, 70, 89, 103, 244; Poland and, 173, 174, 178, 179, 182; Romania and, 185, 187, 189; and Soviet economy, 212–213, 217–218, 220
Gosizdat, 40
Gosnab, 45, 214
Gosplan, 29, 41, 43, 45, 213, 214, 215
Grachev, Pavel, 79, 99

Great Purge, Stalin's, 16, 24, 111
Greece, 112; Albania and, 138, 139, 141–142, 271, 273, 274, 276; Bulgaria and, 145, 148; Yugoslavia and, 199, 200
Gromyko, Andrei, 27, 53, 112
Grosz, Karolyi, 163, 167
Group of Seven, 85, 104
Gulf Cooperation Council, 109
gypsies, 156, 158, 189

Havel, Vaclav, 81, 135, 153, 154, 155, 158, 182
health care: Russian, 112, 237–239; Soviet, 30, 39
Helsinki Accords, 141
Helsinki Final Act, 266
Helsinki Watch Group, 21, 41, 185
historical revisionism, in the Soviet Union, 49
Honecker, Erich, 128, 130, 131, 147
hooliganism, Soviet, 38, 237
housing policy, Soviet, 30
housing, private, in Russia, 88–90
Hoxha, Enver, 138, 140, 142, 270, 272
human rights, 53, 145, 185, 257, 266; in Albania, 139–140; in Eastern Europe, 129, 135; in the Soviet Union, 31, 41, 42, 61
Hungary, 52, 61, 63, 85, 104, 107, 231, 232, 266; and Czechoslovakia, 151, 152, 157–158, 280; economy of, 281–285; Eastern Europe and, 114–136; overview of, 160–168; and Romania, 189, 190, 287, 290

Iliescu, Ion, 95, 187, 188, 190, 276, 287, 288, 289, 290
India, 106, 109, 233, 239
industrial enterprises, Soviet, 29, 41
INF treaty, 61
inflation, in Hungary, 282–283
institutional pluralism, in the Soviet Union, 18
institutions, Soviet economic, 29
interest groups, activity of, in the Soviet Union, 20–21
International Atomic Energy Agency, 64
International Court of Justice, 64
International Monetary Fund, 101, 104, 132, 148, 157, 172, 175, 176, 177, 180, 195, 290; Bulgaria and, 277, 278, 279; Russia and, 85, 87, 231
Iran, 33, 37, 63, 96, 99, 106, 109, 253, 254, 257
Iraq, 63, 82, 90, 91, 97, 148, 182, 205, 276
Islam: Central Asia and, 54, 98–100, 104, 105, 109, 253, 255–258; Soviet Union and, 33, 35, 36, 37, 38, 68, 69, 91, 92; Yugoslavia and, 193–207, 292
Israel, 167, 185
Italy: Albania and, 138, 142, 271, 273; Eastern Europe and, 117, 119, 125; Soviet Union and, 40, 44, 230, 233
Itzebegovic, Alija, 205, 206

Jakes, Milos, 130, 131, 147, 152, 154, 159
Japan, 180; and Russia, 107, 239; and the Soviet Union, 60, 63–64, 91, 230, 231, 232, 233, 234
Jarulzelski, Wojciech, 121, 171, 172–173, 174, 178
John Paul II, Pope, 145, 148, 149, 152, 172–173, 178
Johnson, Ralph R., 206–207
joint ventures, 45, 47–48, 64, 65, 167, 177
Jordan, 63
Judaism, 11, 116, 132, 228; in Hungary, 160, 165–166; in Poland, 170, 178; in Romania,

185, 189, 190; in the Soviet Union, 21, 37, 49, 75, 267
judicial branch, of Soviet government, 24–25, 27–28, 59
juvenile delinquency, in the Soviet Union, 36, 38, 236–237

Kádar, Janos, 161, 162, 163, 166, 167, 168
Kalmykia, 245
Kania, Stanislaw, 171, 172
Karabakh Committee, 54, 55
Karadzic, 295
Karakalpakia, 241
Karimnov, Islam, 75, 100
Katyn Forest massacre, Poland's, 178–179
Kazakhstan, 6, 69, 74, 91, 96, 98, 99–100, 101, 106, 110, 111, 112, 223, 242, 248, 251–252; foreign policy of, 108–110; Islam in, 255–258; Russia and, 252–255
keiretsu, Japanese, 231, 232, 233
KGB, Soviet Union's, 21, 28, 34, 37, 41, 48, 49, 57, 59, 71, 72, 73, 74, 75–76, 97, 145, 148
Khashulatov, Ruslan, 78, 79, 80, 84, 223, 225
Khrushchev, Nikita, 15, 17–18, 23, 24, 31, 40, 42, 49, 62, 93, 112, 136, 170
Klaus, Vaclav, 155, 158, 159, 280
Kohl, Helmut, 63, 105, 128, 134, 158, 167, 180
Komsomol, 20
Kosovo, 120, 138, 142, 193, 197, 198, 199, 202, 272, 274–275, 292–293, 294, 295
Kozyrev, Andrei, 96, 229, 260
Kravchuk, Leonid, 74, 93, 94
Kremlin, 20, 25, 26, 116
Krychkov, Vladimir, 71, 72
kulaks, 17
Kurile Islands, 64
Kuwait, 147
Kyrgyzstan, 7, 101, 112, 242; foreign policy of, 108–110; Islam and, 255–258; Russia and, 252–255

Labed, Aleksandr, 95–96
Landsbergis, Vytautas, 51, 68, 71, 103, 181
Latvia, 9, 35–36, 50–51, 52, 68, 71, 73, 101, 102, 111, 228
Law on Constitutional Powers, Albania's, 140
Law on State Enterprises, Soviet, 214
law, Soviet, 27–28
legislative branch, of Soviet government, 24–26, 57
Lenin, Vladimir, 11, 12, 13–15, 17, 19, 22, 28, 33, 45, 70, 85, 87, 110, 121, 139, 154, 185, 216, 219, 225, 241
Libya, 106, 257, 277
Ligachev, Yegor, 49, 50, 56, 75
Lithuania, 9, 35–36, 49, 50–53, 67, 68, 71, 101–103, 112, 136, 158, 228, 268; and Poland, 180–181; and Yugoslavia, 196, 197
Lukanov, Andrei, 147, 148
Lukyanov, Anatoly, 58, 72, 277, 278

Macedonia, 134, 145, 148, 274, 276. See also Yugoslavia
Mafia, Russian, 87–88, 231
Magadan, 243, 246
Mao Zedong, 138, 196
market economy: in Eastern Europe, 132–133, 148; Russian, 84–90, 102
Markovic, Ante, 195, 197, 200, 293
Marshall Plan, 119
Marx, Karl, 11, 14, 19, 234

Marxism: in Eastern Europe, 121, 134, 139, 154, 163, 194; Soviet Union and, 10–11, 12, 28, 30, 33, 63, 70, 71, 85, 87, 212, 225
Mazowiecki, Tadeusz, 174, 180
Meciar, Vladimir, 158, 159, 280
Meskhetia, 69, 256
Mexico, 63, 233
Michael, Romania's King, 184, 186–187, 190
middle class, in Czarist Russia, 11–12
Middle Europe, 136
military: in Eastern Europe, 127–128, 133; Soviet, 20–21, 23–24, 32, 57, 59–60, 72–73, 75, 90–91, 92–93
Milosevic, Slobodan, 104, 142, 193, 195, 196, 197, 200, 201–202, 274, 276, 291, 293, 294, 296
Missile Control Regime, 106
Mitterrand, François, 63, 134
Moldova, 7, 54, 68, 69, 74, 90, 95–96, 101, 112, 117, 148, 241, 269, 287; and Romania, 189–190
Molotov-Ribbentrop Pact, 181
monarchical socialism, in Romania, 184–185
Mongolia, 64
money crisis, Russian, 86–87
monopoly, Soviet economy and, 215–217, 220, 230
Montenegro, 134, 274, 278. See also Yugoslavia
Moravia, 158–159
Mozambique, 63
Mutalibov, Ayaz, 97, 109, 262

Nabiyev, Rakhman, 98–99
Nagorno-Karabakh, 54–55, 90, 96–97, 98, 112, 261, 267
Nagy, Imre, 161, 167, 168
Nano, Fatos, 140, 141, 272
narodniki, 12
National Wealth Management Funds, Poland's, 176
NATO (North Atlantic Treaty Organization): Eastern Europe and, 105, 107, 108, 119, 127, 128, 129, 133, 136, 148, 158, 166, 167, 179, 182, 196, 200, 203, 207, 227; 229, 254, 265, 272, 296; Soviet Union and, 31, 32, 61, 63, 76, 91, 103, 104
navy, Soviet, 92–93
Nazarbayev, Nursultan, 99–100, 110
Nazi-Soviet Nonaggression Pact, 50
New Economic Mechanism: Bulgaria's, 144; Hungary's, 161, 168
New Economic Policy (NEP), Lenin's, 16, 17
New Thinking, Gorbachev's, 60–64, 101
Nicaragua, 63
Nicholas II, Czar, 11, 12, 13, 37, 110
Nine Plus One Agreement, 67, 72, 73
NKVD, 178–179
nomenklatura, 23, 233, 238
North Korea, 4, 61, 106–107
North Vietnam, 4, 61
Nove, Alec, 216, 217, 219
nuclear energy, 148; Soviet, 43–44, 248–252. See also Chernobyl
nuclear weapons, 106, 108; Soviet, 24, 60, 61, 91, 93, 101

Oder-Neisse line, 180
oil industry, collapse of Russian, 88
Olszewski, Jan, 175, 176, 177
Organization of the Caspian Sea, 254
Ossetia, 69, 91, 92, 94, 262
Overseas Private Investment Corporation, 157

Owen, David, 203–204, 206, 295

Pakistan, 109, 253, 257; Soviet Union and, 33, 37
Pamyat, 49
paradnost, 28
parallelism, Soviet, 21
parasitism, Soviet, 38
Paris Club, 278, 286
parliament, Russian, Yeltsin and, 222–226
parliamentary elections, in Albania, 140
Partisans, Yugoslavian, 118
Pashko, Gramoz, 140, 142, 272
Pavlov, Valentin, 71, 72
Pawlak, Waldemar, 176, 178
Payin, Emil, 91
Peace Corps, 158
people's assessors, Soviet, 27
perestroika, 10, 19, 21, 44–64, 70, 71, 89, 103, 128, 129–130, 131, 145–146, 213, 220, 236, 244; in Hungary, 161–162, 166; in Poland, 173–174, 178
personality cult: Ceausescu's, 184; in Russia, 16–17
Petrakov, Nikolai, 67
Pilsudski, Josef, 175
Pirvulescu, Constantin, 186
pluralization, of Soviet politics, 69–73
Poland, 40, 44, 61, 63, 85, 102, 103–104, 107, 147, 195, 231, 232, 249, 266; Czechoslovakia and, 151, 152, 157–158; Eastern Europe and, 114–136, 167; economy of, 285–286; overview of, 169–182; Romania and, 188, 190
Politburo, Soviet, 18, 21, 22–23, 25, 26, 34
political dissent, in the Soviet Union, 40–41, 49–50
political education, in the Soviet Union, 19–20
political repression, in Central Asia, 123–124
Pollisinski, Kauto, 264
Poltoranin, Mikhail, 228
Pomerania, 180
Popov, Dimitar, 148, 278
Popov, Gavril, 69, 73
popular fronts, Soviet, 56
Powell, Colin L., 205
Prague Spring, 151, 152
Presidium, Soviet, 18, 25, 26, 59
prices, decontrol of, in Russia, 84–85
Primakov, Yevgeni, 66
privatization, economic: in Eastern Europe, 133–134, 140, 155, 271; in Poland, 175, 176, 179, 285, 286; in the Soviet Union, 29–30, 84, 85–86, 229–235
production, decline of Soviet, 64
proletariat, 115
profitability, perestroika and, 45, 46
Pugo, Boris, 71, 72

Rakhmanov, Emomail, 99
Rakosi, Metyas, 161, 168
Rakowski, Miezslaw, 173, 174
Raznatovic, Zeljko, 198
Reagan, Ronald, 129, 167
Redman, Charles E., 203–204
regional cooperation, in the C.I.S., 111–112
Roman Catholic Church, 53, 123, 126, 152; and Poland, 170–172
Roman, Petre, 187
Romania, 54, 61, 94, 112, 178, 205; Bulgaria and, 145, 148, 276; communism in, 287–290; Eastern Europe and, 114–136;

Hungary and, 167–168; overview of, 183–190
Rugova, Ibrahim, 198, 274
Ruli, Genc, 272
Russia, 4, 64, 67, 68, 69, 74, 75, 112, 114, 148; Caucasus and, 259–263; Central Asia and, 252–255; Eastern Europe and, 116–117, 167; economy of, 84–90; emergence of, 75–84; ethnic issues in, 91–92, 94–96, 97; foreign policy of, 101–107, 110, 111; military of, 90–91; Romania and, 189–190; social problems in, 235–240; Yeltsin and, 222–227; Zhirinovsky and, 227–229. See also Commonwealth of Independent States; Soviet Union
Russian Orthodox Church, 11, 12, 37, 40, 49, 144
Russian Socialist Democratic Party (RSDP), 12, 110
Rutskoi, Aleksandr, 71, 76, 77, 78, 80, 93, 224, 226, 240
Ryerson, William, 272
Ryzkhov, Nikolai, 58, 67, 70, 71

Sachs, Jeffrey, 85, 230
Sakha, 242, 245
Sakhalin Island, 107
Sakharov, Andrei, 40, 41, 57, 58, 69, 70
Salik, Muhammed, 109
SALT II arms control agreement, 31
Samizdat, 40, 41
satellization, of Eastern European countries, to the Soviet Union, 114, 118–120, 132, 154
Saudi Arabia, 36, 37, 98, 99, 109, 253, 255
Savostyanov, Yevgeny, 76
Schumpeter, Joseph, 216, 220, 281
SDI (Strategic Defense Initiative), 61
secret police, 11, 17; Stalin's, 16, 178–179, 250
Secretariat, Soviet, 23, 34
Securitate, Romania's, 186, 190
Selami, Eduard, 272
Selyunin, Vasily, 47
Serbia, 91, 104, 105, 134, 142, 267, 268, 274, 276, 278. See also Yugoslavia
serfs, in Russia, 11, 12
Seslj, Vojislav, 201, 202
shadow economy, Soviet, 213
Shaimiyev, Mintimer, 92, 246
Shakrai, Sergei, 80, 81
Shamir, Yitzhak, 167
Shaposhnikov, Yevgeni, 73, 74, 260, 261
Shatalin, Stanislav, 66, 70, 84
Shcharnsky, Anatolyi, 40
Shelov-Kovedyayev, F., 253
Shevardnadze, Eduard, 58, 60, 70, 71, 94–95, 106, 189, 259–260
Shmelyev, Nikolai, 47, 217
Siberia, 41, 43, 80, 105, 107, 242
Silesia, 180
Simonetti, Marko, 232
Singh, Arup, 278
Sinyavsky, Andrei, 41
Slovakia. See Czechoslovakia
Slovenia, 134, 231, 268. See also Yugoslavia
Snegur, Mircea, 95, 96
Sobchak, Anatoli, 69, 73, 81
social contract, Communism and, 44
social policy, in Hungary, 281–285
social problems: in Hungary, 165–166; in Romania, 189; in Russia, 235–240; in the Soviet Union, 36–39
social security, Soviet, 30

social welfare, in Central Asia, 122–123
socialism, 193; in Eastern Europe, 114, 134, 151, 161, 163; in Romania, 184–185; in Russia, 10–11, 14–15, 19, 21, 24, 32, 35, 44, 48, 61, 84
societal organizations, Soviet, 29
Sokolovsky, Marshal, 60
Solidarity, 40, 152, 170, 172, 173, 174, 177, 179, 182
Solzhenitsyn, Alexander, 40
Somalia, 135
Soviet, definition of, 10
Soviet Union, 10–64; Bulgaria and, 144–145, 147–148; collapse of, 64–75; Czechoslovakia and, 151–152, 157, 158; Eastern Europe and, 117–137, 139; economy of, 41–43, 212–221; Hungary and, 160–161, 166–167; nuclear energy and, 248–252; Poland and, 170, 171, 173–174, 178–179, 180, 182; privatization in, 229–235; Romania and, 184–185, 187, 190; Yugoslavia and, 195–196, 207. See also Commonwealth of Independent States; individual countries; Russia
Soviet-German Non-Aggression Pact, 178, 179
space exploration, Soviet Union and, 24
Spain, 40, 125, 200, 233
Stalin, Joseph, 14, 16–17, 18, 19, 22, 24, 31, 45, 49, 50, 54, 62, 69, 91, 100, 101, 105, 111, 118, 120, 125, 130, 138, 151, 161, 170, 178–179, 186, 250; Soviet economy and, 217–220
Starcevic, Fyodor, 262
Starodubstev, V. A., 72
START I arms control agreement, 93, 106, 108, 110
state farms, Soviet, 29
Stojecevic, Stanko, 196
Stolojan, Theodor, 187, 188
Stoltenberg, Thorwald, 204, 206
Strougal, Lubomir, 153
structural constraints, Soviet privatization and, 231–232
Suchoka, Hanna, 176, 177, 286
Sudetenland, 158
Supreme Soviet, 25, 26, 34, 53, 57, 58, 59, 66, 67, 72, 73, 74–75, 77, 78, 79, 214; C.I.S., 243; Russian, 240
Suslov, Mikhail, 18
Syria, 106–107, 277
Szcecin, 180
Szlajfer, Henryk, 286

Tajikistan, 7, 90, 91, 98–99, 101, 111, 112; foreign policy of, 108–110; Islam and, 255–258; Russia and, 252–255
Tammerk, Tarmu, 264
Tatarstan, 53–54, 68, 92, 93, 167, 225, 244, 245–246, 249, 251
Ter-Petrosyan, Levon, 262, 263

terrorism, 41, 64
Thatcher, Margaret, 204
Tito, Joseph Brosz, 118, 119, 120, 134, 138, 144, 193, 194, 195–196, 197, 198, 207, 293
Tizyakov, A. I., 72
Toekes, Laszlo, 186
Tomasek, Frantisek, 153
Tosk people, 138, 140
totalitarianism, in Russia, 16
trade unions, Soviet, 23
Trans-Dniester, 69, 95, 241
Transylvania, 134, 185, 189, 190, 287, 289–290
Travkin, Nikolai, 226
Treaty of San Stefano, 148
Trotsky, Leon, 15, 16, 49, 215
Tudjman, Franjo, 197, 200, 202, 203, 204, 294
Turkey, 69, 96, 97, 100, 109, 112, 114, 115, 167, 233, 253, 257, 258, 287; Albania and, 137, 271, 274, 276; Bulgaria and, 144, 145, 147–148, 275, 276–277; Yugoslavia and, 193, 199, 201
Turkmenistan, 8, 43, 98, 112; foreign policy of, 108–110; Islam in, 255–258; Russia and, 252–255
turnover tax, Soviet, 30
Tuva, 242, 245
Tyminski, Joseph, 174
Tyumen, 246

Ukraine, 8, 22, 41, 43–44, 50, 53, 64, 67, 69, 73–74, 76, 84, 90, 91, 92–93, 101, 106, 110, 111, 112, 167, 181, 223, 241, 249, 287; foreign policy of, 108, 205
unemployment, in Hungary, 282–283
United Nations, 185; Albania and, 138–139, 142; Eastern Europe and, 123, 126, 157; Russia and, 101, 104–105, 106; Soviet Union and, 33, 64, 75, 92; Yugoslavia and, 199, 203–205, 207, 296
United States, 100, 105; Albania and, 271, 274; Bulgaria and, 145, 148; Czechoslovakia and, 156–157; Eastern Europe and, 109–110, 117, 118, 119, 129, 135, 138, 141; Poland and, 176, 179–180, 182; Romania and, 185, 190, 290; Russia and, 105–106, 239; Soviet Union and, 10, 17, 24, 31, 48, 52, 60, 61, 66, 91, 219, 230, 250, 266; Yugoslavia and, 196, 200, 205–207
Urbanek, Karel, 153, 159
USA Institute, 34
Ustinov, Dmitri, 24
Uzbekistan, 8, 43, 69, 75, 84, 98, 99, 100, 101, 111, 112, 241–242; foreign policy of, 108–110; Islam and, 255–258; Russia and, 108–110

Vacariou, Nicolae, 188
Vance, Cyrus, 200, 203, 206, 295
Velliste, Trivimi, 264
Vernon, Raymond, 234

violence, in Russia, 235–236
Vojvodina, 197, 198, 292
Volga Germans, 105
Volsky, Arkady, 80, 85, 226
voting, in the Soviet Union, 20

Wahhabis, 255, 256
Walesa, Lech, 103, 158, 170, 172, 173, 174, 175, 177, 178, 179, 182
War Communism, in Russia, 16
Warsaw Pact, 32, 61, 63, 112, 120, 123, 126, 127, 129, 135, 136, 142, 151, 152, 158, 161, 163, 166, 168, 178, 182, 184, 196, 229
welfare, Soviet, 30
What Is To Be Done? (Lenin), 13
Wiesel, Elie, 189
women, discrimination against, in the Soviet Union, 36, 38–39
Woodruff, Fred, 106
worker incentives, perestroika and, 45, 46
World Bank, 101, 102, 104, 134, 148, 176, 180, 231, 232, 278, 286
World Court, 101
World War I, 115, 160, 185; Soviet Union and, 51, 53, 212, 216
World War II, 197; Eastern Europe and, 114, 115, 117, 123, 135, 151, 158, 171; Poland and, 178–179, 180; Romania and, 184, 190; Soviet Union and, 24, 31, 62, 101, 107, 110, 232, 233
Wroblewski, Andrzej, 286

Yablokov, Alexi, 249
Yacovlev, Aleksandr, 60, 65, 70, 153
Yakutia, 242, 245
Yarin, Viktor, 236
Yavlinsky, Grigory, 67, 80, 81, 84
Yazov, Dmitri, 58, 60, 71, 72–73
Yeltsin, Boris, 55, 57, 58, 66, 68, 70, 71, 72, 73, 111, 112, 136, 148; foreign policy and, 101–107, 108; ethnic issues and, 92, 93, 94–95, 97; market economy and, 84–90; military and, 90–91; new Russia and, 75–84, 222–227, 228, 229
Young Pioneers, 20
Yugoslavia, 32, 104, 158, 168, 267, 268, 269, 274; Albania and, 142, 144, 273; Bulgaria and, 145, 277, 278; collapse of, 291–297; Eastern Europe and, 114–136, 137; overview of, 191–207

Zaslavskaya, Tatiana, 212, 221
zemstovs, 12
Zhelev, Zhelyu, 143, 147, 148, 149
Zhivkov, Todor, 130, 131, 144, 146–147, 275–276
Zhukov, G. D., 17, 24
Zinoviev, Gregori, 16
Zorkin, Valery, 78
Zyuganov, Gennadi, 80